Media and Messages

Media and Messages

Strategies and Readings in Public Rhetoric

Greg Barnhisel
Duquesne University

PEARSON
Longman

New York San Francisco Boston
London Toronto Sydney Tokyo Singapore Madrid
Mexico City Munich Paris Cape Town Hong Kong Montreal

Senior Vice President and Publisher: Joseph Opiela
Vice President and Publisher: Eben W. Ludlow
Development Editor: Katharine Glynn
Marketing Manager: Deborah Murphy
Senior Supplements Editor: Donna Campion
Production Manager: Denise Phillip
Project Coordination, Text Design, and Electronic Page Makeup: WestWords, Inc.
Senior Cover Design Manager: Nancy Danahy
Cover Designer: Nancy Danahy
Cover Photos: © Getty Images, Inc.
Photo Researcher: Photosearch, Inc.
Manufacturing Buyer: Lucy Hebard
Printer and Binder: Hamilton Printing
Cover Printer: Coral Graphic Services

For permission to use copyrighted material, grateful acknowledgment is made to the copyright holders on pp. 523–528, which are hereby made part of this copyright page.

Library of Congress Cataloging-in-Publication Data

Barnhisel, Greg, 1969–
  Media and messages : strategies and readings in public rhetoric / Greg Barnhisel.
    p. cm.
  ISBN 0-321-17975-7 (pbk.)
  1. English language—Rhetoric. 2. Mass media—Authorship—Problems, exercises, etc.
  3. Readers—Mass media. 4. College readers. I. Title.
PE1408.B4316 2005
808'.0472—dc22

                                                              2004004275

Please visit us at http://www.ablongman.com

ISBN 0-321-17975-7

1 2 3 4 5 6 7 8 9 10—HT—07 06 05 04

To Alison and Jack

Contents

What is public writing? How does writing aimed at a public differ from writing aimed at oneself, one's immediate friends, or a class? What sort of ethical and rhetorical responsibilities do we have when composing writing for the/a "public"? What do writers do and how do they change the content of their writing when they are using the media to reach the public?

Can journalism, or any other writing, truly be objective? Is it possible to avoid bias in writing intended for the public? Is the media liberal, conservative, or neither? And if it is biased, how do we get reliable news? How do the stylistic choices made by news writers and editors and producers convey bias—intended or unintended?

Readings

The Writer at Work   What Is an Argument?   112

Style Toolbox   Choosing the Right Verb   117

Chapter 3   What Are You Selling?   122

What is public relations and advertising language? Do they/how do they differ from nonpersuasive language? How has the pervasiveness of promotion and advertising language affected all forms of public communication? How do advertisers and PR people use the conventions of the "objective" media to promote their causes and products?

The Language of Advertising   126

The Language of Public Relations   129

Advertising and PR: The Ethical Dimension   136

Readings

Chapter 6   What's Real?   354

How much of what we understand as "real life" is actually an orchestrated event? What counts as real news, and what is just a photo opportunity? What is a publicity stunt—and how do we all try to orchestrate them for our own benefit?

Alternate Contents

Preface

The genesis of this book, as I suppose is true with all composition text-books, was in the classroom—specifically, in a Southwestern University classroom in 1998. Even in those early days of the Internet I was already apprehensive about students' ability to conduct effective Web research on their own, and so, when we got to the point of learning how to use sources, I took them to a computer classroom and walked them through several ways of researching a topic by using computer-based sources—several wrong ways and several right ways. We didn't finish the exercise that day, though, because the students themselves got into a heated discussion about reliable sources, media bias, and whether or not the Internet was actually valuable or just fun. Their discussion—which I did very little to lead—demonstrated to me how deeply immersed in the media most students are, how curious they are about the media, and how spotty their knowledge is about how the media works. Listening to them, I realized for the first time what many writing teachers quickly learn: teaching academic or persuasive writing without confronting the fundamental changes occurring in communications and the media is a difficult or even impossible task. Moreover, in any course that purports to teach critical thinking and reading, it's increasingly nonsensical not to look closely at the media. *Media and Messages,* then, attempts to do those two things simultaneously.

Features

Media and Messages gives students a broader and a deeper understanding of the most pressing issues regarding the media in contemporary America, but also teaches lessons in appealing, responsible, and ethical public writing. Each feature is designed to support these two goals.

- *Chapter titles* are posed as questions to promote inquiry and cover such topics as public writing, whether any writing can be objective, who owns the media, who owns ideas, and what kind of rhetoric is out of bounds.
- *Informative chapter introductions* discuss the chapter's topics and draw students into the subject by examining current events and previewing the readings. Each chapter includes "Analyzing the Message" questions that give students the opportunity to explore the chapter topic and related issues prior to studying the readings.

- *Readings* are drawn from a wide variety of sources, represent a diversity of genres, and reflect a variety of perspectives. Nearly half of the readings are editorials or features from large-circulation newspapers, opinion journals, or mass-market magazines. There are comic strips, blogs, and student papers as well. If students learn from the readings what debates society is having about media issues and what some of the positions in those debates are, they should also learn from those readings that there are a vast number of different ways to contribute to that conversation.
- *Headnotes* provide helpful background and contextual information for each reading.
- *"Topics for Reading and Writing"* after each selection are useful for class discussion and writing assignments. These questions ask students to explore the argument presented in the reading as well as to make connections between and among the other readings in the chapter.
- *"Writer at Work"* sections in each chapter guide students in developing their rhetorical skills. Starting with a discussion of the personal essay and descriptive writing, the "Writer at Work" lessons ask students to evaluate how writing intended for a public is different both in content and aims from private writing.
- *Each chapter concludes with the "Style Toolbox"* activity which ask students to turn their focus from the global, rhetorical level of writing to the sentence level.
- *"Writing with Style"* exercises focus on grammatical topics: the various methods of constructing a compound sentence, or the effective (as opposed to the erroneous) use of sentence fragments. As with the rest of the book, though, these style tools are taught not in terms of what is "correct," but as tools in effective writing for specific audiences and specific occasions.
- *Flexible organization.* Although in each chapter all of the four sections work well as a unified whole (for instance, the "Writer at Work" and "Style Toolbox" sections use readings in the chapter for examples), the sections are also very much detachable if instructors want to use the book simply as a reader or simply as a rhetoric.
- *Emphasis on audience.* The "Writer at Work" lessons in each chapter stress that students must always understand their audience, its desires and prejudices and emotions, before they can even begin crafting their messages; therefore, many of the exercises in constructing theses or making emotional appeals or assembling evidence specify an audience to whom the student is making an argument. Fortunately, most of the debates surrounding the media also focus on questions of audience: can a highly-concentrated system of media ownership adequately serve a democratic population? To what extent should writers be concerned with offending small segments of their audience? How does a media news outlet find an audience, and how does it then attempt to "construct" that audience?

The readings, as well, have been chosen and organized to help students understand questions of audience in public writing, and several student papers are included that show how student writing, as well, can be informed by and contribute to public discourse. Finally, the "Style Toolbox" lessons in grammar and style are not exclusively concerned with teaching students correct grammar; rather, they briefly outline eight different stylistic choices students must make or flourishes students can use, asking them always to think about whether a particular stylistic choice is appropriate for a particular audience.

▎▎ Organization

Each of the eight chapters in the book is composed of four sections:

- An introduction to the chapter's subject-matter
- A set of four to ten readings
- A "Writer at Work" lesson in writing and rhetoric
- A "Style Toolbox" section

Each chapter's introduction provides a brief overview (anywhere from five to twenty pages) of the media issue in question. Chapter 5, "Who Owns Information," for instance, the introduction includes a summary of the controversy surrounding downloading music or movies from the Internet, then discusses such issues of intellectual property as the Digital Millennium Copyright Act, conflicts between artists and record companies about ownership of songs and recordings, "director's cuts" of films, and companies that provide sanitized versions of movies, and plagiarism. None of the chapters focuses on a single controversy; rather, the chapters take as their subjects broad areas of debate. Instructors can assign these introductions to their classes to ensure that all students have at least a basic understanding of the issues addressed polemically by the readings.

Readings

Because *Media and Messages* is concerned exclusively with public discourse, all of the readings included—even those in the chapter that focuses on the personal essay—were intended for the public sphere. But in the public writing included there is great variety of voice, stance, occasion, and audience. Approximately half of the readings are editorials or features from large-circulation newspapers, opinion journals, or mass-market magazines. Students can compare the use of voice in a *National Review* or *American Prospect* opinion piece to that of an editorial in the *USA Today* or *New York Times*. The feature articles, as well, come from diverse publications, from the *Boondocks* comic strip to the *American Journalism Review*. There are student-written texts and articles from college newspapers, excerpts from scholarly books and from light memoirs, classics (Orwell's "Shooting an Elephant") and new genres (the "blog"), and visual texts. If students learn from the readings what debates society is having about media issues and what some of the positions in those debates are, they should also glean from those readings that there are a vast number of different ways to contribute to that conversation.

Writer at Work

The "Writer at Work" sections teach writing largely rhetorically, but in this they do not exclude genres of writing that aren't necessarily persuasive. Starting with a discussion of the personal essay, the "Writer at Work" lessons ask students to evaluate how writing intended for a public is different both in content and aims from private writing. Chapters 2 and 3 introduce the basic building-blocks of persuasive writing: audience analysis, the construction of a thesis, and the ethical, emotional, and logical components of an argument. The rest of the "Writer at Work" lessons are discussions of particular kinds of claims, focusing on the aim of an often real-world rhetorical occasion. The exercises and questions included in the "Writer at Work" sections reinforce the aims-based nature of the lessons by asking students to construct arguments about the media issues addressed in the book. In the "Writer at Work" section outlining arguments about meanings and definitions, for instance, students write about whether a movie studio or a director is the owner of a film, or whether or not Microsoft should be considered a monopoly.

Style Toolbox

The final section—the "Style Toolbox"—at the end of each chapter turns the book's focus from the global, rhetorical level of writing to the sentence level. In these sections, students are shown how to make decisions about what voice to use in their papers (first or third person? colloquial or formal? analytic or polemical?), about choosing among several verbs with similar meanings but different connotations, and even about the use of the passive voice. There are also exercises on grammatical topics: the various methods of constructing a compound sentence, or the effective (as opposed to the erroneous) use of sentence fragments. As with the rest of the book, though, these style tools are taught not in terms of what is "correct," but as tools in effective writing for specific audiences and specific occasions.

Final Thought

Although the book can be used in many different ways, if taught as a unified whole it will, I hope, train students to write well and responsibly, to critically read both the content and the institutional structure of the media, and to genuinely understand how good, ethical writing still has a very important role to play even in a society that at first glance seems not to value it.

⦀ Instructor's Manual

The instructor's manual for *Media and Messages: Strategies and Readings in Public Rhetoric* provides support and guidance for first-time composition instructors as well as experienced teachers. The learning objectives for each chapter are listed and explained, and a number of in-class exercises (with assessment tools) are provided for each chapter. Finally, the Instructor's Manual provides additional ideas and discussion about each of the readings.

⦀ Acknowledgments

I would like to thank the reviewers, including Jami Carlacio, Ithaca College; Marguerite Helmers, University of Wisconsin at Oshkosh; Toni Randall, Santa Monica College; Susan Romano, University of New Mexico; and Diane Thompson, Harrisburg Area Community College for their helpful and insightful feedback. Jonathan Silverman of Pace University and Dean Rader of the University of San Francisco encouraged me to come up with an idea for a book and helped me conceptualize what it might look like. Roger Anderson and the staff and faculty of the University of Southern California Writing Center and Writing Program were all helpful in the project—often unwittingly. Thanks also to the faculty and graduate students of the Duquesne University English Department and McAnulty College of Liberal Arts for their support and patience during this process. Eben Ludlow of Longman has consistently been a good-humored guiding spirit behind this project, and I am extremely grateful for his wisdom and experience as well as for the help of everyone at Longman. I'm especially indebted to Katharine Glynn, the developmental editor for this project, for her hard work, close readings, and wonderful suggestions; I could not have completed this book without her help. Finally, *Media and Messages* is dedicated to my wife, Alison, and my son, Jack.

Greg Barnhisel
Duquesne University

How Do I Enter the Conversation?

chapter 1

"Contemporary America is a media-driven, image-centered society in which the immediately appealing is more valued than anything of permanent importance or real substance. Today's youth are progressively being dumbed down by a constant diet of television and rap music and violent movies. Even magazines, to which serious-minded people could once turn to inform themselves about the crucial issues of the day, are now dominated by profiles of moronic celebrities and 'news you can use' stories, ignoring serious debate or historical context. At fault are the corporate media, whose relentless calls to buy, spend, and consume have drowned out all other voices in our culture. In short, American society is going to hell, and the media are at fault."

Or so many people would have it. Others celebrate the dizzying array of images and voices and products and ways to communicate that today's world offers. To these more optimistic observers of contemporary America, the **media**—meaning not just electronic journalism **but all means of technological mass communication,** from digital cable television to the Internet to pager networks—give ordinary people ways to communicate with each other and with large audiences that would have been inconceivable just

Writing is done alone and in a community at the same time.

50 years ago, when most people received only three television channels, only one telephone company existed, and a handful of studios in Los Angeles produced essentially every movie an American could see. Today, we get our information from hundreds of different sources—news channels, commercial and nonprofit radio stations, newspapers, and millions of websites. Technology allows us, moreover, to communicate with almost anyone in the world, no matter where we are: standing in line at a grocery store in Normal, Ill., I can call friends in Chicago, in Miami, in Karachi.

"And even," these sanguine defenders of today's media might add, "while the content of communication is shorter, faster, snappier, more visual, and less verbal, that's by no means a bad thing: most of us learn best if there is some visual component to new information. A story told with sound bites, quick cuts, flashing images, and well-chosen music is more memorable and more affecting than one told just with words. And what's wrong with celebrity journalism, reality television, or websites devoted to the mullet hairstyle? If nobody wanted them, they'd disappear; that's the nature of a democratic political system and market-based economy. Laments about the disappearance of long, dry news articles, of motionless and expressionless news anchors sitting at a featureless desk, are based on nothing but disguised class prejudice, a fear of regular people running things, and nostalgia for an imagined world of cultured intellectual discourse that never really existed in the first place."

Whether they curse this new world, glory in it, or simply struggle to make sense of it, few people would deny that the nature of mass communication—both its transmission and its content—has changed fundamentally in the last 25 or 30 years. In this new environment, what place is there for the kind of thoughtful writing that used to play such a central role in public discourse? The virtues of the written word seem to have given way to the visceral impact of the image. Newspaper stories are shorter than ever. Magazines are more dominated than ever by big pictures and splashy layout, and have drastically cut back on long articles. The venerable and venerated *New Yorker,* home of much of the greatest American writing of the twentieth century, advertising itself as "perhaps the best magazine that ever was," named as its editior a British celebrity journalist. Even screenwriting has been affected: television scriptwriters look at unscripted "reality television" with fear, and many movies produced by the major studios seem to have been written by a computer program or by a focus group. The Web publishes writing, but in all of that vastness how does one find the good stuff? Yet students are still required to write, in old-fashioned ways and for old-fashioned forums, in order to graduate from high school or college. In fact, universities today are *increasing* their writing requirements. Are universities dense, or perverse, or prescient? What is the place of writing in a culture that values sensation and the image more highly than the careful use of language? To put it simply, what role does writing have in public discourse in today's America?

III Public Discourse and the Unofficial Public Sphere

To begin to answer that question we must first think about what we mean by "public discourse" and "the public sphere." Democratic or republican societies like ours have always had two kinds of public spheres or public spaces: the official and the unofficial. The most important kind of official public space is, of course, an election. Official public space can also refer to the activities of the government to which all citizens have access—you might think of the Athenian *boule* (assembly of citizens) or our own Congress.[1] The U.S. government is remarkably open, and most of its activities, deliberations, and procedures are available for ordinary citizens to observe. Official public space that takes a physical form includes monuments like the U.S. Capitol, the Smithsonian Institution museums in Washington, D.C., or Alcatraz in San Francisco Bay; everyday buildings like public schools, libraries, post offices, city halls, and police stations; or open space like village greens, county recreation areas, state beaches, national parks, and U.S. Forest Service or Bureau of Land Management land. All of this official public space is owned by all U.S. citizens. Although there are rules as to its use, those rules are created through public debate and democratic choice (we elect the people who appoint the people who make the rules).

Official public space is only one component of the public sphere, though. Much of the debate about what our nation or state or town should do about

---

[1] Of course, "citizenship" in the Athenian state—including only property-owning, nonslave males—was much more restrictive than in today's America.

issues appears in the vast unofficial public space that is often called "public discourse." **Public discourse can be understood as the conversations that take place in front of audiences;** this category encompasses an almost unimaginable variety of communication. Presidential debates held in august halls and televised on every network are one variety of public discourse. Television programs and advertising are another kind of public discourse. Billboards, graffiti, bumper stickers, taunts traded between two athletes in a magazine, or CD covers are also varieties of public discourse. Maybe you post "blog" (journal) entries on your website—that's public discourse, too.

Private and public communication

With the term "public discourse" encompassing so many things, what kinds of communication *don't* qualify as public discourse? If communication is not meant for a public audience, it usually can't be considered public discourse. Personal conversations fit into this, of course, as do letters or e-mails exchanged between friends, communication in a closed forum such as a business meeting or grand jury hearing, or the wave you give another driver at a four-way stop.

Public discourse and private communications differ not only in their intentions, but also in their content. When you are speaking privately with your parents, your friends, or even your professor, you speak differently than you would if you were saying the same things in public. Private communications are often informal, off the cuff, unprepared. They can also be exceedingly formal; the private communications between a person in authority (a police officer, the King of Spain) and a person who needs something from that person can be extremely formal and even ritualized. The essential difference between public and private discourse is that in private communication, the speaker crafts his or her message specifically for the one person or small group he or she is speaking to, taking into consideration that person or group's desires, prejudices, and intellectual capacity.

It is in this calculation that even the best communicators sometimes err. In a famous gaffe, President Ronald Reagan demonstrated how communication that might have been suitable for private conversation can be quite inappropriate in public discourse. As he prepared to give a radio address, the former actor warmed up his voice and tested the microphone by joking, "Ladies and gentlemen, I have just signed legislation outlawing Russia forever. We begin bombing in five minutes." President Reagan didn't know the microphone was on. Although nobody took the president seriously, the idea that he could casually joke about a nuclear holocaust horrified some listeners and confirmed many people's perception that Reagan did not acknowledge the humanity of our adversary. Moreover, this joke lowered people's impressions of Reagan's *ethos,* or personal reliability: how could a man in such an important position and with such grave power be so flippant? (For others, though, Reagan's joke only increased their affection for him—he didn't take himself too seriously, he could joke like an ordinary guy.) Not all such mistakes, though, are so serious; the humorous disjunction of private communication in a public forum has always been the fodder for television and movie screenwriters. The plot device of someone having to shout private communication (usually a declaration of love) over loud background noise only to have that background noise cease so the character ends up shouting loud enough for everyone to hear is trite and familiar.

But private communication can be inappropriate in public for reasons that go beyond personal embarrassment. During the early 1990s, while continuing to engage in a public war of words with each other, the government of Israel and the Palestine Liberation Organization conducted secret negotiations and, without the pressure of their constituencies criticizing or even undermining the ongoing talks, achieved a landmark peace settlement in 1994. (That settlement, the Oslo Agreement, has been made irrelevant because of the violence of the past few years.) Sometimes a speaker can make the same argument in public and in private but make it differently in each case: businesses pursuing a merger will often make bland, nonspecific public statements while communicating privately with very detailed and personal appeals.

Public discourse: The ethical dimension

Public discourse, of course, is conducted quite differently than private communication. Constructing effective public communication, just like private communication, rests heavily on knowing what works with a particular audience. But people who communicate to the public must think very carefully not only about what they are trying to achieve with this communication, but also about how a wide variety of people might respond to or react to this message. Every utterance of a political candidate will be reported and analyzed by a vast number of people with whom that candidate will have no personal contact; she can't explain "what she really meant" when her message is interpreted unfavorably. Advertisers face similar dilemmas all the time—an appeal might work beautifully with one audience but offend another. No message will be effective with every audience: a writer or speaker must carefully calculate how to appeal to the broadest audience and alienate the fewest people.

But public discourse also carries with it some practical and ethical considerations that do not necessarily apply to private communication. Public discourse should be ethical largely because ethical communication is often more appealing and more persuasive than unethical communication. What's different is not necessarily that you can't engage in some of the "tricks" you might use in private communication—using evidence that you know isn't true, for instance, or pushing easy emotional buttons, or bullying the audience with your authority—but that in speaking to a larger audience you will likely be *caught,* and thereby your message will lose effectiveness. Public discourse should be ethical because the questions debated in public discourse affect so many people. Students of rhetoric and public discourse, though, have always known that this ethical imperative is by no means enough to compel everyone to behave ethically.

This all makes our ethical code for public discourse seem pretty instrumental—that is, we're only ethical because it works, not because it's right. To a large extent, this is true. **Rhetoric—the persuasive use of language, especially in public discourse**—has had a complicated and often compromised relationship to ethics going back to the days of ancient Greece. In the Athenian democratic system, like in ours, political decisions were made by a vote of the citizens after sides had presented their arguments. This was a system in which the ability to speak persuasively was very valuable. A group of freelance rhetoric teachers known as "sophists" roamed the *agora* or marketplace, hiring themselves out to prominent young men to teach them how to get what they wanted by speaking persuasively in front of the assembly. In the dialogues of the Athenian philosopher Plato, the character of Socrates (a philosopher who searches only for truth) expresses contempt for these sophists, for whom being persuasive—even if it was misleading or dishonest—was much more important than being right. Rhetoric isn't much different today: some of the most appealing arguments are frequently less than fully ethical.

At this point you might ask yourself what, specifically, would constitute ethical public rhetoric. Is it ethical to appeal to people's emotions? To what degree? Almost every side in a debate will accuse the other side of relying so heavily on emotion that it overwhelms logic—is this a fair accusation? Is there something wrong with making decisions based on emotion rather than on logic? Traditionally, appeals based on emotion have been contrasted with those based on logic or clarity: is this fair? Can an emotional appeal be clear, and a logical argument be obfuscatory?

Another important question to consider is how the speaker's authority or influence plays into these questions of rhetoric and ethics. Several years ago the eminent journalist David Brinkley, who for many years moderated a Sunday morning news discussion program on the ABC television network, retired from his job and began working as a spokesman for various companies, including the Archer-Daniels-Midland (ADM) agricultural conglomerate that had recently been found guilty in a wide-ranging price-fixing criminal investigation. It seemed clear that ADM had sought out the most trustworthy voice it could find, at least partly to counteract public impressions that the company was crooked. Was ADM ethical in doing this, rather than in improving their behavior or explaining it to the public? Did Brinkley act ethically in agreeing to help cleanse ADM's public image? Or, to take another example, what happens to the reputations of such entertainers as Moby, Run-DMC, Sting, or Missy Elliot when *they* do television commercials? Obviously, they don't derive their popularity and authority from being respected, objective journalists, but some—Moby and Sting especially—have been very outspoken activists in favor of environmental and animal-rights causes. When these performers allow their music to be used to sell cars or clothes or soda, are they hypocritical? Can we still take them seriously when they speak about issues? Should we ever have taken them seriously in the first place?

Public rhetoric that is both ethical and effective is pretty easy to spot. First of all, it will treat its audience with respect, neither patronizing nor excessively flattering the audience. Ethical rhetoric lays out its argument clearly, allowing the audience to judge what the speaker is really saying. Ethical arguments will present evidence and will allow audience members to examine the validity of that evidence for themselves. (This is the reason you must cite all your evidence and claims of fact in scholarly papers!) Ethical speakers will present themselves honestly, and not pretend to be something they're not. Moreover, while using emotion as a tool of persuasion is perfectly acceptable, ethical public rhetoric

Rapper Missy Elliot and singer Madonna in a recent Gap clothing commercial.

will not manipulate the audience emotionally. All of this probably seems pretty basic, but as you start to think about all the manifestations of public rhetoric in the world today you'll probably also be surprised at how many of them are fundamentally unethical.

Public discourse versus private communication: The practical dimension

Martin Luther King, Jr.'s "Letter from Birmingham Jail" (included with this chapter) is perhaps the single greatest example of ethical public rhetoric in American history. It also provides us an excellent opportunity to think about the

Martin Luther King, Jr. in the Birmingham Jail.

differences between public and private writing. His letter is, after all, a letter: a piece of private communication between a speaker and a small audience (in this case, several clergymen of the city of Birmingham, Ala.). But King's letter is also an example of an old and honorable genre of public rhetoric, the "open letter." An open letter is written to a specific audience—usually someone in power—but is then published in a public forum as well as being sent to its addressee (if it is actually sent). The goal of an open letter, then, is to make an argument to a specific person—but to allow the public as a whole to "listen in" to that argument.

King's letter bears many of the characteristics of personal correspondence. A clergyman himself, King addresses his audience as a colleague would, establishing a commonality with his audience by assuming their familiarity not only with the Judeo-Christian tradition but also with the daily duties of pastoral office. The intensely personal tone and content of the letter also are typical of private correspondence, for we are often reluctant to "open ourselves up" in front of an audience. Responding to these clergymen's disapproval of "outside agitators" coming to Birmingham to stir up trouble, King adopts a pained tone; he is disappointed in his brothers in the cloth. This tone could come across as condescending were King speaking directly to a wider audience, but here he can implicitly say "you are all men of God: you should know better."

But this meticulously crafted letter was not intended solely for these few clergymen. By its length, by the detail of its analogies and the care taken to defend its moral stands, King shows his desire to make this argument to Birmingham as a whole, to the South, and to the rest of the United States. His argument, after all, cuts deeply at the notion of the responsibilities of a citizen. It is difficult for us today, now that King has become almost a secular saint, to understand just how revolutionary his ideas about justice and the state were—and are. But King is preaching rebellion. He argues that citizens have not only the right but the responsibility to disobey laws they feel are unjust. King even proposes a mechanism for determining whether or not a law is unjust, a mechanism based largely on the common understanding of God he shares with the clergymen. However, understanding that there would be members of the wider audience who do not share this notion of God, he adds secular criteria for determining the justness of a law (whether or not it degrades human personality and whether or not it turns the person into an object). In this open letter, King makes a powerful appeal to clergymen who share most of his core beliefs, but also expands those arguments so they appeal to the laity, and even to atheists.

King's letter was both a private communication and a very formal act of public rhetoric. Momentous occasions and controversies of great importance often call for formal genres like the open letter. Another type of personal writing made public is the essay itself. Pioneered by the French philosopher Michel de Montaigne in the seventeenth century, the *essai,* or "attempt," was initially a meditation of no set form or length on a philosophical, social, or historical topic. Today, outside of school (where student papers are generally called "essays") the essay is still used to explore a topic without a predetermined length or format, but the subject matter is generally personal. These personal essays vary widely: some are reminiscences about one's own history, some describe dreams and aspirations, some describe daily life. Personal essays also have no set voice, tone, level of diction, or much else. What most personal essays have in common is what we might call *generalizability:* the experiences or feelings described in the essay are common to many of us and therefore shed a new light on or help us better understand our own experiences or feelings, or they illustrate a point about an issue, controversy, or problem that affects many. Among the readings included in this chapter are several personal essays, ranging from Sandra Tsing Loh's humorous reminiscence of an entertainment industry party to Richard Rodriguez's serious and thoughtful meditation on his upbringing and education.

In another example of a private genre becoming public discourse, the Internet diary ("weblog" or just "blog") has received plaudits for its exploration of the possibilities of the online forum. More public than a diary, less formal than an article or a press release, the daily postings to a blog exist on the border between private ruminations and public pronouncements. The opportunities the Web offers people to publish their thoughts (or themselves, with a webcam) has either given birth to or exploited an already-existing desire of Americans to observe the most mundane details of other people's daily lives. Included with this chapter is one blog ("Salam Pax's") by a pseudonymous Iraqi who was one of the very few nongovernmental voices documenting everyday life in Baghdad during and after the U.S. bombardment and invasion of early 2003. To what degree are blogs or webcam feeds performances aimed at an audience? To what degree are they unmediated private thoughts and actions? How do the two (private expression and public performance) differ? These are some issues to wrestle with as you read the pieces included in this chapter and as you think about the difference between your own private and public writing.

The spread of the media and the development of new communication technologies have both created new arenas for private and public writing and shifted the boundaries between private and public discourse. As independent, noncorporate voices are increasingly shut out of mainstream commercial media, private-writing-turned-public-discourse is moving to other forums. Anyone can be a published author on the Web. Inexpensive digital video cameras and editing equipment make it possible for a screenwriter to see her script produced without having to raise millions of dollars or give up creative control. Private writing becomes public discourse on the radio, when teenagers living in some of the toughest housing projects in Chicago have produced audio diaries for public-radio programs such as *This American Life* or *All Things Considered.* The consolidation of corporate control over the media may even, paradoxically, increase the amount and variety of public writing, as people search for and open up new outlets for their thoughts.

If you haven't noticed by now, the real theme of this book isn't something as simple as "the media are changing quickly" or "communication technologies are transforming our lives." In almost all the issues and problems and controversies you'll read about in this book, one underlying dialectic recurs: the interaction between the individuals who want to use the media or use communication technologies for their own needs, and the corporations or governments or regulatory bodies who own or want to control the use of those technologies. (I call this an "interaction" or a "dialectic" and not a "conflict" or "struggle" intentionally; many times these two sides can and do work together to satisfy the desires of both parties.) Frequently, though, this interaction does become a conflict, as when a radio host wants to broadcast material the FCC has deemed obscene, or when a college student wants to copy files that a movie studio or record company says it owns. It's also important to remember that the history of the media and the public cannot be told as the perpetual conflict between the virtuous individual and the oppressive group. Often, it is the group—the nonprofit organization, the funding body, the innovative company, the government—that creates the technology and devises ways for individuals to use that technology.

As you read the examples of personal writing for a public audience that are included in this chapter, ask yourself the questions about ethics and rhetoric that are, just as much as the proper use of the semicolon or construction of thesis statements, truly the subject-matter of college writing courses. What is the use of personal writing in the public sphere? How do new technologies change the role, the importance, and the actual appearance of personal writing in the public sphere? Are there new ethical imperatives or responsibilities generated by new technology—do we as individuals actually need to contribute *more* to public discourse to counteract or temper or even reinforce the voices of power?

Readings

Martin Luther King, Jr.
Letter from Birmingham Jail

Martin Luther King, Jr. (1929–1968), has become something close to the United States's secular saint: he represents the best of what Americans aspire to be. We remember his relentlessly nonviolent approach to

Public statement by eight Alabama clergymen:

We the undersigned clergymen are among those who, in January, issued "An Appeal for Law and Order and Common Sense," in dealing with racial problems in Alabama. We expressed understanding that honest dismantling the pervasive system of Jim Crow and segregation in the ex-Confederate states, his melding of religion and political philosophy, and his martyrdom in Memphis. However, his canonization has come at a price. We tend to shy away from engaging his ideas critically, to the extent that even those who would disagree with some of King's fundamental beliefs instead try to link themselves with him. But King was truly a radical. Yes, he opposed segregation and racism, and was nonviolent. However, liberals would be very leery of just how religious a state King would build; it's hard to imagine that Thomas Jefferson's "wall of separation" between church and state would exist in King's dream nation. Those on the right who like to quote King's "content of their character" statement in arguments against affirmative action conveniently look past his almost socialist economic beliefs, his willingness to devalue rights of private property and individual freedom for the common good, and his unequivocal opposition to the war in Vietnam.

In the "Letter from Birmingham Jail," King provocatively argues that he has the right to pick and choose which laws he will obey. Certainly, he proposes a theoretically compelling (if still controversial) philosophical structure for evaluating whether a law is just or unjust, but how comfortable should we be with the notion that religious duty outweighs our obligation to civil society? Isn't this precisely the same argument posed by polygamists and people who bomb abortion clinics? In addition, think about

convictions in racial matters could properly be pursued in the courts, but urged that decisions of those courts should in the meantime be peacefully obeyed.

Since that time there had been some evidence of increased forbearance and a willingness to face facts. Responsible citizens have undertaken to work on various problems which cause racial friction and unrest. In Birmingham, recent public events have given indication that we all have opportunity for a new constructive and realistic approach to racial problems.

However, we are now confronted by a series of demonstrations by some of our Negro citizens, directed and led in part by outsiders. We recognize the natural impatience of people who feel that their hopes are slow in being realized. But we are convinced that these demonstrations are unwise and untimely.

We agree rather with certain local Negro leadership which has called for honest and open negotiation of racial issues in our area. And we believe this kind of facing of issues can best be accomplished by citizens of our own metropolitan area, white and Negro, meeting with their knowledge and experience of the local situation. All of us need to face that responsibility and find proper channels for its accomplishment.

Just as we formerly pointed out that "hatred and violence have no sanction in our religious and political traditions," we also point out that such actions as incite to hatred and violence, however technically peaceful those actions may be, have not contributed to the resolution of our local problems. We do not believe that these days of new hope are days when extreme measures are justified in Birmingham.

We commend the community as a whole, and the local news media and law enforcement officials in particular, on the calm manner in which these demonstrations have been handled. We urge the public to continue to show restraint should the demonstrations continue, and the law enforcement officials to remain calm and continue to protect our city from violence.

We further strongly urge our own Negro community to withdraw support from these demonstrations, and to unite locally in working peacefully for a better Birmingham. When rights are consistently denied, a cause should be pressed in the courts and in negotiations among local leaders, and not in the streets. We appeal to both our white and Negro citizenry to observe the principles of law and order and common sense.

how King has become such a beloved figure after his death, when during his life he was always divisive and at worst suspected of being a communist subversive by the director of the Federal Bureau of Investigation. What are the processes by which a media-saturated society takes control of the meaning of a person's life?

Signed by:

C. C. J. Carpenter, D.D., LL.D., *Bishop of Alabama*
Joseph A. Durick, D.D., *Auxiliary Bishop, Diocese of Mobile, Birmingham*
Rabbi Milton L. Grafman, *Temple Emanu-El, Birmingham, Alabama*
Bishop Paul Hardin, *Bishop of the Alabama-West Florida Conference of the Methodist Church*
Bishop Nolan B. Harmon, *Bishop of the North Alabama Conference of the Methodist Church*
George M. Murray, D.D., LL.D., *Bishop Coadjutor, Episcopal Diocese of Alabama*
Edward V. Ramage, *Moderator, Synod of the Alabama Presbyterian Church in the United States*
Earl Stallings, *Pastor, First Baptist Church, Birmingham, Alabama*

Following is the letter Martin Luther King, Jr., wrote in response to the clergymen's public statement.

April 16, 1963

My Dear Fellow Clergymen:

While confined here in the Birmingham city jail, I came across your recent statement calling my present activities "unwise and untimely." Seldom do I pause to answer criticism of my work and ideas. If I sought to answer all the criticisms that cross my desk, my secretaries would have little time for anything other than such correspondence in the course of the day, and I would have no time for constructive work. But since I feel that you are men of genuine good will and that your criticisms are sincerely set forth, I want to try to answer your statement in what I hope will be patient and reasonable terms.

I think I should indicate why I am here in Birmingham, since you have been influenced by the view which argues against "outsiders coming in." I have the honor of serving as president of the Southern Christian Leadership Conference, an organization operating in every southern state, with headquarters in Atlanta, Georgia. We have some eighty-five affiliated organizations across the South, and one of them is the Alabama Christian Movement for Human Rights. Frequently we share staff, educational and financial resources with our affiliates. Several months ago the affiliate here in Birmingham asked us to be on call to engage in a nonviolent direct-action program if such were deemed necessary. We readily consented, and when the hour came we lived up to our promise. So I, along with several members of my staff, am here because I was invited here. I am here because I have organizational ties here.

But more basically, I am in Birmingham because injustice is here. Just as the prophets of the eighth century B.C. left their villages and carried their "thus saith the Lord" far beyond the boundaries of their home towns, and just as the Apostle Paul left his village of Tarsus and carried the gospel of Jesus Christ to the far corners of the Greco-Roman world, so am I compelled to carry the gospel of freedom beyond my own home town. Like Paul, I must constantly respond to the Macedonian call for aid.

Moreover, I am cognizant of the interrelatedness of all communities and states. I cannot sit idly by in Atlanta and not be concerned about what happens in Birmingham. Injustice anywhere is a threat to justice everywhere. We are caught in an inescapable network of mutuality, tied in a single garment of destiny. Whatever affects one directly, affects all indirectly. Never again can we afford to live with the narrow, provincial "outside agitator" idea. Anyone who lives inside the United States can never be considered an outsider anywhere within its bounds.

You deplore the demonstrations taking place in Birmingham. But your statement, I am sorry to say, fails to express a similar concern for the conditions that brought about the demonstrations. I am sure that none of you would want to rest content with the superficial kind of social analysis that deals merely with effects and does not grapple with underlying causes. It is unfortunate that demonstrations are taking place in Birmingham, but it is even more unfortunate that the city's white power structure left the Negro community with no alternative.

In any nonviolent campaign there are four basic steps: collection of the facts to determine whether injustices exist; negotiation; self-purification; and direct action. We have gone through all these steps in Birmingham. There can be no gainsaying the fact that racial injustice engulfs this community. Birmingham is probably the most thoroughly segregated city in the United States. Its ugly record of brutality is widely known. Negroes have experienced grossly unjust treatment in the courts. There have been more unsolved bombings of Negro homes and churches in Birmingham than in any other city in the nation. These are the hard, brutal facts of the case. On the basis of these conditions, Negro leaders sought to negotiate with the city fathers. But the latter consistently refused to engage in good-faith negotiation.

Then, last September, came the opportunity to talk with leaders of Birmingham's economic community. In the course of the negotiations, certain promises were made by the merchants—for example, to remove the stores' humiliating racial signs. On the basis of these promises, the Reverend Fred Shuttlesworth and the leaders of the Alabama Christian Movement for Human Rights agreed to a moratorium on all demonstrations. As the weeks and months went by, we realized that we were the victims of a broken promise. A few signs, briefly removed, returned; the others remained.

As in so many past experiences, our hopes had been blasted, and the shadow of deep disappointment settled upon us. We had no alternative except to prepare for direct action, whereby we would present our very bodies as a means of laying our case before the conscience of the local and the national community. Mindful of the difficulties involved, we decided to undertake a process of self-purification. We began a series of workshops on nonviolence, and we repeatedly asked ourselves: "Are you able to accept blows without retaliating?" "Are you able to endure the ordeal of jail?" We decided to schedule our direct-action program for the Easter season, realizing that except for Christmas, this is the main shopping period of the year. Knowing that a strong economic-withdrawal program would be the by-product of direct action, we felt that this would be the best time to bring pressure to bear on the merchants for the needed change.

Then it occurred to us that Birmingham's mayoral election was coming up in March, and we speedily decided to postpone action until after election day. When we discovered that the Commissioner of Public Safety, Eugene "Bull" Connor, had piled up enough votes to be in the run-off, we decided again to postpone action until the day after the run-off so that the demonstrations could not be used to cloud the issues. Like many others, we waited to see Mr. Connor defeated, and to this end we endured postponement after postponement. Having aided in this community need, we felt that our direct-action program could be delayed no longer.

You may well ask: "Why direct action? Why sit-ins, marches and so forth? Isn't negotiation a better path?" You are quite right in calling for negotiation. Indeed, this is the very purpose of direct action. Nonviolent direct action seeks to create such a crisis and foster such a tension that a community which has constantly refused to negotiate is forced to confront the issue. It seeks so to dramatize the issue that it can no longer be ignored. My citing the creation of tension as part of the work of the nonviolent-resister may sound rather shocking. But I must confess that I am not afraid of the word "tension." I have earnestly opposed violent tension, but there is a type of constructive, nonviolent tension which is necessary for growth. Just as Socrates felt that it was necessary to create a tension in the mind so that individuals could rise from the bondage of myths and half-truths to the unfettered realm of creative analysis and objective appraisal, so must we see the need for nonviolent gadflies to create the kind of tension in society that will help men rise from the dark depths of prejudice and racism to the majestic heights of understanding and brotherhood.

The purpose of our direct-action program is to create a situation so crisis-packed that it will inevitably open the door to negotiation. I therefore concur with you in your call for negotiation. Too long has our beloved Southland been bogged down in a tragic effort to live in monologue rather than dialogue.

One of the basic points in your statement is that the action that I and my associates have taken in Birmingham is untimely. Some have asked: "Why didn't you give the new city administration time to act?" The only answer that I can give to this query is that the new Birmingham administration must be prodded about as much as the outgoing one, before it will act. We are sadly mistaken if we feel that the election of Albert Boutwell as mayor will bring the millennium to Birmingham. While Mr. Boutwell is a much more gentle person than Mr. Connor, they are both segregationists, dedicated to maintenance of the status quo. I have hope that Mr. Boutwell will be reasonable enough to see the futility of massive resistance to desegregation. But he will not see this without pressure from devotees of civil rights. My friends, I must say to you that we have not made a single gain in civil rights without determined legal and nonviolent pressure. Lamentably, it is an historical fact that privileged groups seldom give up their privileges voluntarily. Individuals may see the moral light and voluntarily give up their unjust posture; but, as Reinhold Niebuhr has reminded us, groups tend to be more immoral than individuals.

We know through painful experience that freedom is never voluntarily given by the oppressor; it must be demanded by the oppressed. Frankly, I have yet to engage in a direct-action campaign that was "well timed" in the view of those who have not suffered unduly from the disease of segregation. For years now I have heard the word "Wait!" It rings in the ear of every Negro with piercing familiarity. This "Wait" has almost always meant "Never." We must come to see, with one of our distinguished jurists, that "justice too long delayed is justice denied."

We have waited for more than 340 years for our constitutional God-given rights. The nations of Asia and Africa are moving with jetlike speed toward gaining political independence, but we still creep at horse-and-buggy pace toward gaining a cup of coffee at a lunch counter. Perhaps it is easy for those who have never felt the stinging darts of segregation to say, "Wait." But when you have seen vicious mobs lynch your mothers and fathers at will and drown your sisters and brothers at whim; when you have seen hate-filled policemen curse, kick, and even kill your black brothers and sisters; when you see the vast majority of your twenty million Negro brothers smothering in an airtight cage of poverty in the midst of an affluent society; when you suddenly find your tongue twisted and your speech stammering as you seek to explain to your six-year-old daughter why she can't go to the public amusement park that has just been advertised on television, and see tears welling up in her eyes when she is told that Funtown is closed to colored children, and see ominous clouds of inferiority beginning to form in her little mental sky, and see her beginning to distort her personality by developing an unconscious bitterness toward white people; when you have to concoct an answer for a five-year-old son who is asking: "Daddy, why do white people treat colored people so mean?"; when you take a cross-country drive and find it necessary to sleep night after night in the uncomfortable corners of your automobile because no motel will accept you; when you are humiliated day in and day out by nagging signs reading "white" and "colored"; when your first name becomes "nigger," your middle name becomes "boy" (however old you are) and your last name becomes "John," and your wife and mother are never given the respected title "Mrs."; when you are harried by day and haunted by night by the fact that you are a Negro, living constantly at tiptoe stance, never quite knowing what to expect next, and are plagued with inner fears and outer resentments; when you are forever fighting a degenerating sense of "nobodiness"—then you will understand why we find it difficult to wait. There comes a time when the cup of endurance runs over, and men are no longer willing to be plunged into the abyss of despair. I hope, sirs, you can understand our legitimate and unavoidable impatience.

You express a great deal of anxiety over our willingness to break laws. This is certainly a legitimate concern. Since we so diligently urge people to obey the Supreme Court's decision of 1954 outlawing segregation in the public schools, at first glance it may seem rather paradoxical for us consciously to break laws. One may well ask: "How can you advocate breaking some laws and obeying others?" The answer lies in the fact that there are two types of laws: just and unjust. I would be the first to advocate obeying just laws. One has not only a legal but a moral responsibility to obey just laws. Conversely, one has a moral responsibility to disobey unjust laws. I would agree with St. Augustine that "an unjust law is no law at all."

Now, what is the difference between the two? How does one determine whether a law is just or unjust? A just law is a man-made code that squares with the moral law or the law of God. An unjust law is a code that is out of harmony with the moral law. To put it in the terms of St. Thomas Aquinas: An unjust law is a human law that is not rooted in eternal law and natural law. Any law that uplifts human personality is just. Any law that degrades human personality is unjust. All segregation statutes are unjust because segregation distorts the soul and damages the personality. It gives the segregator a false sense of superiority and the segregated a false sense of inferiority. Segregation, to use the terminology of the Jewish philosopher Martin Buber, substitutes an "I–it" relationship for an "I–thou" relationship and ends up relegating persons to the status of things. Hence, segregation is not only politically, economically and sociologically unsound, it is morally wrong and sinful. Paul Tillich has said that sin is separation. Is not segregation an existential expression of man's tragic separation, his awful estrangement, his terrible sinfulness? Thus it is that I can urge men to obey the 1954 decision of the Supreme Court, for it is morally right; and I can urge them to disobey segregation ordinances, for they are morally wrong.

Let us consider a more concrete example of just and unjust laws. An unjust law is a code that a numerical or power majority group compels a minority group to obey but does not make binding on itself. This is *difference* made legal. By the same token, a just law is a code that a majority compels a minority to follow and that it is willing to follow itself. This is *sameness* made legal.

Let me give another explanation. A law is unjust if it is inflicted on a minority that, as a result of being denied the right to vote, had no part in enacting or devising the law. Who can say that the legislature of Alabama which set up that state's segregation laws was democratically elected? Throughout Alabama all sorts of devious methods are used to prevent Negroes from becoming registered voters, and there are some counties in which, even though Negroes constitute a majority of the population, not a single Negro is registered. Can any law enacted under such circumstances be considered democratically structured?

Sometimes a law is just on its face and unjust in its application. For instance, I have been arrested on a charge of parading without a permit. Now, there is nothing wrong in having an ordinance which requires a permit for a parade. But such an ordinance becomes unjust when it is used to maintain segregation and to deny citizens the First-Amendment privilege of peaceful assembly and protest.

I hope you are able to see the distinction I am trying to point out. In no sense do I advocate evading or defying the law, as would the rabid segregationist. That would lead to anarchy. One who breaks an unjust law must do so openly, lovingly, and with a willingness to accept the penalty. I submit that an individual who breaks a law that conscience tells him is unjust, and who willingly accepts the penalty of imprisonment in order to arouse the conscience of the community over its injustice, is in reality expressing the highest respect for law.

Of course, there is nothing new about this kind of civil disobedience. It was evidenced sublimely in the refusal of Shadrach, Meshach and Abednego to obey the laws of Nebuchadnezzar, on the ground that a higher moral law was at stake. It was practiced superbly by the early Christians, who were willing to face hungry lions and the excruciating pain of chopping blocks rather than submit to certain unjust laws of the Roman Empire. To a degree, academic freedom is a reality today because Socrates practiced civil disobedience. In our own nation, the Boston Tea Party represented a massive act of civil disobedience.

We should never forget that everything Adolf Hitler did in Germany was "legal" and everything the Hungarian freedom fighters did in Hungary was "illegal." It was "illegal" to aid and comfort a Jew in Hitler's Germany. Even so, I am sure that, had I lived in Germany at the time, I would have aided and comforted my Jewish brothers. If today I lived in a Communist country where certain principles dear to the Christian faith are suppressed I would openly advocate disobeying that country's antireligious laws.

I must make two honest confessions to you, my Christian and Jewish brothers. First, I must confess that over the past few years I have been gravely disappointed with the white moderate. I have almost reached the regrettable conclusion that the Negro's great stumbling block in his stride toward freedom is not the White Citizen's Counciler or the Ku Klux Klanner, but the white moderate, who is more devoted to "order" than to justice; who prefers a negative peace which is the presence of tension to a positive peace which is the presence of justice; who constantly says, "I agree with you in the goal you seek, but I cannot agree with your methods of direct action"; who paternalistically believes he can set the timetable for another man's freedom; who lives by a mythical concept of time and who constantly advises the Negro to wait for a "more convenient season." Shallow understanding from people of good will is more frustrating than absolute misunderstanding from people of ill will. Lukewarm acceptance is much more bewildering than outright rejection.

I had hoped that the white moderate would understand that law and order exist for the purpose of establishing justice and that when they fail in this purpose they become the dangerously structured dams that block the flow of social progress. I had hoped that the white moderate would understand that the present tension in the South is a necessary phase of the transition from an obnoxious negative peace, in which the Negro passively accepted his unjust plight, to a substantive and positive peace, in which all men will respect the dignity and worth of human personality. Actually, we who engage in nonviolent direct action are not the creators of tension. We merely bring to the surface the hidden tension that is already alive. We bring it out in the open, where it can be seen and dealt with. Like a boil that can never be cured so long as it is covered up but must be opened with all its ugliness to the natural medicines of air and light, injustice must be exposed, with all the tension its exposure creates, to the light of human conscience and the air of national opinion before it can be cured.

In your statement you assert that our actions, even though peaceful, must be condemned because they precipitate violence. But is this a logical assertion? Isn't this like condemning a robbed man because his possession of money precipitated the evil act of robbery? Isn't this like condemning Socrates because his unswerving commitment to truth and his philosophical inquiries precipitated the act by the misguided populace in which they made him drink hemlock? Isn't this like condemning Jesus because his unique God-consciousness and never-ceasing devotion to God's will precipitated the evil act of crucifixion? We must come to see that, as the federal courts have consistently affirmed, it is wrong to urge an individual to cease his efforts to gain his basic constitutional rights because the quest may precipitate violence. Society must protect the robbed and punish the robber.

I had also hoped that the white moderate would reject the myth concerning time in relation to the struggle for freedom. I have just received a letter from a white brother in Texas. He writes: "All Christians know that the colored people will receive equal rights eventually, but it is possible that you are in too great a religious hurry. It has taken Christianity almost two thousand years to accomplish what it has. The teachings of Christ take time to come to earth." Such an attitude stems from a tragic misconception of time, from the strangely irrational notion that there is something in the very flow of time that will inevitably cure all ills. Actually, time itself is neutral; it can be used either destructively or constructively. More and more I feel that the people of ill will have used time much more effectively than have the people of good will. We will have to repent in this generation not merely for the hateful words and actions of the bad people but for the appalling silence of the good people. Human progress never rolls in on wheels of inevitability; it comes through the tireless efforts of men willing to be co-workers with God, and without this hard work, time itself becomes an ally of the forces of social stagnation. We must use time creatively, in the knowledge that the time is always ripe to do right. Now is the time to make real the promise of democracy and transform our pending national elegy into a creative psalm of brotherhood. Now is the time to lift our national policy from the quicksand of racial injustice to the solid rock of human dignity.

You speak of our activity in Birmingham as extreme. At first I was rather disappointed that fellow clergymen would see my nonviolent efforts as those of an extremist. I began thinking about the fact that I stand in the middle of two opposing forces in the Negro community. One is a force of complacency, made up in part of Negroes who, as a result of long years of oppression, are so drained of self-respect and a sense of "somebodiness" that they have adjusted to segregation; and in part of a few middle-class Negroes who, because of a degree of academic and economic security and because in some ways they profit by segregation, have become insensitive to the problems of the masses. The other force is one of bitterness and hatred, and it comes perilously close to advocating violence. It is expressed in the various black nationalists groups that are springing up across the nation, the largest and best-known being Elijah Muhammad's Muslim movement. Nourished by the Negro's frustration over the continued existence of racial discrimination, this movement is made up of people who have lost faith in America, who have absolutely repudiated Christianity, and who have concluded that the white man is an incorrigible "devil."

I have tried to stand between these two forces, saying that we need emulate neither the "do-nothingism" of the complacent nor the hatred and despair of the black nationalist. For there is the more excellent way of love and nonviolent protest. I am grateful to God that, through the influence of the Negro church, the way of nonviolence became an integral part of our struggle.

If this philosophy had not emerged, by now many streets of the South would, I am convinced, be flowing with blood. And I am further convinced that if our white brothers dismiss as "rabble-rousers" and "outside agitators" those of us who employ nonviolent direct action, and if they refuse to support our nonviolent efforts, millions of the Negroes will, out of frustration and despair, seek solace and security in black-nationalist ideologies—a development that would inevitably lead to a frightening racial nightmare.

Oppressed people cannot remain oppressed forever. The yearning for freedom eventually manifests itself, and that is what has happened to the American Negro. Something within has reminded him of his birthright of freedom, and something without has reminded him that it can be gained. Consciously or unconsciously, he has been caught up by the *Zeitgeist,* and with his black brothers of Africa and his brown and yellow brothers of Asia, South America and the Caribbean, the United States Negro is moving with a sense of great urgency toward the promised land of racial justice. If one recognizes this vital urge that has engulfed the Negro community, one should readily understand why public demonstrations are taking place. The Negro has many pent-up resentments and latent frustrations, and he must release them. So let him march; let him make prayer pilgrimages to the city hall; let him go on freedom rides—and try to understand why he must do so. If his repressed emotions are not released in nonviolent ways, they will seek expression through violence; this is not a threat but a fact of history. So I have not said to my people: "Get rid of your discontent." Rather, I have tried to say that this normal and healthy discontent can be channeled into the creative outlet of nonviolent direct action. And now this approach is being termed extremist.

But though I was initially disappointed at being categorized as an extremist, as I continued to think about the matter I gradually gained a measure of satisfaction from the label. Was not Jesus an extremist for love: "Love your enemies, bless them that curse you, and persecute you." Was not Amos an extremist for justice: "Let justice roll down like waters and righteousness like an ever-flowing stream." Was not Paul an extremist for the Christian gospel: "I bear in my body the marks of the Lord Jesus." Was not Martin Luther an extremist: "Here I stand; I cannot do otherwise, so help me God." And John Bunyan: "I will stay in jail to the end of my days before I make a butchery of my conscience." And Abraham Lincoln: "This nation cannot survive half slave and half free." And Thomas Jefferson: "We hold these truths to be self-evident, that all men are created equal. . . ." So the question is not whether we will be extremists, but what kind of extremists we will be. Will we be extremists for hate or for love? Will we be extremists for the preservation of injustice or for the extension of justice? In that dramatic scene on Calvary's hill three men were crucified. We must never forget that all three were crucified for the same crime—the crime of extremism. Two were extremists for immorality, and thus fell below their environment. The other, Jesus Christ, as was an extremist for love, truth and goodness, and thereby rose above his environment. Perhaps the South, the nation and the world are in dire need of creative extremists.

I had hoped that the white moderate would see this need. Perhaps I was too optimistic; perhaps I expected too much. I suppose I should have realized that few members of the oppressor race can understand the deep groans and passionate yearnings of the oppressed race, and still fewer have the vision to see that injustice must be rooted out by strong, persistent and determined action. I am thankful, however, that some of our white brothers in the South have grasped the meaning of this social revolution and committed themselves to it. They are still all too few in quantity, but they are big in quality. Some—such as Ralph McGill, Lillian Smith, Harry Golden, James McBride Dabbs, Ann Braden and Sarah Patton Boyle—have written about our struggle in eloquent and prophetic terms. Others have marched with us down nameless streets of the South. They have languished in filthy, roach-infested jails, suffering the abuse and brutality of policemen who view them as "dirty nigger-lovers." Unlike so many of their moderate brothers and sisters, they have recognized the urgency of the moment and sensed the need for powerful "action" antidotes to combat the disease of segregation.

Let me take note of my other major disappointment. I have been so greatly disappointed with the white church and its leadership. Of course, there are some notable exceptions. I am not unmindful of the fact that each of you has taken some significant stands on this issue. I commend you, Reverend Stallings, for your Christian stand on this past Sunday, in welcoming Negroes to your worship service on a nonsegregated basis. I commend the Catholic leaders of this state for integrating Spring Hill College several years ago.

But despite these notable exceptions, I must honestly reiterate that I have been disappointed with the church. I do not say this as one of those negative critics who can always find something wrong with the church. I say this as a minister of the gospel, who loves the church; who was nurtured in its bosom; who has been sustained by its spiritual blessings and who will remain true to it as long as the cord of life shall lengthen.

When I was suddenly catapulted into the leadership of the bus protest in Montgomery, Alabama, a few years ago, I felt we would be supported by the white church. I felt that the white ministers, priests and rabbis of the South would be among our strongest allies. Instead, some have been outright opponents, refusing to understand the freedom movement and misrepresenting its leaders; all too many others have been more cautious than courageous and have remained silent behind the anesthetizing security of stained-glass windows.

In spite of my shattered dreams, I came to Birmingham with the hope that the white religious leadership of this community would see the justice of our cause and, with deep moral concern, would serve as the channel through which our just grievances could reach the power structure. I had hoped that each of you would understand. But again I have been disappointed.

I have heard numerous southern religious leaders admonish their worshipers to comply with a desegregation decision because it is the law, but I have longed to hear white ministers declare: "Follow this decree because integration is morally right and because the Negro is your brother." In the midst of blatant injustices inflicted upon the Negro, I have watched white churchmen stand on the sideline and mouth pious irrelevancies and sanctimonious trivialities. In the midst of a mighty struggle to rid our nation of racial and economic injustice, I have heard many ministers say: "Those are social issues, with which the gospel has no real concern." And I have watched many churches commit themselves to a completely otherworldly religion which makes a strange, un-Biblical distinction between body and soul, between the sacred and the secular.

I have traveled the length and breadth of Alabama, Mississippi and all the other southern states. On sweltering summer days and crisp autumn mornings I have looked at the South's beautiful churches with their lofty spires pointing heavenward. I have beheld the impressive outlines of her massive religious-education buildings. Over and over I have found myself asking: "What kind of people worship here? Who is their God? Where were their voices when the lips of Governor Barnett dripped with words of interposition and nullification? Where were they when Governor Wallace gave a clarion call for defiance and hatred? Where were their voices of support when bruised and weary Negro men and women decided to rise from the dark dungeons of complacency to the bright hills of creative protest?"

Yes, these questions are still in my mind. In deep disappointment I have wept over the laxity of the church. But be assured that my tears have been tears of love. There can be no deep disappointment where there is not deep love. Yes, I love the church. How could I do otherwise? I am in the rather unique position of being the son, the grandson, and the great-grandson of preachers. Yes, I see the church as the body of Christ. But, oh! How we have blemished and scarred that body through social neglect and through fear of being nonconformists.

There was a time when the church was very powerful—in the time when the early Christians rejoiced at being deemed worthy to suffer for what they believed. In those days the church was not merely a thermometer that recorded the ideas and principles of popular opinion; it was a thermostat that transformed the mores of society. Whenever the early Christians entered a town, the people in power became disturbed and immediately sought to convict the Christians for being "disturbers of the peace" and "outside agitators." But the Christians pressed on, in the conviction that they were "a colony of heaven," called to obey God rather than man. Small in number, they were big in commitment. They were too God-intoxicated to be "astronomically intimidated." By their effort and example they brought an end to such ancient evils as infanticide and gladiatorial contests.

Things are different now. So often the contemporary church is a weak, ineffectual voice with an uncertain sound. So often it is an archdefender of the status quo. Far from being disturbed by the presence of the church, the power structure of the average community is consoled by the church's silent—and often even vocal—sanction of things as they are.

But the judgment of God is upon the church as never before. If today's church does not recapture the sacrificial spirit of the early church, it will lose its authenticity, forfeit the loyalty of millions, and be dismissed as an irrelevant social club with no meaning for the twentieth century. Every day I meet young people whose disappointment with the church has turned into outright disgust.

Perhaps I have once again been too optimistic. Is organized religion too inextricably bound to the status quo to save our nation and the world? Perhaps I must turn my faith to the inner spiritual church, the church within the church, as the true *ekklesia* and the hope of the world. But again I am thankful to God that some noble souls from the ranks of organized religion have broken loose from the paralyzing chains of conformity and joined us as active partners in the struggle for freedom. They have left their secure congregations and walked the streets of Albany, Georgia, with us. They have gone down the highways of the South on tortuous rides for freedom. Yes, they have gone to jail with us. Some have been dismissed from their churches, have lost the support of their bishops and fellow ministers. But they have acted in the faith that right defeated is stronger than evil triumphant. Their witness has been the spiritual salt that has preserved the true meaning of the gospel in these troubled times. They have carved a tunnel of hope through the dark mountain of disappointment.

I hope the church as a whole will meet the challenge of this decisive hour. But even if the church does not come to the aid of justice, I have no despair about the future. I have no fear about the outcome of our struggle in Birmingham, even if our motives are at present misunderstood. We will reach the goal of freedom in Birmingham and all over the nation, because the goal of America is freedom. Abused and scorned though we may be, our destiny is tied up with America's destiny. Before the pilgrims landed at Plymouth, we were here. Before the pen of Jefferson etched the majestic words of the Declaration of Independence across the pages of history, we were here. For more than two centuries our forebears labored in this country without wages; they made cotton king; they built the homes of their masters while suffering gross injustice and shameful humiliation—and yet out of a bottomless vitality they continued to thrive and develop. If the inexpressible cruelties of slavery could not stop us, the opposition we now face will surely fail. We will win our freedom because the sacred heritage of our nation and the eternal will of God are embodied in our echoing demands.

Before closing I feel impelled to mention one other point in your statement that has troubled me profoundly. You warmly commended the Birmingham police force for keeping "order" and "preventing violence." I doubt that you would have so warmly commended the police force if you had seen its dogs sinking their teeth into unarmed, nonviolent Negroes. I doubt that you would so quickly commend the policemen if you were to observe their ugly and inhumane treatment of Negroes here in the city jail; if you were to watch them push and curse old Negro women and young Negro girls; if you were to see them slap and kick old Negro men and young boys; if you were to observe them, as they did on two occasions, refuse to give us food because we wanted to sing our grace together. I cannot join you in your praise of the Birmingham police department.

It is true that police have exercised a degree of discipline in handling the demonstrators. In this sense they have conducted themselves rather "nonviolently" in public. But for what purpose? To preserve the evil system of segregation. Over the past few years I have consistently preached that nonviolence demands that the means we use must be as pure as the ends we seek. I have tried to make clear that it is wrong to use immoral means to attain moral ends. But now I must affirm that it is just as wrong, or perhaps even more so, to use moral means to preserve immoral ends. Perhaps Mr. Connor and his policemen have been rather nonviolent in public, as was Chief Pritchett in Albany, Georgia, but they have used the moral means of nonviolence to maintain the immoral end of racial injustice. As T. S. Eliot has said: "The last temptation is the greatest treason: To do the right deed for the wrong reason."

I wish you had commended the Negro sit-inners and demonstrators of Birmingham for their sublime courage, their willingness to suffer and their amazing discipline in the midst of great provocation. One day the South will recognize its real heroes. They will be the James Merediths, with the noble sense of purpose that enables them to face jeering and hostile mobs, and with the agonizing loneliness that characterizes the life of the pioneer. They will be old, oppressed, battered Negro women, symbolized in a seventy-two-year-old woman in Montgomery, Alabama, who rose up with a sense of dignity and with her people decided not to ride segregated buses, and who responded with ungrammatical profundity to one who inquired about her weariness: "My feets is tired, but my soul is at rest." They will be the young high school and college students, the young ministers of the gospel and a host of their elders, courageously and nonviolently sitting in at lunch counters and willingly going to jail for conscience' sake. One day the South will know that when these disinherited children of God sat down at lunch counters, they were in reality standing up for what is best in the American dream and for the most sacred values in our Judaeo-Christian heritage, thereby bringing our nation back to those great wells of democracy which were dug deep by the founding fathers in their formulation of the Constitution and the Declaration of Independence.

Never before have I written so long a letter. I'm afraid it is much too long to take your precious time. I can assure you that it would have been much shorter if I had been writing from a comfortable desk, but what else can one do when he is alone in a narrow jail cell, other than write long letters, think long thoughts and pray long prayers?

If I have said anything in this letter that overstates the truth and indicates an unreasonable impatience, I beg you to forgive me. If I have said anything that understates the truth and indicates my having a patience that allows me to settle for anything less than brotherhood, I beg God to forgive me.

I hope this letter finds you strong in faith. I also hope that circumstances will soon make it possible for me to meet each of you, not as an integrationist or a civil-rights leader but as a fellow clergyman and a Christian brother. Let us all hope that the dark clouds of racial prejudice will soon pass away and the deep fog of misunderstanding will be lifted from our fear-drenched communities, and in some not too distant tomorrow the radiant stars of love and brotherhood will shine over our great nation with all their scintillating beauty.

Yours for the cause of Peace and Brotherhood
Martin Luther King, Jr.

Topics for Reading and Writing

1. Although this is primarily a public document, to some extent King's letter is also a personal letter between clergymen. How does King use those components of this letter—the personal connections he has with men he's never met but with whom he shares a vocation—to help make his case?

2. As an exercise in the analysis of style, choose one particularly rich paragraph and look at the sentences individually, or as a list. Then, compare their structures and describe the rhetorical force of each individual sentence and of the sentences in sequence.

3. How does this elucidation of King's philosophy mesh with or contradict your previous understanding of King's ideas? If you are familiar with the "I have a dream" speech, compare the ideas of justice outlined in each.

George Orwell
Shooting an Elephant

Perhaps no adjective derived from a writer's name is so widely used as "Orwellian." Yet in its pervasiveness the term has almost lost its meaning. In his two most famous books, Animal Farm (1944) and Nineteen Eighty-Four (1948), the English writer George Orwell (1903–1950) mercilessly anatomized the history and structures of control of communist governments, and therefore critics, politicians, and social commentators on the right have taken Orwell as one of their own. Used by these writers, "Orwellian" indicates the sinister systems of control disguised as efforts for the public benefit that were typical of the Soviet Union and its satellite states. However, critics on the left have also claimed Orwell, and have pointed to Orwell's dislike of capitalism, his feelings of solidarity with workers, and especially his savage attacks on the ways that corporations and governments void language of meaning. For these leftists, "Orwellian" describes such evasive or misleading locutions as "collateral damage" (the deaths and destruction in civilian populations resulting from military actions), "downsizing" (firings and layoffs), or "the USA Patriot Act" (a 2001 series of laws, passed in the wake of the September 11 tragedies, vastly expanding the powers of law enforcement and restricting civil liberties, especially for noncitizens).

In Moulmein, in Lower Burma, I was hated by large numbers of people—the only time in my life that I have been important enough for this to happen to me. I was subdivisional police officer of the town, and in an aimless, petty kind of way anti-European feeling was very bitter. No one had the guts to raise a riot, but if a European woman went through the bazaars alone somebody would probably spit betel juice over her dress. As a police officer I was an obvious target and was baited whenever it seemed safe to do so. When a nimble Burman tripped me up on the football field and the referee (another Burman) looked the other way, the crowd yelled with hideous laughter. This happened more than once. In the end the sneering yellow faces of young men that met me everywhere, the insults hooted after me when I was at a safe distance, got badly on my nerves. The young Buddhist priests were the worst of all. There were several thousands of them in the town and none of them seemed to have anything to do except stand on street corners and jeer at Europeans.

All this was perplexing and upsetting. For at that time I had already made up my mind that imperialism was an evil thing and the sooner I chucked up my job and got out of it the better. Theoretically—and secretly, of course—I was all for the Burmese and all against their oppressors, the British. As for the job I was doing, I hated it more bitterly than I can perhaps make clear. In a job like that you see the dirty work of Empire at close quarters. The wretched prisoners huddling in the stinking cages of the lock-ups, the grey, cowed faces of the long-term convicts, the scarred buttocks of the men who had been flogged with bamboos—all these oppressed me with an intolerable sense of guilt. But I could get nothing into perspective. I was young and ill-educated and I had had to think out my problems in the utter silence that is imposed on every Englishman in the East. I did not even know that the British Empire is dying, still less did I know that it is a

Unlike many of his contemporaries of modern literature, Orwell was a professional writer and therefore produced a vast amount of work, much of it for newspapers and magazines. A recent anthology just of his journalism and essays fills almost 1,500 pages. He also wrote several novels and memoirs (notable among which are Down and Out in Paris and London *(1933), an account of the vagrant life, and* Homage to Catalonia *(1938), a personal story of the Spanish Civil War). "Shooting an Elephant," one of Orwell's most famous essays, is frequently anthologized for its insights on the predicament of the foot-soldier in the imperial project. Viewed in the light of the concerns of this chapter, though, "Shooting an Elephant" exemplifies the personal essay that is both an examination of the writer's own feelings and an analysis of larger events and issues.*

great deal better than the younger empires that are going to supplant it. All I knew was that I was stuck between my hatred of the empire I served and my rage against the evil-spirited little beasts who tried to make my job impossible. With one part of my mind I thought of the British Raj as an unbreakable tyranny, as something clamped down, in saecula saeculorum, upon the will of prostrate peoples; with another part I thought that the greatest joy in the world would be to drive a bayonet into a Buddhist priest's guts. Feelings like these are the normal byproducts of imperialism; ask any Anglo-Indian official, if you can catch him off duty.

One day something happened which in a roundabout way was enlightening. It was a tiny incident in itself, but it gave me a better glimpse than I had had before of the real nature of imperialism—the real motives for which despotic governments act. Early one morning the sub-inspector at a police station the other end of the town rang me up on the phone and said that an elephant was ravaging the bazaar. Would I please come and do something about it? I did not know what I could do, but I wanted to see what was happening and I got on to a pony and started out. I took my rifle, an old .44 Winchester and much too small to kill an elephant, but I thought the noise might be useful in terrorem. Various Burmans stopped me on the way and told me about the elephant's doings. It was not, of course, a wild elephant, but a tame one which had gone 'must.' It had been chained up as tame elephants always are when their attack of 'must' is due, but on the previous night it had broken its chain and escaped. Its mahout, the only person who could manage it when it was in that state, had set out in pursuit, but he had taken the wrong direction and was now twelve hours' journey away, and in the morning the elephant had suddenly reappeared in the town. The Burmese population had no weapons and were quite helpless against it. It had already destroyed somebody's bamboo hut, killed a cow and raided some fruit-stalls and devoured the stock; also it had met the municipal rubbish van, and, when the driver jumped out and took to his heels, had turned the van over and inflicted violences upon it.

The Burmese sub-inspector and some Indian constables were waiting for me in the quarter where the elephant had been seen. It was a very poor quarter, a labyrinth of squalid bamboo huts, thatched with palm-leaf, winding all over a steep hillside. I remember that it was a cloudy stuffy morning at the beginning of the rains. We began questioning the people as to where the elephant had gone, and, as usual, failed to get any definite information. That is invariably the case in the East; a story always sounds clear enough at a distance, but the nearer you get to the scene of events the vaguer it becomes. Some of the people said that the elephant had gone in one direction, some said that he had gone in another, some professed not even to have heard of any elephant. I had almost made up my mind that the whole story was a pack of lies, when we heard yells a little distance away. There was a loud, scandalized cry of 'Go away, child! Go away this instant!' and an old woman with a switch in her hand came round the corner of a hut, violently shooing away a crowd of naked children. Some more women followed, clicking their tongues and exclaiming; evidently there was something there that the children ought not to have seen. I rounded the hut and saw a man's dead body sprawling in the mud. He was an Indian, a black Dravidian coolie, almost naked, and he could not have been dead many minutes. The people said that the elephant had come suddenly upon him round the corner of the hut, caught him with its trunk, put its foot on his back and ground him into the earth. This was the rainy season and the ground was soft, and his face had scored a trench a foot deep and a couple of yards long. He was lying on his belly with arms crucified and head sharply twisted to one side. His face was coated with mud, the eyes wide open, the teeth bared and grinning with an expression of unendurable agony. (Never tell me, by the way, that the dead look peaceful. Most of the corpses I have seen looked devilish.) The friction of the great beast's foot had stripped the skin from his back as neatly as one skins a rabbit. As soon as I saw the dead man I sent an orderly to a friend's house nearby to borrow an elephant rifle. I had already sent back the pony, not wanting it to go mad with fright and throw me if it smelled the elephant.

The orderly came back in a few minutes with a rifle and five cartridges, and meanwhile some Burmans had arrived and told us that the elephant was in the paddy fields below, only a few hundred yards away. As I started forward practically the whole population of the quarter flocked out of the houses and followed me. They had seen the rifle and were all shouting excitedly that I was going to shoot the elephant. They had not shown much interest in the elephant when he was merely ravaging their homes, but it was different now that he was going to be shot. It was a bit of fun to them, as it would be to an English crowd; besides, they wanted the meat. It made me vaguely uneasy. I had no intention of shooting the elephant—I had merely sent for the rifle to defend myself if necessary—and it is always unnerving to have a crowd following you. I marched down the hill, looking and feeling a fool, with the rifle over my shoulder and an ever-growing army of people jostling at my heels. At the bottom, when you got away from the huts, there was a metalled road and beyond that a miry waste of paddy fields a thousand yards across, not yet ploughed but soggy from the first rains and dotted with coarse grass. The elephant was standing eighty yards from the road, his left side towards us. He took not the slightest notice of the crowd's approach. He was tearing up bunches of grass, beating them against his knees to clean them and stuffing them into his mouth.

I had halted on the road. As soon as I saw the elephant I knew with perfect certainty that I ought not to shoot him. It is a serious matter to shoot a working elephant—it is comparable to destroying a huge and costly piece of machinery—and obviously one ought not to do it if it can possibly be avoided. And at that distance, peacefully eating, the elephant looked no more dangerous than a cow. I thought then and I think now that his attack of 'must' was already passing off; in which case he would merely wander harmlessly about until the mahout came back and caught him. Moreover, I did not in the least want to shoot him. I decided that I would watch him for a little while to make sure that he did not turn savage again, and then go home.

But at that moment I glanced round at the crowd that had followed me. It was an immense crowd, two thousand at the least and growing every minute. It blocked the road for a long distance on either side. I looked at the sea of yellow faces above the garish clothes—faces all happy and excited over this bit of fun, all certain that the elephant was going to be shot. They were watching me as they would watch a conjuror about to perform a trick. They did not like me, but with the magical rifle in my hands I was momentarily worth watching. And suddenly I realized that I should have to shoot the elephant after all. The people expected it of me and I had got to do it; I could feel their two thousand wills pressing me forward, irresistibly. And it was at this moment, as I stood there with the rifle in my hands, that I first grasped the hollowness, the futility of the white man's dominion in the East. Here was I, the white man with his gun, standing in front of the unarmed native crowd—seemingly the leading actor of the piece; but in reality I was only an absurd puppet pushed to and fro by the will of those yellow faces behind. I perceived in this moment that when the white man turns tyrant it is his own freedom that he destroys. He becomes a sort of hollow, posing dummy, the conventionalized figure of a sahib. For it is the condition of his rule that he shall spend his life in trying to impress the 'natives,' and so in every crisis he has got to do what the 'natives' expect of him. He wears a mask, and his face grows to fit it. I had got to shoot the elephant. I had committed myself to doing it when I sent for the rifle. A sahib has got to act like a sahib; he has got to appear resolute, to know his own mind and do definite things. To come all that way, rifle in hand, with two thousand people marching at my heels, and then to trail feebly away, having done nothing—no, that was impossible. The crowd would laugh at me. And my whole life, every white man's life in the East, was one long struggle not to be laughed at.

But I did not want to shoot the elephant. I watched him beating his bunch of grass against his knees, with that preoccupied grandmotherly air that elephants have. It seemed to me that it would be murder to shoot him. At that age I was not squeamish about killing animals, but I had never shot an elephant and never wanted to. (Somehow it always seems worse to kill a *large* animal.) Besides, there was the beast's owner to be considered. Alive, the elephant was worth at least a hundred pounds; dead, he would only be worth the value of his tusks—five pounds, possibly. But I had got to act quickly. I turned to some experienced-looking Burmans who had been there when we arrived, and asked them how the elephant had been behaving. They all said the same thing: he took no notice of you if you left him alone, but he might charge if you went too close to him.

It was perfectly clear to me what I ought to do. I ought to walk up to within, say, twenty-five yards of the elephant and test his behaviour. If he charged I could shoot, if he took no notice of me it would be safe to leave him until the mahout came back. But also I knew that I was going to do no such thing. I was a poor shot with a rifle and the ground was soft mud into which one would sink at every step. If the elephant charged and I missed him, I should have about as much chance as a toad under a steam-roller. But even then I was not thinking particularly of my own skin, only of the watchful yellow faces behind. For at that moment, with the crowd watching me, I was not afraid in the ordinary sense, as I would have been if I had been alone. A white man mustn't be frightened in front of 'natives'; and so, in general, he isn't frightened. The sole thought in my mind was that if anything went wrong those two thousand Burmans would see me pursued, caught, trampled on and reduced to a grinning corpse like that Indian up the hill. And if that happened it was quite probable that some of them would laugh. That would never do. There was only one alternative. I shoved the cartridges into the magazine and lay down on the road to get a better aim.

The crowd grew very still, and a deep, low, happy sigh, as of people who see the theatre curtain go up at last, breathed from innumerable throats. They were going to have their bit of fun after all. The rifle was a beautiful German thing with cross-hair sights. I did not then know that in shooting an elephant one should shoot to cut an imaginary bar running from ear-hole to ear-hole. I ought therefore, as the elephant was sideways on, to have aimed straight at his ear-hole; actually I aimed several inches in front of this, thinking the brain would be further forward.

When I pulled the trigger I did not hear the bang or feel the kick—one never does when a shot goes home—but I heard the devilish roar of glee that went up from the crowd. In that instant, in too short a time, one would have thought, even for the bullet to get there, a mysterious, terrible change had come over the elephant. He neither stirred nor fell, but every line of his body had altered. He looked suddenly stricken, shrunken, immensely old, as though the frightful impact of the bullet had paralysed him without knocking him down. At last, after what seemed a long time—it might have been five seconds, I dare say—he sagged flabbily to his knees. His mouth slobbered. An enormous senility seemed to have settled upon him. One could have imagined him thousands of years old. I fired again into the same spot. At the second shot he did not collapse but climbed with desperate slowness to his feet and stood weakly upright, with legs sagging and head drooping. I fired a third time. That was the shot that did for him. You could see the agony of it jolt his whole body and knock the last remnant of strength from his legs. But in falling he seemed for a moment to rise, for as his hind legs collapsed beneath him he seemed to tower upwards like a huge rock toppling, his trunk reaching skyward like a tree. He trumpeted, for the first and only time. And then down he came, his belly towards me, with a crash that seemed to shake the ground even where I lay.

I got up. The Burmans were already racing past me across the mud. It was obvious that the elephant would never rise again, but he was not dead. He was breathing very rhythmically with long rattling gasps, his great mound of a side painfully rising and falling. His mouth was wide open—I could see far down into caverns of pale pink throat. I waited a long time for him to die, but his breathing did not weaken. Finally I fired my two remaining shots into the spot where I thought his heart must be. The thick blood welled out of him like red velvet, but still he did not die. His body did not even jerk when the shots hit him, the tortured breathing continued without a pause. He was dying, very slowly and in great agony, but in some world remote from me where not even a bullet could damage him further. I felt that I had got to put an end to that dreadful noise. It seemed dreadful to see the great beast lying there, powerless to move and yet powerless to die, and not even to be able to finish him. I sent back for my small rifle and poured shot after shot into his heart and down his throat. They seemed to make no impression. The tortured gasps continued as steadily as the ticking of a clock.

In the end I could not stand it any longer and went away. I heard later that it took him half an hour to die. Burmans were arriving with dahs and baskets even before I left, and I was told they had stripped his body almost to the bones by the afternoon.

Afterwards, of course, there were endless discussions about the shooting of the elephant. The owner was furious, but he was only an Indian and could do nothing. Besides, legally I had done the right thing, for a mad elephant has to be killed, like a mad dog, if its owner fails to control it. Among the Europeans opinion was divided. The older men said I was right, the younger men said it was a damn shame to shoot an elephant for killing a coolie, because an elephant was worth more than any damn Coringhee coolie. And afterwards I was very glad that the coolie had been killed; it put me legally in the right and it gave me a sufficient pretext for shooting the elephant. I often wondered whether any of the others grasped that I had done it solely to avoid looking a fool.

Topics for Reading and Writing

1. Although he works for the British colonizers—as a member of the police, no less—in this essay Orwell tells us that "I had made up my mind that imperialism was an evil thing" and "I was all for the Burmese and all against their oppressors, the British." What does Orwell mean by "imperialism?" What are the structures of imperialism alluded to in this essay? How does Orwell's place in the colonial enterprise complicate or compromise his opposition to colonialism, and how does his opinion change as a result of the events narrated in this essay?

2. How does Orwell construct his own authority in this essay? How does the personal voice he uses undermine or strengthen his points about the larger issues he wants to examine?

3. What does Orwell do, rhetorically, with the figure of the elephant? If he uses it as a symbol or a metonym, what does it represent? Does its meaning change over the course of the essay?

Richard Rodriguez (b. 1944) is one of contemporary America's foremost practitioners of the personal essay, and continues to work in this vein in his most recent book, Days of Obligation: An Argument with my Mexican Father, *as well as in his short spoken-word pieces for PBS television's nightly*

Richard Rodriguez
"Mr. Secrets" from
Hunger of Memory

I am writing about those very things my mother has asked me not to reveal. Shortly after I published my first autobiographical essay seven years ago, my mother wrote me a letter pleading with me never again to write about our family

NewsHour *(for which he won a Peabody Award in 1997). His "intellectual autobiography"* Hunger of Memory *(1982), from which this excerpt is taken, explores Rodriguez's experiences as a child of working-class Mexican immigrants. Rodriguez excelled in school, eventually going on to earn a Ph.D., and throughout his childhood he lived partially in the world of his parents and their culture and partially in the world of high-achieving, promising young students like himself. In "Mr. Secrets," Rodriguez explores numerous questions about the relationship of private and public writing, about a writer's responsibility to his craft and his responsibility to his family, and about the ethical questions of whether a writer can truly give voice to others.*

life. 'Write about something else in the future. Our family life is private.' And besides: 'Why do you need to tell the *gringos* about how "divided" you feel from the family?'

I sit at my desk now, surrounded by versions of paragraphs and pages of this book, considering that question.

When I decided to compose this intellectual autobiography, a New York editor told me that I would embark on a lonely journey. Over the noise of voices and dishes in an East Side restaurant, he said, 'There will be times when you will think the entire world has forgotten you. Some mornings you will yearn for a phone call or a letter to assure you that you still are connected to the world.' There *have* been mornings when I've dreaded the isolation this writing requires. Mornings spent listless in silence and in fear of confronting the blank sheet of paper. There have been times I've rushed away from my papers to answer the phone; gladly gotten up from my chair, hearing the mailman outside. Times I have been frustrated by the slowness of words, the way even a single paragraph never seemed done.

1

It is to those whom my mother refers to as the *gringos* that I write. The *gringos*. The expression reminds me that she and my father have not followed their children all the way down the path to full Americanization. They were changed—became more easy in public, less withdrawn and uncertain—by the public success of their children. But something remained unchanged in their lives. With excessive care they continue today to note the difference between private and public life. And their private society remains only their family. No matter how friendly they are in public, no matter how firm their smiles, my parents never forget when they are in public. My mother must use a high-pitched tone of voice when she addresses people who are not relatives. It is a tone of voice I have all my life heard her use away from the house. Coming home from grammar school with new friends, I would hear it, its reminder: My new intimates were strangers to her. Like my sisters and brother, over the years, I've grown used to hearing that voice. Expected to hear it. Though I suspect that voice has played deep in my soul, sounding a lyre, to recall my 'betrayal,' my movement away from our family's intimate past. It is the voice I hear even now when my mother addresses her son- or daughter-in-law. (They remain public people to her.) She speaks to them, sounding the way she does when talking over the fence to a neighbor.

It was, in fact, the lady next door to my parents—a librarian who first mentioned seeing my essay seven years ago. My mother was embarrassed because she hadn't any idea what the lady was talking about. But she had heard enough to go to a library with my father to find the article. They read what I wrote. And then she wrote her letter.

It is addressed to me in Spanish, but the body of the letter is in English. Almost mechanically she speaks of her pride at the start. ('Your dad and I are very proud of the brilliant manner you have to express yourself.') Then the matter of most concern comes to the fore. 'Your dad and I have only one objection to what you write. You say too much about the family . . . Why do you have to do that? . . . Why do you need to tell the *gringos?* . . . Why do you think we're so separated as a family? Do you really think this, Richard?'

A new paragraph changes the tone. Soft, maternal. Worried for me she adds, 'Do not punish yourself for having to give up our culture in order to "make it" as you say. Think of all the wonderful achievements you have obtained. You should be proud. Learn Spanish better. Practice it with your dad and me. Don't worry so much. Don't get the idea that I am mad at you either.

'Just keep one thing in mind. Writing is one thing, the family is another. I don't want *tus hermanos* hurt by your writings. And what do you think the cousins will say when they read where you talk about how the aunts were maids? Especially I don't want the *gringos* knowing about our private affairs. Why should they? Please give this some thought. Please write about something else in the future. Do me this favor.'

Please.

To the adult I am today, my mother needs to say what she would never have needed to say to her child: the boy who faithfully kept family secrets. When my fourth-grade teacher made our class write a paper about a typical evening at home, it never occurred to me actually to do so. 'Describe what you do with your family,' she told us. And automatically I produced a fictionalized account. I wrote that I had six brothers and sisters; I described watching my mother get dressed up in a red-sequined dress before she went with my father to a party; I even related how the imaginary baby sitter ('a high school student') taught my brother and sisters and me to make popcorn and how, later, I fell asleep before my parents returned. The nun who read what I wrote would have known that what I had written was completely imagined. But she never said anything about my contrivance. And I never expected her to either. I never thought she *really* wanted me to write about my family life. In any case, I would have been unable to do so.

I was very much the son of parents who regarded the most innocuous piece of information about the family to be secret. Although I had, by that time, grown easy in public, I felt that my family life was strictly private, not to be revealed to unfamiliar ears or eyes. Around the age of ten, I was held by surprise listening to my best friend tell me one day that he 'hated' his father. In a furious whisper he said that when he attempted to kiss his father before going to bed, his father had laughed: 'Don't you think you're getting too old for that sort of thing, son?' I was intrigued not so much by the incident as by the fact that the boy would relate it to *me*.

In those years I was exposed to the sliding-glass-door informality of middle-class California family life. Ringing the doorbell of a friend's house, I would hear someone inside yell out, 'Come on in, Richie; door's not locked.' And in I would go to discover my friend's family undisturbed by my presence. The father was in the kitchen in his underwear. The mother was in her bathrobe. Voices gathered in familiarity. A parent scolded a child in front of me; voices quarreled, then laughed; the mother told me something about her son after he had stepped out of the room and she was sure he couldn't overhear; the father would speak to his children and to me in the same tone of voice. I was one of the family, the parents of several good friends would assure me. (Richie.)

My mother sometimes invited my grammar school friends to stay for dinner or even to stay overnight. But my parents never treated such visitors as part of the family, never told them they were. When a school friend ate at our table, my father spoke less than usual. (Stray, distant words.) My mother was careful to use her 'visitor's voice.' Sometimes, listening to her, I would feel annoyed because she wouldn't be more herself. Sometimes I'd feel embarrassed that I couldn't give to a friend at my house what I freely accepted at his.

I remained, nevertheless, my parents' child. At school, in sixth grade, my teacher suggested that I start keeping a diary. ('You should write down your personal experiences and reflections.') But I shied away from the idea. It was the one suggestion that the scholarship boy couldn't follow. I would not have wanted to write about the minor daily events of my life; I would never have been able to write about what most deeply, daily, concerned me during those years: I was growing away from my parents. Even if I could have been certain that no one would find my diary, even if I could have destroyed each page after I had written it, I would have felt uncomfortable writing about my home life. There seemed to me something intrinsically public about written words.

Writing, at any rate, was a skill I didn't regard highly. It was a grammar school skill I acquired with comparative ease. I do not remember struggling to write the way I struggled to learn how to read. The nuns would praise student papers for being neat—the handwritten letters easy for others to read; they promised that my writing style would improve as I read more and more. But that wasn't the reason I became a reader. Reading was for me the key to 'knowledge'; I swallowed facts and dates and names and themes. Writing, by contrast, was an activity I thought of as a kind of report, evidence of learning. I wrote down what I heard teachers say. I wrote down things from my books. I wrote down all I knew when I was examined at the end of the school year. Writing was performed after the fact; it was not the exciting experience of learning itself. In eighth grade I read several hundred books, the titles of which I still can recall. But I cannot remember a single essay I wrote. I only remember that the most frequent kind of essay I wrote was the book report.

In high school there were more 'creative' writing assignments. English teachers assigned the composition of short stories and poems. One sophomore story I wrote was a romance set in the Civil War South. I remember that it earned me a good enough grade, but my teacher suggested with quiet tact that next time I try writing about 'something you know more about—something closer to home.' Home ? I wrote a short story about an old man who lived all by himself in a house down the block. That was as close as my writing ever got to my house. Still, I won prizes. When teachers suggested I contribute articles to the school literary magazine, I did so. And when I was asked to join the school newspaper, I said yes. I did not feel any great pride in my writings, however. (My mother was the one who collected my prize-winning essays in a box she kept in her closet.) Though I remember seeing my by-line in print for the first time, and dwelling on the printing press letters with fascination: RICHARD RODRIGUEZ. The letters furnished evidence of a vast public identity writing made possible.

When I was a freshman in college, I began typing all my assignments. My writing speed decreased. Writing became a struggle. In high school I had been able to handwrite ten- and twenty-page papers in little more than an hour—and I never revised what I wrote. A college essay took me several nights to prepare. Suddenly everything I wrote seemed in need of revision. I became a self-conscious writer. A stylist. The change, I suspect, was the result of seeing my words ordered by the even, impersonal, anonymous typewriter print. As arranged by a machine, the words that I typed no longer seemed mine. I was able to see them with a new appreciation for how my reader would see them.

From grammar school to graduate school I could always name my reader. I wrote for my teacher. I could consult him or her before writing, and after. I suppose that I knew other readers could make sense of what I wrote—that, therefore, I addressed a general reader. But I didn't think very much about it. Only toward the end of my schooling and only because political issues pressed upon me did I write, and have published in magazines, essays intended for readers I never expected to meet. Now I am struck by the opportunity. I write today for a reader who exists in my mind only phantasmagorically. Someone with a face erased; someone of no particular race or sex or age or weather. A gray presence. Unknown, unfamiliar. All that I know about him is that he has had a long education and that his society, like mine, is often public *(un gringo)*.

2

I write very slowly because I write under the obligation to make myself clear to someone who knows nothing about me. It is a lonely adventure. Each morning I make my way along a narrowing precipice of written words. I hear an echoing voice—my own resembling another's. Silent! The reader's voice silently trails every word I put down. I reread my words, and again it is the reader's voice I hear in my mind, sounding my prose.

When I wrote my first autobiographical essay, it was no coincidence that, from the first page, I expected to publish what I wrote. I didn't consciously determine the issue. Somehow I knew, however, that my words were meant for a public reader. Only because of that reader did the words come to the page. The reader became my excuse, my reason for writing.

It had taken me a long time to come to this address. There are remarkable children who very early are able to write publicly about their personal lives. Some children confide to a diary those things—like the first shuddering of sexual desire—too private to tell a parent or brother. The youthful writer addresses a stranger, the Other, with 'Dear Diary' and tries to give public expression to what is intensely, privately felt. In so doing, he attempts to evade the guilt of repression. And the embarrassment of solitary feeling. For by rendering feelings in words that a stranger can understand—words that belong to the public, this Other—the young diarist no longer need feel all alone or eccentric. His feelings are capable of public intelligibility. In turn, the act of revelation helps the writer better understand his own feelings. Such is the benefit of language: By finding public words to describe one's feelings, one can describe oneself to oneself. One names what was previously only darkly felt.

I have come to think of myself as engaged in writing graffiti. Encouraged by physical isolation to reveal what is most personal; determined at the same time to have my words seen by strangers. I have come to understand better why works of literature—while never intimate, never individually addressed to the reader—are so often among the most personal statements we hear in our lives. Writing, I have come to value written words as never before. One can use *spoken* words to reveal one's personal self to strangers. But *written* words heighten the feeling of privacy. They permit the most thorough and careful exploration. (In the silent room, I prey upon that which is most private. Behind the closed door, I am least reticent about giving those memories expression.) The writer is freed from the obligation of finding an auditor in public. (As I use words that some-one far from home can understand, I create my listener. I imagine her listening.)

My teachers gave me a great deal more than I knew when they taught me to write public English. I was unable then to use the skill for deeply personal pur-poses. I insisted upon writing impersonal essays. And I wrote always with a spe-cific reader in mind. Nevertheless, the skill of public writing was gradually developed by the many classroom papers I had to compose. Today I *can* address an anonymous reader. And this seems to me important to say. Somehow the incli-nation to write about my private life in public is related to the ability to do so. It is not enough to say that my mother and father do not want to write their autobi-ographies. It needs also to be said that they are unable to write to a public reader. They lack the skill. Though both of them can write in Spanish and English, they write in a hesitant manner. Their syntax is uncertain. Their vocabulary limited. They write well enough to communicate 'news' to relatives in letters. And they can handle written transactions in institutional America. But the man who sits in his chair so many hours, and the woman at the ironing board—'keeping busy because I don't want to get old'—will never be able to believe that any description of their personal lives could be understood by a stranger far from home.

3

When my mother mentioned seeing my article seven years ago, she *wrote* to me. And I responded to her letter with one of my own. (I wrote: 'I am sorry that my article bothered you . . . I had not meant to hurt . . . I think, however, that edu-cation has divided the family . . . That is something which happens in most families, though it is rarely discussed . . . I had meant to praise what I have lost . . . I continue to love you both very much.') I wrote to my mother because it would have been too difficult, too painful to hear her voice on the phone. Too unmanageable a confrontation of voices. The impersonality of the written word made it the easiest means of exchange. The remarkable thing is that nothing has been spoken about this matter by either of us in the years intervening. I know my mother suspects that I continue to write about the family. She knows that I spend months at a time 'writing,' but she does not press me for information. (Mr. Secrets.) She does not protest.

The first time I saw my mother after she had received my letter, she came with my father to lunch. I opened the door to find her smiling slightly. In an instant I tried to gather her mood. (She looked as nervous and shy as I must have seemed.) We embraced. And she said that my father was looking for a place to park the car. She came into my apartment and asked what we were having for lunch. Slowly, our voices reverted to tones we normally sound with each other. (Nothing was said of my article.) I think my mother sensed that afternoon that the person whose essay she saw in a national magazine was a person unfamiliar to her, some Other. The public person—the writer, Richard Rodriguez—would remain distant and untouchable. She never would hear his public voice across a dining room table. And that afternoon she seemed to accept the idea, granted me the right, the freedom so crucial to adulthood, to become a person very different in public from the person I am at home.

Intimates are not always so generous. One close friend calls to tell me she has read an essay of mine. 'All that Spanish angst,' she laughs. 'It's not really you.' Only someone very close would be tempted to say such a thing—only a person who knows who I am. From such an intimate one must sometimes escape to the company of strangers, to the liberation of the city, in order to form new versions of oneself.

In the company of strangers now, I do not reveal the person I am among intimates. My brother and sisters recognize a different person, not the Richard Rodriguez in this book. I hope, when they read this, they will continue to trust the person they have known me to be. But I hope too that, like our mother, they will understand why it is that the voice I sound here I have never sounded to them. All those faraway childhood mornings in Sacramento, walking together to school, we talked but never mentioned a thing about what concerned us so much: the great event of our schooling, the change it forced on our lives. Years passed. Silence grew thicker, less penetrable. We grew older without ever speaking to each other about any of it. Intimacy grooved our voices in familiar notes; familiarity defined the limits of what could be said. Until we became adults. And now we see each other most years at noisy family gatherings where there is no place to stop the conversation, no right moment to turn the heads of listeners, no way to essay this, my voice.

Topics for Reading and Writing

1. One of the topics of this essay is the essential subject of this first chapter: the relationship between private writing and a public audience. "My reasons for writing," Rodriguez says, "will be revealed . . . to public readers I expect never to meet." Why does Rodriguez write this for a public audience? What is the nature of the interplay between public and private in this essay?

2. Closely related to this is the notion of secrets. Rodriguez's early efforts at writing were, he makes clear, exercises in keeping secrets: he makes up lies about what happens in his family in order to keep hidden their real lives. The act of writing *Hunger of Memory,* we presume, is an implicit repudiation of this need to keep secrets. How does Rodriguez manage the precarious balance between public writing and secret-keeping?

3. What are the ethical problems raised by Rodriguez's project? Does he betray, in any way, his family's trust by rejecting their need to keep the private private? Or is his primary ethical responsibility to himself?

Sandra Tsing Loh, *born in 1961 to a German mother and a Chinese father, is a writer and performance artist based in Los Angeles—or specifically, the vast suburban tracts of the city's San Fernando Valley. Her writings include* Depth Takes a Holiday; If You Lived Here, You'd Be Home by Now; *and the stage show* Aliens in America. *"Industry Mixer" is taken from her memoir* A Year in Van Nuys, *a humorous look at life in America's archetypal suburb—a suburb whose actual multiracial, multicultural, multilingual population puts the lie to its* Brady Bunch *image. In this excerpt, Loh examines one of the rituals of Los Angeles: the entertainment industry party, a social gathering whose real purpose is to facilitate the desperate, relentless self-promoting and networking in which struggling writers and actors and performers must constantly engage.*

Loh's essay is a great example of the humorous personal anecdote that actually conveys much of the nervousness and insecurity felt by the writer. American writers from Mark Twain to Woody Allen have made fun of themselves and of the discomfort that comes when they are confronted by the unfamiliar or the intimidating; Loh continues in this tradition. As you read this, think about strategies for finding humor in excruciating experiences in your own life. How can you convey the stomach-wrenching anxiety you were feeling at the time while still making an audience laugh?

Sandra Tsing Loh
"Industry Mixer" from
A Year in Van Nuys

Cosmopolitan #1

The Miracle of Me stands, triumphant, in an elegant bistro, just off Sunset and La Cienega. I stand, like a Roman god, at the sparkling center of the world. Our glassed-in atrium is fringed by the victory decorations native to the area—small potted ficuses, twinkly white lights, peach tablecloths, and sparkling crystal goblets stuffed with upward-spuming napkins delicately curled as antique roses.

In my right hand, I hold a ruby-red Cosmopolitan in an icy conical glass so big if inverted it could be used as a hat for the Tin Woodman. I take a sip. So sweet. So tart. So perfect.

My new boss, Chris Freund of Fox, is talking. He is a friendly, unassuming, slightly balding man in khaki pants, flanked by a royal bevy of youthful assistants.

Ours is not like a boss/employee relationship at all.

Chris Freund chats in a warm, unguarded way about how he misses New York. "In fact, Sandra, I was surprised to learn that you *weren't* from New York. Your voice is so hip, urban, edgy, and irreverent."

"Thank you," I say. A canapé tray twirls by. Displayed are tiny, plump packages of lamb and feta. ("Eat!" Chris Freund urges me paternally. "Eat, eat, eat!" "What with the new show, I wouldn't want to be putting on *weight* at this point," I joke back. "Oh, don't be ridiculous," he murmurs, patting my hand. "You look absolutely fine!")

From the next room come sounds of some sort of jazz combo warming up. In the warm glow of the Cosmopolitan, Chris Freund's words continue to float over me, to wash over me, to bathe me.

"As we begin the development process," he says, "I've just got a few quick ideas I'd like to run by you. But remember. It's your show. You're the boss. Feel free to say no."

"No?" I say broadly, feeling the alcohol charge me, burn through me like fire. "How about yes? Yes yes yes!"

He smiles, leans in.

"All right. I have this hilarious, I mean hilarious, young comic, she just killed at Toronto, who does this great monologue about the Safe Guy versus the Cool Guy. You know? It's the classic dilemma of a twenty-nine-year-old woman. . . . She's looking at turning thirty, she knows she should get married, but she's torn between settling for the Perfect Guy or taking a chance with the Fun Guy." Chris Freund is tickled by the memory. "What I love about

Kelly's premise, especially as regards to a series, is that while it's hilarious, and completely fresh, it's still very rooted in reality."

"Absolutely," I, the Goddess of Hip, Funny Neurosis, agree. Even though privately I'm thinking, Never in my life have I met anyone with this particular romantic dilemma. Most of the women I know are happy to be with *any* guy, any guy who will agree to some sort of regular, reasonably monogamous dating schedule. If the fellow's cocktail of antidepressants aren't generating actual impotence, so much the better. But not to worry. I'm the boss. I can say no. I select another feta-and-lamb thing. And a mini-toast, with shrimp.

"I have another kid," Chris continues, "very hot, did some scripts last season for *Just Shoot Me.* Randy has this hilarious pilot idea about a twenty-five-year-old cartoonist in Chicago, like a John Cusack type but a little younger, who has a great career going but his love life is a wreck. Why? Because he just can't commit. It's called *Guy Bachelor* and it's a scream. You'd love it. It's just your sense of humor. Very hip and edgy. Becky?" He turns to his assistant. "Be sure to messenger over—"

"Please do," I say.

Chris chuckles and adds, "Of course, there's a waitress who lives in Guy's building, Katie McNally, who's feisty, funny, and, unlike Guy, completely rooted in reality. Katie and Guy have this incredible sexual chemistry. Every time they're together sparks fly, but they can't help always being at each other's throats—"

As he continues to speak, I can't help thinking that again, in life, I have seen only the opposite. Two lonely, unattractive, *non-feisty* people who meet through Great Expectations or online, both desperate to have a relationship. They get along, their cats get along, but the sex itself is so disappointing that the two people spend most of their evenings sitting on opposite sides of the bed in their sweat socks, crying.

Is *now* the time to bring this up? I wonder. Later?

Chris Freund is on to a new pair of Talent.

"We've signed two girls up who we think would be terrific in a sitcom. They were teen Doublemint Twins, and all but in person, this is the key, they're absolutely down to earth. Because of that, I don't want this series to be too 'wacky' or too broad. Rather, I think the focus should be on their relationship to each other, to explore rich themes of friendship, and sisterhood. Let's pull the 'glamour' curtain back. Let's show these girls as not just models, but real people. Let's ask the question 'What's it like to be twenty-two years old, blond, gorgeous . . . identical twins?'"

Cosmopolitan #2

Chris Freund is still talking. The warmth of his voice is still utterly reassuring. But even swaddled cozily as I am in my Swingy Hair and my Yawp and my great, vast Victory Pelt, all at once, I feel it. The slightest little . . . Icy Stab.

I mean, yes, I'm having fun at this party, but I can't stop asking myself, Why is Chris Freund telling me all these stories? Why should I be concerned about all these feisty twenty-three-year-olds and their sexual chemistry and down-to-earth reality when what we really should be talking about is a sitcom set in the San Fernando Valley about ME! ME ME ME!

"It's just . . ." I suddenly find my voice. I try to match his casual, intimate tone. "Regarding those . . . Twins. Being in my sitcom? I'm just not sure twenty-two-year-old . . . models . . . know what it is . . . to have, you know . . ." I throw my arm wide for my patented Jo Anne Worley-esque kicker: "Eye Bags!"

"To have what?" Chris asks, putting a hand on my arm, smiling.

"Eye Bags!" I repeat, taking another sip of my Cosmopolitan. "Eye Bags. You know. That's my trademark. I'm all about Eye Bags."

"You are not!" he retorts, much too quickly. "What Eye Bags? I don't see any! You're a lovely, lovely person, Sandra. Don't put yourself down."

"Well, okay," I say . . . but like needles of hail, the little Icy Stabs are now coming thicker and faster. Does Chris Freund not know about my Eye Bags? Does Chris Freund not know about *the* Eye Bags? About their Hip, Urban, Irreverent appeal? Didn't Jennifer the VP brief him *about* the comedy "engine" (spokes exploding outward) called SANDRA? Has he not been updated re: the SANDRA project? Has he not been *pitched* . . . that thing . . . called SANDRA?

Apparently not, because for the past twenty minutes, we've been doing nothing but talking about that gal Kelly from Toronto, that kid Guy from *Just Shoot Me*, the Twins. . . .

I have this sudden realization that, like some mythical Greek figure, Chris Freund is a man who goes from meeting to meeting to meeting retelling the story he has most recently heard. But if so, I think quickly, cannily, maybe there's another hapless comedic entity coming up after *me*. And therefore, what I need to do now, in these precious few minutes, is to insert Myself and *My* Stories . . . into the Chris Freund chain. I need to get the comedic possibilities of SANDRA to take hold somewhere in his brain, like a virus, so he can pitch the wonder of ME at his next meeting. "At Fox, you know what we like to say-Everyone Loves SANDRA!" he'll enthuse. "Do you know SANDRA? She's the one with the Koo Koo Roo Chicken! The Miracle Bra! The Eye Bags!"

Loudly—and somewhat drunkenly—rose napkins and crystal goblets and shiny silverware spinning around me like a roulette wheel, I start to pitch.

"It's like, why do we envy Marilu Henner's skin for looking so smooth and featureless?" I burst out. "What if the opposite were true—i.e., what if what was admired in L.A. was the ability to look really HAGGARD? What a sea of change that would be in our town. We'd greet each other at lunch with: 'You're looking wonderfully HAGGARD!' Or, 'She's become so HAGGARD at 49, waiters flock around her like bees to honey.' Or, 'Your eyebrows are so woolly, you should be on the cover of *Vogue!*' Or, 'How do I get to look this FABU-LOUS? Coffee, vodka, cigarettes, and, of course, plenty of sun!' Then again, I can't take ALL the credit. I have to admit, some of it is genetic. By the time my Dad turned twenty-eight he had eyebags like Billy Joel."

But this go-round, it all fails to make sense. And instead of a slave-ring of linen jackets heaving forward and back, forward and back, in my own computer-generated Roman forum, Chris Freund is standing stiffly and wearing what I'd call an . . . Unhappy Face. It's this vague frown that says: "I'm not entirely certain, but I believe . . . you have turned my kidneys to ice."

"Preparation H," I plow on sloppily, trying not to slur my words. "It's like the Apocalypse! I mean, it's like forget the Miracle Bra, how about the Four Horses of the Apocalypse Bra? The Apocalypse Bra. Or you might say, 'Give me a kiss! I just turned forty, saw my own reflection, and decided: I'm going to change my name to Merle T. HAGGARD!' 'Cause you look so . . . HAGGARD—"

"What?" he queries, polite.

Cosmopolitan #3

Chris Freund has very much enjoyed our meeting, but now he has to go see someone named Jeffrey. Also someone named Skip. And Trish.

I have been left alone with the assistants, a veritable sea of Oliver Peoples eyewear and spiked hair and chunky black platform shoes.

And more and more faces and mouths are talking around me, storytelling, narrating, describing, pitching. And as they are, the ages of the vibrant characters limbo-dancing through the *Manhattan co-op! Law firm in L.A.! Sports bar in Chicago!* keep skinching lower and lower and lower. No one in this room utters any words that begin with "thirty." No. We started the evening at twenty-nine, moved down to twenty-five, for a while we were at twenty-two, and now I'm hearing, "High school! They're like the hippest smartest kids in high school! And the female lead is, like, eleven! You know, that awkward age where you know you should settle down with a steady boyfriend, but you can't decide whether to settle for the really Nice Guy or the really Fun Guy!"

Who do I know who's *eleven*? I think. Somebody's niece who lives in Boston.

Indeed, I reflect sadly, accidentally sloshing some Cosmopolitan on my wrist and licking it off (no one seems to care—they're all busy pitching my ear off). Generally I find that people are a lot older in Life than they are in Television and the Movies. A parallel, invisible race—that's the rest of *us*. Padding about in our sweatpants, gray-faced, wanly pushing our carts through the grocery store of Life, eating Lay's potato chips right out of the bag as, unlike our bright, cheerful TV counterparts, we just keep getting older and older and older, year by year by year.

Not that real people don't have *similar* problems to ones characters have on TV. Real people, *too,* can't get a date, they, *too,* have hilariously humiliating jobs, but instead of being twenty-four, they're like forty-four. "I can't get a date and I'm forty-four!" I mean, look at Gwyneth (from Accounting)! She's having more sex than any other living human being and she's fifty-three! Fifty-three!

Cosmopolitan #4

Denise Francis, media consultant from Amelia.com, can't stop talking about how great the party is going, how great the deal is going, how great *we* are going. Denise and I sit together on a floral-patterned window bench. I notice, with a wave of weariness, that her thigh, in its black satin cigarette pant, is about half the size of mine.

"The great thing about Fox," she says, trembling with excitement, as though she is on speed. "The great thing about Chris Freund is that he is about development. He is about *supporting* Talent, about giving that Talent everything it needs, every step of the way. He says he's in this for the long haul."

The band in the next room has started to play. It's swing music, a festive melange of horns, and drums, and bass, and a laughing male singer crooning, "Jump and Jivin'! Jump and Jivin'!" And for the first time this evening, I feel a sudden familiarity, an ease, an unexpected lift of happiness from some long-forgotten place. "Jump and Jivin'"? I love that song! I think. I *love* it! Where do I know that song from?

And then I realize: *It's that Gap commercial!* I'm feeling nostalgic for *the good times I never had,* in that fictional *commercial,* swing-dancing with a bunch of laughing twenty-five-year-olds in Gap pants—aka pants, in reality, that I can't even get *into.* Nostalgia? What nostalgia? The only *actual* life memory Gap has given me is panicking in a Gap dressing room, realizing the only pants in the store that'll pull up over my hips are size REVERSE FIT. You know, for that "rare" woman whose butt is *bigger* than her waist—us *freaks!*

To my right side, Andrea from Casting is busy reassuring Denise and me about . . . some problem I was hitherto unaware of.

"I know what it seems like, reading the trades," Andrea is saying. "It seems like everywhere you look, twenty-four-year-old stand-up comics with five minutes of material—five minutes max—are being given million-dollar deals!"

To my left side, Mark from New Talent Development is agreeing with her. "That's not what we do," he says. "What *we* do is take Hip, Edgy, Irreverent voices and we *grow* them."

"As long as they're FRESH and HIP and YOUNG—"

"And YOUNG and HIP and FRESH—"

What is this with these people and the word *fresh?* I think hysterically. The more they repeat that dreaded phrase, "Fresh YOUNG Talent," the more and more I feel like Haggard OLD Talent. . . .

And the more I feel like Haggard OLD Talent (age thirty-six—I should be shot!), the more this bitterness comes vomiting up, like raw sewage, toward all the FRESH YOUNG TALENTS at age twenty-four with their million-dollar deals and their HIPNESS and their FRESHNESS—

But look. Andrea's hand is on my right arm. Mark's hand is on my left. Every so often, they squeeze me, they pat me, loving, possessive. . . .

Which gives me another idea.

And that is . . .

Who's to *say* I'm not the . . . FRESH YOUNG TALENT they're talking about? Yes, I just turned thirty-six, but (thanks to Denise Francis's brilliant coaching) *Fox* doesn't know that. Indeed, how do they know I'm not, rather than an extremely well-rested (due to the miracle of the sleep mask) thirty-six-year-old, a FRESH (if somewhat tired) YOUNG TALENT of, say, twenty-eight—a twenty-eight-year-old who, hilariously, is a kind of insomniac? Because she's so neurotic . . . about her air miles!

How bad do my Eye Bags look today, anyway? Catching a pale, filmy reflection of myself in the glass, I feel like a yellowed—but wily old—cur. With mottled vampire teeth I can extend—or retract—at will. The debate racks me. Haggard or Fresh? Haggard or Fresh? As my executives speak, I continue to nod, unobstrusively . . . tilting my head over to the left, to catch less of the track lighting from above and more of the shadows of the potted dwarf (dwarf! I didn't notice that before—are they really *dwarf?*) ficuses, so the Eye Bags are a tad more . . . camouflaged. I relax my features into less of a rictus of desperate hilarity and more into an expression that is funny, and yet cheerful and winsome and . . . FRESH! FRESH FRESH FRESH FRESH FRESH!

"That Kelly from the Toronto Comedy Festival," Andrea is agreeing with Mark. "Fox is very high on her. I think she'd be great as the lead in Sandra's sitcom. She's like a young Meg Ryan."

And in that moment, any last vestige of Denial vaporizes, and I know.

That's what "You, you are a sitcom!" means. It means "You're such a hip, urban, edgy, irreverent *person,* you could write jokes for a hilarious sitcom based on *my* life starring the adorable Meg Ryan! (Except ten years younger)."

"Absolutely," I agree, tossing my head boldly. "A young Meg Ryan. Sure!"

Cosmplta&*@n #5

I stumble out onto the patio. Bracing myself with one arm, I look up into the cool night air. I consider the Bermuda triangle the small, foul dinghy called *Sandra* is capsized in, the Bermuda triangle that is Santa Monica, Doheny, and Robertson, three or four or five avenues of boutiques colliding in an illogical V that is less a regular, functional throughway than a kind of Eurotrash *bikini bottom* of an intersection, some little three-hundred-dollar thing a sixteen-year-old would just wear once and throw away . . .

And, looking up La Cienega, I see a flash of something large and white and frightening. It is a brightly lit-up billboard advertising a HEAD. This HEAD. The BIG . . . SCARY . . . PERPETUALLY LAUGHING HEAD that is . . . *THE KING OF QUEENS!* He *is* the king! He *is* the king! THE KING OF QUEENS is so massive and larval and so full of garish, explosive merriment— his teeth alone are like ten feet high—that I open my mouth in a silent scream!

I flash, at that moment, on *Fellini Satyricon,* where Rome is corrupt and foul and rotting and yet horsecarts keep rolling festively down boulevards with big god heads or, in the case of Fellini's *Amarcord,* big Mussolini heads, and I'm thinking instead of big Mussolini heads on La Cienega Boulevard this is what we have . . . THE KING OF QUEENS!

And just beyond, on the great illuminated stage of the next billboard, is Teri Hatcher. In *Cabaret.* "Teri Hatcher!" The name clangs through my head like a jingle ("Bu-u-u-uy Mennen!"). "Teri Hatcher. Te-ri . . . Hatcher!"

Why Teri Hatcher? I wonder, with a profound sense of tragedy. And why *Cabaret?*

I mean, in New York, *Cabaret* starred Tony Award-winning Natasha Richardson. In L.A.: *Teri Hatcher.* What happened there? Couldn't Natasha come do it out here? Was she not offered the booking? Did some linen-clad Beverly Hills agent say, "Oh no, forget Natasha Richardson. L.A.—that's Teri Hatcher country"?

"Te-ri . . . Hatcher!" Why is it every time I hear those syllables I feel like a kicked bunny, about to cry? Because—here you go! "Teri Hatcher" sounds like the name of *every mean girl* in junior high school, doesn't it? You begin with the kittenish, Southern California—sunny TERI (spelled T-E-R-I) . . . and then, just when you're struggling out of your too-tight bell-bottoms into your size-fourteen bathing suit, out from behind the girls' lockers comes . . . HATCHER!!!

Interesting fact: At *my* junior high school, Malibu Park, right here in the L.A. basin, the sizes of the swimsuits we wore for gym practice were color-coded. You had orange, the petites; green, the very slim; red, the struggling with puberty; and then beyond, in no-man's-land, was whale-calf blue. You'd pull this thing up over yourself, open your fleshy arms wide, and say: "Citizens of Malibu Park? You may now begin *stoning* me."

And looking into the window, holding my fifth Cosmopolitan, ring of purple around my lips, dark canyons under my eyes, I see quite clearly that I look one thousand years old. Literally one thousand. I am like this dug-up semi-Asiatic Ice Age man who is walking through the alien planet of La Cienega as if in a dream.

The door bangs open.

It is comedy VP Jennifer. Jennifer the Valley Dweller. Jennifer the Dunkin' Donuts schlepper. Jennifer the Satanic Monologist. She has a hip young man in tow. They've come out here for a smoke.

I look at her and think: I can't hear one more story. I am a wrung-out shell. I have not one more drop of lifeblood to give to the Comedy Slave Galley.

I turn to run. But it is too late. She sees me.

"Hey!" Jennifer says. "It's our favorite comedy writer!"

"Michael Harris," the young man says, leaning forward, putting his hand out. "And you are—?"

"Thirty-six!" I shriek.

"What?" he says, still smiling. Other development kids are arriving, these . . . these identical *stick puppets* in Oliver Peoples glasses and Chinesey tops and chunky black platform shoes. Their shadows skinny, against the scrim of Mexican paver tile. Mine wide.

"Let me say it again," I say to the growing crowd. "I'm thirty-six! Thirty-six! Thirty-six! Thirty-six!" It's like I've been struck with this chronological Tourette's syndrome. Every time I repeat the number, I get this kind of self-destructive thrill. I imagine, each time, all these little Bridges of Opportunity being bombed: Thirty-six! Thirty-six! Thirty-six! Or perhaps I'm more like a renegade Buddhist monk setting himself on fire in a public place, as a kind of protest/performance-art piece. He lights a match; the watching crowd gasps; flames engulf him: thirty-six!

"That's right, Michael," I declare. "I'm out of the game. I can't be hired for anything. I'm as good as dead."

"You don't ever have to say your age," Jennifer says. "Although it's true, over at the WB, they say they don't want any writers over twenty-five."

"But I *want* to say my age, *Jennifer!*" Oh my God, I think. The Id! Breaking forth from its beastie-box! It's out! **"Because I feel I *should* bomb these bridges, the ones to all that great . . . media and entertainment industry . . . *work* out there that is earmarked only for the Young and the . . . the . . . the fucking FRESH!**

"Because you know what? I can't do it anyway! At heart, I'm old, I'm haggard, and I'm angry. As a matter of fact, *get to know me!* I've been like this all my life! Even when I was twenty I couldn't get with the . . . the Youth Program." I wave my arms wildly. "Youth seemed to be this dank pit (with Coors banners fluttering above) into which body after body was flung! Being Young was all standing around for hours and hours at dorm parties that smelled like vomit and Flock of Seagulls thumping and pock-marked beer kegs dispiritedly spurting foam like drool!

"I mean, I *could* do what everyone else in this wretched town does— pretend I'm twenty-six so I can get my next job creating the propaganda that makes our Young People feel that there is no escape from fetid blasts from the poophole of Spuds MacKenzie—but you know what? I don't *want* to be a card-carrying employee of the drecky evil Youth Culture mega DeathStar Spelling Hasselhoff corporation. (Which I think is on Wilshire, isn't it? That big glass building?)"

I am literally screaming at them. Spittle is flying. God, it feels good!

"Because I am *not* full of pep! I am *not* a character America loves. There *is* no Sprite in me. I would rather eat cold beans from a can—very likely what I'll be doing—than apply my few remaining brain cells to some already green-lit twentysomething romantic comedy where Jennifer Aniston goes on a hilarious blind date and has a mistaken identity mishap with—WHO CARES?"

And now, grandly, I pull myself taller and *curse them all.* I notice, on the Mexican paver tile, that now, instead of being merely wide, my shadow is looming vast and black and cavernous. My voice is a deafening harpy screech. My pudgy yellow talon stabs at them.

"And kids, wait till you get to be my age! Then you'll see how as the years go by, those birthdays just come faster and faster and faster! I swear, I had three new birthdays in 1998 alone! And you'll see how, after age thirty, each new birthday hits one like an accusation. With its disastrously higher number, each new birthday is a reminder of something you did wrong. You forgot to do your 'Stay Young' exercises, to take your 'Stay Young' pills! Because of this negligence, you're a year older. You've failed *again.* It's like: 'My God—is there some kind of migrant work crew I could have hired to keep this thing from growing over? They could have come the same day as the gardener and the pool guy. . . .'

"So all right already! Okay? I'm sorry! I'm sorry I forgot to stay young! If I hadn't been so distracted by life and work and whatever else, I'm sure I'd be twenty-six today. *Just like all of you!* But remember this one thing, you guys. Tempus fugit for everybody. Leo DiCaprio or no, you and I are on the *Titanic,* and we are . . . fucking . . . going down together!"

Topics for Reading and Writing

1. Obviously, Loh's primary means for appealing to her audience is through self-deprecation and humor. What are the advantages of self-deprecation when one is trying to make an argument? What are some of the drawbacks or dangers of self-deprecation?

2. Loh divides this piece into sections that correspond to the number of Cosmopolitans (a cocktail) that she drinks at this party—by the fifth one, of course, she has trouble even making sense. How else might she have structured the piece? Can you imagine this piece rewritten as a serious personal essay, and if so, what might the structure look like?

3. At one point (in her fourth Cosmopolitan) Loh starts to feel as if she's in a wonderful group memory, only to realize that what she's remembering is really a Gap commercial. The disconnect between her reality (being a thirtysomething woman living in an unfashionable part of Los Angeles), the reality of the party (hip entertainment-industry people in their twenties), and the patent unreality of what these people create (scripts for *Just Shoot Me,* Gap commercials) is emphasized by her growing intoxication. Examine this theme a little more closely, trying to look clearly at the events that Loh blurs together with alcohol. It might even be interesting to compare the ideas of media unreality in this essay with your own understanding of the creation of an "unreal," sainted Martin Luther King, Jr.

Salam Pax
excerpt from weblog

During the invasion of Iraq in 2003, United States journalists had unprecedented access to the combat operations. "Embedded" in military units, reporters had the chance to see the war from the inside. Critics of this program charged that the "embedding" was simply a ploy to make reporters more sympathetic to the soldiers who protected them; moreover, if reporters actually lived with the soldiers, there would be more than enough stories there to keep the reporters from poking around outside the perimeter. What was lost, for the most part, was news from outside of the U.S. or British military's territory. Only a few reporters stayed in Baghdad, and they were closely monitored by the security forces of Saddam Hussein's regime. It was difficult to learn what the war was like for ordinary Iraqis.

One of the only voices talking about life behind the lines belonged to "Salam Pax,"

:: Friday, May 30, 2003 ::

I really need to get something out of my system.

I got an email. After throwing everything and the kitchen sink at me they ask:

"How are your parents doing?
Ah yes, your parents. Salam, people are wondering."

Actually they are doing very well, thank you. My father was invited to an informal dinner attended by Garner the second week he was in Baghdad; he also met some of Bodine's aides and has met some of Bremer's aides a couple of times too. Not to mention many of your top military people south of Baghdad.

Seriously, not joking there.

Let me make a suggestion. Do not assume, not even for a second, that because you read the blog you know who I am or who my parents are. And you are definitely not entitled to be disrespectful. Not everything that goes on in this house ends up on the blog, so please go play Agatha Christy somewhere else.

the pseudonym for a blogger based in Baghdad (available at www.dear_raed.blogspot.com). At first, nobody knew who "Pax" was, or even if he was a real person—his blog described what it was like to live in Baghdad as the bombs fell and the U.S. forces came through, but how was anyone to be sure that this wasn't written by someone in Nashville, or Kuwait City, or by a functionary of Hussein's secret police? "Pax's" dispatches told a vivid story of privation and hardship but the voice was one of a sophisticated, multilingual, educated, ironic observer. If this was a plant of the U.S. or Iraqi military, people quickly learned, it was a great one, designed to gain the sympathy of journalists and intellectuals. After the war ended, the journalist Peter Maass, writing in Slate.com, revealed that he had discovered that "Pax," who "is chubby and cherubic and hip and speaks beautiful English," was in fact his interpreter! In his article "How do I know Bagdad's famous blogger exists? He worked for me," Maass writes that . . . in early May, I agreed to hand over a fantastic interpreter I had been working with to a colleague who could offer him long-term employment, as I would be leaving the country at the end of the month. I needed a new interpreter to fill the gap for two weeks or so, and the colleague mentioned that he had just met a smart and friendly guy named Salam. I quickly traced Salam to the Sheraton Hotel. Salam—this is his real first name—was sitting in a chair in the lobby, reading Philip K. Dick's The Man in the High Castle. I knew, at that moment, that I would hire him. (http://slate.msn.com/id/2083847, posted June 2, 2003)

My mother, a sociologist who was very happy in pursuing her career at the ministry of education decided to give up that career when she had to choose between becoming Ba'ath party member and quitting her job, she became a housewife. My father, a very well accomplished economist made the same decision and decided to become a farmer instead.

You are being disrespectful to the people who have put the first copy of George Orwell's 1984 in my hands, a heavy read for a 14 year old with bad English. But that banned book started a process and gave me the impulse to look at the world I live in a different way.

go fling the rubbish at someone else.

Have I told you that my father agreed to act as the mediator in the surrendering process between a number of Iraqi government officials and the American administration here? He is a man with sound moral judgment and people listen to his advice. People at the American administration and many of the new political parties had asked him for consultation.

Did I tell you about the time when one of Bremer's aides asked him what the difference between a tribal sheikh and a mosque sheikh is? They send them thousands of miles to govern us here and then ask such questions.

Did I tell you about his unending optimism in what the Americans can achieve here if they were given time? He is so much less of a skeptic than I am, we had our shouty arguments a number of times since the appearance of the Americans on our theatre of events.

You see, there is a lot that I have not told you about, and I don't see an obligation to do so. You all hide behind your blog names and keep certain bits of your life private.

I think the things that were said in the email above and on other sites were out of line.

There is more

"It seems your writing is dedicated to proving two points, first, minimizing the American contribution to removing Saddam and then, proving what terrible things the US did to get rid of Saddam, so as to paint a picture that it wasn't worth it."

As to the first. There is no way to "minimize" the contribution of the USA in removing saddam. The USA waged a friggin' war, how could you "minimize" a war. I have said this before: If it weren't for the intervention of the US, Iraq would have seen saddam followed by his sons until the end of time. But excuse me if I didn't go out and throw flowers at the incoming missiles. As for the second point, I don't think anyone has the right to throw cluster bombs in civilian areas and then refuse to clean up the mess afterwards.

Anyway.

I don't really understand why among the 26 million Iraqis I have to explain everything clearly, are you watching the news? can't you see the spectrum of reactions people have to the American presence in Iraq?.

I was at an ORHA press conference the other day (got in with someone who *had* a press pass) the guy up there on the podium said in an answer to a question, that most probably the people who have had good encounters with the coalition forces were saying things are getting better and those who have had bad things happening to them were saying things are getting worse.

It is still too early to make any judgments, I don't feel that I have an obligation say all is rosy and well.

Iraq is not the black hole it used to be and there are a bazillion journalists here doing better than I can ever do, they have a press ID and they know how to deal with stuff.

As to the question "why are you not documenting saddam's crimes?" Don't you see that this is not the sort of thing that should be discussed lightly in a blog like this one. And what's with "documenting," me tiny helpless salam documenting things that were going on for 30 years? Sorry to blow your bubble, but all I can do is tell you what is going on in the streets and if you think journalists are doing a better job of that then maybe you should go read them. One day, like in Afghanistan, those journalists will get bored and go write about Syria or Iran; Iraq will be off your media radar. Out of sight, out of mind. Lucky you, you have that option. I have to live it.

25/3
10:05am (day5)

one mighty explosion at 12 midnight exactly the raid lasted for 10 minutes then nothing. We had and are still having horrible weather. Very strong winds, hope we don't get a sandstorm.

In the [oh-the-irony-of-it-all] section of my life I can add the unbelievable bad luck that when I wanted to watch a movie because I got sick of all the news, the only movie I had which I have not seen a 100 times is "the American President". No joke. A friend gave that video months ago, I never watched it. I did last night. The American "presidential palace" looks quite good. But Michael Douglas is a sad ass president.

No internet this morning, no internet last night. And we just had an explosion right now [12:21] no siren no nothing. Just one boom. And another.

You can hear the sound of the planes. Look this is what you hear the last two days when a huge explosion is coming. First the droning of what is, I think, a plane then one small boom, followed by a rolling rumble that gets louder and suddenly BOOM, and the plane again. I think this is a proper raid because I can still hear explosions. Laytah.

24/3

9:29pm (day4)

Tonight we didn't notice any news channel reporting anything from fairford about the B52s, but then again the bombardment hasn't stopped the whole day. Last night's bombardment was very different from the nights before. It wasn't only heavier but the sound of the bombs was different. The booms and bangs are much louder; you would hear one big bang and then followed by a number of these rumbles that would shake everything. And there are of course the series of deep dob-dob-dobs from the explosions farther away. anyway it is still early (it is 9:45pm) last night things got seriously going at 12, followed by bombardments at 3,4 and 6am each would last for 15 minutes. The air raid sirens signaled an attack around 12 and never sounded the all clear signal. Sleep is what you get between being woken up by the rumbles or the time you can take your eyes off the news. We hear the same news items over and over. But you can't stop yourself.

The air raid sirens are not really that dependable, when they don't sound the all clear after a whole hour of silence you get fidgety. The better alarm system is quite accidental. It has become a habit of the mosque muezzins (the prayer callers) to start chanting "allahu akbar—la ilaha ila allah" the moment one of them hears an explosion. The next muezzin starts the moment he hears another calling and so on. It spreads thru the city pretty fast, and soon you have all the mosques doing the "Takbir" for five minutes or so. Very eerie but works well to alert everybody.

Below you see one of the emails we got, in English, this is loosely translated the subject line is "critical info"

The world has united in a common cause. These countries have formed an alliance to remove the father of Qusay and his brutal regime. Qusay's father has tyrannized the sons of the Euphrates and exploited them for years and he has to be removed from power.

The coalition forces are not here to hurt you, but they are here to help you. For your safety the coalition forces have prepared a list of instructions to keep you and your families safe. We want you to realize that these instructions are to keep you safe, even if they are, maybe, not (appropriate) [*this is a bit difficult because even in Arabic I don't get exactly what they mean, but it sure got my attention, are they going to ask me to stand naked in the garden or something?*] we add that we don't want to hurt innocent people.

Please and for your safety stay away from potential targets, like TV and Radio stations. Avoid travel or work near oil fields. Don't drive your cars at night. Stay away from military buildings or areas used for storage of weapons. All the mentioned are possible targets. For your safety don't be near these buildings and areas.

For your safety stay away from coalition forces. Although they are here for not your harm [sic] they are trained to defend themselves and their equipment. Don't try to interfere in the operations of coalition forces. If you do these forces will not see you as civilians but as a threat and targets too.

Please for your safety stay away from the mentioned areas. Don't let your children play there. Please inform your family and neighbors of our message. Our aim is to remove he father of Qusay and his brutal regime.

Then they list the frequencies for "Information Radio". They even plan to transmit on FM. What immediately caught my attention is the use of "father of Qusay". We don't say "walid Qusay" in Iraqi-Arabic but use "abu Qusay" and he is usually referred to as "abu Uday", but then again Uday is obviously out of the game. No one sees him in meetings. Four of the emails came from a hotpop account, one from a Lycos and another from a yahoo accounts. I don't think they expect anyone to answer. But it is mighty interesting to see what happens if I write to one of them.

Was watching a report on Al-jazeera a while ago about Mosul and its preparations. The reporter interviewed someone from "fedayeen saddam" he said that he is in Mosul to "kill the Americans and kill anybody who does not fight the Americans", there in one short sentence you have the whole situation in Basra, and most probably many Iraqi cities, explained. Fear is deep and trust in the people-from-foreign is not high.

PS from Diana: before we concluded, I said, "Salam, I just want to say one thing." And I said, "Fuck Saddam Hussein!" as loud as I could w/o disturbing the neighbors. (And, by extension, an entire foreign policy edifice that supported the monster.) Now, I've got nothing personal against the guy, in fact, he strongly resembles my late, dear uncle Artie Feinberg (I tell you, he could be one of those doubles, except he's dead), but I just wanted to make a point. Which is: now we can say those things without fear of getting relatives or friends dragged off and killed. And Salam said, "Everybody on the street is saying this like a mantra, "Fuck Saddam, fuck Saddam, fuck Saddam. . .". Well maybe Salam didn't say the word "mantra" but you get the point, which is: we can't possibly understand what it's like to be Iraqi. It must be like being in a root cellar for 35 years, and now you are stumbling around in the light, blinking your eyes, wondering if what you see is real, or a dream. Note: Evil Boss Unit be tellin' lies. I didn't bug nobody. I sent him one email. And I apologized for that. Evil Boss Unit be a sexist who believes wimmin ought to be seen and not heard. We'll see about that in the new Iraq. We didn't do no liberatin' and pullin' down statues to be told, "get in the kitchen and fry those felafal balls, bitch." Get ready for a wild ride, Iraq.

Topics for Reading and Writing

1. How does Pax's blog demonstrate the potential of the blog format?

2. "Pax" is not a native speaker of English. How does this affect your reading of his blog? Is the blog a format that translates well between languages, or is it likely to remain primarily an English-language phenomenon?

3. "Pax's" story illustrates how quickly the Web can make someone into a minor celebrity. How, precisely, did Pax achieve this celebrity? What are some

other Internet-created celebrities? How has the Internet changed the process by which people obtain rapid renown?

The Writer at Work Exploring Writing About and for Yourself

When do you write about yourself? In e-mails, of course: "oye zoila want to go to starbucks tonight to study? no quiero 2B in dorm tonight. call me on my cell. ;-)" You probably also write about yourself in other similar forums such as text messages on your telephone, notes scribbled in class, or even profiles of yourself for online dating services. In more formal writing, though, you probably don't write much about yourself. The writing you have produced for school, especially in recent years, has been less about you and more about the outside world—about government, about novels, about psychology. It's not appropriate to make your report on *A Tale of Two Cities* focus on you. In fact, for this reason many high school teachers actually forbid their students from using "I" in formal writing.

This prohibition of the first person can seem very arbitrary and even nonsensical given many of the things that high school students read. *Catcher in the Rye,* Maya Angelou's *I Know Why the Caged Bird Sings,* essays by naturalists and scientists, and even works of history often use the first person—why is it wrong for students to do so? The short answer is that it's not. Using the first person is just fine in many kinds of writing and in many forums. The problem is that inexperienced writers generally haven't yet developed the ability to judge when the first person is appropriate, and when it's not. The "Style Toolbox" section of this chapter addresses the question of voice in greater detail, but in simplest terms the reason that students are generally discouraged from using the first person is that the first person calls attention to the writer and to that writer's authority, or lack thereof. Reading an essay about photosynthesis or the Smoot-Hawley Act written in the first person makes the reader consider the writer: who is this person? Why does this person have the authority or knowledge to talk about this subject? The first person also makes the essay *about* the writer to some extent. This is often a perfectly fine thing: a book report describing the effect of a particularly moving novel on readers would be a very suitable place to use the first person, as would a discussion of Civil War history focused on the contemporary appearance of the battlefield of Gettysburg. Writers, though, have to learn to focus readers' attention on the subject matter, and the first step to accomplishing that is to eliminate the first person.

The first person is generally appropriate, though, in the genre of writing known as the personal essay. An "essay," as you learned earlier in this chapter, is literally an "attempt," a stab at a topic. An essay, according to the *Oxford English Dictionary,* is "a composition of moderate length on any particular subject . . . more or less elaborate in style, though limited in range." Essays do not attempt to be exhaustive treatments of a topic; rather, essays explore a topic from one particular angle—often the writer's own personal experience of that topic. To vastly oversimplify the designation, the personal essay tends to explore the encounters of the individual with the complexities or difficulties presented by the outside world. Some personal essay topics are vastly overused—such topics as "what I did on my summer vacation" or "the most memorable person I've ever met" rarely interest the reader or are even capable of eliciting interesting or original observations from the writer. (You may have encountered similar tedious and inevitable topics in your application to college.) However, personal essays on familiar or even clichéd topics, by virtue of their stress on individual experience, can be interesting and original pieces of writing.

Not all essays are personal, of course. The writer generally credited with the invention of the form, the French philosopher Michel de Montaigne, wrote many essays that do not focus on himself. The twentieth-century essayist George Orwell often used the first person in his essays without stressing the personal. The natural world is a frequent subject of essayists, and nature writing can either focus on the writer's response to the natural world or can exclude the human entirely (see the work of John McPhee or Aldo Leopold for examples of nature essays).

Personal writing can also be persuasive writing, or "rhetoric" as we have defined it earlier in this chapter. Martin Luther King's "Letter from Birmingham Jail," of course, is perhaps the paragon of a piece of personal writing used for a rhetorical purpose, but all the other pieces included in this chapter serve both as personal writing and as persuasive arguments. Sandra Tsing Loh's piece makes points about the complicated relationship of a writer to the rituals of Hollywood and about her own feelings about her work, while Richard Rodriguez's serious personal writing argues about the place of the immigrant in American culture. "Salam Pax's" blog is frequently explicit in its rhetorical aims, and just as frequently seemingly pointless when read in retrospect—blogs are immediate forms.

When using the personal essay or any kind of personal writing as rhetoric, though, the writer must be careful about that same issue of authority. Implicitly but inevitably, the personal essay argues that the main source of evidence for whatever point is being made is the personal experience or feelings of the writer. All writers have to be careful about how convincing one's own personal experiences or feelings can be when applied to a vast topic like (to take one example) the war in Iraq. "Salam Pax's" personal opinion and point of view on the war, of course, carries a great deal more power; one of the several justifications of the war offered by the Bush administration was that the Iraqi people *wanted* Saddam Hussein out of power. Since few Americans actually know any Iraqis, "Pax's" accounts of the feelings of the Iraqi people would carry a great deal of persuasive force. As you write, think about these same issues. How much authority do you have on the topic about which you are writing? And what *kind* of authority is it?

Finally, although this book focuses almost exclusively on writing as a task with specific set objectives and an identifiable audience, it is important to consider that the personal essay is also "personal" because its objectives can be interior. That is, one of the goals of the personal essay is frequently the clarification of a writer's thoughts for the writer's own benefit. It is often said, by writing teachers and educational administrators, that writing is a process, not a product, and that the act of writing is inseparable from critical thinking itself. In writing we sort through our ideas, discard faulty ones and polish promising ones, evaluate evidence and choose the argument that will be most convincing both to ourselves and to our audience. But in most writing, this process occurs prior to the product that we see. In a newspaper editorial or scholarly journal article or presidential speech, the brainstorming and idea-wrangling have already taken place. In an essay, though, the writer has the freedom to bring the thought process to the fore. Because the form itself is so concerned with the personal and with the writer's own responses to the world, an essay will frequently describe the intellectual journey the writer traveled to arrive at the conclusions expressed in the essay. An experienced writer develops a sense of whether or not the intellectual journey is interesting or valuable, and based on that will decide whether or not to include it in the final draft.

IDEAS INTO PRACTICE 1-1

Not all personal writing has to take the form of a personal essay; in fact, most personal writing *doesn't* end up taking that form. Come up with a topic of your own choice that can combine something with which you have personal experience and a larger societal issue. You might write, for example, about a recent plane trip you took, thinking about how the post-September 11 security measures affected you. Then write at least one paragraph in all the following formats. After you write each of these paragraphs, think about how the genre of the writing and the audience have determined the different ways you've chosen to make your arguments.

1. A short "script" you might read to a radio call-in show dealing with the topic at hand.
2. A weblog entry on this idea, perhaps including some personal experiences.
3. A letter about this issue to a relative.
4. An e-mail to a friend from high school.
5. A presentation to your writing class.
6. A humorous anecdote.

IDEAS INTO PRACTICE 1-2

Write a first draft of a personal essay without concern to the form or argument of your writing; think primarily about the voice and about your own presence in the writing. You can select from the following topics, or choose your own. As you write, try to strike a balance between the imperative to be honest about your personal experiences and feelings and the imperative to produce a piece of writing that will be interesting and enlightening to an audience of readers who don't know you. For this first draft, let your intellectual journey—the process—determine the structure of the paper. **Do not think about other personal essays or any other forms of writing you have read before and try to structure your paper according to those models.** If you decide to revise the paper, you can then think about it in terms of product, polishing it so that its structure and argument are appealing to an audience.

1. A film or television show that made you realize something you'd never known about your own relationship with your parents.
2. The role of student-run media (websites, the high school paper) in your high school or hometown.
3. When and how you realized that the media were "biased"—and what "biased" means.
4. How society determines what's "cool," what's "in," what's "fashionable."
5. Advertising's effects on you and your friends.
6. The one object or media image or event that absolutely, exactly represents your group or family or religion or subculture—or the one object or image or event that most distorts your group or family or religion or subculture.

Style Toolbox

Choosing a Voice: First Person or Third?

Apart from deciding what to write about, choosing a voice or point of view is probably the most important choice a writer makes. "Voice" is usually broken down into two categories: the first person and the third person. Simply put, the first person uses "I" and the third person doesn't. (The second person, using "you," isn't commonly used outside of very informal writing, instructional manuals, and textbooks like this one.) Think about the kinds of writing you like, and try to remember what voice that writing uses. Autobiographies generally use the first person—in other words, they are written using "I." Much informal writing (letters, e-mail, journals, newspaper columns, and the like) also uses the first person. Creative writing such as novels, songs, stories, and poetry is frequently in the first person.

The third person, on the other hand, characterizes most formal writing. Journalism is almost always in the third person, as are scholarly books, legal writing, business reports, grant applications, and the like. However, not all third-person writing is formal or nonfictional. Much poetry is in the third person, as are many novels.

In determining whether or not a piece of writing should be in the first or the third person, a writer always keeps in mind the **rhetorical situation—or, in other words, the goal of the piece, the occasion (if any) for which it is written, and its intended audience.** If you outline before you start writing, start by writing down what this piece of writing is meant to accomplish. Then, write down the audience. Be as detailed as possible. When you write, for example, a letter to the school newspaper, it's not sufficient to say "I'm writing for a general audience." Who reads the school newspaper? Mostly students, or some faculty? Do parents read the paper? Administrators? People outside of the university community?

Once you've determined who your audience is, think about how you can make your written voice as appealing to them as possible. You make your argument compelling and persuasive by carefully designing the way you come across to your audience. If your audience is likely to respond to passion, you might use an energetic, personal style of writing. If your audience responds to careful reasoning, you would probably tone the passion down and focus on the logic of the argument.

You use the same process in choosing a voice. Generally speaking—and this is by no means a hard and fast rule—the first person will appeal to people's emotions and sympathies, while the third person will appeal to people's logical sense. Using the first person allows you to call upon your own life ("I know about this issue because of my own experiences"), while using the third person makes you sound as if your authority derives not just from you, but from the facts themselves. A first-person voice makes an argument more subjective—which can, depending upon the rhetorical situation, make the argument more or less effective.

Varieties of the First Person

> My dad invented the first authentic wormless Mexican jumping bean with an empty Contac capsule and a ball of mercury he siphoned off a store-bought thermometer. He did it for potential profit in Ciudad Juarez in 1953 in a high-rise complex that the government built for el pueblo out of prefab concrete and reinforced plastic girders. They named it Huertas de Netzhualcoyotl after the Aztec poet-king. (El Huiltlacoche, "The Man Who Invented the Automatic Jumping Bean," *The Pushcart Book of Essays*)

In this excerpt from a personal essay, the writer immediately establishes his authority to tell a story that isn't really about himself by establishing that the central figure in the story is his father. The first-person voice leavens, to some degree, the flat, matter-of-fact tone the writer establishes with his long, prepositional-phrase-heavy sentences. In this excerpt, the personal voice injected by the first-person narrative complements the very fact- and detail-heavy content of the essay—it's easier to keep track of all those facts because we hear the boy in the story telling us about them.

Whereas "El Huiltlacoche's" voice is fairly casual, the first person can also be used in much more formal occasions. In his masterpiece *The Souls of Black Folk,* W.E.B. Du Bois generally uses a very elevated voice derived from classical rhetoric and Biblical language. The introduction to that book's fifth chapter, "Of the Wings of Atalanta," begins with just such a voice:

> South of the North, yet north of the South, lies the City of a Hundred Hills, peering out from the shadows of the past into a promise of the future. I have seen her in the morning, when the first flush of day had half-roused her; she lay gray and still on the crimson soil of Georgia; then the blue smoke began to curl from her chimneys, the tinkle of bell and scream of whistle broke the silence, the rattle and roar of busy life slowly gathered and swelled, until the seething whirl of the city seemed a strange thing in a sleepy land.

The first person here isn't really about establishing the authority of the author to speak about a small personal story, as it does in the previous excerpt. Rather, here the first person is almost ritually invoked; the voice is that of a poet or a preacher or a prophet.

In political discourse, the first person is frequently used in order to make the argument as plain as possible: "I think this should happen," "I'm opposed to that." This kind of plainspoken first-person voice is particularly effective when coming not from a well-known politician but from an ordinary citizen—to use a favorite student expression, it makes it easier to "relate to" the speaker, as in the following opinion piece from the *Philadelphia Inquirer:*

> On Dec. 22, Nizah Morris, an African American transgender woman, was found unconscious with head wounds on Walnut Street in Center City. She died two days later. Although the city medical examiner classified Morris' death as a homicide, it took a month for the police to classify it as a murder. As a transgender person, I find with Nizah Morris' death the same frustrations and official indifference (especially among the police) I've seen with other crimes against transgender people. (Cei Bell, "Danger Across Genders." *Philadelphia Inquirer* 14 Apr. 2003)

Bell's opening paragraph is especially effective because she begins with an objective-sounding third-person recounting of a crime—we don't immediately classify this as "opinion." When she does take these facts and use them as evidence in a statement of opinion, she grounds that opinion not just in one incident but in her own experience by using the first person.

> The more legal and material hindrances women have broken through, the more strictly and heavily and cruelly images of female beauty have come to weigh upon us. Many women sense that women's collective progress has stalled; compared with the heady momentum of earlier days, there is a dispiriting climate of confusion, division, cynicism, and above all, exhaustion. (Naomi Wolf, *The Beauty Myth*)

In this excerpt from her influential study of media images of female beauty, Naomi Wolf argues primarily from a third person point of view, but makes it clear that she is actually writing in a first-person voice by including herself in the class "us." Why doesn't Wolf use the same strategy that Cei Bell does, and argue more forthrightly from the first person? After all, she could talk about how "images of female beauty" affected her feelings about herself. Wolf's argument, though, is different than Bell's in that it is a book-length academic study. Where Bell's argument is a short newspaper editorial in which she is essentially making one point—law enforcement authorities need to pay more attention to how transgender people, as a class, are being victimized—Wolf's argument is much more complicated, wide-reaching, and dependent upon a preponderance of evidence. It doesn't stretch the audience's credulity for Bell to say "the cops don't pay attention to crimes against transgender people—I can attest to this, and if you need more look at Nizah Morris's case." However, if Wolf were to argue that "media images of beauty hurt women—it happened to me!" that would be a much more difficult thesis to prove. By writing in a first-person voice in which the first person ("I" or "we") is rarely invoked, Wolf sounds more fair and even-handed.

Varieties of the Third Person

The third-person voice is just as versatile as the first-person voice. The following examples, like the examples of the first-person voice, are responses to very different rhetorical occasions. For each of the following excerpts, think about why each writer chose to use the third person, and ask yourself what advantages that choice has over the alternative.

> With the Iraq war more or less tucked under the American belt as a success, U.S. leverage to bring about a settlement of the festering dispute between the Israelis and Palestinians is greater than it has been since the end of the first Gulf War in 1991. Increased U.S. influence flowing from the war makes it time to move quickly to seek agreement from the Israelis and Palestinians to the "road map," the proposed two-state settlement developed by the United States, the European Union, the United Nations and Russia. ("Unfold the Map: Get Serious About Israeli-Palestinian Peace." *Pittsburgh Post-Gazette* 10 Apr. 2003)

This excerpt, from an unsigned newspaper editorial, demonstrates a fairly standard use of the third person in persuasive writing. Look for the statement of opinion: "makes it time to move quickly." This is a judgment, not a statement of fact, but whose judgment? The sentence doesn't say "I think it's time" or "the *Post-Gazette's* editors and publisher feel that it's time"; the statement uses the third person to make this statement of opinion seem less like one person's opinion and more like a statement of fact. This isn't an attempt to mislead readers, because the piece is clearly labeled an editorial, but the construction of the sentence can make an opinion sound like a fact—and therefore sound more convincing.

> In the second century of the Christian era the empire of Rome comprehended the fairest part of the earth and the most civilized portion of mankind. The frontiers of that extensive monarchy were guarded by ancient renown and disciplined valor. The gentle but powerful influence of laws and manners had gradually cemented the union of the provinces. Their peaceful inhabitants enjoyed and abused the advantages of wealth and luxury. The image of a free constitution was preserved with decent reverence: the Roman senate appeared to possess the sovereign authority and devolved on the emperors all the executive powers of government. (Edward Gibbon, *History of the Decline and Fall of the Roman Empire*)

This paragraph, from perhaps the best known work of history in the English language, uses the third person as a medium in which to make an argument. Unlike the *Post-Gazette* editorial, Gibbon doesn't make any obvious statements of opinion. Rather, he lets loaded language in ostensibly neutral statements of fact—"renown," "disciplined," "peaceful," "decent reverence," and the like—make his argument (that Rome in that period should be viewed positively). Gibbon's writing demonstrates how one can use the third person to make an argument through coloring the facts with leading adjectives, rather than through making concrete statements of opinion.

The third person can also be used for humorous effect, as in the following excerpts:

> The bus from North Carolina to Oregon takes four days, which breaks down to roughly seventy-five thousand hours if one is traveling without the aid of a strong animal tranquilizer. (David Sedaris, "C.O.G.," from *Naked*)

Organized crime is a blight on our nation. While many young Americans are lured into a career of crime by its promise of an easy life, most criminals actually must work long hours, frequently in buildings without air-conditioning. Identifying criminals is up to each of us. Usually they can be recognized by their large cufflinks and their failure to stop eating when the man sitting next to them is hit by a falling anvil. (Woody Allen, "A Look at Organized Crime," from *Getting Even*)

Many people are surprised to find out that the sledgehammer has only one moving part: it. Yet "Should I buy now or wait for the new models?" is a refrain often heard from the panicky first-timer, who forgets that the number of new sledgehammer innovations in the last three thousand years can be counted on one finger. (Steve Martin, "The Sledgehammer: How It Works," from *Pure Drivel*)

All of the preceding quotes rely on the third person's detached voice and aura of authority for their humor. In each of the excerpts, the writer sets up expectations in the audience that this paragraph will play it straight: each introductory clause has little to indicate that the intention of the piece is humorous. This causes readers to approach the rhetorical situation as if it were simply the transmission of factual information. The comedy resides both in the absurdly hyperbolic nature of the statements that follow and in the fact that they are narrated in precisely the same straight-laced voice.

WRITING WITH STYLE 1-1

For each of the following exercises, write two sentences: one in the first person and one in the third person. You can choose a humorous tone or a serious tone; you can be informal or formal. Then, describe the different rhetorical effect of each sentence and in what rhetorical occasions and for which audiences each sentence might be effective.

Example: 1. An argument in favor of making uniforms mandatory in high schools.

    a. In my high school, just in my senior year, four kids had their basketball shoes stolen, several kids were assaulted for wearing the wrong team's colors, and dozens of kids were teased and ridiculed on a daily basis for wearing the wrong brand names.

    b. School uniforms counteract teenagers' natural desires to classify people into cool and not-cool groups based solely on the clothes they wear; because of this, the adoption of a mandatory uniform for our school will reduce bullying by at least thirty percent.

1. A description of a trip from your campus back to your home.
2. An argument opposed to the opening of the Arctic National Wildlife Refuge for energy exploration (oil drilling).
3. An explanation of how the media have a liberal bias.
4. An appreciation of the talents of Jennifer Lopez.
5. A rebuttal to the editorial in the campus paper this morning.

Whom Can You Trust?

Chapter 2

If we intend to enter the conversation about media and society, and if we seek to make convincing arguments in that conversation, where do we get our information? Or rather, since information (as purveyed to us by an increasingly omnipresent media) seems to be plentiful, where do we get *reliable, unbiased, true* information, as opposed to opinions, rants, lies, sales pitches, spin, disinformation, misinformation, or PR?

We are all familiar with the distinction between facts and opinions, of course. These questions appear very simple—"Madagascar is an island" is a statement of fact, "Madagascar is the best island in the world" is a statement of opinion—but as we begin to think about the media, news, journalism, and how we amass information about the outside world, this simple dichotomy between fact and opinion quickly begins to break down. Even a simple statement of fact like "President Bush led us in a war against Iraq in 2003" isn't as simple as it

The news studio of the Spanish-language network Univision.

seems. The conflict against Iraq wasn't technically a "war," since Congress did not declare war on Iraq. Some readers would question what was meant by "us," since President Bush did not lead the troops of the other members of the "coalition of the willing" (most notably Great Britain). President Bush's administration might quibble with the notion that we were warring against Iraq, for they preferred to argue that the attack was against the Saddam Hussein regime, not against the Iraqi nation. And some particularly embittered people might resist calling Bush "president" because of lingering ill feelings about the disputed election of 2000.

Once you start thinking about these issues it's hard to stop. Every statement on the news, every headline, every sentence in your history professor's lecture starts to seem questionable. It's just not possible to verify independently every piece of information that comes our way. What we learn to do is judge the reliability of the *sources* of information. When we are children, we soon learn that statements by authority figures like parents or teachers or firemen are trustworthy, those made by peers less so. Growing up, in many ways, is the process of gradually learning not only whom to trust, but more importantly how to estimate the potential trustworthiness of the people and messages we encounter every day. Eventually, we develop sophisticated strategies for gauging whether and how much to trust people or messages that directly impact our own lives: you might learn, for instance, that a dress might not be as flattering as the sales attendant says it is, or that when your father expresses disapproval of your ambition

George Stephanopolous

to sky-surf his feelings come primarily from concern for you. These messages are relatively easy to evaluate in terms of trustworthiness.

But what about people and messages that aren't directly related to our lives? How do we learn about the world outside of our immediate circle of experience? What if we don't have the background information necessary to sift intelligently through competing messages about the world? Specifically, how do we learn what is happening in the world, and how do we make sense of what to think about world events?

Many, probably even most, young people did not think about these issues much until September 11, 2001. Then, as the cliché has it, "the world changed." Following the tragic terrorist attacks Americans and people all over the world desperately needed to find out what happened and what it meant. We turned to the media—specifically, the news. Then, after listening to endless commentary, seeing film of the collapsing skyscrapers dozens of times, spending hours watching the "crawl" at the bottom of the screen reporting breaking news and rumors, reading tens of thousands of words in newspapers and magazines about the attacks, and staying up all night Googling sites about Osama bin Laden, many of us stopped and began to think: what of all this can I trust?

We can trust the media, can't we? In the United States, journalism attempts to be as unbiased, or "objective," as possible, and journalists in most formats strive toward pure objectivity. Accusations of bias are a journalist's or publisher's or producer's nightmare, for if a news outlet gets a reputation for being biased, it loses credibility and people will stop turning to it. But we as readers or viewers don't think about that when we turn on the news or pick up a newspaper. In the United States, we take it for granted that the press is, or at least tries its hardest to be, objective.

Even a quick inventory of where we get our news, though, will cause us to complicate that easy assumption. TV news tries to be objective, and for the most part the news directors, editors, producers, and even on-air anchors adhere to standards of journalistic fairness. However, ABC News's George Stephanopolous used to be a member of the Clinton administration, and the same network's Diane Sawyer worked for President Nixon. Does this make them biased? Or do their offsetting biases make ABC News, as a whole, balanced? Do CNN and MSNBC and Fox have a bias, given the increasing amount of airtime they give to such commentators as conservative Bill O'Reilly or liberal Alan Colmes? Newspapers strive even harder to provide the public with just the truth—"All the News That's

Diane Sawyer

Fit to Print" is the *New York Times* motto—except on the editorial pages or in "advertorials" (paid advertisements laid out to look like editorial content) or in pieces labeled "Commentary" or in the recently exposed false stories filed by *Times* reporters Jayson Blair or Rick Bragg. And what about all-news websites like Reuters.com or The Drudge Report? People on the left argue that commercially sponsored, for-profit news organizations will always report the news in a way that supports corporations over the people's interest, while people on the right insist that since more than half of journalists identify themselves as liberal, the journalism they produce can't help but reflect their bias. Given all this, where can we find news that's just *news?*

Let's return to September 11 and look at how actual people used the media to get what they needed. The sources that people consulted to learn more about the causes, events, and effects of the attacks ranged from the seemingly objective to the unabashedly biased. Most people consulted several sources at first, choosing among the most convenient **formats.** In this book I will use "format" to indicate the different ways information can reach us: television, radio, websites, newspapers, magazines, books, flyers, billboards, telephone solicitations, pop-up ads on websites, headlines delivered to pagers and cell phones, readerboards in public places, etc. For instance, many people (especially those in the western United States) first heard about the attacks on their clock-radio alarms that woke them up that morning. Most then turned to the television, choosing either one of the **broadcast networks** or an all-news **cable network** such as CNN, MSNBC, or the Fox News Channel. The broadcast networks are the for-profit commercial entities NBC, CBS, ABC, and Fox. (The WB and UPN also behave like broadcast networks in that they provide programming for a nationwide audience that is available over the air, but as they do not have news divisions they are outside the scope of this discussion.) Unlike cable networks, these companies "broadcast" their programming over the airwaves via affiliated stations in local markets—anyone within range of one of their transmitters can receive their signals for free. For much of the history of television, the networks and their national programming dominated the industry, the only competition being local television stations (whose signals did not reach outside a given geographic area) and, after 1969, "public television," a nonprofit, largely government-funded source of programming that focused on educational and cultural content. Broadcast networks make money primarily by selling advertising during their programming, but they also generate revenue from local stations and, increasingly, are subsidized by the larger conglomerates that own each network.

Cable networks, like broadcast networks, are (with a few exceptions) for-profit companies that provide programming for a national audience. Unlike broadcast networks, though, cable networks do not reach individual homes over the air; instead, their feeds reach consumers directly through an electronic cable. Consequently, cable networks do not need local affiliate stations. Cable networks generate their revenue largely through the sale of advertising, but some "pay" networks such as HBO or Cinemax also require subscribers to pay a fee in order to receive the programming.

On their way to work, many people again listened to the radio, choosing either a commercial AM news station or a National Public Radio affiliate station. In the office, a computer with Internet access brought news from CNN.com, the BBC World Service, or Yahoo!. Many people used several sources of news simultaneously—in the University of Southern California Writing Center, where I worked at the time, we listened to NPR while watching CNN Headline News and reading the online edition of the *New York Times* and even scanning the news bulletins sent via pager networks! That evening, back at home, people returned to the broadcast networks' or cable networks' nonstop coverage of the disaster's aftermath, taking in the horrifying filmed footage for the tenth time. The next morning, **local newspapers** around the country carried **wire-service** stories about the tragedy as well as, perhaps, stories written by their own reporters about local reaction to the attacks. (A local newspaper serves a geographically defined market. Almost every city and town has a local newspaper. Some local newspapers such as the *Daily Oklahoman* (Oklahoma City) or the Portland *Oregonian* also serve a wider geographical area—in these cases, an entire state. A wire service provides news content and photographs for newspapers, magazines, and websites. Local newspapers that subscribe to a wire service such as Reuters or the Associated Press (AP) can print any story from that wire service in their paper. These services are crucial for small papers that do not have reporters covering stories or "beats" far away from the paper's home office.) **National newspapers** (either a newspaper that is not devoted to a particular local market or a newspaper in a local market that is both distributed across the country and nationally recognized for the quality and scope of its journalism) such as the *New York Times* or *USA Today* devoted much of their editions to the story, supplementing the immediacy of television news with the more thoughtful, detailed, informed coverage characteristic of newspaper journalism.

Clearly, there is no shortage of ways to get information. But that forces us to think about the *nature* of this information: where does it come from? Someone observes, someone reports, someone edits, someone filters, someone decides where it goes in the newspaper or in the broadcast, someone lays it out on the page or screen, someone chooses the headlines or accompanying graphics or music. Where do *they* get their information? What information don't they have? How do these people create the stories they report, and how does their own subjectivity affect the stories they tell? And how can we use our knowledge of the process of creating the news to make informed, responsible judgments about where we get our news?

▐▐▐ The "Clinton News Network" Versus "We Report. You Decide."

Although the reports of the demise of newspapers are certainly premature—recent studies show that 77 percent of Americans read their daily local papers an average of five times a week and 54 percent read an additional print news source[1]—newspaper readership is declining. Young people, especially, rely more heavily on television and the Internet than on newspapers: according to a 2002 study by the Pew Research Center for the People and the Press, only 32 percent of Americans under age 50 read newspapers regularly.[2] A huge majority of Americans get some or all their news from television: local broadcast stations, national broadcast networks, and cable networks. Never have there been more outlets for the news on television. At the same time, never have there been more complaints that television news is biased, untruthful, "spun," deceptive, and partisan. With more news and (presumably) more competition, shouldn't quality improve? And—perhaps a more interesting question—does it even make sense to equate "quality" with "objectivity" or "freedom from bias"?

As the coverage of the 2003 invasion of Iraq showed, television news has irrevocably changed the world's relationship to the events of the day. Viewers around the world watched as U.S. forces began an air attack on a foreign country and listened to reports from journalists "embedded" with U.S. combat units as they sped to Baghdad or Basra. Never before could the citizens of a nation actually watch from half a world away as their military began operations. Television's first great news moment, more than a quarter-century before—the coverage of President John F. Kennedy's 1963 assassination, its aftermath, and his funeral—demonstrated the power that television had to connect people with the outside world. The coverage of subsequent news events such as the Vietnam War, the attempted assassination of President Ronald Reagan, the space shuttle Challenger's explosion, the siege of Sarajevo, and the September 11 attacks has taken advantage of new technologies such as satellite transmission, handheld cameras, and digital editing to enable news to be more comprehensive and immediate than the inventors of television could have imagined. The immediacy that television gives to news and the ability of live moving pictures to make us *feel* a story, have an amazing power. And where language can be manipulated, pictures can't lie—can they?

That's obviously a leading question. Of course pictures can be manipulated. As far back as the 1920s, the leadership of the Soviet Union attempted to rewrite their history by painting over the images of out-of-favor figures such as Leon Trotsky in official photographs. More recently, in 1994 *Time* magazine was

---

[1] Smith, Ted, et al. *What the People Want from the Press.*

[2] Kohut, Andrew. "Young People Are Reading: Everything but Newspapers." *Columbia Journalism Review* (Apr. 2002). Available at archives.cjr.org/year/02/ 4/kohutvoice.asp

strongly criticized for deception and potential racism when it artificially darkened a cover photograph of murder suspect O.J. Simpson (see Ch. 6 for more on this). But the arrival of digital photography and video has given even amateurs enormous power over images: with computer applications such as Photoshop or Imovie, anyone can alter a photograph or even a segment of video! In television commercials, advertisers have taken advantage of this technology by inserting images of dead celebrities such as Fred Astaire or John Wayne that make it appear as if the celebrity is interacting with the people in the commercial. Given how much we depend on visual images in the process of making up our minds about controversial issues, the shaky trustworthiness of photography, film, and video is a little scary.

The intentional altering of images for political or commercial purposes is certainly cause for concern. However, instances of this are—we hope!—relatively rare. Almost all the time, in television news coverage bias or "slant" enters largely through how such images are chosen, edited, given a soundtrack, and assembled into a story. This work, in turn, is performed by several people: the reporter who chooses what images and people to focus on, the camera operator who chooses how to film those images and people, the story's producer who orders the images and puts them together with stock footage and music and voice-overs, the video editor who actually assembles the story into a 90- or 120- or 300-second segment, and the executive producer of the news program who chooses whether to broadcast that story at all and how to frame it within the program.

Because news organizations are worried that Americans don't understand or care about foreign news, frequently foreign news will be covered as an example of a "master narrative," or a very large and familiar story or type of story. Some master narratives include an oppressed people rising up against a despotic dictator, the intractable poverty of the developing world, an individual succeeding against all odds, or a person who is selflessly devoted to doing good even in very difficult circumstances. A story about a foreign war—the wars in Bosnia and Kosovo, for example—can create great sympathy for one side based on nothing more than the images when those images are attached to such a master narrative. Most of the media outlets in the United States and Europe covered those conflicts as episodes in the series of wars that followed the breakup of Yugoslavia. According to the master narrative used to explain these wars in the United States, as Yugoslavia fell apart several military strongmen gained power by using ancient cultural and racial resentments to gain support among their people. With the largest army, one of these strongmen (Slobodan Milosevic of Serbia) led his nation in aggressive wars of conquest against the rest of the breakaway republics and even against minority populations in his own nation. American reporters in the ex-Yugoslavia who covered the war tended to interview distraught victims of the Serbs, to shoot video of towns destroyed by Serb artillery, and (most damningly) to find evidence proving that the Serbian program of "ethnic cleansing" relied on Nazi-style concentration camps and hidden mass graves. The American public's sympathy was roused by the horrifying images of what seemed like another Hitler, and many demanded some kind of action against Serbia.

Things were very different in Serbia. There, press coverage focused on a different master narrative: the heroic justice of the Serbian campaign to reclaim their ancestral lands from infidels (the Muslims) and criminals (the Croats, many of whom sided with the Nazis during World War II). Western reports of mass graves and concentration camps were either ignored or explained as actually being the responsibility of Serbian enemies. With televised images of heroic Serbian freedom fighters battling ancient foes and of homeless, hungry Serbian refugees displaced by the military actions of the Muslims or Croats, the Serb media stirred up fanatic patriotism and paranoia in the Serbian populace.

Similar manipulation can happen with issues that are much less grim. During President Clinton's impeachment trial, networks that constantly rebroadcast the image of Monica Lewinsky shaking the president's hand at the rope line were criticized as being anti-Clinton, while others that focused on footage of him looking presidential (at state functions, giving speeches) were criticized as being too favorable toward the president. Many conservatives, who had long felt that the broadcast networks tended to be liberal in their coverage, were angered by what they felt was CNN's insufficiently critical stance toward President Clinton and began calling it the "Clinton News Network." The fact that Ted Turner, an outspoken liberal and then-husband of leftist actress Jane Fonda, owned the network was for them confirmation of CNN's bias. At the same time, the young Fox News Channel gained popularity among conservatives for its self-proclaimed unbiased coverage—"We Report. You Decide" and "Fair and Balanced" became its slogans. The network immediately gained a reputation that differed dramatically from its self-image, due largely to the fact that its founder and owner, News Corp. chairman Rupert Murdoch, is an outspoken conservative who has not hesitated to influence or even direct the political stances of his other media holdings. Few media-watchers were surprised at news that Roger Ailes, Fox News chairman and former Republican strategist, had advised President Bush in the aftermath of September 11, 2001.[3] As you will see in the readings included with this chapter, Fox News truly came into its own during the 2003 invasion of Iraq, when its unabashedly pro-American coverage earned it the highest ratings of any cable news channel, easily outdistancing CNN or MSNBC.

It's not political stories that most strain TV news credibility, though. The last 20 years has seen an unprecedented move toward "media consolidation," or the increasing concentration of media ownership in a few hands. These "hands" are enormous, vastly powerful corporations with interests in everything from communications to liquor to nuclear missiles. Many people suspect that a profit-driven corporation would be reluctant to allow one of its divisions (NBC News, ABC News, CNN) to criticize or air the dirty laundry of another division (General Electric, Disneyland, Interscope Records), and reports of a news division's parent company altering or quashing entirely a story about another division of

---

[3] Stanley, Alessandra. "A Letter from the Boss Contradicts Fox's Creed." *New York Times* 19 Nov. 2002. Before coming to Fox News, Ailes worked as President George Bush's head media strategist and as an adviser to President Reagan.

the company are increasingly and disturbingly frequent. (This topic will be explored in greater detail in Chapter 4.) Nor is the news produced by the non-profit sector (PBS television, National Public Radio, or smaller organizations such as Pacifica or the Christian Broadcasting Network) immune to outside pressures on its objectivity; it hardly seems possible that these broadcasters will cover their corporate or foundation underwriters with a critical eye. Local news programming—that is, the "Eyewitness News" or similar morning, noon, din-nertime, and late-night news produced by a local broadcast network affiliate—rarely even enters into discussions about journalistic objectivity, largely because local stations carry little that can be called "news," preferring to focus on weather, sports, and human-interest stories. Local news broadcasts have been harshly criticized for ignoring local issues such as mayoral and school board elections, zoning and growth controversies, labor issues, poverty, and religion. Instead, most local channels focus their news coverage on the one issue that marketing surveys have suggested draws in more viewers than anything: crime.

These questions about the news are not unique to our time. As far back as 1958, the eminent reporter Edward R. Murrow warned of threats to journalism's objectivity coming from business pressures. In the 1970s, CBS anchorman Walter Cronkite was called "the most trusted man in America," but were people naïve to think that he was any freer from bias or slant than his successors today? While many on the left say that things are worse today than ever because of greater corporate centralization, many on the right say that things are actually getting better when such companies as Fox News seek to balance what they feel is a general liberal slant to news coverage. These questions—like most questions about language and objectivity—are not simple, and they rarely can be defini-tively answered. In the rest of this chapter, we will interrogate our own terms ("objectivity," "bias," "slant") in order to better understand the nature of the categories under discussion.

Analyzing the Message

Where do you get your news? Make a list of the five most important sources you use for news. Be specific: don't say "TV," state the sta-tions and programs you like; don't say "Internet," indicate the actual web-sites you use. What kind of news do you get from each? When an important international event occurs, which of these do you find most reli-able? What about for an important local event? Then think about the process of creating the news for each of these sources. How many people and steps do you think are involved in producing the news story that you are reading or hearing or watching?

▌▌ A Presumption of Objectivity

But as this is a textbook about language and writing, we must now turn our attention to an essentially verbal form of journalism: the newspaper. A careful look at the writing of a newspaper news story can help us understand how sto-ries are constructed and how true "objectivity" is a phantom—a laudable goal to pursue but an impossible ideal to attain. The American Society of Newspaper Editors (ASNE) statement of principles says "Every effort must be made to assure that the news content is accurate, free from bias and in context, and that all sides are presented fairly," and the Society of Professional Journalists (SPJ) Code of Ethics states that journalists must "distinguish between advocacy and news reporting. Analysis and commentary should be labeled and not misrepresent fact or context."[4] Newspapers do contain statements of opinion, but generally reserve a specific place for those statements (the editorial page) and mark them clearly as opinion. The primary business of a newspaper is to report the news, as fairly and comprehensively as possible, and the great majority of stories in the news section of a newspaper attempt to do just that: state the facts, arranged into a story that is easy and appealing for a reader to follow.

But is it possible to state "just the facts"? With some kinds of stories this seems easy:

- "A tornado has been spotted over southeastern Travis County."
- "New housing starts were up 1.8% in the second quarter of 2002."
- "California Governor Gray Davis apologized for making fun of Arnold Schwarzenegger's accent."

Just the facts, right? It would seem so. However, while these headlines cannot really be criticized for bias, they aren't particularly interesting or enlightening. All they tell us are the most basic, rudimentary information about a story.

Headlines, then, lead into news stories. A news story provides more information than a headline can. Typically, the "lead" of a news story (whether written for print, radio, or television format) presents readers or listeners or viewers the five "W's," the who-what-where-when-why and how of a story.

- "Doppler radar indicates tornado-like activity over southeastern Travis County. This storm cell could affect the communities of Montopolis, Del Valle, Webberville, and Pilot Knob. People in these communities should stay indoors in a tornado-safe room. The National Weather Service has issued a tornado warning until 10 p.m. tonight."
- "New housing starts were up 1.8% in the second quarter of 2002. This follows a 1.5% increase from the first quarter of 2002 and is also up 5% over the same period last year."
- "On Wednesday, Gov. Gray Davis apologized on a San Francisco radio show for his comments about Arnold Schwarzenegger's Austrian accent."

---

[4] "ASNE Statement of Principles." http://www.asne.org/index.cfm?ID=888. "Society of Professional Journalists—Code of Ethics." http://www.spj.org/ ethics_code.asp. Note that the term "objectivity" does not appear in either of these statements.

Without explanatory details, a headline is just a bit of information; the writer must add details to make a story. The writer must then make decisions about what details to include—and by including certain details, the writer implicitly says that those details are more important than other details she could have included. In the tornado story, the writer and editor decided this was the kind of story that was of immediate interest to a small group of people. If a tornado was coming (this answers the "what" question), these people needed to know *where* (southeastern Travis County), *who* was affected (the people of Pilot Knob and other towns), *when* this story was relevant (until 10 p.m.), and *how* to stay safe. Other details, such as whether other tornadoes were occurring elsewhere in the United States or the history of tornadoes in southeast Travis County, are left out as not immediately relevant.

So is this "bias"? It would be difficult to find bias in the tornado story, simply because we only think about bias when dealing with an issue about which people might disagree. Nobody *wants* or *supports* tornadoes. This is not the case, though, with most other kinds of stories—the Gray Davis story, for example. In October 2003, California voters faced a general election to decide whether or not to recall, or fire, Governor Gray Davis in the year following his election. Candidates for Davis's job—the ballot also asked voters to decide who should replace the governor—included Lieutenant Governor Cruz Bustamante and assemblyman Tom McClintock as well as actors Arnold Schwarzenegger and Gary Coleman, pornographer Larry Flynt, and comedian Gallagher. Stories about elections deal with controversial questions, opening them to charges of bias. How about the sentence provided about the election—can you spot bias there? Probably not. The story as printed answers the five W's: it tells us what happened, who was involved, when it happened, how it happened, and where it took place. It is impossible to tell from the words themselves whether the writer supports or opposes Davis.

What this story does not tell us is the last W: why. In answering the why question, journalism ventures into contentious territory. In answering this question, too, journalism becomes more than just a headline service and truly starts to enable the people to "make judgments about the issues of the day," again in the words of the ASNE statement. For almost any news story, there are several competing answers to "why"? Murders in Chicago, let's say, are up 10% this year. The Democratic mayor might explain it as a result of growing poverty caused by Republican tax policy, while the Republican governor of Illinois could explain it as a failure of the Chicago police force. Conservative sociologists might explain it as the result of the decline of the nuclear family but liberals might blame it on the easy availability of guns. Just reporting the numerical increase would avoid accusations of bias, but would not tell the full story— which necessarily involves choosing an answer to "why?" How is a news writer supposed to choose among these competing explanations?

Because reporters are presumably experts on their beat (the area or subject they regularly cover), and because editors have years of training and experience in identifying what a news event means in the context of other news events, reporters and editors will often decide what the *real* story behind a story is. It's here—in the framing of a story, in *how* it's used—that slant or bias often enters.

For instance, the headline about housing starts is not, in itself, particularly interesting to anyone outside the financial or home-building industries. An editor might, however, decide that the real story here is the gradual improvement of the economy, and use the new detail about housing starts to illustrate this larger story. Another editor at another paper might see the real story as something different—perhaps as evidence that, contrary to the president's predictions of economic improvement, housing starts are barely up at all.

Let's illustrate this point with a specific example. The following story appeared in the *Los Angeles Times* on September 11, 2003.

Governor Apologizes for Remark About Accent
By Gregg Jones, Los Angeles Times

FRESNO—Gov. Gray Davis on Wednesday bowed to growing pressure and apologized for poking fun at Republican Arnold Schwarzenegger's Austrian accent.

The controversy has been dogging Davis as he campaigns for the support of disgruntled Democrats and independents in an Oct. 7 special recall election.

Davis triggered the flap at a union picnic Saturday when he responded to a comment from the crowd by saying that someone who couldn't pronounce "California" shouldn't be governor.

"I was joking around with someone in the crowd after a speech," Davis said during an interview with KGO-AM radio in San Francisco. "It was a poor joke. I shouldn't have done it."

Davis said he wants people "to know that I'm doing this [apologizing] because I feel so strongly that this is a state that welcomes all people."

Pressed further by KGO's Ed Baxter, Davis said that the remark "was made to one individual in a crowd on the way out. I guess a reporter overheard it. I regret saying it, because I'd rather eat humble pie than have one Californian think that I don't fully appreciate, which I do, the role that immigrants have played in our society."

After Schwarzenegger campaign officials denounced his words as a slur on immigrants, Davis on Sunday said his comment was a "joke" but refused to apologize.

What is the real story here? Certainly, Davis's apology is the actual "news." However, the writer of this piece, Gregg Jones, apparently thinks the real story is Davis's inability to leave this statement behind him after he initially tried to portray it as a harmless joke. Mr. Jones expresses this contention not by explicitly saying that, but by framing the story and choosing words that convey this opinion. In our previous example of a story about this issue, the writer simply reports the facts: Gray Davis apologized for making a statement about Arnold Schwarzenegger's accent. But in these paragraphs, Jones uses several loaded words—"dogging," "poking fun," "growing pressure," "flap"—to emphasize that the real story here was the fact that the issue wouldn't go away. Jones focuses on Davis, quoting him extensively in three paragraphs here (and several in the rest of the story) and burying the response from Schwarzenegger's camp in the seventh paragraph. The repetition of Davis's defense in these early paragraphs immediately shows that Jones wants to emphasize a picture of the governor as defensive, on his heels, not in control of the election.

Is this bias? Certainly. The writer is giving his opinion about why this is a story that merits over 20 paragraphs of coverage. We could easily come up with several other interpretations of these events. Schwarzenegger's celebrity, which Jones barely mentions, made many voters sympathize with—or dislike—him. Another writer might see the real story as Davis's chilly reception from California's voters (these details appear much later in the story). Still another writer could see Davis's statements as evidence of a serious character flaw—bigotry. All these points are undeniably reasonable, yet they all serve to bias or "spin" the news story so that it supports an opinion. Why does an ostensibly objective, well-respected paper like the *Los Angeles Times* allow itself to be biased in a story that should be utterly objective?

The short answer is because the paper wants to answer the "why" question. Historically, newspapers that strove for objectivity simply avoided answering the why question, fearing that in the choice of answers the paper would necessarily show bias and lose credibility. But over the last few decades, more and more newspaper editors and publishers have decided that the job of a newspaper is to provide not just the five W's but also some background to a story and an explanation for why this story is significant enough to be covered. Since the 1930s, most people get their breaking news from immediate sources such as the radio, television, and—recently—the Internet. Since newspapers cannot provide immediate news—even with dozens of "EXTRA!" editions every day, newspapers would still get the news to consumers well after radio and TV did—the important national newspapers have developed a new strength: explaining a story in detail and contextualizing it. Newspapers such as the *New York Times, Los Angeles Times,* and *Washington Post* have distinguished themselves for this and have given the newspaper a new role in the age of immediate mass communication.

Because of their willingness to answer the why question, these papers have also developed a distinct slant to their coverage, tending over the long term to adopt a slightly left-of-center stance. Readers often see the positions taken by the paper on their editorial pages echoed in the tone of the news stories and in the conclusions reached in the news analysis pieces. As a result, conservative readers who want or need the information provided by the superior reporting of these papers will attempt to read past the bias, or will, in instances they find particularly objectionable, complain publicly about the bias in these prominent news sources. Where these three leading national newspapers tend to lean left, many smaller, local newspapers tend to display a conservative, pro-business bias. Some of these papers, especially those in larger markets, are owned by large media conglomerates such as Gannett, Knight-Ridder, or Cox Communications and, according to their critics, support the interests of their parent corporations in their news coverage.[5] Many small-town papers are the de-facto voice of the business interests of that community because they depend on those businesses

---

[5] This topic will be explored in greater detail in Chapter 4.

for advertising revenue. Liberal readers in those small communities do what conservative readers of the national publications do—read past the bias, write letters to the editor, boycott the paper.

⫴ News on the Sentence Level

Let's look at a story in even greater detail. The following story appeared on the Associated Press wire on December 18, 2002.

Judge: Bonds' Home Run Ball Must Be Sold
By Ian Stewart, Associated Press Writer

SAN FRANCISCO—The two fans who claimed ownership of Barry Bonds' record-setting No. 73 home run ball after a brawl in the right-field stands must sell the ball and split its value—an estimated $1 million—a judge ruled Wednesday.

Bonds hit the ball into the record books, and into a long court battle, on the last day of the regular season in October 2001 to set the season record for homers. Since then, the ball has been locked both in legal limbo and a safe-deposit box.

Judge Kevin McCarthy said that both Alex Popov, who gloved the ball for an instant, and Patrick Hayashi, who ended up with the ball, have a legitimate claim—and so neither should get the ball outright.

"Their legal claims are of equal quality and they are equally entitled to the ball," McCarthy ruled. "The ball must be sold and divided equally between the parties."

Is there bias here? Does Ian Stewart favor the claims of either Mr. Popov or Mr. Hayashi? It's difficult to find one. However, there does seem to be bias of another kind in the story. When you read it, context clues tell you the writer doesn't think this is a particularly important story. He does this not by explicitly saying so, but by choosing figurative language and metaphors that give a light-hearted, sporting tone to this story about sports. Barry Bonds "hit the ball into the record books, and into a long court battle," Stewart says. This double metaphor (Bonds didn't *literally* hit that ball into any books or into court) brings with it a tone that lessens the seriousness of the prose. Stewart's use of the word "gloved" also extends the sporting language and the less-than-grave tone. Mr. Stewart's bias, then, is in his attitude toward the story; he tells us this story is not particularly important and can be treated lightly.

Compare this with the figurative language used in another, much more serious story:

Officials Say Declaration Falls Short, but War Not Imminent

WASHINGTON (CNN)—The Bush administration is ready to declare that Iraq's declaration of its weapons programs falls far short of a full and complete accounting, and suggested Wednesday that Iraqi leader Saddam Hussein has missed his "last chance" to disarm.

> Administration officials will present that assessment to the U.N. Security Council, but the officials said the Bush national security team is not pushing for immediate military confrontation.
>
> "The United States will continue to be deliberative in this manner. But this was Saddam Hussein's last chance," White House spokesman Ari Fleischer said. [6]

Is there any figurative language? Not really. The language here is stark, plain, telling readers that this is a very serious story. Still, this story operates on levels beyond the text. Careful readers will ask, "What actually happened that's being reported here?" The reporter states that the Bush administration is "ready to declare" something, but does not identify the forum in which the administration declared this readiness. Perhaps the reporter is drawing his or her own conclusions from evidence not present in the story. It's also possible that reports of the administration's readiness come from an unidentified source within the administration who has told the press something before the administration announces it officially. Such "leaks" or "background sources" are an important source for news.

Both of these stories are news; however, they present their facts in very different ways. The baseball story gives us the facts and tells us, implicitly, that this is a light story. The Iraq story emphasizes its own importance while suggesting that the real story here goes beyond the facts—it takes either a reporter's analysis or a background source to say what's really happening. Both stories are on their surface trustworthy. They come to us from reliable, reputable news organizations (AP and CNN). They give us no reason to doubt them. And yet they are subtly biased.

Analyzing the Message

Look at several different news articles from different sources about the same topic. Carefully pull each of the stories apart to discover their bias or slant or point of view. Can you boil each of these stories down to a thesis—something that the writer is arguing? After you analyze the pieces, write your own news story about the same topic. Can you avoid "bias?"

Bias or "emplotment?"

But even the term "bias" is probably too simplistic, too pejorative. After all, if objectivity is as elusive or illusory as it seems to be, continually criticizing the news for being biased is the equivalent of attacking a "straw man," or a false opponent. (The straw man and other logical fallacies will be discussed extensively in Chapter 4's "Writer at Work" section.) Perhaps it's more productive to think about bias and objectivity in terms of another word, "emplotment." Emplotment names the process of putting details and voice together in order to make a

---

[6] CNN.com. 18 Dec. 2002.

story; all news stories rely on this process in order to make sense of the facts for a reader or a viewer. At the same time, emplotment (as its root word "plot" indicates) also involves the creation of a story *by a writer.* Someone must decide what details go in and which don't, what order the details appear in, which details are emphasized and which downplayed, what kind of voice is used to tell the story. In this process a writer's view or personality or bias or slant (we tend to choose among those words depending on how well we like the story) is manifested.

Let's look at a few more examples of that last element of emplotment, the selection of a voice. The following three passages (all made up by me—not actually from published materials) all utlize different voices. Ask yourself as you read how the voice of the writer helps shape our impressions of the events narrated and how "present" the narrator is in the story.

> Zia Padora breezes into the room, lighting a cigarette as she breathlessly apologizes for her tardiness. She wears a toile halter top, capri pants, and espadrilles—summery, befitting the scene, the back patio at the Urth Café on Melrose in Los Angeles.

> I was born in this town. Today it's as grim as it was then. The empty factories loom over the deserted streets. Where I remember broken Thunderbird bottles are now crack vials, syringes, and other drug paraphernalia. My old schoolyard's soccer fields are entirely mud now in the winter, when they aren't iced over.

> The New Beetle attempts to recapture the spirit of its predecessor, the legendary Bug, the VW born of efficient Nazi imagination that putt-putted a million Woodstock Nation dreams. But it fails. Its cutesy built-in dashboard flower vase feels forced—"I'm whimsical! I'm flower-power, not gasoline-powered!" Its Day-Glo colors try to convince us that they aren't serious, but they can't: they are the gaudy camouflage of multinational capitalism.

The first passage is clearly the passage in which the author disappears most into the background. The focus is on the subject (Zia Padora) from the beginning. The sense of movement the writer conjures up with words like "breezes" and "breathlessly" also keeps us thinking about the thing moving, not about the voice narrating.

The other two examples are both very descriptive, but in different ways. In the second passage, the reader can easily envision this "grim" town, but it's hard to picture it without thinking of the writer—largely because it's written in the first person. We can see the surroundings but we do so while imagining the writer himself, as a young person, growing up there. Although our understanding of subject matter is always mediated by a writer, in a descriptive essay it's important to make sure the reader doesn't feel that the only way to experience the subject matter is through the writer's own eyes.

In the third passage, the first person disappears but the writer is very present. It's hard to concentrate on the car being described when every sentence calls attention to itself. This writer clearly enjoys writing. Each sentence has an exuberance to it, a joy in writing. However, in that the sentences make us think about them *as* sentences. We pay attention to the writing more than to the subject. To use an old metaphor, we look *at* the window rather than *through* it.

In the first passage, the subject is allowed to stand out. The only hint that a writer is even present is the implied meeting-time (for which Zia Padora is late): apart from that, the focus is entirely on the subject. But even while downplaying her own presence, the writer is subtly able to make her presence felt. She wants the reader to see Padora in a particular way. Padora is compared twice to the wind—she "breezes" in, she's "breathless." The writer deftly alludes to a picture with which we are familiar (an outdoor table at a trendy location in ever-summery Los Angeles, home of celebrities) and quickly sketches a flighty actress to fill out the scene. With just a few details and well-chosen adjectives, the writer conveys her first impression of Padora without coming out and saying anything so blunt as "Zia Padora is like the wind."

Why disguise what you're trying to say? Why *not* just come out and state that "Padora is like the wind"? Primarily, in descriptive work writers doesn't do this because they want to stay in the background. By making statements of opinion, the writer reminds the reader of his or her presence, which in turn makes the reader think more about the writer ("What is this writer trying to convince me to believe?") than about the subject matter ("What is Zia Padora like?"). As a writer, when you want the reader to focus on the subject matter, it's generally a good idea to minimize your presence as much as possible.

Voice is by no means the only important element in the emplotment of a piece of writing, journalistic or other. The structure of a piece of writing is also crucial. Structure works much like good camerawork in a movie or a television show or even a commercial. Like a cinematographer (the person behind the camera), a writer controls what we see. A writer can choose to initially show us something interesting and then quickly cut away from it, making us eager to see more. A writer can also focus relentlessly on one thing, describing its many facets and showing it to us from many angles so that we feel we know it very well. Or a writer, faced with a very large topic, might focus on several or even dozens of different things, giving us quick glimpses of each, in an effort to make us understand the large scope of the thing described.

In this passage, Joan Didion uses structure to emplot her story very deliberately:

> Dick Haddock, a family man, a man twenty-six years in the same line of work, a man who has on the telephone and in his office the crisp and easy manner of technological middle management, is in many respects the prototypical South-ern California solid citizen. He lives in a San Fernando Valley subdivision near a freshwater marina and a good shopping plaza. His son is a high-school swim-mer. His daughter is "into tennis." He drives thirty miles to and from work, puts in a forty-hour week, regularly takes courses to maintain his professional skills, keeps in shape and looks it. When he discusses his career he talks, in a kind of politely impersonal second person, about how "you would want like any other individual to advance yourself," about "improving your rating" and "being more of an asset to your department," about "really knowing your busi-ness." Dick Haddock's business for all these twenty-six years has been that of a professional lifeguard for the Los Angeles County Department of Beaches, and his office is a $190,000 lookout on Zuma Beach in northern Malibu. (from "Quiet Days in Malibu")

The effect Didion wants to achieve here is one of surprise, of course. Haddock is described as "the prototypical Southern California solid citizen" and the details we learn about him make us expect him to be a junior executive at IBM or a project supervisor at Northrop. Only at the end do we learn that his solid middle-class career is actually a job that most of us associate with teenagers on summer vacation. The argument Didion makes here with her structure is a familiar one—Southern California can normalize lifestyles that most people would find bizarre—but her structure makes this shopworn observation seem new and interesting.

Let's think about structure more extensively by constructing a piece of writing of our own—an article for your school newspaper on the reality television program *High School Reunion,* in which a group of high school classmates are reunited to live together for two weeks in a Hawaiian beach house. Your initial plan, as is the case with much journalistic writing, is simply to describe the most important aspects of the program and try to identify what makes it unique—what would make it interesting to an audience. Watching the program for several consecutive weeks, you take notes on the lush tropical setting, the attractive people dressed in beachwear, and the "hall passes" and other devices the producers have come up with to give the show some kind of a plot. Sitting down to write your paper, you review your notes and find that the overwhelming impression you get is one of silliness and triviality. The Maui setting is just the kind of fantasyland where these "contestants," celebrating the 10-year reunion of their high school graduating class, can live a pretend life for two weeks. They don't have to wear work clothes, and can show off their bodies for each other and for the viewers. The dates and social outings that the producers of the show arrange, you conclude, are just a desperate attempt to make *something* happen.

With this conclusion, the structure for your article becomes clear: you'll start out by describing the setting, briefly talk about the premise of the show, then move on to descriptions of the contestants. After describing each contestant, you move into the heart of your article: recounting the phony games and contests that the classmates are asked to engage in by the producers. Already, just by sifting through the factual details, you're beginning to come up with an implicit thesis: *High School Reunion* demonstrates the desperate silliness of network programmers. But how can you write this article so it doesn't explicitly state your opinion?

An article on *High School Reunion* focusing on these aspects of the program is easy to imagine. You've probably even seen similar essays about other reality programs, describing the programs and stressing their ultimate silliness—"How can we humiliate these people?" the producers seem to say. As you write the essay, though, you might find yourself thinking more deeply about the program. What starts to strike you, as you watch the interactions again, is not the outward features of the show but the inner workings of the participants' relationships. Contrived as it might be, this program does give a telling glimpse of each personality—and the fact that everyone is identified by their high school designations ("the bully," "the misfit," "the tall girl," "the prom queen") underscores the ways that the roles we play in high school can end up as models for how we live our lives and relate to other people. As you write, you find that your attitude and approach to the show start to change. The important details are no longer the beach and the bodies, but the roles the contestants play. "The pipsqueak" is now a bodybuilder; "the nerd" is now a confident man, "the bully" seems as cocky as he must have always been. But as they confront the people from their past, their roles come alive again: the nerd's hostility toward the bully resurfaces and the two are given boxing gloves for a fight.

As your thinking about what's important in the subject changes, the structure of your paper will change as well. The features of the show itself become less important as the thrust of your argument changes from an attack on the show's creators to an exploration of the show as a forum in which our past is forced to live in the present. Given this, in your writing you will probably talk less about the house, the beach, and the clothes, except as they relate to the personal interactions. The one-time pipsqueak's refusal to button his shirt over his bulging pecs speaks for itself, in your description; you do not have to connect those dots for the reader to understand your point. Most of your paper, in this model, will focus on the events of the show and the interactions between the contestants, and will ultimately make an argument about how our high school personae live on in us even as we try desperately to leave them behind.

The process of sketching out this article should demonstrate at least two important aspects of writing to you. First, the process of putting together an article from scattered details always involves emplotment, the creation of a structure or what Hollywood screenwriters might call a "story arc" for your article. In this process you are already interpreting for your reader. The second important aspect of writing modeled here is that the writing process is just that: a process. As you begin to think about structure, you have to come to grips with the actual nature of your topic and with what you are trying to say about it. It's not necessary to be able to say with certainty, as you sit down to write your article, what the essence of your argument is going to be. Fortunately, most writers do not know what they are really trying to say about something until they start writing. Writing is a form of brainstorming in itself; in writing we try on ideas, see if they fit, and often as not discard them for something better.

Think about these ideas as you watch the television news, listen to the radio news, or read news stories online or in the newspaper. How is the story emplotted? How has the writer taken the details of an event that is extremely complicated and boiled it down to a story? How does this process make the story more appealing, more understandable, more digestible? What might get left out in this process? Does this make the story biased? Is that important? Does this bias invalidate the story? How does one decide what to believe?

A nalyzing the Message

Think about a possible topic for a journalistic article—either choose one from the following list or think of your own. Then, on a separate sheet of paper write down three possible arguments to make or "angles" to take toward the subject matter. For each one of these possible approaches, briefly outline what details you would absolutely need to include in order to make that argument, which details would be absolutely necessary in order to draw a credible or accurate picture of your topic, and what seemingly important details you might downplay or leave out entirely.

Some potential topics:

1. A controversial athlete.
2. The worst movie you saw last year.
3. New York City as portrayed on television.
4. The most elegantly designed object in your bedroom.
5. How to tie your shoes.

Readings

Media Research Center
Media Bias Basics

Taken from the website of the **Media Research Center**, *this excerpt from "Media Bias Basics" lays out the case that U.S. media outlets slant significantly to the left. This piece—not exactly an essay, yet more than just a collection of statistics—demonstrates how writing for the Web can be quite different, yet no less effective, than writing for other forums. It's worth taking a look at the Center's homepage (www.mrc.org) as well.*

The Media Research Center is a nonprofit foundation based in Alexandria, Va. It is headed by L. Brent Bozell, III, a leading voice in conservative circles. The MRC calls itself "the leader in documenting, exposing, and neutralizing media bias."

Seventy million Americans rely on broadcast television for their news. They form opinions based on what they hear and see and to a lesser extent, read. Since citizens cannot cast informed votes or make knowledgeable decisions on matters of public policy if the information on which they depend is distorted, it is vital to American democracy that television news and other media be fair and unbiased.

Conservatives believe the mass media, predominantly television news programs, slant reports in favor of the liberal position on issues. Most Americans agree, as the data below indicate. Yet many members of the media continue to deny a liberal bias.

Evidence of how hard journalists lean to the left was provided by S. Robert Lichter, then with George Washington University, in his groundbreaking 1980 survey of the media elite. Lichter's findings were authoritatively confirmed by the American Association of Newspaper Editors (ASNE) in 1988 and 1997 surveys. The most recent ASNE study surveyed 1,037 newspaper reporters found 61 percent identified themselves as/leaning "liberal/Democratic" compared to only 15 percent who identified themselves as/leaning "conservative/Republican."

With the political preferences of the press no longer secret, members of the media argued while personally liberal, they are professionally neutral. They argued their opinions do not matter because as professional journalists, they report what they observe without letting their opinions affect their judgment. But being a journalist is not like being a surveillance camera at an ATM, faithfully recording every scene for future playback. Journalists make subjective decisions every minute of their professional lives. They choose what to cover and what not to cover, which sources are credible and which are not, which quotes to use in a story and which to toss out.

Liberal bias in the news media is a reality. It is not the result of a vast left-wing conspiracy; journalists do not meet secretly to plot how to slant their news reports. But everyday pack journalism often creates an unconscious "groupthink" mentality that taints news coverage and allows only one side of a debate to receive a fair hearing. When that happens, the truth suffers. That is why it is so important news media reports be politically balanced, not biased.

How the Media Vote: Elite Media

Overview

In 1981, S. Robert Lichter, then with George Washington University, and Stanley Rothman of Smith College, released a groundbreaking survey of 240 journalists at the most influential national media outlets—including the *New York Times, Washington Post, Wall Street Journal, Time, Newsweek, U.S. News & World Report*, ABC, CBS, NBC and PBS—on their political attitudes and voting patterns. Results of this study of the "media elite" were included in the October/November 1981 issue of *Public Opinion*, published by the American Enterprise Institute, in the article "Media and Business Elites." The data demonstrated that journalists and broadcasters hold liberal positions on a wide range of social and political issues. This study, which was more elaborately presented in Lichter and Rothman's subsequent book, "The Media Elite," became the most widely quoted media study of the 1980s and remains a landmark today.

Key Findings

- 81 percent of the journalists interviewed voted for the Democratic presidential candidate in every election between 1964 and 1976.
- In the Democratic landslide of 1964, 94 percent of the press surveyed voted for President Lyndon Johnson (D) over Senator Barry Goldwater (R).
- In 1968, 86 percent of the press surveyed voted for Democrat Senator Hubert Humphrey.
- In 1972, when 62 percent of the electorate chose President Richard Nixon, 81 percent of the media elite voted for liberal Democratic Senator George McGovern.
- In 1976, the Democratic nominee, Jimmy Carter, captured the allegiance of 81 percent of the reporters surveyed while a mere 19 percent cast their ballots for President Gerald Ford.
- Over the 16-year period, the Republican candidate always received less than 20 percent of the media's vote.

Presidential Voting Patterns of Media Elite, 1964–1976

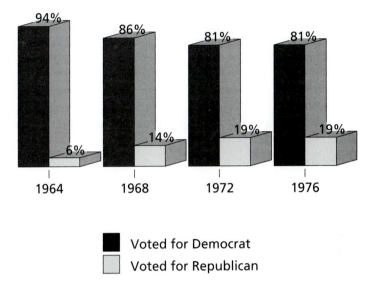

■ Voted for Democrat
□ Voted for Republican

■ Lichter and Rothman's survey of journalists discovered that "Fifty-four percent placed themselves to the left of center, compared to only 19 percent who chose the right side of the spectrum."

■ "Fifty-six percent said the people they worked with were mostly on the left, and only 8 percent on the right–a margin of seven-to-one."

■ Only one percent strongly agreed that environmental problems were ovestated, while a majority of 54 percent strongly disagreed.

■ 90 percent favored abortion.

■ 80 percent supported "strong affirmative action for blacks."

■ 54 percent did not regard adultery as wrong, compared to only 15 percent who regarded it as wrong.

Conservative Reporters Few . . . and Getting Fewer

Overview

In 1996, as a follow-up to a 1988 survey, the American Society of Newspaper Editors (ASNE) surveyed 1,037 reporters at 61 newspapers of all sizes across the nation, asking "What is your political leaning?" Results of the survey were published in ASNE's 1997 report The Newspaper Journalists of the '90s, highlights of which appeared in the MRC's May 1997 *MediaWatch*.

Key Findings

- In 1988, 62 percent of journalists identified themselves as "Democrat or liberal" or "lean to Democrat or liberal." In 1996, 61 percent said they were liberal/Democrat or leaning that way.
- In 1988, 22 percent identified themselves as "Republican or conservative" or "lean to Republican or conservative." By 1996 that figure had declined to 15 percent.

Self-Identified Political Leanings of Newspaper Journalists, 1996

61%

15%

24%

- Conservative
- Liberal
- Independent/Other

- Those identifying themselves as independent jumped from 17 to 24 percent between the two years.
- At newspapers with more than 50,000 circulation, 65 percent of the staffs were liberal/Democrat or leaned that way. The split at papers of less than 50,000 was less pronounced though still significant, with 51 percent of staffs identifying as liberal/Democrat compared to 23 percent who identified as conservative/Republican.
- Women were more likely than men to identify as liberal/Democratic. Only 11 percent identified themselves as conservative or leaned that way.
- Minorities tend to be more liberal/Democrat with a mere three percent of blacks and eight percent of Asians and Hispanics putting themselves on the right.

Most Recent Data: Six Percent of Press Conservative

Overview

The "National Survey of the Role of Polls in Policymaking," completed by Princeton Survey Research Associates for the Kaiser Family Foundation in collaboration with *Public Perspective*, a magazine published by the Roper Center for Public Opinion Research, was released in late June 2001.

The poll questioned 1,206 members of the public, 300 "policymakers" and 301 "media professionals, including reporters and editors from top newspapers, TV and radio networks, news services and news magazines." Significant findings from the survey of media professionals appear below.

Key Findings

- The Kaiser Family Foundation survey found that members of the media were four times as likely to identify themselves as "liberal" than as "conservative:"

Self-Identified Political Leanings of the Press, 2001

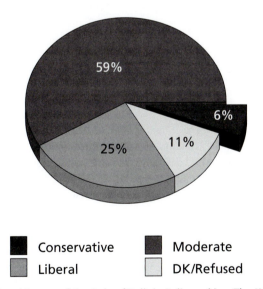

Source: *National Survey of the Role of Polls in Policymaking,* The Kaiser Family Foundation in collaboration with *Public Perspective*, page 27 question D4, June 2001.

- Similarly, the survey found that members of the media were more than seven times more likely to identify themselves as "Democrat" than as "Republican:"

Self-Identified Political Affiliations of the Press, 2001

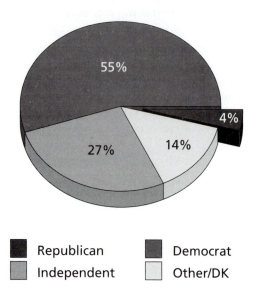

55%

4%

27%   14%

■ Republican   ■ Democrat
□ Independent   □ Other/DK

Source: *National Survey of the Role of Polls in Policymaking,* The Kaiser Family
Foundation in collaboration with *Public Perspective,* page 27 question D3, June 2001.

Worlds Apart: Media And Public Beliefs
Massive Majority of Media Hold Strong Liberal Beliefs

Overview

In 1985, the *Los Angeles Times* conducted one of the most extensive surveys of
journalists in history. Using the same questionnaire they had used to poll the
public, the *Times* polled 2,700 journalists at 621 newspapers across the country.
The survey asked 16 questions involving foreign affairs, social and economic
issues. On 15 of 16 questions, the journalists gave answers to the left of those
given by the public.

Key Findings

- Self-identified liberals outnumbered conservatives in the newsroom
  by more than three-to-one, 55 to 17 percent. This compares to only
  one-fourth of the public (23 percent) that identified themselves as
  liberal.
- 84 percent of reporters and editors supported a so-called "nuclear
  freeze" to ban all future nuclear missile deployment; 80 percent were
  against increased defense spending; and 76 percent opposed aid to
  the Nicaraguan Contras.

- 82 percent of reporters and editors favored allowing women to have abortions; 81 percent backed affirmative action; and 78 percent wanted stricter gun control.
- By a margin of two-to-one, reporters had a negative view of then-President Ronald Reagan and voted, by the same margin, for Walter Mondale in 1984.

Public Beliefs Much More Conservative

According to a 2001 Gallup poll, 41 percent of Americans identify themselves as conservatives, 38 percent as moderates and 18 percent as liberals. On three of four cornerstone political issues, the public overwhelmingly supports the conservative position:

- Americans support the death penalty by 70 to 17 percent, with 53 percent believing it should be imposed more frequently and more than twice as many opposing a temporary moratorium as favoring one (53 vs. 23 percent).
- Americans support gun ownership by 66 to 20 percent, with 58 percent agreeing with the statement that "If guns are outlawed only outlaws will have guns." Almost twice as many believe a ban on guns would make the country more dangerous rather than more safe (55 vs. 27 percent).
- Americans support lowering taxes and government spending by 58 percent, compared to 4 percent who support increasing them and 33% who support the tax and spending status quo.
- When it comes to abortion, 52 percent of Americans support the Roe vs. Wade decision compared to 37 percent who oppose it. Exactly half of Americans identify themselves "pro-choice," compared to 42 percent who identify themselves as "pro-life." Nonetheless, 50 percent believe abortion is "too easy" to obtain, compared to only 16 percent who believe it's "too hard" to obtain.

Not surprisingly, when it comes to political ideology, Americans are almost twice as likely to identify themselves as conservative than liberal.

Public's Opinion of Media Coverage: Are the Media Biased?

The issue of public opinion on media bias is comprised of two subparts: Do Americans believe the news media are biased and, if so, what type of bias is it? The answer to the first subpart is clearly yes.

Overview of the Pew Study

One of the most comprehensive surveys of the public's general opinion of the media was done in 1997 by the Pew Research Center for The People & The Press, formerly known as the Times Mirror Center for the People and the Press. This research compared poll results from the mid-1980s with the late-1990s, (using identical questions) and determined a growing percentage of the public realize the media are biased. This information was also reported in the MRC's April 1997 *MediaWatch*.

Key Findings of the 1997 Pew Study

- 67 percent said that "In dealing with political and social issues" news organizations "tend to favor one side." That was up 14 points from 53 percent who gave that answer in 1985.
- Those who believed the media "deal fairly with all sides" fell from 34 percent to 27 percent.
- Republicans "are more likely to say news organizations favor one side than are Democrats or independents (77 percent vs. 58 percent and 69 percent, respectively)."
- The percentage who felt "news organizations get the facts straight" fell from 55 percent to 37 percent.
- Of respondents with an unfavorable view of network TV news, 50 percent couldn't give a reason for their dissatisfaction, leaving "news is biased" as the most cited reason at 14 percent. Another seven percent listed "give opinions not facts," and three percent offered "too liberal" as their response. Those three reasons totaled 24 percent while conservative bias didn't make the list.

Most Americans View Bias as Liberal

Overview

In 1997, the Center for Media and Public Affairs (CMPA) retained the Lou Harris Organization to poll 3,000 people about their attitudes toward the press. According to the poll, those who saw a liberal bias outnumbered those who perceived a conservative bias by two-to-one. The results of the poll were published in the May/June 1997 *Media Monitor*, the CMPA's newsletter and in the MRC's October 1997 *MediaWatch*.

Key Findings of the CMPA/Harris Survey

- CMPA reported: "Majorities of all major groups in the population, including 70 percent of self-described liberals, now see a 'fair amount' or 'great deal' of bias in the news. In general, perceptions of bias rise along with levels of education and political participation."
- "Those who see a liberal tilt outnumber those who detect a conservative bias by more than a two to one margin. Forty three percent describe the news media's perspective on politics as liberal, compared to 33 percent who see it as a middle of the road, and 19 percent who find it to be conservative."
- "Even self-described liberals agree: 41 percent see the media as liberal, compared to only 22 percent who find the news to be conservative. Among self-designated conservatives, of course, the spread is

even greater: 57 percent say the media are liberal and 19 percent see them as conservative."

Other studies show similar findings:

■ 66 percent agree strongly or somewhat that the news media "favor a liberal point of view." Only 26 percent disagree strongly or somewhat that the news media "favor a liberal point of view." (Yankelovich Partners Poll, July 1996.) This is consistent with an earlier poll that found 65 percent agreed strongly or somewhat that the "mass media seem to favor liberal views on politics and issues." Only 28 percent disagreed strongly or somewhat that the "mass media seem to favor liberal views on politics and issues." (Barna Research Group, August 1993.)

■ 39 percent think national network TV news is biased against conservative political groups such as the Christian Coalition, National Rifle Association, National Right to Life Committee, compared to only 14 percent who believe it is biased in favor of such groups. 41 percent believed TV news was even-handed toward conservative political groups. (ABC News, January 1997.)

■ 32 percent believe the news media coverage of the 1996 presidential campaign was biased to the liberal point of view, compared to only eight percent who believe it was biased to the conservative point of view. (Roper Center, Institute for Social Inquiry, October 1996.)

Topics for Reading and Writing

1. This selection relies very heavily on statistical information. Is the case it makes for the pervasive liberal bias of the U.S. media persuasive? Why? If not, why not?

2. Do you think the MRC believes that an "objective" media is possible, or even desirable?

3. How does the actual format for this piece differ from the more traditional opinion essays and feature articles included in this chapter? How does this piece take advantage of its web-based forum?

*Writing for the leading daily newspaper of America's most liberal major city, San Francisco, **Debra J. Saunders** here argues that although liberal bias is endemic in American journalism, the conservative movement can still remain healthy and in the mainstream of American society. More interesting are*

Debra J. Saunders
Conservatism Can Survive
Despite Liberal Bias

Of course the news media are liberal. A survey of the Washington press corps found that 89 percent of them voted for Bill Clinton in 1992, while 7 percent went for George Bush.

Saunders's examples of stories that "you are very unlikely to read in a mainstream paper." Bias is conveyed just as much through what isn't printed as by what is, and Saunders here argues that although "most journalists . . . strive for balance within a story," it's in the choice of stories that run that the media's liberal slant is most evident. Do you agree?

When I'm with my brethren in the news biz, whether in the newsroom or at a press conference, I know two things: I'm the freak; and 90 percent of the people around me didn't vote for George W. Bush, hate Attorney General John Ashcroft for not letting medical marijuana clubs flout federal drug law, but were furious that the Gonzalez family didn't rush to pack Elian off to Cuba after then-Attorney General Janet Reno told them to.

About the only journalists who won't admit that the news media are filled with liberals are lefties whose big beef is that the media are liberal instead of ultra-left.

I'm not whining, because I know that conservatism can thrive despite liberal bias. Nor do I respect those who quit reading newspapers because of the bias. After all, savvy readers can see through the gauze. Better to get the facts with a little bias than no facts at all.

Besides, most reporters—not columnists, who are paid to be opinionated—try to keep their ideology under wraps. Most also strive for balance within a story.

It's in the story ideas, however, that the bias really shows.

Here are some stories that you are very unlikely to read in a mainstream newspaper, and certainly not on the front page:

Gender gap hurts Democrats. (The better half of the gender gap is that men vote Republican.)

Illegal immigrants cashing welfare checks hit record high. (That's not the case now, but when it was, you really had to dig to read it here.)

Parents and students support standardized tests. (Only stories against testing need apply.)

Alaskan caribou herds thrive near oil pipeline. (If there were a 10 percent decline in the size of the herds, you know that there'd have been a front-page story heralding ecological disaster.)

Senate panel rejects Kyoto global warming pact. (Last year, a Senate committee voted to urge President Bush to return to the Kyoto negotiations, but to reject any treaty that exempts developing nations, which Kyoto does.)

You also see the bias in the stories that papers report on ad nauseum. When Prop. 209, which ended racial preferences in state hiring and admission, was on the ballot in 1996, The Chronicle ran more than 250 pieces (including letters to the editor) on the measure from July to December.

Repetitive stories chronicled the fears of minority students, with next to no recognition of students who might be helped. Poll stories reported that women "surprisingly" supported the measure.

The reportage was similar for Proposition 187, the 1994 measure that denied health care and schooling for illegal immigrants. I voted against 187, but still was appalled at journalists' frequent failure to report relevant information, say, on the costs of illegal immigration.

Prop. 209 won 54 percent of the vote, and 187 garnered 59 percent. Go figure: Many reporters write that support for either measure is politically risky.

Too many reporters saw it as their mission to defeat Propositions 209 and 187. In the end, the constant droning of the same arguments revealed a pitiful lack of imagination, and a herd mentality, in a profession that prides itself in its independence and intellectual curiosity.

The mantra at the modern journalism conference is diversity; but practitioners don't really understand what diversity means.

Topics for Reading and Writing

1. What point does Saunders make with her examples of stories that are ignored by the "liberal media?"

2. Saunders alludes to a concern with "diversity" in the modern media. What does she mean by that? Give examples of this concern for "diversity."

3. Unlike many commentators who argue that the media is liberal, Saunders feels that most journalists actually try to keep their feelings "under wraps"— which suggests that it's at the editorial level that the liberal bias enters news coverage. Do you agree with this? Do reporters or editors or producers or corporate executives set the tone of news coverage for an organization?

Daphne Eviatar, a contributing editor to the trade magazine American Lawyer, *analyzes the content of the Fox News Channel in this piece from the liberal journal* The Nation. *The Fox News Channel—the 24-hour cable news channel owned by conservative Australian businessman Rupert Murdoch— has only become more popular and influential in the years since Eviatar wrote her article, and Fox's coverage of the 2003 conflict in Iraq easily drew higher ratings than either of its competitors. Two real issues are embedded in the conversation about Fox News Channel. The first question is whether or not Fox is actually biased to the right. Roger Ailes, the network's head, fervently denies it, and his supporters insist that the channel only seems right wing because we have grown so accustomed to the liberal bias of the major broadcast networks, the* New York Times, *and CNN. Ailes's critics, though, deride the network's slogans—"We Report. You Decide" and "Fair*

Daphne Eviatar
Murdoch's Fox News

It was the last Sunday in January, and Vice President Dick Cheney was making the morning talk-show rounds. On ABC, Sam Donaldson posed hard-hitting questions about the new Administration's failure to alleviate California's energy crisis, the wisdom of George W. Bush's proposed tax cut and John Ashcroft's elusive answers to questions during his confirmation process. On NBC, Tim Russert challenged Cheney on the President's plans for deterring a recession, his commitment to campaign finance reform and how Ashcroft's pledge to enforce the law on abortion squares with the President's antichoice positions.

And on Fox? Brit Hume and Tony Snow—two of the news channel's most conservative anchors—pitched softballs to the new Vice President, prodding him to denounce the Clinton Administration and positioning him to pronounce the energy crisis in California the product of federal clean-air regulations and evidence of the need for offshore oil drilling. About Ashcroft, in a soundbite replayed on Fox throughout the day, Hume asked: "Do you sense in some of the opposition to him, that his faith and his devotion to it is being held against him? And do you sense in that, perhaps, a kind of anti-Christian bigotry?"

and Balanced"—as the journalistic embodiment of the Big Lie, the idea that a ludicrous idea, repeated fervently and frequently enough, will eventually be accepted as truth.

But beyond this question, and perhaps more important for the soul of American-style journalism, is the question of whether or not there's anything necessarily wrong with biased news. In much of the rest of the world, newspapers and television networks are up front about their political stances; in fact, until recently in Italy the government broadcasting entity (RAI) ran three competing news broadcasts each night, each one affiliated with a different political party's bias.

It was a typical question on a typical Sunday on the Fox News Channel. Although its right-wing talk-show hosts like Bill O'Reilly have received copious press attention, the conservative slant of Fox's regular news coverage has not. And while much has been written about Fox's gaffe on election night involving George W. Bush's cousin (which some think caused the public to regard Bush as the legitimate winner), there's been far less focus on the blatant partiality of Fox's regular staff, contributors and guests. It all combines to create a calculated mouthpiece for the right that remains thinly veiled behind its misleading mantra, "fair and balanced." And Fox could have real influence: According to *Editor & Publisher* magazine, a TV monitor in the White House press briefing room that aired CNN throughout the Clinton Administration was recently switched to the Fox News Channel.

It takes only a few hours on any given day to see Fox's political predilections in action. The Cheney interview, for example, began an ordinary Sunday of conservative cheerleading. Fox Washington correspondent James Rosen, covering the controversy over the Ashcroft nomination, portrayed the Senate opponents as political opportunists "venting" to appease their constituents. The features were no different. A segment about an effort to teach religion in public school was promoted repeatedly with the teaser: "Are we as a nation more or less spiritual today than we were twenty-five years ago? Are we a country that is losing faith?" Viewers were asked to call in answers. Later that same day, a tabloid-style piece on teen abuse of crystal methamphetamine was a virtual banner ad for right-wing policies of strict law enforcement and lengthy incarceration; in the approximately quarter-hour segment, drug treatment or addiction's causes were never once mentioned.

Such slants should come as no surprise, given the cast Rupert Murdoch has chosen to run Fox News Channel, the latest venture of his News Corporation. At the top is Roger Ailes, a onetime strategist to Presidents Nixon, Reagan and the elder George Bush. Ailes's lineup of talent, in addition to Hume and Snow (the latter a former chief speechwriter for the elder Bush), includes David Asman, former Op-Ed editor at the *Wall Street Journal,* and Sean Hannity, whose personal website features links to Rush Limbaugh's show and the National Rifle Association. Frequent Fox contributors include Fred Barnes, executive editor of *The Weekly Standard;* Monica Crowley, former assistant to Nixon; Jim Pinkerton, former Reagan and Bush staffer; John Podhoretz, editorial page editor of the *New York Post* and former Reagan speechwriter; and John Fund, a member of the *Wall Street Journal*'s editorial board and collaborator on Limbaugh's political diatribe, *The Way Things Ought to Be.*

Of course, paying lip service to its "fair and balanced" refrain, Fox is careful to include token moderates on its talking-head shows. But the middle of the road is routinely pitted against the ultraconservative. So-called liberal contributors, who are at best centrists, include NPR's Juan Williams and Mara Liasson and *Roll Call*'s Morton Kondracke. Murdoch has never been shy about using his news outlets, which include the *New York Post* and *The Weekly Standard,* to disseminate his politics. What's particularly insidious about the Fox channel, though, is that Murdoch has gone out of his way to cloak its politics in slogans like "We Report, You Decide" that lull the audience into believing it's hearing not a conservative viewpoint but the unadulterated truth.

The heights of distortion are reached on prime time. Since December, *The O'Reilly Factor,* a shout-show starring Bill O'Reilly, has been a top-rated talk show on cable, frequently surpassing MSNBC's *Hardball With Chris Matthews, Rivera Live* and even CNN's *Larry King Live.* O'Reilly is a step up from Rush Limbaugh—better looking and more reasonable—but he's an equally staunch conservative. The evening of January 16 was typical. To debate the controversial Ashcroft nomination, O'Reilly pitted the powerful Christian Coalition's Pat Robertson against Annie Laurie Gaylor, co-founder of an obscure Wisconsin-based atheist advocacy group. When Gaylor expressed concern about Ashcroft's position on abortion, O'Reilly cornered her into making the irrelevant pronouncement that she wouldn't personally support anyone for public office who was antichoice. Now O'Reilly could dismiss her entirely: "That's an extreme view, Miss Gaylor, so you're an extremist." And so, by implication, was everyone else who opposed Ashcroft's nomination.

If you can make it through O'Reilly, stick around for *Hannity & Colmes,* Fox's higher-decibel version of CNN's *Crossfire.* Though the idea is to pit left against right, Alan Colmes, the awkward-looking designated lefty of the pair, is no match for his right-wing matchup, Sean Hannity. Hannity smugly rolls right over Colmes and his Democratic guests while coaxing conservatives to pontificate without interruption. During Fox's postelection coverage Hannity bellowed repeatedly that "the Vice President because of his blind ambition has brought us to the brink of a constitutional crisis" and charged that the Democrats were trying to "steal the election" by demanding a vote recount. Meanwhile, "they might as well have a scarecrow in the liberal seat," says media critic and University of Illinois professor Robert McChesney.

Even Fox's supposedly "straight" nightly news anchors take regular swipes at Democrats. Covering the postelection litigation in Florida, for example, anchor John Gibson railed that "the Democratic lawyers have flooded Florida" because "they are afraid of George W. Bush becoming President and instituting tort reform and their gravy train will be over." Fox further blurs distinctions between news and opinion by having anchors and political commentators switch roles from one day to the next. O'Reilly, for instance, played anchor just after the Supreme Court handed down the decision that ended Gore's fight for the presidency.

Fox's murkiest judgment call may have been hiring John Ellis, the President's first cousin, to analyze election exit-poll results. Lo and behold, Fox was the first network to declare erroneously that Bush had won the election, prompting the avalanche that followed. We now also know that Ellis was discussing confidential exit-poll information with his cousins throughout election night. At

Congress's mid-February hearings on election night coverage, Ailes said in his prepared testimony that Ellis was merely acting as "a good journalist talking to his very high-level sources."

But the bias didn't stop there. Peter Hart of Fairness & Accuracy in Reporting notes that after Bush was named the winner of the election, "on Fox, the question was posed as, 'Will Bush compromise or will he stand tough on his principles?'" On December 17, for example, Snow asked Bush Chief of Staff Andrew Card: "Now, the President-elect says that he wants to reach across the partisan divide, and a lot of people are interpreting that as meaning that he has got to water down his views to appease liberal Republicans and Democrats. Is that what he's going to do?"

This blending of news with right-wing partiality dismays many Fox employees. Although staffers say they don't receive direct orders to include or ignore stories for political purposes, "I've been at editorial meetings," says one Fox News Channel employee who did not want to be named. "Certain stories fly and certain stories don't. I'm not blind and neither are my colleagues. Everyone is aware that something is at work. There's a reason that there's a perception that Fox leans to the right."

A manager at the Fox News Channel who's been in broadcast news for six years and who also declines to be identified says the tilt is reflected in the enterprise pieces aired. "The ideas come from the bureau chiefs, and they want to get their reporters on the air, so they're going to pitch stories that management will approve." Says Sarah Barrows, a former production assistant and booker at the Fox News Channel, "They know who their audience is, and they pick stories based on that." Barrows, now an associate producer at Oxygen Media, says that during the Clinton impeachment investigation, for example, "that story probably led nine out of ten times." The Whitewater investigation was another popular front-runner. "Fair and balanced? Give me a break," says a former Fox producer. "During the Clinton impeachment—which they were just loving—it was OK to run a Newt Gingrich soundbite by itself. But if you ran a soundbite by a Democrat you also had to run a soundbite by a Republican." Though this producer had worked at CBS News and at an ABC affiliate, "I had never experienced a newsroom that was that conservative." Fox management's far heavier hand than at other networks is in part a reflection of the fact that Murdoch owns 30 percent of the stock of News Corporation; the other major television networks are all owned by large corporations with widely held shares.

The Fox spin has even crept into its website; each week it posts a new "PC Patrol," in which columnist Scott Norvell bashes liberal organizations like the ACLU for trying to separate church from state or ridicules feminist organizations for criticizing the comments of Fox favorite Rush Limbaugh.

So there's no question that under Fox's guise of neutrality lurks the right-wing designs of its management. But is that a problem? Contributors don't think so. "Fox reports the news from a more conservative mindset than conventional journalism," says Kondracke, a Fox regular. "And that's good. Because if you only have the perspective of the standard liberal outlook, that distorts reality too. Fox is an antidote to conventional news media." NPR's Juan Williams says that at Fox, "I've never felt so intellectually free." Sure, it's slanted, he says, but "the widespread perception of the American people is 'all these people have bias.'" Fox management, meanwhile, denies any partiality. "We feel that other networks have a liberal bias to them," says Bill Shine, executive producer for the Fox News Channel. "But Mr. Ailes pounds this into us at every staff meeting, every time we get together: 'fair and balanced.'" Ailes declined to comment.

True, studies have shown that Washington journalists are more likely to vote Democratic and identify themselves as liberal. One frequently cited survey by the Freedom Forum/Roper Center in 1996 found that 61 percent of the 139 Washington-based journalists queried professed to being either "liberal" or "liberal to moderate," while only 9 percent said they were "conservative" or "moderate to conservative." But how that plays out in news coverage is a different matter. A study by the Project for Excellence in Journalism found that in the last weeks of the presidential campaign, Bush was twice as likely to receive positive coverage as Gore. And the group's study examining five scattered weeks between February and June revealed that more than three-quarters of the campaign coverage included discussion that Gore lies and exaggerates or is tainted by scandal, while the most common theme about Bush was that he is a "different kind of Republican." No Democratic bias there.

Still, Fox is obviously filling a niche. Since it started in 1996, ratings have soared, climbing more than 200 percent in the last quarter of 2000 from the same period the year before. During the fourth quarter of 2000 it started turning a profit, a year ahead of schedule. And in December, its ratings beat CNN in prime time, even though CNN reaches about 22 million more homes. So does Fox's success attest to a huge conservative audience out there? Not necessarily. Sure, there's the Limbaugh crowd, which wants to hear right-wing vitriol. But plenty of people tune in to be titillated by the news channel's brash, infotainment style. "People come up to me on the street and say, 'I hate that Sean Hannity,'" says University of Southern California law professor and frequent Fox contributor Susan Estrich, one of the news channel's few truly liberal regular commentators. "But I say, 'Do you hate him five days a week?' They say, 'Yes.' They watch it."

Murdoch has done something ingenious: He's created an entertaining news channel that disseminates his viewpoint far and wide and also makes good business sense. It costs far less to get two people to snipe at each other on the air than to pay reporters and producers to dig up real news. And although Fox may be leading the transformation to econo-news, it is not alone. The pressure to attend to the bottom line is yielding a watered-down form of journalism at all TV news outlets. "My views of contemporary journalism are so disheartening at the moment that I find it very difficult to point just to Fox and say, 'Tsk, tsk, look what they're doing,' without pointing at the same time to all of the networks and saying, 'Tsk, tsk, what have you done?'" says Marvin Kalb, Washington-office director of the Shorenstein Center on the Press, Politics and Public Policy and a former broadcast journalist for CBS and NBC.

Murdoch may be the most blatant, though, about putting profits above principles. In the mid-1990s he eliminated the BBC from his Hong Kong-based

Star Satellite news service because the Chinese government didn't like the channel's critical programming. And his publishing house, HarperCollins, dropped former Hong Kong governor Chris Patten's *East and West,* which included less than flattering descriptions of Chinese leaders. At a Fox-owned station in Florida, award-winning reporters Jane Akre and Steve Wilson claim their contract was canceled in 1997 because they refused to soft-pedal their investigative story about the effect of bovine growth hormone on the state's milk supply after BGH producer Monsanto complained directly to Roger Ailes. They sued. Wilson couldn't prove his case, but Akre won hers, which charged that Fox fired her for threatening to blow the whistle on its action.

But every network has its closetful of stories killed, buried or neutralized to serve the owners' or advertisers' interest. A study last year by the Pew Research Center for People and the Press and *Columbia Journalism Review* found that more than 40 percent of nearly 300 journalists surveyed said they had intentionally avoided newsworthy stories or softened the tone of stories to benefit the interests of their news organizations. That fear of offense radically restricts the range of opinion that makes it onto the news networks, redefining the center and relegating left speakers to the fringe, seemingly out of touch with their audience.

So what to do? Media critic McChesney proposes stepping up FCC regulations, boosting funding for public radio and television, and revamping the antitrust laws to set limits on media ownership. Lawrence Grossman, former president of NBC and PBS, advocates making broadcast companies pay to use the public airwaves and using that money to fund public service programming and a stronger public broadcasting system. Realistically, however, given Bush's picks at the FCC and the Justice Department, additional fees and stricter antitrust scrutiny are unlikely to happen anytime soon. And it's hard to imagine this sharply divided Congress putting significantly more money into public broadcasting.

Can liberals compete? Yes and no. "I hope there's a revolt out there that wants to have ten liberal *O'Reilly Factor*s," quips Fox contributor Estrich. "Where are these guys on the left who can do a news channel that covers the news well and also provides an opportunity to get their views across?"

These days, that's an enormously expensive proposition. When Murdoch entered the game, on top of capital and production costs he paid cable operators $10 per household to carry the Fox News Channel. "That escalated the cost of starting a channel to $500 million," estimates Jay Levin, founder and former owner of the alternative *LA Weekly,* who tried to launch an environmental cable channel in 1993 that was ultimately unsuccessful. But there are alternatives. Digital television is finally becoming a reality and should vastly increase the number of channels, at least temporarily reducing startup costs. And the newest broadband technology creates an opportunity for an endless number of televisionlike stations via the Internet.

Fox started in 1996, when anti-Clinton sentiment burned bright. The new Bush Administration offers ample targets for left-wing fire. And there's a market for it, insists John Schwartz, president of Free Speech TV, a nonprofit station based in Boulder, Colorado, that's carried on the satellite Dish Network and reaches 5 million homes. "There's a fanatical viewership," says Schwartz.

Of course, without a media magnate like Murdoch behind it, an independent station's reach will never rival Fox's. But done with intelligence and wit, left TV could at least be a potent thorn in its side. For now, though, Murdoch and Fox remain unchallenged.

Topics for Reading and Writing

1. How does Eviatar begin the article? Why does she use this approach instead of a more traditional introduction to a piece of persuasive writing?

2. Read Eviatar's and Saunders's articles together. How do they differ in aim and tone? What audience is each writer addressing?

3. Should we just accept that objectivity is a phantom goal and get news from the sources most congenial to our own biases? What effect might this have on democracy?

One of America's most respected political columnists and commentators, E.J. Dionne currently writes for the Washington Post *(from which this article was taken) and has also worked for the New York Times. A senior fellow at the Brookings Institution, Dionne is generally considered a liberal writer. In this piece Dionne takes another look at conservatives' accusations of liberal media bias. Dionne's point, briefly, is that conservatives are (to borrow a sports metaphor) "working the refs," or complaining so much and so loudly that the arbiters of bias start bending their way. Dionne argues that this has resulted in a notable shift to the right in American news coverage, as news organizations that weren't liberal in the first place start making more and more efforts to mollify their conservative critics.*

E.J. Dionne
The Rightward Press

The fat is in the fire on the issue of media bias, and that is a good thing. It's time to revisit a matter on which the conventional wisdom is, roughly, 180 degrees off.

You hear the conventional wisdom all the time from shrewd conservative commentators who understand that political pressure, relentlessly applied, usually achieves its purposes. They have sold the view that the media are dominated by liberals and that the news is skewed against conservatives.

This belief fueled the construction of a large network of conservative institutions—especially on radio and cable television—that provides conservative viewpoints close to 24 hours a day. Conservatives argued that hopelessly left-wing establishments news sources needed to be balanced by brave, relentless voices from the right.

But the continuing attacks on mainstream journalists have another effect. Because the drumbeat of conservative press criticism has been so steady, the establishment press has internalized it. Editors and network executives are far more likely to hear complaints from the right than from the left.

To the extent that there has been a bias in the establishment media, it has been less a liberal tilt than a preference for the values of the educated, professional class—which, surprise, surprise, is roughly the class position of most journalists.

This meant that on social and cultural issues—abortion and religion come to mind—journalism was not particularly hospitable to conservative voices. But on economic issues—especially free trade and balanced budgets—the press tilted toward the center or even toward moderate conservatism. You might say that the two groups most likely to be mistreated by the media were religious conservatives and trade unionists.

But even that view is out of date, because the definition of "media" commonly used in judging these matters is faulty. And that's why you are beginning to hear liberals and Democrats make a new argument. Earlier this week, former president Bill Clinton contrasted what he called an "increasingly right-wing and bellicose conservative press" with "an increasingly docile establishment press." A couple of weeks back, Senate Democratic Leader Tom Daschle lashed out at radio talk show host Rush Limbaugh. He said Limbaugh's attacks were so "shrill" that "the threats against those of us in public life go up dramatically, against us and against our families."

Note the response of the so-called liberal media. Rather than join an outcry against Limbaugh, the establishment commentary was mostly aimed against Daschle and picked up the conservative cry that he was "whining." Limbaugh was invited for lengthy and respectful interviews on CNN's "Reliable Sources" and Tim Russert's show on CNBC.

Now, television hosts are free to invite anyone they wish (they've even had me on), and cable networks long for a piece of Limbaugh's large audience. But that is the point: Limbaugh's new respectability is the surest sign that the conservative talk network is now bleeding into what passes for the mainstream media, just as the unapologetic conservatism of the Fox News Channel is now affecting programming on the other cable networks. This shift to the right is occurring as cable becomes a steadily more important source of news.

All this constitutes a genuine triumph for conservatives. But rather than rest on their laurels, they continue to pound away at any media deviation from their version of political correctness. When Katie Couric had the nerve to ask some tough questions of EPA Administrator Christine Todd Whitman on Monday's "Today" show, the ever-alert conservative Media Research Center trashed Couric for bias. When the Chicago Tribune ran an unflattering picture of President Bush on its Nov. 14 front page, it was assailed for a lack of patriotism. Editors who worry about conservative criticism are not paranoid. You just wonder: Where have the liberals been?

It took conservatives a lot of hard and steady work to push the media rightward. It dishonors that work to continue to presume that—except for a few liberal columnists—there is any such thing as the big liberal media. The media world now includes (1) talk radio, (2) cable television and (3) the traditional news sources (newspapers, newsmagazines and the old broadcast networks). Two of these three major institutions tilt well to the right, and the third is under constant pressure to avoid even the pale hint of liberalism. These institutions, in turn, influence the burgeoning world of online news and commentary.

What it adds up to is a media heavily biased toward conservative politics and conservative politicians. Kudos to the right. Now, what will the rest of us do about the new bias?

Topics for Reading and Writing

1. How does Dionne's essential argument (or thesis) differ from Eviatar's? Do you think each argument is aimed at a different or the same audience? And if they are aimed at different audiences, what are those respective audiences?

2. Dionne's piece appeared on the editorial page of one of America's most important daily newspapers, while Eviatar's appeared in a journal with a clear political leaning. How does Dionne's differ from the other opinion pieces in terms of how it constructs its authority and how it derives its authority from the publication in which it appears?

3. Dionne argues that the "liberal" bias is less a bias in favor of left-wing positions than it is a bias in favor of "the values of the educated, professional class . . . the class position of most journalists." Do you accept this argument? Comparing Dionne's argument to the description of the voting patterns of journalists appearing in "Media Bias Basics," which do you find a more compelling account of the "slant," if any, of the mainstream media?

NRO (*National Review Online*) Debates
Are The Media Liberal?

*Making another appearance in this book, media watchdog group MRC offers up its leader, **Brent Bozell**, to debate **Eric Alterman**, author of the recent book* What Liberal Media? ***Jack Schafer** of the online journal Slate.com responds to both, after the fact. Here we have a fine example of the kinds of snippy arguments made by all the participants in this debate. Both Alterman and Bozell have valuable points to make about bias, but it's unlikely that anyone's mind will be changed by their debate—it sheds more heat than light, as the old cliché has it. However, what is particularly interesting about this debate is Schafer's response. Too often, the contemporary media, especially the liberal-versus-conservative shouting programs that began on PBS* (The McLaughlin Group) *and CNN* (Crossfire) *and now dominate Fox News, attempt to boil issues down to binary questions: either you're for it or against it, either you hate it or love it. This debate exemplifies*

No: Eric Alterman

I will admit I don't have great hopes for convincing NRO readers to see the error of their ways. After all, this is only 500 words. You people are too smart to change your minds about a bedrock belief over just 500 words. For that to happen, I'm afraid, you'd have to buy the book. Do it HERE, if only to give your blood pressure a shot in the arm.

But of course we all know that quite a few of you are too smart to believe that silly nonsense about the media being "liberal." I'm here on this site to tell you guys the jig is up. It's time to come clean. You've milked this cow long enough and she done died. Here's how I put it in the book: (And for you Goldberg/Coulter fans, those little numbers are called "footnotes." They allow other people to check your work.)

While some conservatives actually believe their own grumbles, the really smart ones don't. They know mau-mauing the other side is a just a good way to get their ideas across—or perhaps *how questions are oversimplified by the voices debating them, simply because it's easier to win over the public by making an issue easy than it is by showing an issue in all its contradictions and complications. Schafer's contribution is very valuable here; he shows there are all sorts of stripes of conservatism, all kinds of striations among leftists. Moreover, he shows how apparently "objective" statistics can be used to slant or misrepresent the facts.*

prevent the other side from getting a fair hearing for theirs. On occasion, honest conservatives admit this. Rich Bond, then the chair of the Republican Party complained during the 1992 election, "I think we know who the media want to win this election—and I don't think it's George Bush.[1] The very same Rich Bond also noted during the very same election, however, "There is some strategy to it [bashing the 'liberal' media]. . . . If you watch any great coach, what they try to do is 'work the refs.' Maybe the ref will cut you a little slack on the next one."[2] Bond is hardly alone. That the so-called liberal media [hereafter "SCLM"], were biased against the administration of Ronald Reagan is an article of faith among Republicans. Yet James Baker, perhaps the most media savvy of them, owned up to the fact that any such complaint was decidedly misplaced. "There were days and times and events we might have had some complaints [but] on balance I don't think we had anything to complain about," he explained to one writer."[3] Patrick Buchanan, among the most conservative pundits and presidential candidates in Republican history, found that he could not identify any allegedly liberal bias against him during his presidential candidacies. "I've gotten balanced coverage, and broad coverage—all we could have asked. For heaven sakes, we kid about the 'liberal media,' but every Republican on earth does that,"[4] the aspiring American ayatollah cheerfully confessed during the 1996 campaign. And even William Kristol, without a doubt the most influential Republican/neoconservative publicist in America today has come clean on this issue. "I admit it," he told a reporter. "The liberal media were never that powerful, and the whole thing was often used as an excuse by conservatives for conservative failures."[5] Nevertheless Kristol apparently feels no compunction about exploiting and reinforcing ignorant prejudices of his own constituency. In a 2001 subscription pitch to conservative potential subscribers of his Rupert Murdoch-funded magazine, Kristol complained, "The trouble with politics and political coverage today is that there's too much liberal bias. . . . There's too much tilt toward the left-wing agenda. Too much apology for liberal policy failures. Too much pandering to liberal candidates and causes."[6] (It's a wonder he left out "Too much hypocrisy.")

Over to you, Brent. I'd love to hear how you explain the above. . . .

---

[1] See David Domke, Mark D. Watts, Dhavan C. Shah, and David. P Fan, "The Politics of Conservative Elites and the 'Liberal Media' Argument," *Journal of Communication*, Autumn, 1999, 46.

[2] *Washington Post*, August, 20, 1992, C1.

[3] Mark Hertsgaard, *On Bended Knee: the Press and the Reagan Presidency* (New York: Farrar, Straus & Giroux, 1988) 4.

[4] In an interview with the *Los Angeles Times*. March 14, 1996.

[5] The *New Yorker*, May 22, 1995.

[6] The author received this subscription mailing in June 2001.

Yes: Brent Bozell

These are fascinating times for polemical debate. Are we right to invade Iraq? Will tax cuts weaken or strengthen the economy? On these and so many other issues a conservative can enjoy energetic discourse with the political left.

Just don't ask a liberal if there is a liberal bias in the national news media. In answer to that question you'll continue to hear what conservatives have been hearing for decades. No matter how many times the obvious is proven, and no matter how many ways that evidence is documented, the response from the liberal elites is always the same.

Noise.

For decades conservatives have charged that a liberal bias dominated the press; at every turn the liberals in the press have denied it. But when irrefutable evidence is presented—say, a national survey of the Washington-based media commissioned by the Gannett media organization showing that in 1992, by 89-7 percent, they voted for Bill Clinton over George Bush; that by 50-14 percent they see themselves as Democrats over Republicans; and that while 61 percent describe themselves as liberal, only two percent dare call themselves "conservative"—how do they respond? OK, they concede, we may be philosophically liberal, but it doesn't prove our philosophy affects our performance. But how can such an overwhelming bias *not* affect the work product? Noise.

The Media Research Center has produced dozens of scientific studies, often examining tens of thousands of stories at a time, proving the liberal bias dominating the news media. Not once has a single study ever been refuted, or any of the hundreds of thousands of data been disputed. Much in the same vein that Saddam denies the existence of his weapons of mass destruction, the liberal media simply deny the evidence proving their bias. And if pressed they'll fall to the next line of defense: it speaks to a *general* bias, but doesn't prove anyone's *specific* bias. More noise.

What, exactly, is a liberal denying when he denies a liberal bias in the media? Most journalists continue to promote the mythology that bias is nonexistent in the news business, an amazing proposition given that it is *impossible* not to be biased. What is news? What is the day's top news story? What is to be the lead? Who is to be cited? What ought to be the conclusion? These and so many others are the daily questions a reporter faces, and every single one demands a subjective, biased response. So why do so many journalists deny the obvious? First and foremost, because they really do believe their liberalism is mainstream.

But wait! Stop the presses! Extra! Extra! Bias has been found! After all these years suddenly these same journalists are finding that a conservative bias—yes, indeedy, a *conservative* bias dominates the press because the Fox News Channel and Rush Limbaugh control the world, or something.

Assuming Fox were as conservative as liberals charge—and it's an assumption I am not willing to make—it would now be one against CBS, NBC, ABC, CNBC, MSNBC, CNN, CNN Headline News, and on and on and on. Some conservative dominance. What about Rush and the seemingly endless list of conservatives in the media today, men and women like Cal Thomas, Bob Novak, Michael Reagan, Laura Ingraham, and the like? All have two things in common: All openly, cheerfully acknowledge their biases; and all are commentators. Not a one is a member of the "news" media.

But if you're on the other side of the political fence the rules are very different. If you're a liberal, you're objective. And if you are promoting an agenda, you're a reporter.

Making noise.

Jack Shafer
The Varieties of Media Bias, Part 2

Whenever conservatives talk to liberals about press bias—or vice versa—they talk right past one another. Both factions seem to work backward from their conclusions to the evidence and damn what the other side says. For a prime example, see the "Are the Media Liberal?" debate in *National Review Online* from last week. In it, conservative L. Brent Bozell III of the Media Research Center spars with lefty journalist Eric Alterman, author of *What Liberal Media?*

In his first response to Alterman, Bozell calls liberal media bias "obvious," "documented," and "proven" and cites a "national survey of the Washington-based media commissioned by the Gannett media organization" to demonstrate the press corps' essential liberality. (Actually, the survey was commissioned by the Freedom Forum foundation, which grew out of a foundation started by publisher Frank E. Gannett but is completely independent from the Gannett news corporation.) Bozell writes that the study found that:

> in 1992, by 89-7 percent, [press members surveyed] voted for Bill Clinton over George Bush; that by 50-14 percent they see themselves as Democrats over Republicans; and that while 61 percent describe themselves as liberal, only two percent dare call themselves "conservative.". . .

Such lopsided numbers would turn anybody's head. But how accurate are they? Not very. Reporter Robert Parry exposed the survey's weaknesses in a 1997 piece: The polling group that conducted the survey sent its questionnaires to 323 journalists covering some aspect of Congress. Only 139 completed surveys came back, and nine of them left the question about their presidential vote blank.

While you *might* reap accurate results from a Vulcan mind probe of just 130 members of the Washington press corps, you'd want to make sure the 130 surveyed were the right 130. But that's not the case with this survey. Only 60 of the 323 questionnaires went to journalists at the elite organizations that set the news agenda: the *New York Times, Washington Post, Los Angeles Times, USA Today, Wall Street Journal,* CBS, NBC, ABC, CNN, PBS, National Public Radio, *Time,*

Newsweek, U.S. News, the Associated Press, and Reuters. Instead, the pollster told Parry, most of the surveys were sent to Washington staffers at regional newspapers (the *Boston Globe, Denver Post, Dallas Morning News*) or at the chain wire services (Knight-Ridder, Newhouse), with a quarter of the questionnaires going to pipsqueak pubs like *Indian Country Today, Hill Rag, Washington Citizen,* and *Government Standard.*

The survey guaranteed its respondents anonymity, so nobody knows who, exactly, returned surveys. But we can guess: Self-important big-shots surely round-filed the nosy Q & A, and flattered small-fry probably obliged. I'd be astonished if more than 10 of the 60 elite journos surveyed bothered filling out the form.

What's more, Bozell and Co. ignore the changing face of politics when they attempt to prove the liberality of the press corps by rounding up Clinton voters. Clinton ran as a controversial (within his own party) centrist—not a Carter, Mondale, or Dukakis liberal. He also governed from that slice of the political spectrum. Conclusion? Case most definitely *not* closed.

Alterman matches Bozell's lameness by "disproving" liberal bias with quotations from leading Republicans and conservatives—Rich Bond, James Baker, Pat Buchanan, and Bill Kristol. These figures either confess that they "work the ref" (the press) in hopes of winning favorable coverage for conservatives or concede that press bias really isn't that big a deal. Bozell zings Alterman for ignoring the content-analysis work he and other conservatives have done and for plucking a quotation here and a quotation there from the vastness of Lexis-Nexis to make his point.

The ongoing sermons about media bias from right and left stink mostly because they rely on the ideological frameworks constructed by the bias-hunters of the early '70s. In the old days, it was easy to sort Washington journalists into left and right by lining them up against the wall and giving them a dozen litmus test issues—for or against, say, *reproductive rights; gay rights; civil liberties; gun control; national health care; school prayer; capital punishment; arms control; free trade; welfare; crime; civil rights; the drug war; corporate power; the environment; porn;* and *deficit spending.* Anybody who took the liberal line 75 percent of the time qualified as a liberal.

But the old litmus paper has lost its magic. While the media-bias interlocutors' positions remain fixed—have any political views at the *Nation* changed in the last half-century?—the views of Washington journalists have shifted, as have those of the public. The journalists-formerly-known-as-liberals (TJFKNAL) are no longer reflexively *against* free trade, the drug war, and corporations, thanks, in part, to the centrist teachings of Bill Clinton. And they're no longer reflexively *for* deficit spending, welfare, and porn. Likewise, traditional conservative views about the environment, civil liberties, the deficit, arms control, and health care have morphed, allowing President Bush unilaterally to cut the nuclear arsenal, propose new drug subsidies for the codgers, and budget for deeper deficits.

The litmus paper doesn't work perfectly on conservatives, either, who no longer conform to the convenient stereotypes. The *Weekly Standard* national greatness conservative is a different breed than the orthodox conservative writing at *National Review* and the paleoconservative barking at Buchanan's *American Conservative,* all of whom can quarrel with the Bartleyite neocon *Wall Street Journal* editorial page.

Are Alterman and Bozell dense about the new politics or just loyal apparatchiks?

Some liberal markers endure—feminism (though it's waning), separation of church and state, and labor, for example. But the average Washington TJFKNAL I come into contact with doesn't fall neatly along old-school divisions/lines. Where the liberal reporter of 1979 would no sooner phone a Heritage Foundation analyst for a comment than he would somebody from the John Birch Society, today's average TJFKNAL willingly speed-dials the Heritage Foundation, American Enterprise Institute, or Cato Institute without wincing—in most cases without labeling the organization as right-leaning.

This is not to argue that there are no liberals in the press. Obviously there are. The *New York Times'* Robert Pear still channels the ghost of Hubert H. Humphrey. But most modern reporters swear fealty to the story. (Case in point: If a conservative offered Pear an anti-lib story that got him Page One, he'd take it, but that's not the side of the street he typically works.) If they have to savage a Clinton or a Gore or a Reich in the process, them's the breaks. If there is an overarching bias in the press corps, it's one in favor of official sources in government and business, the powerful people who hold the keys to information. The election of Ronald Reagan gave credence to conservative ideas, not because he turned liberals into conservatives but because liberals couldn't get the story unless they approached conservative ideas with some semblance of balance. (I'll get to the paucity of conservative reporters, lapsed or otherwise, in the reporter ranks, and I'll also write about the profusion of conservatives in the commentariat.)

In his new book, Alterman archly dismisses the existence of the liberal media, writing, "Even the genuinely liberal media is not so liberal," especially compared to the liberal media of Europe. (Of course, the European press follows a tradition in which a newspaper explicitly supports one political party over another while American pressmen are supposed to subordinate their personal views to objectivity.) According to Alterman, the top Washington journalists are social liberals and fiscal conservatives, not card-carrying Americans for Democratic Action members from the days of yore. Alterman credits this critique to the lefty critics at Fairness and Accuracy in Reporting, which commissioned a survey and study—no less flawed in design, participation, and execution than the poll cited above—to assert *the public's views are to the left of the press corps'!*

Bozell's Media Research Center team counters with less than transparent studies they say prove the American public perceives an overwhelmingly liberal bias in the news. Could it be the public automatically thinks the media is liberal because the right wing has hammered away on this point ever since Nixon declared war on the press 35 years ago?

Once again, left and right talk past one another.

Topics for Reading and Writing

1. Sketch out the essential theses of Schafer, Alterman, and Bozell. Then, describe the kinds of evidence they use: statistical, anecdotal, a close reading of one example, a list of a large number of examples, etc. What kind of evidence is most convincing?

2. After reading all the arguments about bias in the American media, compare these ideas with your own experience as a media-watcher. Where do you think the biases, if any, lie? Is objectivity possible? If not, what sort of standard should journalists aspire to attain—or should they be nothing more than propagandists for their positions?

3. What role does the public have to play in policing journalists, in supporting "good" journalism, or in ensuring that the press gives us accurate information about current events? How can new technologies affect the relationship between the people, the press, and power?

Al Neuharth's brief article is his own characteristically USA Today-style contribution to the debate about journalism and bias. Ever since its inception, USA Today has been criticized for its lack of depth and its TV-style coverage of serious news stories. However, in the last few years the newspaper has gained a great deal of respect for its business and sports reporting— not surprisingly, considering that the overwhelming majority of USA Today readers consume the newspaper while traveling, and turn to the paper to keep up with their stocks or their sports teams. The newspaper has, moreover, been a rare recent success story in an industry undergoing painful business contractions, resource cuts due to corporate ownership, and losses in readership.

Al Neuharth
Why Your News is
Sometimes Slanted

Your picture of what's going on in the world depends mostly on which newspapers you read or which TV or cable channels you watch. Nearly all professional journalists try to be objective. But sometimes slants or spins cross the line between skepticism (good) and cynicism (bad).

This week, on the same day, the country's three biggest newspapers had these contrasting page-one headlines on the latest developments concerning drugs for AIDS:

- USA TODAY: "Vaccine for AIDS shows promise."
- *The New York Times:* "Large Trial Finds AIDS Vaccine Fails To Stop Infection."
- *The Wall Street Journal:* "Steep Price of Roche AIDS Drug May Put It Out of Patients' Reach."

AIDS aside, those headlines illustrate distinctly different approaches. USA TODAY is middle-of-the-road, properly skeptical, yet generally upbeat. *The Wall Street Journal* is ultra-conservative, especially cautious on money matters. *The New York Times* is ultra-liberal, often cynical about establishment things.

Some years ago, the first editor in chief of USA TODAY, John Quinn, jested before a National Press Foundation audience that this is how the country's four top newspapers might headline the biggest possible news story—the end of the world:

- *The New York Times:* "World Ends. Third World Countries Hardest Hit."
- *The Wall Street Journal:* "World Ends. Dow Jones Industrial Average Hits Zero."
- *The Washington Post:* "World Ends. White House Ignored Early Warnings, Unnamed Sources Say."
- USA TODAY: "We're Dead. State-by State Demise, pg. 8A. Final, Final Sports Scores, pg. 6C."

Moral: If you understand the philosophy, policy and style of your news dispensers, it helps you balance the baffle and B.S. with the right stuff.

Topics for Reading and Writing

1. What is Neuharth's outlook on media bias? Where can we find objectivity? Many have criticized his paper for its "Don't worry—be happy" approach to the news. Does he respond the same way to questions of bias?

2. Is it fair to characterize the *Wall Street Journal* as "ultraconservative" or the *New York Times* as "ultraliberal"? Do these designations serve Neuharth's business interest in any way?

3. Neuharth's last point almost seems to embody the European idea of journalism—understand the bias of your favorite news source but don't lament it. What does it mean for journalism that such a prominent figure appears to sanguinely accept the omnipresence of bias?

Garry Trudeau
Doonesbury cartoons about *USA Today*

For many people, Doonesbury makes getting out of bed worth the trouble. **Garry Trudeau's** *smart, frankly liberal comic strip began as a student cartoon while Trudeau was at Yale (which itself appears frequently as "Walden College" in the strip), but Trudeau gained fame as one of President Nixon's sharpest and funniest critics during Vietnam and Watergate. Trudeau's characters—dateless wonder turned Internet entrepreneur Mike Doonesbury, arrogant jock/soldier/coach B.D., soulful bimbo Boopsie, clueless Zonker, and many others—have reflected America's last 30 years in their lives. The fatuous, self-important TV reporter Roland Hedley stars in these postmodern panels, which satirize the relentlessly trivial and upbeat USA Today newspaper, then in its early years. Trudeau has never been shy about taking on the media and journalism, even though this has often meant parodying the very newspapers that carry his cartoons.*

DOONESBURY © G. B. Trudeau. Reprinted with permission of Universal Press Syndicate.

DOONESBURY © G. B. Trudeau. Reprinted with permission of Universal Press Syndicate.

DOONESBURY © G. B. Trudeau. Reprinted with permission of Universal Press Syndicate.

DOONESBURY © G. B. Trudeau. Reprinted with permission of Universal Press Syndicate. All rights reserved.

Topics for Reading and Writing

1. What are the characteristics of the *USA Today* that *Doonesbury* highlights here? What sort of criticism do you think is implied by the peppy prose and snappy graphics?

2. What's wrong, in essence, with the kind of journalism that Trudeau belittles in these strips?

3. What has Trudeau been able to accomplish with graphic layout and images that might not be possible in a purely textual analysis/critique of *USA Today?*

Timothy D. Pollard
Yo, Yo, Yo! This is the Hip-hop CNN

*In this article, **Timothy Pollard** points out what many might call the "pandering" of an august cable news network to the most lucrative demographic: young people. The important question that arises from Pollard's article is one that always arises in debates about television or the movies in a capitalistic society: to what degree should the media pursue disinterested standards of quality (determined by powerful bodies of critics or professionals) and to what degree should the media pursue the audiences that will bring it the most profit? Does it "dumb down" the content of the news when middle-aged writers and producers try to use—and often misuse—the slang of people 40 years younger? Does it detract from the dignity and importance of the news? Or is this really an attempt to make current events relevant to a generation that seems to feel increasingly disconnected from the great events of the day?*

Prior to entering academia, Pollard (b. 1959) spent 15 years at CNN in Atlanta and Washington, D.C. He currently teaches at Ball State University in Muncie, Ind.

There is one holy grail in advertising: the 18-to-49-year-old market. This demographic is responsible for the bulk of advertising purchases on television these days. If you do not have this group, you are considered old-fashioned and out of touch with today's hip culture.

To reach this audience, CNN Headline News has adopted a list of terms from "hip-hop" language for use by anchors, in the "crawl" (the news strip that runs at the bottom of the television screen), and in graphics. On this list are words such as *bling-bling* ("jewelry"), *flava* ("style"), *fly* (an older term meaning "attractive") and *freak* ("dance provocatively" or "have sex").

With advertising budgets stretched thin by more and more "niche" television channels on satellite or cable, networks have to refine their missions. The theory is that hip-hop lingo will influence younger audiences to view CNN Headline News and not the other news networks. In fact, CNN Headline News has beaten MSNBC in the key 18-to-49-year-old group for the past two months.

Two questions: Is CNN Headline News pandering to get this age group, or is it simply ahead of the curve? And will the other news networks follow suit?

The question of using current vernacular to replace standard English has been debated for years. Is it OK to use language common to a certain group to get the story across, or is it pandering to the lowest common denominator? If the bottom line is to get people to watch your station or network, then you need to find a way to attract viewers. In an increasingly crowded market, where broad-based networks are losing audience share to niche networks, the thinking goes that segmenting an audience, and going after that audience, is the way to go.

The biggest question is whether young people, who are used to talking in street language, will be attracted to news shows if their language is used on the air. Will getting a young audience to watch the news and learn about the world make those viewers more fluent in the world, less ignorant than many of us old coots think they are?

Those who take the opposing view will see the hip-hoppification of CNN Headline News as pandering. The responsibility of a news organization, they argue, is not to bring street language to the business—it's to present the news in a traditional way, using broadly accessible, standard language that allows the audience to make up its own mind. We shouldn't bring in hip hop; we should give the audience the story as it should be: straight, using proper English. This, in turn, will allow the viewer to increase his or her vocabulary. More learned viewers improve the overall intelligence level of the country.

This argument has a fatal flaw: Young people are not watching news. It is scary how illiterate our children are concerning world and national events. If bringing in their own language puts them in seats in front of the TV and helps them learn about the world, then so be it.

We oldsters used to have our own language. Remember *groovy?* Remember *far out?* Our parents must have had a heart attack when we started talking like that. Now, these words are found in many dictionaries. Twenty years from now, when today's kids are running the country, the same will be true of their youthful slang. Here's hoping they will have watched enough news to know what's going on.

Topics for Reading and Writing

1. Where else have you seen journalists attempt to adopt the language of young people? What is your reaction? Do you feel that you're being pandered to, or does it make the news more significant or understandable?

2. Do you agree with Pollard that "It is scary how illiterate our children are concerning world and national events"? Why has this happened? What can we do to remedy this?

3. Is this a news feature article or an opinion piece? Why?

Gloria Goodale, the arts and culture correspondent of the Christian Science Monitor, writes in this article that a growing number of young people get their news not from traditional sources (TV news, newspapers) or even new media (the Internet), but have started gravitating to comedians as

Gloria Goodale
All the News That's
Fit for Monologue

UCLA student Andrew Bodrogligeti will occasionally watch the evening news, but when he really wants to know what's going on, he tunes into Jay Leno's "The Tonight Show."

purveyors of the news. David Letterman, Jay Leno, Jon Stewart—these, she argues, are the new generation's Walter Cronkite or Tom Brokaw. Is she right? How might this change the way young people relate to and involve themselves in current events? Where do you get your news?

"Jay deflates the main news," he muses from a coffee-house table, peering over the lid of his laptop. "It high-lights the irrelevance of most of the main news shows."

Faster than an Associated Press reporter, the denizens of late-night TV daily serve up all the news that's fit for monologue—and a growing share of the public, particularly young people, are drawing their understanding of current events from Jay, David, and Conan.

For better or worse, the trend increases the ever-strengthening hold of pop culture on the consciousness of America. And while lack of editorial oversight in the world of comedy raises concerns, many media analysts laud this democratization of the news.

"Deep down, people feel they're getting something closer to the truth from the comedians," says Robert Thompson of the Center for the Study of Popular TV at the University of Syracuse in New York. "There's no institutional need to protect, no double speak, no stonewalling to cover up high-level misdoing."

For Mr. Bodrogligeti, the Los Angeles college student, laughs are the first draw to the late-night comedy shows. "They make the news fun," he says.

A Gallup poll in July showed that 17 percent of respondents ages 18 to 29 turn to talk shows every day to get their news. Forty-four percent "occasionally" ingest their information about the world from the late-night crowd.

The comics themselves are aware of their role in bringing this generation face to face with the news. Late-late-night host Conan O'Brien submerses himself in it, even referring to what he does as "journalism."

"I watch documentaries, I watch the news," he says. "I watch anything that will help me bring something to the table when I do the show the next day."

"Tonight Show" host Jay Leno doesn't like to discuss the mechanics of his show, saying too much talk about comedy ruins the laugh. But through a spokesman he confirms that he and his writers rifle leading news sources for material. Mr. Leno won't describe his strategy, but he does call himself an "equal opportunity offender," meaning that nobody and nothing are above being fodder for a joke.

Mr. Thompson says the current interest in late-night talk shows can be traced to the night in 1992 when presidential candidate Bill Clinton played his saxophone on "The Arsenio Hall Show."

The candidates, he says, were picking up the scent of an important sea change in this younger generation. "In a lot of ways, the political consciousness of today's younger people is set by these programs much more than by the leaders," Thompson says. Since then, others have picked up the cue, such as Al Gore when he went on "The Late Show With David Letterman."

But if late-night shows become a primary source of information, there's some risk to the public. Fact-checking and confirmation of sources, practices employed in traditional news outlets, are nonexistent in comedy.

Seated in a North Hollywood coffee shop, resident David Nagy agrees. If everything's a joke, he asks, what's to prevent cynicism from setting in, undermining important democratic institutions such as voting and volunteerism? "If you only got your view of the world from David Letterman," he says, "it would be a pretty twisted one."

It's not just the under-30 crowd watching these shows. Mr. Nagy, who belongs to a generation that has "Saturday Night Live" to thank for finally clarifying President Bush's 1,000 Points of Light campaign, tunes in often to late-night TV. But he offers a practical reason for watching: efficiency.

"It's like a Reader's Digest version of the news," agrees media analyst Thompson. These days, he says, people are overwhelmed by the 24-hour news channels, and they welcome anything that will compress all these sources into a manageable size.

"You listen to the five-minute monologue and you get what you need," he adds. In many ways, the professor points out, this tidy narrative is what the 15-minute national news roundup used to be on television, before the explosion of television outlets changed all that. And it's fun, to boot.

Comic Sandi Shore, who has trained many top comedians, says it's no surprise that politics and comedy are coming closer together in what she calls confusing times. "Humor can be a good way of covering up the hurt," she says, speaking of public response to president Clinton's affair with Monica Lewinsky. "People are hurt that the president lied, and a good laugh can help heal that hurt."

Topics for Reading and Writing

1. If Goodale is right, what does this mean? Is she identifying a shift that actually means something, or is this one of those "fad stories" common to the contemporary media that seek to identify a trend that will ultimately fade into oblivion?

2. If more and more viewers and readers have given up on the notion of "objective" news, what's wrong with choosing comedians to provide that news? Can't we select our news programs based on our tastes—conservatives to Fox News, liberals to NPR, kids to *The Daily Show?*

3. Does Goodale's piece make an argument, or is it simply a descriptive piece? If that distinction means anything—and we probably should preserve that distinction to some degree, just to differentiate between outright editorial comment and straight news—where would this fall on the spectrum of argument?

Taking a significantly different tack on the issue of the trustworthiness of the media is **Paul Saffo,** *who in this article asks us to question the very nature of information in an electronic age. How does it change the reliability of information to know that much of it never takes physical form? How does it change the process of creation and composition of the news (which is famously*

Paul Saffo
Quality in an Age of Electronic Incunabula

A long-forecast information future is arriving late and in utterly unexpected ways. Paper and its familiars—books, magazines, and newspapers—were supposed to become obsolete, quickly replaced by new forms of electronic media. In fact, the consumption of communications paper in the United States has grown at a rate greater than the *called "the first draft of history") that it is often done carelessly, on a screen, with the knowledge that editing or changing language is a very simple task? Medieval writers or copyists, knowing that their work would last centuries, took much more care in committing information to paper than we do today—or did they?*

Several years ago, novelist Nicholson Baker undertook a crusade to preserve as much information on paper as he could. Starting with the card catalog at the San Francisco Public Library, Baker then fought to save the bound print copies of many 1800s and 1900s newspapers from being pulped, as many libraries were doing after they microfilmed the publications. Baker argued that there is unique information contained in the physical state of printed matter that cannot be transferred to an image: the type of paper used, the appearance of the woodcuts or early photographs, the penciled notes on the library's catalog cards. Saffo is less alarmist than is Baker, but what are Saffo's specific fears of what we may lose as we leave print behind for the electronic world?

growth in gross national product for virtually every year since World War II. Electronics didn't replace paper; it enabled the production of greater volumes of print-based media than ever.

Meanwhile, the diffusion and consumption of new media—the incunabula of our time—have occurred more rapidly yet. From television to Nintendo, wave after wave of electronic novelty has invaded our homes, utterly changing our media habits and desires. Thanks to cable and global news services, consumers today have better access to information on breaking events than President Kennedy enjoyed from the situation room in the White House during the Cuban missile crisis. The average home today holds more computing power embedded in its appliances than existed in the entire District of Columbia before 1963.

The relationship between burgeoning paper and even more rapid electronic diffusion resembles an expanding sphere, in which volume increases more rapidly than surface area. The information business has become a kind of piñata: a thin paper crust surrounding an enabling electronic core. Paper has become an artifact of electronic media, but we barely notice because the paper crust conceals the core.

For example, the *Wall Street Journal* is written and edited on computer screens, electronically typeset, and then bounced off satellites to remote printing plants across the country. It assumes its familiar paper form only hours before it appears in our mailboxes. In offices and academic departments, the same pattern explains why we merely create greater volumes of documents than ever; xerographic copiers automate what once was laboriously copied with typewriter and spirit master.

For the moment at least, the social impact of this shift remains hidden beneath the paper skin. For instance, the way we use paper changed fundamentally in the mid-1980s with desktop publishing and new storage technologies. We think of paper as a communications medium, but in fact it has been primarily a storage medium. Consider your favorite book sitting on your bookshelf: how little time it spends in your hands being read, and how much gathering dust. Even a Bible in the hands of the most devout Christian fundamentalist spends more time shut than open.

By 1985, it had become cheaper to store information electronically than on paper, while desktop publishing makes it easier than ever to produce printed copy. The result is that paper is now interface—an increasingly volatile, disposable medium for viewing information on demand. We are solidly on the way to a future where we will reduce information to paper only when we are ready to read it—the phenomenon demonstrated by the *Wall Street Journal*—and then recycle it when done.

Evidence of paper as interface is everywhere. For example, facsimile machines also promote paper as interface. One can subscribe to a growing number of daily customized fax "newspapers" containing only the stories that interest each individual subscriber. The "database publishing" technologies that make these services possible are being used by others to profitably publish everything from customized textbooks to personalized ads in weekly magazines. In four hundred years, our universities have gone from the Stationari of Bologna to the printing press, to the copier, and now the computer to serve up course material.

The forces that made paper as interface possible will have even greater impact in the 1990s. As the communications piñata continues to expand, holes and thin spots are appearing, making paper more transitory yet. Researchers in theoretical physics and other disciplines have abandoned academic journals for electronic mail to keep up with breaking events in their fields. Meanwhile, financial exchanges have traded electrons for paper as the globe's primary transaction medium. Less than a quarter of our money supply is represented by greenbacks; the rest exists only as phantom memory patterns in huge computer data banks.

The term "electronic book" has suddenly become the hottest buzz-word in the media community, and everyone is getting into the act. One company is selling "expanded books"—computer versions of popular novels like *Jurassic Park*—designed to run on laptop portables. Electronic games-maker Broderbund Software is promoting "living books" on CD-ROM disks, leading with a clever children's title, *Just Grandma and Me.* Another company, Mathcad, is offering interactive technical "electronic handbooks" in partnership with academic publishers.

Software companies aren't the only would-be electronic book publishers. IBM has debuted "illuminated books," interactive educational works developed by Bob Abel. Sony is launching its "BookMan" portable CD-ROM player, and other consumer electronics players are furiously developing electronic book platforms of their own.

All of these products share an emphasis on text as their primary information delivery vehicle. Presumably this is why they have been defined as "books," but the vast penetration of these new media belies their apparent aesthetic inferiority to the best of conventional print. Nothing created on a fax, PC, or laserprinter can match letterpress for sheer sensuous quality. More importantly, the experience offered by electronic media is fundamentally different from anything offered by traditional books.

This latter aspect holds an important clue regarding the prospects for these new media. Our new media will not replace existing media directly; rather, they will penetrate by offering experiences that traditional print does poorly, or cannot do at all. A case in point is hypertext, which is simply a superior electronic alternative to the sort of tasks previously relegated to thesauri and encyclopedias.

The term "electronic book" is misleading, however, because these products are not books at all but something new: the incunabula of our own age. We are living in a moment between two revolutions: one of print, four centuries old and not quite spent, and another of electronics, two decades young and just getting underway. Today's "electronic books" amount to a bridge between these two revolutions, and the term's historic associations can help us through a mind-bending shift in much the same way that "horseless carriage" once eased our grandparents into the age of the automobile.

Of course, just as practical automobiles lay decades beyond the first horseless carriages, it will be some time before our new electronic media even begin to approach the sophistication and subtleties of traditional print. Traditionalists will howl at the vulgarity of it all, much as fans of manuscript writing shuddered at the ugly and unreliable monochrome works that came off the earliest presses.

In fact, events today are unfolding much as they did in the time of the original incunabula, between the 1450s and Aldus's publication of the first modern book in 1501. Recall that the very first books off Gutenberg's press were slavish imitations of what scriveners produced by hand. Just as the inventors of plastic first struggled to make the stuff look like wood and tortoise shell, printing pioneers worked to conceal the novelty of their new books. Mercifully, our new electronic media seem to have passed rapidly through this phase with the first wave of CD-ROM titles.

The current crop of "electronic books" recalls what emerged once the early medieval "print nerds" tired of making simple copies of manuscript works. It takes time to turn raw, untamed information technologies into compelling media that touch user imaginations. It took fifty years in the age of printed incunabula; it is likely to take at least a decade for the first wave of electronic books to be reduced to integral and unremarkable artifacts in our lives.

This period of diffusion will mask a deeper debate about quality. Are the new electronic books inferior because they remain in their infancy? Or is there something about electronics that is intrinsically inferior to print? Though I welcome today's electronic innovations, I am beginning to suspect that the latter concern has some basis.

It is possible that the very flexibility of our new electronic media constitutes their essential flaw. Several years ago, designer Milton Glaser observed that each new print technology has been infinitely more flexible than its predecessor—and has produced new conventions that were much worse. For Glaser, the essential determinant of aesthetic quality is the "resistance" of a medium; the harder an artist or craftsperson must work, the better the final product is likely to be. Thus, desktop publishing will always tend to produce results inferior to Linotype output, and no matter how hard publishers try, they will never match the quality of letterpress with digital technologies. Moreover, Glaser says, "the computer bears as close a relationship to the production of quality design as the typewriter does to the production of good poetry."

The uneasy traditionalist in me agrees, even as I enter these words into my labor- and aggravation-saving word processor. Of course, "quality" is only one measure of value when it comes to information and society. Cost and availability round out the equation, and virtually every innovation since the printing press has favored both at the expense of quality. The books printed by Aldus in the early 1500s were nothing to look at compared to the work of medieval copyists, but they made information infinitely more accessible and affordable. While a privileged intellectual minority lamented the vulgarity of books in the market-place, a newly literate population proceeded to change the course of European history.

Today's expanding electronic technologies also serve up an unprecedented explosion in the sheer volume of information assaulting us. A single copy of the Sunday *New York Times* contains more information than a sixteenth-century Venetian merchant was likely to read in a lifetime. Today, more information is stored digitally than on all the shelves of all the libraries in the world.

The resultant "information overload" has fascinated and infuriated us all, but it is something of a red herring; we have been coping with varying degrees of overload for centuries. We will deal with overload in new media in the same way we have always dealt with it—by creating new sense-making tools and social structures tailored to ever richer information environments. Recall that the Di Medicis built their financial empire on a tool for coping with the avalanche of numbers in their brave new world of commerce. Invented by a Benedictine monk, this critical tool was double-entry bookkeeping. Today, the traders of Wall Street are finding increasingly arcane mathematical tools to be essential to survival in what has become an electronic-age "casino of the gods." This ongoing information explosion will have direct effects on our educational structures; continued emphasis on providing students with the intellectual tool kits to cope with information overload is but the most obvious implication.

The *indirect* impacts are far more important. The effect on quality of this explosion in volume is more subtle and worrisome. Quality, by its very nature, tends to be scarce. History suggests that the total amount of quality material in all media has grown slowly over the centuries, but it seems increasingly scarce because the volume of inferior work has grown so much faster. I have little doubt that Gresham's Law applies to media: All things being equal, technological advances will cause the very best to be lost in a burgeoning flow of mediocre works.

Ultimately, quality and quantity in this electronic age converge around changing notions of what constitutes an "original." When a thing is created in a digital environment, every copy made is the equal of the original. In fact, there are no "copies" at all—just multiple originals. This alone guarantees that the information explosion will continue expanding exponentially for the indefinite future. More importantly, though, it may extinguish the very notion of what constitutes an "original" to begin with.

We praise "original" works, and we scorn anything that is "merely derivative." As Picasso once observed, the first man to compare his lover's lips to a rose was quite probably a genius—but everyone to make the comparison thereafter was almost certainly an idiot. The volume of truly original works is actually minuscule; what passes as original is simply a product of our bad memories. Recall that Picasso's "original" work borrowed heavily on themes from African art he observed while a young man. This link, however, is made only by a hand-ful of specialists, while the rest of us consider his work wildly unique.

The search and access power of the digital world will bring our memories back with brutal clarity. Scholars may quickly discover that *nothing* is original and everything is derivative, bordering on plagiarism. Imagine a future electronic book with the ability to link to remote hyperbases and search for sources and content similar to what is being read. The headaches that digital sampling are causing the music industry today are about to be propagated at a much larger scale among scholars. Eventually, we will discover that originality is a myth and that what lifts the great from the merely derivative is not originality at all but passion.

We are entering an age of infinite recall; much more than our information tools are changing. We will become paperless in the same way we once became horseless: Horses are still around, but they are ridden by hobbyists, not commuters. Similarly, new electronic media will creep into our lives, gradually displacing the time we spend with print.

"Electronic books" will mature into new media forms as the age of electronic incunabula comes to a close. Eventually, we will find ourselves in a world that for all intents and purposes will be paperless. We will hardly notice the shift, though, for it will so transform our intellectual lives that comparisons with even the recent past of this century will seem quaint and pointless.

Topics for Reading and Writing

1. Saffo's article cuts to the heart of an essential issue in this chapter as a whole: what does "quality" mean when we talk about the news? Does it mean "the most accurate"? "The most objective"? "The most appealing"? "The most similar to my point of view"? "The most likely to survive into history"?

2. How does Saffo's notion of quality compare with the ideas (implicit or explicit) of some of the other writers included in this chapter?

Tom Tomorrow
Who Watches the Watchers?

Tom Tomorrow's comic strip "This Modern World" runs in many weekly newpapers and occasionally on the New York Times *editorial page. Tomorrow's cartoons—many starring a sassy penguin named Sparky—frequently express a sense of outrage directed both at politicians and at a gullible public that seems willfully, even gleefully, ignorant of what's really going on in the world. In this piece, Tomorrow pokes fun at the tendency of Americans to look for outlets to complain about the media; he remarks on his website (www.thismodernworld.com) that this strip is "sort of about blogging."*

Topics for Reading and Writing

1. The cartoonist here uses the economic concept of diminishing returns to make his case about the media's relationship to citizens. What does "diminishing returns" mean?

2. What is the cartoonist's view of Americans' tendency to complain about the media they willingly consume? Do you agree?

© Tom Tomorrow

The Writer at Work

What Is an Argument?

Undoubtedly, you're familiar with the term "argument." An argument is a disagreement, even a fight, conducted with language. You argue with your parents about whether you should clean your room. You might argue with your boyfriend about where to have lunch. Anyone who has had siblings has had arguments with them, often about nothing. Arguments in this sense are not, however, the subject of this book.

The English term "argument" derives from the Latin word *arguere,* which means "to assert, to make clear, to blame or accuse." (People who talk and write about rhetoric tend to use many Greek and Latin words because the study of the persuasive use of language—or "rhetoric"—reached great heights in ancient Greece and Rome.) This meaning—asserting something or making a claim—survives to this day, and throughout *Media and Messages* we will be using "argument" to mean precisely that. Your argument is the claim you make, it is the point you are trying to get across, it's the thesis or idea you want to convince me to accept. Many people who write about rhetoric will say that (in the words of one well-known textbook) "everything's an argument"; they feel that every message existing in the world, even those that aren't obviously statements meant to persuade, are arguments of some kind. The statement "I like strawberry ice cream" is an argument because it tries to convince an audience of something about the speaker. A stop sign argues that you should stop your car; it's persuasive because it represents the whole system of traffic laws that keep you safe and punish violators. Steven Soderbergh's movie *Erin Brockovich* argues that great things can be accomplished even by a misfit who speaks truth to power. None of these arguments are "claims" or "theses" in the traditional sense that, say, "Shakespeare is the finest Elizabethan poet" is a thesis. However, it is hard to deny that essentially every message is, in some sense, an argument.

This point—that everything's an argument—is probably true. For the purposes of this book, though, we are going to limit our sights to more traditional kinds of claims and arguments. The subject matter of this book is the contemporary media; the chapters and readings included all talk about issues and controversies surrounding the media; the goal of the book is to help you to understand those issues and controversies and to start to contribute to society's conversations about them. Because of that, in *Media and Messages* the terms "argument" and "thesis" (they will be used interchangeably) will mean not all messages existing in the world but rather those claims and theses intended specifically to persuade.

Finding the Arguments in an Issue

From grade school to the SATs and AP tests, you've been trained in reading comprehension. Reading comprehension asks more than that you simply understand words and sentences, or even that you comprehend the main point of a piece of writing. As you have grown up and become a more sophisticated reader you've probably moved past just looking at an editorial piece or a letter for its thesis, the one-sentence statement of its main idea. For instance, the letters on the editorial page of a big-city newspaper might make arguments like:

> We should elect Thomas P. Hairspray to Congress.
> The intersection of Palmdale Avenue and 10th Street is dangerous and the city should install a stoplight there.
> The astronauts on the *Challenger* were heroes.
> Why do the police persecute me for my parking tickets when dozens of murderers go free?
> I'd like to commend Principal Sharyn Gross of Central High School for her good work over the last 20 years.

These are all arguments, clearly—or are they? You have probably learned that a thesis is a complete, declarative sentence that states an opinion. While that's a good rule of thumb, it's important to think about thesis in more exact terms— and to differentiate the thesis of a piece of writing from all the separate things that piece of writing is meant to achieve.

So what is a thesis? A good definition of a thesis might look like this: **a thesis is a statement intended to convince an audience to believe something.** A thesis cannot simply be a statement of fact. Given that, let's see if the previous statements qualify as theses. What is the argument of "We should elect Thomas P. Hairspray to Congress"? That's an easy one: the writer wants to convince the reader that Hairspray should be elected to Congress. But the intention is a little more complicated than that. This argument tries to get the reader first to believe something (Thomas P. Hairspray should be the congressman from this district) and then to act on that belief by voting for Hairspray. In our second example, the argument is clear: a stoplight should be placed at Palmdale and 10th. But what is the writer trying to accomplish by publishing this claim in a newspaper? Stoplight placement is rarely a matter for public vote, especially in a city of any size. This writer is likely trying to accomplish several things with this argument—she wants to show other readers who may have been worried about this intersection that someone shares their concern, she wants this concern expressed in a public forum so everyone knows that the city council or county commission have been made aware of this supposed problem, and she likely also wants to encourage other citizens to exercise pressure on the council or commission to remedy the situation.

The other letters to the editor are all similar to the previous examples in that the explicit argument is not necessarily the same as what the writer wants to accomplish with the letter. The writer of the parking-tickets letter, for instance, probably is less interested in an actual answer to his question than trying to convince the people and the police that his transgressions are not very important in the large scheme of things. Ultimately, though, he knows that nothing will change because of his letter; the intention, then, is primarily to use the letter as an outlet for his frustrations. Often, public writing is intended not just to convince a public of something about an issue, but also to convince the public of something about the *writer*—that the writer is a concerned citizen, that the writer is a patriot, that the writer is unjustly persecuted by the parking patrol.

This leads us to another important idea about theses and the arguments they summarize: **the speaker or writer is always a factor in the argument he or she is making.**

IDEAS INTO PRACTICE 2-1

In the following examples, write all the different things the writer might be trying to accomplish with the following arguments from letters to the editor, essays, and bumper stickers. Think about everything that is packed into these statements—the different opinions that might accompany the main one, the actions the arguments encourage readers to take, the feelings the writer wants us to have about him or her.

1. Corporate Rock Still Sucks.
2. The Iran-Iraq war of the 1980s, in which Saddam Hussein was supported by the United States, provided Saddam with an important testing ground for many of his weapons and battle tactics that he would later use against his own people and against the United States.
3. I can't believe that the city council caved in and gave Wal-Mart a zoning variance.
4. Without a doubt, Julia Roberts is the most glamorous movie star in the world today.
5. Britney Spears is not a good role model for children because she gets by wholly on her sexuality.

Arguments Versus Arguable Issues

An argument can be made about anything in the world. The following are perfectly legitimate arguments:

Texas is the greatest state in the Union.

Miguel Estrada should be confirmed for a seat on the Federal District Court of Appeals.

Eminem, like the Beastie Boys and 3rd Base before him, is just a white boy who takes advantage of African-American culture and gives nothing back.

Only boring people major in pre-law.

Just because these are legitimate arguments—**remember, an *argument* is a claim or thesis intended specifically to persuade**—does not mean they are *arguable points.* Just because people disagree about something does not mean their point of contention is an arguable one. **An *arguable point* is a statement of opinion about which reasonable people can disagree.** The following are not arguable:

■ **provable facts**
   Delaware is north of Georgia.

However, some of the most important arguments in history have been made challenging provable facts. What makes these points arguable is that the person making the argument has unearthed factual proof that the accepted fact is not actually true. Arguments like "the earth is not flat" or "tiny creatures cause sickness" challenged the facts of the time—and proved to be true. If you intend to make an argument challenging an accepted fact, though, you must have a great deal of verifiable evidence.

∎ **personal preferences**
> *Friends* stunk after the third season.
> A rainy day at home is better than a sunny day on the beach.

This should be fairly clear. It's pretty much impossible to convince someone they don't like something if they actually do like it, or to persuade them to like something they hate. A personal preference can become an arguable point, though, when you attempt to show someone aspects of features of the thing they do or don't like that they might not have known about before—aspects that are appealing to him or her.

∎ **issues about which there is insufficient information**
> The Etruscans communicated with extraterrestrials.
> The universe began in a "big bang."
> God created the Earth and all its creatures.

This one is especially tough. Who is to determine how much information is "sufficient" to make a good argument? Like much in rhetoric, this depends largely on the credibility of the speaker. When Stephen Hawking makes a speculative argument about the workings of the universe, we're likely to take him seriously; when your 12-year-old nephew makes a similar argument, you probably dismiss him. At the same time, the sufficiency of given evidence also depends on the beliefs and predispositions of the audience. Religious beliefs, or the lack thereof, can profoundly affect what constitutes "sufficient information" for particular audiences (especially regarding arguments like the last two examples).

In addition to the criteria listed, is it also important to keep in mind that **arguable points center on issues about which reasonable people can disagree.** Some typical kinds of arguments (with their designations and some examples) are:

∎ **whether or not multiple things are essentially the same (argument about identity)**
> There are no important differences between state universities and private colleges.
> Varsity letters should be awarded for participation in drama and honor society as well as for sports.
> Rush Limbaugh and Bill O'Reilly are not the same kind of talk show host.

∎ **whether a specific thing belongs in a given category (argument about definition)**
> Gun control is unconstitutional.
> Jennifer Lopez's music isn't really Latin.
> Oprah Winfrey is a feminist.

- **to what degree a specific thing manifests a given quality (argument about judging or evaluating)**

    Saving Private Ryan is the best war movie ever made.

    A Super Bee is faster than any Lamborghini.

    Matisse's paintings exude greater calmness than Courbet's.

- **whether or not a certain cause produces a given result (argument about causation)**

    Sex education in public schools leads to promiscuity.

    When people receive welfare all their life, they learn not to work.

    If you don't want the networks to produce "reality" shows, don't watch them.

- **whether or not someone should engage in an activity, and why (proposal)**

    The city council should rename this street after Martin Luther King, Jr.

    Ruby, don't take your love to town.

    The United States must attack Iraq in order to eliminate the danger of weapons of mass destruction.

- **how something works or what something means (analysis)**

    In his speeches, George Bush hijacks the language of his opponents; this makes him seem more moderate.

    The movie *Chicago,* with its cynical focus on the quest for fame, attacks today's celebrity-driven culture.

    The craze for boba drinks is just one manifestation of the penetration of Asian tastes into American youth culture.

IDEAS INTO PRACTICE 2-2

Look at the following claims and decide whether or not each is an arguable point. If it is, identify what type of argument it is. If not, explain why.

1. If there's a stupider game than "Sorry," I haven't seen it.
2. You can't call Sarah Hughes an "amateur" athlete—she's definitely a professional.
3. Fluoride in the drinking water is a communist plot.
4. Jaywalking, vandalism, spitting on the sidewalk—they're all victimless crimes.
5. Reinstituting school prayer will do nothing to improve public education.
6. Bill Gates has given a lot of money to promote vaccinations in Africa, but he really should focus his efforts on AIDS prevention.
7. The Sony VAIO is by far the best Wintel laptop on the market.
8. Ralph Ellison's novel *Invisible Man* explores the themes of isolation and prejudice through its use of the unnamed, "invisible" narrator.
9. Civilizations on Mars use hydrogen, not petroleum, as their primary energy source.
10. We should have exited at Washington Boulevard, not Broadway!

As you are probably realizing, whether or not a point is arguable depends upon the context, the situation, and the audience. I constantly have to remind myself and my students **that rhetoric, or the use of language to persuade, is radically situational.** All this means is that the content of your attempts to persuade people of various points, and sometimes even your points themselves, will vary depending upon the audience and the occasion. Let's say you get a summer job working for the admissions office of your university, and one of your responsibilities is to visit area high schools to promote your school. You will make a very different kind of argument to an audience of juniors and seniors than you will to an audience of parents. How might those two **arguments** be different even though the **thesis** is the same? It's the same even with television commercials: ads for the same product (a soft drink, jeans, a computer) aimed at different audiences will be quite different because different audiences respond to different appeals. Although at first this might just seem like a complication— even though I'm saying the same thing, I have to write differently depending on the audience?—it is actually one of the most valuable and powerful features of the art of rhetoric, for it mirrors the diversity of people and ideas in the world.

IDEAS INTO PRACTICE 2-3

Read all the readings included with this chapter, including Tom Tomorrow's cartoon "Who Watches the Watchers?" Then, write down what you think the thesis of each piece is. For each thesis, answer the following questions:

1. Is this an arguable point?
2. If not, what makes it unarguable?
3. What kind of evidence does the writer employ?
4. Does the writer use his or her own special authority on the topic as evidence?
5. Is this thesis something on which you can be persuaded, or is your mind already made up?

Style Toolbox: Choosing the Right Verb

Most student writers are familiar with the idea of diction, or word choice. Writers and speakers choose their diction according to the audience they are addressing and the occasion: speaking on Memorial Day at a national cemetery, President Bush will use very formal diction, while when speaking at a political rally he may use slang phrases and expressions that reflect his Texas upbringing. The vast variety of words that the English language provides us gives us the ability to say the same thing in many different ways, allowing us to achieve different effects. Using exaggeratedly elevated diction, one might say "It appears to me that our collection of athletic warriors is unlikely to make a triumphal exit from this venue of competition"; using ordinary conversational diction, one might say

"I don't think our team is going to win this tournament"; using very colloquial, slangy diction, one might say "We're going to get waxed today."

Almost all the classes of words in the English language—nouns, adjectives, adverbs, even prepositions—provide writers with a wide variety of choices for creating shades of meaning. However, the most powerful class of words in terms of achieving a rhetorical effect is probably verbs. Nouns also carry a great potential for meaning, but audiences often are wary of the distortion or "spinning" of meaning that comes with giving a name to something—were the members of Saddam Hussein's administration "terrorists" or simply "thugs," did we use "precision-guided munitions" or "devastating bombs and rockets"? Writers who use loaded nouns so much that they seem to be name-calling lose significant credibility. However, perhaps because audiences don't listen as closely to verbs, those words can often get across precisely the same nuance of meaning as a noun without calling as much attention to themselves. Look at the following two sentences:

> American liberators achieved victory in Iraq.
> U.S. soldiers liberated Iraq.

Of the two sentences, the first sounds a little more like propaganda. The characterization of U.S. soldiers as "liberators" stands out a little more as an attempt to persuade than does the verb "liberated," even though each sentence says almost exactly the same thing. This is not to say that the careful selection of a verb is just a sneaky way to persuade people without letting them know that you are doing it. Ethical writers and speakers always make it clear when they are trying to persuade. Letting verbs rather than nouns do rhetorical work can make the speaker or writer seem more evenhanded and less outwardly biased, even in the act of trying to sway an audience.

WRITING WITH STYLE 2-1

In the following sentences, list all the verbs (including forms of "to be"). Then, characterize the verbs as a group—what level of diction do they indicate? What information, apart from the indication of the action itself, do they convey about the sentence's subject? What information do they give you about the writer's attitude toward the subject?

1. There was "Back Door Men" by the Shadows of Knight, who were really good at copping the Yardbird riffs and reworking 'em, and "Psychotic Reaction" by Count Five, who weren't so hot at it actually but ripped their whole routine off with such grungy spunk that I really dug 'em the most! (Lester Bangs, "Psychotic Reactions and Carburetor Dung")

2. Where, in what relationships, are they denied or confirmed? These questions, and surely both must be answered, are bound to lead into the whole complex of action which is the practice of living, and which we cannot reduce to such an abstraction as "the contemporary situation." (Raymond Williams, *Culture and Society 1780–1950*)

3. In an appearance on CBS's *Early Show,* actress Susan Sarandon claimed to possess information the public doesn't and cited the example of veter-

ans' benefits. According to Sarandon, the benefits will be cut by "two hundred and some billions of dollars" over the next ten years. A quick check of federal budget numbers proved that her claim was ludicrous. (Media Research Center, "MRC Spotlight" Apr. 22, 2003)

4. In a surprising reversal, appeals court judges scoffed at Vice President Dick Cheney's team of lawyers when they requested intervention in a two-year old case regarding the anonymity of Cheney's energy task force . . . One of the appeals court judges chided Cheney's advocates for trying to evade the district court's ruling. ("Cheney's Secrets," *Mother Jones "Daily Briefing"* Apr. 22, 2003)

5. Forget the excuses. Elite colleges charge an arm and a leg because they can . . . Princeton boasted average returns of more than 15% per year on its endowment in the 25-year period leading up to 2001. It uses about 4% of the endowment in its annual budget. That leaves a lot to fiddle with. (Laura Vanderkamp, "Reduce College Sticker Shock." *USA Today*)

Because English is so rich in vocabulary, it's often harder to select a verb that will move an audience in precisely the right way than it is to find any kind of alternate way to say something. For example, assume that you are trying to convince a friend that you have come to really enjoy driving as an activity rather than just as a means to get from Point A to Point B. You could just say "I really like driving around," but what about your other options? Let's look at a few.

Drive: to control an automobile.

Motor: to drive, but has a connotation of old-fashioned luxury (one "motors" in a Rolls-Royce or Bentley), of leisure, of Sunday drives in the country.

Race: to drive fast, with a definite destination in mind.

Steer: to drive, focusing on the direction rather than the speed.

Travel: to drive at no great speed, enjoying the trip.

Careen: to drive recklessly, weaving through traffic, hitting obstacles and bouncing off them, with a connotation of being out-of-control or intoxicated.

Tool around: to drive idly with no particular destination in mind, as a form of recreation. Slang term.

Burn rubber: to drive extremely fast, especially by accelerating quickly after stops. Slang term.

(You can think of probably 20 other terms for driving, each indicating a particular variety of this activity and degree of formality.) To best convey the kind of driving you enjoy, you'd probably say something like "I really like just tooling around." You could also use the term "motor," but the sentence "I really like just motoring" sounds funny—in casual American English, "motor" means to leave someplace quickly, not necessarily by automobile. You certainly wouldn't say "I really like just racing" or "I really like just traveling" to express this particular idea—they describe a totally different type of driving.

Consulting a thesaurus is the easiest way to come up with a variety of verbs, but it's also one of the riskiest—using a word whose connotation just doesn't fit what you are trying to say makes you look silly. Before using a word that you find in the thesaurus, make sure you have a good sense of how that word is used in common English. English has a wealth of words for similar activities; yet each individual word indicates a specific variety of that activity and is appropriate for specific rhetorical situations. English teachers all have stories about particularly inappropriate words their students have chosen when using the thesaurus, like this one:

> The car that ran into my bike didn't desist at the stop sign.

The student here obviously didn't want to use the word "stop" twice in one sentence. Her instinct was good, but you probably won't end up with a good choice if you just select a verb from a thesaurus entry. In addition, you don't always have to find a fancier or longer or "smarter" word. Just because you're now writing for a more sophisticated audience doesn't mean that you have to always use a more sophisticated vocabulary. The essence of good word choice is appropriateness: sometimes the simplest language is best.

WRITING WITH STYLE 2-2

Change the relatively neutral verbs in the following sentences to verbs with stronger or more persuasive connotations. Then, describe how your change affects the rhetorical impact of the sentence.

1. Drunk drivers cause thousands of deaths a year in America.
2. However, in states such as Montana and Mississippi it is still legal for a driver to consume alcoholic beverages while operating his or her vehicle.
3. The state legislature in Montana, in fact, recently failed again to pass an open-container law.
4. It's unfortunate that this legislative decision will probably result in dozens of deaths on the highways.
5. Ordinary citizens should join with groups like MADD to offer education about the perils of drunk driving—maybe this will eventually influence the legislatures of these states.

Finally, one of the easiest and most effective ways to improve your writing is to use action verbs as much as possible in the place of forms of "to be" like "is," "are," "were," "will be," and so on. Instead of "Avoiding large-scale infection is a reason that travelers from regions where SARS is spreading are quarantined when they come to Canada," say "Canada quarantines travelers from SARS-infested regions to prevent large-scale infection." "Raising the driving age to 18 is a terrible idea" has much less impact than something with a strong action verb—something like "The proposal to raise the driving age to 18 boggles the mind with its idiocy." (Granted, that's not a great sentence, but you get the idea.) "To be" verbs flatten your writing, while action verbs call attention to your prose and to the actions you are describing. Although it's neither desirable nor probably even possible to eliminate all forms of "to be" from your writing, it's definitely worth revising each draft with an eye to reducing your use of those words—especially in important thesis statements and topic sentences, which need to stand out to the reader. Pay special attention to sentences beginning with "There is/are" or "A reason for . . . is"; such sentences, which usually introduce crucial elements of an argument, stand out much more when rewritten with action verbs.

WRITING WITH STYLE 2-3

Rewrite the following passages, changing the "to be" verbs to make the prose more vivid and active.

1. Wasserman was the very personification of the maxim that information is power. His appetite for information was insatiable, and his employees were amazed at his powers of retention.
2. In times of global uncertainty, a sense of safety is more important than ever. Children, especially, can be tense and anxious and parents are their best sources for comfort.
3. The ideal hostess is dressed appropriately and is cheerful. Drinks should be in hand by 6 and dinner is on the table precisely at 7 p.m. No dinner party can be successful without these elements.
5. It isn't just her irrepressible perkiness but her underlying strength that makes Reese Witherspoon a movie idol.
6. There are several reasons why we should drill for oil in Alaska.

What Are You Selling?

In the previous chapter, we learned that the notion of "objectivity" in journalism or the media is less an attainable goal than a direction or pole toward which most American journalism orients itself. If nothing can actually be wholly objective, in other words, American journalism at least tries its best to minimize the bias or slant or subjectivity that necessarily comes when people try to tell stories to each other. The philosophy of minimizing slant is not uncontroversial, either; many critics argue that the most ethical course for journalism to take would be frankly to acknowledge its biases, so as not to mislead readers or viewers. It's hard to imagine what this would look like in practice—would every news story begin with "This is only one reporter's view of things, but . . ."—but certainly in other parts of the world the media and journalists are outwardly ideological, and critical viewers or readers simply sift through a number of versions of the

New York City's Times Square is famous for its billboard advertisements.

same event, critically reading each account in an effort to find the most congenial truth.

Ironically, most Americans have the most experience exercising their critical reading skills not on journalism but on the types of communication openly intended to convince us to do or buy or believe something. Most of us actively resist the messages of promotion and persuasion, subconsciously separating them from advertising messages that provide us with useful information. To counteract this, the people who create those messages constantly must improve those messages to make them more appealing. They do this in dozens of ways—sometimes they even disguise those persuasive messages as the very types of "objective" messages that we are inclined to trust. We often don't know when we are being persuaded of something. Conservatives and liberals complain about this kind of bias in news coverage, but in fact politicians and journalists are amateurs at the art of persuasion when compared to the true professionals in the field: advertisers, promoters, and publicists. Even though almost all of us are aware that the messages of advertising and promotion might be misleading, we must constantly hone our skills at critical reading. In this chapter, we will examine how new technologies and today's media environment have changed the ways advertising and promotion try to reach us. In addition, we will examine issues of ethical rhetoric, both for the advertisers and for ourselves. And although we will certainly talk extensively about the power of images, the main focus of this chapter will be on the *language* of selling.

It would be difficult to say categorically that communication today is more dominated by selling and advertising and promotion than ever before. Certainly, people have always used language and images in these ways. What's different today is that there is just so much *more* communication. New technologies make it possible for people to communicate with us almost anywhere, anytime—and the people most eager to take advantage of this tend to be advertisers.

Think about the last time you were truly cut off from messages that were trying to reach you. In your dorm room? The television, the radio, the computer, your telephone all bring messages to you—not to mention your roommate's "Absolut" advertisement collection and your own poster of Allen Iverson. The utopian dreams of the Internet as the virtual home for millions of virtual communities, as a haven for truly free speech, have been thwarted, to some extent, by the colonization of the Internet by commercial interests. Anyone with an e-mail account has certainly received spam, or junk commercial e-mail. In fact, some spam is so unavoidable that it has become a joke: penis enlargement, Nigerian financial scams, pornographic websites, refinanced home loans, and many others. Spam is irritating, certainly, and companies offering antispam software (much of which is itself sold via spam) have sprung up, but technology tends to allow spammers to keep one step ahead of those trying to stop them—and constitutional guarantees of free speech protect spammers' rights to advertise.

The Internet isn't the only space being taken over by ads. Look around your writing classroom. Unless you attend a school in which uniforms are mandatory, you can probably spot several advertising messages on your classmates' clothes. Companies like Coca-Cola give away free book covers to students so their messages can get out. Travel agents selling spring break trips to ski or beach destinations might have posted brochures in your classroom. In high school, you might have watched the Channel One current events television news service—which includes advertisements that schools are contractually obligated to make the students watch. (See Mark Crispin Miller's article "How To Be Stupid," included in this chapter.) Ads reach you at home, in your car, at work . . . just about everywhere.

Recently, advertisers have colonized spaces that would have seemed unlikely just 10 years ago. In supermarkets, checkout lines now have television screens, shopping carts carry advertising, and even stickers on bananas promote movies or websites. On airplanes, in-flight movies have been replaced by network television programming (complete with commercials), airline food is being phased out in favor of branded snacks, the *Skymall* catalog offers products from dozens of retailers, and if you can't find anything you like in *Skymall* your flight attendant may come down the aisle with a cartload of duty-free products. Advertisements appear not only on free postcards given out in nightclubs and bars, but on the walls of restrooms and even at the bottom of urinals. Companies rent out time on their telephone lines so that callers to customer service have to listen to ads. Television shows now incorporate advertising—the prizes on *Survivor,* the cell phone brand used on *Alias,* the products "spontaneously" discussed by the hosts of *The Best Damn Sports Show Period,* are all there because of product placement deals between the sponsor and the show's producer. New shows are being developed purely as vehicles for sponsored products, as Frazier Moore points out in his article "Shill-o-vision" (included in this chapter). Digital cable not only brings you all the advertising on television channels, but includes advertising on its program guide screens and special "messages" that advertise upcoming events.

Ironically, the very pervasiveness of advertising may be making the ads themselves less effective — when we are constantly bombarded by messages, we tend to tune them out. To counteract consumers' desire to avoid advertising, advertisers engage in an endless struggle to stay one step ahead of us. They accomplish this by moving to space that was previously ad-free and by disguising ads so they don't look or sound or feel like ads. "Product placement" is the term for the sponsored insertion of brands into movies or television shows or radio programs; this kind of advertising has gone on for decades, ever since advertisers realized the ineffable power of movie glamour. And while most people have given up on trying to pressure movie studios not to use product placement, the sponsored inclusion of one product—tobacco—has been the target of attacks by consumer and health groups. Although both the tobacco companies and the movie studios deny that they have any product-placement agreements, antismoking groups argue that smoking in the movies is on the rise even as it is declining in the population as a whole—they suspect an under-the-table arrangement, but the movie studios and tobacco companies strenuously deny it.

Advertising and promotion even sneak into more journalistic media. Large companies will often use one of their businesses to promote another. Readers of the *New York Post,* a daily tabloid, in the winter of 2002–2003 might have noticed a great deal of coverage of the television program *Joe Millionaire*— both the *Post* and the network that aired *Joe Millionaire* are divisions of the large media company News Corporation. Publicists like to arrange for splashy, celebrity-laden parties when a new product is released, for the coverage of the party in the gossip or society pages will inevitably mention the occasion for the party—sometimes this is even a condition of a reporter receiving a pass to the party! Companies benefit when a celebrity uses their product, so companies will send expensive goods as gifts to famous people in the hopes that those celebrities will use those products—an Apple iPod, a Burberry scarf, a Cadillac Escalade—in public. Promoters and publicists engage in publicity stunts to get their clients' names in the newspaper or on television, or they might even plant stories with friendly reporters. Many infomercials, or program-length commercials, are produced to look like news broadcasts and are then aired by local broadcast stations or cable networks. And as Eugene Marlow points out (see Chapter 6), the video news release—a promotional video shot to look like real news, then sent to local or national news stations in the hopes that those stations will air them—are making steady inroads into local news broadcasts. The goal of all these efforts is to get that brand or that product or that person into the news, for presumably consumers are less likely to tune "news" messages out than they are to ignore messages coded as "advertising."

Analyzing the Message

Think a little bit about the pervasiveness of advertising. Go to a public space of some kind—a park, the quad at your school, a city bus, the library—and take notes all of types of advertising you can find there. Then, freewrite on the following topics: how have the advertisers crafted these messages for this forum (a T-shirt, a book cover, a flyer, the Goodyear blimp)? Should there be public space that is unavailable to advertisers, or do prohibitions on advertising violate the right to freedom of speech?

The Language of Advertising

Advertisements are so pervasive today that it's often difficult to step back and try to think about the category of advertising without thinking of specific advertisements. But in order to discuss the language of advertising, it's important to get a handle on what we're talking about. **Advertising is public communication intended to inform the public about a good or service or event and to convince the public to buy that good, make use of that service, or attend that event.** Advertising often provides us with extremely valuable information. Car ads that list an automobile's features allow us to make an intelligent decision about whether a Toyota Camry or a Dodge Spirit is better suited for our needs. Advertisements for drugs make us aware of conditions we might have—hay fever, arthritis, depression—and let us know that there may be a pharmaceutical solution for those problems. Advertising can also give us clues about which of two similar products we can afford.

Advertising, like every other kind of writing discussed in this book, is also a form of rhetoric. As such, it is specifically designed to persuade us to do or think or feel something, and in order to accomplish its aims advertising relies on similar kinds of strategies. Everything is the biggest, the best, the most glamorous, the most extreme, and so on. Even young children quickly learn to see behind such pitches as:

Four out of five doctors recommend . . .
The hottest new toy of the season!
The choice of a new generation.

Advertisers are caught in a difficult bind: they need to promote their product or service as being more desirable than the competitors', but they can't lie in advertising. The solution, much of the time, is to make claims that are not provable, to rely on nebulous categories, and to appeal to the audience's emotions, not their intellects. Much advertising makes a science out of employing "weasel words" that sound good but that actually mean nothing.

Advertising's appeals, like any form of rhetoric, can be analyzed according to the categories laid out in the Writer at Work sections of this chapter and the previous one. An ad's claim or thesis is usually pretty simple—"buy this product"—but as consumers have grown more savvy and suspicious of sales pitches, many companies have recently put less stress on such hard-sell approaches and have concentrated instead on an approach known as "brand building" in their advertisements. The goal of brand building, rhetorically, is quite sophisticated. Basically, brand building seeks to use a heavy pathos appeal to get you to feel something about a particular product; then, once an emotional connection has been made with the product, the company uses that as a type of ethos—you can trust this product because you feel this way about our brand.

Nike, the athletic shoe and apparel manufacturer, has been a pioneer in the kind of advertising that stresses the brand, not the product. The company's "Just Do It" campaign sought to make consumers associate Nike with determination, with the desire for top performance at all costs, with total devotion to sports. Its commercials frequently did not feature famous athletes, instead focusing on ordinary peoples' (especially women's) dedication to their chosen sport. When Nike did feature athletes, the company used athletes who were both perceived as the best at their sport (Marion Jones, Tiger Woods, Lance Armstrong, soccer's Ronaldo) and who were largely uncontroversial. The company wanted consumers to associate the name "Nike" and the swoosh logo with this kind of devotion and excellence—and then to use those emotional associations to create ethos or authority for every product the company made.

This kind of brand-building advertising often relies much more heavily on image than on language; many Nike commercials, for instance, have no words at all. Images can be much more powerful than words in creating emotional resonance. Words also invite the audience to talk back, even if only in their minds. A recent campaign by the soft-drink company Sprite adopted a unique approach, in that it actually argued *against* the brand-building tactics of other beverage manufacturers. Most soft-drink campaigns employ glamorous stars or images of very attractive, athletic, happy people consuming the beverage, arguing implicitly that consuming this beverage will somehow make you like those people. Some recent commercials for Sprite explicitly stated that their drink won't make you taller, won't make you better-looking, won't make you an "extreme" person. You won't play basketball like Grant Hill if you drink Sprite. The campaign's tagline, "Obey your thirst," also seemed to appeal to consumers' desire to be individuals. The implicit message was that individuals, those who see through the misleading marketing of the other companies, drink Sprite. However, many viewers were not impressed by the apparent contradiction in this message— "Sprite's marketing tells me that I'm not a sucker for marketing if I drink Sprite."

Even once a brand has been established in consumers' emotional memories, reshaping that brand for changing times is a constant concern for marketers. In 1991, Kentucky Fried Chicken changed its official corporate name to KFC, in an attempt, according to corporate spokespeople, to emphasize the variety of food available at the restaurant. The name change was also certainly motivated by the growing health consciousness in the American public, who might shy away from restaurants boasting fried food. Later in the 1990s, the company adopted a new spokescharacter for its TV and print ads. This cartoon version of their traditional Colonel Sanders character (a Southern gentleman in a white suit and string tie) exhibited a new attitude, one that had been gaining popularity in marketing efforts aimed at teenage boys: street smart, in-your-face, extreme, aggressive. Most viewers found this transformation of one of the most familiar corporate spokesmen to be ridiculous, a transparent attempt by a company to jump on a marketing bandwagon by using advertising executives' idea of "attitude." One reaction, from the Jackson, Miss., *Clarion-Ledger,* was typical:

> In this commercial, the white-haired Colonel, in all of his finger-lickin' glory, had been reduced to a funky little cartoon character that was rapping and dancing to bass-thumping hip-hop music. He was spinning around like a break-dancer in a cheesy 1980s rap movie. The singers in the background were chanting, "Go Colonel. Go Colonel." Colonel Sanders looked more like Deion Sanders doing an end zone dance after returning an 86-yard interception for a TD. My, how times have changed. What's next, Ronald McDonald freak dancing with the red-haired, freckle-faced Wendy's girl?[1]

Dealing with public ridicule of your carefully-crafted image makeover is one thing, but attempting to stop the viral spread of malicious rumors about your company is another. Soon after KFC's name change, a story began racing around the Internet that explained the name change as the result of a legal problem. Specifically, the rumor held that KFC was using an unidentified genetically modified organism, not a chicken, as its primary product—and because of this the FDA forbade the company from advertising itself as selling chicken. The story was utterly false and is now memorialized as an urban legend, but it is hard to tell how much immediate or lasting damage it did to KFC.

Analyzing the Message

Find five kinds of advertisements: a television ad, a radio ad, a full-page advertisement in a national popular magazine such as *People* or *Rolling Stone,* a billboard, and an Internet pop-up. For each of these advertisements, copy down all the language used. Then answer the following questions:

1. Look at it on the paper: how does its impact differ on the screen or on your paper from when it is spoken or laid out with graphics and a well-chosen typeface? If it is spoken (for instance in a radio or television spot), how much does the voice matter—is it in an accent, does the sex or age of the spokesperson matter, does a recognizable celebrity speak the words? What is the "attitude" or tone of the ads?

2. What claims, both explicit and implicit, are being made? Think about this question: often many claims (about the product, about the company, about the users) are contained in a very simple ad.

3. What is the target audience? Be sure to take into consideration where this ad appeared (in which magazine, during which television program, on which radio station).

---

[1] "Oh, the Good Ole Days of Simple Commercials." Jackson *Clarion-Ledger,* 12 Dec. 2001.

4. What specific words seemed targeted at this audience that might not be used with another audience?

5. To what degree does the advertisement promote the particular product? To what degree does it promote the brand itself?

⫴ The Language of Public Relations

Public relations is a form of communication very similar to advertising and is frequently used for the same purposes. But where advertising is essentially bought and paid for, PR includes all the forms of public communication that do not involve purchasing time or space in the mass media. Press conferences, statements in the newspaper, news releases, stunts, interviews—all of these are forms of public relations. While advertising generally attempts to convince consumers to buy a particular product or service, public relations (when practiced by a corporation) has broader aims: to ensure a company's health by putting the best face on a quarterly loss, describe a new venture, explain the firing of a high-ranking executive. It's not just corporations that use PR, either. Universities employ PR specialists (often in the "University Relations" office), as do city governments, police departments, nongovernmental organizations, school boards . . . just about any body that wants to communicate its message to the public.

Because PR is a form of public rhetoric like any other, its practitioners engage in the same process of audience analysis that others use. What differentiates PR from advertising, though, is that the rhetorical goals are often latent or even hidden. PR practitioners generally want to seem like they are just providing objective information; good PR practitioners are able to present that information so it puts their client in the best light. This practice is called "spinning," and it is arguably the central concern of public relations. Viewers of political talk shows such as *Face the Nation* or *The O'Reilly Factor* are probably familiar with this notion of "spinning" the news—commentators with a political stance (such as Bill O'Reilly) or advocates of a particular position (guests of these shows who might be politicians or representatives of groups being discussed) purport to just be presenting facts when they are actually trying to make an argument with these facts.

Our relationship to this kind of rhetoric is contradictory. Political commentators and spokespeople routinely dismiss opposing points as spin, and in fact O'Reilly's own book was called *The No-Spin Zone*. His contention was that he does not allow people to spin the facts on his watch. Of course, O'Reilly himself is among America's most successful spinners of the day's events. It's important to recognize that the dichotomy between factual statements and spin is a misleading one: as we saw in the previous chapter, it is almost impossible to make a statement that is completely free of bias or opinion, and truthfully, such purely factual statements rarely tell us much about the world. Good readers must learn how to spot bias, how to understand what a particular bias or spin may be omitting or overly emphasizing, and how to search out multiple sources of information that complement each other.

While "spin" is usually used to describe rhetoric about political issues or explanations of a fact or event, "PR" generally refers to any information provided on behalf of an individual, group, or corporation. PR by no means is restricted to the written or spoken word, either; one of the pioneers of the field, Edward Bernays, defined PR as the science of "creating circumstances," of producing events that are designed to be "newsworthy" but that do not appear to be staged.[2] Bernays was a master at the publicity stunt, the happening that would draw media and public attention without seeming like advertising. (Our focus here, though, is the language of PR, especially as used in the contemporary media, so we will not be examining publicity stunts in any detail.)

Let's look at three examples of PR conducted through journalism. Our first example, from the February 24, 2003 *New York Times,* is a typical feature story reporting on a change in advertising strategy by a large fast food company.

Arby's Tries a Talking Mitt
By Sean Mehegan

Arby's has spent several years carving out a position for itself as "adult fast food." But now Arby's is turning to a cartoonish kitchen implement to help rescue its sagging brand recognition.

The chain's new animated character is named Oven Mitt. Goofy, assertive and a bit of a ham—much like Tom Arnold, the celebrity who is providing its voice—Mr. Mitt is Arby's new spokesthing and will appear in an $85 million national advertising campaign, beginning Sunday. W. B. Doner & Company of Southfield, Mich., has the account.

The emergence of Oven Mitt signals a sharp creative change for Arby's, a 3,200-store system franchised by the Triarc Companies, based in New York. Previously, Arby's used a voice-over from the singer Barry White in spots called Appetite Man, to highlight specific products on its menu. Oven Mitt is more about building the Arby's brand, company executives said.

In one commercial, Oven Mitt is running the Arby's kitchen and lectures the staff to "take care of the oven mitt," not like the previous day, when Oven Mitt was trapped under a heavy pan. In another spot, Oven Mitt introduces Arby's Italian beef and provolone sandwich, then begins belting out a version of the song "Volare." The tagline for the campaign is, "What Are You Eating Today?"

With the ads, Arby's is trying to emphasize that it oven-roasts its beef, a method of preparation that the company says sets it apart from the competition.

Consumers saw a lot of value in oven roasting, said Michael Howe, Arby's president. "It took them back to a time that was more honest, more trusting."

"This is something we've always provided to consumers," he said. "Now we're putting it in a fun, exciting, modern communication."

---

[2] Stuart Ewen, *PR! A Social History of Spin.* New York: Basic Books, 1996. The best explanation of Bernays's principles of public relations can be found in Bernays's own article "The Engineering of Consent," available in many public relations textbooks.

"Clearly, consumers are migrating away from burgers," he said, "but what they're really looking for is high-quality, high-flavor sandwiches. They're looking for good food. It's about food quality more than anything else."

[John] Lauck, [president of the Arby's Franchise Association] added: "The heart of this isn't to go out and say, 'This is a better-for-you product.' The higher order is to establish a brand personality. You're buying a higher-quality sandwich, with the implied benefit that it's going to be better for you."

First of all, the existence of this story itself is the result of PR. In order to make the *New York Times* aware of the change in the Arby's spokescharacter, Arby's (or its advertising agency) sent the newspaper a press release. The editors of the business section then decided that this change was newsworthy, so they assigned a reporter to write a story. (Smaller papers and television or radio outlets may simply insert the company press release as the story—and the company will encourage this by making their press release sound as little like advertising as possible—but the *New York Times* holds itself to higher standards of journalistic independence.)

The language that the two spokespeople use is typical of corporate PR. Michael Howe, the company president, states that "consumers saw a lot of value in oven roasting" because "it took them back to a time that was more honest, more trusting." How Howe might know this he doesn't indicate; it is likely that this "information" is either the result of focus group surveys or simply of boardroom brainstorming. Howe is careful to get in words like "value," "trusting," and "honest," for the new campaign for Arby's clearly seems designed to remind consumers of a myth of home: Mom roasting dinner in the oven, her oven mitts on her hands as she removes the roast. Nowhere does Howe bring up the corporate machinery that went into deciding on the character change—the marketing surveys and focus groups, the careful search for a celebrity voice involving dozens of talent agencies and marketing consultants and personal managers and casting directors, the test kitchens and laboratories searching for the best way to mass produce meat products that must be efficiently shipped and stored. He then goes on to state that "this is something we've always provided to consumers," but he does not say what "this" is. The grammar of the previous sentence would seem to indicate that the antecedent of "this" is "a time that was more honest, more trusting." This statement sounds good at first, but when examined closely it is meaningless. How has Arby's provided consumers with a time that "was more honest, more trusting"? The restaurant does not have old-fashioned decor, and has always made use of up-to-date technologies. The restaurant cannot transport people to a different time. In this statement, Howe simply is trying to link pleasant adjectives to his company without making any actual argument about that link.

Corporate PR, like political advertising, frequently relies on one very important rhetorical trick: the assertion that "the American people" want something and that this corporation or politician is just responding to that desire. Think about how many political ads feature the candidate saying something like "The American people want . . ." or "the people of Wisconsin need . . ." Speakers using this rhetorical trick never detail how they know what the American public wants and never portray the speaker as anything but the faithful servant of this public. "Clearly," Howe continues, "customers are migrating away from burgers." This assertion has no evidence backing it up, but for many years the media has talked about a growing health consciousness in the American public, so it's a generalization we are likely to initially accept. "What they're really looking for," he continues, "is high-quality, high-flavor sandwiches." This is hard to contest, especially if sandwiches can also mean pitas, tacos, wraps, and other bread-and-filling products that have recently proliferated on fast food menus. Consumers certainly aren't looking for low-quality, low-flavor anything. "They're looking for good food." This is again true—who could argue that consumers are looking for bad food? The debatable proposition here—the absent thesis—is that Arby's sells the "high-quality, high-flavor sandwiches" that consumers want, but Howe does not actually make that statement. Instead, talking around this real claim by making ancillary claims that seem plausible allows him to act like he's convinced us that Arby's sandwiches are the "high-quality, high-flavor" nonburger sandwiches he claims consumers want.

It's hard to argue with any of Howe's individual points: sure, oven roasting reminds us of home-cooked meals, and Americans like good food, and people are probably looking for something besides burgers, and sandwiches are popular. None of these points actually says anything of real consequence, though. PR relies on these kinds of inarguable propositions in order to encourage the audience to trust the speaker—who wouldn't believe that Americans are looking for good food?—which then makes it easier to convince us of a claim that, often as not, is never explicitly made, for an explicit claim is open to a counterclaim.

At this point it's almost hard to remember that this story concerned a new spokescharacter for Arby's, because the company president has used this forum to advance the interests of Arby's in general—he's engaging in PR like a pro. But what about this character? According to Howe, it's great, it's a "fun, exciting modern communication." Again, this is a meaningless statement. Consumer reaction will determine whether or not this character is "fun" or "exciting" and as for "modern," it's hard to even tell what he means by that. Didn't he just want us to believe that the oven mitt was supposed to remind us of a more honest, more trusting time that is presumably in the past? Is this a modern character or one that evokes the past?

This kind of argument uses a logical fallacy called "begging the question": stating that the oven mitt is "fun" and "exciting," when that is exactly the point that consumers will later determine, takes the arguable question as an already-proven fact. (See the Writer at Work section of this chapter for more discussion of logical fallacies.) Interestingly, John Lauck of the franchisee's association doesn't seem to have received the memo about the new advertising strategy, because his statement sounds more like he is analyzing the campaign from the outside. Making it clear that Arby's isn't going to actually *say* that their sandwich is "better for you" than the competitors, Lauck asserts flatly that this new move is all about implying rather than actually stating: "The heart of this isn't to go out and say, 'This is a better-for-you product.' The higher order is to establish a brand personality. You're buying a higher-quality sandwich, with the implied benefit that it's going to be better for you."

Corporate PR, because the end goals always tend to be the same (to increase sales or to increase the stock price of a company), frequently boils down to this kind of rhetoric: implication rather than actual assertion, an avoidance of statements of fact that can be contradicted, a reliance on meaningless statements like "Americans want good food" or "Americans want good value," and "begging-the-question" tricks in which we are told to accept as given statements that need to be proven. In another kind of PR these kinds of salesman-like tricks are much more rare. Celebrity publicity has a much more nebulous and therefore interesting task: to promote a person. Certainly, the promotion of a person often involves selling, for that person is generally involved with movies or books or music or speaking appearances that need to be sold, but celebrity publicity tends not to openly sell the celebrity's products. Rather, celebrity publicity generally tries to construct public understanding of the celebrity as a person who is so appealing that we want to consume any products associated with that person.

Celebrity publicity comes in thousands of forms: red-carpet walks at movie premieres, appearances on late-night talk shows, press releases about political issues, roles in films, guest slots on records and CDs, "drop-ins" on another celebrity's show, segments on entertainment-oriented TV shows, and many others. For those interested in the written word, perhaps the most interesting form of celebrity publicity is the magazine profile. There have been celebrity-oriented magazines for as long as there have been celebrities, of course, and today there are more than ever: *People, Teen Beat, Gear, Us Weekly, In Touch, InStyle,* and dozens of others focus on the doings of famous people. Moreover, recently many magazines that have traditionally not focused on celebrities have started to do so in order to increase newsstand sales—both fashion magazines and news-magazines have started to put film and television personalities on their covers to spur impulse purchases.

But the celebrity profile as a genre probably reaches its apex in those magazines that claim to put a premium on good writing rather than just on the inclusion of as many celebrities as possible. *Vanity Fair, Esquire, GQ, Rolling Stone, Spin, Interview, Details,* and a few others dominate this market. In these magazines' celebrity profiles, the writer allows him or herself to have a personality; and the writing stands out as something important in its own right. The writer will often use the first person and explicitly express opinions. These articles can be especially effective PR because of the illusion of critical distance and objectivity. Where the articles in *People* or *Us* are frequently approved by the celebrity in question (or the publicist) before they go to press, and therefore rarely include anything unflattering, these "quality" celebrity profiles appear to be free of the control of the publicist, and therefore hold out the promise of being truly revealing. This, unfortunately, is generally not the case—most celebrity publicists provide interviewers with ground rules before the interview ever begins, specifying which topics may not be covered. (See Catherine Seipp's article in this chapter for a longer discussion of the role of celebrity publicists in magazine journalism.)

This is not to say that these profiles are boring. Many of them are a hoot to read, even though the celebrities are invariably smarter than we think, more carefree than we think, earthier than we think, just really down-to-earth people with amazing talent and striking good looks. A recent profile of the actors Edward Norton and Ralph Fiennes begins this way:

> Here is who we are: We are men at work who know life and also know each other because we have now worked together, playing good and evil. We are men who act because we must. We are American and British, thirty-three and thirty-nine, lean and intense and acclaimed and humble. We are not pretty, but women do not mind at all. We are particular about how we are addressed: It is *Edward,* never *Ed;* it is *Rafe,* never *Ralph.* (We favor the Old English pronunciation, if you please, because that is how the family intended it to be.) So don't even think about calling us Eddie or Ralphy, if it's not too much to ask. Our work together was executed during the year's first four months, but rarely were we in the same place at the same time, since the point of the exercise was for one of us to appear in desperate pursuit of the other and vice versa.[3]

The conceit is clever: the two actors in the profile are made to speak in the first person plural. The profile gives us much the same information as any other, but its narrative voice is unique, making us think that this profile might somehow get more deeply under the skin of these celebrities than a 500-word piece in *Us Weekly* or a 90-second segment on *Entertainment Tonight.*

Here's another paragraph from a recent profile, this one more traditional:

> It's a long way from the Five Points to the courtyard of the Chateau Marmont, in Hollywood, where if you saturate your handkerchief with camphor you will only miss the scents of jasmine and bougainvillea, along with the occasional waft of exhaust from Sunset Boulevard. As careful readers of this and other magazines already know, the hotel's courtyard is where nearly all show-business interviews take place. (The remaining handful occur while swerving in and out of traffic on La Cienega in someone's BMW X5.) And so here is Cameron Diaz herself, dressed casually but crisply in blue jeans and heels and a half-off-the-shoulder black sweater, swaying her way out of the lobby's Old Hollywood gloom and looking every bit the easygoing, long-limbed dazzler she typically plays on-screen. When she smiles, her eyes and teeth react to the hazy, early-afternoon light with the same electricity you might have thought cinematographers and lighting designers spend hours to confect. This is not a movie star of whom it is said, "She's so much smaller and washed-out-looking in person." This is a woman whose genetic blessings are as manifest as her lack of affection.[4]

In this profile, the author makes fun of the genre of the profile just as much as the author of the Norton-Fiennes profile does. "Here we are," he implies, "in the same place where every other interview happens, I've done this a million times . . ." The point of this world-weary, seen-it-all voice is then to note just

---

[3] Bill Zehme, "Portrait of the Actor as Two Men," *Esquire* Sept. 2002: 160.

[4] Bruce Handy, "Buenos Diaz," *Vanity Fair* Jan. 2003: 68. Copyright © 2003 Conde Nast Publications. All rights reserved.

how much Cameron Diaz stands out from this clichéd setting. This writer, seeking to find a new way to say exactly what everyone else says about this particular celebrity (she's luminous, she's unaffected by her celebrity), does so by emphasizing the routine nature of the celebrity profile.

The aim of both of these profiles, as of most of the other celebrity coverage that saturates the media today, is to promote the celebrity as a brand, something greater and more complicated and more enduringly fascinating than any individual project. This kind of coverage is generally orchestrated, in the case of very famous people, by a small army of publicists and assistants and agents and managers who arrange not only for the coverage itself but also for how the coverage will be conducted.

Celebrity promotion is also taking up greater space in the news. In recent years, the mainstream television and magazine news outlets, which have historically been reluctant to engage in the promotion of individual products or services, have embraced what we might call "the culture of celebrity." Reckoning that linking news stories with celebrities will draw viewers or readers, editors and producers attempt to link almost every kind of story with a recognizable celebrity. The 2003 California gubernatorial recall election became a story not about the democratic process but about Arnold Schwarzenegger and Gary Coleman. Gun control becomes "Charlton Heston versus Susan Sarandon." Race and justice become "O.J." Issues, of course, are drastically oversimplified when covered as spats between famous people. But even more interesting is that these arguments about public policy can become vehicles—risky ones, of course, because stars with political ideas will inevitably alienate some fans who don't share those ideas—for the promotion of celebrity itself. It's worth thinking about these kinds of issues in the abstract. Ask yourself why stories about celebrities seem so much more interesting than other kinds of stories. Can celebrity angles be a way for news programmers to get us to pay attention to real issues in the world—did Janeane Garofalo's opposition to the war in Iraq make people think about the war? Can a celebrity's presence in the middle of a sordid crime story make you think more about the issues that might lie behind that crime?

A nalyzing the Message

Find three celebrity profiles: one from *GQ, Esquire, Vanity Fair,* or *Vogue;* one from *People, Entertainment Weekly, TV Guide,* or *Us* and one from a TV source such as *Entertainment Tonight* or the TV Guide Channel's "90 Second Life Story." Compare the three stories in terms of their use of point of view, setting, and language. Specifically, answer the following questions for each profile:

1. Who is the writer? What does he or she tell us (explicitly or implicitly) about him or herself in the article?

2. Was this article based on personal contact between the writer and subject, or did the writer use previously published material or statements by publicists for source material? If it was an interview, does the writer say where was it conducted? Does the writer use the setting for a rhetorical purpose? If there was no contact between writer and subject, where did the writer obtain his or her facts?

3. What factual details does the writer tell us about the celebrity?

4. What judgments or statements of opinion does the writer make about the celebrity?

5. How would you characterize the language used by the writer—what adjectives does he or she use to directly describe the celebrity, what does he or she compare the celebrity to, what verbs does the writer use to describe the celebrity's actions?

6. If this celebrity has controversial or problematic events in his or her life that *you* know about (e.g., Tom Cruise and Scientology, Billy Bob Thornton and domestic violence, Halle Berry and her hit-and-run accident), does the writer deal with them? If so, does the writer deal with them sufficiently? If not, is it clear that these questions were off-limits?

Advertising and PR: The Ethical Dimension

Although we have been taking a somewhat adversarial stance in talking about the practices of promoting, advertising and PR are not somehow compromised or corrupt or evil because their primary impetus is to persuade or convince or sell. As you have already seen, almost all language is rhetoric—an attempt to persuade. It's valuable to examine ads and PR as separate phenomena because their characteristic tactics and techniques constantly grow more sophisticated, and because the mass media is dominated by the messages of advertising and PR. Understanding those tactics and techniques makes us more selective consumers of the media, smarter judges of messages in general, and better citizens of a democracy in which everyone is guaranteed the right to free speech—even if that speech consists of nothing but advertising and promotion.

What this discussion leaves untouched, though, is the question of ethics and its relationship to rhetoric. If rhetoric's fundamental purpose is to persuade, to make people believe something they didn't believe before or do something they wouldn't have done before, how can it be ethical? Isn't it true that the most effective rhetoric in fact relies on tricks we might consider unethical—the misrepresenting of one's own aims (as in the "no-spin zone" idea), the misrepresentation of arguable points as facts, the selective suppression of relevant information, the appeal to emotions instead of (rather than along with) logic? Given this, isn't all advertising and public relations unethical?

These are very difficult questions, of course. Rhetoric has always been ethically suspect; as long ago as ancient Athens the philosophers Socrates and Plato derogated rhetoric as a poor substitute for what should be humanity's real concern, the search for truth. But for Plato's student Aristotle an ethical rhetoric was possible. There is a great deal of ethical advertising and PR: in fact, the great majority of advertising and PR is ethical. If it's impossible to tell a story without constructing that story according to our own biases, there is no such thing as purely objective, purely truthful communication. Everything, in other words, is rhetoric. American journalism implicitly acknowledges this but tries as hard as possible to balance all sides of a question and to give readers or viewers the *fairest* account of a story. It would not be just of us to hold advertising or PR to an ethical standard higher than the one to which we hold journalism just because persuasion is the *purpose* of these industries. Ethical advertising or public relations, in turn, should be open about its desire to persuade, should not misrepresent or lie about or omit significant details that might be inconvenient or damaging, and should not appeal to our harmful prejudices.

In 1993, hundreds of children in Washington, Idaho, and Nevada fell gravely ill after eating at Jack in the Box fast food restaurants; three died. The bacteria E. coli, present in contaminated or undercooked meats was quickly identified as the cause. Initially, Jack in the Box denied responsibility and "stonewalled" the press, refusing to offer any information and even blaming the Washington state department of health. As evidence mounted that the children had been infected from eating Jack in the Box hamburgers, the company realized that this crisis could put it out of business permanently. After a month of relentlessly bad publicity, the CEO of the company replaced his PR firm. The new firm (headed by Jody Powell, who had been President Jimmy Carter's press secretary) quickly turned the problem around, taking responsibility for the outbreak and talking openly with the public about the company's plans for avoiding any future contamination of its meat. The company not only survived, but in recent years has thrived and expanded, and today its health and safety standards are among the most stringent in the industry. The Jack in the Box episode is a wonderful case study of the efficacy of ethical PR. The company's initial strategy of refusing to take responsibility and of attempting to shift attention and blame to others backfired; the public could tell the company wanted to hide something. After Jack in the Box changed its strategy, the public responded well. We appreciate it when people communicate ethically with us, especially when they don't necessarily have to.

As you read the articles included with this chapter, ask yourself these questions about the ethical responsibility of publicists and advertisers and marketers. Can we come up with rules—not laws but generally accepted standards of practice—for those who are in the business of selling or promoting? Should we just accept that everything is a sales pitch, and adopt a flinty cynicism toward the world's messages? And are there any causes that are so beyond acceptability, so reprehensible, that there can be no such thing as ethical rhetoric on their behalf?

Analyzing the Message

What is ethical advertising? What ethical responsibilities do advertisers or publicists or promoters have to the audience they are addressing? For the purposes of this exercise, practice being an advertiser or PR professional. Think about the following situations, and come up with a strategy that reflects some sort of ethical structure.

1. The launch of a new $200 basketball sneaker.
2. The discovery that your political candidate embezzled $1 million from his campaign funds to pay off his former lover.

3. News reports that a saboteur is poisoning your products before they arrive on store shelves.

4. The fact that your college has just been named the number 1 best value in your region by a national magazine.

Readings

*Ads have always been present on television. From its earliest days, television was a commercial medium, allowing for-profit stations and networks to rent a piece of the broadcast spectrum in order to try and turn a profit. Even television executives frankly admit that the real business of TV is not producing programming but selling advertising; popular programs are important not because the network benefits directly from having millions of people watch them but because the network can then sell advertising space on those programs for a premium, by demonstrating to those advertisers that millions of people will see their ads. Nor is the penetration of advertising into programming a recent development. Many early programs (Texaco Star Theater, General Electric Theater) were sponsored by one company whose logo and name were repeated throughout the program, and late night talk show hosts such as Jack Paar did ads for their sponsors during the program. In this article, Associated Press media critic **Frazier Moore** complains that those early days of heavy sponsor presence seem to be returning—that devices such as digital video recorder services, which allow consumers to fast forward through or simply not tape commercials, are forcing the TV networks to again weave the sponsors into the shows themselves.*

Frazier Moore
Shill-o-vision: The Ads Take over TV

New York (AP)—Last night, I watched four hours' worth of TV in a little over three hours. As the kids say: Sweet!

Count me among the fans of digital video recorders (commonly known by the brand name TiVo), which allow us to watch programs on our schedule, not the networks'. I can even stop and restart a show while it airs!

But that's not really news. Nor is what I consider the sweetest thing about so-called personal TV: the time I save by rocketing through commercial breaks and other clutter.

No wonder the networks and their advertisers are panicked by the onset of the TiVo Age, a post-VCR paradise when zapping commercials is so easy as to be almost irresistible. And no wonder they are fighting back with increasingly drastic countermeasures.

Sure, I get the picture: There is no such thing as a free show. With broadcast TV, commercials pay the bills. On basic cable, too, advertising pays much of the freight. So, even though there's no admission charge for me to see "The West Wing" or "Joe Millionaire," when the ads come on, my bill comes due. Then, I am expected to pay with my attention.

My problem is, the price for this "free" TV is soaring.

During the past decade on the networks, the time devoted to commercial breaks has swollen by more than 15 percent in prime time, where currently it's about 16 minutes of every hour. It's nearly 21 minutes of each daytime hour.

And that's assuming I haven't stumbled on a show rammed through the Time Machine, which, for any broadcaster who uses it, "easily creates up to 30 seconds of extra commercial time in a 20–30 minute program" by selectively eliminating frames from the program—compression sorcery "virtually undectable (sic) to viewers," according to the Web site of the company that sells it.

Eventually, of course, every commercial break will end. But with television turning into shill-o-vision, the commercials need never end.

Buying in

Advertisers can buy their way into programs like CBS' "Survivor" and Fox's "American Idol," where "product integration" deals treat a thirsty castaway to a certain brand of beer or plop a wannabe star into a room named for a certain make of car to spill her guts.

This summer, the WB plans to air a weekly variety series that will take the inevitable next step. It will do away with commercial breaks while it weaves advertising throughout the show. Voila! A seamless hour of entertainment and hucksterism. I can almost hear the networks jeering, "TiVo THAT!"

Meanwhile on scripted programs, more and more product plugs are peddled, then plugged right into a scene.

For instance, there's no mistaking (nor is it any accident) that a certain brand of cell phone is all the rage with the characters on ABC's "Alias"—yet that cell phone, however conspicuous in the action, never announces itself as a product being pitched. Thus does storytelling commingle with selling on the sly.

Once upon a time, "Seinfeld" made hilarious use of real-life product brands—from Junior Mints and Snapple to J. Peterman and the New York Yankees. "Seinfeld" creators understood how, in a consumer society, brands are part of our vernacular and our self-identity. And that's how they served Jerry and friends, whose product preferences were purely character-driven—not the result of bought-and-paid-for insertions.

These days, the potential windfall is often too tempting for producers and networks to resist. A gold rush beckons. And number-crunches scramble to devise a practical pricing plan.

Product placement

One market-analysis firm ranks the value of a product placement "based on how central the product was to the plot, which character used it and for how long," says an article in Advertising Age.

According to the formula arrived at by another research firm, a close-up shot of the product in a hit sitcom, plus "hands-on" interaction from one of its characters, might fetch the network on which it appears nearly $250,000—and even more, to get the character to say the product's name out loud.

The networks insist these new revenue streams are essential to their future.

Besides, viewers like me were just asking for it. With our TiVos and VCRs, we've been jumping the turnstile to get a free ride far too long.

How much longer? The networks are cracking down and cashing in. Shill-o-vision is on the rise. But only in this way, or so the networks insist, will TV stay free. It will be worth every penny.

Topics for Reading and Writing

1. Brands are undoubtedly, as Moore argues, "part of our vernacular." When characters drink from unbranded milk cartons or eat unbranded candy, it stands out. So what is wrong with sponsors taking advantage of our natural desire to see the world on TV more accurately represent the brand-saturated real world?

2. Is Moore in favor of or opposed to the increasing presence of ads in television shows? What does this have to do with keeping television free?

3. If you could pay $10 a month for 6 completely commercial-free channels, but all access to commercially sponsored free television were eliminated, would you do it? $20 for 10? $80 for 300?

What is the place of for-profit endeavors in our underfunded public schools? If a company is willing to provide media content for schools—current events programming, created with a youth audience in mind— what's wrong if they want a return on their investment? And if students are bombarded by commercials every minute of their lives, what's so bad about watching a few commercials in school? The rise of the Channel One news service has made all these questions urgent. Channel One, which provides a short current events news show complete with commercials to high schools, certainly produces programming that's "relevant" to high school students, which helps schools educate students in their responsibilities as citizens of a democracy. However, schools that use Channel One must also show the accompanying commercials, which appears to compromise the traditional place of schools outside the commercial arena. Both of these articles oppose Channel One, but for different reasons. As you read these articles, think not only about the reasons they choose to write about Channel One, but also about how each author constructs his or her authority to speak on the topic.

Jessica Gelt is a graduate student in the University of Southern California's school of print journalism; her article appeared in USC's Daily Trojan *newspaper.*

Jessica Gelt
Commercials in Class Are No Surprise

What do *Seventeen* magazine and Osama bin Laden have in common? They both want the attention of teenagers. And they can receive it jointly through the Channel One Network, a company that broadcasts news and commercials to 8 million students in 12,000 middle, junior and high schools across America.

Channel One, which began broadcasting in 1990, is owned by PRIMEDIA Inc. On its company Web site, PRIMEDIA Inc. describes itself as, "the leading targeted content and integrated marketing solutions company in both the consumer and business-to-business sectors." PRIMEDIA Inc. is also the "#1 special interest magazine publisher in the U.S.," with 250 titles including: *Seventeen, Teen Beat, Automobile, Shooting Times, Shotgun News, Today's SUV* and *Soap Opera Digest.*

How does Channel One work? It preys on poorly subsidized schools by offering a television set for each classroom, two VCRs and a satellite dish—as long as the school agrees to show 12 minutes a day of Channel One in the classroom. A daily dose of Channel One includes 10 minutes of teen-oriented "news" and one to two minutes of commercials. During the course of a year, Channel One takes up a full week of school time, with about one full day of that week spent watching ads.

A Channel One trade ad published in *Advertising Age* read: "Channel One is viewed by more teens than any other program on television. Channel One reaches . . . nearly 40 percent of all 12- to 17-year-olds. Every day Channel One is seen by as many teens as the Super Bowl. Channel One's audience exceeds the combined number of teens watching anything on television during Primetime! Huge ratings. Unsurpassed reach. Unparalleled impact among teen viewers."

Most of the ads on Channel One are for junk food, entertainment and sports equipment. Graphic anti-drug public service announcements are also regularly aired. A recent one showed two teen boys getting high on marijuana. One of the giggling boys pulls his father's gun out of a desk drawer and says, "It's not loaded." The announcement ends with the boy blowing his friend away.

This public service announcement proves that Channel One is partially subsidized by federal money. The Office of National Drug Control Policy is not the only federal advertiser seen on Channel One. The U.S. Navy, Air Force and Marines also run ads on the station, making parallels between Channel One and the "Two Minutes Hate" in George Orwell's book *1984,* too easily drawn.

The ethic of Channel One's distribution is fraught with class-war implications. In a recent interview with Robert W. McChesney, author of *Rich Media, Poor Democracy: Communication Politics in Dubious Times,* Sharon Bloyd-Peshkin, editor of Chicago Parent magazine, asked how Channel One operates. McChesney's response highlights one of the most disturbing aspects of Channel One's "modus operandi."

"It's notable that in affluent schools, you're much less likely to find Channel One. This is simply for those children of the masses who go to public schools; they're the ones who get this commercial education. I'd have a lot less concern about Channel One if the children of the George Bushes of the world were getting a full dose of this. But they're not. The further down you go on the class chain, the more likely kids are to be seeing Channel One in school," McChesney said.

McChesney says that besides the Center for Commercial-Free Public Education, based in Oakland, Calif., not many groups have forged a resistance to Channel One.

"If parents saw this and were aware of it, there would be more concern," McChesney said. "But parents don't generally know what their kids are being exposed to. It's out of sight, out of mind for many parents. That's one of Channel One's selling points: They get in under the radar."

When people who have never heard of Channel One are told about it, they inevitably react with surprise. Why? U2 played during halftime of Super Bowl XXXVI while the names of those who had just died in the World Trade Centers scrolled on a large screen behind them. That flagrantly commercial use of tragedy didn't bother us. So how can we feign astonishment at the fact that commercials have slithered their way to the forefront of public education?

Teens are perfectly trained consumers; we live in a society constructed to ensure this. The dawning of commercially subsidized public education was as inevitable as the release of *Men in Black II.* The Constitution ensures that church and state remain separate, but it says nothing about corporate America and education. Trying to fight the spread of Channel One without the help of the Constitution, in a country that prides itself on its cultural imperialism, is like trying to suck the cream out of a Twinkie.

America would do well to examine why Channel One is so successful. It's not because people don't know about it—it's because it seems so natural.

Mark Crispin Miller is a professor of media studies at New York University and wrote this article for Extra!, *the journal of Fairness and Accuracy in Reporting (FAIR).*

Mark Crispin Miller
How To Be Stupid: The Lessons of Channel One

News, of course, is not the point of Channel One—any more than it's the point of those commercial TV newscasts that many of us watch at home night after night. If the basic aim of all such TV shows were really journalistic, it might be possible to glean from them some simple daily understanding of the world; but what we get these days from TV news is loud, speedy filler, which—with minimal background, and no context—leaves the mind with nothing but some evanescent numbers, a helpless sense of general disaster, a heavy mental echo of official reassurance and (not too surprisingly) an overwhelming vague anxiety.

The news on Channel One leaves this impression—for it looks and sounds a lot like what we get on regular TV, only more so. Genially presented by its very young and pretty (and meticulously multiracial) team of anchors, the "news" is even more compressed and superficial than the stuff the networks give us: big accidents and major snowstorms, non-stories about the Super Bowl, horse-race coverage of domestic politics, bloody images of foreign terrorism, the occasional nerve-wracking and largely unenlightening visit to some scary place like Haiti or Tibet, and features—either grim or inspirational—on teens suffering from various high-profile torments (cancer, AIDS, addiction).

Of course, it being TV news, much of it is starkly painful—gory corpses in the streets of Tel Aviv, stretchers hefted from a midnight train wreck in suburban Maryland, survivors weeping after Oklahoma City, etc. When, on the other hand, it isn't horrible or sad, the news on Channel One is just confusing: a blast of isolated factoids about very distant and extremely complicated fights (e.g., Bosnia) and the equally complex—and, for that matter, distant—wrangles in the federal limelight (e.g., Clinton's budget vs. the Republicans'), all of it dressed up with the usual brilliant, zippy graphics, but none of it made clear or relevant enough to bear in mind. A student with a photographic memory might be able to retain those random facts and figures, but most kids wouldn't be, nor is there any reason why they should.

As inane as it may seem, however, the news on Channel One, by turns horrific and confusing, does serve an important purpose—just like the news on regular TV. In either case, the news is, to repeat, no more than filler. Its real function is not journalistic but commercial, for it is meant primarily to get us ready for the ads. What this means is that the news must, on the one hand, keep us sitting there and watching, as an M.C. has to keep his audience mildly entertained between the acts; but it must also constantly efface itself, must keep itself from saying anything too powerful or even interesting, must never cut too deep or raise any really troubling questions, because it can never be permitted to detract in any way from the commercials. Its aim must be, in short, to keep our eyes wide open and our minds asleep, so that the commercial will look good to us, sound true to us, and thereby work on us.

The Ads in Context

If the news on Channel One often seems perplexingly abstract, offering no clear impression from those many sudden, pointless names and numbers, that perplexity enhances the effect of the commercials. So brightly focused and so dazzlingly insistent, each stands out luminous and sharp in the bewildering murk of factoids like a high-tech lighthouse in a blinding fog. The routine horror of the news on Channel One also indirectly bolsters the commercials, which proffer their young viewers a fantastic antidote to all those tragic woes and bloody dangers. Skeletal and nearly bald, a real teenager with leukemia suffers through the agonies of chemotherapy—just after a fictitious teenaged girl (full-bodied, and with all her hair) finds happiness by using Clearasil. Buildings explode and people mourn in Bosnia (with its "brutal and complex story of ethnic hatreds and violent nationalism")—and then we see the Buffalo Bills, locked up and deprived of lunch by their demanding coach, chomp with furtive relish on their Snickers bars ("Hungry? Why wait?"). And so on.

Surely all the mass advertising on the TV news thus benefits from such delicious contrast with the uglier images of telejournalism (as long as those other images are not too ugly). The ads on Channel One would seem to be especially powerful, however, because they thrive by contrast not just with the news before and after them, but with the whole boring, regimented context of the school itself.

Imagine, or remember, what it's like to have to sit there at your desk, listening to your teacher droning on, with hours to go until you can get out of there, your mind rebelling and your hormones raging. It must be a relief when Channel One takes over, so you can lose yourself in its really cool graphics and its tantalizing bursts of rock music—and in the advertisers' mind-blowing little fantasies of power: power through Pepsi, Taco Bell, McDonald's, Fruit-A-Burst and/or Gatorade ("Life Is a Sport. Drink It Up!"), power through Head 'n' Shoulders, Oxy-10 and/or Pantene Pro-V Mousse (". . . a stronger sense of style!"), power through Donkey Kong and/or Killer Instinct ("PLAY IT LOUD!") and/or power through Reebok ("This is my planet!").

Buy the Power!

Of all the promises that advertising makes us, this promise of a certain rude empowerment—personal, immediate and absolute—is now the one that comes at us most often. Although it comes at all of us countless times each day, we see the promise used most often in those ads that are directed at the weakest of us: the poor, women generally—and kids, as Channel One makes clear. Over and over, the product flashes into view as something that you ought to pay for not because you might enjoy it but because it promises to make you indestructible, as tough as nails, as hard as steel: a Superman or Superwoman.

"I'm a guided missile," grunts the famous football player—so big and strong because of Reebok, evidently, so if you buy those shoes you'll be that big and strong (and famous). A hot babe beams at us and pops a stick of Doublemint—and then she's happily kissing this buff guy, whose hands are out of sight while she has her arms wrapped around this neck, so that it's obvious—just from a glance—who's in control. (Then there's a different babe, and same thing happens.) Such fantasies appear to answer—and, of course, also exacerbate—the ferocious longing of their captive audience for freedom, independence, confidence and strength, which adolescents generally lack, and know they lack.

It isn't necessary to pay close attention to those loaded images in order for their message to get through to you. Indeed, mass advertising tends to be devised on the correct assumption that its audience will not be studying it carefully, but merely flipping through the magazines, driving right on past the billboards, and only half-watching—or even fast-forwarding—the TV spots. Thus the kids required to sit through Channel One, although they might appear to zone out during the commercials, are still likely to get the point, which is conveyed explosively enough to register through their peripheral vision, and which thus comes at them repeatedly—as all successful propaganda must.

And that point, again, is very simple (which is, of course, another requisite of winning propaganda). That point is: "Buy the power." As simple as it sounds, however, there is much more to the ads than that—for advertising never merely makes its most apparent pitch, but at the same time always offers up a vision of how you should live, and of how the world around you ought to be. It's one thing to say that the ads idealize power and identify the products with that power. But what exactly is that "power"? And what precisely is it that the advertising asks its teenaged audience to do, and think, in order to attain that "power"? These are crucial questions, since Channel One is, after all, by now required in thousands of our nation's schools, as a daily part of the curriculum. What, then, are its lessons?

Lesson #1: "Watch."

This is in fact the fundamental teaching of each ad, expertly hammered home by every virtuoso shot, every pointless, jarring cut, every stupefying jangle of computer graphics. It's also the most basic teaching of the ads en masse: for everybody in those ads is always staring at something (either at the product or at us), and is also himself or herself spectacular: as icy-cool and drop-dead gorgeous as the product. Now and then we see a kid contentedly waiting in line, but no kid depicted in the ads is ever reading, ever thinking, nor ever even unself-consciously conversing with some other kid(s). Sometimes—briefly, just before their rescue by the product—they might look anxious, lonely, doubtful. Otherwise, they are all alike continuously rapt in a Spielbergian state of blithe, wide-eyed wonderment, watching it all, and loving every minute of it—just as the student audience is meant to do. (Of course, Channel One includes many a loud ad for movies and TV from Fox, Time Warner, Universal and other such educators.)

The ads sometimes baldly celebrate that posture of euphoric gaping—as in an amazing spot for Skittles, a 30-second masterpiece that might be taken as an accurate dream-vision of what Channel One itself is all about. On the slate-gray face of a dead planet, under a luminous night sky, a bevy of cartoonish reptiles (each a different Skittle-color) slowly poke their cute, round, bleary dino-faces out of their respective hidey-holes, like prairie dogs just waking up. "Yum?" each one says groggily: "Yum?" Suddenly a shimmering wave of multicolored light hits the horizon and then flares across the sky—and all the little dinos perk right up and follow its swift course in pop-eyed wonder, together swaying from left to right in perfect unison.

In the wake of that celestial surge there is a shower of—meteors? No: Skittles, which drop and bounce amid the rooted crowd like day-glo-colored balls of manna, and the critters noisily gulp them down. "Yum," they now say, getting sleepy: "Yum." They sink back down into their holes. Finally, there's a long shot of the ruined planet and its many-hued Saturnian ring, which—we now see—constantly revolves around the sphere, so that that same exhilarating surge of colored light must dazzle those hole-dwellers regularly every day. We then hear this command, uttered in a childish whisper (and also printed on the screen): "Skittles. Taste the rainbow!"

The groggy little ones, their empty world, the daily light-show and its putatively yummy vision of the product: In its grotesque way the vision functions as a tidy allegory of Channel One itself, whose viewers are likewise always being promised an immediate reward for their continued watching.

Lesson #2: "Don't Think."

The sort of watching that is urged on teenagers by Channel One (and also urged on all of us by advertising generally) involves no reflection, no interpretation: on the contrary. First of all, the spectacle is much too fast and noisy to permit, much less encourage, any thoughtfulness; and yet the ads discourage thinking not just automatically, because of their distracting visuals and manic pace, but also, it would seem, deliberately, by taking every opportunity to celebrate stupidity. While forever hyping its commitment to the endless sharpening of the teenaged mind ("Imagine knowing everything," etc.), Channel One continually assures its audience, through the commercials, that it's really cool to be an idiot.

This is partly a result of the great corporate interest—prevalent throughout the entertainment industries—in exploiting the inevitable rebelliousness of adolescent boys. Whether on Channel One or regular TV, the ads aimed at that uneasy group appeal to a defiant boorishness that, in the real world, routinely lands a lot of young men in jail, and that the movie studios and video-game manufacturers endlessly glamorize in works like *Happy Gilmore, Ace Ventura 2: When Nature Calls* and *Down Periscope* ("See it and Win!"), Virtual Boy, Donkey Kong 2 and Killer Instinct ("PLAY IT LOUD!"), among many others advertised on Channel One. Since that loutish posture is as anti-intellectual as it is anti-social, the celebration of stupidity in Channel One's commercials owes a lot to that particularly noxious form of target marketing.

And yet it isn't only Channel One's male-oriented ads that say it's cool to be an idiot: All the advertising makes that point repeatedly, and makes it to the viewers of both sexes—for advertising (which is, of course, a form of propaganda) must forever tell its audience not to think.

Those cuddly reptiles gulping Skittles are just one species of the many simple, hungry organisms that Channel One's commercials represent as excellent consumers. Such beings know all you need to know: Any higher inquiry—or any inquiry at all—is laughable, the ads imply. "Woah!" breathes a frenetic youngster, having just wolfed down a very crunchy spoonful of the cereal in the bowl he's gripping: "How do they cram all that graham into Golden Grahams?" A halo of bright multicolored question marks pulsates and jiggles all around his head as he engages in moronic speculation—rendered for us in high-speed cartoons—about exactly how they cram all that graham. ("But how?" he finally asks again, then shrugs and takes another mouthful.)

Although portrayed as god-like, the big celebrities who do the ads on Channel One are likewise hailed for having heads of near-perfect emptiness. "Some people say I've got too much on my mind," Shaquille O'Neal murmurs at us, sitting tall in an expensive leather lounger (slick hip-hop bopping in the background). "Movies, music, toys. Correction: There's only one thing in my head: the championship." (Quick shots of Shaq looking like a winner.) "That's what's in my head," he says, then adds, "This is my planet." (And that's the Reebok logo on his chest.)

Over and over, the ads idealize ignorance: like the kid who wonders about nothing but how "they" make that cereal so sugary, and like the famous athlete in whose mind (he says) there's nothing but the fact that he's a famous athlete, the ads' countless momentary heroes each know only what the advertisers want their audience to know. The beauties talking earnestly about their faces and Noxema, or about their hair and Pantene Pro-V Mousse, and the dog who drinks a Pepsi (in a happy dream he's having about drinking Pepsi), and the animated M&M's who would do anything to get into that ad for M&M's ("I wanna be in that commercial!"): All those empty-headed figures speeding through the ads on Channel One are nothing but role models for the spread of Channel One's commercial propaganda, which wants its youthful audience to be just as thoughtless, easily distracted and obsessed. Those speedy figures are, in fact, the opposite of proper students (and therefore don't belong in schools).

Lesson #3: "Let Us Fix It."

The ads on Channel One also promote stupidity by representing all of life as nothing but a series of extremely simple problems, each soluble through the immediate application of some very smart commodity or other. To all your problems, Channel One keeps telling its young audience, we have the solutions. This myth promotes stupidity, first of all, by ruling out all problems any higher, deeper, more complex or general than, say, your boredom or your dandruff. Such trivialization must make students blind not only to the daunting truths and major questions of philosophy and history, but also to the harder, richer pleasures still available beyond the screaming little world of Channel One (where, for example, "nothin's more intense than slammin' a Dew!").

While grossly oversimplifying everything, moreover, that myth of the advertisers' total competence, of their ability to solve, at once, your every "problem," also promotes stupidity by suggesting that there is no worthwhile knowledge other than the knowledge of elite technicians (who are, of course, all working for Nintendo, Reebok, Mars, AT&T and the other major corporate advertisers, while you're just sitting there in front of that TV). Channel One's commercials are all, finally, celebrations of technology: not only are the ads themselves mind-bending feats of digital f/x, but they all tout the video games and pimple creams and running shoes as masterworks of technical design. Even tasty treats like Golden Grahams ("But how?"), and that "scorching new four-alarm, double-decker taco from Taco Bell," are sold primarily as the efficient and ingenious products of those corporations' labs.

It is their mystique of high technology that finally makes those ads and goods alike appear so very powerful—and that is meant to make the rest of us feel helpless, needy, stupid. (The news on Channel One continually reconfirms that view, through numerous awe-struck reports on seeming scientific break-throughs.) If you have any power at all, you can thank us for it, the ads tell their young viewers: "All that stuff your parents never dreamed of . . . AT&T is bring-ing it all within your reach!" proclaims a commercial for AT&T ("Your true choice"), which ends by asking for submissions to an essay contest on the theme "How Technology Has Benefited My Education."

Just as ads have done for well over a century, the ads on Channel One rou-tinely try to wow their audience with brisk bits of pseudo-scientific hooey, along with many clever mock-explanatory visuals. "The exclusive pro-vitamin formula penetrates, improving your hair," we're assured by a sweet, breathy female voice, as we watch a fleet of gently tumbling golden pellets disappear into the auburn scalp of an expensive-looking redhead. In another ad, an exuberant "science teacher," posed before his bunsen burners and reports, tells how he managed to teach "Chad" (whom we see repeatedly in handsome close-up) that "science is a beautiful thing," because "science is the key to clear skin." ("The medicine in Oxy–10 penetrates, it helps eliminate pimples fast," the "teacher" says by way of explanation.) He concludes: "Scientific equation: Oxy–10 equals great skin!"

Again, these are devices—the fake "authority," the vaguely scientific-sounding mumbo-jumbo—that advertising has been using on the public since the 19th Century. Their patent falseness makes them grossly inappropriate for use inside our schools—where children ought to learn to think, not to be taken in.

Lessons #4: "Eat Now."

While you need almost nothing in your head, you must put this—and lots of this—into your mouth. Of all the lessons taught day after day on Channel One, this one may have the most immediate effect, because that visual stimulus—watching someone chewing, sipping, gulping, licking his/her lips—is irresistible, especially when you're hungry and/or thirsty.

The same tantalizing tactic is routine on Channel One. Because teens tend almost always to be hungry, and because they're not allowed to eat in school, the many spots for candy, pizza, chewing gum, tacos, cereal and burgers, for Pepsi, Gatorade and Mountain Dew, are probably the most successful ads on Channel One, which shows—by far—more ads for drink and munchies than for any other category of product. Stuck there with their stomachs growling, the viewers of Channel One must feel downright tormented by the last shot in those ads for Snickers (with its dark nougat, chunks of peanut, gooey caramel, rippling choco-late): "Hungry? Why wait?"

Thus those sleepy critters gulp their Skittles, that curious kid scarfs down his Golden Grahams, those happy diners at McDonald's chow down on their Big Macs, and so on. And yet there's evidently more to the appetite(s) aroused by Channel One than the mere biological need for carbohydrates. The teenagers are hungry not for bread alone but for autonomy, security, control; and so the ads don't simply make the munchies look delicious, but represent them as a tasty means to personal "empowerment." "How does Shaquille O'Neal get fired up for a game? With a scorching new four-alarm double-decker taco from Taco Bell!"—and, after tearing into one of those hot, gloppy, crunchy little beauties, Shaq goes tearing down the court—in flames! (And he scores!)

And yet it is the girls more than the boys who are endlessly assured that eating makes you powerful. "Well duh, of course it's delicious!" snaps a pretty adolescent blonde about her Frosted Cheerios, and then a pert (and light-skinned) African-American pre-teen confides, "It's way too good for adults!" (Each girl hefts a spoon and holds a giant bowlful of the stuff.) And it's the girls who are enticed by Channel One's commercials for such cheap treats as Doublemint and Winterfresh, which taste so good that they'll make you taste good, and therefore make you overpoweringly delectable, just like the product (a promise made through countless careful images of slender, lovely chewers variously "in control").

Lesson #5: "You're Ugly."

Although it hypes itself as a brave new instrument of teenage "mind expansion," Channel One—that is, its owners and its sponsors—would certainly prefer that its young audience not become acute enough to grasp certain glaring contradictions in each broadcast.

For example, there's a huge—and highly profitable—contradiction within many of the ads themselves: between the likely physical effects of all that grease and sugar advertised so festively, and the tiptop physical condition of those great-looking hunks and babes and famous athletes doing all the eating and the drinking in the ads. In fact, the diet advertised on Channel One would—and actually does—make kids obese: fatter nowadays than ever, the statistics tell us. But such reports cannot compete with those deliciously misleading images of, say, the Buffalo Bills all eating Snickers, or Shaquille O'Neal getting "fired up for a game" by eating stuff from Taco Bell.

Such images insist, obliquely, that all that fattening food won't make you fat at all but (magically!) exceptionally fit—just as the images aimed at the girls imply that a diet of M&M's and fries and Pepsi won't inevitably make you tubby, give you zits and cavities and dull your hair, but will somehow help to make you just as slender, buxom, bright-eyed, radiant and peppy as those primping, winking models, who seem to have those buff boys under control.

Although they certainly don't want their viewers to be unattractive, the advertisers do want all of us to feel as fat, zitty, flaky, haggard, flabby, pale and smelly as it takes to get us buying what we're told we need so as to come across like winners. As old as advertising itself, this subversive tactic too has no place in the classroom, whose adolescent inmates generally feel bad enough about themselves already—as Channel One reminds them often. "NERVOUS about going back to school?" demands an ad for Clearasil in one September broadcast. "No wonder. With those ZITS." The numerous teen-oriented spots for skin creams, dandruff shampoos, mousse, breath-sweeteners and conditioners (the second biggest product category on Channel One) make clear exactly how the students are advised to see themselves: as horrors, in dire need of the assurances, advice and goods pitched "free" in each day's broadcast.

Lesson #6: "Just Say Yes."

Aside from the upbeat commercial spots for edibles, cosmetics, sportswear and entertainment, Channel One's broadcasts also include a number of solemn public service ads (PSAs) made mostly by the Ad Council on behalf of various pro bono enterprises. Such sound directives—telling kids to use their seat belts, work for charitable outfits, wear their helmets when they go skateboarding, stay away from crack, recycle—might appear to justify those daily broadcasts in our nation's schools, by making Channel One appear morally impeccable and socially progressive. (There can be little doubt that Channel One includes those PSAs for that very purpose, as a way to disarm resistance and muffle criticism.)

For all their apparent civic-mindedness, however, the PSAs actually make Channel One a more effective means of selling teenagers on all that dubious merchandise—for those kinder, gentler spots actually enhance the crass commercial pitch by masking its true character. Thanks to them, the students can more readily half-believe that all of this is "educational"—that this relentless daily come-on has some "higher purpose." Channel One can't really be telling us to think about nothing but ourselves (can it?), if it includes that moving voluntarist promo for the Points of Light Foundation: "Do Something Good. Feel Something Real." Nor could the program really be requiring us to sit here gaping at TV commercials, just like at home—because Channel One is also urging us to try some jazz, check out some modern art: "Arts And Humanities. There's Something In It For You," concludes a spot for the National Cultural Alliance.

And of course there are all those scary messages from the Partnership for a Drug-Free America, played every week on Channel One: crafty teenaged pushers lurking in the schoolyard, or even in the hallways, offering their wares—and all the younger kids, so tough and self-possessed, just tell those predators to beat it! Channel One must really want us to have independent minds if it keeps on warning us like that.

And yet the contradiction here is total, for the only moral difference between the individual drug-dealers and the corporate advertisers in our nation's schools is one of scale: The advertisers are immeasurably richer, and have done a lot more harm. Both work full-time to lure the children into absolute and permanent dependency, and both do so exclusively for profit's sake. Both, therefore, would prefer that their young targets be ill-educated on the subject of addiction. Thus the advertisers help put out that cautionary propaganda, which demonizes the individual (black) pusher—and thereby helps obscure the advertisers' own addictive mission.

Addiction 101

For it is addiction that the advertisers sell on Channel One (and everywhere else): They want to hook the kids forever, to have them needing all that junk forever, to have them all forever paying for it. While the stuff they sell does not, of course, induce a catastrophic physical dependency like heroin or crack, the way they sell it powerfully glamorizes the destructive spiritual condition of all addicts, whatever they may crave: the desperate neediness (you need it now!) and ever-more-acute insatiability (now you need more!). Thus, despite their many stern denunciations of the illegal market in the streets, the advertisers only make such drug use all the likelier and more widespread, by urging children—daily, hourly—into just the sort of appetite that, in many people, must be fed, in one way or another.

First of all, the ads teach that you can and should surrender to your craving right away: "Hungry? Why Wait?" The jokey tone of the solicitation (which is the usual tone of advertising to the young) cannot quite hide the deadly earnestness of that appeal, which the commercials make incessantly, both verbally and visually. You may be told to "Do the Dew" or "Bite the Burst" or "Taste the Rainbow," but the imperative is quite the same in every case, and reconfirmed in image after image: Eat it, drink it, wear it, play it now. With their extreme compression and extraordinary vividness, the ads present a world in which there isn't any saving, any planning toward the buying of the product, nor any pleasurable anticipation of the buying of the product—nor even any savoring of that product in itself (which once gone is forgotten, and you want another one). In that fantastic world, the only things are you and it; and since it's yours—and even if it isn't yours—you take it, and you take it now ("Why wait?").

While thus continuously urging your immediate self-indulgence, and ads on Channel One also promote the addict's attitude through the usual psychotic overestimation of the modest items that they sell. It isn't just a candy bar, it isn't just a pair of pants—it's a delirium, an orgasm, an apocalypse of fun. The admakers use every visual and aural means available to make the everyday experience of tasting this or wearing that seem like a sort of psychedelic wet dream, in which you feel like you've never felt before: ecstatic and all-powerful.

Thus the products are routinely advertised as working just like drugs: You swallow them, and go delightfully insane. Kids gulp candy or chomp into burgers or take crunchy bites of cereal—and their eyes light up, they beam and laugh and dance like lunatics. A ballerina pops a stick of Winterfresh, and breaks into exuberant motion (and a line of little girls in tutus imitates her buoyant steps). A quartet of hip-looking guys take slugs of Mountain Dew ("nothin's more intense!")—and lift off, wearing rocket belts, each one embracing an exotic-looking babe.

A blase youngster sitting on his bed, and bored out of his skull by his Dad's earnest lecture on the birds and bees, discreetly pops a Starburst—and then obviously comes. While Dad obliviously natters on, the kid imagines a tremendous wave, then sits bolt upright with a look of wired euphoria, and then he's suddenly a joyous swimmer in deep bright blue waters, amid giant floating chunks and slices of fresh fruit. ("The juice is loose!" screams out the all-male chorus as the boy settles back looking slyly satiated and that big fool leaves the room.)

Such images can only lead to a widespread sense of disappointment (and have no doubt contributed to cases of emotional disorder among teenagers). The problem here is not that kids will actually believe that munching Skittles is like dropping acid. Rather, it's the likelihood that all that wild music and intoxicating imagery, inappropriately linked with mere consumer goods, has established an impossible standard of enjoyment. Every pleasure, the commercials say, must be a major kick such as you've never felt in all your life (and such, of course, as you can only get from PepsiCo or Mars or Reebok or Nintendo). Thus that propaganda makes it ever harder to recall what actual pleasures should be like; and so it's only natural that the kids bombarded by those ads would come to feel ever more jaded, ever more blase—numb enough, perhaps, to need those still more dangerous stimulants that Channel One so piously deplores.

To recognize the falseness of that propaganda, to learn to read its images, and also to read widely and discerningly enough to start to understand the all-important differences between a good life and a bad one: such are the proper aims of school. Which is why Channel One should not be there.

Topics for Reading and Writing

1. Should schools be commercial-free zones? Why? Is it possible to teach skills like critical thinking if schools also purvey advertisements, which ask us to defer critical thinking?

2. Both of these pieces are clearly marked as opinion pieces: one ran on the editorial page of a university newspaper, while the other appeared in the journal of a nonprofit organization with a strong political mission. Given these similarities, how are the articles rhetorically different? What does this have to do with their respective audiences?

3. Miller is very explicit about what he sees as the habits of thought and behavior created or encouraged by Channel One. Is his analysis too "deterministic" (that is, is he too certain about exactly what effect these programs and ads have)? If so, does this completely or only partially undermine his core argument?

*In this article from the American Journalism Review, **Catherine Seipp** (a writer and columnist for such magazines as Jewish World Review, Mediaweek, and Forbes) provides a behind-the-scenes view of the publicists' roles in the creation of magazine articles. With several vivid anecdotes, Seipp sketches out*

Catherine Seipp
The Puppet Masters

Here's a typical skirmish from the Hollywood journalists vs. Hollywood publicists wars: Bruce Bibby, a senior editor at E! Online, used to write the Ted Casablanca column at Premiere. For his last column, there he was covering the opening party of the Arnold Schwarzenegger shoot-'em-up "Eraser." At the time, Bob Dole was complaining about *the shift in the balance of power between celebrities and journalists, a shift that now seems to favor the celebrities more than ever.*

the Hollywood product's excessive violence and vulgarity. So Bibby asked Schwarzenegger, a Republican indelibly associated with mindless onscreen violence, what Dole would think of his latest action-packed vehicle.

"Five times he asked me to repeat the question," Bibby says. "Finally he looked at one of his bodyguards and said, 'Who is this guy?'" Apparently that was the signal for some mindless off-screen violence, because next thing Bibby knew, the bodyguard had shoved him up against the outdoor heating lamp with instructions to get out.

Bibby immediately went up to the Warner Brothers public relations person, Vivian Boyer, to tell her what had happened. Boyer was sympathetic, but Bibby was no longer invited to Warner Brothers screenings after that. "That's the hypocrisy of this town I both love and hate," he says equably. "It's just an example of how used to puffery they are."

In any case, such events are fairly routine, and Bibby is back in Warner Brothers' good graces. "I let them have their space and then called and got back on the list," he shrugs.

The dance of mutual dependence between magazines and celebrities has long been a tense tango, with a media culture so carefully choreographed by publicists that celebrities can be shocked when they encounter a rare unpuffy question. It's the equivalent of getting stomped on by a clod trying to lead. But these days the tango seems to be performed by marionettes, manipulated from above by celebrity publicists. That's because stars and their handlers are less willing to participate in noncover stories and, in a glutted, increasingly homogenous market, editors are more fearful about risking covers that may not sell.

The setting for all this is today's celebrity-saturated newsstand, which lately has become so competitive that even fashion magazines like *Vogue* and *Harper's Bazaar* regularly feature actresses instead of model on their covers. Then there's the currently hot "lad" market of guys-being-guys titles (*Maxim, FHM, Details*), which has created a whole promotional landscape for busty starlets, as well as a slew of new magazines (*Teen People, Cosmogirl*) catering to the celebrity-centered fantasies of adolescents.

So on a stage where all eyes are fixed on one glittering object—the famous face that can magically transform newsstand browsers into newsstand buyers—is it any wonder that the celebrity publicist now controls every tiny detail of the scene?

"As the editors get more desperate, the publicists get more powerful," says Lisa Granatstein, *Mediaweek*'s magazine industry reporter. Thus the recent assortment of who-he? young faces on *Vanity Fair*'s last Hollywood issue. As James Meigs, editor in chief of *Premiere,* told Granatstein in her *Mediaweek* column: "We're defining celebrity down."

The publicists are now in fact so powerful they resemble the Puppet Masters in the Robert Heinlein novel—alien creatures that embed themselves into human spines and control their victims' every move. Even when you don't see

"The Puppet Masters" by Catherine Seipp from *American Journalism Review*, October 1999. Reprinted by permission of *American Journalism Review*.

the Puppet Masters themselves, you see their work in the magazines you read: the generically innocuous, limited-access celebrity profile, for instance, typically centered around a short meal at a restaurant.

Sometimes, in desperation to add atmosphere, bits of business are imagined by the editor and inserted into the scene: ". . . Lisa Kudrow said, toying with the last of her scrambled eggs," is an example that made one writer I know pull her name from her story. In this Puppet Master-controlled planet of celebrity journalism, the celebrity reveals little except liberal use of the word "amazing"—the favorite all-purpose adjective these days of people who can't be bothered to think of anything else to say.

The full force of the Puppet Masters, though, is felt in the unsaid but prickly question of what they would think—even when the subject at hand is so tame you wonder why anyone would worry about it at all. The new *McCall's StarStyle* is a publication that may give *InStyle*—"the publicist's friend" as it's called in the trade—a run for its money as most innocuous magazine on the block. The cover story in the February 23 debut issue featured "100 Get Glam Tricks" from Jennifer Aniston, Gwyneth Paltrow and half-a-dozen other stars. Since the story relied on information from stylists and costumers, not the stars themselves, the magazine presumably didn't have to worry about dealing with the stars' gatekeepers.

"We wanted to report on her look," *StarStyle* Editorial Director Sally Koslow says of cover girl Aniston. "We weren't looking for cooperation."

Still, Koslow froze up when asked how *StarStyle* got the cover picture if Aniston didn't cooperate by posing for it. "I don't want to discuss that," Koslow said firmly. Why not? "Because I don't. It's private." From her tone, you'd think she'd been asked to divulge her medical records. "Sometimes," she added finally, "beautiful photos already exist."

Well, yes: The cover credit listed NBC as well as the photographer's name, so presumably it came from the NBC publicity department—hardly a shocking or unusual situation. Still, Koslow evidently felt nervous enough about the whole thing to send along a letter explaining. "I'm sorry I couldn't have been more forthcoming with you, but I'm reluctant to give helpful hints to the competition.

"Also, I regret using the popular term 'write-around' (a piece done without interviewing the subject) in connection with our celebrity reporting," she added. "I prefer the term 'profile.'"

The Puppet Masters' power is fearsome because of the celebrity-driven dynamic of the modern magazine market. "I don't know how much longer we can go on with it," says Lesley Jane Seymour, who recently took over as *Redbook*'s editor in chief after a stint at *YM*. "I mean, *Popular Mechanics* had Jay Leno on the cover, which was clever. But when you have all these smaller magazines siphoning off celebrities, what's going to happen? I'm worried we're all going to look the same. Maybe we'll go back to models, and models will hopefully be more humble."

Celebrity publicists, meanwhile, don't have to be humble. "I had someone try to dictate what we could say in the cover lines," Seymour recalls. "I was just flabbergasted."

The assumption used to be that PR power couldn't possibly get any more iron-gripped. To cite one oft-repeated example from when the press really began griping about such things: A few years ago Pat Kingsley, the doyenne of the Hollywood über-publicity machine PMK, asked freelancers to sign agreements promising not to sell their round-robin Tom Cruise interviews to anyone other than the publications they were representing at the studio-sponsored press junket. No signature, no interview—and maybe even no more invitations to junkets, the bread-and-butter of Hollywood coverage.

This summer, PMK's fist came down again with an elaborate consent agreement for TV access to Cruise in connection with publicity for "Eyes Wide Shut." Shows like ABC's "20/20" and "Good Morning America" had to agree that Cruise interviews would run only in their entirety and only for those particular programs, thus barring interview clips from being sold to archival-dependent shows such as E!'s "True Hollywood Story" or A&E's "Biography." The waiver, obtained by the Los Angeles Times, also specified that Cruise not be presented "in a negative or derogatory manner" and that unaired interview footage must be destroyed (with PMK provided "evidence of such destruction") if its client so requested. In other words, no "blooper" clips of Mr. Cruise.

Understandably, no editor wants to give examples of concessions he or she is making to publicists these days. But the honest ones admit it does happen.

"The game has changed so much," sighs Lori Berger, for most of her career an entertainment writer for magazines like *Cosmopolitan* and *Marie Claire* but now editor in chief of the year-and-a-half-old teen magazine *Jump*. For one thing, handlers for teen idols like Claire Danes and Katie Holmes have recently decided they don't want their clients degraded by appearing in teen magazines. Instead they want them in *Vanity Fair*, which in its recent focus on the young and semi-famous seems to be courting the *Teen People* demographic.

"I remember years ago, when you were an editor, you had power," Berger adds. "But publicists are now making editing decisions, and I am just astonished by it. It used to be that you were selling the celebrity, but that was it. Now you're not getting the story you want, or the picture you want, or even the hair and makeup you want, because the publicist approves all that. I always say to publicists now: 'I want your job!'"

As a reaction against such all-controlling tactics, *People* magazine began finessing the art of the write-around in the early '90s. This is the profile based on interviews with the subject's friends and enemies but not the subject. Lanny Jones, *People*'s top editor from 1989 to 1997 and now vice president of strategic planning at Time Inc. in New York, says the write-around became necessary because without it, "we were no longer practicing good journalism. I don't want to name names, but there are big glossies that are compromised."

At the same time, Jones had become frustrated with what he saw as "the complete lack of trust between publicists and magazines, and the mind-set—on either side—that they're all wrong and we're all right. The whole atmosphere had been filled with razor blades because of the rise of tabloids and tabloid TV." Jones organized lunch meetings of West Coast editors doing business with Hollywood. About a dozen regulars attended, representing magazines that included *TV Guide, Premiere, Entertainment Weekly, Newsweek* and *Playboy*, among others.

Since many there had complaints about publicists' demands, one or two hardliners suggested presenting a united front of resistance against PR power, recalls attendee Stephen Randall, executive editor of *Playboy*. This notion was quashed by the second meeting, however, when Jones read a statement from Time Warner attorneys.

"Apparently we'd be in violation of the RICO statutes," Randall says. "It was akin to antitrust." Actually, it wasn't quite that colorful: "We were advised by lawyers it wasn't a good idea," noted Jones, who says the idea was never seriously considered. "Not because of RICO—that's gangsters—but because of restraint of trade."

Still, I haven't heard of any similar rebellions since. So have things improved?

Jack Kelley, *People*'s West Coast bureau chief since 1990, says that, contrary to rumor, there are no publicists who refuse to work with the magazine.

There was a flurry of reaction after *People* ran a cover story detailing the breakup of Robin Williams' first marriage and the actor's subsequent romance with his nanny-cum-second-wife. But Kelley noted that this happened more than 10 years ago, and "Robin's talked to us at least three times since then."

Because of *People*'s mass audience (plus the fact that the magazine has the dreaded write-around down to a science), Kelley says he hasn't had much difficulty dealing with celebrities and their publicists these days. The only outrageous anecdotes he could think of happened years ago. One was when Annie Potts, at the height of her "Designing Women" fame, was getting married for the third time and her publicist offered *People* an exclusive on the story for $500,000. The other was when Michael Jackson was marrying Lisa Marie Presley and his representatives wanted complete approval of everything from cover photos to inside text. "We just said, 'Thanks, but we'll wait for the divorce,'" Kelley recalls.

"For A-list celebrities, we will occasionally bend the rules," he adds, "but for 95 percent of the cases, it's our way or the highway." That means: a "hometake" (*People* jargon for a photo taken at the subject's home, usually with family) and no questions off-limits during the interview.

But *People,* a news-driven weekly magazine, has enough circulation and resources that publicists can't afford to completely alienate it. The situation is different for the typical monthly glossy, which relies on the quick and friendly freelance-written interview. The type of time-consuming profile that Gay Talese wrote for *Esquire* in the '60s—such as "Frank Sinatra Has a Cold," which evolved over a leisurely expanse of time hanging out with Sinatra—just isn't affordable anymore, either for magazines or for writers.

In a glutted market, it's the ordinary writers at ordinary magazines who acutely feel the new iron-fisted reign of the personal publicist. "In my opinion, it's gotten worse in the past five years," Ivor Davis says heatedly. David, who is English, is a veteran Hollywood freelancer for various foreign publications. He and his wife, Sally Ogle Davis, wrote a rant against the power of Hollywood publicists for *Los Angeles* magazine in the early '90s. Ivor Davis is still invited to junkets but feels the fallout, even when it's misdirected.

"I tried to do an interview with Jon Favreau"—(Who? Exactly.)—"he was playing Rocky Graziano in a Showtime movie," Davis continues. "And the publicist said, 'Yes, I remember you. Weren't you involved in litigation with Geena Davis?'" Actually, no; the publicist must have been thinking of another entertainment journalist, unauthorized celebrity biographer Frank Sanello, who got in trouble with Geena Davis because of an article he wrote about her for *Woman's World*. No matter: interview denied. "Now here's a young actor who presumably wanted publicity, and she's using this against me, which will only hurt him," Ivor Davis says, his voice rising in outrage.

"Most actors want to sit down and have an exchange," says Annett Wolf, partner in Wolf-Kasteler Public Relations and a high-powered Hollywood publicist. But despite the litany of complaints writers have about arrogant, ignorant publicists, it seems publicists have some legitimate complaints about arrogant, ignorant writers. "A lot of these writers are people in their 20s and 30s" with little knowledge of film history, Wolf points out. For instance, she says, if the topic is a new war movie, "sometimes the actor will bring up some scene from 'Apocalypse Now' or 'The Deer Hunter' and there's dead silence. The writer has no idea what he's talking about. And then the client tells me later, 'So, why am I doing this again?'"

Thus, the "surfeit now of the kind of snap-shot celebrity reporting, where someone just sits down with the person over salad and then just kind of regurgitates it," as *People*'s Kelley describes it. Of course, there are some who have raised this sort of thing to a fine art. "It might be that I have a particularly charming group of writers, but we don't seem to have problems with access or time," says David Granger, editor-in-chief of *Esquire* for the past two years and *GQ* executive editor before that. "But then, I've seen someone like Tom Junod do wonderful things with just two or three hours spent with John Travolta."

Granger adds that he doesn't have much of a problem with publicists blackballing writers—perhaps because he tends to use writers who don't only interview celebrities. This doesn't mean he isn't asked to submit the writer's clips for approval. Take the profile of Robert DeNiro that writer Mike Sager did for *Esquire* a couple of years ago. "DeNiro's sort of famously picky, and the publicist wanted to see everything [Sager] had even written," Granger recalls. "But they ended up being very comfortable with him."

For his part, DeNiro's publicist, Stan Rosenfield, says: "We ask for writer approval because, A, we can get it, and B, why should I set myself up with someone who is not a good writer or has a reputation for being 'balanced,' and you and I both know what that means. We have to protect the client's best interests."

Those who break the rules of the game can find themselves blackballed, albeit in a smooth way. A Hollywood journalist told me: "One day, Pat Kingsley took me to lunch, casually mentioned some other journalists and said, 'You know, we just take people like that off our list.' And I am off the list. I realized I hadn't been invited to a screening of 'Celebrity.' So I called up Miramax and they said, 'PMK handles that, because it's Woody Allen.' I just thought, 'Oh . . . .'"

Sometimes you're not *off*, but *on* a list, which can be worse. Michael Gross, who contributes regularly to *New York* magazine and *GQ*, and who wrote the first Madonna cover for *Vanity Fair* back in 1985, was assigned by a British magazine in the mid-1990s to do a cover story on Tatum O'Neal. "A PR person came to the shoot and said Tatum would not be doing the shoot if Michael Gross did the article," Gross says. "The magazine asked if I minded and I said I didn't, and to their credit the PR firm, Baker Winokur Ryder, sounded abashed. I did make the point to them that they were interfering with a contract, but I've had good dealings with them later. It all clarified when some big account executive in Hollywood told me there is a list and I'm on it."

The irony is that the Tatum O'Neal assignment wasn't meant to be anything but a puff piece, and that's what Gross would have delivered. But because of his reputation for digging up dirt on stars, he's been involved in intricate games of strategy with publicists. For his 1997 interview with Alec Baldwin for *New York* magazine, the first thing public relations firm Wolf-Kasteler asked was if he planned to go ahead with the article even if they didn't grant him an interview.

"Then there was this whole six-week-long dance," Gross recalls. "They weren't obstructive, but neither were they helpful. When you operate as a journalist instead of as part of the entertainment marketing machine, you won't get the cooperation the tame writers will, but you'll get some, because it provides a way for them to keep track of what you're doing. Finally with Baldwin, on the Sunday night before I was going to write the piece, I had an interview."

Gross continues: "The last celebrity profile I wrote before Baldwin was Richard Gere for *Esquire*. The first thing I did was call PMK. No one called me back, so I dropped off a letter to Gere's doorman. In 24 hours I had Pat Kingsley breathing fire down my neck." Gross never got an interview with Gere, although he did get an off-the-record lunch with him and access to the actor's friends. Gere and his publicist never agreed to a photo shoot, though. So Gross casually mentioned to Gere's agent, Ed Limato, "Oh, by the way, your boy lost the cover." Limato immediately yelled to an assistant: "Get Gere on the phone!"

"Somehow," continued Gross, "the next thing you know, Gere's in Greg Gorman's studio, and somehow, the pictures got to *Esquire*." Result: a cover story, without any uncool appearance of cooperation.

But these days Gross has shifted his attention away from celebrity interviews to concentrate on books. "I respect Pat Kingsley," he says, echoing a common sentiment of the entertainment press. "The people I don't respect are the so-called journalists who think they're on the same side of the fence as Pat Kingsley. I think it's institutionalized now. These glossy magazines only do hard, critical journalism on people who are dead, dying or out of favor. They only bare their fangs at signs of weakness."

The old guard actually had less patience for celebrities and their peccadilloes than you might think. Helen Gurley Brown, *Cosmopolitan*'s grande dame emeritus, used to get extremely annoyed about the whole business. "Celebrities have become more crazy and over-the-top than I can ever remember," she says. "People who should know better are worshipful." Brown didn't feature stars on the cover much, partly because she found their demands too irritating. Raquel Welch, for instance, refused all the clothes prepared for her *Cosmo* shoot. Sharon Stone didn't like the way she looked, and since she had been given the right to approve the picture, the cover wasn't used.

These days, however, media spin has seeped past the machinations that go into producing magazine covers; now it's a skill practiced by the editors themselves. After I talked to Brown, I tried to talk to her successor at *Cosmopolitan* at the time, Bonnie Fuller. But Fuller wouldn't take the call without a list of questions submitted beforehand, as if she were Sharon Stone herself. Eventually I reached *Cosmo*'s entertainment editor, Jennifer Kasle Furmaniak, who came in under the new editor, Kate White. And while Furmaniak notes that "the more other magazines give leeway—saying you can have whatever you want—the harder it is for the rest of us," she adds that this is really more of "a trend for other magazines, but fortunately not for *Cosmo*. A small magazine . . . with circulation an eighth or a quarter of ours might have problems."

Some writers have simply gotten out of the hard-hitting game altogether. "After 25 years I got tired of talking to people about what they did," says Jesse Kornbluth, who used to do dirt-digging Hollywood stories for *Vanity Fair* and *New York* magazine but now is editorial director at America Online. "I wanted people to talk to me."

As writer at large for *Madison* magazine, Kornbluth still does some celebrity interviews. But he has ground rules: "I only do Q&As, which kind of levels the playing field. I don't do follow-up interviews, I don't interview their friends; it's just two hours. I send everyone I interview a copy of the transcript, and then we edit for clarity. It's a simple, clean transaction—and there's no room for anyone to complain later. It's really very different from those nauseating pieces in which the writer suddenly inserts himself, while still pretending that the piece isn't really all about his own perception. This idea that the star should participate in his own destruction is just so ridiculous."

At the other end of the scale is Toby Young, co-founder of the witty and bitchy *Modern Review* in London, who lately has been deconstructing his misadventures in the world of celebrity journalism for the *New York Press* (where I also have a column). Graydon Carter, the *Vanity Fair* editor in chief and well-known Anglophile, brought Young over to work at the mother ship of celebrity cover stories in the mid-'90s. But Young couldn't seem to learn the rules of the game. When he was assigned to interview Nathan Lane, he asked the actor first if he was Jewish, and then if he was gay, at which point the publicist stepped in and declared the interview over.

Afterward, Young recalls, Carter summoned him to his office. "Toby," Carter sighed, "You can't ask Hollywood celebrities whether they're Jewish or gay. Just assume they're both Jewish and gay, OK?"

Young was finally fired after a drunken dispute over a restaurant bill landed him on the *New York Post*'s Page Six, which the long-suffering Carter decided wasn't good publicity for *Vanity Fair*. Nor were the antics that didn't get reported, such as Young cornering Mel Gibson at the Vanity Fair Oscars party—this was when the actor-director had swept the Oscars for "Braveheart," his film about the Scottish national hero—and asking why Gibson had such a grudge against the English.

"Suddenly I felt this tug on my collar," Young told me. "It was Graydon yanking me back, hissing, 'Toby! Stop bothering celebrities!'"

A.J. Benza, who was a gossip columnist for the New York *Daily News* before moving to Los Angeles last year to host E!'s "Mysteries and Scandals" show, has another point of view. "I always got along with publicists; I dated a lot of them—I'm not gonna lie," he says. "But what really gets me sick is these publicists dropping dimes on the people they work for.

"Say you're a publicist," he continues. "Maybe you've got an actress as a client and some shoe store—I'm just using this as an example of how it works, because I've been out of it for a couple of years. So you call up asking me to do something on this shoe store. I say, 'I don't wanna do something on some stupid shoe store, baby, what else ya got?' Oh, the actress is anorexic. OK, so I agree to mention the shoe store if I can get the anorexia story."

Now that Benza is in Hollywood and working occasionally as an actor, he sees the same publicists who used to call him with dirt, but from the other side of the fence. When young actors tell him they've just hired a publicist, he typically says only: "Uh-huh, that's great. They sure use the phone a lot."

Most publicists contacted for this story didn't call back, which is understandable. But eventually I had pleasant and enlightening chats about how things seem from the PR side with three veterans in the field.

Henri Bollinger is president and a founding member of EPPS, the 6-year-old Entertainment Publicists Professional Society, which has about 220 members. He's also a past president of the Publicists Guild, and personally represents mostly corporate entertainment clients, like the lobbying group Entertainment Industries Council. He says that the two major issues publicists are concerned about these days are controlling access to clients and placement of clients.

"The problem is a lot of publications flat out don't discuss publicity deals," Bollinger says, "And then we find out deals were made" with other stars. It all depends, of course, on how badly the publication wants someone. "But there are no secrets in this industry," he notes, "and certainly no secrets among publicists." One agency that always gets criticized is PMK. Well, PMK asks nothing others don't ask. But PMK more often gets their way. And if they'd behaved in all the ways they'd been accused of having behaved, they'd be out of business by now.

"The hottest button in the industry right now is placement," he continues, "because publications will not often be interested in second-tier stars. To put it in perspective, in Los Angeles alone there are some 3,000 entertainment publicists. So you have this vast army out there trying to get some space. That's the reason you have a lot of negotiating going on, when you have all these publicists with a few hot clients and maybe 20 other clients each who are not so hot. Magazine editors hate it with a passion, but they have to deal with reality."

Then there is the matter of how publicists are seen (and often treated) by the media—as irritating middlemen who get in the way of the writer and his subject. "*TV Guide* even went so far as to say that no publicist could be present at the interview," notes Bollinger. "That lasted maybe three weeks at the most. These policies were brought up at the Publicists Guild meeting, and word spread we were not to accept these conditions. It belittles you."

Annett Wolf of Wolf-Kasteler is celebrating her company's 10th anniversary this year. She and Lisa Kasteler run something of a boutique business, with just 50 clients but some very sought-after ones, including Nicolas Cage, Meg Ryan, Cate Blanchett, Alec Baldwin, Jenna Elfman, Samuel L. Jackson and Angela Bassett. Despite her company's somewhat fearsome reputation, she projects a friendly and relaxed persona over the phone.

"Our job description was created to be helpful," she says, laughing, "and I do take pride in trying to adhere to that. I really do want people to trust me, as much as they can, given my job description." But, she adds, she has some qualms about how the entertainment media work now. "I don't like that every person now knows how a movie is put together. The suspension of disbelief is eroded. It takes away from the magic of going to the movies." Thus her reluctance to let writers hang around on the set and ask any question that occurs to them.

"Actors are not running for public office," she points out. "They don't owe the public every detail about their personal lives. I don't go in saying, 'Don't ask about that,' because, A, I know it pisses off the journalists more than anything, and, B, they kind of become like a dog with a bone with it. The only thing I do sometimes is step in and say, 'Please don't answer that question if it makes you uncomfortable.' Because the world has changed so much, especially in the past year, there really isn't anything they won't ask now.

"I have to tell you, I am not that confrontational. The only time I get very forceful is with some hideous story, reported by some drunk, about something that supposedly happened in some bar. It might start off in the tabs, but it ends up in *USA Today,* or *Morning Report,* or *Entertainment Weekly.* That's changed in the past couple of years."

What's also changed is the increased use of celebrities to sell glossy magazines. "In order to get them, the magazines have to be fairly nice about it. It's as simple as that," Wolf says. "And, as you can see, they are willing to present these actors in a very friendly way. You know, these are people who have had sometimes very difficult lives, and the media presents them as these big, beautiful, exotic flowers." But there's a downside to all this, even from the PR side.

"Really talented people get overlooked now, because the turnover is so much bigger and so much faster," Wolf says. "You can barely remember who was famous three years ago. It wasn't that way in the early '90s." Which is why she sometimes plays hardball with placement involving inside pieces, saying, "OK, then, who's going to be on the cover and is not going to be completely insulting to the talent of my client? If it's some young adorable bunny who's done a film and a half, then we'll do TV instead, because a lot of people watch it, and they'll show a clip."

Stan Rosenfield has been in the public relations business for 35 years, 24 as head of his own company. His clients include Robert DeNiro, Danny DeVito, John Goodman, Will Smith, George Clooney, Joan Lunden and Christian Slater. He has been around long enough that his recollections of how public relations used to be—when the memory of Walter Winchell still cast a shadow on the land—offer a colorful glimpse of a vanished world.

"In the '60s and parts of the '70s, PR firms used to be able to make a living just representing actors who make a living just doing guest shots on TV," Rosenfield says. "You could easily get trade coverage in the industry papers of these actors. We quote unquote 'planted the column.'" Rosenfield started out working for legendary publicist Jay Bernstein. "I was copy chief—I wrote up and planted five to seven items per week. No one does that anymore. And you'd give them an outside item [a piece of news not on a client] for every three planted ones. Here we called them 'outside items'; on the East Coast they called them 'freebies.'"

"It used to be more creative," he continues. "About 25 years ago, there was an old flack by the name of Dave Epstein, who went overboard with PR on his client." The trades in those days were filled with announcements of fictitious, European-based producers who had just hired someone's client. Epstein, it was felt, carried this too far. The trades struck back. "So one day on page one, one of the trades ran an obit: Epstein's favorite phony producer had been killed in a car crash. But Epstein was undeterred. He came up with the producer's brother."

Now, of course, the emphasis has shifted from old-fashioned hijinks in the trades and gossip columns to dead-serious maneuvering for glossy magazine celebrity covers. "Well, we call it 'fine tuning,' or 'protecting one's position,' " Rosenfield remarks, "but if you want to call them 'celebrity covers,' that's fine with me. Anyway, unless you can get a guarantee of a cover, you can really hurt a client. To go from the cover to the inside . . . well, there are a lot of gray areas. Or 'amber lights' as I call them.' " One of those amber lights might be the touchy area of approving the writer assigned to do the story.

"Yeah, absolutely we're more careful about looking at that," Rosenfield says. "I always say this: Clients hire us as much for our judgment as for our ability to execute a plan. Sometimes you just don't have the leverage, and sometimes there are times when you horse trade. A good PR person is more than someone who comes to the phone and says, 'Yes, we'll do this' or 'No, we won't.' "

Still, even a publicist can get irritated with that immediate, unthinking "No!" publicists these days are known for. "I don't think they're in it for the long haul," he says of his crowd. "These people who just give the emphatic, quick 'No,' you better do it with the blessing of your client." One time Rosenfield asked another publicist if his client would do something for a charity Rosenfield was involved with. "He said, 'No,' and I said, 'Why don't you do this? Because I know it's his favorite charity. Why don't you ask him? Before I ask someone on the board to ask him.'

"And you have to keep that in mind, when you say no to a journalist," he adds. "Sometimes the journalist knows other people in the client's life." But Rosenfield was careful to give the publicist he'd approached for his charity an opportunity to reconsider. "Despite that line in 'Butch Cassidy and the Sundance Kid,' there are rules to a knife fight," he says.

And what does Rosenfield think of the media now? He has three big irritations: privacy issues, inaccuracy and negativity. "Freedom of the press doesn't mean you have to be vitriolic," he points out. "It is why they invented the word 'symbiotic.' But you know, the magazines, in their rush to be super-competitive, gave the control to us. Any power, eventually we're going to lose it. But right now we've got it."

Topics for Reading and Writing

1. What does this article show about the relationship between the producers of entertainment and producers of journalism? What is the role of publicists in this relationship?

"I'm not spinning—I'm contextualizing."

2. Does this article change your view of the "dance of mutual dependence between magazines and celebrities"? Is it proper for magazines to relinquish this degree of control to celebrities and their publicists?

3. Seipp uses primarily anecdotal information in this article but clearly wants it to be taken seriously as an argument about the nature of journalism and publishing today. What other kinds of evidence might she use that she hasn't here? Does she leave any question unanswered?

4. What Seipp sees as dangerous, others might see as liberating: celebrities are now in control of their images instead of at the mercy of the media. Is this power shift a fundamentally democratic one?

Calvin Naito, a public relations and corporate communications professional based in Los Angeles, argues in this rebuttal piece from the Los Angeles Times *that the constant portrayal of PR professionals as weasels and bottom-feeders is unfair. Responding to a feature article in the* Times *that surveyed movie images of sleazy press agents in such movies as* Phone

Calvin Naito
Not a Publicist but a Problem-solver

I could barely contain myself after reading Juan Morales' article, "Movies Turn Press Agents Into Evil, Conniving Sultans of Spin" (April 28). No cup of coffee needed that morning to get me going.

As someone who works with the media for a living, I have to take exception to the popular portrayals of publicists in movies. Furthermore, the publicists quoted in the

Booth, *Naito argues here that his job is to "make positive news" for his clients. "Good publicists," he states, "ensure that their clients' stories make the news in an informative and entertaining way." Most of this article is taken up with a basic overview of the responsibilities of the publicist and of the practical difficulties that confront the PR professional, but Naito does end his article by stating that most publicists would love to work for clients who are "topical, socially redeeming and human."*

article did not sufficiently explain the true role of PR and defend what is a difficult but noble profession.

We have a hard life. Society is in an "age of public relations." I agree with some of the quoted sources that publicists are "all-purpose" and "the most harried and anxious and traumatized" of people in a work setting. If you want to consistently make positive news for your clients in, for example, Los Angeles—the nation's second-largest media market—you need a valuable repertoire of skills. In a setting so large, diverse and distracted, it is difficult to cut through the clutter and noise and ensure that your story is seen and heard.

Good publicists ensure that their clients' stories make the news in an informative and entertaining way. Despite performing this vital function for a vast audience, the profession—ironically—has a bad image. PR has bad PR. Many people view PR as a dishonest specialty, a field that spins clients out of awkward situations and flat-out lies when necessary. Even I am reluctant to describe myself as a publicist, so negative is its connotation. And actor Al Pacino in movies like "People I Know" doesn't help!

If others are willing to use swords to rid the world of Saddam, then I will not hesitate to use a pen to help slay the stereotype of public relations.

A publicist is on a leash held by the client and can roam only as far as the principal allows. If unfettered, the publicist would, in dealing with reporters, run in harmony with these basic guidelines: Be honest but discreet. Hustle and get back to them as soon as you can. Help them sort out and visualize the story by providing them with information that is timely, clear, accurate and useful.

Effective media relations pros are pragmatic problem-solvers who know that fixing is better than faking. For example, they advise chief executives to operate under the assumption that the media will investigate their organizations. Such problem-solving publicists speak truth to power and lead the CEOs' minds to actively identify shortcomings, for example, in business plans, workplace practices and personal conduct. The aim is to correct such deficiencies before walking the media gantlet.

The publicist occupies an inherently political role between the executive and celebrity (who often has a mammoth ego) and the media/public. If astute, the publicist will have the clearest picture of reality. The PR person knows what the star looks like without the makeup on. He or she is talking directly with the press, senses the nature of the story and has enough detachment not to get overly emotional, as many celebrities and executives invariably do.

In an ideal situation, the quality publicist's perspective and skills are fully utilized. Unfortunately, this is rarely the case. Sometimes the principal irrationally kills the messenger. Often, the client ignores the counsel, and the publicist may be put in the awkward spot of trying to pitch and defend the indefensible. They are forced to be loyal soldiers and follow orders, even though they know better. In spite of this, the best publicists do not lie. You don't have to tell the public everything, but everything you tell them must be true. We do the best we can with what we are given.

The publicist often operates in the cross-fire between image and truth. We dream of days when we can persuade clients to be largely what they strive to project. When this happens, we can smell the "sweet smell of success."

The fundamental facts are: The best way to make positive news is to do something positively newsworthy. The best way not to get bad press is not to do something bad. Publicist Tony Angellotti is right when he says, "You cannot control the press." However, he should have added that celebrities and other principals can control their personal behavior.

We crave working on a product launch (be it a movie, government social service program or whatever) or for a company or decision-maker that is topical, socially redeeming and human. But when there are limitations, as there usually are, we still try to do our job for the client, truthfully. Managing relations with the public is a difficult and honorable profession—you just haven't seen it in the movies yet.

Topics for Reading and Writing

1. Obviously, Naito hopes to counter what he sees as the flood of negative images of publicists by saying what their job is *really* like. But does he really answer the criticisms of PR and promotion leveled by William Lutz and Catherine Seipp? What does Naito leave unexamined? Where is Naito's argument most convincing?

2. What is your opinion of the profession of public relations? Does it simply boil down to "professional liar" or is there an unsung ethical component to public relations? Does society really need these people?

In this article Charles O'Neill (a former advertising executive, who originally wrote his essay for the textbook Exploring Language) *presents a much less negative view of advertising than many of our other writers. Focusing on language strategies without presumptively assuming that those strategies are dishonest, O'Neill describes the actual linguistic reasons that advertising language seems so different than the language we use to communicate among ourselves. Advertising is simply a way of using language, O'Neill argues; it is in itself neither ethical nor unethical. Only when examined along with its intentions can we make an ethical judgment about particular advertisements.*

Charles O'Neill
The Language of Advertising

In 1957, a short dozen years after World War II, many people had good reason to be concerned about Science. On the one hand, giant American corporations offered the promise of "Better Living Through Chemistry." Labs and factories in the U.S. and abroad turned out new "miracle" fabrics, vaccines, and building materials. Radar and other innovative technology developed during the War had found important applications in the fast-growing, surging crest of consumer-centric, late 1950s America.

But World War II American Science had also yielded The Bomb. Specialists working in a secret desert laboratory had figured out how to translate the theoretical work of Dr. Einstein, and others, into weapons that did exactly what they were intended to do, incinerating hundreds of thousands of civilian Japanese men, women and children in the process. The USSR and USA were locked in an arms race. Americans were told the Soviets held the advantage. Many families built bomb shelters in the yard, and millions of school children learned to "Duck and Cover."

So when Vance Packard wrote a book about a dark alliance of social scientists with product marketers and advertisers, an alliance forged in order to gain a better understanding of "people's subsurface desires, needs, and drives," to "find their points of vulnerability," he struck a resonant chord. The scientists who had brought us the weapons that helped win the war had now, apparently, turned their sights on the emerging consumer society. By applying the principles of laboratory experimentation and scientific reasoning to learn about the fears, habits and aspirations of John and Mary Public, they would help businesses create products whose sales would be fueled by ever-more powerful advertising. In the view of Virginia Postrel, (writing in the *Wall Street Journal* in August 1999), the book "envisions consumers as passive dupes who never catch on even to the most obvious manipulations." Among many examples cited, Mr. Packard noted that what he called "depth probers" had learned that "fear of stern bankers was driving borrowers to more expensive loan companies. Banks began training their employees to be nice so as to attract more business." We were led to believe the banker's smile was a form of manipulation, a contrived courtesy. The book was itself a bestseller.

Mr. Packard is certainly not alone as a critic of advertising. Every decade has brought a new generation of critics. We recognize the legitimacy—even the value—of advertising, but on some level we can't quite fully embrace it as a "normal" part of our experience. At best, we view it as distracting. At worst, we view it as dangerous to our health and a pernicious threat to our social values. Also lending moral support to the debate about advertising is no less an authority than the Vatican. In 1997, the Vatican issued a document prepared by the Pontifical Council, titled "Ethics in Advertising." Along with acknowledgement of the positive contribution of advertising (e.g., provides information, supports worthy causes, encourages competition and innovation), the report states, as reported by the *Boston Globe,* "In the competition to attract ever larger audiences . . . communicators can find themselves pressured . . . to set aside high artistic and moral standards and lapse into superficiality, tawdriness and moral squalor."

How does advertising work? Why is it so powerful? Why does it raise such concern? What case can be made for and against the advertising business? In order to understand advertising, you must accept that it is not about truth, virtue, love, or positive social values. It is about money. Ads play a role in moving customers through the sales process. This process begins with an effort to build awareness of a product, typically achieved by tactics designed to break through the clutter of competitive messages. By presenting a description of product benefits, ads convince the customer to buy the product. Once prospects have become purchasers, advertising is used to sustain brand loyalty, reminding customers of all the good reasons for their original decision to buy.

But this does not sufficiently explain the ultimate, unique power of advertising. Whatever the product or creative strategy, advertisements derive their power from a purposeful, directed combination of images. Images can take the form of words, sounds, or visuals, used individually or together. The combination of images is the language of advertising, a language unlike any other.

Edited and Purposeful

In his book, *Future Shock*, Alvin Toffler described various types of messages we receive from the world around us each day. Much of normal, human experience is merely sensory, "not designed by anyone to communicate anything." In contrast, the language of advertising is carefully engineered, ruthlessly purposeful. Advertising messages have a clear purpose; they are intended to trigger a specific response.

The response may be as utterly simple as "Say, I *am* hungry. Let's pull right on up to the drive-through window and order a big, juicy Wendy's burger, fast!"

In the case of some advertising, our reactions may be more complex. In 1964, the Doyle Dane Bernbach agency devised an elegantly simple television add for President Lyndon Johnson's campaign against his Republican challenge, Barry Goldwater. A pretty young girl is shown picking petals from a daisy, against the background of a countdown. The ad ends with the sound of an explosion. This ad, ranked number 20, among TV Guide's assessment of the 50 greatest TV commercials of all time, was broadcast once, but it had succeeded in underscoring many voters' greatest fear: a vote for the GOP was a vote for nuclear war; a vote for Johnson was a vote for peace. The ad's overwhelming, negative message was too much even for President Johnson, who ordered it replaced.

This short TV spot reached well beyond hunger—"Fast food—yummy!"—into a far more sacred place: "Honey, they want to kill our kids!"

Rich and Arresting

Advertisements—no matter how carefully "engineered"—cannot succeed unless they capture our attention. Of the hundreds of advertising messages in store for us each day, very few will actually command our conscious attention. The rest are screened out. The people who design and write ads know about this screening process; they anticipate and accept it as a premise of their business.

The classic, all-time favorite device used to breach the barrier is sex. The desire to be sexually attracted to others is an ancient instinct, and few drives are more powerful. A magazine ad for Ultima II, a line of cosmetics, invites readers to "find everything you need for the sexxxxiest look around . . . ." The ad goes on to offer other "Sexxxy goodies," including "Lipsexxxxy lip color, naked eye color . . . Sun-sexxxy liquid bronzer." No one will accuse Ultima's marketing tacticians of subtlety. In fact, this ad is merely a current example of an approach that is as old as advertising. After countless years of using images of women in various stages of undress to sell products, ads are now displaying men's bodies as well. A magazine ad for Brut, a men's cologne, declares in bold letters, "MEN ARE BACK"; in the background, a photograph shows a muscular, shirtless young man preparing to enter the boxing ring—a "manly" image indeed; an image of man as breeding stock.

Every successful advertisement uses a creative strategy based on an idea that will attract and hold the attention of the targeted consumer audience. The strategy may include strong creative execution or a straightforward presentation of product features and customer benefits.

■ An ad for Clif Bars, an "energy bar," is clearly directed to people who want to snack but wouldn't be caught dead in a coffee house eating ginger spice cake with delicate frosting, much less ordinary energy bars—the kind often associated with the veggie and granola set: The central photograph shows a gristled cowboy-character, holding a Clif Bar, and asking, in the headline, "What 'n the hell's a carbohydrate?" Nosiree. This here energy bar is "bound to satisfy cantakerous folk like you."

■ Recent cigar ads attract attention through the use of unexpected imagery. An ad for Don Diego cigars, for example, shows a bejeweled woman in an evening dress smoking a cigar, while through the half-open door her male companion asks, "Agnes, have you seen my Don Diegos?"

■ A two-page ad for Diesel clothing includes a photo showing the principal participants in the famous Yalta conference in 1945 (Churchill, Roosevelt, and Stalin) with one important difference: Young models in Diesel clothing have been cleverly added and appear to be flirting with the dignitaries. The ad is presented as a "Diesel historical moment" and "the birth of the modern conference." This unexpected imagery is engaging and amusing, appealing to the product's youthful target audience.

Even if the text contains no incongruity and does not rely on a pun for its impact, ads typically use a creative strategy based on some striking concept or idea. In fact, the concept and execution are often so good that many successful ads entertain while they sell.

Soft drink and fast-food companies often take another approach. "Slice of life" ads (so-called because they purport to show people in "real-life" situations) created to sell Coke or Pepsi have often placed their characters in Fourth of July parades or other family events. The archetypical version of this ad is filled-to-overflowing with babies frolicking with puppies in the sunlit foreground while their youthful parents play touch football. On the porch, Grandma and Pops are seen quietly smiling as they wait for all of this affection to transform itself in a climax of warmth, harmony, and joy. In part, these ads work through repetition: How-many-times-can-you-spot-the-logo-in-this-commercial?

These ads seduce us into feeling that if we drink the right combination of sugar, preservatives, caramel coloring, and secret ingredients, we'll join the crowd that—in the words of Coca-Cola's ad from 1971—will help "teach the world to sing . . . in perfect harmony." A masterstroke of advertising cemented the impression that Coke was hip: not only an American brand, but a product and brand for all peace-loving peoples everywhere!

If you don't buy this version of the American Dream, search long enough and you are sure to find an ad designed to sell you what it takes to gain prestige within whatever posse you do happen to run with. As reported by the *Boston Globe,* "the malt liquor industry relies heavily on rap stars in delivering its message to inner-city youths, while Black Death Vodka, which features a top-hatted skull and a coffin on its label, has been using Guns N' Roses guitarist Slash to endorse the product in magazine advertising." A malt liquor company reportedly promotes in 40-ounce size with rapper King T singing. "I usually drink it when I'm just out clowning, me and the home boys, you know, be like downing it . . . I grab me a 40 when I want to act a fool." A recent ad for Sasson jeans is a long way from Black Death in execution, but a second cousin in spirit. A photograph of a young, blonde (they do have more fun, right?) actress appears with this text: "Baywatch actress Gene Lee Nolin Puts On Sasson. OOLA-LA. Sasson. Don't put it on unless it's Sasson."

Ads do not often emerge like Botticelli's Venus from the sea, flawless and fully grown. Most often, the creative strategy is developed only after extensive research. "Who will be interested in our product? How old are they? Where do they live? How much money do they earn? What problem will our product solve?" Answers to these questions provide the foundation on which the creative strategy is built.

Involving

We have seen that the language of advertising is carefully engineered; we have discovered a few of the devices it uses to get our attention. Coke and Pepsi have caught our eye with visions of peace and love. An actress offers a winsome smile. Now that they have our attention, advertisers present information intended to show us that their product fills a need and differs from the competition. It is the copywriter's responsibility to express, exploit, and intensify such product differences.

When product differences do not exist, the writer must glamorize the superficial differences—for example, differences in packaging. As long as the ad is trying to get our attention, the "action" is mostly in the ad itself, in the words and visual images. But as we read an ad or watch it on television, we become more deeply involved. The action starts to take place in us. Our imagination is set in motion, and our individual fears and aspirations, quirks, and insecurities, superimpose themselves on that tightly engineered, attractively packaged message.

Consider, once again, the running battle among the low-calorie soft drinks. The cola wars have spawned many "look-alike" advertisements, because the product features and consumer benefits are generic, applying to all products in the category. Substitute one cola brand name for another, and the messages are often identical, right down to the way the cans are photographed in the closing sequence. This strategy relies upon mass saturation and exposure for impact.

Some companies have set themselves apart from their competitors by making use of bold, even disturbing, themes and images. For example, it was not uncommon not long ago for advertisers in the fashion industry to make use of gaunt, languid models—models who, in the interpretation of some observers, displayed a certain form of "heroin chic." Something was most certainly unusual about the models appearing in ads for Prada and Calvin Klein products. A young woman in a Prada ad projects no emotion whatsoever; she is hunched forward, her posture suggesting that she is in a trance or drug-induced stupor. In a Calvin Klein ad, a young man, like the woman in the Prada ad, is gaunt beyond reason. He is shirtless. As if to draw more attention to his peculiar posture and "zero body fat" status, he is shown pinching the skin next to his navel. One well-recognized observer of public morality, President Clinton, commented on the increasing use of heroin on college campuses, noting that "part of this has to do with the images that are finding their way to our young people." One industry maven agreed, asserting that "people got carried away by the glamour of decadence."

Do such advertisers as Prada and Calvin Klein bear responsibility—morally, if not legally—for the rise of heroin use on college campuses? Does "heroin chic" and its depiction of a decadent lifestyle exploit certain elements of our society— the young and clueless, for example? Or did these ads, and others of their ilk, simply reflect profound bad taste? In fact, on one level, all advertising is about exploitation: the systematic, deliberate identification of our needs and wants, followed by the delivery of a carefully constructed promise that Brand X will satisfy them.

Symbols offer an important tool for involving consumers in advertisements. Symbols have become important elements in the language of advertising, not so much because they carry meanings of their own, but because we bring meaning to them. One example is provided by the campaign begun in 1978 by Somerset Importers for Johnnie Walker Red Scotch. Sales of Johnnie Walker Red had been trailing sales of Johnnie Walker Black, and Somerset Importers needed to position Red as a fine product in its own right. Their agency produced ads that made heavy use of the color red. One magazine ad, often printed as a two-page spread, is dominated by a close-up photo of red autumn leaves. At lower right, the copy reads, "When their work is done, even the leaves turn to Red." Another ad—also suitably dominated by a photograph in the appropriate color—reads: "When it's time to quiet down at the end of the day, even a fire turns to Red." Red. Warm. Experienced. Seductive.

Advertisers make use of a great variety of techniques and devices to engage us in the delivery of their messages. Some are subtle, making use of warm, entertaining, or comforting images or symbols. Others, like Black Death Vodka and Ultima II, are about as subtle as MTV's "Beavis and Butt-head." Another common device used to engage our attention is old but still effective: the use of famous or notorious personalities as product spokespeople or models. Advertising writers did not invent the human tendency to admire or otherwise identify themselves with famous people. Once we have seen a famous person in an ad, we associate the product with the person: "Britney Spears drinks milk. She's a hottie. I want to be a hottie, too. 'Hey Mom, Got Milk?'" "Guns 'N Roses rule my world, so I will definitely make the scene with a bottle of Black Death stuck into the waistband of my sweat pants." "Gena Lee Nolin is totally sexy. She wears Sasson. If I wear Sasson, I'll be sexy, too." The logic is faulty, but we fall under the spell just the same. Advertising works, not because Britney is a nutritionist, Slash has discriminating taste, or Gena knows her jeans, but because we participate in it. In fact, we charge ads with most of their power.

A Simple Language

Advertising language differs from other types of language in another important respect; it is a simple language. To determine how the copy of a typical advertisement rates on a "simplicity index" in comparison with text in a magazine article, for example, try this exercise: Clip a typical story from the publication you read most frequently. Calculate the number of words in an average sentence. Count the number of words of three or more syllables in a typical 100-word passage, omitting words that are capitalized, combinations of two simple words, or verb forms made into three-syllable words by the addition of *–ed* or *es*. Add the two figures (the average number of words per sentence and the number of three-syllable words per 100 words), then multiply the result by . 4. According to Robert Gunning, if the resulting number is 7, there is a good chance that you are reading *True Confessions*. He developed this formula, the "Fog Index," to determine the comparative ease with which any given piece of written communication can be read.

Let's apply the Fog Index to the complete text of Britney Spears' 1999 ad for the National Fluid Milk Processing Board ("Got Milk?")

> "Baby, one more time isn't enough.
> 9 out of 10 girls don't get enough calcium. It takes about 4 glasses of milk every day. So when I finish this glass, fill it up, baby. Three more times."

The average sentence in this ad is 7.4 words. There is only one three-syllable word, *calcium*. Counting *isn't* and *don't* as two words each, the ad is 40 words in length. The average number of three syllable words per hundred is 2.5.

7.4 word per sentence
+ 2.5 three syllable words/100
9.9
X.4
3.96

According to Gunning's scale, this ad is about as hard to read as a comic book. But of course the text is only part of the message. The rest is the visual; in this case, a photo of pop star Britney Spears sprawled across a couch, legs in the air, while she talks on the phone. A plate holding cookies and a glass of milk is set next to her.

Why do advertisers generally favor simple language? The answer lies with the consumer: The average American adult is subject to an overwhelming number of commercial messages each day. As a practical matter, we would not notice many of these messages if length or eloquence were counted among their virtues. Today's consumer cannot take the time to focus on anything for long, much less blatant advertising messages. Every aspect of modern life runs at an accelerated pace. Overnight mail has moved in less than ten years from a novelty to a common business necessity. Voice mail, pagers, cellular phones, e-mail, the Internet—the world is always awake, always switched on, and hungry for more information, now. Time generally, and TV-commercial time in particular, is now dissected into increasingly smaller segments. Fifteen-second commercials are no longer unusual.

Advertising language is simple language; in the ad's engineering process, difficult words or images—which in other forms of communication may be used to lend color or fine shades of meaning—are edited out and replaced by simple words or images not open to misinterpretation. You don't have to ask whether King T likes to "grab a 40" when he wants to "act a fool," or whether Gena wears her Sassons when she wants to do whatever it is she does.

Who Is Responsible?

Some critics view the advertising business as a cranky, unwelcomed child of the free enterprise system—a noisy, whining, brash kid who must somehow be kept in line, but can't just yet be thrown out of the house. In reality, advertising mirrors the fears, quirks, and aspirations of the society that creates it (and is, in turn, sold by it). This factor alone exposes advertising to parody and ridicule. The overall level of acceptance and respect for advertising is also influenced by the varied quality of the ads themselves. Some ads, including a few of the examples cited here, seem deliberately designed to provoke controversy. For example, it is easy—as President Clinton and others charged—to conclude that clothing retailers deliberately glamorized the damaging effects of heroin addiction. But this is only one of the many charges frequently levied against advertising:

1. Advertising encourages unhealthy habits.
2. Advertising feeds on human weaknesses and exaggerates the importance of material things, encouraging "impure" emotions and vanities.
3. Advertising sells daydreams—distracting, purposeless visions of lifestyles beyond the reach of the majority of the people who are most exposed to advertising.
4. Advertising warps our vision of reality, implanting in us groundless fears and insecurities.
5. Advertising downgrades the intelligence of the public.
6. Advertising debases English.
7. Advertising perpetuates racial and sexual stereotypes.

What can be said in advertising's defense? Advertising is only a reflection of society. A case can be made for the concept that advertising language is an acceptable stimulus for the natural evolution of language. Is "proper English" the language most Americans actually speak and write, or is it the language we are told we should speak and write?

What about the charge that advertising debases the intelligence of the public? Those who support this particular criticism would do well to ask themselves another question: Exactly how intelligent is the public? Sadly, evidence abounds that "the public" at large is not particularly intelligent, after all. Johnny can't read. Susie can't write. And the entire family spends the night in front of the television, channel surfing for the latest scandal—hopefully, one involving a sports hero or political figure said to be a killer or a frequent participant in perverse sexual acts.

Ads are effective because they sell products. They would not succeed if they did not reflect the values and motivations of the real world. Advertising both reflects and shapes our perception of reality. Consider several brand names and the impressions they create: Ivory Snow is pure. Federal Express won't let you down. Absolut is cool. Sasson is sexxy. Mercedes represents quality. Our sense of what these brand names stand for may have as much to do with advertising as with the objective "truth."

Advertising shapes our perception of the world as surely as architecture shapes do our impression of a city. Good, responsible advertising can serve as a positive influence for change, while generating profits. Of course, the problem is that the obverse is also true: Advertising, like any form of mass communication, can be a force for both "good" and "bad." It can just as readily reinforce or encourage irresponsible behavior, ageism, sexism, ethnocentrism, racism, homophobia, heterophobia—you name it—as it can encourage support for diversity and social progress. People living in society create advertising. Society isn't perfect. In the end, advertising simply attempts to change behavior. Do advertisements sell distracting, purposeless visions? Occasionally. But perhaps such visions are necessary components of the process through which our society changes and improves.

Perhaps, by learning how advertising works, we can become better equipped to sort out content from hype, product values from emotions, and salesmanship from propaganda.

Topics for Reading and Writing

1. O'Neill argues here that language used by advertisers may be particularly alluring but cannot be held responsible for all the pernicious effects cultural critics ascribe to advertising. Do you accept his argument? Is advertising language ethically neutral, or is this kind of language by its very nature—by its fundamental appeal to the emotions rather than to logic—unethical? And if so, what does that say about the ethical nature, in general, of pathos appeals?

2. "Advertising," O'Neill argues, "is only a reflection of society." Is this a sufficient argument? What other phenomena are just "reflections of society"?

During the 1990s, many members of a generation of young people that had been dismissed as apathetic organized themselves for radical action. The great causes of the past—Vietnam, the civil rights movement—being past, these young people coalesced around a much more nebulous and complicated issue: what is often innocuously termed "economic development," or the spread of corporate

Naomi Klein
"The Branding of Learning"
from *No Logo*

A democratic system of education . . . is one of the surest ways of creating and greatly extending markets for goods of all kinds and especially those goods in which fashion may play a part.

—Ex-adman James Rorty, *Our Master's Voice,* 1934

Although brands seem to be everywhere—at kids' concerts, next to them on the couch, on stage with their multinational capitalism to the developing world. This loose organization (whose primary meeting place was the Internet) physically came together at several important summits and conferences of world leaders, especially the meetings of the World Trade Organization and the so-called "G–8" group of leading industrial nations. Violent protests ensued at meetings in Seattle, Genoa, and Quebec City.

What were these protests about? The protesters had a vast array of concerns, but perhaps the best umbrella concept is "globalization," or the way that capitalism (embodied both as capitalist nations and as corporations) is spreading around the world. These protesters feel, for instance, that global capitalism endangers the environment, threatens the uniqueness of cultures, devalues spiritual life in favor of material well-being, exacerbates the divide between rich and poor, makes the lives of the poor worse, and is a profoundly damaging trend. One of the voices that emerged from this loose confederation of activists has been that of the Canadian journalist **Naomi Klein** (b. 1970), who published No Logo: Taking Aim at the Brand Bullies in 1999. Klein's book analyzes the political and economic effects of globalization as it is embodied in branding, or the association of identity and emotions with a corporate name.

heroes, in their on-line chat groups, and on their playing fields and basketball courts—for a long time one major unbranded youth frontier remained: a place where young people gathered, talked, sneaked smokes, made out, formed opinions and, most maddeningly of all, stood around looking cool for hours on end. That place is called school. And clearly, the brands had to get into the schools.

Marketers and cool hunters have spent the better part of the decade hustling the brands back to high school and pouring them into the template of the teenage outlaw. Several of the most successful brands had even cast their corporate headquarters as private schools, referring to them as "campuses" and, at the Nike World Campus, nicknaming one edifice "the student union building." Even the cool hunters are going highbrow; by the late nineties, the rage in the industry was to recast oneself less as a trendy club-hopper than as a bookish grad student. In fact, some insist they aren't cool hunters at all but rather "urban anthropologists."

And yet despite their up-to-the-minute outfits and intellectual pretensions, the brands and their keepers still found themselves on the wrong side of the school gate, a truly intolerable state of affairs and one that would not last long. American marketing consultant Jack Myers described the insufferable slight like this: "The choice we have in this country [the U.S.] is for our educational system to join the electronic age and communicate to students in ways they can understand and to which they can relate. Or our schools can continue to use outmoded forms of communications and become the daytime prisons for millions of young people, as they have become in our inner cities." This reasoning, which baldly equates corporate access to the schools with access to modern technology, and by extension to the future itself, is at the core of how the brands have managed, over the course of only one decade, to all but eliminate the barrier between ads and education. It was technology that lent a new urgency to nineties chronic underfunding: at the same time as schools were facing ever-deeper budget cuts, the costs of delivering a modern education were rising steeply, forcing many educators to look to alternative funding sources for help. Swept up by info-tech hype, schools that couldn't afford up-to-date textbooks were suddenly expected to provide students with audiovisual equipment, video cameras, classroom computers, desktop publishing capacity, the latest educational software programs, Internet access—even, at some schools, video-conferencing.

Of course the companies crashing the school gate have nothing against education. Students should by all means learn, they say, but why don't they read about our company, write about our brand, research their own brand preferences or come up with a drawing for our next ad campaign? Teaching students and building brand awareness, these corporations seem to believe, can be two aspects of the same project.

When students aren't watching Channel One or surfing with ZapMe!, an in-school Internet browser first offered free to American schools in 1998, they may turn their attention to their textbooks—and those too may be sending out more messages to "Just Do It" or "CK Be." The Cover Concepts company sells slick ads that wrap around books to 30,000 U.S. schools, where teachers use them instead of plastic or tinfoil as protective jackets. And when lunchtime arrives, more ads are literally on the menu at many schools. In 1997, Twentieth Century-Fox managed to get cafeteria menu items named after characters from its film *Anastasia* in forty U.S. elementary schools. Students could dine on "Rasputin Rib-B-Cue on Bartok Bun" and "Dimitri's Peanut Butter Fudge." Disney and Kellogg's have engaged in similar lunch-menu promotions through School Marketing, a company that describes itself as a "school-lunch ad agency."

Competing with the menu sponsors are the fast-food chains themselves, chains that go head-to-head with cafeterias in 13 percent of U.S. schools. In an arrangement that was unheard of in the eighties, companies like McDonald's and Burger King now set up kiosks in lunchrooms, which they advertise around the school. Subway supplies 767 schools with sandwiches; Pizza Hut corners the market in approximately 4,000 schools; and a staggering 20,000 schools participate in Taco Bell's "frozen burrito product line." A Subway sandwich guide about how to access the in-school market advises franchisees to pitch their brand-name food to school boards as a way to keep students from sneaking out at lunch hour and getting into trouble. "Look for situations where the local school board has a closed campus policy for lunch. If they do, a strong case can be made for branded product to keep the students on campus." The argument works for administrators such as Bob Honson, the director of nutritional services for the Portland, Oregon, school district. "Kids come to us with brand preferences," he explains.

Not all students' brand preferences, however, are accommodated with equal enthusiasm. Since the fast-food outposts don't accept vouchers from kids on the federal lunch program and their food is usually twice as expensive as cafeteria fare, kids from poor families are stuck with mystery meat while their wealthier classmates lunch on Pizza Hut pizza and Big Macs. And they can't even look forward to days when the cafeteria serves pizza or cheeseburgers, since many schools have signed agreements with the chains that prohibit them from serving "generic versions" of fast-food items: no-name burgers, it seems, constitute "unfair competition."

Students may also find that brand wars are being waged over the pop machine outside the gym. In Canada and the U.S., many school boards have given exclusive vending rights to the Pepsi-Cola Company in exchange for generally undisclosed lump sums. What Pepsi negotiates in return varies from district to district. In Toronto, it gets to fill the 560 public schools with its vending machines, to block the sales of Coke and other competitors, and to distribute "Pepsi Achievement Awards" and other goodies emblazoned with its logo. In communities like Cayuga, a rural Ontario tobacco-farming town, Pepsi buys the right to brand entire schools. "Pepsi—Official Soft Drink of Cayuga Secondary School" reads the giant sign beside the road. At South Fork High School in Florida, there is a blunt, hard-sell arrangement: the school has a clause in its Pepsi contract committing the school to "make its best effort to maximize all sales opportunities for Pepsi-Cola products."

Similarly bizarre and haphazard corporate promotions arrangements are thrown together on college and university campuses around the world. At almost every university in North America, advertising billboards appear on campus bicycle racks, on benches, in hallways linking lecture halls, in libraries and even in bathroom stalls. Credit-card companies and long-distance phone carriers solicit students from the moment they receive their orientation-week information kit to the instant after they receive their degree; at some schools, diplomas come with an envelope stuffed with coupons, credit offers and advertising flyers. In the U.S. Barnes & Noble is rapidly replacing campus-owned bookstores, and Chapters has similar plans in Canada. Taco Bells, KFCs, Starbucks and Pizza Huts are already fixtures on university campuses, where they are often clumped together in food courts inside on-campus malls. Not surprisingly, in the U.S and Canada the fiercest scholastic marketing battles are fought over high-school gym class and university athletics. The top high-school basketball teams have sponsorship deals with Nike and Adidas, which deck out teenagers in swoosh- and stripe-festooned shoes, warm-ups and gym bags. At the university level, Nike has sponsorship deals with more than two hundred campus athletics departments in the U.S. and twelve in Canada. As anyone familiar with college ball well knows, the standard arrangement gives the company the right to stamp the swoosh on uniforms, sports gear, official university merchandise and apparel, on stadium seats and, most important, on ad banners in full view of the cameras that televise high-profile games. Since student players can't get paid in amateur athletics, it is the coaches who receive the corporate money to dress their teams in the right logos, and the amounts at stake are huge. Nike pays individual coaches as much as $1.5 million in sponsorship fees at top sports universities like Duke and North Carolina, sums that make the coaches' salaries look like tokens of appreciation.

As educational institutions surrender to the manic march of branding, a new language is emerging. Nike high schools and universities square off against their Adidas rivals: the teams may well have their own "official drink," either Coke or Pepsi. In its daily broadcasts, Channel One makes frequent references to the goings-on at "Channel One schools." William Hoynes, a sociologist at Vassar College who conducted a study on the broadcaster, says the practice is "part of a broader marketing approach to develop a 'brand name' consciousness of the network, including the promotion of the 'Channel One school' identity."

Hey, Kids! Be a *Self*-Promoter!

In a corporate climate obsessed with finding the secret recipe for cool, there are still more in-school resources to tap. After all, if there is one thing the cool hunters have taught us, it's that groups of kids aren't just lowly consumers: they are also card-carrying representatives of their age demographic. In the eyes of the brand managers, every lunchroom and classroom is a focus group waiting to be focused. So getting access to schools means more than just hawking product—it's a bona fide, bargain-basement cool-hunting opportunity.

For this reason, the in-school computer network ZapMe! doesn't merely sell ad space to its sponsors; it also monitors students' paths as they surf the Net and provides this valuable market research, broken down by the students' sex, age and zip code, to its advertisers. Then, when students log on to ZapMe!, they are treated to ads that have been specially "micro-targeted" for them. This kind of detailed market research is exploding in North American schools: weekly focus groups, taste tests, brand-preference questionnaires, opinion polls, panel discussions on the Internet, all are currently being used inside classrooms. And in a feat of peer-on-peer cool hunting, some market researchers have been experimenting with sending kids home from school with disposable cameras to take pictures of their friends and family—returning with documented evidence, in one assignment conducted for Nike, "of their favorite place to hang out." Exercises like these are "educational" and "empowering" the market researchers argue, and some educators agree. In explaining the merits of a cereal taste test, the principal of Our Lady of Assumption elementary school in Lynnfield, Massachusetts, said: "It's a learning experience. They had to read, they had to look, they had to compare."

Channel One is pushing the market-research model even further, frequently enlisting "partner" teachers to develop class lessons in which students are asked to create a new ad campaign for Snapple or to redesign Pepsi's vending machines. In New York and Los Angeles high-school students have created thirty-second animated spots for Starburst fruit candies, and students in Colorado Springs designed Burger King ads to hang in their school buses. Finished assignments are passed on to the companies and the best entries win prizes and may even be adopted by the companies—all subsidized by the taxpayer-funded school system. At Vancouver's Laurier Annex school, students in Grades 3 and 4 designed two new product lines for the British Columbia restaurant chain White Spot. For several months in 1997, the children worked on developing the concept and packaging for "Zippy" pizza burgers, a product that is now on the kids' menu at White Spot. The following year, they designed an entire concept for birthday parties to be held at the chain. The students' corporate presentation included "sample commercials, menu items, party games invested by the students and cake ideas," taking into account such issues as safety, possible food allergies, low costs "and allowing for flexibility." According to nine-year-old Jeffrey Ye, "it was a lot of work."

Perhaps the most infamous of these experiments occurred in 1998, when Coca-Cola ran a competition asking several schools to come up with a startegy for distributing Coke coupons to students. The school that devised the best promotional strategy would win $500. Greenbriar High School in Evans, Georgia, took the contest extremely seriously, calling an official Coke Day in late March during which all students came to school in Coca-Cola T-shirts, posed for a photograph in a formation spelling Coke, attended lectures given by Coca-Cola executives and learned about all things black and bubbly in their classes. It was a little piece of branding heaven until it came to the principal's attention that in an act of hideous defiance, one Mike Cameron, a nineteen-year-old senior, had come to school wearing a T-shirt with a Pepsi logo. He was promptly suspended for the offense. "I know it sounds bad—'Child suspended for wearing Pepsi shirt on Coke Day,'" said principal Gloria Hamilton. "It really would have been acceptable . . . if it had just been in-house, but we had the regional president here and people flew in from Atlanta to do us the honor of being resource speakers. These students knew we had guests."

In May 1996, students and faculty at the University of Wisconsin at Madison found out what was in the text of a sponsorship deal their administration was about to sign with Reebok—and they didn't like what they discovered. The deal contained a "non-disparagement" clause that prohibited members of the university community from criticizing the athletic gear company. The clause stated: "During and for a reasonable time after the term, the University will not issue any official statement that disparages Reebok. Additionally, the University will promptly take all reasonable steps necessary to address any remark by any University employee, agent or representative, including, a Coach, that disparages Reebok, Reebok's products or the advertising agency or others connected with Reebok." Reebok agreed to nix the demand after students and faculty members launched an educational campaign about the company's patchy record on labor rights in Southeast Asia. What was exceptional about the Wisconsin clause is that the university community found out about it before the deal was signed. This has not been the case at other universities where athletic departments have quietly entered into multimillion-dollar deals that contained similar gag orders. The University of Kentucky's deal with Nike, for instance, has a clause that states that the company has the right to terminate the five-year $25 million contract if the "University disparages the Nike brand . . . or takes any other action inconsistent with the endorsement of Nike products." Nike denies that its motivation is to stifle campus critics. "If people could get away from this attitude that Nike is in this to control these universities, they would better understand what these things are all about," says Steve Miller, Nike's director of colleges sports marketing.

Regardless of the intentions when the deals are inked, the fact is that campus expression is often stifled when it conflicts with the interests of a corporate sponsor. For example, at Kent State University—one of the U.S. campuses at which Coca-Cola has exclusive vending rights—members of the Amnesty International chapter advocated a boycott of the soft drink because Coca-Cola did business with the since-ousted Nigerian dictatorship. In April 1998, the activists made a routine application to their student council for funding to bring in a human-rights speaker from the Free Nigeria Movement. "Is he going to speak negatively about Coca-Cola?" a council member asked. "Because Coca-Cola does a lot of positive things on our campus like helping organizations and sports." The representatives from Amnesty replied that the speaker would indeed have some negative comments to make about the company's involvement in Nigeria and funding for the event was denied.

These are extreme examples of how corporate sponsorship deals re-engineer some of the fundamental values of public universities, including financial transparency and the right to open debate and peaceful protest on campus. But the subtle effects are equally disturbing. Many professors speak of the slow encroachment of the mall mentality, arguing that the more campuses act and look like malls, the more students behave like consumers. They tell stories of students filling out their course-evaluation forms with all the smug self-righteousness of a tourist responding to a customer-satisfaction form at a large hotel chain. "Most of all I dislike the attitude of calm consumer expertise that pervades the responses. I'm disturbed by the serene belief that my function—and more important, Freud's, or Shakespeare's, or Blake's—is to divert, entertain, and interest," writes University of Virginia professor Mark Edmundson in *Harper's* magazine. A professor at Toronto's York University, where there is a full-fledged mall on campus, tells me that his students slip into class slurping grande lattes, chat in the back and slip out. They're cruising, shopping, disengaged.

Where Was the Opposition?

Many people, upon learning of the advanced stage of branded education, want to know where the university faculty, teachers, school boards and parents were while this transformation was taking place. At the elementary and high-school level, this is a difficult question to answer—particularly since one is hard-pressed to find anyone but the advertisers who is actively *in favor* of allowing ads into schools. Over the course of the decade, all the large teachers' unions in North America have been quite vocal about the threat to independent instruction posed by commercialization, and many concerned parents have formed groups like Ralph Nader's Commercial Alert to make their opposition heard. Despite this, however, there was never one big issue on which parents and educators could band together to fight—and possibly win—a major policy battle on classroom commercialization.

Unlike the very public standoffs over prayer in schools or over explicit sex education, the move to allow advertisements did not take the form of one sweeping decision but, rather, of thousands of little ones, Usually these were made on an ad hoc, school-by-school basis, frequently with no debate, no notice, no public scrutiny at all, because advertising agencies were careful to fashion school promotions that could slip between the cracks of standard school-board regulations.

There is, however, another, more ingrained cultural factor that has helped the brands get inside the schools, and it has to do with the effectiveness of branding itself. Many parents and educators could not see anything to be gained by resistance; kids today are so bombarded by brand names that it seemed as if protecting educational spaces from commercialization was less important than the immediate benefits of finding new funding sources. And the hawkers of in-school advertising have not been at all shy about playing upon this sense of futility among parents and educators. As Frank Vigil, president of ZapMe! Computer systems, says: "America's youth is exposed to advertising in many aspects of their lives. We believe students are savvy enough to discern between educational content and marketing materials." Thus it became possible for many parents and teachers to rationalize their failure to protect yet another previously public space by telling themselves that what ads students don't see in class or on campus, they will certainly catch on the subway, on the Net or on TV when they get home. What's one more ad in the life of these marked-up and marked-down kids? And then again . . . what's another?

But while this may explain the brands' inroads in high schools, it still doesn't explain how this process has been able to take such a firm hold on the university campuses. Why have university professors remained silent, passively allowing their corporate "partners" to trample the principles of freedom of inquiry and discourse that have been the avowed centerpieces of academic life? More to the point, aren't our campuses supposed to be overflowing with troublemaking tenured radicals? Isn't the institution of tenure, with its lifelong promise of job security, designed to make it safe for academics to take controversial positions without fear of repercussion? Aren't these people, to borrow a term more readily understood in the halls of academe, *counter-hegemonic?*

Sadly, part of the explanation for the lack of campus mobilization is simple self-interest. Until the mid-nineties, the growing corporate influence in education and research seemed to be taking place almost exclusively in the engineering departments, management schools and science labs. Campus radicals had always been prone to dismiss these faculties as hopelessly compromised right-wing bastions: who cared what was happening on that side of campus, so long as the more traditionally progressive fields (literature, cultural studies, political science, history and fine arts) were left alone? And as long as professors and students in the arts and humanities remained indifferent to this radical shift in campus culture and priorities, they were free to pursue other interests—and there were many on offer. For instance, more than a few of those tenured radicals who were supposed to be corrupting young minds with socialist ideas were preoccupied with their own postmodernist realization that truth itself is a construct. This realization made it intellectually untenable for many academics to even participate in a political argument that would have "privileged" any one model of learning (public) over another (corporate). And since truth is relative, who is to say that Plato's dialogues are any more of an "authority" than Fox's *Anastasia?*

This academic trend only accounts for a few of the missing-in-actions, however. Many other campus radicals were still up for a good old political fight, but during the key years of the corporate campus invasion they were tied up in a different battle: the all-consuming gender and race debates of the so-called political correctness wars. As we will see in the next chapter, if the students allowed themselves to be turned into test markets, it was partly because they had other things on their minds. They were busy taking on their professors on the merits of the canon and the need for more stringent campus sexual-harassment policies. And if their professors failed to prevent the very principles of unfettered academic discourse from being traded in for a quick buck, this may also have been because they were too preoccupied with defending themselves against their own "McCarthyite" students. So there they all were, fighting about women's studies and the latest backlash book while their campuses were being sold out from under their feet. It wasn't until the politics of personal representation were themselves co-opted by branding that students and professors alike began to turn away from their quarrels with each other, realizing they had a more powerful foe.

But by then, much had already been lost. More fundamentally than somewhat antiquated notions of "pure" education and research, what is lost as schools "pretend they are corporations" (to borrow a phrase from the University of Florida) is the very idea of unbranded space. In many ways, schools and universities remain our culture's most tangible embodiment of public space and collective responsibility. University campuses in particular—with their residences, libraries, green spaces and common standards for open and respectful discourse—play a crucial, if now largely symbolic, role: they are the one place left where young people can see a genuine public life being lived. And however imperfectly we may have protected these institutions in the past, at this point in our history the argument against transforming education into a brand-extension exercise is much the same as the one for national parks and nature reserves: these quasi-sacred spaces remind us that unbranded space is still possible.

Topics for Reading and Writing

1. Klein clearly is opposed to the spread of branding; she does not even make an attempt to write this chapter from an objective point of view. Does this weaken her argument or strengthen it? How? To what degree must an argument be fair in order to be persuasive?

2. What's wrong with brands in universities? Isn't it *good* that college students can have the food or shoes or coffee they are already used to when they visit the student union or bookstore? And when the United States is so controlled by corporations, isn't excluding them from universities just a way to create an artificial world for students? Shouldn't we be training them for the world they'll live in after graduation?

3. How do you see the corporate influence at your own school? What is your opinion of how it affects the curriculum, the academic freedom of the professors, and the social life of the students?

One of the most respected newsmagazines in the world, **The Economist** *often surprises its American readers by its cheeky tone and often frankly opinionated "news" stories. This British magazine generally supports unfettered economic freedom, globalization, and the rights of corporations and of individuals against the powers of government. Yet it cannot be dismissed as merely an ideological journal like* National Review *or* The American

The Economist
"Who's Wearing the Trousers?" and "The Case for Brands"

Brands are in the dock, accused of all sorts of mischief, from threatening our health and destroying our environment to corrupting our children. Brands are so powerful, it is alleged, that they seduce us to look alike, eat alike and be alike. At the same time, they are spiritually empty, gradually (and almost subliminally) undermining our moral values.

This grim picture has been popularised by a glut of anti-branding books, ranging from Eric Schlosser's "Fast

Spectator. The Economist *is probably the world's best newsmagazine for those who care about news; as its American counterparts* Time *and* Newsweek *shift their focus to celebrity stories, lifestyle features, and "news you can use,"* The Economist *continues to do cover stories on issues like the Venezuelan elections or European Union monetary policy.*

Food Nation" and Robert Frank's "Luxury Fever" to "The World is Not for Sale" by Francois Dufour and Jose Bove—a French farmer who is best known for vandalising a McDonald's restaurant. The argument has, however, been most forcefully articulated in Naomi Klein's book "No Logo: Taking Aim at the Brand Bullies".

Not since Vance Packard's 1957 classic "The Hidden Persuaders" has one book stirred up so much antipathy to marketing. Its author has become the spokesman for a worldwide movement against multinationals and their insidious brands. Britain's Times newspaper rated her one of the world's most influential people under 35. Published in at least seven languages, "No Logo" has touched a universal nerve. Its argument runs something like this. In the new global economy, brands represent a huge portion of the value of a company and, increasingly, its biggest source of profits. So companies are switching from producing products to marketing aspirations, images and lifestyles. They are trying to become weightless, shedding physical assets by shifting production from their own factories in the first world to other people's in the third.

These image mongers offer "a Barbie world for adults" says Ms Klein, integrating their brands so fully into our lives that they cocoon us in a "brandscape". No space is untouched: schools, sports stars and even youth identity are all being co-opted by brands. "Powerful brands no longer just advertise in a magazine, they control its content," says Ms Klein.

Now they are the target of a backlash. A new generation of activists is rising up and attacking, not governments or ideologies but brands, directly and often violently. Coca-Cola, Wal-Mart and McDonald's have been rounded on over issues ranging from racism to child labour to advertising in schools.

Less a Product, More a Way of Life

In one sense it is easy to understand why Ms Klein and her camp feel as they do. The word "brand" is everywhere, to the point where Disney chairman Michael Eisner calls the term "overused, sterile and unimaginative". Products, people, countries and companies are all racing to turn themselves into brands—to make their image more likeable and understandable. British Airways did it. Target and Tesco are doing it, while people from Martha Stewart to Madonna are branding themselves. Britain tried to become a brand with its "Cool Britannia" slogan, and Wally Olins, a corporate-identity consultant and co-founder of Wolff Olins, a consultancy, even wants to have a crack at branding the European Union.

At the very least, Ms Klein overstates the case. Brands are not as powerful as their opponents allege, nor is the public as easily manipulated. The reality is more complicated. Indeed, many of the established brands that top the league tables are in trouble, losing customer loyalty and value. Annual tables of the world's top ten brands used to change very little from year to year. Names such as Kellogg's, Kodak, Marlboro and Nescafe appeared with almost monotonous regularity. Now, none of these names is in the top ten. Kellogg's, second less than a decade ago, languishes at 39th in the latest league table produced by Inter-brand, a brand consultancy.

Of the 74 brands that appear in the top 100 rankings in both of the past two years, 41 declined in value between 2000 and 2001, while the combined value of the 74 fell by $49 billion—to an estimated $852 billion, a drop of more than 5%. Brands fall from grace and newer, nimbler ones replace them.

Meanwhile, consumers have become more fickle. A study of American lifestyles by DDB, an advertising agency, found that the percentage of consumers between the ages of 20 and 29 who said that they stuck to well-known brands fell from 66% in 1975 to 59% in 2000. The bigger surprise, though, was that the percentage in the 60−69 age bracket who said that they remained loyal to well-known brands fell over the same period, from 86% to 59%. It is not only the young who flit from brand to brand. Every age group, it seems, is more or less equally disloyal. The result is that many of the world's biggest brands are struggling. If they are making more and more noise, it is out of desperation.

As they move from merely validating products to encapsulating whole lifestyles, brands are evolving a growing social dimension. In the developed world, they are seen by some to have expanded into the vacuum left by the decline of organized religion. But this has made brands—and the multinationals that are increasingly identified with them—not more powerful, but more vulnerable. Consumers will tolerate a lousy product for far longer than they will tolerate a lousy lifestyle.

Brands past

Historically, building a brand was rather simple. A logo was a straightforward guarantee of quality and consistency, or it was a signal that a product was something new. For that, consumers were, quite rationally, prepared to pay a premium. "Brands were the first piece of consumer protection," says Jeremy Bullmore, a long-time director of J. Walter Thompson, an advertising agency. "You knew where to go if you had a complaint." Even the central planners in the old Soviet Union had to establish "production marks" to stop manufacturers cutting corners on quality.

Brands also helped consumers to buy efficiently. As Unilever's chairman Niall FitzGerald points out: "A brand is a storehouse of trust. That matters more and more as choices multiply. People want to simplify their lives."

This implicit trade-off was efficient and profitable for companies too. Building a brand nationally required little more than an occasional advertisement on a handful of television or radio stations showing how the product tasted better or drove faster. There was little regulation. It was easy for brands such as Coca-Cola, Kodak and Marlboro to become hugely powerful. Because shopping was still a local business and competition limited, a successful brand could maintain its lead and high prices for years. A strong brand acted as an effective barrier to entry for others.

In western markets, over time, brand building became much trickier. As standards of manufacturing rose, it became harder for firms to differentiate on quality alone and so to charge a premium price. This was particularly true of packaged goods like food: branded manufacturers lost market share to retailers' own brands, which consumers learned to trust.

Nor were traditional branded products any longer the only choice in town. As shoppers became more mobile and discovered more places to buy, including online websites, they switched products more often. Brands now face competition from the most unexpected quarters, says Rita Clifton, chief executive of Interbrand: "If you were a soap-powder company years ago, your competition would come from the same industry and probably the same country. Now it could be anyone. Who'd have thought that Virgin would sell mobile phones, Versace run hotels or Tesco sell banking services?"

Even truly innovative products can no longer expect to keep the market to themselves for long. Gillette spent $750m and seven years developing its three-bladed Mach 3 men's razor, for which it charged a fat premium. But only months later it was trumped by Asda, a British supermarket that came out with its own version for a fraction of the price.

Consumers are now bombarded with choices. They are "commercials veterans," inundated with up to 1,500 pitches a day. Far from being gullible and easily manipulated, they are cynical about marketing and less responsive to entreaties to buy. "Consumers are like roaches," say Jonathan Bond and Richard Kirshenbaum in their book "Under the Radar—Talking to Today's Cynical Consumer." "We spray them with marketing, and for a time it works. Then, inevitably, they develop an immunity, a resistance."

Some of the most cynical consumers, say the authors, are the young. Nearly half of all American college students have taken marketing courses and "know the enemy." For them, "shooting down advertising has become a kind of sport."

Consumers are also harder to reach. They are busier, more distracted and have more media to choose from. And they lead lives that are more complicated and less predictable. A detergent can no longer count on its core consumer being a white housewife. Against this background, it has never been harder to develop or even just sustain a brand. Coca-Cola, Gillette and Nike are prominent examples of the many that are struggling to increase volumes, raise prices and boost margins.

Marketing Mistakes

Marketers have to take some of the blame. While consumers have changed beyond recognition, marketing has not. Elliott Ettenberg, author of a forthcoming book on the decline of marketing says: "Everything else has been reinvented—distribution, new product development, the supply chain. But marketing is stuck in the past." Even in America, home to nine of the world's ten most valuable brands, it can be a shockingly old-fashioned business. Marketing theory is still largely based on the days when Procter & Gamble's brands dominated America, and its advertising agencies wrote the rules. Those rules focused on the product and where to sell it, not the customer.

The new marketing approach is to build a brand not a product—to sell a lifestyle or a personality, to appeal to emotions. But this requires a far greater understanding of human psychology. It is a much harder task than describing the virtues of a product.

Sweden's Absolut Vodka, one of the world's biggest spirits brands, demonstrates this well. Its clever, simple ads featuring its now famous clear bottle were dreamt up long before the vodka was fermented. Goran Lundqvist, the company's president, says that Absolut's wit, rather than its taste, is the reason for the spirit's success: "Absolut is a personality," he claims. "We like certain people, but some people are just more fun and interesting." Other products have also succeeded in touching the emotions. Fans of Ben & Jerry's ice cream, for example, think that it is hip for its ethical stance, while many Harley Davidson owners are literally in love with their machines.

The trouble is that most marketers have to struggle to create such feelings for their brands. Many firms, most notably banks, mistake inertia for liking. Others, such as Coca-Cola and McDonald's, complacent from past success, find it difficult to admit that their customers are drifting away to newer offerings. Yet others, panicking that they need to do something, reinvent themselves and unwittingly lose the essence of their appeal. Old-fashioned market-research methods help explain such mistakes. Focus groups, for example, are poor at rooting out the real reasons why people like brands, but they are still heavily used.

The attempt by brands to adopt a social component—to embrace a lifestyle—is giving consumers a lever to influence the behaviour of the companies that stand behind them. The "No Logo" proponents are correct that brands are a conduit through which influence flows between companies and consumers. But far more often, it is consumers that dictate to companies and ultimately decide their fate, rather than the other way round. Think of the failure of such high-profile product launches as "New Coke"; the disastrous effect on Hoover of a badly-designed sales promotion in Britain a few years ago; or the boycott of genetically modified foods by Europe's consumers.

The Internet also provides some telling examples. Dotcoms such as Webvan and Kozmo were lauded for the speed with which they built their brands. Unconstrained by the need to make profits, however, such companies built customer loyalty artificially. Once business reality returned, they were revealed as unsustainable promises. Consumers, it turned out, were not gullible. As Mr. Olins says: "Is the brand immoral, can it get us to do things we don't want to? No. When we like a brand we manifest our loyalty in cash. If we don't like it, we walk away. Customers are in charge."

Levers for Lifting Standards

The truth is that people like brands. They not only simplify choices and guarantee quality, but they add fun and interest. "In technocratic and colourless times, brands bring warmth, familiarity and trust," says Peter Brabeck, boss of Nestle. They also have a cultish quality that creates a sense of belonging. "In an irreligious world, brands provide us with beliefs," says Mr. Olins. "They define who we are and signal our affiliations."

Jim McDowell, head of marketing at BMW North America, says that when young people visit a 3Com-sponsored baseball stadium or a Continental Airlines' hockey arena, they realise that "some of the best things they have ever experienced have come through brands."

Since brands and their corporate parents are becoming ever more entwined—both in the public perception and commercial reality—it follows that consumers can increasingly influence the behaviour of companies. Arrogance, greed and hypocrisy are swiftly punished. Popular outrage forced Shell to retreat over the scrapping of its Brent Spar oil platform and its activities in Nigeria. Nike has had to revamp its whole supply chain after being accused of running sweatshops.

Even mighty Coca-Cola has been humbled. Told of a contamination incident in Belgium, its then-boss, Doug Ivester, is said to have dismissed it with the comment: "Where the fuck is Belgium?" A few months later, after a mishandled public-relations exercise that cost Coke sales across Europe, he was fired. "It is absurd to say that brands can be too powerful," concludes Interbrand's Ms Clifton. "Brands are the ultimate accountable institution. If people fall out of love with your brand, you go out of business."

This ultimately makes brands highly effective tools through which to bring about change. Rafael Gomez, professor of marketing at the London School of Economics, points out that companies like Nike have been forced to invest heavily in improving their manufacturing standards in order to protect their brands. World Bank studies show that brands have been a boon for developing economies, because it is the branded multinationals that pay the best wages and have the best working conditions. Those countries that are more open to trade and foreign investment, such as the Asian tigers, have shown faster increases in living standards than relatively closed countries such as much of Africa.

Brands of the future will have to stand not only for product quality and a desirable image. They will also have to signal something wholesome about the company behind the brand. "The next big thing in brands is social responsibility," says Mr. Olins, "It will be clever to say there is nothing different about our product or price, but we behave well." Far from being evil, brands are becoming an effective weapon for holding even the largest global corporations to account. If we do not use them for that purpose, as Mr. Olis puts it, "we are lazy and indifferent and we deserve what we get."

Fittingly, brands will then have come full circle. The founders of some of the world's oldest—Hershey, Disney, Cadbury and Boots, for example—devoted their lives and company profits to social improvements, to building spacious towns, better schools and bigger hospitals. The difference in the future will be that it will be consumers, not philanthropists, who will dictate the social agenda.

Imagine a world without brands. It existed once, and still exists, more or less, in the world's poorest places. No raucous advertising, no ugly billboards, no McDonald's. Yet, given a chance and a bit of money, people flee this Eden. They seek out Budweiser instead of their local tipple, ditch nameless shirts for Gap, prefer Marlboros to home-grown smokes. What should one conclude? That people are pawns in the hands of giant companies with huge advertising budgets and global reach? Or that brands bring something that people think is better than what they had before?

The pawn theory is argued, forcefully if not always coherently, by Naomi Klein, author of "No Logo", a book that has become a bible of the anti-globalization moment. Her thesis is that brands have come to represent "a fascist state where we all salute the logo and have little opportunity for criticism because our newspapers, television stations, Internet servers, streets and retail spaces are all controlled by multinational corporate interests." The ubiquity and power of brand advertising curtails choice, she claims; produced cheaply in third-world sweatshops, branded goods displace local alternatives and force a grey cultural homogeneity on the world. Brands have thus become stalking horses for international capitalism. Outside the United States, they are now symbols of America's corporate power, since most of the world's best-known brands are American. Around them accrete all the worries about environmental damage, human-rights abuses and sweated labour that anti-globalists like to put on their placards. No wonder brands seem bad.

Product Power or People Power

Yet this is a wholly misleading account of the nature of brands. They began as a form not of exploitation, but of consumer protection. In pre-industrial days, people knew exactly what went into their meat pies and which butchers were trustworthy; once they moved to cities, they no longer did. A brand provided a guarantee of reliability and quality. Its owner had a powerful incentive to ensure that each pie was as good as the previous one, because that would persuade people to come back for more.

Just as distance created a need for brands in the 19th century, so in the age of globalisation and the Internet it reinforces their value. A book-buyer might not entrust a company based in Seattle with his credit-card number had experience not taught him to trust the Amazon brand; an American might not accept a bottle of French water were it not for the name of Evian. Because consumer trust is the basis of all brand values, companies that own the brands have an immense incentive to work to retain that trust.

Indeed, the dependence of successful brands on trust and consistent quality suggests that consumers need more of them. In poor countries, the arrival of foreign brands points to an increase in competition from which consumers gain. Anybody in Britain old enough to remember the hideous Wimpy, a travesty of a hamburger, must recall the arrival of McDonald's with gratitude. Public services live in a No Logo world: attempts at government branding arouse derision. That is because brands have value only where consumers have choice, which rarely exists in public services. The absence of brands in the public sector reflects a world like that of the old Soviet Union, in which consumer choice has little role.

Brands are the tools with which companies seek to build and retain customer loyalty. Because that often requires expensive advertising and good marketing, a strong brand can raise both prices and barriers to entry. But not to insuperable levels: brands fade as tastes change (Nescafe has fallen, while Starbucks has risen); the vagaries of fashion can rebuild a brand that once seemed moribund (think of cars like the Mini or Beetle); and quality of service still counts (hence the rise of Amazon). Many brands have been around for more than a century, but the past two decades have seen many more displaced by new global names, such as Microsoft and Nokia.

Now a change is taking place in the role of brands. Increasingly, customers pay more for a brand because it seems to represent a way of life or a set of ideas. Companies exploit people's emotional needs as well as their desires to consume. Hence Nike's "just-do-it" attempt to persuade runners that it is selling personal achievement, or Coca-Cola's relentless effort to associate its fizzy drink with carefree fun. Companies deliberately concoct a story around their service or product, trying to turn a run-of-the-mill purchase (think of Haagen-Dazs ice cream) into something more thrilling.

This peddling of superior lifestyles is something that irritates many consumers. They disapprove of the vapid notion that spending more on a soft drink or ice cream can bring happiness or social cachet. Fair enough: and yet people in every age and culture have always hunted for ways to acquire social cachet. For medieval European grandees, it was the details of dress, and sumptuary laws sought to stamp out imitations by the lower orders; now the poorest African country has its clothing markets where second-hand designer labels command a premium over pre-worn No Logo.

The flip side of the power and importance of a brand is its growing vulnerability. Because it is so valuable to a company, a brand must be cosseted, sustained and protected. A failed advertising campaign, a drop-off in quality or a hint of scandal can all quickly send customers fleeing. Indeed, protesters, including Ms. Klein's anti-globalisation supporters, can use the power of the brand against companies by drumming up evidence of workers ill-treated or rivers polluted. Thanks, ironically enough, to globalisation, they can do this all round the world. The more companies promote the value of their brands, the more they will need to seem ethically robust and environmentally pure. Whether protesters will actually succeed in advancing the interests of those they claim to champion is another question. The fact remains that brands give them far more power over companies than they would otherwise have. Companies may grumble about that, but it is hard to see why the enemies of brand "fascism" are complaining.

Topics for Reading and Writing

1. Read these two pieces in conjunction with Klein's. How does *The Economist* respond directly to Klein's arguments? Are its counterpoints convincing? What are the assumptions underlying Klein's piece, and what assumptions underlie these pieces?

2. How does this article make its rhetorical case? Where does it resemble a news article and where does it resemble an opinion piece? What methods do the writers use to carry their argument—word choice, point of view, choice of evidence?

3. "The founders of some of the world's oldest [brands] . . . devoted their lives and company profits to social improvements, to building spacious towns, better schools and bigger hospitals." Do you agree with this? Does this mean that corporations in general have had this effect on society?

Academic researchers use evidence to make arguments, just like all other writers do. However, academic discourse—especially that kind of writing that is for specialists and aimed at an audience of specialists—is quite different from editorial, feature, or student writing. In this article (which appeared in the American Journal of Public Health, *an academic journal with a readership composed primarily of Ph.D.s, health care administrators, government officials, and specialists in public health),* **Elizabeth Smith** *and* **Ruth Malone** *provide a short history of Philip Morris's (now Altria) advertising of tobacco products to gay men. Using previously secret internal company documents, Malone and Smith show that Philip Morris sought to profit from the lucrative gay market but at the same time feared that public recognition of these efforts would bring attacks from antitobacco activists, who would accuse the company of targeting gays with their dangerous product. The company also sought to minimize its association with the gay community, fearing a backlash from conservatives.*

Both Elizabeth A. Smith, Ph.D., and Ruth E. Malone, Ph.D., teach in the school of nursing at the University of California, San Francisco. Dr. Malone also teaches in the Center for Tobacco Control Research and Education at the same university.

Elizabeth A. Smith and Ruth E. Malone
The Outing of Philip Morris: Advertising Tobacco to Gay Men

Numerous studies suggest that gay men have higher smoking prevalence rates than the population as a whole.[1-3] Why gay men are likelier to smoke has not been established. Hypotheses include the stresses of coming out and identity formation, depression, antigay victimization, and a desire to fit into a subculture traditionally formed around gay bars, where both drinking and smoking are the norm.[4] Little previous work has explored tobacco industry influences on the gay community.

Just as it has approached other minorities,[5-7] the tobacco industry has advertised in gay media,[8] sponsored gay community events,[9] and contributed to gay and AIDS organizations.[10,11] The normalizing effects of the tobacco industry's presence in the community may contribute to a higher smoking prevalence[12] and predispose the community to view the industry positively, support industry policy positions, and discourage tobacco control measures.[13] Advertising may have particular salience in the gay community, where it represents social validation.[14]

This study used internal tobacco industry documents and secondary historical media sources to explore the origin and reception of the first tobacco advertising in the gay press. As a "first," the campaign and events surrounding it generated discussion at the company and in the press. This historical analysis shows how the tobacco industry's approach to the gay community differs from its approach to racial minorities and suggests that tobacco control advocates have an opportunity to intervene before the relationship between the industry and the gay community becomes fully developed.

Methods

Data were collected from the Philip Morris Incorporated document Web site (http://www.pmdocs.com/), which provides access to millions of company documents released as a result of the multistate attorneys general settlements and other cases. Between June 1, 2001, and October 1, 2001, we searched the Philip Morris Web site for documents pertaining to the industry's relationship with the gay community. We used a variety of search terms, including *gay, homosexual, queer,* and names of gay publications. We extended the searches by using names of individuals, dates, and other indexing information, in a "snow-ball" search strategy. Further information on document collection and searching strategies was provided previously.[15] In addition, major national newspapers and the lesbian and gay press were reviewed for the relevant period. This case study is based on review of 70 industry documents, Lexis/Nexis searches of more than 50 major newspapers, and examination of 13 lesbian and gay periodicals.

Advertising and the Gay Press

The gay press in the United States emerged in the 1950s, but it was not until the 1990s that national-circulation gay men's periodicals that appealed to mainstream advertisers were established.[16–18] One of these was *Genre*, established in 1991, which was less political and more focused on fashion and "lifestyle" than the previous generation of gay periodicals.[19] At the same time, gay marketing firms, using dubious data,[20] were "pitching" the community to advertisers by claiming that gay households had an average income up to two thirds higher than the national average.[21,22] Gay men also were reputed to have high levels of brand loyalty to companies that advertised directly to them.[23] "This is a dream market," one gay marketer said.[22]

Philip Morris Enters the Gay Market

The combination of gay self-promotion, the availability of appropriate periodicals, the increasing public awareness and acceptance of the gay community, and the desire for larger markets tempted Philip Morris to enter the market. By early 1992, Leo Burnett, Philip Morris's advertising agency, was urging the company to include the gay press in a larger campaign promoting a Benson & Hedges brand extension.[24] (A brand extension is a variation, such as low tar, king size, or soft pack, of an established brand.) A Leo Burnett media supervisor told Philip Morris that the gay community was "an area of opportunity for the brand." As "one of the first (if not the first) tobacco advertiser[s] ," Philip Morris could "'own the market' and achieve exclusivity."[24] Leo Burnett also suggested being "cautious . . . since this is . . . a brand launch" (i.e., a new product), and "the number of viable gay [publications] is limited." On Leo Burnett's recommendation, Philip Morris bought space in the October/November 1992 and December/January 1993 issues of *Genre*.[25]

Philip Morris did not expect the *Genre* advertisements to attract attention. The advertisements had no gay-specific content, and the company did not publicize them, aiming instead for a business-oriented story about how the advertising campaign would revitalize the Benson & Hedges brand. Philip Morris gave the story exclusively to Stuart Elliott, a business reporter for the *New York Times*.[26] Although Elliott was openly gay and was interested in gay marketing efforts,[21] the Philip Morris brand manager's notes[27] and Elliott's article[28] suggest that Elliott was willing to frame the story as an introduction of the brand to the business community, with no gay angle. However, the exclusive arrangement, designed to help Philip Morris control the press coverage, had the opposite effect.

The Outing of Philip Morris

Don Tuthill, the publisher of *Genre*, "outed" Philip Morris. Tuthill was thrilled to land the Philip Morris account. To publicize his accomplishment, he contacted Joanne Lipman, the advertising columnist at the *Wall Street Journal.* When Lipman asked Philip Morris to comment on its *Genre* advertising, company spokespeople declined because of the exclusive arrangement with the *Times.* "Needless to say," Philip Morris documents report, "she [Lipman] was not happy." Lipman's resulting story in the *Wall Street Journal,* headlined "Philip Morris to Push Brand in Gay Media,"[29] was, according to Philip Morris "nasty headlined with a damaging tone that could have . . . reposition[ed] the brand."[26]

Lipman's story was picked up widely in the national media. Versions appeared in at least 7 big-city daily papers and on national and local television and radio news across the country.[30-49] This story had several elements that probably displeased Philip Morris. First, some reporters implicitly contrasted the masculine Marlboro Man with presumably effeminate gay men. The *Wall Street Journal* characterized the advertisements as "unprecedented for . . . Philip Morris, the very company behind the macho Marlboro Man."[29] NBC-TV commented that "when Philip Morris created a macho Marlboro Man, the gay man was probably not what [it] had in mind, but he is now."[42] The *New York Post*'s lead was even more jocular. "Don't look now, Marlboro Man—but you've got a brand-new gay partner."[34] *All Things Considered* treated this aspect seriously, discussing the Marlboro Man's popularity among gay men.[40]

Second, some reports suggested that the new product would be a "gay cigarette." Fox News in New York asked, "Well, just when you thought you had heard it all, how about a cigarette manufactured specifically for gays?"[44] The *New York Post*'s headline screamed, "New cigs aimed at gay smokers."[34] Most of the stories were more nuanced, claiming that the cigarette would be "targeted" to the gay community.[36,39-42,44] Some reports mentioned targeting only in Philip Morris's denial—for example, "Philip Morris denies that it is targeting any specific consumer group."[31,47,48,50]

Probably most troubling from Philip Morris's point of view, many reports brought up R.J. Reynolds' Uptown fiasco.[31,33,34,44,49] In 1989, when R.J. Reynolds' plans to market a new, high-nicotine brand called Uptown to African Americans were revealed, African American community health activists, including US Department of Health and Human Services Secretary Louis Sullivan, reacted with outrage. R.J. Reynolds dropped the brand.[51] Philip Morris could hardly have been happy to have this story rehashed in connection with its product launch.

The accusation of targeting was not entirely accurate. The impetus for advertising in *Genre* came from the advertising agency.[24,25] The agency, in turn, had been actively wooed by *Genre*.[30,52] Philip Morris had not been especially eager. Senior Vice President of Marketing David Dangoor said that there were "long discussions up the line" about the decision. Despite these reservations, Philip Morris ultimately decided that taking this "measured risk" was "the right thing to do."[53] Philip Morris apparently did no market research in the gay community before placing these advertisements, although it recognized some of the market's distinctive qualities. In 1993 the Benson & Hedges budget was slashed, but advertisements remained in *Out* and *Genre* because the space had already been purchased and was "unsuitable for other brand usage."[54]

Philip Morris took pains to emphasize that it was *not* targeting gays. The notes prepared for Michael A. Miles, chairman and chief executive officer of Philip Morris Companies Inc to use at the 1993 shareholders' meeting suggested that he respond to questions with, "We did not develop separate advertising, nor did we attempt to position the brand specifically for gays."[59] Some gay men found this to be an effective defense. Elliott, the *Times* reporter, remarked, "It's not as though you did a special ad with two hunky guys who [had] just has sex with cigarettes in their mouths."[56]

Little evidence exists of how the story impressed the public. No visible response resembling the anti-Uptown campaigns came from either the gay community or tobacco control advocates. We could locate no newspaper articles or company documents that suggest that the exposure damaged the reputations or market share of the brand or company.

Gay Reaction

Gay leaders had a variety of reactions to the advertisements. Jerry Williams, the associate publisher of the weekly *Gay Chicago*, felt that the advertisements meant that "barriers are beginning to fall. It says 'we respect you as consumers and we want your business.'" He said he would "gladly" accept tobacco advertisements.[37] *Genre's* Tuthill was ecstatic. "I'm just celebrating being part of the mix," he said. "We're not being excluded any longer."[30] Tuthill strongly objected to the angle of the *Wall Street Journal's* story, which he said described "the tobacco industry . . . turning its marketing muscle on another minority." The real story, he asserted, was one of "inclusion" and of "how a conservative American company fights discrimination against homosexuals by putting its money where its mouth is."[57]

Others were more ambivalent. *The Advocate's* editor, Jeff Yarbrough, remarked that it was difficult for gay publications to turn down advertisements because they were still "in a beggar's position, rather than a chooser's position."[40] The publisher of Chicago's *Outlines* newsmagazine said that she "might accept a cigarette ad, but balance it with equal space for a public-service message on cancer risks."[37] Another Chicago publisher of a gay periodical said that accepting cigarette advertisements "could damage [his] publication's image." He added, "To me, cigarettes kill."[37] Hal Offen, a spokesman from the Coalition of Lavender Americans on Smoking and Health—possibly the only gay tobacco control group then in existence—said, "This is community already ravaged by addiction. We don't need the Marlboro Man to help pull the trigger."[58,59] A Lambda Legal Defense and Education Fund spokeswoman said, "I don't see how this can be construed as any kind of victory for gay rights."[30]

Philip Morris's internal account of the gay reaction appears flattering to the company but is not entirely convincing. A media relations brief recounted that Philip Morris had "fielded a variety of calls viewed from the gay community . . . . All callers viewed [Philip Morris' advertising] as a very positive

TABLE 1	Phillip Morris's Damage Control Strategies: African American Community and Gay Community	
Strategy	**African American Community**	**Gay Comunity**
Deny targeting specific communities	"Phillip Morris does NOT target specific groups in society."[63]	"We market all of our products to adult smokers, and we don't discriminate. Adult smokers includes both genders, all races and sexual preferences."[32]
Attack accusers	"Underlying the charge that . . . minorities make easy targets for marketing is the chauvinistic belief that they are incapable of making informed personal decisions for themselves."[64]	"People who have a problem with" Philip Morris's advertising in *Genre* "should really question their own levels of bigotry."[65]
Co-opt individuals or organizations	"Dr. Benjamin Hooks, former executive director of the National Association for the Advancement of Colored People, said 'critics of tobacco marketing efforts believe women and blacks are not capable of making their own free choice.'"[64]	GLAAD "has been very effective in facilitating [the] transition" of the [*Genre*] story toward "inclusion."[66]
Emphasize ties to the community	"The question shouldn't be 'why is PM advertising in the minority community?' but rather, 'where are the other major companies?' . . . PM cares enough to compete for minority business."[63]	
Distance the company from the community		"We have no plans to advertise Benson & Hedges Special Kings— or any of our other cigarette brands—in any other supposedly homosexual publications."[67]

Note. PM = Philip Morris. GLAAD = Gay and Lesbian Alliance Against Defamation.

step."[60] The appreciative feedback is plausible, given the response of Tuthill and Williams and the eagerness of some segments of the gay community for commercial recognition. The company also claimed that it "saw a lot of good stories come out of the gay media praising Philip Morris."[26] This claim is not confirmed by a review of the gay press. Of 13 gay papers from across the country, only 4 had any coverage of the incident. The *San Francisco Bay Times* and the *San Francisco*

Sentinel both quoted Offen. The *San Francisco Bay Times* headlined its story "Queers to Philip Morris: Drop Dead."[58,59] Two papers in Chicago also briefly covered the story.[61,62] The *Windy City Times* was the most industry-favorable, quoting Philip Morris's denial that it was "targeting" gays and mentioning market research about Benson & Hedges' popularity among gay men.[66] None of these stories praised Philip Morris.

Damage Control

Philip Morris's response to the media included 3 well-established techniques for coping with protests from racial minorities: deny, attack, and co-opt. In contrast to the company's usual emphasis on its close relationship with the community in question, however, Philip Morris chose to distance itself from the gay community (Table 1). As Philip Morris outlined them a few years later, the first key points to make "re: targeting minorit[ie]s" are that "Philip Morris does NOT target specific groups in society" (deny) and that "Anyone who believes that members of minority groups are more influenced by ads than [other] people is really saying that [they] are not as capable of making rational informed choices as other adults" (attack).[63] Philip Morris made similar remarks to the media in regard to the *Genre* advertisements. The industry has frequently paid apparently independent spokespeople and front groups to represent it (co-opt), and Philip Morris made donations[68] and referred reporters who called about the *Genre* story to the Gay and Lesbian Alliance Against Defamation (GLAAD).[69]

Philip Morris had additional responses to minority group protests in its arsenal; these went unused. For example, the company liked to remind people that it had long supported the African American community by advertising in that community's publications, using African American models, hiring and promoting African Americans, and supporting institutions such as the United Negro College Fund and others "Working for [civil] rights and equal opportunity because it is the right thing to do, not because of any ulterior motives."[63] Philip Morris could not have invoked any such long-standing relationship with or support for the gay community because little such support existed. In 1991, Philip Morris agreed to donate $1 200 000 To AIDS groups.[70–72] The company could have used this donation as evidence of its support of the gay community. It also could have mentioned its financial contributions to GLAAD.[68]

Instead, Philip Morris spokeswoman Karen Daragan emphasized that the *Genre* advertisements were an insignificant part of the larger Benson & Hedges marketing plan, saying that the advertisements would appear in "nearly 60 other magazines" besides *Genre*.[30] The "nearly 60" figure was designed to underscore Daragan's assertion that Philip Morris marketed to all adults. Daragan also specifically mentioned *Playboy* and *Penthouse* as examples,[30] emphasizing the "heterosexuality" of the cigarette and the advertisements.

Philips Morris was especially eager to avoid any connections to gay sexuality, declining to advertise in *The Advocate* because that publication contained "sexually explicit ads."[25] At the shareholder meeting, Miles was coached to assure his audience that *Genre* "does not carry personal ads or ads for explicitly sexual products."[55] One gay publisher characterized this policy as "homophobia. They don't care about phone-sex ads in *Playboy*."[37] The company disavowed any knowledge of the gay community, telling 1 shareholder that it had "no marketing data specific to the 'homosexual market'—if such a market even exists."[73]

Denial, attack, and co-option are strategies the company used specifically to respond to accusations of target marketing. Another strategy the company used in a variety of contexts to control the flow of information was concealment. In this case, the company refused to provide a picture of the new brand or its advertisng.[64] Thus, the story became one about "gay cigarettes," not Benson & Hedges.

Philip Morris's management was pleased with the company's recovery from the unwanted press coverage. Five days after the *Wall Street Journal* story, spokeswoman Daragan remarked that "the news has moved on to the much broader issue of 'inclusion' and does not mention the new cigarette by name."[69] And by early September, Senior Vice President of Marketing Dangoor concluded that the "Corporate Affairs Department did an excellent job with 'damage control.'" The initial *Wall Street Journal* article, Dangoor said, was "very unfortunate and 'unfair'"—but again, the brand was not strongly associated with the story, and "the reporting got fairer with time."[53]

Discussion

One lesson from the *Genre* incident is that tobacco control activists should disrupt the industry's tactic of concealment. Philip Morris was pleased that no pictures of the new product or its advertising reached the public and that the association between the "gay targeting" story and the new cigarette was lost. Keeping the focus on Benson & Hedges, ideally in such a way as to threaten its image or sales, might have been effective. A new product is likely the most vulnerable to any kind of negative publicity, as the Uptown episode demonstrated; activists should monitor business and advertising media closely to anticipate such introductions.

The *Genre* story also suggests that timing is a key aspect of combating concealment. Tuthill's press release came out a month before the advertisements were in print, so health advocates had time to respond. Advocates could have spent that month developing their own campaign designed for release when the advertisements appeared.

Advocates should be ready to capitalize on any attention to the tobacco industry. In this instance, Philip Morris was getting press it did not initiate with an angle that was unexpected, and an opportunity arose to build on the story. On August 15, 1992, a day after the *Genre* story broke, Doctors Ought to Care, a tobacco control advocacy group of physicians and medical students, released a batch of Philip Morris documents that focused on the company's donations to minority organizations,[74] but no link was made to the previous day's story. Doctors Ought to Care or other tobacco control activists could have made that link and potentially extended the life of both stories, as well as facilitating alliances among marginalized groups. The desire for acceptance that makes the gay community vulnerable to tobacco advertising also makes it eager to be regarded as a legitimate minority, and this opportunity could have been used to build tobacco control alliances.

The *Genre* episode also illustrates the complexity of the industry's relationships with marginalized groups. With its advertisements in *Genre*, Philip Morris was entering a lucrative new market and establishing new alliances with little investment. By not developing any gay-specific products or campaigns, Philip Morris protected itself both financially and socially. The company's only expense was for the advertisement itself, and when it was outed, the generic nature of the advertisement made the distancing strategy plausible. At the same time, by establishing itself in the vanguard of companies willing to market to gays, Philips Morris stood to gain valuable brand loyalty.

However, *Genre* was not simply waiting for Philip Morris. *The Advocate*'s Yarbrough pointed out that the gay media were beggars, not choosers, but even beggars act on their own behalf. Simply castigating Philip Morris for "targeting" ignores the publisher's decision to actively seek tobacco advertising. Tuthill did not see himself as a victim of a predatory industry; rather, he believed that he had elevated the status of the gay community by gaining support from a major corporation. Nor was Tuthill unique. As gay publications such as *Genre* became mainstream, they were more likely to get tobacco advertising and to become dependent on the revenue once they had it, and they were less likely to develop a critique of any advertiser, including the tobacco industry.[18] It was no accident that Philip Morris chose this moment to enter the gay market—and no coincidence that it was welcomed.

Thus, the relationship between Philip Morris and Tuthill was a negotiation, though not one between equals. Tuthill was eager for the company's money, but Philip Morris was reluctant to be identified with gay men. And *Genre* was struggling for social acceptance and financial success, whereas the company was hungry for new markets.

This complex of factors means that public health would be well served by the development of an active gay and lesbian tobacco control movement. Objections from outsiders could be dismissed as attempts to keep gay periodicals and the gay community marginal. Health advocates would be unpersuasive if they addressed Tuthill and his ilk as mere victims, rather than acknowledging their agency. Thus, the most effective efforts would come from within the gay community, from those who share the same status and face the same choices as those accepting or courting industry support.

The time to formulate this response is now, while the relationship between the industry and the gay community is still relative young. The contrast with the African American community makes the developmental stage of this relationship clear. Philip Morris, now The Altria group,[75] was, and apparently still is, reluctant to identify or even be associated with the gay community. For instance, it does not publicize its contributions to gay (as opposed to AIDS) organizations such as GLAAD on its Web site (http://www.altria.com). The tobacco industry advertises to the gay community, but unlike other mainstream advertisers, it has yet to develop overtly gay-specific campaigns. The cigarette advertisements in gay magazines do not features gay couples or symbols. Furthermore, these advertisements do not appear to be the primary support of gay periodicals. Few gay organizations are as publicly linked to the industry as GLAAD. These factors suggest that industry links to the gay community are still relatively weak, so advocates could intercede before community dependence on tobacco money becomes widespread and while public skepticism about the industry is still high.

Gay and lesbian tobacco control activists have already developed guidelines to help community organizations make the choice not to accept tobacco money.[76,77] These efforts should be nurtured by funding agencies, which could make community-level interventions a priority. Such programs should encourage activists to monitor and challenge tobacco industry support for gay media and organizations. These programs also should forge connections with tobacco control activism in other communities, and with other health activism in the gay community, such as that surrounding AIDS. The *Genre* story represents an opportunity lost, but it provides useful lessons for tobacco control in the gay community and other marginalized communities just beginning to come the attention of the tobacco industry.

References

1. Skinner WF. The prevalence and demographic predictors of illicit and licit drug use among lesbians and gay men. *Am J Public Health*. 1994; 84: 1307–1310.
2. Ryan H, Wortley PM, Easton A, Pederson L, Greenwood G. Smoking among lesbians gays, and bisexuals: a review of the literature. *Am J Prev Med*. 2001; 21: 142–149.
3. Stall RD, Greenwood GL, Acree M, Paul J, Coates TJ. Cigarette smoking among gay and bisexual men. *Am J Public Health*. 1990; 89: 1875–1878.
4. Harris CE. Out in life; still up in smoke? *J Gay Lesbian Med Assoc*. 1998; 2: 91–92.
5. Pollay RW, Lee JS, Carter-Whitney D. Separate, but not equal: racial segmentation in cigarette advertising. *J Advertising*. 1992; 21: 45–58.
6. Cummings K, Giovino G, Mendicino A. Cigarette advertising and black-white differences in brand preference. *Public Health Rep*. 1987; 102: 698–701.
7. Yerger VB, Malone RE. African American leadership groups: smoking with the enemy. *Tob Control*. 2002; 11: 336–45.
8. Geobel K. Lesbians and gays face tobacco targeting. *Tob Control*. 1994; 3: 65–67.
9. Conkin D. Tobacco $$ for the gay community: a Lucky Strike–or a cancer? *Bay Area Reporter*. December 5, 1996: 18–19.
10. Offen N. Demonstrators booted from GLAAD soiree. *Bay Area Reporter*. June 14, 2001: 2.
11. Engardio JP. Outing the Marlboro Man. *San Francisco Weekly*. February 16–22, 2000: 16.
12. Tye JB, Warner KE, Glantz SA. Tobacco advertising and consumption: evidence of a causal relationship. *J Public Health Policy*. 1987; 8: 492–508.
13. *Tobacco Use Among US Racial/Ethnic Minority Groups–African Americans, American Indians and Alaska Natives, Asian Americans and Pacific Islanders,*

and Hispanics: A Report of the Surgeon General. Atlanta, Ga: National Center for Chronic Disease Prevention and Health Promotion, Office on Smoking and Health; 1998. Report S/N 017–001–00527–4.

14. Penaloza L. We're here, we're queer and we're going shopping! A critical perspective on the accommodation of gays and lesbians in the US marketplace. *J Homosex.* 1996; 31: 9–41.

15. Malone RE, Balbach ED. Tobacco industry documents: treasure trove or quagmire? *Tob Control.* 2000; 9: 334–338.

16. Harris D. Out of the closet, and into never-never land. *Harpers.* December 1995: 52–53.

17. Streitmatter R. *Unspeakable: The Rise of the Gay and Lesbian Press in America.* Boston, Mass: Faber & Faber; 1995.

18. Sender K. Gay readers, consumers, and a dominant gay habitus: 25 years of *The Advocate* magazine. *J Commun.* 2001; 51: 73–99.

19. Enrico D. Bucking trends, gay lifestyle magazine debuts. *New York Newsday.* March 21, 1991: 49.

20. Fejes F, Lennon R. Defining the lesbian/gay community? Market research and the lesbian/gay press. *J Homosex.* 2000; 39: 25–43.

21. Elliott S. Advertisers bypass gay market. *USA Today.* July 17, 1990: B1.

22. Rigdon JE. Overcoming a deep-rooted reluctance, more firms advertise to gay community. *Wall Street Journal.* July 18, 1992: B1.

23. San Francisco Examiner. Survey shows gays have brand loyalty. *Tampa Tribune.* April 28, 1997: 22.

24. Makuch M. Gay-oriented publications. 1992.03.05. Bates No. 2041794319/4320. Available at: http://www.pmdocs.com. Accessed July 16, 2001.

25. Upchurch T. Letter. 1992.06.25. Bates No. 2041794318/4322. Available at: http://www.pmdocs.com. Accessed July 11, 2001.

26. [Speech on media affairs]. 1992.09.00. Bates No. 2025893465/3471. Available at: http://www. pmdocs.com Accessed September 12, 2001.

27. Han V. David Dangoor interview with NYT. 1992.08.12 Bates No. 2025887538/ 7540. Available at: http://www.pmdocs.com. Accessed September 12, 2001.

28. Elliott S. Benson & Hedges shrinks in a bid to regain growth. *New York Times.* August 27, 1992: D18.

29. Lipman J. Philip Morris to push brand in gay media. 1992.08.13. Bates No. 2073723375/3376. Available at: http://www.pmdocs.com. Accessed September 13, 2001.

30. Associated Press. Philip Morris to advertise in magazine for gay men. 1992.08.13 Bates No. 2023439131. Available at: http://www.pmdocs.com. Accessed September 13, 2001.

31. Associated Press. Philip Morris set ads in gay mag. 1992.08.14. *Philadelphia Daily News.* Bates No. 2023439126. Available at: http://www.pmdocs.com. Accessed September 25, 2001.

32. Associated Press. Cigarette giant plans its first campaign in gay magazine. 1992.08.14. *Detroit News.* Bates No. 2023439127. Available at: http://www.pmdocs.com. Accessed September 13, 2001.

33. Associated Press. Cigarette firm targets gay magazine for ads. 1992.08.14. *San Francisco Examiner.* Bates No. 2023439128. Available at: http://www. pmdocs.com. Accessed September 13, 2001.

34. Hoffman B. New cigs aimed at gay smokers. 1992.08.14. Bates No. 2023439130. Available at: http://www.pmdocs.com. Accessed September 17, 2001.

35. McIntyre B. Tobacco company targets gay men. *London Times.* August 15, 1992: 8.

36. Scott J. Targeting gay groups a touchy issue. 1992.08.18. Bates No. 2023439139. Available at: http://www.pmdocs.com. Accessed September 13, 2001.

37. Sall J. Gay magazine gains cigarette ad—and debate. *Chicago Sun-Times.* August 18, 1992: 43.

38. Video Monitoring Services of America. *Day Break* 1992.08.13. Bates No. 2023439117. Available at: http://www.pmdocs.com. Accessed September 14, 2001.

39. Video Monitoring Services of America. *The News at Noon.* 1992.08.13. Bates No. 2023439119. Available at: http://www.pmdocs.com. Accessed September 14, 2001.

40. Video Monitoring Services of America. *All Things Considered.* 1992.08.13. Bates No. 2023439120/9121. Available at: http://www.pmdocs.com. Accessed September 14, 2001.

41. Video Monitoring Services of America. WINS AM radio program [transcript]: 1992.08.13. Bates No. 2023439118. Available at: http://www.pmdocs.com. Accesssed September 20, 2001.

42. Video Monitoring Services of America. *News at Sunrise.* 1992.08.14. Bates No. 2023439136. Available at: http://www.pmdocs.com. Accessed July 20, 2001.

43. Video Monitoring Services of America. Monitoring report Philip Morris Special Kings schedule of broadcast activity. 1992.08.14. Bates No. 2023439122/9123. Available at: http://www.pmdocs.com. Accessed September 20, 2001.

44. Video Monitoring Services of America. *Good Day New York.* 1992.08.17. Bates No. 2023439140/9141, Available at: http://www.pmdocs.com. Accessed July 20, 2001.

45. Radio TV Reports. *Today* (National News) broadcast excerpt. 1992.08.14. Bates No. 2023439137/9138. Available at: http://www.pmdocs.com. Accessed July 20, 2001.

46. *Business Tonight* broadcast excerpt. 1992.08.14. Bates No. 2023439134/9135. Available at: http:// www.pmdocs.com. Accessed July 20, 2001.

47. Radio TV Reports. Headline news broadcast excerpt. 1992.08.14. Bates No. 2023439133. Available at: http://www.pmdocs.com. Accessed September 20, 2001.

48. Rosato D. Cigarette ads. 1992.08.14. Bates No. 2023439129. Available at: http://www.pmdocs.com. Accessed September 13, 2001.

49. Cigarette firm plans ads in gay magazine. 1992.08.14. Bates No. 2023439124. Available at: http://www.pmdocs.com. Accessed September 24, 2001.

50. *Washington Post* coverage of *Genre* advertising [memo]. 1992.08.14. Bates No. 2023439125. Available at: http://www.pmdocs.com. Accessed September 14, 2001.
51. Smith NC. Uptown, Dakota, and PowerMaster. In: Donaldson T. Gini A, eds. *Case Studies in Business Ethics.* Upper Saddle River, NJ: Prentice Hall: 1996: 53–58.
52. Levin G. Mainstream's domino effect: liquor, fragrance, clothing advertisers ease into gay magazines. *Advertising Age.* January 18, 1993: 30.
53. Dangoor DER. Benson and Hedges Special Kings—*Genre* media coverage. 1992.09.02. Bates No. 2023439109. Available at: http://www.pmdocs.com. Accessed September 17, 2001.
54. Schneider R. B&H Kings revised media plan. 1993.06.04. Bates No. 2044361518/1519. Available at: http://www.pmdocs.com. Accessed September 14, 2001.
55. Annual meeting questions and answers for Michael A. Miles PM USA. 1993.01.00. Bates No. 2022989437/9448. Available at: http://www.pmdocs.com. Accessed September 14, 2001.
56. Peterson W. NY Times interview. 1992.08.21. Bates No. 2025887508/7509. Available at: http:// www.pmdocs.com. Accessed September 12, 2001.
57. Tuthill D. Letter from Don Tuthill to Joann Lipman. 1992.08.17. Bates No. 2025887474/7475. Available at: http://www.pmdocs.com. Accessed September 13, 2001.
58. Philip Morris targeting cigarettes to gays. *San Francisco Sentinel.* August 20, 1992: 9.
59. Avicolli Mecca T. Queers to Philip Morris: drop dead. *San Francisco Bay Times.* August 27, 1992: 10.
60. Media relations/employee communications. 1992.08.00. Bates No. 2047319345/9346. Available at: http://www.pmdocs.com. Accessed September 13, 2001.
61. Baim T. Ad news. *Outlines.* September 1992: 35.
62 Philip Morris places ad in gay magazine. *Windy City Times.* August 27, 1992: 10.
63. Asbury Park Press. 1995.05.00. Bates No. 2047319798/9799. Available at: http://www.pmdocs.com. Accessed September 6, 2001.
64. PM USA corporate affairs issues handbook. 1995.01.19. Bates No. 2044183393/3423. Available at: http://www.pmdocs.com. Accessed April 10, 2002.
65. PM USA media affairs (920814–920821). 1992.08.21. Bates No. 2025897821/7826. Available at: http://www.pmdocs.com. Accessed September 13, 2001.
66. Daragan K. Benson and Hedges Special Kings/*Genre* media coverage. 1992.08.19. Bates No. 2023439110. Available at: http://www.pmdocs.com. Accessed September 17, 2001.
67. Consumer response letter re: Genre advertising. 1992.08.21. Bates No. 2046522585/2586. Available at: http://www.pmdocs.com. Accessed September 14, 2001.

68. Internal documents detail aggressive tobacco industry campaign. 1993.01.00. Bates No. 2047896864/6867. Available at: http://www. pmdocs.com. Accessed November 7, 2001.

69. Daragan K. Special Kings/*Genre* coverage. 1992.08.18. Bates No. 2023439113 Available at: http://www.pmdocs.com. Accessed September 14, 2001.

70. Bartlett D. Q&As at 900000 and 910000 shareholders meetings. 1992.04.10. Bates No. 2023004427. Available at: http://www.pmdocs.com. Accessed September 27, 2001.

71. Offen N, Smith EA, Malone RE. From adversary to target market: the ACT-UP boycott of Philip Morris. *Tob Control.* In press.

72. Ramirez A. Philip Morris to increase AIDS donations. *New York Times.* May 30, 1991: D4.

73. Parrish SC. Letter to shareholder Campos re: *Genre* advertising. 1992.08.25. Bates No. 2022844169/4170. Available at: http://www.pmdocs. com. Accessed September 14, 2001.

74. Babcock CR. Philip Morris donations target minority groups. *Washington Post.* August 15, 1992: A6.

75. Smith EA, Malone RE. Altria means tobacco: Philip Morris's identity crisis. *Am J Public Health.* 2003: 553–556.

76. Drabble L. *Ethical Funding for Lesbian, Gay, Bisexual, Transgender and HIV/AIDS Community-Based Organizations: Practical Guidelines When Considering Tobacco, Alcohol, and Pharmaceutical Funding.* San Francisco, Calif: Coalition of Lavender Americans on Smoking and Health and Progressive Research and Training for Action; 2001.

77. Gay and Lesbian Medical Association. *Healthy People 2010 Companion Document for Lesbian, Gay, Bi-Sexual, and Transgender (LGBT) Health.* San Francisco, Calif: Gay and Lesbian Medical Association; 2001.

Topics for Reading and Writing

1. What are the characteristics of academic writing in this article? How do Smith and Malone aim this article at specialists in the field? What assumptions do they make about their audience, and how are these assumptions reflected in the text?

2. How might this article be different had it been written for a different audience? If Smith and Malone wanted to make the same argument on the editorial page of the *San Francisco Chronicle,* for instance, what adjustments would they make for their audience? What evidence might they leave out as being too esoteric and specialized? What evidence would they leave in for its value to persuade even a general audience?

3. Why, according to Malone and Smith did Philip Morris target the gay market? Why did *Genre* publisher Don Tuthull publicize Philip Morris's advertising in his magazine? Why was Philip Morris unhappy when this targeting was publicized?

4. An important subtext of this argument concerns the effects of the settlement between many states and the tobacco industry. What evidence was available to these researchers as a result of this settlement that would otherwise not have been open to public examination? What does this tell you about some of the difficulties of doing research?

5. What are Malone and Smith trying to accomplish with this article? What is its thesis?

In 2001, the Houston energy trader Enron collapsed due to massive financial mismanagement. Tens of thousands of employees lost their jobs and, more importantly, their retirement savings when the value of the company's stock plunged. As information about Enron reached the public, the company's questionable dealings became fodder for public debate. Was Enron responsible for the California energy crisis of 2000–2001? Did Enron's economic gaming have the eventual effect of raising the cost of energy for everyone? Why was Enron so intimately involved with Texas governor, then President, George W. Bush? What did Enron have to do with the development of the Bush-Cheney energy policy?

*Desperate to save at least some of the company's value, Enron hired a new PR team to publicize it after many of its top executives left the company in the wake of the scandal. In this paper, University of Southern California senior **Christopher Stout** examines those PR efforts.*

Christopher Stout
Enron PR: Snake Oil I.V. or Balm?

Whether you're pacing the floor of the New York Stock Exchange or riding a reindeer across ANWR, it's unlikely you've missed the bad news about the Enron Corporation. But, as *London Times* columnist Stephen Hoare wrote in "When Plain Speaking Can Help Limited Bad Publicity in a Crisis"—". . . investor relations is not just about managing bad news; it can involve drip-feeding positive stories."

Hoare then offers the advice of Stephen Benzikie, head of financial communication at Edelman PR: ". . . stories coming out of companies must focus on three things—management, strategy and performance. Stories should focus on personalities, the track record of the people running the company and how they are contributing to the business model" (Hoare). Having ceased paid advertising after their collapse last December, Enron now relies solely on such "stories" to rebuild their tarnished reputation. Showing a keen understanding of Benzikie's PR tactics, the company carefully "drip-feeds" positive tidbits through whatever outlets that will quote them, publicizing subjects and using words which work to woo back investors (and ultimate regain the trust of a nation). As Benzikie states: "Newsflow drives share prices" (Hoare).

The reputation of former CEO Ken Lay having been severely tarnished, Enron's first major public relations feat was the selection of Interim CEO Stephen Cooper. His proven track record and distance from last year's debacle combined with his winning personality make him not only a prime choice for interim CEO, but for spokesman. Thus, conspicuously absent from the media is spokesman and head of Enron public relations Mark Palmer who allows Cooper to become the new, trustworthy voice and face of Enron, (the latter especially necessary since the face of former CEO Ken Lay recently appeared on a magazine cover with his nose digitally lengthened a la Pinocchio).

Thanks to Palmer's public relations work with *The Houston Chronicle* and *USA Today*, the papers virtually advertised the choice traits of Enron's new "spokesman." As Bensikie suggested, the stories focus firstly on the person-alities then the track record of those running the company. The most glowing reports of Cooper's personality come from Enron's hometown paper, suggesting the largest PR push (and influence) was local. In the January 30, 2002, *Houston Chronicle* article, "Enron choice known for charisma; Interim CEO brings proven record," David Ivanovich quotes, "He's almost a genius, if not a genius with just an amazing sense of humor . . . . He's absolutely superb" (1). Descrip-tions of Cooper's winning personality continue: "He is very funny and knows how to get the job done . . . He'll light you up." Again, "'He's a piece of work,' said an executive at a company Cooper helped lead out of bankruptcy" (1). Ivanovich's personal assessment: "Cooper, 55, may possess the charisma and expansive personality necessary for just such an assignment" (1).

Though not always as exuberant, descriptions of Cooper's charisma, humor and people skills spread to dozens of other magazines around the country. In their February 18th article, "New Enron CEO turns company focus to future," *USA Today* journalist Noelle Knox reports that his paper is "the first to get a tour inside Enron since its collapse late last year and spend time with Stephen Cooper . . ."(Knox 3B). *USA Today* may have seen this as a journalistic coup, but it was really a custom-made page from Benzikie's playbook. While many stories rely on descriptions of Cooper from colleagues, this publicity event allowed the personal skills of the new spokesman to be directly illustrated to the public. "Once a week," Knoll reports, "he sends out a lengthy voice mail, telling employ-ees what has happened during the past week, explaining management changes and timetables." He discovers that, "When employees call or send him e-mail, he will go find them in the building to answer their questions" (3B).

Cooper's strong relational skills established, both articles turn to the second aspect of Benzike's prescription for affirmative company stories—the positive points of Cooper's track record. In the span of an article, Cooper's ethos is established not just as a "people-person," but as a practiced and competent "restructurer" of failed businesses. Ivanovich cites Cooper's twenty-five years spent "restructuring and rehabilitating troubled businesses, including Polaroid Corp,. TWA, Boston Chicken and Pegasus Gold Corp" (1). He even provides his educational credentials, (which include a masters from Penn's acclaimed Wharton School of Business).

Such statistics are supplemented by quotes which give the impression that for a pro like Cooper, Enron's restructuring is old hat. He is "a very well-respected and popular figure in the restructuring world," Rosenberg said. Again, "Cooper, a former partner with what was then known as Touche Ross & Co., 'has been in the restructuring business a long, long time'" (Ivanovich 1). *USA Today* allows Cooper to speak for himself, "I've probably been in more Chapter 11s than anybody in the United States, literally" (Knox B3).

Often, when Cooper speaks, he fulfills the other purposes suggested by Beneskie, disseminating information on the strategy, performance and manage-ment of the company. Describing such information, Cooper's words often form positive, re-assuring phrases. The CEO first openly spoke of his strategy in a January 30th conference call, which spread the specifies of his business plans to the press. As *The Houston Chronicle* reported, Cooper "plans to rebuild the com-pany around a number of international and domestic power plants and natural gas facilities, operations that will have predictable revenues and cash flow" (Fowler 1).

Phrases like "predictable revenue" dot Coopers' speech, adding a seeming security to a potentially volatile—if not already incendiary—situation. In the same article, Cooper's words again confirm the stability of the company, stating that chapter 11 "will give us the opportunity to put the company back in equilibrium with its capital structure" (1). Cooper seems well aware that the focus of his words should foster security, stating in a later speech, "it is not right or fair for anyone to be in a state of ongoing uncertainty about their future, their future compensation, and any financial safety net, so we are going to have to move on this at light speed" (Goldberg A21).

The speed of performance (the second point of concentration in Benzikie's list) seems another focus for Cooper in both his actions and words. *The Houston Chronicle* reported, "Cooper seemed to waste little time in getting to work at Enron. He had met with the Enron board of directors even before being named to the job" (Fowler 1). Cooper himself repeats his "light speed" metaphor, this time regarding company restructuring (Folwer 1). He asserts that the company will re-structure so quickly that "Enron can emerge healthy from bankruptcy within a year" (Knox B3).

While many articles quote hopeful phrases regarding the competency of Cooper and the new management team, just as many words seem to be spent in distancing the new CEO and the current employees from the previous management. One of Cooper's more powerful statements focuses the blame clearly away from the people current forming the corporation:

> The lives and reputations of 20,000 people shouldn't be trash-canned because a handful of geniuses decided to run wild," he says. "People ought to keep in perspective that we've got a lot of really tremendous people here, and for the sake of a couple bad apples, we shouldn't blowtorch the entire field. (Knox 3B)

This comment, and many like it that defend the current work force, seem necessary when battling such vehement public statements from former employees as "Enron does not need to exist, because the other CEOs and managers who betrayed us are still there" (Mack A15).

It may have been such vocal reactions that caused Cooper to even further vilify the previous management team, veering from his original strategy to simply focus on the future of the company. In a January 31st article, the first words written to describe the tactics of the then fresh CEO were that he had "no interest in finding out who's to blame for what went wrong . . . but will instead focus on revitalizing the business and preserving jobs" (Fowler 1). It was only three weeks after, through, that an article in the *Houston Chronicle* was solely devoted to Cooper' assessment of the past. The CEO revealed that, "he expects some of the millionaires who used to run the company will end up behind bars" (Kennedy 16). While this may not seem to fall into Bensikie's model, it actually suggests Cooper's "performance" will not in any way be motivated to cover up past sins.

Such a switch also reflects Cooper's and Palmer's keen understanding of their threefold target audience: Houston Enron employees (former and current), a population so large that their opinions seem to directly affect the attitudes, or at least the press, of the city; the general public; and finally, investors.

One Houston reporter found that ex-Enron employees seemed "more interested in getting their severance pay than hearing about potential legislation and company restructuring that is far down the road" (Mack A15). Thus, several articles in the *Houston Chronicle* appear to be specifically designed to foster reconciliation, keeping the 20,000-plus employees, as well as the countless Houstonites personally connected to them, updated on the likelihood of future payments.

One particularly notable article, a PR vehicle, which was eagerly adopted by the *Chronicle,* begins with the statement, "After meeting Thursday with Enron interim Chief Executive Stephen Cooper, the Rev. Jesse Jackson said he sensed movement toward an agreement to provide additional severance payments to ex-employees" (Snyder 21). This nebulous "sense" is followed by the murkier statement, "'Clearly, there is a move toward a settlement,' Jackson said. 'There will be a settlement reached in time'" (21). When and how are not discussed in the article, but Jackson's presence—and more importantly Cooper's readiness to work with him—are duly noted.

In the mind of the general public, though, Enron seems more concerned with restoring its tarnished image—an image on which Cooper noted, "when anything is bad now, it's because somebody's been Enronized or Enronated or Enroned" (Murphy A13). Thus, articles like *USA Today*'s "inside" story offer a fresh look at the once faceless giant, painting the picture of a suffering, human and hope-filled team. The story begins with a pathos-stirring description:

> HOUSTON—Inside Enron headquarters, employees walk by stacks of moving boxes as they scrounge for pens and Post-it Notes from the empty desks of their laid-off co-workers. On one desk, an employee finds a note that reads: "I'm not gone, don't take my stuff!"
>
> Forgotten behind the headlines of smoking guns, Aspen ski homes and shredded documents are almost 18,000 employees who work on Enron's power plants and pipelines. (Knox 3B)

The article then places specific names and faces on the corporation, telling individual tales of wounded souls. "'I've lost 30 pounds in the last six months from long hours and lack of sleep,' says Mark Palmer, vice president of communication." Again, "Downstairs in the company gym, Kathy Kissner, a massage therapist, says that as the company fell apart, employees would call begging for any open appointment or even just five minutes between appointments" (3B).

Rallying these wounded workers together is the sympathetic Cooper who "knows his employees have been hurt financially and emotionally. It's the hardest part of his job" (3B). Not only does the article express Cooper's compassion for his employees, but the article effectively distances Cooper (who appears here a champion for the underdog) and the current Enron staff (who now consist of fearful and tired human beings) from the old Enron who bankrupted countless homes.

This painstaking cultivation of positive public opinion directly impacts Enron's third demographic. Once the vocal employees are contented and America has lost its mistrust, investors can return funds to the healing corporation. Until then, Enron seems to assume that investors desire specifics. The Enron website (www.enron.com) has been redesigned specifically for the fact-seeking backer. The main feature of the home page is now an arrow which points to the phrase "latest news." Underneath, subjects are followed by hyperlinks which state, "read the release." Another nearby link reads, "investor relations." It leads to specific financial statements, filings and conference calls.

The site does also service its former employees, with links leading to both "General Information" and "Career Services." This connects to a page bearing the sentence: "COMPANIES: Sign up for career fair!"—an attempt to entice Houston corporations to hire now jobless employees.

Such attempts add a sobering reality to the situation made so optimistic in the press. It is on the site that unguarded truth is forced, legally, to the surface. In the swirl of Cooper's optimism and the pathos-stirring pages of countless PR prompted articles, the harsh reality still stares future investors in the face. It is here that the drip-fed, positive stories sound more like a bitter pill to be swallowed in the disclaimer:

> This press release contains statements that are forward-looking within the meaning of Section 27A of the Securities Act of 1933 and Section 21E of the Securities Exchange Act of 1934. Investors are cautioned that any such forward-looking statements are not guarantees of future performance . . .

Works Cited

Fowler, Tom; Berger, Eric. "E is for energetic; Cooper hits ground running." *Houston Chronicle* 31 Jan 2002: Business 1

Goldberg , Laura; Feldstein, Dan. "Retention, severance program top priority for Enron's CEO." *Houston Chronicle* 02 March 2002: A21

Hoare, Stephen. "When plain speaking can help limit bad publicity in a crisis." *The Times* (London) 19 Feb 2002: Features

Ivanovich, David. "Enron choice known for charisma; Interim CEO brings proven record." *Houston Chronicle* 30 Jan 2002: Business 1

Kennedy, Helen. "New Enron CEO sees prison for ex-chiefs." *Houston Chronicle* 21 Feb 2002: News 16

Knox, Noelle. "New Enron CEO turns company focus to future." *USA Today* 18 Feb 2002: 3B

Mack, Kristen. "Interim CEO says Enron can still be thriving firm." *Houston Chronicle* 26 Feb 2002: A15

Murphy, Bill. "The fall of Enron; New retention bonuses likely so key personnel will remain." *Houston Chronicle* 21 Feb 2002: A13

Snyder, Mike. "Jackson: Progress in Enron pay issue." *Houston Chronicle* 08 March 2002: A21

Topics for Reading and Writing

1. What was Enron's overall strategy in the wake of its scandalous collapse?

2. Stout uses many journalistic sources in his paper, and quotes frequently from news reports about Enron. What other sources might he incorporate in this paper?

3. What is the essential argument advanced by Stout here? Is this primarily a persuasive paper or simply a descriptive analysis?

*Citizens of Los Angeles are treated to some of the oddest billboards in America, but few rivaled the bizarre, nightmare-kitsch images produced by the Diesel jeans company that appeared in 1999–2002. In the fiercely competitive designer jeans marketplace, Diesel has set itself apart by relying less on sexy models than on strange imagery and fantasy worlds, both in its advertising and even in its retail outlets. In his paper, University of Southern California senior **Calvin Callaway** performs a rhetorical analysis of the Diesel ad campaign, its billboards, websites, and stores.*

Calvin Callaway
Irreverent Post-Modernism in Contemporary Apparel

A cascade of Technicolor brilliance hits the consumer entering the Beverly Center's seventh floor Diesel boutique. Vintage designs and self styled rock star clothing cover the racks while a 50's jingle pipes over the speakers in candy striped cheeriness. The salesmen are tattooed and pierced, worn hard like the carefully faded denim sold at a premium on the wall to the left. DIESEL SPONSORS HAPPINESS pops a 60's valentine typeface. One might jump slightly as their eyes catch the menacing tooth-filled grin of Donald, Diesel's new happy mascot who peers from a floor display. His blazing red Mohawk and unblinking stare evoke chilling coulrophobic nightmares of youth. Though unsettling, the irrational reaction to the monstrous Donald suddenly seems inappropriate when considered against the vibrant green backdrop of love and merriment surrounding his clownish visage. Happy pretty people dressed to the Diesel nines laugh and frolic while the lascivious Donald looks on in glee. Pleasure, Innocence, Lust, Fun, Romance and Denim—buyer beware, you are entering the strange acid-dream that is Diesel's Happy Valley.

For over a decade, Diesel Clothing Company has managed to distinguish itself in an increasingly jaded marketplace. Adopting off-beat and surreal advertising campaigns, Diesel appeals to consumers who would prefer to purchase their rebelliousness and creativity as a pair of designer faded jeans. The company's latest campaign, featuring the new mascot Donald and his fictional playground Happy Valley, prances across this spring's billboards and magazines as both a continuation of its long term marketing goals and a reaction to the contemporary consumer climate. Happy Valley provides an ideal geography for an exploration of how Diesel, a company praised for its striking and innovative advertising, employs its unique voice in aiming at its consumers.

Diesel can trace its advertising developments as a consistent vision since its inception. The Italian-based company began advertising in 1991 under the slogan "Diesel for Successful Living," a mantra it has retained with little deviation ever since (PRESS PACKET). The idea parodies the post-war consumer atmosphere of the 1950's that promised better living through new shiny products. Diesel overtly promises the same, but manages to do so with a hipper-than-thou attitude that plays upon consumer savvy, drawing them with the very appeal they are presumably too hip to fall for. Diesel seems to revel in this ironic anti-consumerism, crafting one campaign after another that viciously mocks the artifice of mainstream marketing.

But Diesel's obstinate up-stream swimming has caused quite a wake. Much of the company's advertising history is colored by controversy: Diesel has caught flak for degradation of women, unblinking appeals to gay audiences, and for exploiting death with morbid ads claiming "At least you'll have a beautiful corpse" (HONAN). But the company has also consistently been favored at advertising awards, winning this year's *Grand Prix* at the Cannes Film festival for a Print or Poster campaign (VAGNONI), and similar awards annually since 1994 (PRESS PACKET). However, the company is not immune from societal opinion. After September 11th's attacks, the "Save Yourself" headline in an ad campaign mocking the length people go for beauty, with laconic quips like "eat algae," "drink urine," and "don't move," was quickly changed to "Stay Young," to avoid any misinterpretation of its sentiment (ABEL).

Similarly, the newest campaign, "Happy Valley," seems to consciously distance itself from the somber post-9/11 climate with dreamlike escapism. By making Diesel ". . . the proud sponsor of all the positive emotions in the world . . ." Amsterdam-based ad agency Kessels Kramer has created a bizarre world of green pastures, emerald forests, and endless happiness to stage the new spring line (EUROVIAE). But though Happy Valley responds in many ways to post-terrorist sentiment, it also fits well into the company's historical marketing scheme. By overtly sponsoring happiness, adventure, love, and fun (to name just a few) Diesel pokes directly at corporations who attempt the same associations obliquely.

"McDonald's and Coca-Cola are trying to create a world of positive emotion," says advertising director Maurizio Marchiori, "but it's a fake world. We wanted to create a mascot that would identify those 'fake' values" (DNR). But identification doesn't mean nullification. Indeed, Diesel manages to align its product with these emotions in any case—making one ponder what real (if any) difference exists between Diesel and the corporate giants it seeks to ridicule. This irony, though consistent with the company's typically anti-establishment identity, emphasizes the brand's clear marketing hypocrisy: Happy Valley advertises by making fun of advertising. But Diesel pulls off this paradox with an arty audaciousness, disguising its real goals of product promotion by appealing to an audience more concerned with its image than true consumer awareness.

The Diesel customer likes the *idea* of being a Diesel customer. It's the image that is worth buying. The Happy Valley Campaign in particular aims at both men and women of an urban, trend-conscious audience. The weird, glazed imagery and tatterdemalion fashion have no obvious appeal for rural consumers—urban hipsters who want to dress like rock star are more interested. They are a young (under thirty) consumer base ranging from high school and college students to urban professionals in liberal vocations (actors, musicians, waiters, etc), that consider themselves active in personal expression. They are politically liberal and ethnically Caucasian—Happy Valley evokes a lilywhite optimism of 1950's America, with scant ostensible appeal to black consumers. Drug influences are rife in the ad's subtext: beyond the patently surreal imagery, Happy Valley's inhabitants frolic with the glazed eyes and euphoric grins of a terminal soma paradise. But this is not to say Diesel's intended consumers are necessarily drug addicts; on the contrary, the ads play upon the mystique of drug culture for those who find the *idea* attractive. Again, image and attitude are key ingredients above literalism or practicality. As far as its audience's sexual preference, Happy Valley seems at first consciously heterosexual. However, its presentation certainly remains accessible to homosexual audiences. The nature of the men's fashion (motley combinations with flowered prints and ascot scarves), suggests a more gay appeal, despite the heterosexual situations in which the models are featured. By this dichotomy, Diesel retains its gay consumer base, while making itself a viable choice for straight customers as well.

But more than anything else, Diesel appeals to the *attitude* of its consumers. They are an audience who consider themselves artistically savvy and politically aware. And Happy Valley adeptly exploits these desires directly with both surreal pop-culture kitsch, and the conceit of faux anti-consumerism satire.

And personifying this disturbing dreamland of happy thoughts and high fashion sits the grinning figurehead of Donald Diesel. His huge carnivorous smile juts from an impish, fleshy face marked only by his crazed eyes and severely painted eyebrows. Atop his otherwise bald pate stripes a fire-red Mohawk to match his identically colored Teletubbie body. His only clothes are a white open collar, cartoonish striped tie and red latex gloves. He is simply terrifying, a nightmarish compilation of all the reasons children are afraid of clowns. He is your happy friend spawned in hell. But Donald's ancestry suggests a more immediate conception spawned from the unholy alliance of the Teletubbie "Po" and the leviathan of corporate mascots, Ronald McDonald himself. This postmodern conglomeration of weirdness provides an artistically creepy and bizarre image for audiences to have fun with, while typifying the anti-corporate commentary running throughout the campaign.

No better character epitomizes corporate imperialism than McDonald's iconographic red-haired, happy clowns; he provides the perfect source for Diesel's parody. In addition to the two clowns' physical (if some what distorted) similarities, the Ronald McDonald references extend to Donald Diesel's merchandised appropriation onto balloons, lollipops, blow-up dolls and above all, fast food imagery. In one such ad sponsoring *"Satisfaction,"* a couple sits with sedated grins behind scores of half chewed french-fries, hamburgers, and chicken nuggets. And on each spent container in monochromatic red and white smiles Donald's devilish grin. With this parody, Diesel wants its consumers to feel good about themselves by recognizing the corporate duplicity of companies like McDonalds. But elsewhere, with unflinching irony, the Diesel ads wholeheartedly advocate consumerism, inviting their audience to join with them in laughing at the extent they will submit to marketing's deception.

The ads' text provides evidence for this tacit submission on the part of the consumer. In one example, the spring catalog opens with an introduction from Donald explaining why Happy Valley is ". . . the happiest place on earth . . . So what are we waiting for? Bring a smile on your face, a song in your heart and a major credit card in your pocket. And let's take a ride through the wonders of Happy Valley." Diesel feels no reason to hide its ultimate goals of convincing the consumer to spend lots of money—tongue in check or otherwise. Money is, after all, subjugated to all the grander things promoted by the ads. In a typical chain of logic, the caption above a magazine advertisement sponsoring *"Freedom"* tells the consumer that "FREEDOM is a feeling you celebrate with the world. Let's visit the plastic surgeon and replace our arms with wings! This may cost a lot of money." But for somewhat less, the ad implies, one could buy a pair of Diesel jeans and experience Happy Valley's freedom as a state of mind. A similarly humorous caption adorns each of Diesel's emotion sponsorships. For the *"Happiness"* ad, Donald tell us that "HAPPINESS is a gift you give for free. Break into a neighbor's house and paint all of the walls pink. Or tell a stranger you have an angel in your pocket—then ask them to touch it." These captions continue a tradition of Diesel wit, mixing irreverence with sexuality and rebellion. And when flipping to one in a fashion magazine, these glossy appeals just ache with coolness. The Diesel customer feels hip "getting" the clever, dazed advice, adding to the mystique of Diesel attitude that they can share vicariously by wearing the company's designs.

Many of Diesel's contemporaries, like Calvin Klein, and recently Kenneth Cole, have sought similar edginess to sell their product. Klein met controversy over its allegedly child-pornographic campaign that posed young models provocatively in front of trailer-park wood paneling. Media watchdogs were in an uproar, and Calvin Klein pulled the ads. But ultimately, the chic designer brand got the publicity it hoped to spark. Kenneth Cole's name has recently sprung up on billboards with uncharacteristically daring declaration of "GOD DRESS AMERICA" in block letters—an ironic play on post-September 11 patriotism. But neither Klein's typically modish detachment, nor Cole's new attempts at pluck, (nor indeed anyone else in the apparel industry) come close to Diesel's unique brand of marketing surrealism. Moreover, this eccentricity seems indicative of the company's overarching philosophy of consciously ". . . turning its back . . . on the fashion establishment," in an attempt to create a truly inimitable and individual product (PRESS PACKET). Diesel refuses to follow industry trends, in either fashion or marketing.

But Diesel's absurdist edginess is not intended for all audiences. Diesel only broadcasts Happy Valley and Donald's beady-eyed grin through specialty niche channels. The company purchased eight billboards in Los Angeles and New York (DNR), at such hip fashion addresses as Fountain and La Brea to stage the spring campaign—further emphasizing its urban chic demographic. And only the more expensive high fashion magazines carry the ads, including Nylon, Details, Fader, and Black Book—while they are conspicuously absent from more mainstream titles like GQ or W. This distribution indicates aims for an artier and more cultured stratum of consumer culture (or at the very least, one that considers itself artier and more cultured!). These are periodicals read by only the most trend-conscious consumer: a young, urban consumer base.

Diesel's web presence at www.diesel.com offers a veritable playground—a virtual Happy Valley in which to play. Asking the casual surfer "How are you feeling today," against Donald head lets him or her pick from the lexicon of sponsored emotions that will bring up an appropriately themed page. Or one may click "The Happy Anarchist Challenge" video game in "Satisfaction Café," where points can be earned whacking protesting vegetarian anarchists who would seek to paint-bomb the happy fast-food establishment. All the while the haunting Happy Valley theme sings from the Happy Player, "*Hap, Hap, Happy Days, fun, fun happy days with Donald . . . who can make your pants tight with pleasure? Donald! . . . Who has a team of lawyers ready to sue? Donald that's who!*" and a dozen or so additional verses to match, all sung with the emphatic emotion of a 1950's product jingle. Diesel again presents the consumer with a dichotomy between ironic social awareness (anarchist vegetarians) and the twisted surreal.

Finally, the spring catalog offers the cap to this season's marketing campaign. This coffee-table styled glossy pamphlet collects each emotion sponsorship into one book, adding a Donald centerfold for flair. The content remains largely the same as the billboard and magazine advertisements; however, one key element becomes more obvious: the purely incidental presentation of Diesel clothing. It's almost as if the inhabitants of Happy Valley just happen to be wearing Diesel apparel, a significance that the ad's other compelling imagery far downplays. A spring catalogue would presumably showcase its new spring line, but in fact Diesel subordinates its merchandise for the sake of its ads' aesthetic goals. Predictably, Diesel's advertisements market a mystique far above their product. Diesel is a company in the business of selling image. Though its customers purchase clothing, they seek to buy an attitude.

Diesel consumers thrive on irony. The company's paradoxical brand of anti-consumerist advertising works because it plays upon the postmodern zeitgeist of modern consumer culture. The young customers Diesel targets have grown up in an atmosphere of escalating media: from the time kids are now born, they are inundated with television, radio, and magazine advertisements; billboards, bench ads, and bus stop posters; corporate websites, internet banners, and junk e-mail; product placement in film, merchandizing and cross marketing with bath towels, bed sheets and appropriately themed Happy Meals—there is no escape. But instead of breeding a blindly submissive populace this saturation has instead numbed consumers. Modern customers are aware of advertising's artifice, but accept its ubiquity as a given. Diesel plays upon this new consumer consciousness, providing an outlet for its unspoken skepticism. And by ridiculing the blatant appeals of 1950s-styled advertising, Diesel invokes the height of consumer naiveté, letting its youth audience rebel against the squareness of its' parents' generation, and "the establishment" of corporate America. This artful deconstruction distracts the audience from Diesel's paradoxical corporate interests, and fully realizes postmodern tendencies in the advertising industry. A savvy consumer gets a thrill deconstructing and undermining the reflexivity of advertisements; consequently, they accept Diesel as a company "on their side," separate from the greedy manipulative mainstream.

The efficacy of this false empowerment points to a new trend of what could be termed *Metaphysical Advertising,* that is, forefronting the advertising behind advertising. The Happy Valley series particularly seems like a twisted subconscious dream of an advertising campaign somehow bubbled to the empirical surface and captured on film. And like a dream, the audience is left with only tenuous strings of meaning and strange bits of hyper-realized, often frightening viscera to engage. A hallucinatory, but fashionable existence: Hooray for Successful Living.

"Hap Hap Happy Days, Fun, Fun, Happy Days With Donald . . ."

Works Cited

Abel, Katie. "Post-Terrorism Ads Evoke Somber Spin." *FN*. 1 October 2001: 6.

Cunningham, Thomas. "Diesel's Ads to Feature New 'Mascot.'" *DNR*. 14 January 2002: 6

DIESEL PRESSPACKET. 2 March 2002. <http://www.diesel.com>

"New Diesel Campaign Stars 'Donald Diesel' Clown in Happy Valley." *Euromarketing Via E-mail*. 15 February 2002

Zargani, Luiza. " Diesel Changes Advertising Campaign." *DNR*. 24 September 2001: 8

Topics for Reading and Writing

1. How does Callaway link his particular observations of the details of the Diesel campaign to larger assertions about the overall *point* or *thesis* of the campaign itself? Is this linkage effective, or could it be improved?

2. How do other jeans companies construct their own images? How does this compare to the Diesel campaign? Why do you think Diesel chose this approach?

The Writer at Work

Shaping Your Appeal

Going from Argument to Rhetoric

In the last chapter we talked about arguments: what constitutes an argument, what kinds of points are arguable and what aren't, and what the broad categories of arguments are. Rhetoric, or the use of language to persuade, begins with an argument. A writer must have an argument that he or she is trying to convince the audience to believe or accept. As you saw in the last chapter, the actual thesis or argument may not exhaust all the intentions of a piece of writing, but effective rhetoric must begin with a clear, easily understandable claim.

Once a writer has a thesis, the process of constructing rhetoric begins. Although it may seem sometimes like good speakers and writers are intuitively able to construct effective arguments, even the most sophisticated writers begin the same way: by thinking systematically about how to make a specific argument appeal to a specific audience or audiences. Audience analysis is the most important element in building a persuasive argument. With a clear idea of the audience being addressed, a writer will then move to decisions about the three basic building blocks of rhetoric, which are known collectively as the "rhetorical triangle":

appealing to the audience's feelings, constructing the speaker's authority, and using logic accurately and responsibly.

Knowing the audience

In order to be effective, an argument must be geared to its audience. The speaker or writer has to know what the audience feels about things, what kind of authority the audience is going to find credible and believable, and exactly what kind of logic the audience will be willing and able to accept. Let's look at a couple of examples. In the 2000 presidential election, the candidates (Texas Governor George W. Bush and Vice President Albert Gore) had to appeal to the broadest conceivable array of audiences. Convincing voters depended on knowing not only what those voters *wanted,* but also on knowing how those voters *felt.* Speaking to an audience of oilmen, George W. Bush wore cowboy boots and played up his Texas childhood and talked about the need for energy exploration. He knew that this audience felt an affinity with him—after all, Bush himself had been an oilman—and he wanted to prove to them that although he had an East Coast, Ivy League pedigree he understood their concerns and way of life perfectly. Bush could not use the same approach with other, more skeptical audiences. Without necessarily glossing over his core beliefs, Bush needed to play up his commonalities with groups such as the National Association for the Advancement of Colored People or a group of suburban mothers. In fact, many commentators felt that an important factor in Gore's defeat was because of his ineffective rhetoric, his inability to change his message and persona for different audiences.

Audience analysis—the technical term for studying an audience in order to find out what that audience thinks, feels, and wants—doesn't always take place in such formal contexts. Probably the most advanced and exact audience analysis comes from the field of advertising. Advertisers need to have exact and up-to-the-minute data on their target markets—or, to put that in real terms, Nike needs to know whether LeBron James appeals to white upper-middle-class suburban 18-year-old hip-hop fans more or less than Tim Duncan does close up, and it is crucial for Hasbro to know if the popularity of Japanese-animation-inspired toys has peaked among 7-year-olds who watch at least 10 hours of television a week. In order to do this, advertisers constantly study what's called demographic data—information about people grouped by location, age, race, economic status, religion, political leanings, and any other variable you could imagine.

Marketers and politicians have access to a whole army of professionals who can conduct audience analyses for them, but what about ordinary people who want to make appealing arguments? Admittedly, it's much tougher for the rest of us to target our audiences as well as advertisers can, but we can certainly make a game attempt just based on our knowledge about the world. Let's say, hypothetically, that the food in your dining hall isn't particularly good—in fact, it's awful. Being a natural student leader, you have taken upon yourself the task of persuading the administration to break its food-service contract with Company A and to accept bids from other companies. After you make an appointment with the vice president of student services to discuss this matter, you realize that you've never done anything like this before! How do you prepare to make your argument?

First of all, you have to think about your audience (in this case, the vice president of student services) and brainstorm about what this person is like and what you think this person might value or respond to. Your list might look like this:

Businesslike
Wants to satisfy student needs but also must keep financial constraints
    in mind
Won't respond to what feels like everyday student complaining
Requires facts and figures in order to make a decision
Can't be too informal with him
Doesn't have to eat the food
Wants students to be happy

This is a good start; from here, you could start to sketch out what to include in your argument. Let's say, then, after you speak to the vice president he tells you that he hears your concern, but that he'd like to see some hard data on students' feelings about food service. You need to return to him with a petition signed by at least a quarter of the students in the college asking for a new food-service contractor.

How do you make this same argument to the students at your school? Now you're dealing not with one person but with, maybe tens of thousands. You should still think about what all the students in your school have in common and what might appeal to them. You know they tend to be dissatisfied with the food service, but many don't feel like taking the step of signing a petition. How do you convince them? Again, begin by thinking about the audience.

Don't like the food
Don't really want to get involved; would rather this be solved without
    work on their part
Many students want greater variety in the food—organics, non-
    genetically modified, vegan, kosher, low-fat
Some students won't live on campus because food is so bad

Some of these characteristics are shared by almost all the students; some (like a desire for kosher food or a refusal to live on campus because of the food) probably only apply to a few. In your argument, then, you'll probably start out by talking about the most general things: "I bet you don't like the food in this dining hall, but you also don't think that there's anything you can easily do to change things. Just by signing this petition, you can take a very serious step toward getting better food service at this college." Then, in speaking to the individual students, you can ask them why they don't like the food and assure them their desires will be taken into consideration when a new contractor is selected.

This, then, is audience analysis. In their speeches and commercials, politicians generally include elements to which almost everyone will respond positively (smiles, the American flag, children and families) before aiming their appeal to the specific audience in question (Chinese-American war veterans, the

Louisville Chamber of Commerce, the National Abortion Rights Action League). Even in your academic papers you do the same thing. You use formal prose and avoid contractions and vulgarities, you cite reputable scholarly sources rather than random websites, you spellcheck your essay and print it on clean paper. All of these are rhetorical techniques by which you are encouraging your professor or your instructor to take you and your paper seriously.

IDEAS INTO PRACTICE 3-1

In a small group, draft a one-paragraph audience analysis on the following audiences. Talk about who these people are, what their gender or racial or economic or age makeup is, what feelings this group shares, and where they might be very diverse. Think about what kinds of rhetorical appeals would appeal to them.

1. Fans of *Buffy the Vampire Slayer*
2. Fans of the *NBA on TNT*
3. Demonstrators at a right-to-life march in Tulsa, Oklahoma
4. Demonstrators at a Falun Gong protest outside the Chinese consulate in San Francisco
5. Readers of *Vibe*
6. Readers of *Convenience Store News*
7. Attendees of the Sisters (Oregon) Quilting Fair
8. Attendees of the tractor pull at the Jefferson County (Oregon) Fair
9. Students at Beverly Hills High School
10. Students at Raton (New Mexico) High School

Pathos: The Audience's Emotions

In the process of identifying your audience you have certainly thought a great deal about the desires, feelings, and emotions of that audience. What do they love? To what are they loyal? What do they dislike or even hate? What symbols represent comfort to them, and what symbols represent danger? Are they more likely to respond to appeals based on anger and aggression, or appeals based on concern and caring? **The way a writer takes into consideration the emotions of his audience and uses them to make his or her appeal is called *pathos*.** *Pathos* is a Greek word meaning "suffering or feeling"; this Greek root has given rise to such English words as "pathetic," "sympathetic," "antipathy," and "pathology."

All capable writers use pathos, but the degree to which an appeal relies on pathos depends on the type of argument being made and on the audience being addressed. In his "Letter from Birmingham Jail" (See Chapter 1), Martin Luther King, Jr., made very effective use of *pathos*. Arguing to a wide cross-section of citizens of Birmingham, Alabama, King brought home the emotional pain of segregation by describing his own "six-year-old daughter's" tearful reaction to being "told that Funtown is closed to colored children." By doing this, King attempted to find common ground with his opponents by appealing to emotions (the desire of a parent to make his child happy) even more deep-seated than racism. "Remember the pain you feel when your child cries?" King implicitly asks his audience. "Segregation makes me feel that pain all the time." In his speech immediately after the September 11 attacks, rather than lashing out in fury President Bush spoke calmly, resolutely, and with unshakable purpose, trying to make Americans feel that someone would lead us when we all felt so lost and frightened. Every detergent commercial with a baby or a teddy bear tries to play on our fond memories of being a loved child wrapped in clean soft blankets; most beer commercials try to appeal to young men's sense of themselves as fun-loving, popular, and just a little bit naughty. Politicians constantly try to convince audiences that their policies will ultimately benefit children—who could be against children? (Mocking this sanctimonious, and frequently disingenuous, appeal to "think of the children," the writers of the television show *The Simpsons* have made it a catch phrase.)

The media controversies outlined in this book, as well, have emotional dimensions. All the arguments about these issues use *pathos* to make their appeals. In the debate about Napster and music file swapping, the Recording Industry Association of America (RIAA) and some musicians ask us to feel their outrage that anyone can steal the work they have created, while those on the other side try to encourage disgust at the greed of record companies. We feel emotionally violated when we learn that "objective" news outlets have been slanting their coverage. Advertisers use the tools of pathos to make us feel good about what they are selling—soap, movies, or politicians. In response, Naomi Klein (whose book *No Logo* is excerpted in this chapter) tries to convey to her readers her own anger at what she calls "brand bullies."

The key to using *pathos,* just as it is the key to any rhetorical technique, is knowing the audience and knowing how they will respond to your argument. *Pathos* is especially important when a writer is trying to convince a group of people to do something: emotion can impel us to action much more powerfully than pure logic can. For thousands of years, leaders have persuaded their people to go to war by using emotional appeals—demonizing the enemy and telling an audience that their own families are at risk has been an effective tactic since the days of the Babylonians. During World War I, British newspapers told stories (later proven to be fabricated) about babies being thrown from second-story windows onto German bayonets. Stories about the horrors of the Nazi regime and rumors about extermination camps convinced many Americans that war against Hitler was necessary. More recently, in 1990 an ordinary Kuwaiti girl (known at the time only as "Nayirah") testified in front of the U.S. Congress that Iraqi invaders were yanking babies out of incubators in Kuwaiti hospitals. Only after the Gulf War ended was it proven that this was also a fabrication created by a public relations firm, and the girl was in fact the daughter of a high Kuwaiti official who wanted America to rescue his country from Saddam Hussein. (See Chapter 6.) From the beginning of his presidency, George W. Bush argued to Americans that another war against Hussein was necessary because his weapons of mass destruction threatened us in our homes. This argument is particularly effective today, because the September 11, 2001, attacks showed us that terrorists not only can but will attack Americans on our own soil—by making such arguments about Iraq, Bush attempted to transfer our fear and hatred of the September 11 terrorists onto Hussein.

IDEAS INTO PRACTICE 3-2

Sketch out a *pathos* appeal for the following arguments. Remember to keep in mind that although many emotions (patriotism, love of family and children) are universal, different audiences must be reached by appeals aimed specifically at their feelings, desires, and interests.

Example

Argument: Music companies have the right to make it impossible to "rip" MP3 music files off of their CDs, thus preventing consumers from trading music without paying for it.

Audience: College students

Pathos appeal: Since trading music files is especially popular among college students, this is a very difficult argument to make. You first might want to think about what is *not* going to work: an argument about the rights of large media conglomerates, a statement that stockholders of those companies will see their shares' values fall as revenues remain flat. What emotional appeals could work? Many college students treasure the idea of private property and feel that the right to property is one of the fundamental rights of American citizens. A discussion of how this kind of trading is simply stealing might work with them—and perhaps a comparison of MP3 traders with shoplifters or kids who break into cars to steal stereos will make them feel that such activity is beneath them. Other college students with less reverence for property rights might have great respect for artists. Sure, many artists are already rich enough, but what about the struggling young singer who needs the royalties from each and every single in order to survive?

1. Argument: SUV drivers should have to pay extra gasoline taxes in order to clean up the environment.
   Audience: Suburban mothers
2. Argument: SUV drivers should have to pay extra gasoline taxes in order to clean up the environment.
   Audience: The fraternity brothers at Kappa Tappa Kegga, most of whom drive SUV's.
3. Argument: The United States should exert greater pressure on Israel to reach a settlement to the Palestinian conflict.
   Audience: The residents of a Jewish retirement home.
4. Argument: Skateboarding is not a crime.
   Audience: Parents who feel that skateboarders are drug-dealing vandals.
5. Argument: The FCC should allow radio stations to broadcast songs with some minor profanity.
   Audience: Parents of high school students.
6. Argument: Division 1-A universities and colleges should cut their football scholarships from 80 to 53 and the money should be used to support smaller sports like wrestling or women's soccer.
   Audience: The alumni athletic booster club at a Division 1-A university.

Establishing the speaker's credibility

Appealing to the emotions of your audience is only one of the three central tactics of good rhetoric. You might be able to push emotional buttons in your audience, but unless you can make them trust you, you won't be able to *convince* them of anything. An effective writer must be credible, must be believable, must carry some kind of authority with his or her audience. **The Greek term used to describe the way that a speaker or writer establishes authority with a particular audience is** *ethos.*

Like *pathos,* ethos is utterly dependent upon the audience being addressed. (Remember in Chapter 2 when we established that **rhetoric, or the use of language to persuade, is radically situational?** This chapter's lesson should be making that very clear.) A speaker or writer can establish credibility in many different ways. When you evaluate a movie you saw last night, part of your *ethos* is simply that you've seen the film in question—you're more credible than someone who only saw an advertisement for the film. A sociologist who has studied gang culture in East Los Angeles has a great deal of credibility when making arguments about the cause of crime in that neighborhood. So does a young man who grew up on those streets. The sociologist's credibility differs from the young man's, though, and each would appeal to different audiences in different ways.

You can establish credibility by being knowledgeable about a topic, by being passionate about a topic, by having personal experience of a topic, by having read about a topic, by having experienced something similar or analogous, by being similar to the audience being addressed, or simply by being a charismatic, attractive, or appealing person. One's job or rank can also create *ethos:* leaders of any sort (from the president of the United States to the college rugby team's assistant captain) gain credibility by virtue of their position. Where an argument appears affects its *ethos;* an essay appearing on the opinion page of the *New York Times* has much more authority than would the same essay appearing on a personal homepage, because reputable publications carry with them a great deal of authority. Conversely, sometimes a speaker will establish *ethos* by denying his own knowledge or intelligence: on the television program *Matlock,* the title character, a small-town lawyer, often established his credibility by stressing his lack of sophistication, saying "well, I'm just a small-town lawyer, I'm not as smart and sophisticated like my big-city opponent, but one thing I do know is . . ." As with *pathos,* an effective writer must take two factors into consideration when he or she starts thinking about *ethos:* the argument being made and the audience in question.

Let's return to the presidential election of 2000. Each of the two candidates, George W. Bush and Al Gore, had very particular strengths and weaknesses in how they were perceived by the public. Bush was widely seen as a "good guy," even a "good ol' boy," and as the kind of person who would be fun to spend time with. However, Bush had to overcome some significant handicaps: specifically, the widespread notion that he was not particularly intelligent or curious about the world, and the perception that all his accomplishments could be attributed to the pull of his wealthy and powerful family (his father, after all, had been president, and his grandfather a U.S. senator). Al Gore's problems were almost exactly the opposite, for he was seen as too smart for his own good, a boring, stiff, humorless pedant who tended to take credit for things (inventing the Internet) that he hadn't actually done. On the positive side, Gore had long experience in government, was undeniably brainy, and had been the vice president in a popular administration whose scandals had left him largely untarnished. In crafting their appeals to the public, Bush and Gore's campaign teams had to play on each candidate's strengths without reinforcing the negative perceptions held by the public. Of course, each man's strength is closely linked to his weakness: the public wants Bush to be just like them, but they also want a smart man to be president; the public wants a smart man to be president, but they don't want to elect the smug smartest kid in the class whom they didn't like in high school.

The candidates' handlers sent them out into public with the mission of counteracting the negatives and accentuating the positives. Bush spoke to small business owners (too much time spent in front of executives of large corporations would have reminded the public of Bush's privileged upbringing) and drilled home his "common sense," probusiness policies: "I'm just like you, I went to school in a small Texas city, I ran a business—hell, I ran a baseball team, who doesn't like baseball?—and I understand where you folks are coming from." Commentators and late-night comedians made endless fun of Bush's sometimes tortured use of language, but this did not seem to affect many people's opinion of Bush as a candidate. Al Gore appeared on the late-night talk shows and joked with the hosts, attempting to show that he wasn't as stiff as people thought, but in the debates his irritation with Bush's oversimplified and sometimes factually incorrect answers showed on his face—and people remembered Gore's sneer more than Bush's mistakes. *Ethos* also comes from one's associates. Attempting to distance himself from President Clinton's personal scandals, Gore brought aboard as vice-presidential candidate Joe Lieberman, a conservative senator who had publicly spoken out against Clinton's behavior. Similarly, Bush tried to counteract his image as a callow lightweight by running with the serious, nononsense, detail-oriented Dick Cheney.

Ethos depends entirely on the audience. Bush's down-home, Christian, Texan persona appeals to many Americans but offends many Europeans (as was evident in the debates preceding the invasion of Iraq). The U.N. feared that President Bush was determined to go to war in Iraq no matter what, and resisted Bush's call for action. In order to persuade these audiences, the Bush administration changed its public face and its arguments, sending Secretary of State Colin Powell (a man respected in Europe) to make the case to the United Nations that Iraq was not complying with requirements to disarm. *Ethos* in this case also depended on complete command of the facts, because the United States was in essence telling the U.N. that it knew more about Iraq's actions than did the U.N. weapons inspectors. Powell bolstered his *ethos* by bringing photographs of weapons sites, recordings of Iraqi weapons engineers discussing forbidden armaments, and massive amounts of data.

Speakers establish their credibility in other ways, too. Advertisers, for instance, construct their *ethos*—the "personality" of the product—in different ways for different audiences. To young men and boys, Nike is Michael Jordan,

Tiger Woods, Lance Armstrong—superstar athletes whose celebrity is inseparable from the brand's. The company achieves this by advertising on television programs, in magazines, and on websites aimed at an audience of young males. To women in their thirties and forties, Nike is different: it is empowering, it is prowoman, it is self-reliant, it is about fitness for its own sake. Advertising aimed at these women relies much less on celebrity and much more on images of what these women aspire, even subconsciously, to be. You have probably noticed that advertising for personal products like deodorants, tampons, and cosmetics is very different when it airs on MTV than when it airs on Lifetime— again, advertisers must decide what each particular audience will find credible. Advertisers choose celebrity spokespeople, moreover, based on the target market's preferences. Ed McMahon and Wilford Brimley push products used by senior citizens, while Britney Spears and Carrot Top hawk products for teens. These advertisers are engaging in exactly the same strategizing you do when you choose your voice and tone for your audience.

Ethos takes place on other levels, too. When you apply for a job, you put on nice clean clothes and type up your résumé neatly—this is an appeal to your audience just as much as Bush's speeches are. In an argument for your writing class, you back up your claims with evidence and write clearly and correctly, because your teacher finds that kind of communication credible. You might make the same argument to your roommate, but you'll probably make it very differently to him or her: you'll use slang, you'll stress your own passion about the idea, and you'll rely more on anecdotes and less on evidence cited from academic sources. Look at the student papers included in this chapter—they rely very heavily on factual evidence because the ethos of a student making an argument about Enron or marketing or Channel One's effects on education is shaky. Our other writers also pay attention to *ethos,* as well; the authors of the study of tobacco marketing adopt a very academic ethos in their article because they are writing for an audience of specialists, while Frazier Moore, writing a very informal piece about television, uses slangy terms and focuses much of the article on his own personality.

Finally, choosing an *ethos* appeal also necessitates that you pay close attention to the argument you are making. Bush and Powell's arguments to the U.N. about war on Iraq were extremely formal because the argument they are making was so serious. Even in a speech to close Texas business associates, Bush would have been unlikely to be informal or humorous about this grave topic. On the other hand, when you argue to your friends that you should go bowling instead of playing miniature golf on Friday night, a grave and serious demeanor is unlikely to be convincing—in fact, because you are trying to convince them to do something fun, seriousness on your part is probably counterproductive!

IDEAS INTO PRACTICE 3-3

Sketch out an *ethos* appeal for the following arguments. Think about not only what kind of speaker this audience will generally find credible, but also how that speaker should come across—should the speaker use formal or informal language, be humorous or not, seem detached or passionate, etc.

Example

Argument: The government should outlaw spam e-mail advertising.

Audience: College students

Ethos appeal: This shouldn't be hard. Many college students have yahoo.com or hotmail.com or aol.com accounts that fill up with annoying unsolicited advertising, while few college students actually have an interest in marketing via spam. A credible speaker could be a college student complaining about spam—the "I'm just like you, and this is so irritating!"—appeal. Humor would work here because so many of the messages are themselves funny as well as annoying; also, spam is not a particularly serious topic.

1. Argument: Taxes should be cut dramatically to stimulate the economy.
   Audience: Public-school teachers.
2. Argument: Taxes should be cut dramatically to stimulate the economy.
   Audience: A gathering of C.E.O.s of large corporations.
3. Argument: Fashion magazines' images of impossibly thin models cause many young girls to have eating disorders.
   Audience: The editor of *Vogue.*
4. Argument: Fashion magazines' images of impossibly thin models cause many young girls to have eating disorders.
   Audience: 20-year-old readers of *Vogue, Elle,* and *Harper's Bazaar.*
5. Argument: People suffering from cancer, AIDS, and other certified maladies should be allowed to use marijuana for medicinal purposes.
   Audience: Parents of high school students.
6. Argument: People suffering from cancer, AIDS, and other certified maladies should be allowed to use marijuana for medicinal purposes.
   Audience: The state legislature.

The reasoning of your argument

Springfield, U.S.A. A bear wanders down from the mountains and lumbers up quiet Evergreen Terrace, mauling the Simpson mailbox in the process. Responding to the increase in bear sightings, the city council passes a new tax in order to pay for bear patrols and a 24-hour bear-spotting helicopter crew. No more bears are seen. Mr. Homer Simpson, speaking to his daughter Lisa, remarks that the new bear tax, although painful, sure had done its job—it got rid of the bears. Lisa, picking up a rock, tells her father he's being ridiculous, that by his logic the rock she has in her hand keeps away tigers. Impressed by the power of his daughter's rock, Mr. Simpson offers to purchase it.

Admittedly, using Homer Simpson to illustrate faulty logic is too easy—he's the very embodiment of faulty logic. But Lisa's point is a good one. For Homer, there was a simple chain of events in play:

1. Bears on the street (initial problem for which we need a solution).
2. Patrols are sent out to find and catch bears (proposed and implemented solution).
3. No more bears (effect of the solution).

Homer thinks the patrols have caused the desired effect—the eradication of bears on the streets of Springfield. Logical Lisa, though, is skeptical. She does not deny any of the three conditions outlined; what she doubts is the causal relationship between the two. She knows that the bear in Item 1 was itself an anomaly: there was no "bear problem" in Springfield, just one confused bear. The bear patrol didn't stop the bears from coming, because (she suspected) no more bears were going to come. There was no relationship whatsoever between Items 2 and 3, any more than there is a relationship between her rock and the absence of tigers.

As you've probably guessed, the third element in our triangle of rhetorical techniques is logic (*logos* in Greek). All arguments, in order to be effective and responsible, must have a logical structure to them. However, many arguments existing in the world in fact rely not on logic, but rather on two much more powerful factors: the emotional state of the audience and the charisma and power of the speaker. Because of this, *logos* is often the poor sister of the powerful *pathos* and *ethos* when it comes to making an effective argument. An angry audience persuaded by a convincing speaker will often be persuaded by illogical and even immoral ideas, but even these kinds of arguments rely on logic—although the logic may be faulty. *Logos,* then, is similar to the other points on the rhetorical triangle in that it has to appeal to the specific audience being addressed. However, since not all of us think clearly and because we can all be swayed by emotions or a persuasive speaker, the *logos* content of a particular message does not need to actually be truly logical in order to be convincing. "Logical fallacies," or the faulty or intentionally misleading use of logic, characterize many arguments.

Just a quick look at a few notable historical arguments can demonstrate the dangers inherent in faulty logic:

Case: The *Dred Scott* decision (U.S. Supreme Court decision stating that a slave who had escaped to the North and gained his freedom must be returned to his master and to slavery).

Argument: Dred Scott is not a full human being, but is rather an object to be owned.

Audience: Citizens of the United States.

Pathos appeal: anger of citizens who have possessions taken away from them; racist feelings; fear of allowing slaves to become U.S. citizens; fear of acknowledging that slavery was based on a falsehood.

Ethos appeal: the authority of the Supreme Court; the power of the laws passed by Congress; the traditions of slavery and the plantation system; the perceived superiority of the White race.

Flaws in logos structure: the unexamined assumption that Africans were not quite human; the refusal to confront the moral contradiction of slavery in a purportedly Christian nation. Only because of the assumption about Africans could slavery have been instituted in the United States; only because of the refusal to apply moral standards to this question could it have lasted.

Case: The massacre of ethnic Tutsis by ethnic Hutus in the central African nation of Rwanda in 1994.

Argument: All Hutus should rise up and kill Tutsis.

Audience: Ethnic Hutu people of Rwanda.

Pathos appeal: resentment of Hutus, the majority group, toward Tutsis, who although a minority held most of the positions of power in the nation; generalized personal anger of individual Hutus at individual Tutsis who may have wronged them; fear that if one didn't take part one would be in trouble.

Ethos appeal: ethnic solidarity; the power of the mass media (these appeals were made largely over the radio); charisma of Hutu leaders.

Flaws in *logos* structure: argument that the only way to remedy the past ethnically based injustice was to murder the Tutsi people; oversimplification of blaming an entire people for the acts of a few leaders.

Certainly, none of us would fall for logical fallacies so blatant—or would we? The logic of the message behind recent Mountain Dew commercials is that "extreme athletes and wild dudes drink Mountain Dew; if you drink Mountain Dew, you will be like those people." When we think about that, it's a silly message. But watching the commercials can be seductive, and this logic, faulty as it is, can seep into our subconscious: "maybe I am a little cooler if I drink this Dew . . ."

Logical fallacies, like rhetoric itself, have been studied for millennia, and because of this we actually have a very useful taxonomy of their types. Listed here are many of the major kinds of logical fallacies with examples.

Hasty Generalization. A hasty generalization is just what it sounds like. In this kind of logical fallacy, the speaker makes a generalization or blanket statement about a whole class of things or people based just on a few examples. "That's the third Lincoln Navigator I've seen run a red light today. People who drive those cars just can't obey the traffic laws."

Red Herring. A "red herring" argument—named after the rotten, or "red," fish criminals would drag over their trails to distract tracking dogs—is a piece of evidence, usually completely unrelated to the issue at hand, intended to distract the audience from the real question. "I realize that you caught me stealing money from the till, but I'd like to remind you that I have been Employee of the Month three times in my tenure here at Jiffy Burger."

Begging the Question. This fallacy asks the audience to accept as factual evidence a statement that is itself in question. "It's impossible that I would steal money from the till—I am a very honest person!"

Non Sequitur. Latin for "it does not follow," a non sequitur is a conclusion that does not follow logically from a premise. "I can't believe Winona Ryder could possibly be guilty of shoplifting—she is such a good actress!"

Faulty Analogy. In order to get an audience to understand an experience or situation that might be foreign to them, writers often use analogies, saying that an unfamiliar thing or activity is like a familiar one. Frequently, businessmen with no political experience run for high political office, arguing that running a city or state or nation is the same as running a corporation, and that their success in the business world will translate precisely to the political realm. However, this analogy is a faulty one because running a government is not, in fact, exactly like running a corporation (although there are a great number of similarities between the two). "Michael Jordan will be a great basketball executive because he was such a leader on the court."

Faulty Causality or ad hoc, ergo propter hoc. As it indicates, the faulty causality argument makes a false cause-effect relationship between two phenomena. ("Ad hoc, ergo propter hoc" simply means "after this, therefore because of this" in Latin.) Homer Simpson's understanding of the bear issue is one example of this fallacy. "Ever since it stopped raining, I've been very happy. I need to move somewhere where it never rains."

Ad hominem attack. An ad hominem ("to the man") attack is an argument that does not confront the issue at hand but rather attacks the opposing speaker or leader. "Who cares what Masterson has to say about universal health care? I hear he never gives to charity and doesn't even recycle."

Ad misericordiam. Meaning not "to misery" but "to mercy," the ad misericordiam argument can be a responsible component of a larger argument—or it can be a logical fallacy. In an appeal to support women's sports at your university, the athletic department may send out a flyer outlining its appeal and adding several stories about scholarship female athletes who were forced to leave college when their sports were cut. However, many arguments that rely exclusively on our sense of pity or mercy can be misleading or fallacious. An old joke tells of a man who murdered his parents, then threw himself upon the mercy of the court because he was an orphan; this is perhaps the most extreme extension of the ad misericordiam fallacy. "Augusto Pinochet may have tortured and murdered thousands of people when he led Chile, but he is a poor old sick man today."

Ad populum. Ad populum attacks are appeals to the prejudices of the people. Many of Hitler's arguments were in fact ad populum arguments—"We all know the Jews are responsible for our economic misery," he argued to a population with a strong history of anti-Semitism. Ad populum attacks usually depend on resentments held by the population against a group. "Lawyers don't want tort reform because those greedheads want to keep suing McDonald's for making coffee too hot and food too fattening." "Although we have no evidence about who vandalized the school, we're fairly convinced that it was no-good teenagers."

Bandwagon. Join the group! Do what everyone else is doing! These are the premises of the bandwagon fallacy. "*Kangaroo Jack* is a great movie—everyone loves it!" "You don't want to propose that our class go to the museum on the field trip; nobody else wants that."

Circular reasoning. Like begging the question, arguments characterized by circular reasoning chase their own tails, metaphorically speaking. "Exercise is good for you because it improves your health." By definition, things that improve your health are good for you; essentially, this statement says "Exercise is good for you because it's good for you."

False Dilemma.   This kind of either-or argument proposes that there are only two possible choices; these arguments are fallacious when there are more than two possible choices. "If you don't go to college, you'll end up sleeping on the streets." "We need to ban gangsta rap music if we don't want all our young men to end up criminals."

Faulty Use of Authority.   If someone is an expert in one thing, they're an expert in everything, right? Of course not. Just because Bono of U2 knows a great deal about rock and roll, he is a credible speaker about Third World debt, right? (In this case, it might be true, because Bono has spent many years working for Third World debt relief.) However, other rockers—Fred Durst or Shakira—might not carry the same kind of authority. The faulty use of authority is especially effective because of our tendency to take very seriously the statements of experts, no matter what their field of expertise is. "If Rudolph Giuliani supports the weakening of the Endangered Species Act, so do I!"

Slippery slope.   Like the false dilemma, the slippery slope fallacy proposes that if we don't perform (or refrain from performing) an action, a series of progressively more terrible outcomes will occur. These arguments today are generally made regarding constitutional rights. "If you let them outlaw submachine guns, they'll take away all our deer rifles and .22s next!" "Unless we successfully defend all forms of legal abortion everywhere in the nation, we will lose the right to any legal abortions anywhere."

Stacking the deck.   A particularly common fallacy among beginning college writers, "stacking the deck" means including only that evidence that supports one's own point—even while ignoring a large amount of evidence for the other side. Candies that advertise themselves as "Fat Free!" make the implicit argument that they are healthy—in fact, these candies never included fat, but are still composed exclusively of sugar and artificial colorings. "There is no evidence whatsoever that marijuana does any harm. Cigarettes and alcohol are much worse."

The logical structure of your argument depends on much more than simply avoiding these fallacies, of course. Sketched out in the rest of the Writer at Work sections of this book are the basic logical requirements for many kinds of arguments—what kind of evidence you must have to prove that something causes something else, how you should construct a definition for a term you want to put into discussion, and the like. Logic also depends heavily on the type of evidence you provide your reader: the evidence must actually illustrate the point you say that it illustrates, the evidence must be factual if you assert that it is, the evidence must be verifiable. Constructing a logical argument contributes to your ethos, as well; if the audience sees that your argument makes logical sense, then you gain credibility as a reasonable and sensible person. Nobody wants to be Homer Simpson, after all.

IDEAS INTO PRACTICE 3-4

1. Find several logical fallacies in arguments you find in public discourse. The best place to start is probably in advertising, but see if you can't find some logical fallacies in political speeches, in letters to the editor of your

local or college paper, or even in the ideas of characters in a movie or novel or television program. Outline the structure of fallacy and describe what type of fallacy it is.

2. Construct your own logical fallacies. Thinking about issues that are important in your school, city, or state, sketch out an argument that relies on faulty logic, then identify what type of fallacy you are using.

Style
Toolbox

The Passive Voice

The passive voice, bane of writing teacher and perplexer of writing students. What is it? Why do teachers hate it so much? How can you—or why should you—avoid it?

The passive voice, most simply explained, is a construction in which instead of the doer (or what we'll call the "agent") *doing* something, something *is done by* the agent. In terms of grammar, the passive voice reverses the typical order of the active voice (agent-action-thing acted upon). Confusing? Let's look at two examples of the active voice:

Serena Williams won the French Open this year.
The university raised tuition again.

In those sentences, the agents—the nouns that actually perform the action—are "Serena Williams" and "the university." Grammatically, those nouns are also the *subjects* of the verbs ("won" and "raised," respectively). Both verbs are transitive—that is, they take a direct object—and so each sentence has an object that is being acted upon. In the first sentence, the object is "the French Open," in the second sentence the object is "tuition." Finally, each sentence has what we'll call an "adverbial," a word or phrase that describes when or where or how the action is performed; in these sentences the adverbials are "this year" and "again."

In the passive voice, the order isn't doer-action-object. Rather, passive sentences proceed like this: thing acted upon-action-(doer). (Because they rely on an object, passive sentences must be created from transitive verbs.) "Doer" is in parentheses here because a passive sentence doesn't have to include the thing or person that performs the action. Transformed into passive sentences, our previous examples would look like this:

The French Open was won by Serena Williams this year.
Tuition was raised by the university again.

The essential change in these sentences is in the verb: from "won" to "was won," from "raised" to "was raised." Passive sentences flatten out the action and take much of the emphasis off the verb, which generally isn't something you want to do. Much good writing relies on the effects of verbs, as you've seen in the previous chapter's Style Toolbox. When we listen to or read something that's in the passive voice, it often feels like nobody's actually doing anything and that things are just happening . . . passively.

You'll also notice that in the sentences given the agents go from the head of the sentence to the middle, and are preceded by the word "by." In the passive voice, it's actually not necessary even to identify who is doing the action. Grammatically, the sentence has a subject ("the French Open" and "tuition") but the subject isn't actually doing the action—the subject conjugates not the action verb "win" or "raise" but the linking verb "be." So what happens to the original subject—the agent, the doer of the action? In the previous sentences, the agents are identified with a phrase beginning with "by," and indeed this is the only way to identify the agent in a passive sentence: the election was stolen *by* my opponent, the car was driven *by* James Bond, the book was written *by* Louise Bogan. Rhetorically, this takes the emphasis off the action and places it on the recipient of the action.

What's particularly problematic—and also valuable—about passive sentences is that the writer doesn't even have to identify the agent. In some sentences, doing this results in a sentence that really says nothing: "The French Open was won." "The book was written." Other sentences, though, really don't require an agent to make sense—and actually, they can be just as rhetorically effective, albeit for a different aim, without the agent being identified.

Tuition was raised, again. (It would be obvious who raised tuition.)
The election was stolen! (One can make an inflammatory charge without actually *accusing* anyone of anything.)
All of a sudden, Arthur was being dragged into the alley. (The writer wants to keep the identity of Arthur's assailant a mystery.)
Mistakes were made. (The classic bureaucratic voice. So that nobody has to take responsibility for these "mistakes," the identification of the agent is omitted.)

Writing teachers dislike the passive voice for many reasons, but chief among them has to be the way they allow writers who don't have much information about a topic to sound like they know what they're talking about. The bureaucratic voice of the sentence "mistakes were made" embodies this kind of writing, in which the writer doesn't have to know who actually is doing anything. It's also a way for a writer or speaker to avoid personal responsibility: "My paper was turned in late" rather than "I turned in my paper late," "the keys to my car were misplaced" rather than "I lost my car keys."

In addition to ethical objections, writing teachers have stylistic objections to the overuse of the passive voice. "To be" verbs—and by definition all passive sentences must include a form of "to be"—tend to make writing less vivid, dryer, flatter, grayer, and duller. Even a vanilla sentence like "John McPhee loved fishing and the outdoors" is much more memorable and pointed than "Fishing and the outdoors were loved by John McPhee," and when you start writing about subjects that are themselves active (and you want to convey that active sense) the active voice is a necessity.

This is not to say, of course, that you should never use the passive voice. The passive can be very rhetorically effective, especially when a writer or speaker wants to focus not on the causes but on effects, as in the following passage:

Our oceans are heating up. Our climate is being changed. Our mountains are being torn down and our rivers are being filled with chemicals. Our entire world is being changed for the worse and nobody will take charge of fixing it!

As you become a more experienced and comfortable writer, you will learn how to use the passive more effectively. What you should keep in mind now is that most of the time you are tempted to use it, the passive voice is the wrong choice. Sometimes—rarely, yes, but sometimes—it works. Using the passive or the active voice is, like everything else in this book, a rhetorical choice, and as I keep repeating, rhetoric is radically situational.

WRITING WITH STYLE 3-1

Change the passive voice sentences among the following to active, and vice-versa. If, in a passive sentence, no agent is included, devise your own.

1. Of all this that was being done to complicate his education, he knew only the color of yellow. (*The Education of Henry Adams* Chapter 1)
2. Joe Lindsay is said by Lum Boger to be the largest manufacturer of prevarications in Eatonville. (Zora Neale Hurston, "The Eatonville Anthology")
3. The American economy now exhibits a wider gap between rich and poor than it has at any time since World War II. (Robert B. Reich, "Why The Rich Are Getting Richer and the Poor Poorer")
4. Now he would never write the things he had saved to write until he knew enough to write them well. (Ernest Hemingway, "The Snows of Kilimanjaro")
5. Inanimate objects are classified into three major categories—those that don't work, those that break down and those that get lost. (Russell Baker, "The Plot Against People")
6. Senator Brock Adams, a respected Democrat, was known to make sexual advances toward young women assistants. (Patty Fisher, "The Injustice System: Women Have Begun to Fight")
7. One stifling mid-July day of 1912 I was summoned to a Grand Street tenement. (Margaret Sanger, "The Turbid Ebb and Flow of Society")
8. Barbara Walters visits Regis and Kathie Lee to impart backstage chatter about the celebrities she has interviewed for her latest special, to be broadcast that evening. (Tom Schactman, "What's Wrong with TV? Talk Shows")
9. All of us have similar experiences. We share in the life journey of growth, development, and transformation. (Linda Seger, "Creating the Myth")
10. Before the trial of this prisoner, several of her own children had frankly and fully confessed not only that they were witches themselves, but that this their mother had made them so. (Cotton Mather, "The Trial of Martha Carrier")

WRITING WITH STYLE 3-2

Using a body paragraph of your last graded essay, rewrite the paragraph, changing the voice from active to passive or vice-versa. Given the audience, aims, and rhetorical situation, which works better?

Who Owns the Public Sphere?

Chapter 4

In the previous chapters, we've looked very specifically at language: how private and public language differ, how objectivity may be unattainable through language, and how the language of hype and marketing pervades the public sphere. Now we are going to set our sights on a broader topic: ownership. Remember the term **"public sphere" (the space—virtual or physical—where individuals and groups interact in order to exchange opinions)** from Chapter 1? In this chapter, we are going to consider the media's portion of that space, who owns or has control over it, and what impact that ownership has on what can be debated and on how debates are conducted.

As discussed in Chapter 1, the official public sphere consists of governmental space—everything from the halls of Congress to the national forests to your public library. A great deal of the conversation necessary in a democratic society takes place in those arenas, of course, as do the discussions with the most impact on

City newstands like this one in Cambridge, Mass., provide readers with a wealth of different perspectives on current events.

law and policy (such as congressional hearings or trials). But where else does the conversation of a democratic society occur?

You might, right now, be in one such place: a university. Of course, many schools are themselves governmental—the U.S. Naval Academy in Maryland, Evergreen State College in Washington, Rutgers University in New Jersey, and hundreds of others are all public schools. But many other schools are private, with little or no affiliation with the government. Yet certainly college campuses and classrooms and conferences and publications are part of the public sphere—they are, in fact, one of the most important arenas in the public sphere. Professors and graduate students produce research in history, biotechnology, gender studies, and other fields with public policy implications. Guest speakers come to campus to talk about subjects of public interest—your college might even sponsor debates between public figures. In your classes, you and your classmates learn about the issues of the day and discuss them. Many people, looking back at their college years, see their late-night dorm-room debates as their introduction to the world of politics!

The public sphere includes dozens of such arenas. Churches, bowling leagues, book groups, concerts, even shopping malls are all part of the public sphere, for they are arenas in which people interact and discuss issues of importance. You can probably think of others: schoolrooms and playgrounds, corporate stockholder meetings, Internet chat rooms. These spaces can be either physical or virtual, or both. One of the broadest and most powerful arenas in the public sphere is that virtual place belonging to what we call the "media." A word we use frequently and variably, "media" derives from the Latin *medium* meaning "middle"—a fitting etymology for a word that denotes the means by which communication travels between a speaker or writer and an audience. As most often used, **"the media" refers to all the vehicles of mass communication— newspapers, telephone, television, radio, Internet, billboards, and so on— and the psychic space between speaker and audience they occupy or have created for themselves in our public sphere.**

But increasingly, **"the media" also refers to the speakers themselves— the bodies that produce content to be transmitted via those means.** In this second sense, "the media" encompasses thousands of different types of entities, from giant radio station owners such as Clear Channel Communications to a single religious AM station in Kansas; it refers to self-published 'zines and to *TV Guide;* it includes both the massive News Corporation conglomerate and small marketing companies. The media hold a central position in our public sphere, for while there are innumerable arenas in which people can gather (physically or virtually) and exchange ideas, only the media can reach a truly mass audience.

"A mass audience"—let's think about this. What is the biggest group of people you've ever seen gathered in one place? A Saturday night movie audience can number in the hundreds. Large theaters for plays and concerts might have a capacity of 10,000. Some athletic stadiums can hold over 100,000 people. Outdoor gatherings can be even larger—the 1963 March on Washington (at which Martin Luther King, Jr., gave his "I Have a Dream" speech) drew a quarter of a million people to the Washington Mall to hear speakers on civil rights; 500,000 people probably attended the 1981 concert in New York's Central Park by Paul Simon and Art Garfunkel; and some estimates had the London demonstrations of Feb. 15, 2003, against the invasion of Iraq at over a million people. The numbers that the media reach, though, dwarf even the largest physical gathering you can imagine. Web pages on obscure topics might count tens of thousands of visitors, while millions visit Yahoo.com every day. Low-rated television shows still draw Nielsen ratings indicating that millions of people are watching. Important speeches, like the address given by President Bush after September 11, 2001, are broadcast around the world on radio and television. Every year the Super Bowl reaches more than a billion people.

Clearly, the media can reach numbers of people that would have been unfathomable before the twentieth century. Because of their vast reach and its ability to communicate exactly the same message to all these people simultaneously, the twenty-first century media are the most powerful means of mass communication ever imagined. Before radio, politicians who wanted to reach a mass audience could only do so via printed matter (pamphlets, flyers, or even campaign buttons) or through personal appearances. In the 1930s, President Franklin Roosevelt began to use the mass media—specifically, the radio—to communicate directly with the American people, and by this produced a new sense of intimacy, a closeness that had never existed between a president and his citizens. Later presidents have all taken advantage of the intimacy that radio and, later, television gave them, to the extent that today we feel like we know our president down to his speech patterns and typical facial expressions. The mass media's power is not limited to use by political leaders, of course. Without the technology to reach millions of people, there can be no such thing as a "celebrity." And while celebrities certainly predate television and the movies—the English poet Lord Byron was an international celebrity as far back as the 1820s—instantaneous telecommunications reproduce the images of celebrities in our homes until we feel we know them.

This ability to provide instant communication and infinite reproduction of images brings with it power, a power that grows as we become more and more dependent on the media in our daily lives. Almost everything we know about the outside world comes to us through the media. Most of the decisions we make about who to vote for, what causes to support, what celebrities to admire, even what products to buy are informed by the media. But who are we talking about when we talk about "the media"? Who owns these channels of communication? What interests and biases do they have? How do these interests and biases affect the information we receive? And how can ordinary citizens reach a mass audience?

lll Conglomerates and Media Consolidation

Today, thousands of corporations and private nonprofit organizations are involved in the business of producing media content and conveying that content to consumers. However, in reality, only a very few companies (10 as of early 2003) utterly dominate the mass media: movies, broadcast and cable and satellite television, Internet access, radio, newspapers, magazines, recorded music, book publishing, theaters and concert venues, billboard advertising, movie theaters, and so on. Because they are composed of a large number of very different companies yoked together under central ownership, these companies are called "conglomerates."[1]

These conglomerates own a truly dazzling array of properties. Just to take one example, the Walt Disney Company owns all the properties branded with the Disney name: Walt Disney Studios for movies, the Disney Channel on cable television, Radio Disney, Disneyland theme parks, the Disney cruise lines, Disney Children's Book Group, and so on. But Disney's presence in the media only begins with its eponymous ventures. ABC, one of the three original broadcast television networks, is a division of Disney, as is the ABC Radio Network. So are the television sports channels ESPN, ESPN2, ESPN Classic, and ESPNews; *ESPN The Magazine;* ESPN Radio; and the ESPN Zone restaurant chain. Miramax Film Corp., one of the leading art-film producers and distributors, is also an arm of Disney. The same goes for the Hyperion book publisher, the cable channel A&E, the Anaheim Mighty Ducks hockey team, the New Amsterdam

---

[1] An up-to-date accounting of these constantly changing corporate affiliations can be found on the *Columbia Journalism Review*'s "Who Owns What" page (www.cjr.org/tools/owners).

The Big Ten (April 2004)

AOL/Time Warner. Major properties: America Online, Netscape Communications, Warner Brothers Studios, Atlantic Records, Time Life Books, WB network, HBO, CNN, *Time, People,* Atlanta Braves baseball team.

General Electric. Major properties: NBC, Bravo, Telemundo, General Electric consumer products, 13 major-market television stations.

Viacom, Inc. Major properties: Paramount Pictures, Blockbuster Video, Simon & Schuster publishers, MarketWatch.com, Infinity radio network, CBS, MTV, 39 TV stations, subway and bus and billboard advertising.

Walt Disney Company. Major properties: Disneyland, Disney Studios, Disney Cruise Lines, *Us Weekly,* ABC, ESPN, Buena Vista Television productions, Anaheim Mighty Ducks, Radio Disney.

Liberty Media Corporation. Major properties: USA Films, Denver Nuggets, PRIMEDIA magazines, Citysearch, Discovery Channel, Sprint.

AT&T Corporation. Major properties: AT&T Cable provider, long-distance and cellular service provider, part owner of Warner Bros. Properties.

News Corporation. Major properties: Los Angeles Dodgers, Fox television network, National Geographic Channel, HarperCollins publishers, *New York Post,* Twentieth Century Fox studios, Fox Sports Radio, Staples Center, Sky and BskyB satellite TV systems.

Bertelsmann. Major properties: largest TV broadcaster in Europe, Lycos Europe, Random House publishers, Arista Records, *Family Circle, YM.*

Vivendi Universal. Major properties: *Rolling Stone* magazine, Larousse publishers, Universal Studios Hollywood theme park, USA Network, Cineplex Odeon theatres, October Pictures, Cegetel cell phone service in France, Interscope Records.

Sony. Major properties: Sony consumer electronics, Columbia Pictures, Game Show Network, PlayStation, Epic records, Loews Theaters.

NOTE: The Big Ten might soon become the Big Nine; as this book goes to press, General Electric and Vivendi Universal have agreed to merge.

Theater on Broadway in New York City, various radio and television stations, and dozens of other assets.

Disney and its media competitors want to be so big because they are gambling on big profits as the result. With so many potential sources of revenue, the earnings can be vast. There is also security in size. The large number of divisions allows some branches of the company to be temporarily unprofitable—a bad year at Disneyland, for instance, might be offset by exceptional profits for ESPN or the *Beauty and the Beast* stage musical (another Disney property). It's a model that has proven to be a very powerful and compelling way to do business.

Of course, size can also be dangerous. In hard economic times, large companies can suffer enormous losses. It is also difficult to maintain control over or foster a common culture in immense companies. To counter these problems, the companies constantly shuffle the properties under the umbrella of the conglomerate: an unprofitable division may be sold off, while another company might be purchased. Frequently, the conglomerate may enter into a joint venture with another company in which the companies share expenses. The film *Titanic,* for instance, was a joint production of News Corporation's 20th Century Fox division and Viacom's Paramount Pictures. In that case, neither company wanted to risk the almost $200 million investment in the picture—but in the end, when the movie ended up with profits of almost $1 billion, both companies probably wished they'd been the sole investor! It's not just movies, either. Risky or innovative technologies are also often joint ventures of many media companies. TiVo, the provider of digital recording for live television, is owned jointly by five of the Big Ten conglomerates!

Another perceived benefit of size for these conglomerates is what is known as "synergy," or the benefits produced by cooperation between divisions. Since these companies own outlets in many different kinds of media, they can save money by using the same content in many different media. Let's take Disney as our example again here, for Disney has successfully exploited synergy with many of its properties. The 1991 Walt Disney Pictures movie *Beauty and the Beast* (itself taken, like many of Disney's properties, from a fairy tale that was in the public domain, or legally ownable by no one) helped usher in a new golden age of animation, and Walt Disney Pictures followed up on *Beauty and the Beast's* success with *Aladdin, The Lion King, Mulan,* and others. The characters and story of *Beauty and the Beast,* then, served as the raw material for attractions at Disneyland, for books published by Disney Children's Book Group, for cartoons on the Disney Channel and Toon Disney, for stories in *Disney Adventures* magazine, and for a Broadway show (that ran at the New Amsterdam Theatre). Disney's movie *The Mighty Ducks* (1992) served as the introduction for the Anaheim Mighty Ducks professional hockey team as well as for the sequels *D2: The Mighty Ducks* and *D3: The Mighty Ducks.* This relationship ran in reverse with the film *Angels in the Outfield* (1994), a remake of a 1951 movie of the same name with the then-Disney-owned Anaheim Angels as the featured team. These Disney teams received exposure from ESPN, which broadcast the games of both teams and showed highlights of their games on *SportsCenter,* and from ABC, which broadcasts professional hockey games.

Synergy doesn't always work, of course, and if the initial property isn't popular with the public the conglomerate's other divisions can't take advantage of it. But in the preceding examples, the synergy has largely been successful—the properties reinforced each other's identities, and this more powerful brand identity probably helped each property be more profitable. And in the end, the examples of *Beauty and the Beast* and the Disney-owned sports teams, sports-themed films, and sports programming have little social importance. These examples deal with entertainment properties, and although the content of entertainment can certainly be controversial, it rarely has much immediate political or social impact.

▐▐ Conglomerates, Synergy, and the News

That is not the case with the news—where people get their information about the outside world. Synergy has had an impact on the news just as much as on entertainment, but the conglomerates tend not to like to talk about this kind of synergy. Almost all of our Big Ten conglomerates have journalism divisions of some kind. Traditionally, the news division of a radio station or newspaper or television network has had little or nothing to do with the business side of the company—many newspapers would put the two divisions on separate floors of the building or actually build a physical wall of separation between the two so there would be no chance of a conflict of interest between reporting the news and making the organization profitable. In the 1960s and 1970s, the news divisions of the major television networks regularly lost money, but the network heads felt that the profitable entertainment divisions should subsidize the news—and that the prestige that accompanied a reputable news division was its own profit. CBS, ABC, and NBC took pride in the quality of their news, and maintained large corps of reporters to ensure that both foreign and domestic news were adequately covered. But increasingly, news divisions are being told that their mission does not end with informing the public in an unbiased fashion. The heads of our Big Ten conglomerates, seeking increased profits, are now demanding that even the news side of the operation be profitable—and this can be a tough task for news organizations. Revenue in television news comes from advertising, and advertising rates are pegged to a program's Nielsen ratings. In their search for profits, the news has become ratings-driven—that is, the producers try to cover subjects that make people *want* to watch.

This change has not been met with approval in some quarters. Many media critics, educators, and even your parents have probably pointed out that the things we want to watch are often not the things we should be watching. By using methods such as surveys and focus groups, media consultants (the people hired by news organizations to do research on what people want to watch) have concluded that certain subjects garner big ratings for the news: crime, celebrities, sex, sensationalism, and "news you can use" (generally health or consumer topics). I'm sure you can think of any number of stories of this type just from this week's TV news—a grisly local murder, the Kobe Bryant sexual-assault case, a new weight loss pill. And while television news still covers topics of great importance like the economy, elections, health care, poverty, and religion, the time given to these stories, and the depth with which they are covered, is diminishing.

According to these same media consultants, other topics cause people to tune the news out. Chief among these is foreign news. Responding to this discovery, national TV news networks slashed foreign coverage in the 1990s. A 1997 Harvard University study found that foreign stories comprised 13.5% of television news in 1995, as opposed to 45% in the 1970s. Another report found that in 2000, the three major broadcast networks aired 1382 minutes of foreign news—a drop of 65% in just 10 years.[2] The lack of attention in the public sphere to the outside world has consequences, too: prior to September 11, 2001, studies showed that most Americans could not find Afghanistan or Iraq on a globe, a fact for which both the media and the American educational system bear responsibility.

Media consultants and their network clients have also concluded that familiar subjects, covered differently, can get different ratings. Covering a political campaign as if it were a horse race or popularity contest seems to get better ratings—and is often easier and cheaper—than covering the same campaign with a careful focus on the issues. For this reason, we tend to remember impor-

---

[2] David Shaw, "Foreign News Shrinks in Era of Globalization." *Los Angeles Times* 27 Sept. 2001.

Massachusetts Governor Michael Dukakis during the 1988 Presidential election

tant elections not in terms of the issues of the day, but in terms of the politicians as people. The election of 2000, for instance, was the contest between the stiff smartest-guy-in-the-class (Gore) and the not-so-bright good ol' boy (Bush). The 1988 election seemed to turn on the ridiculous, endlessly reproduced image of the nerdy, bushy-browed Democratic governor of Massachusetts, Michael Dukakis, perched uncomfortably on a tank with a combat helmet on his head. Other stories about complicated issues tend to get oversimplified or skipped over by news producers nervous that the public won't sit still for a nuanced and complicated story. Difficult and multifaceted issues such as health care, Social Security, and economic or foreign policy are covered briefly if at all. On the other hand, easy-to-understand stories that combine sex and violence and celebrity, such as O.J. Simpson or Michael Jackson are covered out of proportion to their importance.

This becomes an issue when we think about what the news is for. Journalism—and television news falls under this category—is meant to inform us about topics of importance in the world. Furthermore, a democracy depends on an informed public. When a network shirks its responsibility to educate the public, it commits a grave disservice to its audience and to the nation that grants it the use of the airwaves (which are legally, in the United States at least, public property). Moreover, the news organizations' moves to cut foreign coverage in response to a perceived lack of public interest may be itself ill-informed: a 1996 study by the respected Pew Research Center for the People and the Press that asked what kinds of stories Americans followed found 15 percent indicated foreign news, just 1 percent below national politics and 2 percent *ahead of* celebrity news.[3] And the very young people so avidly pursued by TV news still seem to be turning away from traditional news programs—a 1998 Gallup poll showed that

---

[3] *Ibid.*

17 percent of 18–29-year olds got their news not from Dan Rather or CNN or the *New York Times,* but from late-night comedians such as Jon Stewart or Conan O'Brien (see Gloria Goodale's article on this subject in Chapter 2). Of course, these trends are still just that—trends—and it is too early to write off TV news. After all, in times of crisis or during important events most of us still turn on the television to get crucial information. But that the nature of television news is being radically transformed is incontrovertible. *How* the news—local, national broadcast, and cable—will change in the next few years is the real question.

We can already see many of these changes. Synergy's demands, many critics have pointed out, have caused the very idea of the "news" to be blurred. Most of the conglomerates that own national news organizations—Viacom (CBS), Disney (ABC), AOL-Time Warner (CNN), News Corp (Fox News)—are primarily in the business of producing entertainment. And entertainment products need promotion. Synergy demands that the AOL-Time Warner magazines *Entertainment Weekly, People,* and *Time* put stars of Warner Brothers movies on the covers as much as possible, that AOL promotes these movies on its Web portal, and that the WB and HBO television networks air promotional programming for these movies. This synergy also demands that these movies be covered as news: a profile of a Warner Brothers actor on CNN, for instance, or a feature on the CNN.com website. None of this means that these companies *only* feature their own properties, of course; it would not be in the best interests of any of these companies to appear so blatantly biased. The differences we see on the air are subtle, while the difference behind the scenes—the introduction of the concerns of the owning conglomerate into the editorial room of the news division—are profound.

One effect the push for profits has had on television news has been the proliferation of "newsmagazine" programs. The paragon of this kind of programming, CBS's *60 Minutes,* covers three stories in depth every Sunday evening. Generally, one of the stories is hard news, one is a feature story, and one is a celebrity profile. *60 Minutes* pioneered "attack journalism," a form of investigative reporting in which the story's subject—a corrupt politician, or the head of a company that is committing a crime or producing a dangerous product—is ambushed by the reporter. The pleasure of watching these stories derives from seeing the villain (and this kind of story always makes its sympathies and hostilities very clear) squirm as the reporter asks him the questions *we* wish we could ask. In the 1990s, the other networks began producing their own newsmagazines. Shows like *Dateline NBC* and *Primetime Live* (ABC) took a similar approach—long-form stories, ambush journalism—but tended to concentrate even more on celebrity and on profiles of ordinary people triumphing over terrible odds. Critics lambasted these newsmagazines, joking that the shows would have to be cancelled after all the good diseases and tragedies were already covered. But people watched—and the shows were relatively inexpensive to produce, making them ultimately more profitable to the network than an entertainment show with similar ratings. They are, moreover, undeniably compelling at times, and their investigative journalism has broken many important stories.

The newsmagazines have also, though, provided examples of the potential conflicts inherent in journalism produced by media conglomerates. In a growing number of cases, news organizations produced stories critical of corporations

AOL-Time Warner executive Steve Case gestures during a 2003 news conference in New York.

only to have those stories squelched by higher-ups in the conglomerate. Perhaps the most famous of these examples was documented in the movie *The Insider*. In that incident, a tobacco industry scientist named Jeffrey Wigand went to *60 Minutes* with evidence that cigarette manufacturer Brown & Williamson tinkered with the nicotine levels in cigarettes in order to foster addiction in smokers, and that the company was well aware of the health problems associated with tobacco even though its executives had consistently denied to Congress that they did or knew any such thing. *60 Minutes* completed the story, but before it could air the network executives stepped in and stopped it from airing, fearing a lawsuit from Brown & Williamson, for Wigand had signed a nondisclosure agreement with his former employer. The real concern for the CBS executives, though, was that a costly lawsuit could jeopardize the impending purchase of CBS by the industrial conglomerate Westinghouse. Journalists across the country were furious once reports of this surfaced—CBS had clearly gagged its own journalists who were pursuing a story that could have stalled or scuttled a business deal.[4]

Although the CBS-Brown & Williamson episode is the most famous example of this kind of conflict of interest, it is by no means the only one. In 1994,

---

[4] For a detailed summary of the entire CBS-Brown & Williamson episode, see Lawrence Grossman's "Lessons of the Sixty Minutes Cave-In," *Columbia Journalism Review* Jan./Feb. 1996, also available at www.cjr.org/archives.asp?url=/ 96/1/60minutes.asp.

ABC's newsmagazine *Day One* did a similar story about manipulated nicotine levels in cigarettes. Philip Morris (now Altria), the tobacco company, investigated in this story, immediately sued ABC for $10 *billion* and demanded an apology. ABC complied—and paid Philip Morris's $15 million legal fees. Just like CBS, ABC was in negotiations to be purchased (by Disney, which eventually did buy the network) and feared the damage that would be caused by a protracted legal battle. (Recently, Disney has also been criticized for squelching an ABC News story about working conditions at Disneyland.) NBC frequently covers consumer-oriented stories about faulty products—but since its purchase by General Electric, investigations of that company's products and policies (in the 1980s defense procurement scandal, GE was one of the companies singled out for drastically overcharging the federal government for such products as toasters) do not air on NBC or its affiliated networks.

One of the biggest stories the corporate media ignores is media conglomeration itself. Even before this age of media concentration, few people would expect an individual media organization to report on itself with anything like pure objectivity. Rather, free-market advocates have traditionally argued that the media companies would want to critically cover each other, hoping to find stories that might undermine the credibility of competitors. However, study after study shows these media organizations refuse to cover the effects of conglomeration in other companies, even when such a story might give the reporting organization an advantage over competitors. One possible explanation for this is that all the national television networks, all the all-news cable channels, and many of the country's leading newspapers are owned by conglomerates whose main business is not news. Reporting on stories being stopped at ABC might lead readers or viewers to an easy conclusion—if it happens at Disney's subsidiary ABC, why wouldn't it happen at GE's subsidiary NBC? Or AOL-Time Warner's subsidiary CNN? Or Viacom's subsidiary CBS? Many critics and scholars of the press (and, increasingly, even conservatives like Arizona Senator John McCain or *New York Times* columnist William Safire) point out that the conglomerates today act more like a cartel than like competitors—what's good for one, in other words, is good for all.

It would not be fair to paint media concentration and conglomeration as simply an evil. Conglomeration does benefit the public in many ways. Because they are divisions of giant, wealthy companies, media organizations today have access to resources they simply did not have 30 years ago—and that money has paid for capital investments in new technologies like high-definition imagery and satellite transmitters that allow us to get live pictures from the battlefields of Iraq. Most of the news outlets that provide the content for television news programs also operate websites where many of us obtain our news. And while it diminishes the variety of voices available through the mainstream media, corporate concentration does act as a sort of quality control guarantor. We all enjoy a good blockbuster movie, but before conglomeration no studio could afford to risk $100 million or more on a movie. Conglomeration and synergy also allow us to enjoy many products similar to ones we enjoy already. I knew, for instance, that since I enjoy ESPN's *Sportscenter* sports news program I might also like *ESPN The Magazine* and the ESPN Zone restaurants—and I do. Finally, synergy and conglomeration are often boons to a company's stockholders, and many of these companies have millions of stockholders who constitute a significant segment of the American public.

The concentration of ownership of the mainstream corporate media is unlikely to stop anytime soon. It is overly cynical to dismiss the corporate media for being corporate, though. For all the problems and conflicts of interest described, the media is still populated by dedicated, ethical, professional journalists and editors and camera operators and producers and writers who honestly want to inform the public about the important issues of the day. Nor are the corporate media the only news organizations that feel pressure. Because of this, *all* media, not just corporate media, must be heard and seen and read critically.

Analyzing the Message

1. Apart from the problems described, what are some of the potential dangers of media conglomeration on the news? On entertainment? Are there advantages to conglomeration and synergy? How does this issue affect your daily life—or does it?
2. What other examples of synergy can you identify?
3. What venues do ordinary citizens have to get their thoughts and feelings about media consolidation heard?

▌▍ Public Obligation and Media Regulation

What obligation does the media have to society? And what power should the government have to regulate the media? As the media pervade our daily lives more and more and become ever more central to the political process, these questions are more pressing. But in the United States, where early on the press was given an almost unprecedented degree of freedom, we are especially reluctant to place any restrictions on the actions of the media—for the media's business is to exercise one of America's fundamental freedoms, the right of free speech.

Notwithstanding the great importance we give to free speech, the power inherent in the ability to communicate with millions of people has caused the government to regulate the use of technologies of mass communication. Libel laws, for instance, state that the media cannot tell damaging lies about people. For many years, the government (through its Federal Communications Commission, or FCC) required television and radio stations to cover controversial issues and, in doing to, to present opposing views. All broadcast television stations are required to air at least some educational programming for children. Broadcast television stations are forbidden from televising nudity and radio stations cannot play songs that include profanity. And until recently, companies were strictly limited as to how many media outlets—newspapers, television stations, radio stations—they could own in a single local market.

Over the last 15 years, though, media deregulation has gained momentum. Led by both Republican and Democratic presidents (Ronald Reagan, George

Bush, Bill Clinton, and George W. Bush) suspicious of big government and by an increasingly conservative Congress, the weakening or elimination of regulations on media companies began in earnest in 1987. In that year, the FCC eliminated its Fairness Doctrine that required television and radio stations to cover controversial issues in a fair and balanced matter. Although efforts were made in Congress to reinstate the doctrine, President Bush vetoed the bill in 1991. Stations were now free to present only one side of an issue, with the only check on their partisanship or bias now the audience's willingness to believe them.

At the same time, because of the efforts of such media figures as Howard Stern and television producer Stephen Bochco, standards for broadcast profanity and obscenity came under attack. The crude subject matter of Stern's morning radio show earned the host several FCC fines and legions of imitator "shock jocks," while Bochco's *NYPD Blue* charged into controversy in its first season with its own harsh language and glimpses of unclothed male and female bodies. Sexual subject matter, once reserved for the 10 p.m. hour, is now a staple on "family hour" shows such as *Friends,* and on cable, programs like *Beavis and Butt-Head* and *South Park* brought a new level of crudity to television. At the same time, other cable programs such as *The Sopranos* and *Six Feet Under* have used their freedom to include sex, violence, and profanity to make extremely compelling television.

The Fairness Doctrine's demise and the loosening of strictures on language and subject matter have had a profound impact on what we see on television and hear on the radio. However, neither of these two changes have had a fraction of the impact that the concentration of media ownership into just a few hands will have—and has already had. As a few media companies have swallowed many of the others, we have already seen a marked decrease in the diversity of voices on the radio and on television. Media-watchers on the left and the right are pointing out that the vitality of democracy itself is at risk if we do not defend our efforts to maintain a well-informed populace.[5]

Critics of the media are especially frightened of the effects of the Telecommunications Act of 1996, the first large-scale effort to come to terms with the rapidly changing media landscape. The Act had dozens of sections and provisions on topics ranging from long-distance telephone service to digital television. However, its most sweeping effects will probably be felt from its changes in restrictions on ownership. Fearing the effects of a powerful media on the public, in its first years the FCC prohibited one company from owning many media outlets, especially in one market. If the same company owned several radio stations and the newspaper in a small town, reasoned the FCC, that town's citizens would have little access to information or opinions that company did not want to provide. A free and diverse press has always been one of America's strengths;

---

[5] See, for instance, the op-ed piece "On Media Giantism" by conservative columnist William Safire (*New York Times* 20 Jan. 2003), in which Safire argues against the FCC's loosening of media ownership regulations.

the FCC sought to foster that environment in the new world of radio and (later) television.[6]

The Telecommunications Act of 1996 eliminated most of those restrictions. Reasoning that cable television, cable radio, the Internet, and desktop publishing had dramatically expanded the number of potential media outlets, the Act's authors sought to free up media companies to own as many outlets as they wanted—given the number of potential "microphones" out there, it seemed inconceivable that one company could dominate the media to the detriment of democracy. The conglomerates immediately responded, shrinking their number from dozens to the Big Ten we have today.

The FCC took up deregulation again in 2002–2003, as Chairman Michael Powell (son of Secretary of State Colin Powell) sought to modernize some of the FCC's rules on media ownership. Citing the changes in the industry as a result of new technologies and the 1996 Act, Powell proposed loosening the strictures on ownership and concentration even more, and sought public and industry comment before putting the rules changes before the FCC board for a vote. Public advocates and many politicians objected to Powell's decision-making process, pointing out that the chairman met hundreds of times with industry figures but only twice with the public. In the end, the commission approved the new rules, which allowed media companies to own more media outlets in the same market than before. Powell defended these rule changes as overdue, citing the explosion in media outlets in the last 20 years, but advocates for the public disagreed, pointing out that while there are more stations and networks on TV than ever before, most of those stations and networks are owned by the same companies—potentially undermining the FCC's mission of making sure that numerous voices are heard over the airwaves. Powell's decision has been met by a surprising amount of resistance, even in traditionally conservative quarters. Because of this bipartisan suspicion of what the ultimate effects of the new rules might be, in Summer 2003 both the House and the Senate voted to block the rules from taking effect, and a federal court ruled in September 2003 that the rules could not be implemented before undergoing a full judicial review. Although media concentration may well continue or even accelerate, the degree of opposition to the FCC's rule change—and the diversity of the new rules' adversaries—demonstrates that the public is aware of this issue and is demanding that its voice be heard about it.[7]

---

[6] The Telecommunications Act of 1996 was extremely wide-ranging and complicated. Two valuable resources to help you understand the exact nature of the Act are the Federal Communications Commission's website (www.fcc.gov) and the Benton Foundation's homepage on the Act (http://www.benton.org/publibrary/policy/96act/home.html).

[7] It's important to remember, however, that the *entire* public is by no means opposed to these rules. Many would like the FCC to loosen its strictures even further. For one argument of this sort, see the conservative Heritage Foundation's article "The Myth of Media Concentration: Why the FCC's Media Ownership Rules Are Unnecessary," available at www.heritage.org/ Research/InternetandTechnology/wm284.cfm.

▮▮ Independent Voices: Left of the Dial

In 1985, the Minneapolis punk rock band the Replacements recorded a song called "Left of the Dial." In this wistful song, sung to a young woman in an underground band, the narrator takes it for granted that her music would only be heard on the "left of the dial"—that is, on the college or community radio stations typically broadcast on the lower FM frequencies. Although nominally a song of romantic longing, in the song the singer also wonders "how can I get my music played on the radio?" Why, the Replacements wanted to know, won't radio stations play our music? Perhaps you have wondered about that. Why does it seem like commercial television and radio and magazines are dominated by the same kinds of information, the same kinds of music, the same kinds of programming? Where can I find a truly independent voice?

The easiest answer is the one the Replacements resignedly offer: "left of the dial." Because the airwaves (those portions of the electromagnetic spectrum over which television and radio are broadcast) are officially public property, in the United States the federal government has asserted its rights to reserve some of that space for voices of social value that otherwise might not be heard. On FM radio, the frequencies from 87.9 to 91.9 megahertz are reserved for noncommercial stations. Usually, those frequencies are dominated by religious stations, by college radio stations, and by affiliates of National Public Radio, the quasigovernmental radio network. On television, the FCC has generally reserved one channel per market for use by a station whose programming is "primarily educational" in nature.[8]

The limited range of the broadcast spectrum has always meant that there is a finite number of television or radio stations that can be broadcast over the air; because of this, the government proactively ensured that at least some of these stations would have an educational mission. But today, many if not most people do not receive television over the air. Instead, programming comes into our houses via a cable or a satellite receiver, and instead of 13 channels a cable company can offer hundreds. With this opening up of television in the late 1970s and early 1980s, dozens of new independent channels were born: MTV, ESPN, HBO, CNN, USA, and many others. Hundreds more followed, each targeting a more specific audience. This was, finally, a true diversity of programming, a wealth of independent voices. Or so it seemed. These stations were soon bought up by the conglomerates, and by the late 1990s the new cable stations were no longer independent startups—they were projects conceived and financed by the conglomerates. Cable's promise of hundreds of different voices quickly gave way to the reality of the Big Ten—who, not surprisingly, also tend to own the cable providers. However, even in this age of concentration, a few pockets of independent voices exist on television. Most cable providers are required to reserve at least one channel for "community access television," or for programs produced by ordinary members of a community. While the programs themselves

---

[8] Again, see the FCC's website (www.fcc.gov) for more information on the rules governing the airwaves.

are often amateurish, community access television remains one of the few places on television not under corporate control.

Radio has gone much the same way. As a result of the Telecommunications Act of 1996, caps on radio ownership (once limited to 46 total stations) were eliminated. Today, one company—Clear Channel Communications, based in San Antonio, Texas—now owns over 1200 radio stations. The FCC retained some limits on how many stations a company can own in one market, but the result of the 1996 Act and the 2003 FCC rules change has been (and will continue to be) the growth of centralized ownership. Consumer activists claim that radio's offerings, both in terms of the variety of talk and music programming, grow narrower every day, and that corporate centralization and cost-cutting will undermine radio's important role in small towns and rural areas as the only forum for local news. Spokesmen for Clear Channel and other radio conglomerates respond that a larger company will be better able to satisfy consumer desires by pooling the resources of many radio stations, and that such a large company will be able to ensure standardized quality across all its stations in all its markets. Clear Channel is frank and unembarrassed by its priorities. Clear Channel CEO Lowry Mays told *Fortune* magazine in an interview in 2003 that "if anyone said that we're in the radio business, it wouldn't be someone from our company. We're not in the business of providing news and information. We're not in the business of providing well-researched music. We're simply in the business of selling our customers products."[9]

Synergy and cost-cutting have had major effects here, as well. Clear Channel's stations promote each other, but since the company also owns concert venues and billboards and has an interest in music promotion, certain artists receive disproportionate "spins" and attention on Clear Channel's stations. Much local programming, moreover, is no longer local. The morning DJ in your town might be recording his patter in Chicago or Dallas, with an occasional local reference thrown in for each market.

Whether we are talking about radio, television, the movies, or even print journalism, the progress is toward centralization, consolidation, and sameness. When it comes to music or movies, this is rarely more than annoying: it's hard to find an alternative sound or an independent cinema. But these television and radio stations also provide us with the news and with analysis of the news, and that can be dangerous. Clear Channel and Infinity Broadcasting and the ABC Radio Network may be in competition, but on political questions their interests are very similar. Even though Fox News Channel and CNN snipe at each other, in the end their stances on laws about the media are probably identical.

So where can you find a truly independent voice? That's difficult. Newspapers can offer viewpoints that differ from the voices of the media conglomerates, but newspapers themselves are probably owned by conglomerates such as Gannett, Newhouse, or the Tribune Company. Most cities have an alternative weekly such as the *LA Weekly,* the *New York Press,* the *Chicago Reader,* or *The*

---

[9] Christine Chen, "Not the Bad Boys of Radio." *Fortune* 18 Feb. 2003. Available at www.fortune.com/fortune/ceo/articles/0,15114,423802,00.html.

Stranger in Seattle; these weeklies generally provide a nonmainstream (if generally leftist) take on current events. However, even some of these alternative weeklies are owned by large companies that own many such papers. Left of the dial radio news is also valuable. National Public Radio maintains very high journalistic standards on its programs *All Things Considered* and *Morning Edition* (but conservatives feel that NPR's news often skews to the left). Many cities have affiliates of Pacifica Radio Network, an unabashedly leftist alternative to NPR. On the right, the nonprofit groups Family Research Council and Focus on the Family both provide current events and news programming, generally to religious radio stations on the AM dial. Television offers the unmediated congressional coverage of C-SPAN, the highly regarded public television news program *Newshour with Jim Lehrer,* and the unpredictable, often raucous programming available on cable-access stations. Those with expanded cable can also view the news as seen from foreign countries; the British Broadcasting Corporation is an especially reliable and evenhanded purveyor of news.

So there are a few places where Americans can go to consume "independent" news. But what about forums for producing or commenting on the news? Where can we go to get our voices out? Surprisingly, even in an environment of such concentrated ownership there are many ways to write for a public even if you don't work for Viacom or Vivendi Universal. Write for your college newspaper. Submit an editorial (remembering the lessons you've learned about audience analysis and effective rhetoric) to your hometown newspaper. Write a letter to National Public Radio responding to one of their stories. Get a show on your college or community radio station. Volunteer at the NPR affiliate station in your town—often after working at the station for several months you can write or produce a segment of local news. If you're more visually minded, buy or borrow a digital video camera and make your own footage: you can create news, comedy, or even a feature film. You could produce a show for the cable-access station. Write a play for a community theater group. Start a blog and submit it to one of the blog clearinghouse sites like blogspot.com. Write a piece for a religious radio station in your community. Write an article for the alternative newsweekly in your town or in the nearest city. Or start your own local news website. The articles on Dave Eggers, on the antiwar activists who use the Internet to organize, and on the conservative student newspapers included with this chapter might provide you with some ideas or inspiration. Especially interesting is Gloria Steinem's article "Sex, Lies, and Advertising," which discusses the pressures felt by the owners of *Ms.* magazine when they debated whether or not to make the magazine ad-free. How independent can a magazine be, Steinem asks, when the advertisers can determine content? Who then really "owns" that magazine?

Analyzing the Message

1. What are the dominant media voices in your community? Which of these have a national audience and which are aimed at a local or regional audience? How do the local or regional media outlets reflect the concerns of the community?

'Extra!...Extra!...Read some about it!'

2. Who owns the television and radio stations in your community? Are any of them owned locally?

3. What are the forums for independent voices in your community? Are there independent newsweeklies, community radio stations, cable-access television stations? How can you make your voice heard in those forums?

Readings

In this short article from the Columbia Journalism Review, **Janet Kolodzy** *looks at some of the practical ramifications of media conglomeration and centralization and finds much to cheer. Media outlets can pool their resources and draw upon the strengths of each format's reporters to strengthen their joint offerings.*

Janet Kolodzy
Everything That Rises

The fear of Big Media has overpowered much of the debate on cross-ownership of newspapers and television in local markets. But the issue isn't who owns the media; it's what those owners do with it. Journalists tend to believe in competition, but when we stop to consider, competition hasn't always brought diversity and quality in news. Convergence can—if done right.

Convergence means cooperative relationships between television, online, and print media. In places where this already exists, good journalism still flourishes. In some cities, local or regional cable news networks have developed relationships with newspapers, and diversity of opinion hasn't suffered.

Yet some critics equate convergence with a loss of jobs, heavier workloads for journalists, and monolithic news and opinion. They see it as the manifestation of the dark side of media consolidation. Convergence can indeed be all those things, if journalists let it.

But convergence can also harness the benefits of online, broadcast, and print to provide news to people when and where they want it. Few people get their news from one source anymore. Just look at all the ways people got news about the war in Iraq. They used TV for immediacy, online for diversity, and print for context. Journalism's adaptation to that fragmentation has been sluggish. Convergence is one way to keep up.

So far, television and the Internet have reaped the biggest benefits of convergence. Hundreds of print reporters operate in major cities with only handfuls of television reporters and few, if any, online reporters. With convergence, TV and the Internet get the depth of reporting and expertise that newspapers offer. In exchange, newspapers reach people who would never buy a newspaper, let alone subscribe to one.

Example: The *Hartford Courant* collaborates with a Fox affiliate. The Tribune Company, which owns the *Courant* and WTIC Fox 61, has placed its own stamp on convergence. Instead of trying to turn its print reporters into TV journalists, the *Courant* hired a television producer, Ellen Burns, to turn newspaper stories into TV stories. One example: reports on how New York's Cardinal Edward Egan handled priest sex-abuse cases when he was the bishop in Bridgeport, Connecticut. While the *Courant* wrote its reports, Burns packaged them for Fox 61. Instead of a weak, hurriedly produced and day-late TV story, WTIC viewers saw a well-researched, quality report. The TV version also was aired in New York, and the *Courant* piece made it into *Newsday*, both Tribune properties. More people learned of the story in different ways. The winner: the public.

Meanwhile, local and regional cable news networks have succeeded by using the depth of newspaper reporting to bring more government watchdogging and analysis to television. Newspaper reporters realize the reach of television when they go on the regional cable news networks to talk about their stories or to provide analysis.

Convergence's unfulfilled potential is in redistributing reporting resources. Watching dozens of media organizations descend on West Warwick, Rhode Island, after the recent deadly nightclub fire left me wondering about all the other wasted reporting opportunities. After the first day, all those reporters kept repeating the same two basic stories: who was to blame, and how the survivors and victims' families were faring. Convergence could have freed up some of those reporters to pursue investigative or other angles, providing some diversity and depth.

The key is to play to the strengths of each medium, and to respect those strengths. We saw some of that in the war with Iraq. *New York Times* reporters provided updates on CNN and PBS, adding depth and nuance. We heard the *Los Angeles Times* on NPR or someone from MSNBC on *Imus in the Morning*. NBC and Fox News reporters were filing Weblogs. The war tested the ingenuity of news organizations to manage resources to get the most diverse coverage.

But convergence, clearly, can be mismanaged. As one Tampa reporter put it, "We need managers who know the value of all media so that this new tactic can be harnessed properly." A carbon copy of a story in print, online, and on television doesn't cut it. Nor does a single perspective.

Journalists can devote their energy to debate the red herring of cross-ownership or they can channel it to make convergence work.

Topics for Reading and Writing

1. Is Kolodzy being naïve to ignore the dangers of media conglomeration and centralization that so many of our other writers point out? Or is she looking past the media's general liberal bias to see the positive effects of the free market on news coverage?

2. Who is the audience for this article? How does Kolodzy appeal to this specific audience? (Think about where this article originally appeared, and who reads that publication.)

---

*In this article, **Marc Fisher** engages in what is essentially a rhetorical analysis, analyzing the content of the journalism produced by the large media companies. Fisher, a columnist at the* Washington Post *who has also written* After the Wall: Germany, Germans, and the Burdens of History, *contributed this article to the* American Journalism Review, *a journal aimed at practicing journalists that examines current issues in journalism in a critical or theoretical light.*

For Fisher, one of journalism's raisons d'etre— "reasons for being"—is to perform the "filtering and synthesizing of information" citizens need in order to inform themselves about the issues of the day. But in today's "information age," when we all have access to the kinds of information that only a few people would see just 20 years ago, do we need journalists to perform this filtering and synthesizing for us? Doesn't

Marc Fisher
The Metamorphosis

The first clue came in New Hampshire, during the 1996 presidential campaign, when, no longer able to tolerate the inanity of Steve Forbes' Total Message Control, I stopped off in a picturesque town to take the local temperature. Among the first people I interviewed were 1) a C-SPAN junkie who wanted only to talk about the zen of Brian Lamb, 2) a talk-radio fanatic who refused to let me write down a word of his rant because he knew from listening to Rush ("I'm a megadittos man," my new friend told me) that I would only twist his views to match my liberal homosexual agenda, and 3) a bakery manager who was slackjawed over the fact that I neither read nor had ever heard of his favorite news source, Media Bypass, a monthly magazine (and now Web site and radio show, too) that reveals the "uncensored national news."

Of course, I still didn't really get it. Several more years went by before I finally realized that the essence of journalism had changed: The revelation arrived on a sunny afternoon in suburban Maryland, where I traveled to interview an elementary school principal, who had prepared for me by writing a short, neat list of "Talking Points," which now sat front and center on his desk. "Here's my sound bite," the man offered lamely. Luckily, I was able to persuade the *that just grant them the power they deny craving? Can't we be our own filters?*

principal to leave his list behind, join me on a leisurely walk, and tell me what was really happening in fourth grade.

But whether or not I got any morsel of truth out of that principal, something big has happened. The past 25 years have brought not only vast changes in the technology and corporate structure of journalism, not only a revolution in the definition of news and the expectations of both news consumers and news providers, but a startling rejiggering of the basic elements of what we do. Truth, fact and information seemed fairly straightforward concepts to most people in the news business a quarter century ago. Today, they're entirely up for grabs.

In the 1970s, news people could still be heroes—in our own minds and in the public imagination. In 1976, we flattered ourselves with comparisons to Jason Robards as Ben Bradlee and Robert Redford and Dustin Hoffman as Woodstein. Those were heady days: In "The Parallax View," only the reporter sees the huge conspiracy that is asphyxiating the nation, but he is killed before he can publish the story. In "Three Days of the Condor," the press is the last defense against the eternal Them.

But by 1979, postmodernism had poked its prickly finger into the national imagination: In "Apocalypse Now," Dennis Hopper was a freelance photographer who was our window onto the madness of Kurtz, the insanity of Vietnam, but Hopper was strung out, no longer able to synthesize information. He was our eyewitness, still shooting pictures, still sending us messages, but he was beyond judging. The observer had become an idiot.

It wouldn't be long before Hollywood picked up on the growing antipathy toward those who would dare to tell the people what the news was. The next decade brought an endless parade of reporters with loose morals, zero ethics and a paralyzed, misshapen view of what America should be.

Bye-bye, Woodward! Bye-bye, Murrow! Hello, "Dirty Laundry," the Don Henley song from 1983:

> I make my living off the Evening News
> Just give me something—something I can use
> People love it when you lose,
> They love dirty laundry . . . .
>
> We got the bubble-headed bleach-blonde
> comes on at five
> She can tell you 'bout the plane crash with a gleam in her eye
> It's Interesting when people die
> Give us dirty laundry . . . .
>
> Kick 'em when they're up
> Kick 'em when they're down
> Kick 'em when they're up
> Kick 'em all around

"The Metamorphosis" by Marc Fisher from *American Journalism Review,* November 2002. Reprinted by permission of *American Journalism Review.*

The Era of Journalistic Good Feeling that prevailed in AJR's early years, when disco was king and the imperial presidency was being dismantled by a cardigan-clad peanut farmer, was replaced by the unease and rancor of 1988's "Die Hard"—in which the reporter character was a self-obsessed buffoon who finally got a punch in the mouth, winning cheers from moviegoers. The press, now more routinely lumped into an unkempt mass called the "media," took on a collective identity; instead of hero reporters, we often saw ourselves depicted as a faceless throng, a clot of shouting, hectoring goons—The Pack. When we had any individual character, it wasn't exactly exemplary. In "Absence of Malice," audiences sided with the besieged businessman(!) Paul Newman against the conniving careerist Miami Sentinel reporter Sally Field.

But our image wasn't all that had changed. The audience was different, too. One other verse of "Dirty Laundry" demonstrates that for all the cynicism and aggression that came to dominate the image of the media mob, this souring of the relationship between the media and the public was a two-way street:

> You don't really need to find out what's going on
> You don't really want to know just how far it's gone
> Just leave well enough alone
> Keep your dirty laundry.

The public, Henley knew, no longer had much appetite for serious news. Of course, they weren't getting as much of the hard stuff as their parents had. Time and People, once wholly different, even antagonistic cousins, now seemed hard to tell apart. The late '70s hand-wringing about the increasing presence of analysis pieces and interpretive reporting in the nation's newspapers soon gave way to the decline of beats, the wholesale evisceration of newsroom staffs and newsholes by chains that sold their souls to Wall Street, and the evolution of broadcast news operations from the glory days of "CBS Reports" and NBC's "White Papers" to a state in which "Network," Paddy Chayefsky's 1976 satire on the creeping ascendancy of entertainment values, could easily be taken as a documentary.

This industry has reacted to powerful changes in what we produce and how it's received by focusing on some ailing trees, missing the fact that the forest is being paved over by developers. We pronounce ourselves determined to solve the Case of the Shrinking Sound Bite or the Mystery of Our Lack of Diversity or the Tragedy of the Missing Young Readers. And to be sure, these mini-crises exist. Political candidates' sound bites, which averaged 43 seconds on the network newscasts back in 1968, were down to 9.8 seconds by 1988 and squeezed to 7 seconds by 1996. But this debate, like most of those we've obsessed over through these 25 years, misses the larger point: You could hardly broadcast longer bites if you wanted to now, because politicians, like business people and even the proverbial man on the street, barely speak in complete sentences anymore. Of course, neither do TV newsfolk, whose language has devolved into a bizarre staccato of phrases and gerunds: "Mayor Smith rejecting tonight new allegations. Kathy Daly, on the night beat, with the mayor." Who's the chicken, who's the egg, who can figure out what's going on?

The harsh truth is that fewer people care what we do than did 25 years ago. And fewer think there's anything essential about the filtering and synthesizing of information that we perform.

We've made it all the easier for consumers to spurn our products because we've bought into the notion that all voices are equal, that a blowhard on talk radio has as valid a reading of political events as does the Washington bureau chief of the New York Times, or that opinions dumped onto a random Web site are as useful as a story written by a reporter who knows every deputy secretary in the agency he covers.

We have moved ever further from the basics of journalism. In the magazine world, the '70s now seem an impossibly rich period of serious reporting and adventuresome writing—in general mags such as New Times, in an edgy sports book called Jock, in an irreverent journalism review called MORE. The next era in magazine journalism explored new horizons in glitz, celebrity worship and a telegraphic style that virtually precludes storytelling.

Many newspapers at some point in the '80s or '90s declared government coverage boring, announced that they would cover the issues readers really care about and, under the guise of redeployment, proceeded to cut beat coverage and overall staffing to the point that nothing gets covered well. TV networks shuttered bureaus around the globe and nation, the nation's second tier of newspapers bowed out of national and foreign coverage, editorial and op-ed pages grew blander and more ideologically constricted.

And then we declared the decline in popular interest in our products unfathomable.

But news consumers didn't go away, they just found more interesting ideas. While we were busy dumbing down, the public was deconstructing the basic concept of news. Consumers couldn't buy our presses or transmitters, but some of them found ways to express their skepticism: They questioned our methods and even our belief in facts. Encouraged by new technology that promised the most raw and open of information democracies, consumers developed a crush on "unmediated" news: Personalize your Yahoo! News page. Watch C-SPAN. Listen to congressmen and joumos alike cutting loose with Imus. Get your politics from your college roommate's occasional e-mails about the Outrage of the Week.

Reasonably intelligent people today can and do report that they trust the "news" on the Howard Stem show or Jay Leno's monologue or the Drudge Report or their favorite blog more than the product of self-appointed arbiters of accuracy and fairness. The more "professional" and glitzy the corporate media became, the more attractive seemed Brian Lamb's 1979 stroke of genius, C-SPAN's purposefully dull and quiet approach.

Has the audience grown less discriminating, accepting Greta Van Susteren, Ann Coulter and George Stephanopoulos as journalists, or more sophisticated—sifting through the cacophony of the Web to draw their own conclusions about current affairs?

The only possible answer: Yes.

When I worked in Miami, there was an editor who made a big show of posting on the wall of his office a large, handwritten poster listing the things readers really care about. As you might expect, this did not bode well for nuts-and-bolts reporting. The list included sex, money, children, schools, home, cars—and the governing idea was that we would shape our coverage to match the list. There is, of course, nothing wrong with this list, nor with using the pages of a newspaper to reflect and illuminate readers' passions. But newspaper companies were only too eager to use such lists as an excuse to scale back on journalism's other obligation, the one enshrined in the Constitution: to serve as a check on government and other institutions. This involves providing information that the audience may not be clamoring for. This involves doing something well beyond mirroring popular taste. This involves spending money that may not produce an immediate return.

News executives in this country like to portray the past 25 years as a period of adjusting to changing audience desires. This has created the spectacle of editors and publishers claiming that they cannot control their own content because they are required to follow the public's demands. But there is no such natural law, and proof is available in other countries, particularly in Western Europe, where the definition of news has not changed nearly as severely as it has here. Newspapers and broadcast operations in those countries retain the same news agenda of a quarter century ago—a sometimes dull, easily lampooned mix of government, diplomatic and foreign reporting. Our news is more interesting—far more varied, far more entertainingly presented. But the contrast is worth noting, if only to show that there was nothing inevitable about our dumbing down.

Some changes of the past 25 years were, however, unstoppable. Thanks to the rise of the computer and the Web, the dreary spread of punditry has forced out real reporting like so many snakehead fish devouring other species in a pond. The rise of cable TV news channels, the Web's infinite newshole and corporate mandates to spend less on newsgathering have pushed managers to turn to the easiest and cheapest form of content—mouthing off. The handful of Web news ventures that engaged in original reporting didn't last long; those that survived consist primarily of commentary and analysis. Even CNN, which for years responded to the broadcast networks' cutbacks by increasing its fleet of reporters around the globe, has joined the rush to bloviate, replacing many hours of reporting with talkmeistars such as Connie Chung to go up against such "news" programming as Phil Donahue and Bill O'Reilly on MSNBC and Fox News Channel.

But amid all the on-air shouting and online chatter, the Web has also revolutionized reporting in exciting and encouraging ways. I shake my head just trying to reconstruct a day of reporting circa 1985—hours of phone calls just to find a good source on some new topic; long afternoons at me library, combing through the Reader's Guide to Periodicals; days spent at the courthouse, sifting through property records. All gone, like magic. But given the literally thousands of hours of drudge work that any reporter has saved over the past decade thanks to computers and the Web, how is it possible that we do not live in a golden age of reporting?

Popular culture has splintered in dozens of directions over these 25 years. A common national conversation became harder than ever to achieve. Cable ballooned into 100 choices, including three increasingly similar news operations. New magazines and e-zines now cater to every sliver of interest and identity. But a wave of consolidation and closings also narrowed outlets for news—radio largely bowed out of the news business, a tragedy that became most apparent on September 11, when most stations, without even a single news person on staff, ended up simulcasting the audio of TV coverage. In too many places, newspapers became monopoly operations, with coverage reflecting the arrogance and laziness that that status too often brings.

Every traditional news medium concluded that it is in grave danger of losing an entire generation of readers, viewers, listeners. Young people graze on the edges of the news empire, picking up headlines from the crawl on cable TV, tasting meatier stories highlighted on their favorite Weblogs, dipping into Yahoo! on the theory that it is something different, even though it's the same AP copy that's in their local newspaper.

Certainly the quality of people going into the business has only improved, at least on paper. The past 25 years saw the increased professionalization of journalism—more and more smart kids from fancy schools, ever fewer blue-collar types whose résumés featured more street sense than sheepskin. But expensively educated reporters didn't turn out to be any more aggressive, humane or artistic in their craft; if anything, the new crop was more malleable, more easily handled by corporate managers.

With ever fewer family-owned news operations, managers fell under the thumb of the short-term and shortsighted demands of Wall Street analysts, who made it clear that the journalism they liked best was tasty little morsels of stories, done on the cheap: TV newsmagazine minidramas that play on the emotions, a lite menu of news-you-can-use in print. I've been haunted for years by the sick feeling that overcame me in the mid-'80s after I received a lecture from a former schoolmate who had become a media analyst at a big Wall Street firm. "The Miami Herald has no business having foreign or domestic bureaus," he told me. "It's financially irresponsible. They should be using wires." Not long after that, to a much greater extent, they were.

All of which brings us back to the central question—what went wrong? In 1976, the editor of my high-school newspaper was suspended from his post after he published an article documenting marijuana sales and use on the school's campus. The story was a model of restraint well-reported, played inside the paper with discreet art. A quarter century later, student editors around the country routinely find themselves prevented from reporting on sensitive topics such as drugs, sex and race. The Student Press Law Center says complaints about censorship jumped from 478 in 1996 to 859 in 2000, and the trend continues (see "High School Confidential," June). Students have been prohibited from writing about lawsuits against their schools, criminal charges against students, student pranks, homosexuality, discrimination, even the debate over explicit teen dancing.

In the schools, as in the professional arena, lawyers and managers have gained the upper hand over reporters and editors. We all work in a narrower field of play—restrained by libel concerns, ethnic sensitivities, fiduciary responsibilities, all leading to less bold reporting, fewer chances taken.

For a brief, shining moment, it appeared that the Web could be an end run around those heightened sensitivities. For a couple of years, there was even a site dedicated to publishing the censored work of student reporters. But

BoltReporter.com is no more. And with ever more students being suspended or even expelled for their writings, it's no wonder that many schools—as many as 20 percent of U.S. high schools, according to the High School Journalism Institute at Indiana University—don't publish newspapers. A few brave young people continue to publish their censored work online—a splendid example resides at www.geocities.com/feature7777—but high-school students do not have the legal tools to be the vanguard of press freedom.

They do, however, have the righteous energy to show us what needs to be done. Have the traditional media consigned themselves to a grim future of narrowed possibilities and dull responsibility? Is dumbing down the only response we can concoct to our thinning audience? Or can journalists in the next 25 years reassert our sense of purpose and direction? All those people who have turned to other, seemingly less reliable sources are still searching for meaningful and compelling information. A trustworthy and fair filter that tells great stories and holds the nation's institutions accountable will always find an audience.

Topics for Reading and Writing

1. Fisher is a columnist for the *Washington Post,* but in this article he trades in the short, pithy, personal observations typical of a column for a more expansive, analytical tone. How does this article differ in style from the newspaper columns included in this book? How does this affect its rhetorical impact?

2. "The essence of journalism [has] changed," Fisher writes. What *was* journalism's "essence" before this change? What has caused this change? What is journalism like now?

Eric Boehlert
Radio's Big Bully

Clear Channel Communications, the radio station owners based in San Antonio, have embarked on a vigorous project of expansion over the last few years, and currently the chain owns over a thousand stations, as well as interests in concert promotion, theaters, and billboard advertising. The company has also been active politically, organizing pro-Bush rallies during the lead-up to the invasion of Iraq and preemptively issuing "do not play" lists for its DJs during that military conflict. Politically conservative, well-connected within the Bush administration, and ruthlessly centralized in its corporate control over its vast empire, Clear Channel is the

In the late 1990s, while no one was looking, a corporate behemoth became the largest owner and biggest force in America's most venerable mass medium: commercial radio.

Radio stations that once were proudly local are now being programmed from hundreds of miles away. Increasingly, the very DJs are in a different city as well.

Want your record played on one of those stations? Be prepared to pay—dearly—for the privilege. Want your band's concert to be sponsored by a radio station? Be careful: If you pick a competitor, the behemoth might pull your songs off its playlists overnight—from two, 10, 100 stations.

Looking for classy radio programming? Don't look here. The company is known for allowing animals to be killed live on the air, severing long-standing ties with *very embodiment of what critics of media consolidation fear.*

*But are these fears justified, or are they just another example of the antibusiness attitude so often displayed by liberals? Writing in the generally liberal online magazine Salon.com, senior writer **Eric Boehlert** (who has followed the radio and music industries for years), Boehlert argues that these fears are in fact more than fair. As you read Boehlert's article, though, test it for the logical fallacies outlined in Chapter 3. Does Boehlert try to use the boorish behavior of Clear Channel's executives as grounds for arguing that the company is bad? Does he fall into the traps of ad hominem or bandwagon or circular-reasoning fallacies?*

community and charity events, laying off thousands of workers, homogenizing playlists and a corporate culture in which dirty tricks are a way of life.

Welcome to the world of Clear Channel—radio's big bully.

It was a bittersweet night last June for the 40 to 50 radio executives and on-air personalities from the AMFM Network, including countdown king Casey Kasem. The scene was the famous Spago restaurant in West Hollywood for a night of eating and drinking on the company tab.

It was sweet: Everyone was in town for the annual R&R trade magazine industry convention, and it was a rare opportunity to schmooze with colleagues face to face at the plush Sunset Boulevard eatery.

Bitter though, as well, because the dinner marked the end of 460-station AMFM as an independent entity. Its parent company was being purchased by Clear Channel Communications—for a stunning $24 billion.

Many in the room recognized that in the compressed world of radio consolidation, AMFM as they knew it would cease to exist and many of them would soon be squeezed out of jobs.

Indeed, that same night at Spago, Clear Channel's radio chief, Randy Michaels, just happened to be holding court along with half a dozen minions of his own. A true radio original, Michaels had achieved legendary status inside the business as a shock jock (before there was a Howard Stern), and an effective but often tasteless programmer.

Michaels moved into management in the 1990s. Today, as Clear Channel's guardian of the airwaves, the bombastic exec is among the most powerful, not to mention colorful, men running the music business.

"Everything's a food fight with him," says one radio executive, who says Michaels is still a morning man at heart. "He's paranoid, disingenuous, pathological. That's what makes him so lovable."

The mood at Spago was cordial. Michaels even wandered over to the AMFM party to give a rah-rah speech about the upcoming AMFM/Clear Channel partnership.

As the party wound down and the crowd cleared out, two AMFM producers were unexpectedly waved over to the Clear Channel table by Michaels and his friend Kraig Kitchin, who runs Premiere Radio Networks, Clear Channel's powerful syndication arm.

According to industry sources, Michaels and Kitchin proceeded to grill the producers about AMFM shows and personnel. The producers, somewhat loquacious after an evening of food and spirits, spoke frankly, disparaging many AMFM initiatives and radio personalities.

Within days, AMFM Network president David Kantor heard from Kitchin. Kantor was told that once the merger was through, the two producers who'd spoken so bluntly would be let go. Michaels, Kitchin said, was not happy. Kantor was even given proof of the producers' bad-mouthing; the conversation at Spago had been surreptitiously recorded by a cellphone on the table. Kantor had been played parts of it.

"These guys didn't even work for Clear Channel yet and they were set up," says a former AMFM employee. "They used that conversation to fire them. Here's the head of Clear Channel and he's taping conversations? It's insane. It was a classic Randy Michaels dirty trick. He was just fucking with their heads; that's what they do."

Radio companies used to be severely constrained from owning what from the government's perspective was too many stations. Companies could own only two in any one market and no more than 28 nationwide. Government policy enforced the notion that radio was broadcast on the public airwaves and had an accompanying public trust. Local stations were supposed to be assets to local communities. The ownership rules were designed to keep ownership as diverse as possible and keep the stations' focus as local as possible.

All that changed in the 1990s. Five years ago, President Clinton, pressured by a GOP-controlled Congress, signed into law the Telecommunications Act, which essentially did away with ownership restrictions on radio. Now, just a handful of companies control radio in the 100 largest American markets.

Of these, Clear Channel rules the horizon with 1,200 stations, which generate more than $3 billion annually in revenues.

How big is Clear Channel? The company owns stations in 247 of the nation's 250 largest radio markets. Clear Channel in particular dominates the Top 40 format (KIIS-FM in Los Angeles, WHTZ and WKTU in New York, KHKS in Dallas, WXKS in Boston, WHYI in Miami, etc.) and controls 60 percent of rock-radio listening.

While radio's mad dash of consolidation was perhaps inevitable, it has still sent shock waves through the industry. Indeed, it's hard to say which puzzles the industry more—that one company has so quickly amassed such an enormous, 1,200-station roster or that a former shock jock like Michaels is running it.

The Wall Street Journal recently toasted Michaels as the never-grow-up "Peter Pan" of radio. An anonymous straw poll among radio and record pros, though, would probably reveal more who now see Michaels as Captain Hook. (He and other top Clear Channel executives declined to be interviewed for this story.)

Michaels has become the symbol of Clear Channel's dominance of an entire, multibillion-dollar media industry. What's made that adjustment so difficult for some is Clear Channel's litigious, cost-cutting, arrogant style of business.

And it's an attitude Michaels sets from the top.

Ever since Clear Channel's AMFM acquisition was completed, a simmering discontent has been brewing, prompted by some particularly heavy-handed moves on Clear Channel's part. "They were on their best behavior before AMFM, but now they're getting nasty," says Robert Unmacht, former editor and publisher of the M Street Journal, which tracks the radio business.

For instance, Clear Channel owns Premiere Radio Networks, which syndicates popular talk shows like those of Rush Limbaugh and Laura Schlessinger to hundreds of stations across the country.

Earlier this year Clear Channel sent out letters to non-Clear Channel stations that used Premiere features, informing them that their popular talk shows, including Limbaugh's and Schlessinger's, would be summarily yanked and moved immediately to Clear Channel competitors across town.

(Other large radio-owning conglomerates own syndicated shows as well, but as yet none have been wielding the programming in such a blatantly domineering way.)

"We spent hundreds of thousands of dollars over the past 12 years promoting the Rush Limbaugh show locally and we're paid back with a letter telling us it's being moved to our direct competitor," laments Glenn Gardner of talk station WTDY and rock outlet WJJO, both in Madison, Wis.

"We weren't even given a chance to bid and hang onto the show. Clearly what they're trying to do is squeeze everybody else out. We contacted [Wisconsin Sen.] Russ Feingold and told him this really needed to be looked at."

An even more recent example of Clear Channel's hardball style: On the very day radio-ratings company Arbitron went public with a Wall Street offering this month, Clear Channel decided to announce to Arbitron—and its investors—that the behemoth would not be renewing its contracts for the company's ratings surveys in 130 markets that were then under negotiation. The announcement represents a huge hit that could cost Arbitron tens of millions of dollars in lost revenues annually—not to mention dampen the company's newly public stock.

Over the past few years, there has been no shortage of industry players who would rail about Clear Channel and argue that the company was "ruining radio in so many different ways."

Off the record, that is.

"People in this business don't know who they're going to be working for next week. So a lot of them are just plain afraid to speak out," says Gardner. "It's a conspiracy of silence. It's really bizarre."

That silence is now being broken.

"They're definitely bullies, no question about that," says Ed Levine, chairman of Galaxy Communications, whose stations compete with Clear Channel in several upstate New York markets. "They've truly become the evil empire. Like everything else, Clear Channel has gone too far, gotten too greedy and too powerful. As a broadcaster who grew up in the business I don't believe their overall net effect for radio has been positive."

Marv Nyren, the marketing manager for four Phoenix stations of Emmis Communications, the nation's sixth-largest station owner, echoes that idea: "Most don't believe what they've done is good for the industry. They're all about quantity, not quality. They've taken the value out of radio and turned it into a commodity."

Clear Channel does have its share of supporters. "Ultimately these are people who will do what's right for the industry," insists Larry Roberts, president of Fisher Regional Radio Group.

Adds one Clear Channel programmer: "It's an aggressive company with foresight. They want to be the pioneers. The industry is going through fundamental change right now and some people are threatened by that."

It's not just the sheer number of stations that upsets so many people. Thanks to laissez-faire regulators in Washington, Clear Channel quickly has put together a stunning piece of vertical integration in big-money pop culture. Last year, the company spent $4.4 billion to purchase SFX Entertainment, the nation's dominant concert venue owner and touring promoter. Clear Channel also owns a radio research company, a format consultancy, regional radio news networks, an airplay monitoring system, syndicated programming, radio trade magazines like the Album Network, 19 television stations and 700,000 outdoor billboards worldwide. With so many resources at hand, the company has all but cut off its business with outside vendors.

"Clear Channel's not looking to be part of an industry, but rather a world unto themselves, and a lot of people resent that," says Unmacht.

Record company executives are particularly resentful about how Clear Channel stations leverage their playlists to make sure its SFX concert-promotion division lands certain tours.

Since concert fans listen to the radio a lot, there has long been a symbiotic relationship between concert venues and local radio stations. Ceaseless radio promotion helps sell concert tickets; and association with the hottest concert tours gives the stations concert tickets to give away and valuable P.R. identification with the best shows in town.

Clear Channel, the company's critics say, has been using its size to wrestle away tours from competitors by leveraging its size against record companies and artists.

"Clear Channel comes into markets and says to record companies, 'Don't give that station a concert or band promotion or there will be no business with us across our platform of stations,'" reports Hal Fish, program director at WBZX and WEGE in Columbus, Ohio.

Representatives from two platinum-selling rock bands confirm that their acts were pulled from Clear Channel stations over concert-promotion disputes, and not just pulled locally. The bands were yanked off playlists from a coalition of aligned Clear Channel stations stretching over several states. "It did happen; it was real," reports one label executive.

The groups' representatives spoke on condition the artists' names not be used, for fear of further irritating Clear Channel.

"Clearly the FCC [Federal Communications Commission] and the Department of Justice do not understand the connection and the power [Clear Channel] has" from owning so many radio stations and concert outlets, complains one concert promoter.

That controversy, though, pales in comparison to the one that's brewing over Clear Channel's second major power grab.

Pressured by Wall Street to find new streams of nontraditional revenue, Clear Channel, as Salon reported several weeks ago, is busy forging an exclusive alliance with a radio promotion company called Tri State Promotion & Marketing. The unprecedented deal could reap Clear Channel tens of millions of dollars.

Radio promotion firms—or "indies"—serve as well-paid middlemen or lobbyists, paid by record companies to get their songs played on radio stations. (The middlemen are necessary as "cut-outs": If labels paid directly for the airplay and stations didn't notify listeners, both would be in violation of payola laws.) The indies pay radio stations amounts in the six figures in return for an exclusive relationship—and invoice record companies thousands of dollars every time a station adds a new song to its playlist.

This multimillion-dollar promotions game has of late become less about salesmanship and more about market control. Now, say industry sources, Clear Channel, through Tri State, wants a piece of that lucrative pie.

By gaining exclusive access to Clear Channel's roster of playlists, Tri State, run by Michaels' old Cincinnati friend Bill Scull, could create steep new tolls for record companies wanting to get songs on the air on the nation's biggest broadcaster. And a part of those tolls will presumably find their way back to Clear Channel's corporate bottom line.

"They're going to gouge us," fears a record label rep.

The exclusive alliance would come at the expense of other indies who would likely lose their Clear Channel stations as clients. "For guys who are basically in the underbelly of consolidation, who probably got more than they should have, and are right on the cusp of anti-competition, I wouldn't be quite so aggressive. They're going to get their tit caught in the wringer."

"They're starting to rain all over everybody's parade and take food off people's tables, and that's when you get in trouble," says one radio veteran who has dealt with both Michaels and Clear Channel for years.

Michaels' career has been remarkable. Born as Benjamin Homel, he's a broadcasting enthusiast who has been known to rebuild old radios in his spare time. Fellow programmers credit him for helping create modern country radio back in the 1970s with WDAF in Kansas City, Mo., where he spun country songs at a Top 40 pace. And he's given credit for bringing legendary AM stations back to life, like WLW in Cincinnati, by reinvesting in news departments.

Behind the mike he made a name for himself back in the '70s and '80s farting on the air, cracking jokes about gays and tantalizing listeners with descriptions of "incredibly horny, wet and ready" naked in-studio guests. Along with getting hit with a sexual harassment suit, Michael pulled in big ratings wherever he went.

Ten years ago, he was an officer of a Cincinnati company called Jacor, which was founded in 1981 when Terry Jacobs bought up three religious radio stations. By 1990 it was a little-known radio outfit teetering on bankruptcy whose shares were trading for 75 cents.

But in 1993, Michaels made a key move. He persuaded self-described "vulture capitalist" Sam Zell to invest $70 million in the ailing Jacor. The swashbuckling investor, once described by Fortune as an "elfin billionaire who tools around Chicago on a motorcycle the size of an armored car," quickly bonded with the freewheeling Michaels. Soon Jacobs announced he was "retiring"; Michaels was given the Jacor reins and the OK to start buying stations.

"We're big. We're bad. We're back. We're rich," he bragged to the Cincinnati Enquirer in 1994.

Together, Michaels and Zell banked on their belief that legislators would soon ease ownership restrictions on radio owners. Back in 1995, station owners, represented by the mighty lobbying arm of the National Association of Broadcasters, found lots of friends in Washington busy drafting the telecommunications bill.

"The problem was the Republican Congress wanted not to rewrite the rules but eliminate them," recalls former FCC chairman Reed Hundt, who, along with the Clinton White House, opposed such drastic action. "The question was, 'Who's your constituency, the listener or the owner?' There was no question of who the Republican constituency was."

Hundt and President Clinton favored easing ownership restrictions, but at a more go-slow pace. In the end, says the former FCC commissioner, "the White House position on radio got rolled."

Corporate broadcasters were jubilant. Others in the business were not: "They gave the forest to the clear cutters," says one.

The ink on the Telecommunications Act was barely dry in January 1996 when Jacor, which at the time owned just 25 stations, started scooping up properties. Three years later Jacor had added 425 more stations to its roster.

In the meantime, another aggressive company, Clear Channel, was buying up stations as well. The company was built by Lowry Mays, a Texas A&M graduate who studied petroleum engineering and later got a degree from Harvard Business School. Mays fell into the radio business in 1972 when he guaranteed a bank note for a friend buying a San Antonio station. When his friend bailed, Mays, then an investment banker, took over the station himself. Over the years he continued to grow the company with acquisitions.

Like Zell at Jacor, Tom Hicks at Chancellor Media and Mel Karmazin at Infinity Broadcasting (he's now president of mighty Viacom), Mays went on a post-deregulation buying spree. With his bold $24 billion move in 1999 for AMFM, the deal that essentially marked the end of the consolidation spree, Clear Channel reigned as king of radio's hill. "Nobody in Vegas would have handicapped that—Clear Channel finishing in the No. 1 position," notes one radio pro.

Along the way, Clear Channel fixed its eyes on the smaller Jacor. Zell sold his company to Clear Channel in 1998 for $3.4 billion; his Jacor investments reaped a $1 billion profit.

But as part of the deal, Michaels and his cliquish team were put firmly in control of the new operation's radio properties. If they hadn't been, it would have cost the new owners more than $100 million in executive payouts.

"What's amazing is that Jacor swallowed up Clear Channel," says Levine at Galaxy Communications. "Older Clear Channel guys are still scratching their heads. They can't figure out how it happened."

Almost overnight Clear Channel's corporate culture changed. "It's really a Jacor company," notes one radio syndicator. "Even though it's called Clear Channel, it's just the Jacor mentality."

"Clear Channel before Randy [Michaels] was not hated," says Jerry Del Calliano, publisher of Inside Radio. (Del Calliano and Michaels have had a running range war for years. The two are currently facing off in court.) "But with the addition of the Jacor boys, Clear Channel became another company entirely," Del Calliano says.

What buttoned-down Clear Channel inherited, says Unmacht, were "basically good ol' boys from the frat house. They want to see who can be the rudest and crudest. Everything is done with the attitude of 16-year-olds in gym class, but with modern-day business smarts. They're definitely a rough lot." A few years ago Unmacht had dinner with an entourage of Jacor executives, including Michaels, at a Cincinnati restaurant, where they pointed out the still-visible stains from butter patties they had thrown at light fixtures.

That corporate culture extends down to the stations in various ways. It was given national exposure in the '90s when Jacor jock Liz Richards, working out of WFLA in Tampa, Fla., sued the company, including Michaels personally, for sexual harassment.

Interviewed on ABC's "20/20" program in 1992, Richards alleged that male co-workers dubbed her president of the "Cunt Club," that on the employee sign-in board someone drew a caricature of her with a penis ejaculating in her mouth and that a station manager falsely bragged to colleagues at a business dinner about getting head from Richards in a limousine.

Gary Kelly, a friend of Richards', appeared on camera to tell about the time he showed up at a station event to meet Richards and was told by her boss that the single mother of two was busy giving blow jobs in the parking lot.

At the time, Michaels was vice president of programming and an on-air personality at WFLA. Richards said he had a hand in setting the station's tone—she told ABC he once roamed the station halls with a flexible rubber penis tied around his neck, accosting female employees.

Michaels would not be interviewed on the show, and rejected the charges.

Jacor's response? "We are going to be forced to make public certain things about [Richards'] behavior which are going to further tarnish her reputation," Dave Reinhart, WFLA station manager and close friend of Michaels, told the St. Petersburg Times. Richards' suit was settled out of court in 1995.

More recently, Jacor's Tampa stations were back in the news in February, when WXTB morning man Todd Clem, who has the on-air handle "Bubba the Love Sponge," broadcast the killing of a live boar from the station's parking lot. WXTB posted pictures of the blood-soaked stunt on its Web site. It was the third time in a year that an animal was killed or tortured on-air at a Clear Channel station.

"They are not the most original people in the world, so if something works and gets a reaction they'll do it all over the place," notes Greg Mull, who programmed WXTB before Jacor bought the station.

Back in the Jacor days, the boar-killing incident likely would have been laughed off. But now Michaels has to answer to a boss—Mays, who besides being the patriarchal founder and chairman of Clear Channel, is also a friend of former President Bush's.

"I'm sure all of that made Lowry really uncomfortable," says Unmacht. Mays declined to comment for this story.

While Mays and his two investment banking sons, Mark and Randall, keep a tight rein on Clear Channel's financials, Michaels runs the radio properties. But broadcasters say there's a reason even the company's own employees refer to it as "Cheap Channel"; the Mays family demands high returns for Wall Street through Draconian cost cutting.

Michaels has become a believer in cost cutting; one of his innovations is the implementation of centralized, bureaucratic control over stations. Most Clear Channel stations are now overseen—and programmed—by regional, not local, programmers.

"Randy's afraid of Lowry," says Del Calliano at Inside Radio. "If Lowry wants budgets cut, Randy cuts budgets. He can't reinvest in the stations."

Unmacht agrees: "It's clear that Lowry Mays has changed him. He's a very different Randy. Now it's all business—profits, losses and trying to stay in the good graces of the Mayses. Randy would like to have good programming. We're just not seeing what he could do with a free hand. We saw that at Jacor and it was very good. But the pressure is now on to do more with fewer people. Everything needs to show a profit yesterday."

"It's difficult to do good radio and I think Clear Channel is overworking people, which ultimately drives down morale and success," worries the head of radio promotion at a major record label.

Through a process known as "cyber-jocking," Clear Channel has eliminated hundreds, if not thousands, of DJ positions (and saved tens of millions in salary) by simply having one company jock send out his or her show to dozens of sister stations. Thanks to clever digital editing, the shows still often sound local. And this isn't just for the graveyard shifts but for midday and even morning-drive shows.

Today, traveling across the country, radio listeners hear not only the same songs over and over but the same jocks from coast to coast. For instance, the midday show by a DJ named Randi West has aired simultaneously on Clear Channel stations in Cincinnati; Louisville, Ky.; Des Moines, Iowa; Toledo, Ohio; Charleston, S.C.; and Rochester, N.Y.

According to radio sources, though, the Clear Channel jocks used in this fashion often receive little or no extra money for filling on-air vacancies in dozens of extra markets.

The company claims that it's a way to broadcast major-market talent in small-town stations. But do FM stations in Phoenix really need help landing major talent? Apparently they do: Clear Channel's Top 40 station there, KZZP, has been rebroadcasting Rick Dees' morning show from KIIS-FM in Los Angeles.

Why? The only expense for the Phoenix station is paying a board operator. "They've got a morning show for $6 an hour. That's not programming for the listeners," says Nyren at Emmis.

After purchasing WNUA in Chicago, Clear Channel last year shut down the WNUA Cares for Kids Foundation, which had raised hundreds of thousands of dollars for charity.

For more than 20 years in Louisville, AM mainstay WHAS had exclusively aired the Great Balloon Race during the Kentucky Derby Festival. Late last year the Clear Channel station, which in the past had paid a rights fee for the community event, informed derby officials the station now wanted to get paid for airing the event. "What this signaled to me was that there was a change in the way that they are choosing to promote community events," Derby Festival president Mike Berry said at the time.

To be fair, Clear Channel is not alone when it comes to heavy-handed cost cutting in radio these days. Two weeks ago the Chicago Sun-Times reported that local Infinity country station WUSN told its on-air jocks they had to attend the George Strait Music Festival and work the crowd.

What was wrong with that? The jocks had to buy their own tickets!

The station's management suggested they buy lawn seats, which started at $30. How much money did the penny-pinching WUSN bill in ad sales last year? Nearly $50 million.

Will Clear Channel, radio's big bully, get away with all this?

Can national programmers impose their prefab formats on local radio stations? Won't audiences revolt?

There is some evidence that consolidation economics has damaged radio's popularity. Desperate for additional revenue, stations have substantially increased the number of commercials aired, often cramming 15 or 20 minutes' worth of ads in each hour.

Listeners have taken note of the onslaught. In just the past seven years radio listening has declined nearly 15 percent, according to Arbitron. One in three listeners between the ages of 12 and 24 recently told Arbitron they were listening to less radio specifically because of the commercial overload.

"It pains me to say it, but radio sucks and it has sucked for the better part of consolidation," says Del Calliano at Inside Radio. "And anybody who loves radio knows that. You'd have to be working for Randy Michaels to say otherwise."

Topics for Reading and Writing

1. The radio business is getting more centralized by the day. What's wrong with that? What is the upside of playlists generated by consulting firms? Why shouldn't record companies be involved in deciding what artists get played? Are we nostalgic for an era of noncorporate radio and independent music that really never existed?

2. Boehlert's piece appeared in Salon.com, one of the Web's most popular and well-respected cultural journals. How does Boehlert's writing differ from how he might compose this argument for a newspaper? For a magazine? For a television segment on *60 Minutes* or *Frontline?* What are the essential differences between writing for the Web and writing for a paper-based publication?

Brent Staples, author of Parallel Time: Growing Up in Black and White *(1993), here contributes an editorial to the* New York Times *about what he sees as one of the dangers of corporate ownership of radio stations. Popular music, Staples feels, used to be a political barometer, reflecting the feelings of young people.*

Brent Staples
The Trouble with Corporate Radio: The Day the Protest Music Died

Pop music played a crucial role in the national debate over the Vietnam War. By the late 1960's, radio stations across the country were

Today, songs that challenge corporate authority would never be heard on the corporate radio. In fact, bands who write political music might even have trouble finding a venue for their concerts.

crackling with blatantly political songs that became mainstream hits. After the National Guard killed four antiwar demonstrators at Kent State University in Ohio in the spring of 1970, Crosby, Stills, Nash and Young recorded a song, simply titled "Ohio," about the horror of the event, criticizing President Richard Nixon by name. The song was rushed onto the air while sentiment was still high, and became both an antiwar anthem and a huge moneymaker.

A comparable song about George W. Bush's rush to war in Iraq would have no chance at all today. There are plenty of angry people, many with prime music-buying demographics. But independent radio stations that once would have played edgy, political music have been gobbled up by corporations that control hundreds of stations and have no wish to rock the boat. Corporate ownership has changed what gets played—and who plays it. With a few exceptions, the disc jockeys who once existed to discover provocative new music have long since been put out to pasture. The new generation operates from play lists dictated by Corporate Central—lists that some D.J.'s describe as "wallpaper music."

Recording artists were seen as hysterics when they complained during the 1990's that radio was killing popular music by playing too little of it. But musicians have turned out to be the canaries in the coal mine—the first group to be affected by a 1996 federal law that allowed corporations to gobble up hundreds of stations, limiting expression over airwaves that are merely licensed to broadcasters but owned by the American public.

When a media giant swallows a station, it typically fires the staff and pipes in music along with something that resembles news via satellite. To make the local public think that things have remained the same, the voice track system sometimes includes references to local matters sprinkled into the broadcast.

What my rock 'n' roll colleague William Safire describes as the "ruination of independent radio" started with corporatizing in the 1980's but took off dramatically when the Telecommunications Act of 1996 increased the number of stations that one entity could own in a single market and permitted companies to buy up as many stations nationally as their deep pockets would allow.

The new rules were billed as an effort to increase radio diversity, but they appear to have had the opposite effect. Under the old rules, the top two owners had 115 stations between them. Today, the top two own more than 1,400 stations. In many major markets, a few corporations control 80 percent of the listenership or more.

Liberal Democrats are horrified by the legion of conservative talk show hosts who dominate the airwaves. But the problem stretches across party lines. National Journal reported last month that Representative Mark Foley, Republican of Florida, was finding it difficult to reach his constituents over the air since national radio companies moved into his district, reducing the number of local stations from five to one. Senator Byron Dorgan, Democrat of North Dakota, had a potential disaster in his district when a freight train carrying anhydrous ammonia derailed, releasing a deadly cloud over the city of Minot. When the emergency alert system failed, the police called the town radio stations, six of which are owned by the corporate giant Clear Channel. According to news accounts, no one answered the phone at the stations for more than an hour and a half. Three hundred people were hospitalized, some partially blinded by the ammonia. Pets and livestock were killed.

The perils of consolidation can be seen clearly in the music world. Different stations play formats labeled "adult contemporary," "active rock," "contemporary hit radio" and so on. But studies show that the formats are often different in name only—and that as many as 50 percent of the songs played in one format can be found in other formats as well. The point of these sterile play lists is to continually repeat songs that challenge nothing and no one, blending in large blocks of commercials.

Senator Russell Feingold of Wisconsin has introduced a bill that would require close scrutiny of mergers that could potentially put the majority of the country's radio stations in a single corporation's hands. Lawmakers who missed last month's Senate hearings on this issue should get hold of the testimony offered by the singer and songwriter Don Henley, best known as a member of the Eagles, the rock band.

Mr. Henley's Senate testimony recalled the Congressional payola hearings of 1959–60, which showed the public how disc jockeys were accepting bribes to spin records on the air. Now, Mr. Henley said, record companies must pay large sums to "independent promoters," who intercede with radio conglomerates to get songs on the air. Those fees, Mr. Henley said in a recent telephone interview, sometimes reach $400,000.

Which brings us back to the hypothetical pop song attacking George Bush. The odds against such a song reaching the air are steep from the outset, given a conservative corporate structure that controls thousands of stations. Record executives who know the lay of land take the path of least resistance when deciding where to spend their promotional money. This flight to sameness and superficiality is narrowing the range of what Americans hear on the radio—and killing popular music.

La Cucaracha © 2003 Lalo Alcaraz. Dist. by Universal Press Syndicate. Reprinted with permission. All rights reserved.

Topics for Reading and Writing

1. Baby boomers like to romanticize the role of music in creating the activism of the 1960s, but are they overemphasizing its importance? And even if protest music doesn't get played on Clear Channel stations, won't people still hear it? Is radio the only way to promote music?

2. What does Staples mean by "payola"? And what does this have to do with protest music?

3. One of Staples's implicit arguments is that it's wrong for a company to use its corporate power over the media to promote political viewpoints. How does he reconcile this idea with his celebration of the radio stations that played the 1970s protest song "Ohio"?

---

*Dave Eggers is one of the most fascinating young writers in America today. At once drawn to and repelled by the mass media, Eggers has founded two very influential underground journals (*Might *and* McSweeney's*), started extracurricular programs for young people in the troubled Mission District of San Francisco, edited collections of contemporary writing, been rejected as a potential cast member of MTV's* Real World: San Francisco *cast, and served as a sort of unofficial scoutmaster to a group of young writers who look at the media and the culture of celebrity in a sardonic but appreciative way. Eggers is also the author of the best-selling* A Heartbreaking Work of Staggering Genius *(2000) (a memoir about raising his younger brother after both parents died) and the novel* You Shall Know Our Velocity *(2002). Although rarely strident or even public about his beliefs or desires, one of the motivations underlying many of Eggers's projects is the desire to circumvent or undermine the corporate mass media and its growing control over avenues for writing. In this piece from the liberal journal* The

Lorraine Adams
The Write Stuff

There is a long, slow line. The queue of narrow-shouldered boys in thrift-store shirts and black-tighted girls with Emily Dickinson stares is blocking aisles in a Washington bookstore. The faithful look to be just out of college or just past 30. They thread through the door and onto the sidewalk.

They are waiting for Dave Eggers to sign copies of his first novel. Eggers' charisma is not readily apparent. His hair is frizz, his eyes scrunched, his shirt untucked. He looks vitamin deficient. "I think," says bookstore clerk Keltie Hawkins, "his appeal has something to do with being a combination of cool and approachable." His is an unsexy cool—it comes from a mawkish life story. When Eggers was 21, his parents died of cancer within a month of each other, leaving him to raise his 8-year-old brother. Seven years later, Eggers' 2000 memoir, *A Heartbreaking Work of Staggering Genius,* became a best seller. Its story of a near-child raising a child resonated with a generation marked by divorce, working parents and what Eggers terms "a loose weak human chaos of emotion."

A Heartbreaking Work was published by Simon & Schuster, but the novel he is signing in the Washington bookstore is a product of his own publishing company. Eggers, who once

American Prospect, *Lorraine Adams profiles Eggers, focusing on how he uses—or tries to avoid—his celebrity as a way to promote the political and literary projects he truly cares about.*

quit a plum editing job at *Esquire* magazine in disgust, abhors corporate publishing. His first novel is available only on his Web site and at independent bookstores. Despite these handicaps, *You Shall Know Our Velocity* has been on *The Washington Post*'s best-seller list for months. An *On the Road* for the millennial generation, it follows two young men dispensing $32,000 to impoverished people across Africa and Eastern Europe. Most reviewers have either derided its puerility or raved about its prose. Few have taken seriously its characters' confrontation with economic inequities.

Most observers see Eggers and his fans as existing outside politics. But Eggers' literary superstardom is prompting an alternative culture that has grown up around him over the last five years. It is a San Francisco- and Brooklyn-based community of writers, artists, designers and, increasingly, children—with a growing national following. They are the readers, contributors and designers of the literary journal-cum-Web site *McSweeney's* (first published in 1998) and *McSweeney's* Books. (Eleven have been published so far.) They are, especially in the last year, the audiences at *McSweeney's*-sponsored conferences, readings and concerts across the country. They are idealistic about education, sentimental about children and impatient with the homogeneous culture that corporations produce.

You Shall Know Our Velocity is dedicated to Beth, Eggers' older sister who was a law student at the time their parents died and also contributed to the parenting of the youngest Eggers, Christopher. In 2001, Beth took a fatal overdose of an anti-depressant combined with an over-the-counter pain reliever, acetaminophen. Once a family of six, the Eggers clan now numbers three. How many other upper-middle-class, suburban midwestern families can claim such familiarity with premature death and the parenting improvisations that have largely been the province of the precarious poor?

That familiarity may bear some relationship to Eggers' creation last April of a way station for the less parented in San Francisco's Mission District, a working-class Hispanic neighborhood.

Called 826 Valencia (after its street address), the learning emporium has a reading room done in Moroccan-style furnishings where young people can study. There is also a college-scholarship program for students interested in writing. Eggers and about 400 volunteers teach writing and comics creation, run workshops on SAT preparation and help kids launch student publications. They deploy 20 to 30 tutors at a time into classrooms at the request of teachers for one-on-one work on student writing. "They're great," said James Kass, executive director of Youth Speaks, a San Francisco, New York and Seattle nonprofit program for teenagers that fosters the literary arts. "They have a real belief that they can help teachers and public schools that are overextended and underfunded, because they can attract a lot more volunteers than most nonprofits because of Dave Eggers. They've done a lot in a short time." (Eggers and *McSweeney's* President Barb Bersche declined to be interviewed. "With our tight deadlines for our upcoming books, tutoring and teaching classes at 826 Valencia, and juggling traveling for speaking engagements, we really haven't been able to participate in any interviews all year," Bersche wrote in an e-mail.)

Beyond confirming how the center works, 826 Director Nínive Calegari also declined to be quoted, saying, "We've been asking people not to focus on us. There are so many nonprofits in San Francisco doing such great things, we're kind of shying away from any publicity." She has a point. The Mission Learning Center, for example, in existence for 30 years, tutors students who read below their grade level. Aim High, in its 16th year, is an academic- and cultural-enrichment program for motivated middle-school students. Less than a year old, 826 may merely be another well-intentioned but ultimately micro attempt to solve a macro social problem—the failure of urban education.

The nine issues of *McSweeney's*, lined up on a shelf, are a curious collection. One is composed of 14 color pamphlets in a box. One is a short-spined, cloth-covered oblong. One's front cover is blank. Inside, the graphics are luscious, funny and playful, culled from children's illustrations, scientific drawings, museum catalogues and flea-market memorabilia. This mishmash is the *McSweeney's* aesthetic. There is an implied *McSweeney's* economics: What is valuable is made in batches, the hand of its maker much in evidence. There is a *McSweeney's* psychology: Previously outmoded warmth is defended with a force field of self-consciousness. And there is *McSweeney's* endorsed music: Exemplified by the band They Might Be Giants, it is a cross between understated rock and nursery chant, with quizzically cerebral lyrics. The band appeared with Eggers and other *McSweeney's* writers at performances last fall in Washington, Philadelphia, New York and elsewhere.

But until recently, there was only the most primitive *McSweeney's* politics. In his memoir, Eggers writes proudly of the idiotic magazine he founded in the early 1990s, *Might*. He describes Lead . . . or Leave and Third Millennium, two national advocacy groups designed to mobilize a youth version of the AARP to fight for Social Security reform, writing, "We make contact with these organizations, pledge solidarity, though to be honest we have absolutely no idea what they're talking about."

Eggers writes that the magazine lionizes Wendy Kopp, "at twenty-five the founder of Teach for America, which places recent college graduates in under-staffed or financed schools, mostly urban. We love people like this, those who are starting massive organizations, trying new approaches to age-old problems and getting the word out about it, with great PR, terrific publicity photos, available in black and white or color transparency." The smirk at the end is a lot like Eggers' take on political engagement: "It's like the '60s! 'Look! Look,' we say to one another, 'at the imbalances, the glaring flaws of the world, aghast, amazed. Look how things are! Look at how, for instance, there are all these homeless people! Look at how they have to defecate all over the streets, where we have to walk! Look at how high rents are! Look at how the banks charge these hidden fees when you use their ATMs!'"

Eggers' novel *Velocity* has a different outlook. Here the narrator criticizes his mother for mocking his madcap globalized charity:

You're the type that won't give to a street person; you'll think you're doing them harm. But who's condescending then? You withhold and you run counter to your instincts. There is disparity and our instinct is to create parity, immediately. Our instinct is to split our bank account with the person who has nothing. But you're talking behind seven layers of denial and justification. If it feels good it is good, and today, at the ocean, we met a man living in a half-finished hut, and he was tall and had a radio and we gave him about $700 and it was good. It can't be taken from us, and you cannot soil it with words like condescending and subjective, fey and privileged words, and you cannot pretend that you know a better way. You try it! You do it! We gave and received love! How can you deprive us of that?

The *McSweeney's* generation brings to mind another that thought parents had it all wrong—the London counterculture of the early 1960s. As Shawn Levy points out in his book *Ready, Steady, Go! The Smashing Rise and Giddy Fall of Swinging London,* at first there was little that was political about iconoclastic fashion (Mary Quant and Twiggy), new music (the Beatles and the Rolling Stones) and defiant lifestyles (illegal drugs and sexual license). These trends spread to the United States, but there they became, as they did not in the United Kingdom, transformative political movements—civil rights, feminism and Vietnam War protest.

Could *McSweeney's* alternative culture be a precursor, as swinging London was, to a new political physics? Could *McSweeney's* be analogous to the 1950s *City Lights Journal,* City Lights Publishers and the Beats—Allen Ginsberg, Lawrence Ferlinghetti, Jack Kerouac?

There is not a protest flavor to *McSweeney's*. This, along with its relative indifference to drugs and sex, separates it from the Beats, the forerunners of Haight-Ashbury's hippies. But there is, as there was in swinging London, inventiveness. Some of this comes from *McSweeney's* "why not?" sense that there *are* ways around the mega-consolidated culture manufacturers. "Perhaps Dave's most political act is his attempted rebuke of the publishing industry and the chains," says a New York editor.

Until recently, archness had been the hallmark of *McSweeney's*. A recent issue shows that attitude to have softened. At the top of its cover are the words "thankful" and "emboldened." Right below the magazine's title are the words, "The hot-blooded life-saving presumption of perpetual, irrational or more likely, irreducibly rational good will." The motto for this issue, also on the cover, reads, "We give you sweaty hugs." The issue is dedicated to the students of 826 Valencia.

There are more overtly political stories and essays, among them William T. Vollmann's "Three Meditations on Death," about Yugoslavia, the Holocaust and Vietnam; K. Kvashay-Boyle's "Saint Chola," about a Muslim girl's vilification in junior high; and Gabe Hudson's "Notes from a Bunker Along Highway 8," about the Gulf War.

One of the touchstones *of McSweeney's* has been Eggers' expansion of the obligatory copyright language into an expanded jujitsu lampooning the media. In the recent issue, Eggers devotes this section to the work at 826 Valencia:

The students have been astounding. Many of the stories written by our younger visitors involve nautical themes, because directly in front of the writing lab is our new store, where we sell quality pirate supplies at reasonable prices. The store's proceeds pay the rent at 826 Valencia, in toto, because we expected and have been correct in thinking that people were sick of having to drive all the way to the mall to buy swabbing mops, planks and millet. Behind the store and the reading lab are our new editorial offices where we assemble all the *McSweeney's* books and journals, with our full-time staff of two and the help of many outstanding interns. These three pieces—the publishing, the lab, the store—interact in wonderful and unexpected ways and can't be explained here. We feel very thankful for the life that exists at 826 Valencia each day, the noise it generates and the kids who come in to learn or laugh or, for some, to sit and read quietly.

In 1840, Ralph Waldo Emerson and Margaret Fuller, founding editors of the *Dial,* published a letter to readers. The journal, Emerson wrote, was united against any convention that was "turning us to stone, which renounces hope, which looks only backward, which asks only such a future as the past, which suspects improvement, and holds nothing so much in horror as new views and the dreams of youth . . . . And so with diligent hands and good intent we set down our Dial on the earth. We wish it may resemble that instrument in its celebrated happiness, that of measuring no hours but those of sunshine. Let it be one cheerful rational voice amidst the din of mourners and polemics."

While *McSweeney's* is hardly the *Dial,* and Eggers is no Emerson, there are interesting similarities. Optimism is only one. There are also commonalities between 826 Valencia and Bronson Alcott's Temple School, founded in 1834, with its colorblind admissions and emphasis on imagination to foster learning among children.

McSweeneyites also seem related to the pragmatist tradition, described in Louis Menand's *The Metaphysical Club,* a collective biography of Oliver Wendell Holmes Jr., Charles Sanders Peirce, William James and John Dewey. While not their intellectual equals by any means, the McSweeneyites do seem to share that quartet's belief that ideas are, as Menand writes, "tools—like forks and knives and microchips—that people devise to cope with the world in which they find themselves. They believed that ideas are produced not by individuals, but by groups of individuals—that ideas are social . . . . Ideas should never become ideologies—either justifying the status quo, or dictating some transcendent imperative for renouncing it."

Ferlinghetti, the Beat poet who founded the City Lights bookstore, explained in a 1997 interview that ideology, indeed political engagement, were at first taboo to him and his peers. "The Beat . . . is the cool citizen, the cool cat who will not stick his neck out far enough to be engaged," he said. Today, the Beats are associated with revolutionary politics. But the Beats never wrote about racial segregation or the second-class status of women. Today, the Transcendentalists (who *did* write about abolishing slavery and women's rights) have been drained of their engagement, becoming in the popular imagination little more than nature lovers extolling the beauty of Walden Pond and renouncing society.

No matter where Eggers and *McSweeney's* stand in relation to these important parts of American intellectual and cultural history, it is hard to ignore their new direction toward the political. There is a link between what Eggers experienced personally and his sensitivity to the need for mentoring that honors the connection between the seriousness of learning and play. He challenges—in his graphic innovations at *McSweeney's*, in his shunning of corporate control of writing, in his desire to teach children to write, not just read—accepted rules of publishing and pedagogy. Maybe he is an opportunist and a huckster. Very soon, like Jay McInerney and Tama Janowitz, the so-called voices of my generation, he may fall into oblivion and inconsequence. But the readers who wait in line for him will remain, and so will the hopes they harbor for innovation.

Topics for Reading and Writing

1. Celebrity activism always generates a backlash—from Martin Sheen and Janeane Garofalo to Charlton Heston and Ronald Reagan, actors-turned-activists spur resentment in many people, who feel that privileged celebrities have no business speaking on behalf of "regular people." Eggers seems very aware of this, and is not interested in becoming another celebrity spokesperson for a political cause. How does Eggers's celebrity or notoriety interact with or undermine his activist projects?

2. Adams's article is a fine example of a profile with an agenda. How does her profile differ from the others in this book (for example, George Packer's "Smart-Mobbing the War" in this chapter)? What strategies does Adams use to convey her argument?

Edward R. Murrow (1908–1965) of CBS News is probably, along with Walter Cronkite of the same organization, one of the most beloved broadcast journalists in American history. Murrow was based in London during World War II and Americans still remember his radio dispatches from that city as German bombs fell. Murrow covered the Korean War but also helped develop, through his programs See It Now, Person to Person, *and* I Can Hear It Now, *some of the templates for radio and television news coverage that still endure today. Murrow's 1952* See It Now *program about the "Red Scare" and Wisconsin Senator Joseph McCarthy is widely*

Edward R. Murrow Address to RTNDA Convention, October 15, 1958

This just might do nobody any good. At the end of this discourse a few people may accuse this reporter of fouling his own comfortable nest, and your organization may be accused of having given hospitality to heretical and even dangerous thoughts. But the elaborate structure of networks, advertising agencies and sponsors will not be shaken or altered. It is my desire, if not my duty, to try to talk to you journeymen with some candor about what is happening to radio and television.

I have no technical advice or counsel to offer those of you who labor in this vineyard that produces words and pictures. You will for-

credited with turning the tide of public opinion against the controversial senator. Murrow's well-known address to the Radio-Television News Directors Association is included in this book to demonstrate that the concerns about centralization, corporate control, the dumbing-down of news for ratings, and the power of advertisers aren't by any means new.

give me for not telling you that instruments with which you work are miraculous, that your responsibility is unprecedented or that your aspirations are frequently frustrated. It is not necessary to remind you that the fact that your voice is amplified to the degree where it reaches from one end of the country to the other does not confer upon you greater wisdom or understanding than you possessed when your voice reached only from one end of the bar to the other. All of these things you know.

You should also know at the outset that, in the manner of witnesses before Congressional committees, I appear here voluntarily—by invitation—that I am an employee of the Columbia Broadcasting System, that I am neither an officer nor a director of that corporation and that these remarks are of a "do-it-yourself" nature. If what I have to say is responsible, then I alone am responsible for the saying of it. Seeking neither approbation from my employers, nor new sponsors, nor acclaim from the critics of radio and television, I cannot well be disappointed. Believing that potentially the commercial system of broadcasting as practiced in this country is the best and freest yet devised, I have decided to express my concern about what I believe to be happening to radio and television. These instruments have been good to me beyond my due. There exists in mind no reasonable grounds for personal complaint. I have no feud, either with my employers, any sponsors, or with the professional critics of radio and television. But I am seized with an abiding fear regarding what these two instruments are doing to our society, our culture and our heritage.

Our history will be what we make it. And if there are any historians about fifty or a hundred years from now, and there should be preserved the kinescopes for one week of all three networks, they will there find recorded in black and white, or color, evidence of decadence, escapism and insulation from the realities of the world in which we live. I invite your attention to the television schedules of all networks between the hours of 8 and 11 p.m., Eastern Time. Here you will find only fleeting and spasmodic reference to the fact that this nation is in mortal danger. There are, it is true, occasional informative programs presented in that intellectual ghetto on Sunday afternoons. But during the daily peak viewing periods, television in the main insulates us from the realities of the world in which we live. If this state of affairs continues, we may alter an advertising slogan to read: LOOK NOW, PAY LATER.

For surely we shall pay for using this most powerful instrument of communication to insulate the citizenry from the hard and demanding realities which must be faced if we are to survive. I mean the word survive literally. If there were to be a competition in indifference, or perhaps in insulation from reality, then Nero and his fiddle, Chamberlain and his umbrella, could not find a place on an early afternoon sustaining show. If Hollywood were to run out of Indians, the program schedules would be mangled beyond all recognition. Then some courageous soul with a small budget might be able to do a documentary telling what, in fact, we have done—and are still doing—to the Indians in this country. But that would be unpleasant. And we must at all costs shield the sensitive citizens from anything that is unpleasant.

I am entirely persuaded that the American public is more reasonable, restrained and more mature than most of our industry's program planners believe. Their fear of controversy is not warranted by the evidence. I have reason to know, as do many of you, that when the evidence on a controversial subject is fairly and calmly presented, the public recognizes it for what it is—an effort to illuminate rather than to agitate.

Several years ago, when we undertook to do a program on Egypt and Israel, well-meaning, experienced and intelligent friends shook their heads and said, "This you cannot do—you will be handed your head. It is an emotion-packed controversy, and there is no room for reason in it." We did the program. Zionists, anti-Zionists, the friends of the Middle East, Egyptian and Israeli officials said, with a faint tone of surprise, "It was a fair count. The information was there. We have no complaints."

Our experience was similar with two half-hour programs dealing with cigarette smoking and lung cancer. Both the medical profession and the tobacco industry cooperated in a rather wary fashion. But in the end of the day they were both reasonably content. The subject of radioactive fall-out and the banning of nuclear tests was, and is, highly controversial. But according to what little evidence there is, viewers were prepared to listen to both sides with reason and restraint. This is not said to claim any special or unusual competence in the presentation of controversial subjects, but rather to indicate that timidity in these areas is not warranted by the evidence.

Recently, network spokesmen have been disposed to complain that the professional critics of television have been "rather beastly." There have been hints that somehow competition for the advertising dollar has caused the critics of print to gang up on television and radio. This reporter has no desire to defend the critics. They have space in which to do that on their own behalf. But it remains a fact that the newspapers and magazines are the only instruments of mass communication which remain free from sustained and regular critical comment. If the network spokesmen are so anguished about what appears in print, let them come forth and engage in a little sustained and regular comment regarding newspapers and magazines. It is an ancient and sad fact that most people in network television, and radio, have an exaggerated regard for what appears in print. And there have been cases where executives have refused to make even private comment or on a program for which they were responsible until they'd heard the reviews in print. This is hardly an exhibition confidence.

The oldest excuse of the networks for their timidity is their youth. Their spokesmen say, "We are young; we have not developed the traditions nor acquired the experience of the older media." If they but knew it, they are building those traditions, creating those precedents everyday. Each time they yield to a voice from Washington or any political pressure, each time they eliminate something that might offend some section of the community, they are creating their own body of precedent and tradition. They are, in fact, not content to be "half safe."

Nowhere is this better illustrated than by the fact that the chairman of the Federal Communications Commission publicly prods broadcasters to engage in their legal right to editorialize. Of course, to undertake an editorial policy, overt and clearly labeled, and obviously unsponsored, requires a station or a network to be responsible. Most stations today probably do not have the manpower to assume this responsibility, but the manpower could be recruited. Editorials would not be profitable; if they had a cutting edge, they might even offend. It is much easier, much less troublesome, to use the money-making machine of television and radio merely as a conduit through which to channel anything that is not libelous, obscene or defamatory. In that way one has the illusion of power without responsibility.

So far as radio—that most satisfying and rewarding instrument—is concerned, the diagnosis of its difficulties is rather easy. And obviously I speak only of news and information. In order to progress, it need only go backward. To the time when singing commercials were not allowed on news reports, when there was no middle commercial in a 15-minute news report, when radio was rather proud, alert and fast. I recently asked a network official, "Why this great rash of five-minute news reports (including three commercials) on weekends?" He replied, "Because that seems to be the only thing we can sell."

In this kind of complex and confusing world, you can't tell very much about the why of the news in broadcasts where only three minutes is available for news. The only man who could do that was Elmer Davis, and his kind aren't about any more. If radio news is to be regarded as a commodity, only acceptable when saleable, then I don't care what you call it—I say it isn't news.

My memory also goes back to the time when the fear of a slight reduction in business did not result in an immediate cutback in bodies in the news and public affairs department, at a time when network profits had just reached an all-time high. We would all agree, I think, that whether on a station or a network, the stapling machine is a poor substitute for a newsroom typewriter.

One of the minor tragedies of television news and information is that the networks will not even defend their vital interests. When my employer, CBS, through a combination of enterprise and good luck, did an interview with Nikita Khrushchev, the President uttered a few ill-chosen, uninformed words on the subject, and the network practically apologized. This produced a rarity. Many newspapers defended the CBS right to produce the program and commended it for initiative. But the other networks remained silent.

Likewise, when John Foster Dulles, by personal decree, banned American journalists from going to Communist China, and subsequently offered contradictory explanations, for his fiat the networks entered only a mild protest. Then they apparently forgot the unpleasantness. Can it be that this national industry is content to serve the public interest only with the trickle of news that comes out of Hong Kong, to leave its viewers in ignorance of the cataclysmic changes that are occurring in a nation of six hundred million people? I have no illusions about the difficulties reporting from a dictatorship, but our British and French allies have been better served—in their public interest—with some very useful information from their reporters in Communist China.

One of the basic troubles with radio and television news is that both instruments have grown up as an incompatible combination of show business, advertising and news. Each of the three is a rather bizarre and demanding profession.

And when you get all three under one roof, the dust never settles. The top management of the networks with a few notable exceptions, has been trained in advertising, research, sales or show business. But by the nature of the coporate structure, they also make the final and crucial decisions having to do with news and public affairs. Frequently they have neither the time nor the competence to do this. It is not easy for the same small group of men to decide whether to buy a new station for millions of dollars, build a new building, alter the rate card, buy a new Western, sell a soap opera, decide what defensive line to take in connection with the latest Congressional inquiry, how much money to spend on promoting a new program, what additions or deletions should be made in the existing covey or clutch of vice-presidents, and at the same time—frequently on the same long day—to give mature, thoughtful consideration to the manifold problems that confront those who are charged with the responsibility for news and public affairs.

Sometimes there is a clash between the public interest and the corporate interest. A telephone call or a letter from the proper quarter in Washington is treated rather more seriously than a communication from an irate but not politically potent viewer. It is tempting enough to give away a little air time for frequently irresponsible and unwarranted utterances in an effort to temper the wind of criticism.

Upon occasion, economics and editorial judgment are in conflict. And there is no law which says that dollars will be defeated by duty. Not so long ago the President of the United States delivered a television address to the nation. He was discoursing on the possibility or probability of war between this nation and the Soviet Union and Communist China—a reasonably compelling subject. Two networks CBS and NBC, delayed that broadcast for an hour and fifteen minutes. If this decision was dictated by anything other than financial reasons, the networks didn't deign to explain those reasons. That hour-and-fifteen-minute delay, by the way, is about twice the time required for an ICBM to travel from the Soviet Union to major targets in the United States. It is difficult to believe that this decision was made by men who love, respect and understand news.

So far, I have been dealing largely with the deficit side of the ledger, and the items could be expanded. But I have said, and I believe, that potentially we have in this country a free enterprise system of radio and television which is superior to any other. But to achieve its promise, it must be both free and enterprising. There is no suggestion here that networks or individual stations should operate as philanthropies. But I can find nothing in the Bill of Rights or the Communications Act which says that they must increase their net profits each year, lest the Republic collapse. I do not suggest that news and information should be subsidized by foundations or private subscriptions. I am aware that the networks have expended, and are expending, very considerable sums of money on public affairs programs from which they cannot hope to receive any financial reward. I have had the privilege at CBS of presiding over a considerable number of such programs. I testify, and am able to stand here and say, that I have never had a program turned down by my superiors because of the money it would cost.

But we all know that you cannot reach the potential maximum audience in marginal time with a sustaining program. This is so because so many stations on the network—any network—will decline to carry it. Every licensee who applies for a grant to operate in the public interest, convenience and necessity makes certain promises as to what he will do in terms of program content. Many recipients of licenses have, in blunt language, welshed on those promises. The money-making machine somehow blunts their memories. The only remedy for this is closer inspection and punitive action by the F.C.C. But in the view of many this would come perilously close to supervision of program content by a federal agency.

So it seems that we cannot rely on philanthropic support or foundation subsidies; we cannot follow the "sustaining route"—the networks cannot pay all the freight—and the F.C.C. cannot or will not discipline those who abuse the facilities that belong to the public. What, then, is the answer? Do we merely stay in our comfortable nests, concluding that the obligation of these instruments has been discharged when we work at the job of informing the public for a minimum of time? Or do we believe that the preservation of the Republic is a seven-day-a-week job, demanding more awareness, better skills and more perseverance than we have yet contemplated.

I am frightened by the imbalance, the constant striving to reach the largest possible audience for everything; by the absence of a sustained study of the state of the nation. Heywood Broun once said, "No body politic is healthy until it begins to itch." I would like television to produce some itching pills rather than this endless outpouring of tranquilizers. It can be done. Maybe it won't be, but it could. Let us not shoot the wrong piano player. Do not be deluded into believing that the titular heads of the networks control what appears on their networks. They all have better taste. All are responsible to stockholders, and in my experience all are honorable men. But they must schedule what they can sell in the public market.

And this brings us to the nub of the question. In one sense it rather revolves around the phrase heard frequently along Madison Avenue: The Corporate Image. I am not precisely sure what this phrase means, but I would imagine that it reflects a desire on the part of the corporations who pay the advertising bills to have the public image, or believe that they are not merely bodies with no souls, panting in pursuit of elusive dollars. They would like us to believe that they can distinguish between the public good and the private or corporate gain. So the question is this: Are the big corporations who pay the freight for radio and television programs wise to use that time exclusively for the sale of goods and services? Is it in their own interest and that of the stockholders so to do? The sponsor of an hour's television program is not buying merely the six minutes devoted to commercial message. He is determining, within broad limits, the sum total of the impact of the entire hour. If he always, invariably, reaches for the largest possible audience, then this process of insulation, of escape from reality, will continue to be massively financed, and its apologist will continue to make winsome speeches about giving the public what it wants, or "letting the public decide."

I refuse to believe that the presidents and chairmen of the boards of these big corporations want their corporate image to consist exclusively of a solemn voice in an echo chamber, or a pretty girl opening the door of a refrigerator, or a horse that talks. They want something better, and on occasion some of them have demonstrated it. But most of the men whose legal and moral responsibility it is to spend the stockholders' money for advertising are removed from the realities of the mass media by five, six, or a dozen contraceptive layers of vice-presidents, public relations counsel and advertising agencies. Their business is to sell goods, and the competition is pretty tough.

But this nation is now in competition with malignant forces of evil who are using every instrument at their command to empty the minds of their subjects and fill those minds with slogans, determination and faith in the future. If we go on as we are, we are protecting the mind of the American public from any real contact with the menacing world that squeezes in upon us. We are engaged in a great experiment to discover whether a free public opinion can devise and direct methods of managing the affairs of the nation. We may fail. But we are handicapping ourselves needlessly.

Let us have a little competition. Not only in selling soap, cigarettes and automobiles, but in informing a troubled, apprehensive but receptive public. Why should not each of the 20 or 30 big corporations which dominate radio and television decide that they will give up one or two of their regularly scheduled programs each year, turn the time over to the networks and say in effect: "This is a tiny tithe, just a little bit of our profits. On this particular night we aren't going to try to sell cigarettes or automobiles; this is merely a gesture to indicate our belief in the importance of ideas." The networks should, and I think would, pay for the cost of producing the program. The advertiser, the sponsor, would get name credit but would have nothing to do with the content of the program. Would this blemish the corporate image? Would the stockholders object? I think not. For if the premise upon which our pluralistic society rests, which as I understand it is that if the people are given sufficient undiluted information, they will then somehow, even after long, sober second thoughts, reach the right decision—if that premise is wrong, then not only the corporate image but the corporations are done for.

There used to be an old phrase in this country, employed when someone talked too much. It was: "Go hire a hall." Under this proposal the sponsor would have hired the hall; he has bought the time; the local station operator, no matter how indifferent, is going to carry the program—he has to. Then it's up to the networks to fill the hall. I am not here talking about editorializing but about straightaway exposition as direct, unadorned and impartial as falliable human beings can make it. Just once in a while let us exalt the importance of ideas and information. Let us dream to the extent of saying that on a given Sunday night the time normally occupied by Ed Sullivan is given over to a clinical survey of the state of American education, and a week or two later the time normally used by Steve Allen is devoted to a thoroughgoing study of American policy in the Middle East. Would the corporate image of their respective sponsors be damaged? Would the stockholders rise up in their wrath and complain? Would anything happen other than that a few million people would have received a little illumination on subjects that may well determine the future of this country, and therefore the future of the corporations? This method would also provide real competition between the networks as to which could outdo the others in the palatable presentation of information. It would provide an outlet for the young men of skill, and there are some even of dedication, who would like to do something other than devise methods of insulating while selling.

There may be other and simpler methods of utilizing these instruments of radio and television in the interests of a free society. But I know of none that could be so easily accomplished inside the framework of the existing commercial system. I don't know how you would measure the success or failure of a given program. And it would be hard to prove the magnitude of the benefit accruing to the corporation which gave up one night of a variety or quiz show in order that the network might marshal its skills to do a thorough-going job on the present status of NATO, or plans for controlling nuclear tests. But I would reckon that the president, and indeed the majority of shareholders of the corporation who sponsored such a venture, would feel just a little bit better about the corporation and the country.

It may be that the present system, with no modifications and no experiments, can survive. Perhaps the money-making machine has some kind of built-in perpetual motion, but I do not think so. To a very considerable extent the media of mass communications in a given country reflect the political, economic and social climate in which they flourish. That is the reason ours differ from the British and French, or the Russian and Chinese. We are currently wealthy, fat, comfortable and complacent. We have currently a built-in allergy to unpleasant or disturbing information. Our mass media reflect this. But unless we get up off our fat surpluses and recognize that television in the main is being used to distract, delude, amuse and insulate us, then television and those who finance it, those who look at it and those who work at it, may see a totally different picture too late.

I do not advocate that we turn television into a 27-inch wailing wall, where longhairs constantly moan about the state of our culture and our defense. But I would just like to see it reflect occasionally the hard, unyielding realities of the world in which we live. I would like to see it done inside the existing framework, and I would like to see the doing of it redound to the credit of those who finance and program it. Measure the results by Nielsen, Trendex or Silex—it doesn't matter. The main thing is to try. The responsibility can be easily placed, in spite of all the mouthings about giving the public what it wants. It rests on big business, and on big television, and it rests at the top. Responsibility is not something that can be assigned or delegated. And it promises its own reward: good business and good television.

Perhaps no one will do anything about it. I have ventured to outline it against a background of criticism that may have been too harsh only because I could think of nothing better. Someone once said—I think it was Max Eastman—that "that publisher serves his advertiser best who best serves his readers." I cannot believe that radio and television, or the corporation that finance the programs, are serving well or truly their viewers or listeners, or themselves.

I began by saying that our history will be what we make it. If we go on as we are, then history will take its revenge, and retribution will not limp in catching up with us.

We are to a large extent an imitative society. If one or two or three corporations would undertake to devote just a small traction of their advertising appropriation along the lines that I have suggested, the procedure would grow by contagion; the economic burden would be bearable, and there might ensue a most exciting adventure—exposure to ideas and the bringing of reality into the homes of the nation.

To those who say people wouldn't look; they wouldn't be interested; they're too complacent, indifferent and insulated, I can only reply: There is, in one reporter's opinion, considerable evidence against that contention. But even if they are right, what have they got to lose? Because if they are right, and this instrument is good for nothing but to entertain, amuse and insulate, then the tube is flickering now and we will soon see that the whole struggle is lost.

This instrument can teach, it can illuminate; yes, and it can even inspire. But it can do so only to the extent that humans are determined to use it to those ends. Otherwise it is merely wires and lights in a box. There is a great and perhaps decisive battle to be fought against ignorance, intolerance and indifference. This weapon of television could be useful.

Stonewall Jackson, who knew something about the use of weapons, is reported to have said, "When war comes, you must draw the sword and throw away the scabbard." The trouble with television is that it is rusting in the scabbard during a battle for survival.

Topics for Reading and Writing

1. Murrow complains that the television networks want to "shield" the American public from anything that is "unpleasant." Why do they do this, according to Murrow? Do they still do this?

2. Murrow argues for the benefits of the "free-enterprise system," but insists that it must be "free and enterprising." What do you think his opinion of the state of media today would be? And if free enterprise has brought us to our current state of highly centralized control of media, is free enterprise to blame? Or is this state not something to be worried about?

This profile of young antiwar activist Eli Pariser isn't about who owns the media exactly, but it sheds some interesting light on questions of the nature of ownership. In its early years, the decentralized Internet seemed to be the very epitome of democracy, or even anarchy: there were no rules, no governing bodies, and no police, just a community of (mostly) like-minded people who wanted to exchange information without going through familiar channels. Determining who "owns" the Internet is particularly difficult,

George Packer
Smart-Mobbing the War

You can find America's new antiwar movement in a bright yellow room four floors above the traffic of West 57th Street—a room so small that its occupant burns himself on the heat pipe when he turns over in bed and can commute to his office without touching the floor. Eli Pariser, 22, tall, bearded, spends long hours every day at his desk hunched over a laptop, plotting strategy and directing the electronic traffic of an instantaneous movement that was partly assembled in his computer. During the past three months it has gathered the numbers that took three years to build during Vietnam. It may be the fastest-growing protest movement in American history.

because it doesn't exist in any central place: the Internet is every computer logged on, every server providing information, every T1 line or WiFi connection or phone jack. The number of owners, then, is immeasurable. Given this, is the Internet still a good place for activists to go when they want to communicate without being spied upon, without having restrictions on what they can talk about? Do they "own" any part of the Internet just by squatters' rights?

On the day after Sept. 11, Pariser, who was living outside Boston at the time, sent an e-mail message to a group of friends that urged them to contact elected officials and to advocate a restrained response to the terror attacks—a police action in the framework of international law. War, Pariser believed, was the wrong answer; it would only slaughter more innocents and create more terrorists. Friends passed his letter on to more friends, it replicated exponentially, as things tend to do on the Internet, and Pariser woke one morning to find 300 e-mail messages in his in-box. A journalist called him from Romania. "I've received this from five different people," he said. "Who are you?"

Almost simultaneously, a recent University of Chicago graduate named David Pickering was posting a petition with a similar message on a campus Web site. By Sept. 14, Pickering's petition had almost 1,000 signatures. On Sept. 15 it reached Pariser, who got in touch with Pickering and proposed that they join forces, with Pickering's petition posted on a Web site that Pariser set up as a conduit for responses to his own e-mail. Pariser called it 9-11peace.org. On Sept. 18, 120,000 people from 190 countries signed the petition. By then, the server was beginning to crash.

By Oct. 9, when Pariser finally lugged four copies of the petition to his local post office—one each for George W. Bush, Tony Blair, Kofi Annan and the secretary general of NATO—it was more than 3,000 pages long, with more than half a million signatures. There was no response from the White House, which had already begun the war in Afghanistan. But Pariser had happened upon an organizing tool of dazzling power. "It was word of mouth," he says. "This is why this system of organizing works."

In the fall of 2001 the idea of a measured response to the attacks along the lines of a criminal-justice model was a distinctly minority view. Only one member of Congress, Barbara Lee of California, voted against the war resolution. The petition created a network for the war's isolated and beleaguered opponents that let them know they were not alone as history rolled over them.

A little more than a year later, the pressure of a war with Iraq has turned the underground spring into a genuine social convulsion. At the end of 2001, Pariser was approached by another dot-org that had been watching the heavy traffic on his Web site—a group called moveon.org. started in Berkeley in 1998 by married software entrepreneurs, Wes Boyd and Joan Blades, to stop the impeachment of Bill Clinton. Pariser joined them as a consultant and merged the two sites. Last fall moveon.org, caught the growing wave of antiwar feeling, and its membership doubled, so that it now counts almost 1.3 million worldwide and 900,000 in this country. Moveon.org became known as the mainstream of the growing movement, joining a larger coalition called Win Without War, whose name seems expressly designed to ward off any charges of anti-Americanism.

Moveon.org organized meetings around the country between members and politicians, calling for tough inspections as a rational alternative to war, and its influence began to be felt in Congress. Its Political Action Committee raised more than $700,000 for Paul Wellstone's re-election last October after the Minnesota senator voted against the Iraq war resolution, and when Wellstone died in a plane crash, moveon.org used its database to raise $200,000 for his replacement on the ballot, Walter Mondale, in just two hours.

All this electronic activity went largely unnoticed by the press. The nationwide antiwar rallies on Oct. 26 and Jan. 15 were dominated by far more radical groups, like International Answer, that had gotten out in front of the protest movement, turning out a core of activists under the perennial anti-American slogans. But as the threat of war frayed nerves across the country, moveon.org formed a tactical alliance with the radical groups, with which it had nothing in common other than opposition to war in Iraq. "We've changed the way that we do organizing in the last eight months," Pariser told me. "One of the things is to move past e-mailing and phone calls and get people back out on the street and use the Internet as a backbone for catalyzing that."

Last November, at the European Social Forum in Florence, antiwar groups chose Feb. 15 as a day of continent-wide protest. The American wing of the movement learned of the plan through e-mail from European groups like Stop the War Coalition and Attac France. United for Peace and Justice decided to sign on in December, though organizing here only started on Jan. 7, a mere five weeks before the date set for the demonstrations. To anyone who hadn't been paying attention—not least, those in the mainstream media—the hundreds of thousands who braved the cold near the United Nations on Feb. 15, and the millions more around the world, came as a revelation.

But popularity has had a way of killing American protest movements. When history refuses to bend to their will, frustration leads the majority to drift away, while grouplets in the vanguard grow more extreme in their ideas and their tactics. On the left in particular, from the Popular Front of the 1930's to the antiwar mobilization of the 60's, mass movements tend to self-destruct in factional fights just when they've begun to acquire a national following. These are old ghosts, and 22 is young for anyone to have to figure them out.

When Pariser had his 90 seconds onstage at the Feb. 15 rally, he seemed literally to bounce on his toes in the frigid air, unable not to smile. "For each person who's here, there are a hundred who weren't able to make it," he told the throng that filled First Avenue from 51st to 72nd Street. "I know—I get e-mail from them. They're ordinary, patriotic, mainstream Americans."

Eli Pariser seems to exist so that patriotic, mainstream, duct-tape-buying Americans can't dismiss the antiwar movement as a fringe phenomenon of graying pacifists and young nihilists. He has a copy of the Constitution on his bookshelf. He says things like "It's not the Internet that's cool—it's what it allows people to do." He is unfailingly polite and thoughtful, careful to acknowledge what he doesn't yet know, and only the way he holds his face away and fixes you with a sidelong look as he speaks tells you that this is an ambitious and slightly cagey young man.

Pariser says that when he was 5, he picketed in his own driveway in rural Maine with a sign that said. "Nature's great—don't take it away." He descends on his father's side from Zionist Jews who helped found Tel Aviv, and on his mother's from Polish socialists. His parents, co-founders of an alternative school and amicably divorced when Pariser was 7, were Vietnam protesters. But an interesting generational split inverts the 60's order of things: the son is less rebellious, less estranged from his country, than the parents. His mother used to argue with him to do *less* homework, and after Sept. 11 his parents couldn't understand Pariser's willingness to call himself a patriot.

In 2000, after graduating from Simon's Rock College of Bard in western Massachusetts, Pariser and a handful of friends toured the country for three months in a renovated school bus, recording the stories of ordinary people in order to find out what makes Americans tick politically. The idea was yet another Web project (americanstory.org—it hasn't happened yet), but the effect on Pariser was much larger: in the midst of a national campaign that left most people bored and disenchanted, he found that opinion polls and political rhetoric didn't come close to doing justice to Americans' beliefs. "There's all this gloss and spin and whatever, and then there's actually what people think," he told me. "Even when we talked to people who are racists, pro-gun folks, I couldn't make myself dislike them just because of their political views."

Internet democracy solves the problem of how to focus political activity in a vast country of extremely busy and distracted citizens, because what keeps so many Americans busy and distracted these days is the Internet. In late February, my in-box received a forwarded message with the subject line "Virtual March: Heading to 200,000 SEND FAX~a5646u63431t0~." The "Virtual March on Washington" was a campaign that Win Without War staged on Feb. 26: hundreds of thousands of Americans around the country flooded the Washington offices of their elected officials with antiwar messages, timed by electronic coordination so that phone lines wouldn't jam up. Internet democracy allows citizens to find one another directly, without phone trees or meetings of chapter organizations, and it amplifies their voices in the electronic storms or "smart mobs" (masses summoned electronically) that it seems able to generate in a few hours. With cellphones and instant messaging, the time frame of protest might soon be the nanosecond.

Dot-org politics represents the latest manifestation of a recurrent American faith that there is something inherently good in the *vox populi*. Democracy is at its purest and best when the largest number of voices are heard, and every institution that comes between the people and their government—the press, the political pros, the fund-raisers—taints the process. "If money is what it takes to get attention, we'll do that," Pariser says. "But we'll do it the grass-roots way."

Pariser says that he and other organizers are less political propagandists than "facilitators" who "help people to do what they want to do." Even the structure of moveon.org—more than a million members and only four employees—embodies the idea that a simple and direct line connects scattered individuals and the expression of their political will. With an interactive feature on the Web site called the Action Forum, members regularly make suggestions and respond to the staff's and one another's ideas. Automated reports arc generated by the server every week, moveon.org's staff looks at the top-rated comments—and somehow, out of this nonstop frenzy of digital activity, a decision gets made. And, in a sense, no one makes it. Dot-org politics confirms what Tocqueville noticed more than a century and a half ago: that Americans, for all our vaunted individualism, tend to dissolve in a tide of mass opinion.

Behind the stage at the Feb. 15 rally, Pariser made a point of introducing himself to Dennis Kucinich, the boyish-looking Democratic congressman from Cleveland who is planning to run for president on an antiwar platform. Kucinich has followed Pariser's rise, and he declared: "Eli has proven we're in a new era of grass-roots activism. The basis for human unity is not just electronic—the human unity precedes the electronic, and then is furthered by it. Eli represents 'the advancing tide,' which Emerson said 'creates for itself a condition of its own. And the question and the answer are one.'"

The spirit of Emerson was on First Avenue, and it hovers over the new antiwar movement as it has infused so much protest politics in American history. There is a very old American type of protester—think of Emerson's friend Thoreau, or of John Brown—who sees politics as an expression of personal morality. This spirit belongs to President Bush as much as to his antiwar opponents, who mirror one another in viewing the world through a lens of moral polarity.

Part of the success of the Feb. 15 demonstrations, and of the movement itself, lies in the simplicity of the message. L.A. Kauffman, a staff organizer at United for Peace and Justice, the coalition of more than 200 organizations that endorsed the rally, designed leaflets and banners rending, "The World Says No to War." The slogan says nothing about oil, or inspections, or Israel—or Saddam. "It's not a paragraph of analysis," she points out. "It's not a lengthy series of demands." The simplicity allows groups that have nothing else in common politically—that might even be opponents—to work together.

Leslie Cagan, a founder of United for Peace and Justice (which is only four months old) and a veteran antiwar activist, says that in 1991, during the gulf war, the ideological infighting was much more bruising. The attitude in this movement, for now, is to submerge political disagreement. "We all see what a nightmare this war would be," she says. "That's bigger than any of the differences between us."

When a group like International Answer—whose leader, Ramsey Clark, has defended many of the world's dictators, including Saddam—calls for a march on the White House on March 15, United for Peace and Justice doesn't make its decision about whether to join based on the politics of the original sponsor. A leader of the most mainstream coalition in the movement, Win Without War, of which moveon.org is a part, is urging members to participate in the Answer demonstration.

This strategy of openness is unquestionably the best way to increase numbers in the short run. But it has its perils, and inevitably it forces ideological choices even when the movement seeks to avoid them. In the planning for Feb. 15, for example, a Bay Area coalition of groups refused to include Michael Lerner, a rabbi and editor of Tikkun magazine, among the speakers because he had publicly criticized one of the groups, International Answer, for its anti-Israel views. The coalition's policy was to exclude anyone who had attacked a member group—which meant that the peace movement had to choose between Lerner and Answer.

The night before Feb. 15, Bob Wing of United for Peace and Justice told me: "Anti-Semitism is not tolerable. I don't think it's a huge problem, but it is a problem and something to be aware of. But we're not talking about thought control—we're talking about making this as big as we can." When I asked Leslie Cagan whether pro-Saddam speakers would have been allowed onstage, she said, "We try not to edit them." Pariser put it this way: "I've always been a real believer that the best ideas win out if you let them happen. I'm personally against defending Slobodan Milosevic and calling North Korea a socialist heaven, but it's just not relevant right now."

The strongest tendency at the Feb. 15 rally (and in the movement generally) was not anti-Americanism or anti-globalism or pro-Arabism; it was simply a sense that war does more harm than good. A young woman from Def Poetry Jam shouted: "We send our love to poets in Iraq and Palestine. Stay safe!" The notion that there is no real safety in Iraq and, strictly speaking, there are no poets—that the Iraqi people, while not welcoming the threat of bombs, might be realistic enough to accept a war as their only hope of liberation from tyranny—was unthinkable. The protesters saw themselves as defending Iraqis from the terrible fate that the U.S. was preparing to inflict on them. This assumption is based on moral innocence—on an inability to imagine the horror in which Iraqis live, and a desire for all good things to go together. War is evil, therefore prevention of war must be good. The wars fought for human rights in our own time—in Bosnia and Kosovo—have not registered with Pariser's generation. When I asked Pariser whether the views of Iraqis themselves should be taken into account, he said, "I don't think that first and foremost this is about them as much as it's about us and how we act in the world."

For now, clarity and a sense of righteousness have created the most potent American protest movement in a generation. What isn't clear is how the new movement will sustain itself once a war begins. Ask movement organizers about their planning for the next few crucial weeks, with a war seemingly imminent, and the answers are vague. "We don't think a month in advance," Pariser says. "We can capture the energy of the moment better at the moment"—a notion echoed by Wes Boyd, who explains that moveon.org's great strength is flexibility and speed, not "scenario planning." L.A. Kauffman of United for Peace and Justice says, "If war does break out, you are going to see a global day of action like you've never seen." Coalition leaders stay in touch with their European counterparts, e-mailing every few days, but for now the movement seems to be trying to catch up with its own success. Other than the demonstration planned for March 15, no mass mobilization was scheduled as of last week.

After an invasion, moveon.org's Wes Boyd says, the movement may become more polarized. Groups like Answer will continue to oppose American foreign policy in its totality, while moveon.org's membership might turn its fund-raising power to Democratic presidential politics. A number of potential Democratic antiwar candidates have started to emerge, including Kucinich, former Gov. Howard Dean of Vermont, former Senator Carol Moseley Braun of Illinois and the Rev. Al Sharpton. While Pariser is too cautious to declare any political ambitions of his own, the party would be foolish not to pursue a young activist with his talents.

In the yellow room on West 57th Street, Pariser's bookcase is heavy with fiction that tends toward large, bleak visions: Orwell's "1984," DeLillo's "Underworld," David Foster Wallace's "Infinite Jest." The literature seems out of tune with Pariser's optimism about democracy and his own temperament. Pariser says he reads the books "as a way of kind of seeing what it's like to not be happy. There's a part of me that's drawn to kind of big stories, sort of epicness—this sense of this sweeping narrative. If I want to get an instant adrenaline rush, that's the way that I do it—thinking about my work now: this is huge, we've got so many people and there's such big stakes."

Topics for Reading and Writing

1. Does the Internet really put us in a "new era of grass-roots activism"? Read this in conjunction with William S. Klein's piece "Faking the Voice of the People" in Chapter 6—how can we determine what the voice of the people really is?

2. "There is a very old American type of protester . . . who sees politics as an expression of personal morality," Packer writes. What does he mean? How can Pariser and President Bush share this? What other ways are there to approach politics? And who should be allowed to determine—in other words, who "owns"—the rules about how political debates are conducted?

Gloria Steinem—writer, activist, journalist, icon—is America's most famous feminist, and her magazine Ms. *has been a leader in feminist writing and reportage since the 1970s. But can feminism coexist with American-style consumer capitalism? Do consumer products and the advertising that promotes those products necessarily work against the goals of feminism, or can the two cooperate? And to what degree should advertisers be involved in determining the editorial direction of a political magazine?*

This essay could just as easily have been included in the previous chapter on advertising because it examines the way that the images and language of advertising work; placed with this chapter, though, it raises interesting questions about media ownership as it applies to noncorporate,

Gloria Steinem
Sex, Lies, and Advertising

About three years ago, as *glasnost* was beginning and *Ms.* seemed to be ending, I was invited to a press lunch for a Soviet official. He entertained us with anecdotes about new problems of democracy in his country. Local Communist leaders were being criticized in their media for the first time, he explained and they were angry.

"So I'll have to ask my American friends," he finished pointedly, "how more *subtly* to control the press." In the silence that followed, I said, "Advertising."

The reporters laughed, but later, one of them took me aside: How *dare* I suggest that freedom of the press was limited? How dare I imply his newsweekly could be influenced by ads?

I explained that I was thinking of advertising's media-wide influence on most of what we read. Even newsmagazines use "soft" cover stories to sell ads, confuse readers with "advertorials," and occasionally self-censor on subjects known to be a problem with big advertisers.

But, I also explained, I was thinking especially of women's magazines. There, it isn't just a little content noncommercial enterprises. In the essay, Steinem examines "ownership," broadly defined: when advertisers have a great deal of say in the survival of a magazine, do they "own" that magazine to some degree? And since Ms. was originally intended to be owned, in a sense, by the feminist community, how does the inclusion of advertising undermine that intention?

that's devoted to attracting ads, it's almost all of it. That's why advertisers—not readers—have always been a problem for *Ms.* As the only women's magazine that didn't supply what the ad world euphemistically describes as "supportive editorial atmosphere" or "complementary copy" (for instance, articles that praise food/fashion/ beauty subjects to "support" and "complement" food/fashion/beauty ads), *Ms.* could never attract enough advertising to break even.

"Oh, *women's* magazines," the journalist said with contempt. "Everybody knows they're just catalogs—but who cares? They have nothing to do with journalism."

I can't tell you how many times I've had this argument in 25 years of working for many kinds of publications. Except as moneymaking machines—"cash cows" as they are so elegantly called in the trade—women's magazines are rarely taken seriously. Though changes being made by women have been called more far-reaching than the industrial revolution—and though many editors try hard to reflect some of them in the few pages left to them after all the ad-related subjects have been covered—the magazines serving the female half of this country are still far below the journalistic and ethical standards of news and general interest publications. Most depressing of all, this doesn't even rate an exposé.

If *Time* and *Newsweek* had to lavish praise on cars in general and credit General Motors in particular to get GM ads, there would be a scandal—maybe a criminal investigation. When women's magazines from *Seventeen* to *Lear's* praise beauty products in general and credit Revlon in particular to get ads, it's just business as usual.

I.

When *Ms.* began, we didn't consider *not* taking ads. The most important reason was keeping the price of a feminist magazine low enough for most women to afford. But the second and almost equal reason was providing a forum where women and advertisers could talk to each other and improve advertising itself. After all, it was (and still is) as potent a source of information in this country as news or TV and movie dramas.

We decided to proceed in two stages. First, we would convince makers of "people products" used by both men and women but advertised mostly to men—cars, credit cards, insurance, sound equipment, financial services and the like—that their ads should be placed in a women's magazine. Since they were accustomed to the division between editorial and advertising in news and general interest magazines, this would allow our editorial content to be free and diverse. Second, we would add the best ads for whatever traditional "women's products" (clothes, shampoo, fragrance, food, and so on) that surveys showed *Ms.* readers used. But we would ask them to come in *without* the usual quid pro quo of "complementary copy."

We knew the second step might be harder. Food advertisers have always demanded that women's magazines publish recipes and articles on entertaining (preferably ones that name their products) in return for their ads; clothing advertisers expect to be surrounded by fashion spreads (especially ones that credit their designers); and shampoo, fragrance, and beauty products in general usually insist on positive editorial coverage of beauty subjects, plus photo credits besides. That's why women's magazines look the way they do. But if we could break this link between ads and editorial content, then we wanted good ads for "women's products," too.

By playing their part in this unprecedented mix of *all* the things our readers need and use, advertisers also would be rewarded: ads for products like cars and mutual funds would find a new growth market; the best ads for women's products would no longer be lost in oceans of ads for the same category; and both would have access to a laboratory of smart and caring readers whose response would help create effective ads for other media as well.

I thought then that our main problem would be the imagery in ads themselves. Carmakers were still draping blondes in evening gowns over the hoods like ornaments. Authority figures were almost always male, even in ads for products that only women used. Sadistic, he-man campaigns even won industry praise. (For instance, *Advertising Age* had hailed the infamous Silva Thin cigarette theme, "How to Get a Woman's Attention: Ignore Her," as "brilliant.") Even in medical journals, tranquilizer ads showed depressed housewives standing beside piles of dirty dishes and promised to get them back to work.

Obviously, *Ms.* would have to avoid such ads and seek out the best ones— but this didn't seem impossible. *The New Yorker* had been selecting ads for aesthetic reasons for years, a practice that only seemed to make advertisers more eager to be in its pages. *Ebony* and *Essence* were asking for ads with positive black images, and though their struggle was hard, they weren't being called unreasonable.

Clearly, what *Ms.* needed was a very special publisher and ad sales staff. I could think of only one woman with experience on the business side of magazines—Patricia Carbine, who recently had become a vice president of *McCall's* as well as its editor in chief—and the reason I knew her name was a good omen. She had been managing editor at *Look* (really *the* editor, but its owner refused to put a female name at the top of his masthead) when I was writing a column there. After I did an early interview with Cesar Chavez, then just emerging as a leader of migrant labor, and the publisher turned it down because he was worried about ads from Sunkist, Pat was the one who intervened. As I learned later, she told the publisher she would resign if the interview wasn't published. Mainly because *Look* couldn't afford to lose Pat, it *was* published (and the ads from Sunkist never arrived).

Though I barely knew this woman, she had done two things I always remembered: put her job on the line in a way that editors often talk about but rarely do, and been so loyal to her colleagues that she never told me or anyone outside *Look* that she had done so.

Fortunately, Pat did agree to leave *McCall's* and take a huge cut in salary to become publisher of *Ms.* She became responsible for training and inspiring generations of young women who joined the *Ms.* ad sales force, many of whom went on to become "firsts" at the top of publishing. When *Ms.* first started, however, there were so few women with experience selling space that Pat and I made the rounds of ad agencies ourselves. Later the fact that *Ms.* was asking companies to do business in a different way meant our saleswomen had to make many times the usual number of calls—first to convince agencies and then client companies besides—and to present endless amounts of research. I was often asked to do a final ad presentation, or see some high decision-maker, or speak to women employees so executives could see the interest of women they worked with. That's why I spent more time persuading advertisers than editing or writing for *Ms.* and why I ended up with an unsentimental education in the seamy underside of publishing that few writers see (and even fewer magazines can publish).

II.

Do you think, as I once did, that advertisers make decisions based on solid research? Well, think again. "Broadly speaking," says Joseph Smith of Oxtoby-Smith, Inc., a consumer research firm, "there is no persuasive evidence that the editorial context of an ad matters."

Advertisers who demand such "complementary copy," even in the absence of respectable studies, clearly are operating under a double standard. The same food companies place ads in *People* with no recipes. Cosmetic companies support *The New Yorker* with no regular beauty columns. So where does this habit of controlling the content of women's magazines come from?

Tradition. Ever since *Ladies Magazine* debuted in Boston in 1828, editorial copy directed to women has been informed by something other than its readers' wishes. There were no ads then, but in an age when married women were legal minors with no right to their own money, there was another revenue source to be kept in mind: husbands. "Husbands may rest assured," wrote editor Sarah Josepha Hale, "that nothing found in these pages shall cause her [his wife] to be less assiduous in preparing for his reception or encourage her to 'usurp station' or encroach upon prerogatives of men."

Hale went on to become the editor of *Godey's Lady's Book*, a magazine featuring "fashion plates": engravings of dresses for readers to take to their seamstresses or copy themselves. Hale added "how to" articles, which set the tone for women's service magazines for years to come: how to write politely, avoid sunburn, and—in no fewer than 1,200 words—how to maintain a goose quill pen. She advocated education for women but avoided controversy. Just as most women's magazines now avoid politics, poll their readers on issues like abortion but rarely take a stand, and praise socially approved lifestyles, Hale saw to it that *Godey's* avoided the hot topics of its day: slavery, abolition, and women's suffrage.

What definitively turned women's magazines into catalogs, however were two events: Ellen Butterick's invention of the clothing pattern in 1863 and the mass manufacture of patent medicines containing everything from colored water to cocaine. For the first time, readers could purchase what magazines encouraged them to want. As such magazines became more profitable they also began to attract men as editors. (Most women's magazines continued to have men as top editors until the feminist 1970s.) Edward Bok, who became editor of *The Ladies' Home Journal* in 1889, discovered the power of advertisers when he rejected ads for patent medicines and found that other advertisers canceled in retribution. In the early 20th century, *Good Housekeeping* started its Institute to "test and approve" products. Its Seal of Approval became the grandfather of current "value added" programs that offer advertisers such bonuses as product sampling and department store promotions.

By the time suffragists finally won the vote in 1920, women's magazines had become too entrenched as catalogs to help women learn how to use. The main function was to create a desire for products, teach how to use products, and make products a crucial part of gaining social approval, pleasing a husband, and performing as a homemaker. Some unrelated articles and short stories were included to persuade women to pay for these catalogs. But articles were neither consumerist nor rebellious. Even fiction was usually subject to formula: if a woman had any sexual life outside marriage, she was supposed to come to a bad end.

In 1956, Helen Gurley Brown began to change part of that formula bringing "the sexual revolution" to women's magazines—but in an ad-oriented way. Attracting multiple men required even more consumerism, as the Cosmo Girl made clear, than finding one husband.

In response to the workplace revolution of the 1970s, traditional women's magazines—that is. "trade books" for women working at home—were joined by *Savvy, Working Woman,* and other trade books for women working in offices. But by keeping the fashion/beauty/entertaining articles necessary to get traditional ads and then adding career articles besides, they inadvertently produced the antifeminist stereotype of Super Woman. The male-imitative, dress-for-success woman carrying a briefcase became the media image of a woman worker, even though a blue-collar woman's salary was often higher than her glorified secretarial sister's, and though women at a real briefcase level are statistically rare. Needless to say, these dress-for-success women were also thin, white, and beautiful.

In recent years, advertisers' control over the editorial content of women's magazines has become so institutionalized that it is written into "insertion orders" or dictated to ad salespeople as an official policy. The following are recent typical orders to women's magazines:

> ∎ Dow's Cleaning Products stipulates that ads for its Vivid and Spray'n Wash products should be adjacent to "children or fashion editorial"; ads for Bathroom Cleaner should be next to "home furnishing/family" features; and so on for other brands. "If a magazine fails for 1/2 the brands or more," the Dow order warns, "it will be omitted from further consideration."
> ∎ Bristol-Myers, the parent of Clairol, Windex, Drano, Bufferin, and much more, stipulates that ads be placed next to "a full page of compatible editorial."

■ S.C. Johnson & Son, makers of Johnson Wax, lawn and laundry products, insect sprays, hair sprays, and so on, orders that its ads *"should not be opposite extremely controversial features or material antithetical to the nature/copy of the advertised product."* (Italics theirs.)

■ Maidenform, manufacturer of bras and other apparel, leaves a blank for the particular product and states: "The creative concept of the _____ campaign, and the very nature of the product itself appeal to the positive emotions of the reader/consumer. Therefore, it is imperative that all editorial adjacencies reflect that same positive tone. The editorial must not be negative in content or lend itself contrary to the _____ product imagery/message (e.g., *editorial relating to illness, disillusionment, large size fashions, etc.*)" (Italics mine.)

■ The De Beers diamond company, a big seller of engagement rings, prohibits magazines from placing its ads with "adjacencies to hard news or anti/love-romance themed editorial."

■ Procter & Gamble, one of this country's most powerful and diversified advertisers, stands out in the memory of Anne Summers and Sandra Yates (no mean feat in this context): its products were not to be placed in *any* issue that included *any* material on gun control, abortion, the occult, cults, or the disparagement of religion. Caution was also demanded in any issue covering sex or drugs, even for educational purposes.

Those are the most obvious chains around women's magazines. There are also rules so clear they needn't be written down: for instance, an overall "look" compatible with beauty and fashion ads. Even "real" nonmodel women photographed for a women's magazine are usually made up, dressed in credited clothes, and retouched out of all reality. When editors do include articles on less-than-cheerful subjects (for instance, domestic violence), they tend to keep them short and unillustrated. The point is to be "upbeat." Just as women in the street are asked, "Why don't you smile, honey?" women's magazines acquire an institutional smile.

Within the text itself, praise for advertisers' products has become so ritualized that fields like "beauty writing" have been invented. One of its frequent practitioners explained seriously that "It's a difficult art. How many new adjectives can you find? How much greater can you make a lipstick sound? The FDA restricts what companies can say on labels, but we create illusion. And ad agencies are on the phone all the time pushing you to get their product in. A lot of them keep the business based on how many editorial clippings they produce every month. The worst are products," like Lauder's as the writer confirmed, "with their own name involved. It's all ego."

Often, editorial becomes one giant ad. Last November, for instance, *Lear's* featured an elegant woman executive on the cover. On the contents page, we learned she was wearing Guerlain makeup and Samsara, a new fragrance by Guerlain. Inside were full-page ads for Samsara and Guerlain antiwrinkle cream. In the cover profile, we learned that this executive was responsible for launching Samsara and is Guerlain's director of public relations. When the *Columbia Journalism Review* did one of the few articles to include women's magazines in coverage of the influence of ads, editor Frances Lear was quoted as defending her magazine because "this kind of thing is done all the time."

Often, advertisers also plunge odd-shaped ads into the text, no matter what the cost to the readers. At *Women's Day,* a magazine originally founded by a supermarket chain, editor in chief Ellen Levine said, "The day the copy had to rag around a chicken leg was not a happy one."

Advertisers are also adamant about where in a magazine their ads appear. When Revlon was not placed as the first beauty ad in one Hearst magazine, for instance, Revlon pulled its ads from *all* Hearst magazines. Ruth Whitney, editor in chief of *Glamour,* attributes some of these demands to "ad agencies wanting to prove to a client that they've squeezed the last drop of blood out of a magazine." She also is, she says, "sick and tired of hearing that women's magazines are controlled by cigarette ads." Relatively speaking, she's right. To be as censoring as are many advertisers for women's products, tobacco companies would have to demand articles in praise of smoking and expect glamorous photos of beautiful women smoking their brands.

I don't mean to imply that the editors I quote here share my objections to ads: most assume that women's magazines have to be the way they are. But it's also true that only former editors can be completely honest. "Most of the pressure came in the form of direct product mentions," explains Sey Chassler, who was editor in chief of *Redbook* from the sixties to the eighties. "We got threats from the big guys, the Revlons, blackmail threats. They wouldn't run ads unless we credited them."

"But it's not fair to single out the beauty advertisers because these pressures came from everybody. Advertisers want to know two things: What are you going to charge me? What *else* are you going to do for me? It's a holdup. For instance, management felt that fiction took up too much space. They couldn't put any advertising in that. For the last ten years, the number of fiction entries into the National Magazine Awards has declined.

"And pressures are getting worse. More magazines are more bottom-line oriented because they have been taken over by companies with no interest in publishing.

"I also think advertisers do this to women's magazines especially," he concluded, "because of the general disrespect they have for women."

Even media experts who don't give a damn about women's magazines are alarmed by the spread of this ad-edit linkage. In a climate *The Wall Street Journal* describes as an unacknowledged Depression for media, women's products are increasingly able to take their low standards wherever they go. For instance: newsweeklies publish uncritical stories on fashion and fitness. *The New York Times Magazine* recently ran an article on "firming creams," complete with mentions of advertisers. *Vanity Fair* published a profile of one major advertiser, Ralph Lauren, illustrated by the same photographer who does his ads, and turned the lifestyle of another, Calvin Klein, into a cover story. Even the outrageous *Spy* has toned down since it began to go after fashion ads.

And just to make us really worry, films and books, the last media that go directly to the public without having to attract ads first, are in danger, too. Producers are beginning to depend on payments for displaying products in movies, and books are now being commissioned by companies like Federal Express.

But the truth is that women's products—like women's magazines—have never been the subjects of much serious reporting anyway. News and general interest publications, including the "style" or "living" sections of newspapers, write about food and clothing as cooking and fashion, and almost never evaluate such products by brand name. Though chemical additives, pesticides, and animal fats are major health risks in the United States, and clothes, shoddy or not, absorb more consumer dollars than cars, this lack of information is serious. So is ignoring the contents of beauty products that are absorbed into our bodies through our skins, and that have profit margins so big they would make a loan shark blush.

Topics for Reading and Writing

1. Why does Steinem choose this personal, narrative voice to make her case? Why not write a more standard opinion piece about the role of advertisers in determining editorial content? Rhetorically, what does she lose by making this a story, and what does she gain?

2. What is Steinem's argument in this piece? Who is her audience? Look at a few issues of *Ms.*—what is the rhetoric of the magazine like? Does it reflect Steinem's own voice?

3. One of Steinem's concerns, and one of the concerns of feminism, is to redefine the idea of a "women's magazine." Rather than a magazine dominated by articles about and advertisements for products that women might use, *Ms.* is a magazine dominated by articles about issues that affect women. Steinem, through this magazine, reminds us that a demographic group—women, Latinos, White men—shouldn't be defined solely by what they consume in the economy. Compare this idea as embodied in *Ms.* with several other women's magazines— some examples might be *Lucky, InStyle, Jane, Vogue, Allure, Shape.* How do each of those magazines construct the idea of "women"?

The Writer at Work

Analyzing and Interpreting

How Does an Argument "Mean"?

"How does a poem mean?" In 1959, the poet and literary scholar John Ciardi (and his collaborator, poet Miller Williams) wrote a well-known book of literary analysis whose title asked this strange question. The book, widely used in high school English courses, does not introduce students to poetry by posing poems as puzzles to be solved or as questions to be answered. Rather, Ciardi and Williams show that poems are magnificent little feats of engineering, with dozens of systems working jointly to create a whole. The job of the reader or of the critic, then, is not to find the secret meaning of the poem, but to understand and explain how it works—how the words, the images, the sounds, even the appearance of the poem on the page create reactions and catalyze interpretive acts on the part of a reader.

Essays, editorials, position papers, and other arguments are not poems, of course. But these different forms of verbal communication do have some important similarities. They use language to communicate and convince. They take into consideration the emotions and beliefs of the audience. They construct a speaker that will convey, as effectively and persuasively as possible, the writer's argument. Finally, they can all be taken apart so a reader can see how they work—or, in Ciardi and Williams's words, "how they mean." Often the best way to begin learning how to write effective arguments is to reverse engineer others' arguments—to analyze other pieces of writing to see how, or if, they accomplish their aims. This kind of writing task, not surprisingly, is generally called a **rhetorical analysis.** Undoubtedly you have done this kind of intellectual work many times before; every time you analyze a poem or a novel or a song or a painting you are engaging in the same kinds of processes that you will use in analyzing rhetoric. The only difference is that with rhetoric, the explicit intention of the text is to persuade; therefore, in a rhetorical analysis your job is to find out how—or whether—that persuasion works, and for what audiences. Sometimes your job is also evaluative: you may also be asked to judge how well that rhetoric achieves its aim with its target audience.

Outside of the academic world (where the analysis of language is a constant concern), these kinds of analytical arguments, by themselves, are fairly rare. The rhetorical analysis is often a component of or a precursor to another kind of argument. The contention that "the media is liberal" relies on a rhetorical analysis, for the person arguing this must take apart—"unpack"—the message or messages in question and demonstrate to the audience that the message in question works in such a way that it advances the liberal viewpoint. (See Dionne's "The Rightward Press" or the Media Research Center's "Media Bias Basics" in Chapter 2 for examples of rhetorical analysis.) With that point established, the writer can then move on to her other task—proposing that a conservative network should be founded to counter the liberal bias, or comparing the liberal bias in the American media to bias in other nations' media. A rhetorical analysis is also valuable when employed as part of a rebuttal to a competing claim. Let's say your opponent makes an argument to an audience of high school seniors that Congress should pass a constitutional amendment prohibiting flag burning. In his argument, your opponent brings up the World War II veterans who died for the flag, the war widows who saw their husbands' coffins draped in the flag, even the famous image of young of John F. Kennedy, Jr., saluting his assassinated father's coffin—which was covered in a flag. Because your opponent's images are so powerful and evocative, it would behoove you to rob them of some of their power by analyzing them. Beginning your rebuttal with a rhetorical analysis, you could talk about how your opponent was seeking to use the most powerful, most hallowed possible emotions—emotions that can only be denied at the risk of seeming unpatriotic—because his point lacked logic. Pointing out to your audience that you respect them enough to argue to their brains as well as their hearts, you could continue by saying that the soldiers and President Kennedy died not for the flag but for the nation it represented—a nation that enshrines freedom in its Constitution.

Identifying the Audience—in Reverse

Remember in the last chapter where you learned about how to identify your audience and how to start constructing an argument that would appeal to that audience? When you are analyzing an argument, the writer who made that argument—a politician, an advertising agency, your roommate—went through this process. This doesn't mean he or she did it *well*. Many advertising campaigns have failed miserably because they misjudged their audience, and many political gestures have appeared ludicrous because the politicians didn't understand how their audience would see or understand those gestures. When you analyze a piece of rhetoric, it's worth pointing out if the writer has made notable miscalculations either in identifying the audience he or she is addressing, or in identifying the beliefs and desires of that audience.

Let's look back again to King's "Letter from Birmingham Jail," one of the touchstones of twentieth-century rhetoric. As we discussed earlier, King's audience is actually two audiences. He specifically writes to the members of the Birmingham clergy who signed a letter opposing "outside agitators," but because this was an open letter, published for all to read, he was also addressing all the citizens of Birmingham and the South. How did he aim his argument at this audience?

- ■ Audience: clergymen
- ■ Strategies: addresses them as "Brothers"; refers to the Bible; alludes not just to Christian but also to Jewish thinkers (one of the signatories of the original letter was a rabbi); humbly compares himself to St. Paul because he writes letters about Christian ethics while in jail; argues that this crusade is not for self-glorification but for the fulfillment of God's commands, etc.
- ■ Audience: White Birmingham residents/Southerners
- ■ Strategies: makes it clear that he is a Southerner, not an "outsider"; grounds his argument in beliefs and emotions—Christianity, love for one's children—he holds in common with his audience; does not attack them with anger; stresses the patience of his people; emphasizes to the audience that racial equality will not threaten the freedoms of White Southerners

IDEAS INTO PRACTICE 4-1

An analytical argument must explicitly discuss the intended audience of the argument (or work of art) in question. But it's not always so simple to decide who the intended or actual audience of a piece of writing might be. To do so, it's often valuable to brainstorm for a while. Where did this argument appear?

On television? On what network? During what program? What time did it air? Who generally watches this program? If it was in a newspaper, was it a national or local paper? What is the readership of the paper—affluent Southern California suburbanites in Orange County, working-class people in East St. Louis, farmers in Canyon, Texas?

Find arguments—advertisements, letters, articles, editorials, or the like—appearing in the following places. For each, write down a brief description of the audience for the argument, including several adjectives describing this audience. Example:

  ■ An advertisement for the Sony Vaio laptop computer, appearing in *Business Week* magazine.

The audience for this advertisement is probably involved in a leadership position in business—either as an executive or as an entrepreneur of some type. Low-level employees might read this magazine, as well, in order to educate themselves about the world of business. This advertisement is probably aimed at the businessperson who is looking for a personal computer; it's unlikely that the Vaio would be purchased in large quantities to be used as the work terminals for large numbers of employees. The ad itself stresses the versatility of the computer and specifically states that it plays DVDs and games as well as crunches numbers and prepares persuasive presentations, reinforcing the message that this computer will probably be used as a personal computer.

1. An issue of *Business Week.*
2. A commercial airing during the television program *60 Minutes.*
3. A billboard on top of a building downtown.
4. An advertisement on a shopping cart in a large grocery store.
5. The lead editorial in your local newspaper.
6. A congressional speech delivered on C-SPAN.
7. An advertisement included inside a CD you recently bought.
8. The president's latest speech.

Analyzing the Rhetorical Triangle

Once you have identified the target audience of a piece, the real reverse engineering begins. Think back to those three Greek terms from chapter four: ethos, pathos, and logos. How does the argument in question use each of those? King's letter, for instance, uses emotions in several different ways. He seeks the audience's sympathy in the story about his daughter and Funland. He seeks the audience's respect as a pastor. He seeks solidarity from his fellow clergymen. He wants to appeal to the audience's desire for cooler heads to prevail in this emotional issue, and so makes his argument in well-reasoned points. An analysis of an advertisement can work in much the same way. The recent television commercials for the 1-800-COLLECT calling plan have used comic celebrities such as David Arquette and Carrot Top as pitchmen. These goofy commercials are set in fun, recreational settings—basketball courts, the beach, in the movies, at a football game—reassuring consumers that collect calling is a casual kind of activity, not an emergency last resort most of us associate with runaways, hospitals, and police stations. Your analysis might note that the emotional appeal of the argument is actually inappropriate for the situation or for the audience—a stirring tribute to Korean War veterans will move an audience of septuagenarians, but it's likely that a discussion of the sacrifices of Gulf War soldiers would appeal more to people in their twenties.

Certain kinds of arguments are most convincing when they are made with a heavily emotional appeal, while others rely almost entirely on the impeccable credibility of the speaker. Edward R. Murrow's 1958 speech to the Radio-Television News Directors Association has only gained in ethos as it has aged, for the recent changes in journalism make people more and more convinced that Murrow, one of the pioneers of broadcast reporting, represents a golden age of journalism that will never return. The folk singer Janis Ian, whose article "Music Industry Spins Falsehood" appears in Chapter 5, derives credibility from her personal experiences working with record companies. Other arguments are almost entirely logical. A good writer must put together the proper combination of logic, authority, and emotion for his or her audience. A good analyst must unpack that argument and show how each element has been constructed. In essence, such an analysis attempts to read the mind of the writer, to figure out what was going on "behind the curtain" while this message was being constructed. Calvin Callaway's paper on the Diesel jeans marketing campaign (included in Chapter 3) is an especially good student example of such an analysis.

Although most analyses contain almost identical elements, such arguments can serve any number of purposes. At times they are just explications, descriptions of how this message makes its appeal. The presence of the writer in such arguments is generally limited to being an objective voice pointing out how something works. However, analyses of this type can also serve as the basis for other kinds of arguments. An analysis of a politician's remarks can serve as evidence for a charge that the politician is a racist—as happened in late 2002 to the Mississippi senator Trent Lott, who praised the segregationist 1948 presidential campaign of Strom Thurmond at Thurmond's birthday party. Boiled down to its basics, this argument (a rhetorical analysis leading into a definitional argument and then a proposal argument) would look like this:

> Although Lott denies he is a racist, an analysis of his remarks at Thurmond's birthday party, as well as on many other occasions, shows that Lott uses the same kind of subtly disguised, racially based appeals that have characterized public racism since the success of the civil rights movement made outward bigotry unacceptable. We cannot have a proven racist as Senate Majority Leader, so Lott needs to be deposed.

An analysis of an advertising campaign such as the Mountain Dew "extreme sports" spots can serve other advertisers as a model for their own campaigns.

> Mountain Dew sells its sodas to young people by associating the brand with the "extreme sports" trend, a trend that appeals to large numbers of young males

who like to feel "extreme" and rebellious even if they do not engage in those activities.

These analyses can also be used as the basis for ethically based arguments about a speaker or a claim.

As you've no doubt discovered from using the rhetorical triangle in constructing your own arguments, none of the categories (ethos, pathos, or logos) is entirely separable from the others. In advertising, for instance, using a spokesperson such as Lance Armstrong or Isabella Rossellini establishes a particular kind of ethos, of course (Armstrong represents fortitude, determination, and athletic excellence, while Rossellini represents grace, beauty, and European sophistication), but it also works as a pathos appeal—we have *feelings* about these people that the advertisers want to use. Similarly, logic enters into the equation: if Product X is good enough for Lance Armstrong, who is a very demanding person and relies on his equipment, it follows that Product X is good enough for me. For this reason, it's often too simplistic to divide an analysis paper up simply by the three categories of the rhetorical triangle. Rather, look at the larger picture: talk about how the primary strategy of the ad is to use Armstrong (or to present us with governmental statistics, or to make us feel for the victims of this tragedy, or whatever the primary appeal happens to be) and then break that appeal down by how it appeals to our emotions, our need for credible authority, and our desire for a logical solution.

IDEAS INTO PRACTICE 4-2

1. Take four of the arguments that you chose in the Ideas into Practice 4-1 exercise, and sketch out an outline for a rhetorical analysis of each of them. Building on your own experience constructing arguments, unpack or reverse engineer these arguments, constantly asking yourself what strategies the writer has employed to appeal to the target audience you have already identified. Try to use the rhetorical triangle in your analysis without making it the structuring principle of your argument.

2. Outline a rhetorical analysis for one of the shorter opinion pieces in this book—especially good for this would be Janis Ian's "Music Industry Spins Falsehood" in Chapter 5, E. J. Dionne's "The Rightward Press" in Chapter 2, or Derek Shaw's "Punks, Bums, and Politicians," included in Chapter 7.

3. Write your own rhetorical analysis of a news program, a feature article in a magazine, or a newspaper editorial. A particularly interesting way to approach this question would be to choose a piece of straight news—that is, not an opinion piece—and to answer whether or not that piece exhibits the kind of bias or slant we have talked about in this book. Does the front-page article on rebuilding Afghanistan that appeared in the *New York Times* show a liberal bias? Does the feature on new television programs appearing on Fox News Channel favor the Fox network's

programs? Prove your claim by using specific examples from the text you analyze.

Style **T**oolbox

Adverbials

An adverb, you probably already know, is a word that modifies a verb. Some adverbs designate time and place: "then," "now," "never," "often," "here," "there," "everywhere." Many designate the manner in which an action is performed; these adverbs typically end with the suffix "-ly": "quickly," "inadvertently," "reluctantly," "probably." But adverbs are not the only way to modify a verb. Both phrases (combinations of words) and clauses (structures with subjects and predicates) can provide information that modifies a verb. When used in this way, those phrases and clauses are called "adverbials." It's easy to identify adverbials: they provide information about the time, place, reason, and manner of a sentence's action.

Let's look at a few examples of adverbials:

> The mayor responded <u>angrily</u> (*adverb*) <u>when accused of financial malfeasance</u> (*subordinate clause*).
>
> <u>Later</u> (*adverb*) <u>that evening</u> (*noun phrase*), Nupur ended up ordering a pizza <u>because all that studying made her extremely hungry</u> (*subordinate clause*).
>
> <u>Without acknowledging the students' laughter</u> (*subordinate clause*), Professor Kim <u>stiffly</u> (*adverb*) stalked <u>out of the classroom</u> (*prepositional phrase*).

These constructions provide additional information about the action—how, when, where, or why it was performed. Sometimes this information is the heart of the sentence, as in the first example: "The mayor responded" says little, but the adverbials describing the manner and occasion of his response are the essential contribution of this sentence. Adverbials are the most memorable components of many famous sentences, in fact:

> It's better to die <u>on your feet</u> than live <u>on your knees</u>.
>
> <u>Four score and seven years ago</u>, our fathers brought forth <u>on this continent</u> a new nation, conceived in liberty, and dedicated to the proposition that all men are created equal.

When used well, adverbials can make pedestrian writing into superior writing. Apart from their ability to add critical information to a sentence, an important element of their value is that unlike most other English parts of speech, they can often be moved around within a sentence. Look at the first example sentence provided. Broken down into its elements, the sentence looks like this:

SUBJECT: The mayor
VERB: responded
ADVERBIAL 1 (manner): angrily
ADVERBIAL 2 (time): when accused of financial malfeasance

We can rewrite that sentence in several ways:

> The mayor, when accused of financial malfeasance, responded angrily.
> When accused of financial malfeasance, the mayor responded angrily.
> When accused of financial malfeasance, the mayor angrily responded.
> Angrily, the mayor responded when accused of financial malfeasance.
> Angrily, when accused of financial malfeasance the major responded.
> The mayor, when accused of financial malfeasance, angrily responded.

Some of these options are certainly better stylistically than others, but they are all grammatically correct and they all make sense. Adverbials are particularly versatile, because they can be moved around within the sentence as long as the subject and verb being modified are clear. Herein also lies their rhetorical power. As you will learn further in the Style Toolbox for Chapter 6, the rhythm of your sentences is an important part of their rhetorical impact—and moving adverbials around within a sentence changes a sentence's rhythm.

But how can the placement of an adverbial have a rhetorical effect? Let's look at some specific examples, starting with the well-known first sentence of Abraham Lincoln's Gettysburg Address:

> <u>Four score and seven years ago</u>, our fathers brought forth <u>on this conti-
> nent</u> a new nation, conceived in liberty, and dedicated to the proposi-
> tion that all men are created equal.

The two adverbials underlined in the sentence give information about the time and place of the action (the "bringing forth" of the "new nation" by "our fathers"). What about if we move them around?

> Our fathers brought forth <u>on this continent</u> a new nation, conceived in
> liberty, and dedicated to the proposition that all men are created
> equal <u>four score and seven years ago</u>.

This sentence, although it contains precisely the same information as Lincoln's, lacks the gravity and sense of occasion of the original. Why? It's hard to say exactly, but certainly the placement of the time adverbial at the start gives the sentence a feeling of importance, of setting the stage for a profound statement. Also, introducing a sentence with an adverbial of time is always subconsciously reminiscent of storytelling: a traditional way to start a story is with an adverbial like "Once upon a time" or "A long time ago in a galaxy far, far away." So let's keep the time adverbial at the beginning and move the place adverbial around. Let's try

> <u>Four score and seven years ago</u>, <u>on this continent</u> our fathers brought
> forth a new nation, conceived in liberty, and dedicated to the propo-
> sition that all men are created equal.

This isn't as jarring a change as the previous one, but we still lose something. Certainly we are forced to wait another beat or two for the introduction of the subject. In addition, Lincoln placed the phrases "on this continent" and "a new nation" together: the two mirror each other in several ways, even though they have different rhythms and grammatical functions (one an adverbial, one the object of the main verb). Let's try one other change:

> <u>Four score and seven years ago</u>, our fathers brought forth a new nation
>   <u>on this continent</u>, conceived in liberty, and dedicated to the proposi-
>   tion that all men are created equal.

Not bad, but still missing something. Perhaps the placement of "on this continent" before "a new nation" is crucial to Lincoln's meaning. After all, he wants to emphasize how these "fathers" created something political and social (a nation) out of something geographical (a continent). "Continent" then needs to stand out as a preexisting fact that "our fathers" acted upon. The term "continent" is resolutely nonhuman; to place this term before "nation" underscores its vastness and the difficulty of humans influencing it, making the creation of a "nation" even more impressive.

Sometimes an adverbial can't be so free-floating. No doubt you've heard of the term "dangling" or "misplaced modifier"; these grammatical errors are common—and often quite amusing. Although a number of different kinds of grammatical constructions can become misplaced modifiers, often misplaced is a particular type of subordinate clause called an "elliptical" (because something has been left out—an "ellipsis" is the typographical mark . . . , used to indicate that something has been deleted). Ellipticals generally are clauses from which the subject and part of the verb have been deleted, as in the following:

> <u>While watching the last episode of *American Idol*</u>, I placed several suc-
>   cessful wagers on the outcome.

The elliptical implies but leaves out two words—"While [I was] watching the last episode of *American Idol*." In this sentence, it isn't a problem: it's very clear that "I" was watching television. However, in many cases of dangling or misplaced modifiers, this relationship isn't obvious:

> <u>Falling from a height of 100 feet</u>, our principal pointed out the beauty
>   of the waterfall.

It's certainly conceivable that a dedicated educator might make even his plunge to a watery death into a learning opportunity, but it's unlikely this is what the writer intends to say. The confusion comes because the omitted parts of the elliptical aren't clear. What is falling? Clearly the writer meant to say that the waterfall falls from a height of 100 feet, but grammatically the sentence contradicts this. Why? It's quite simple, actually. Think of an elliptical as a decapitated body (the elliptical phrase or clause) looking for its head (the subject and the rest of the verb that will make it make sense). Desperate to "recapitate" itself, the elliptical always takes *the very next candidate* as its head. (This type of confusion can even alter what a phrase or clause does grammatically in the sentence. In fact, in this sentence the elliptical is performing the grammatical function of an adverbial—it's modifying the verb "pointed out"—when the writer intends it to be an adjectival construction, modifying the noun "water-fall.") In these cases, the elliptical is often changed into a different kind of clause and moved to another place in the sentence. Revised, the sentence would proba-bly read

> Our principal pointed out the beauty of the waterfall, which fell from a
>   height of 100 feet.

If the writer wanted to keep the original elliptical, he or she might revise the sentence to read

> Falling from a height of 100 feet, the waterfall's beauty was pointed out
>   by our principal.

This sentence, though, clumsily and unnecessarily uses the passive voice and is, strictly speaking, inaccurate—it's the waterfall, not the waterfall's beauty, that falls from a height of a hundred feet.

Adverbial ellipticals are great tools to use in your writing, but they need to be used carefully and accurately. Just to reinforce the point (and because writing teachers love to collect humorous examples of dangling or misplaced modifiers), here are a few more: think of these whenever you start out a sentence with an elliptical!

> Smashed flat by a passing truck, my dog sniffed at what was left of a
>   half-eaten hamburger. (Is the dog or the burger smashed flat?)
> As a child, my mother used to take me to the sheep barns in the spring
>   to see the new lambs. (When my mother was a child, or when I was a
>   child?)
> Before going to class this morning, the breakfast line was crowded.
>   (The breakfast line has to attend class?)

WRITING WITH STYLE 4-1

Rewrite each of the following sentences, moving the adverbials around in the sentence. How does the different order change the meaning of the sentence or its rhetorical effect?

1. Then, catching sight of Stephen Dedalus, he bent towards him and made rapid crosses in the air, gurgling in his throat and shaking his head. (James Joyce, *Ulysses*)
2. I stared at it in the swinging lights of the subway car, and in the faces and bodies of the people, and in my own face, trapped in the darkness which roared outside. (James Baldwin, "Sonny's Blues")
3. I was, unfortunately, lolling in a hot tub when word arrived that the police would be by shortly to hang me. (Woody Allen, "Viva Vargas!")
4. Weakly, feebly, powerlessly, I stretched my hand out to just barely reach the packet of antihistamines.
5. The nation must bravely face up to its responsibilities today.

6. On her very first day of work at the White House, my friend Marianella brought the president some papers to sign.
7. In the 1980s, my parents sold tofu burgers outside Grateful Dead concerts for several years to get money to get in the shows.
8. We will barely break even this year.
9. SARS is spreading rapidly throughout several Asian nations because of inadequate response from governmental health authorities.
10. After the party, Tom Cruise's character has to furiously clean the house before his parents return home.

Who Owns Information?

Chapter 5

Shawn Fanning loved computers. From his dormmates at Northeastern University in Boston, Shawn learned about the MP3, a format in which music could be transformed into a digital file, loaded onto a computer, and traded like e-mail. In his first year at Northeastern, Shawn seemed even more interested in computers than in school. Concerned, Shawn's uncle gave him a project: develop a computer program for use with these music files. Shawn threw himself into the project. By May 1999, he had completed a beta (or test) version of his application, which—he hoped—would be a super-efficient method of searching for MP3 files on the Internet. He was right. Within a year, Shawn became a national celebrity, and his creation was both celebrated for exploiting the democratic nature of the Internet and reviled for undermining fundamental rights to property and ownership.

The program Shawn wrote was, of course, Napster. In its short lifetime, Napster—which

Musicians Don Henley and Courtney Love testify before the California State Assembly.

allowed individual users to seek out MP3 files from servers across the world and download those files to the user's own computer—became a sensation, first on college campuses and then across the country. Almost overnight, it seemed senseless to spend money on music. Why would you, when you could get it for free?

You probably know the end of this story. The Recording Industry Association of America (RIAA), the trade group for record companies, filed suit against Shawn and his company, alleging copyright violation. Napster allowed people to steal music, the RIAA said—what could possibly be legal about this? The controversy went public in a major way, with famous musicians on both sides. Metallica's drummer Lars Ulrich became one of the most visible spokesman for the anti-Napster side, pointing out that royalties from record sales constituted a significant portion of his income, while other musicians (including rapper Chuck D of Public Enemy and folk singer Janis Ian, whose article on the subject is included with this chapter) argued that Napster gave exposure to bands the corporate music industry ignored. In July 2001, a federal judge ordered Napster to stop allowing users to trade music—in effect shutting down the company. And although the Bertelsmann media conglomerate quickly bought Napster, hoping to use Napster's technology eventually to charge users for music, the federal injunction ended the brief but spectacular career of Fanning's startup. (In 2002, Bertelsmann sold Napster to Roxio, a manufacturer of CD burners; the company

Metallica's Lars Ulrich testifying before Congress about Napster.

now offers downloadable music that users can purchase. Meanwhile, the RIAA has continued in its aggressive stance against "pirates," and has begun filing suit against individuals for copyright violation.)

The Napster controversy evokes an issue in which almost each of us has a stake: who owns information? Who has the right to own or profit from ideas or art? In the Napster controversy, the recording industry, musicians, and consumers faced off, each claiming ownership over the music being traded. Each had a good claim. The record companies pointed to their legal ownership of the recordings in question. Musicians, whether they sided with or against the RIAA, emphasized their legal ownership of the songs and performances and their ethical right to ownership over their own recordings. Consumers insisted that they owned the actual CDs or MP3 files in question and had the right to do what they wanted with those disks or MP3s. Who was right?

The Three Claims to Ownership

These conflicting claims need to be viewed in a more general light. Napster simply resurrected an old argument in Western societies, one that has cropped up periodically since the printing press made it possible for information to be quickly, accurately, and infinitely reproduced and sold. Before the age of mechanical reproduction, the transmission of written information or of art was generally a one-to-one transaction between the creator and the consumer. The writer of a medieval book (St. Thomas Aquinas, say, or Geoffrey Chaucer) read his work aloud to an audience. The book might be copied, but that copy had to be made by hand, making mass production of any scale unfeasible. The printing press changed everything. Accurate copies of books could now be produced cheaply and in great numbers. With more books available, more people learned to read. More people then began writing books for this new audience of the literate. Increasingly, intellectual debates took place not in aristocratic houses or the royal court or universities, but in print. Art, too, changed. Poets could now write for a broader public of the newly literate (who were both middle-class and aristocratic), and as a result their subject matter changed. A new form of writing— the novel—was born as a result of the printing press.

The printing press *democratized* art and information—it made them available to the people. But at the same time, the printing press (and such descendants as the lithograph, the photograph, the phonograph, the photocopier, the scanner, the CD burner . . .) created a new class of entrepreneurs: the *re*producers and distributors of creative work. Artists and writers, rarely rich folk themselves, need to find someone who *owns* the expensive machinery of reproduction and distribution before they can get their work out to the public. In the early days of printing, an author would present his manuscript to a printer, who made a judgment about whether or not the book would sell. If the printer thought the book could make money, he would agree to print it. Things are no different today. In the process of making this book, I took my idea to the publisher, who made a judgment about whether or not anyone would buy it. When he decided enough people would buy the book to offset the expenses he would incur in publishing it, he accepted the manuscript.

Where it gets tricky is in the question of ownership—both in terms of who owns and what is owned. For example, when a writer gives his manuscript to a publisher and that publisher prints 50,000 copies, who owns those copies? In most cases, the contract between the writer and the publisher says that the writer is given a certain number of free copies of his book and the right to purchase additional copies at a large discount. All the rest of the copies belong to the publisher, until the publisher sells those copies to a bookseller or to a reader. The book then belongs either to a bookseller or to its end user.

But who owns *the book?* Who has the right to buy and sell and use and excerpt and quote from and turn into a movie the contents of the book? Those rights are set out in the contract between the publisher and the writer; surprisingly, the publisher maintains a great deal of ownership over the ideas that the writer produced because most book contracts specify that the publisher owns the *copyright* to the book. Generally, the publisher can sell pieces of the book (excerpts) to magazines, owns the right to sell the book to a paperback publisher, controls foreign rights over the book, and perhaps even reserves the right to sell the book's story to a movie or television producer. When another author wants to quote from the book, he or she must ask the publisher for permission, and will often have to pay a fee. Of course, in most of these cases the writer receives money (in the form of royalties), but you are probably surprised to learn that the publisher actually owns most of the rights to do things with a writer's work.

Why should a publisher retain so many rights over someone else's creative work? Primarily, the answer is that the publisher has invested a great deal of money into producing the work. When working with most publishers, a writer invests nothing, monetarily. (Her investment of time and effort is another matter.) The publisher assumes all the risk that the book will lose money. If a writer wants to be published, she must give up some, or even most, of her rights over what will happen with her book. In exchange, she receives the satisfaction of seeing her work in print, as well as the knowledge that she will make money if the book sells thousands of copies or is made into a successful movie. If the book is a success and does make a lot of money for the publisher and author, she can then use this as leverage for better terms when she negotiates the contract for her next book.

The ownership of the right to reproduce a particular book is known as "copyright." Copyright law is an enormously complicated subject, but in its simplest sense, the United States adopted copyright so that writers would be assured of having the sole authority to determine who can profit from their work. In the 1700s and 1800s, before copyright was generally accepted by the American and European governments, it was quite common for a printer to obtain an author's book, copy it down, and produce his own "pirate" edition, with no money going to the author. Under our system of copyright, an author legally lends his or her copyright to a publisher; both parties must then abide by the terms of the contract they sign (e.g. the author cannot then publish that same book with another publisher, and the publisher cannot sell copies of the book without paying royalties to the author). No other publisher may legally produce an edition of that book.

But what about the ideas contained in a book? Who owns those? This gets even more complicated. Ideas are, by their nature, intangible and nebulous. If you've ever watched a movie and thought, "I had that idea already!" you've no doubt known how hard it is to own an idea. In the types of professions where ideas are of supreme importance—creative fields or academia, for instance—ideas themselves are the most important products. Because ideas are so important in those fields, rules and laws have been written to determine who owns ideas and who has the right to profit from them.

By now, you are certainly familiar with the concept of "plagiarism." **In simplest terms, plagiarism is taking credit for someone else's work.** Copying a report out of the encyclopedia and turning it in as your own is an example of plagiarism, of course. So is buying a term paper on the Internet instead of writing your own. It might surprise you to know that when you quote someone without indicating the source, even if you put it in quotes, this is also plagiarism. When you read an article and use its argument in your paper without giving credit to the author, you are plagiarizing. When you cut and paste something from the Web into your paper, you are plagiarizing. Professors take plagiarism extremely seriously, and you must be extremely careful always to give proper credit to your sources. It's not just students who plagiarize, either. In their best-selling books of American history, Doris Kearns Goodwin and Stephen Ambrose actually inserted whole paragraphs copied from their source materials. Goodwin and Ambrose both defended themselves by claiming that this was an oversight, an error committed by research assistants, but the charges stuck and their reputations have suffered. In 2003, the *New York Times* admitted that Jayson Blair, one of its reporters, had plagiarized some stories (from sources such as the San

Antonio *Express-News*) and made up others. Blair was fired, but in the aftermath of the Blair incident two of the paper's highest-ranking editors also resigned as a way to take responsibility for Blair's trangressions.[1]

What happens, though, when someone isn't plagiarizing (copying or quoting without giving credit to the original author), but instead is stealing ideas? The repercussions vary depending on what kinds of ideas we're talking about. In the academy these matters tend to be judged in a rather old-fashioned way—within the community. Generally, in academic research the community of scholars who might be interested in new research is so small (a few thousand people at the most, sometimes only dozens) that they tend to know already who has had an idea. Taking credit for someone else's research is a particularly grievous transgression in the academy, for in many fields everything depends on producing and publishing new scholarship. A scholar found to have plagiarized likely will lose it all—position, pay, prestige.

In a creative field like the movies, the accuser must provide evidence that he or she already had this idea, made this idea public somehow, and that the accused thief had access to the idea. In a famous case, writer Art Buchwald sued Paramount Studios, claiming that the studio had stolen his idea and turned it into the Eddie Murphy movie *Coming to America.* Buchwald argued that he had written a "treatment" (a basic outline of the story) and had given that treatment to an executive at the studio, who had simply hired someone else to write the movie without giving any credit to Buchwald. The studio denied this, saying that another writer had come up with the idea. In the end, the studio settled with Buchwald (that is, it paid him money in order to get him to drop his claim). Because the environment in Hollywood makes such cases so likely (ideas circulate around constantly, many ideas are very similar, and the original writer of an idea has very little say in what eventually happens), the professional organizations that govern writers, directors, and studios have adopted strict rules about idea theft.

Other creative fields don't have such well-defined rules. Novelists use each other's ideas constantly; in fact, a defining characteristic of postmodern fiction is the use of and commentary on other writers' work and ideas. Much of the history of Western literature consists of the conversation writers have with each other through their books and characters. Some writers feel this goes too far—in 2001 Alice Randall wrote *The Wind Done Gone,* a retelling of Margaret Mitchell's *Gone With the Wind* story from the point of view of the African-American characters. The Mitchell estate sued Randall, arguing that she had violated their copyright on the scenes and characters in *Gone With the Wind.* Certainly, they wanted exclusive ownership over this fictional world—they had already commissioned a sequel to the 1936 novel and perhaps had plans to

---

[1] Plagiarism is even more complicated when examined across cultures, as many teachers have learned. In many Asian cultures, copying the writing of an eminent source is not considered plagiarism; rather, it is a sign of deserved respect. Many students who come from these cultures have great difficulty adjusting to the high premium U.S. educational institutions put on scholarly originality. No matter what culture you are from, though, it is incumbent upon you to know the rules of plagiarism and scholarly integrity as they are codified at your school and to follow them.

produce others—but they also did not want Mitchell's characters or novel to be thrown into an unfavorable light. The Mitchell estate failed in their attempt to stop Randall's novel. In another recent case, *Harry Potter* author J.K. Rowling was the target of accusations that she stole all her ideas from the published novels of struggling writer Nancy Stouffer. Stouffer disputed Rowling's well-known story that she came up with the idea for Harry's universe while riding a train, and pointed to her own novels, which featured a magical protagonist named "Larry Potter" and characters known as "Muggles" (a name also used in Rowling's books). Stouffer claimed that her self-published books had sold hundreds of thousands of copies. In 2002, though, a federal district court judge ruled for Rowling, noting that much of Stouffer's evidence appeared to be falsified.

In music, too, ideas can be stolen—and there are consequences. The late Beatle George Harrison became embroiled in a decades-long lawsuit over his 1971 song "My Sweet Lord." In 1976, a court determined that Harrison had stolen the melody from the Chiffons' 1963 hit "He's So Fine" in writing "My Sweet Lord." Harrison successfully argued that he had not consciously stolen anything, but the court decided that even if Harrison's intentions had not been to steal, in the end his song was too close to the Chiffon's song and could not be fairly credited to him—Harrison was found liable for "unconscious plagiarism" and had to pay royalties to the copyright holder of "She's So Fine."

Rap and hip-hop music have experienced numerous copyright disputes because of their reliance on previously recorded music. Early rap recordings featured a rapper, or "MC," rapping over records manipulated by a DJ. As soon as rap began to gain popularity, the artists who made the records rapped over by the MC began to demand that the rap artists obtain their permission and sometimes even pay royalties for the use of their records. Sampling—the digital recording of sounds that are then inserted into performances—also became widespread in rap, with similar results. Even such famous and well-established artists as the Beastie Boys have been involved in lawsuits resulting from their use of samples.

Even when the legal issues are settled in advance, the question of artistic originality in rap music remains. Many of rap's most popular songs have been built on instantly recognizable samples from well-known pop hits. Rap's first hugely successful song, Run-DMC's "Walk This Way," used the Aerosmith song of the same name—and Aerosmith themselves appeared on the record, performing their trademark song in rap style. MC Hammer's 1990 hit "U Can't Touch This" used the familiar bass line from Rick James's 1981 song "Superfreak," and Puff Daddy's 1998 tribute to Biggie Smalls, "I'll Be Missing You," relies entirely on the Police's 1983 "Every Breath You Take." Responding to criticism that their music isn't really *theirs,* rappers will often answer that the artistry and originality of rap lies not in the creation of original melodies, but in the expert use of language and in the manipulation of preexisting beats and musical phrases.

Ａ nalyzing the Message

1. What does it mean for a work of art to be "original"? Is rap music original when it uses previously recorded music? Is a movie remake like *Ocean's Eleven* original? What about a movie based on a Disney theme-park attraction like *The Country Bears* or *Pirates of the Caribbean?* Or what about a book like Helen Fielding's *Bridget Jones' Diary*, which is a retelling of Jane Austen's classic *Pride and Prejudice?*

2. What value should be put on artistic originality? Should art be judged on a different standard because it is derived from a previous work? Or do we live in a historical epoch when everything has already been said, making originality impossible?

3. Think about a time in your own scholarly career when you have committed or been accused of or been tempted to commit plagiarism. Was the violation clear-cut—for example, did you copy and try to conceal that you had copied? Or was it more complicated?

Who owns a creative work?

Questions about the ownership of ideas and words plague the writer's and song-writer's trades, but recent technological advances have made issues of copyright violation in other media—specifically music and the movies—even more pressing. In these media, the companies that produce and distribute the work of artists play a more central role, simply because it's prohibitively expensive for a single person to make and distribute a movie or even a CD. In order to produce a CD, musicians must have instruments, microphones and amplifiers, and time in a recording studio—none of which is cheap. Movies are even more expensive, with some costing well over $100 million and even "low-budget" films rarely produced for under a million dollars. Musicians and directors, therefore, must find someone to help them with money and resources: that's where the record companies and movie studios enter the picture. And with such large investments in the artists' products at stake, the record companies and movie studios are reluctant to relinquish any control over the product or rights to the profits. This desire often comes into conflict with artists' wishes to make the decisions about their own creations.

Let's look at some specific examples from the world of recorded music. For many years, musicians have complained about what they felt to be the inordinate amount of ownership record companies could claim over their music. In fact, such musicians as Sheryl Crow, Don Henley, and Courtney Love have likened record contracts, perhaps hyperbolically, to indentured servitude: most record contracts require the musician to record exclusively for the record company for a period of up to seven years, while giving the record company the right to cancel the contract at any time. Furthermore, the "masters" (the actual studio recordings that become singles or albums) belong to the record company. Young, struggling musicians sign these contracts when they are poor and eager for any exposure. If the musician is successful, he or she cannot renegotiate the contract to obtain more favorable terms; if the musician is not successful, the record company is under no obligation to produce any more of his or her records. When a record company signs a musician or a band, the company advances that musician or band money to be used in renting a studio, hiring a producer and engineers, recording masters, pressing a CD, and promoting the music. After that CD begins to sell, the record company takes out its own expenses before the musician or group is entitled to any royalties. In fact, even after a successful record a musician can end up owing the record company money. (Many African-American artists of the 1940s, 1950s, and 1960s were victims of abusive record company contracts that took advantage of those artists' second-class legal status and lack of social power, and dozens of artists whose records sold hundreds of thousands of copies saw little or no money from their recording careers.) Certainly, the record company, like a book publisher, puts a great deal of money at risk when it commissions a new album from a struggling band. However, the *sums* of money involved in music are so much greater than in publishing, frequently amounting to hundreds of thousands of dollars, that it is often impossible for a small band with a small following ever to repay the record company.

In recent years, many artists have decided entirely to avoid becoming entangled with record companies and have used the Internet and digital technology to produce and distribute their own music. Such revolts against record companies by major rock and roll artists date from the early 1970s, when the Beatles and Led Zeppelin both started their own record companies (Apple and Swan Song, respectively) for their own bands. However, in recent years, since it has become so inexpensive to produce music digitally and because the Web allows anyone to open a mail-order store, such startups have proliferated. Prince, Fugazi, Ani DiFranco, Public Enemy, the Grateful Dead, and large numbers of underground rappers bypass the big record companies completely.

What especially angers many musicians is the fact that the record companies own their music. John Fogerty, the songwriter and bandleader of the 1960s folk-rock band Creedence Clearwater Revival, fought Fantasy Records for decades over royalties and ownership of his enduringly popular and lucrative recordings, but the company did not relent. Adding insult to injury is the fact that the company can use Creedence songs in ways that Fogerty would never want. In 2001, Fantasy licensed Wrangler Jeans to use a Creedence song, "Fortunate Son," for a television commercial. The commercial celebrated patriotic images over Fogerty's words "some folks are born, made to wave the flag/ Oh that red white and blue." Fogerty wrote the song as an attack on young people who, in the Vietnam era, loudly proclaimed patriotism but still tried to avoid military service. Ironically, the commercial's imagery (a parade of flags and blue jeans) was in direct contradiction of the song's message. Even though he wrote the song and performed the version used in the commercial, Fogerty has no say over how it can be used.[2]

The ownership of movies is just as complicated. Recently, DVDs that include the "director's cut" of films have become very popular. But what is the "director's cut"? Movie studios (the companies that finance the movies and often provide sets, office space, and equipment to moviemakers) want more than anything for their movies to be profitable—to reach the widest possible audience. In order to accomplish this, the studio will often force a filmmaker to make changes in the movie: everything from the script to the star to the amount of profanity is often determined by the studio, not the producer or director. Directors, though, frequently resent what they see as interference from people who don't

---

[2] Bob Baker, "No 'Fortunate Son' of corporate America." *Christian Science Monitor* 22 Nov. 2002.
(http://www.cmonitor.com/stories/a&e2002/fogerty_fortunate_son_1122_2002.shtml)

understand the artistic process and whose primary allegiance is to money. As a result, directors will "recut" a movie after a studio has released it to the public, in effect making the movie they wanted to make in the first place. Many films exist in both original and "director's cut" versions—Francis Ford Coppola's *Apocalypse Now,* Oliver Stone's *Natural Born Killers,* and Ridley Scott's *Blade Runner* are all available in both versions. While those director's cuts reflect the desires of the director at the time the film was originally released, sometimes directors change their minds after decades. George Lucas recently inserted new material into his 1977 classic *Star Wars* for a theatrical rerelease. These short scenes were created entirely digitally with technologies unavailable when the movie was originally made. It is hard to say what the "real" movie is—the original studio version that became a classic, the version that most accurately reflects the creator's intentions at the time he or she made the film, or the version that reflects the director's desires today.

Digital technology has taken the concept of director's cut even further. In 1999, one of the most eagerly awaited films in history was finally released: *Star Wars Episode 1: The Phantom Menace,* directed by George Lucas and produced by Twentieth Century Fox and Lucas's company, Lucasfilm. Thousands of *Star Wars* cultists camped outside theaters for weeks before the movie's premiere, but reaction to the film was at best lukewarm. Fans didn't like the pace of the movie, felt that the acting was stilted, saw the script as juvenile, and especially hated one of the characters, a computer-generated creature named Jar-Jar Binks. Soon after the film left theaters, though, a pirate or unauthorized version started circulating among Internet denizens and film buffs. Called *Star Wars: The Phantom Edit,* this version of Lucas's film was shorter and faster paced than the "real" version of the film, and to many fans' delight essentially eliminated the Binks character. Because of digital technology, the "Phantom Editor" (as he became known) was able to turn an entire movie into a computer file and to recut it. No longer does an editor need the actual celluloid film—a movie can be digitized, turned into a long series of 1s and 0s, and manipulated like any other computer data file. (In fact, some movies are "filmed" entirely on digital video, bypassing film entirely.)

So is the Phantom Editor a thief? A vandal? A rogue genius? Both the studio and Lucas attacked the film as theft—the film belonged to them, they argued, and altering it in any way was tantamount to defacing someone else's property. The case brings up several interesting issues. First of all, who does a movie really belong to—if this is theft, in other words, who is the victim? The studio, the producers, and the director all share parts of the copyright of the film, and because Lucas is a famous and powerful director it's likely that the studio cannot make any arrangements to promote or distribute or alter the film without his input. (This would not be the case with less powerful directors.) The Phantom Editor's actions certainly affected Lucas's creation, and in this sense Lucas is the injured party—but how is the Phantom Editor's movie different from a novel like Randall's *The Wind Done Gone?* Artists always use each other's work—commenting on it or even blatantly "stealing" it in the pursuit of their own artistic vision. But what about the rights of the studio that provided the initial investment and may rely financially on the movie's enduring popularity? And, going further with this idea, do the fans have any rights of ownership over

Lucas's story? Without their devotion to and love for *Star Wars,* after all, these films would never have been made. Does this give the fans any ethical rights to the story or how it is made?

What are the limits of copyright?

The questions about what the "real" film is and the distinction between the song (owned by the songwriter) and the recording (owned by the record company) bring up an even more fundamental question about copyright: what can be copyrighted, and for how long? Obviously, a book can be copyrighted, as can a poem or article or recording or movie . . . but what about a character? A design? A sentence? What is the limit of ownership? And how long should the creators of works be able to control those works?

In recent years the purview of copyright has been expanded dramatically, largely because of scientific advances. Biotechnology and chemical companies have patented (a legal status similar to copyright) molecules and even life forms, and the U.S. legal system has supported the claim that these unique creations can in fact be owned by a commercial entity. Even human genes can be patented. Characters and images, as well, are subject to copyright—nobody can legally use Bugs Bunny or sell products with the NBA logo on them without the permission of the copyright holder. Even certain combinations of words can be copyrighted: most advertising slogans you can think of ("The Choice of a New Generation," "Fair and Balanced," "It's Everywhere You Want To Be") belong to the company that owns the copyright. This is not to say that if you utter the phrase "Be All You Can Be" you are obliged to pay royalties to the U.S. Army, though; copyright in this case has been defined to mean that no other entity can use those phrases or sentences for their own commercial gain or for the purposes of confusing consumers.[3] Songs, even short jingles, are subject to copyright, as well. Many people do not know that "Happy Birthday to You" is actually copyrighted: legally, any performance of the song in public or for profit is prohibited without the permission of the copyright holders (a foundation representing the two sisters who wrote the song, and Summy-Birchard Music, a division of AOL-Time Warner). According to the president of Summy-Birchard, the song brings in about $2 million a year.[4]

Control over images can be much more tightly held. The estates of Elvis Presley and Martin Luther King, Jr., both exert complete control over commercial and noncommercial use of the images of the King and Dr. King. People who want to use images of either person must obtain the permission both of the copyright holder of the particular image (usually the photographer who took the

---

[3] In summer 2003, News Corporation, owner of the Fox News Channel (see Chapter 4), filed suit against the liberal writer and comedian Al Franken over his book *Lies and the Lying Liars Who Tell Them: A Fair and Balanced Look at the Right.* Fox claimed that Franken was illegally using its copyrighted slogan "Fair and Balanced" and had also illegally placed a photograph of Fox News employee Bill O'Reilly on the cover of the book. Fox claimed that consumers would be misled by the book's title and cover picture and might think that it was an actual Fox News product. A judge disagreed and threw the suit out of court.

[4] Bruce Anderson, "Beyond Measure." *Attaché* Jan. 2002.

image) and of the estates of Presley or King. The International Olympic Committee is notoriously protective of both the name "Olympics" and the five-ring logo of the Olympic Games. Several athletic organizations (such as the Special Olympics and Gay Olympics) ended up in court battles with the Olympics about use of the name and logo, with only the Special Olympics being granted permission to use the term.

Arguing, reasonably, that a great deal of the value of the company is tied up in the power and familiarity of the images of Mickey Mouse and Donald Duck, the Walt Disney Company is perhaps the epitome of the protective copyright holder. Often Disney has marshalled all its legal might and financial leverage to fight even the smallest mom-and-pop business that used any Disney character or image in its advertising. In fact, Disney's obsession with copyright protection has probably cost it some public goodwill, for press coverage of some of these fights has portrayed Disney, fairly or not, as a ruthless profiteering behemoth instead of the family-friendly company it likes to appear to be. But can Disney be faulted for wanting to protect its most valuable asset?

Companies like Disney or AOL-Time Warner or Sony, although they continue to generate a huge number of new products every year, still rely very heavily on public fondness for what they have produced in the past—whether that is the back catalog of popular recording artists, or the company's familiar characters and franchises, or simply the values and feelings that the public associates with that brand name and its logos and slogans. Disney and AOL-Time Warner (which owns the characters of the Looney Tunes cartoon lineup) rely on the ability to control what Mickey or Bugs does, where he appears, what products he endorses. Disney has always sought to expand its purview beyond its own characters, as well, and to bring other popular children's characters and stories into the Disney tent. Because of Disney's cartoons, most children associate Winnie the Pooh, Mowgli, Peter Pan, Tarzan, Beauty and the Beast, Uncle Remus, Cinderella, Snow White, and many others only with Disney—the company gets to the children before A. A. Milne or Rudyard Kipling or Edgar Rice Burroughs or the Brothers Grimm can, ensuring that people's main experiences with these children's stories will be "Disneyfied."

Very recently, though, these companies endured an extremely close call about their copyrights. As it was originally conceived, copyright was not perpetual. Authors were granted the exclusive right to profit from their works only for a limited period of time. In fact, the U.S. Constitution enshrines the limited nature of copyright:

> the Congress shall have power . . . to promote the progress of science and useful arts, by securing for limited times to authors and inventors the exclusive right to their respective writings and discoveries.

Over the history of copyright, the term for which creators could hold copyright has consistently grown. The 1790 Copyright Act specified that this term was 14 years, with the possibility of renewal for another 14; 41 years later the original term of 14 years was doubled. Late in the nineteenth century European nations signed the Berne Convention, which set the term of copyright as the life of the author plus 50 years (the U.S. passed its own law to this effect in 1976). In 1998, the "Sonny Bono Copyright Term Extension Act" (named after the California congressman who had performed with, and was married to, the singer Cher) added another 20 years to the term of copyright. In that same year the Digital Millennium Copyright Act made it illegal for consumers to disable anti-copying technologies.

Almost immediately upon the passage of the Bono act, a small Internet publisher named Eric Eldred, supported by eminent academics such as Stanford law professor Lawrence Lessig, filed a legal challenge to the new law. Eldred's and Lessig's argument was quite simple: the term of copyright must be limited, because that was what copyright's inventors wanted. The Constitution's language, after all, stated that the goal of copyright was "to promote the progress of science and useful arts"; Eldred and Lessig and others argued that that progress is best advanced when the creator is allowed to profit from a creation for a period of time, after which the rest of society may use that creation.

Eldred and Lessig had formidable opponents, though. Big money was at stake, as were properties belonging to some of America's largest corporations. Among the creations that would have gone out of copyright without an extension were films like *The Wizard of Oz,* songs such as "It Had To Be You," and books such as *The Great Gatsby.* Most importantly, the cartoon character Mickey Mouse (who appeared first in the 1928 cartoon "Steamboat Willie") would have become public domain. The Walt Disney Company unleashed an all-out lobbying campaign in Congress to help pass the Bono bill. As the Eldred case neared the Supreme Court, Disney stepped up its lobbying in Congress (to ensure a new law in case Bono was declared unconstitutional) and in public (to persuade Americans that copyright extensions were in everyone's interest). In early 2003, the Supreme Court upheld the Bono act with only two justices dissenting, reasoning that since Congress had consistently extended copyright (11 times just since 1943), there was no reason that the Bono act was any different than its predecessors.

Public reaction has been stronger than anyone expected, given the essentially arcane and legalistic matters at issue. Editorial writers across the political spectrum condemned the decision as they had attacked the act itself. The left argued that Congress and the Supreme Court were simply handing out welfare to giant media corporations, while many writers on the right attacked the decision as a setback for ingenuity and the free market. Most of those who oppose the act and the Supreme Court decision fear that copyrights will continue to be extended indefinitely—every time Mickey Mouse nears public domain, the powerful lobbying apparatus of Hollywood will go into action to lengthen copyright yet again. The dissenters on the Court itself agreed. Justice John Paul Stevens noted in his dissent that over the last 80 years only one year's worth of books, musical compositions, movies, or other works of visual art has entered the public domain. By allowing Congress to continue to extend existing copyrights, Stevens said, the majority ignored "the central purpose" of the Copyright Clause.[5]

Issues of copyright extension are closely related to issues of how consumers can circumvent copyright, and the Digital Millennium Act attempted to

---

[5] If you are interested in the particulars of this case (*Eldred* v. *Ashcroft*), including the majority and dissenting opinions, consult the Supreme Court's website—www.supremecourtus.gov—where you can download documents from the case.

deal with those problems of unauthorized copying. Media companies have always been suspicious of technologies that allow consumers to copy information. Publishers fought against the installation of photocopying machines in university libraries—in fact, publishers initially opposed public libraries!—and the movie studios fought tenaciously against the VCR, fearing that if consumers could watch films in their homes theater attendance would fall. (The studios did not take into consideration the money they could make from home video, though: for years, movies have earned far more from videocassette and DVD sales than they do in theaters—totals from the first half of 2002 were $4.2 billion from DVD and video sales and rentals, and $1.7 billion at the box office.[6]) Record companies fought against blank recordable cassette tapes in the 1970s and 1980s just as, today, they fight against CD burners and MP3 trading software. Even as they pursue legislative responses to copying, companies will continue to try and develop technological solutions. However, in the digital age it is likely that clever users will stay at least one step ahead of any security technology. In one famous example, CDs were encoded with information that made it impossible to play them on (and, presumably, copy their songs onto) a computer. However, users discovered that drawing a line around the outer edge of the disk with a felt-tip pen prevented the computer from reading this anticopying software.

Questions about who owns information or creative work are much more complicated than they might seem at first, and in writing about these questions it is of crucial importance not to oversimplify them. At first glance it probably seems as if there are two easily stereotyped sides squaring off in these debates: the large corporations who have steadily extended their control over more and more creative work (which is generally created by others), and the public that wants more, cheaper, and freer access to those works. It's not that clear-cut, though, and when examining any particular issue it is worth thinking about whose interests are really served by any given position—sometimes the interests of independent musicians and large media corporations are at odds, but at other times they mesh. And since these arguments are being made in public, readers have to be aware of the rhetoric being used. Appeals to "freedom" and "the natural circulation of information" might simply be camouflage for an argument stating that consumers shouldn't ever have to pay for anything if don't feel like it. Similarly, a focus on the tribulations of a struggling musician might actually be rhetoric meant to hide the real argument: that consumers should never be able to copy anything for free, no matter what it is or what it's being used for.

Even if it is an oversimplification to boil down these arguments to two sides, it is valuable to think of this debate as being driven by two large general tendencies in society today—not just in American society, but around the world. The first large tendency or development is what we might call the accretion of private ownership of the public sphere. Not just in the areas of media and information but in almost every sphere, properties and powers and rights are more and more held by large for-profit entities. Radical critics point to

---

[6] Frank Ahrens, "Hollywood Sees the Big Picture with DVDs." *Washington Post* 7 Oct. 2002: A1.

international bodies like the World Trade Organization, which has the right to overrule a nation's own laws in the interests of international trade. In developing nations and in the so-called "First World" alike, public resources like water and roads are increasingly privately owned. Across the world, government-owned phone companies, television networks, power authorities, and even prisons are being transferred into the hands of private entities. The growth of private ownership of information and media products, and the increasing duration and scope of that ownership, is only a small area of this world-historical development.

Opposing this development is what we might call the diffusion and devolution of power via technology. Modern technology allows citizens to communicate with each other more quickly, more efficiently, more cheaply, over greater distances, and more frequently than ever before. Having a pen pal in Pakistan or Egypt used to be exotic; now it's mundane to log onto bulletin boards and comment on Joe Millionaire's choices or bemoan Manchester United's losses with people from Texas, Mexico, Russia, and Paraguay. New vectors of communication allow us to establish a wider variety of communities than ever before. Technology gives people power: we can cheaply and easily publish books, make movies, and organize movements. Technology makes it easier to oppose the growth of centralized corporate ownership, too. Many writers and musicians have bypassed the corporate music industry entirely and attempt to produce and distribute their music themselves. Technology also makes it easier to steal, as anyone who has seen the music and movies and fake IDs for sale at a Los Angeles or Mexico City or Bangkok street market knows. Technology doesn't only work on one direction, either; the same technologies that allow protesters to come together and organize demonstrations against repressive governments in Serbia or China can also be used by those governments to find and imprison protesters. And we must not forget that these same technologies of communication are tools of groups like Al Qaeda, and allow those groups to operate in secrecy. Technology itself rarely has an ethical nature: it's how we use it that matters.

Analyzing the Message

1. What should be the limits of copyright—are there creations that should not be copyrightable? New words? Sentences? Musical phrases?

2. What is a reasonable principle for determining the length of copyright? How can lawmakers balance the public's interest with the Founders' desire for limited terms of copyright and the interests of corporations and creators to continue profiting from their creations?

3. Many Napster users argued that they did not use the service to avoid buying CDs, but instead downloaded new music so they could decide whether or not to buy that musician's recordings. Many artists who have been shut out of commercial radio supported Napster for that reason, as well—the service got their music out to the people. How should this affect public policy about copyright law? Can people be trusted not to use Napster to just steal music they'd otherwise buy? Should the law reflect that?

Readings

*What is the nature of "free speech"? More to the point, what kinds of abuses are disguised by appeals to free speech? In this editorial, **Amy Peikoff** argues that the (ultimately unsuccessful) challenge brought against the Sonny Bono Copyright Act and the Digital Millennium Act is a thinly veiled attack on private property cloaked in rhetoric about free speech. Peikoff, a writer for the libertarian Ayn Rand Institute, typifies the libertarian intellectual approach to public policy in that she opposes any governmental efforts to legislate the "public good." Peikoff supports the law, but not because it will be ultimately in the public interest; only the marketplace can determine the public interest, she implies.*

Amy Peikoff
Would-Be Intellectual Vandals Get Their Day in the Supreme Court

In 1998 Congress, pursuant to its Constitutional power to determine the duration of federal copyright protection, passed a law extending the term of that protection by 20 years. This law brought United States copyright protection in line with that already afforded in Europe. In addition, as the average life expectancy in the United States now exceeds 70 years, the law brings copyright protection in line with the legal vehicle for the posthumous control of tangible property—the law of testamentary trusts, which bases the term of such control on a human lifespan.

Despite the reasonableness of this law, Stanford professor Lawrence Lessig is spearheading a legal challenge to it, culminating in his argument before the Supreme Court this Wednesday. Lessig, who seems to have become, in the words of *New York Times* writer Amy Harmon, "a rock star for the digital liberties set," is expected to argue that the law is "overly restrictive of the free-speech rights of would-be users of copyrighted material that previously would have been in the public domain."

In the recent decades we have already seen the "right to free speech" extended to mean the "right" to be provided with a free platform for one's speech. Anyone who dares to be successful enough to own a property where the public enjoys gathering—e.g., a shopping mall—is for that reason compelled to allow people to speak on that property. "Free" speech thus means: free of any need to earn one's own physical instrumentalities or audience, of even to pay for the right to borrow someone else's achievements.

Lessig would have the Supreme Court extend this perversion of free speech to mean: free of any need to pay for the borrowing of someone else's greatest achievement: original thought. Or worse: free of any need sufficiently to digest that original thought so as to be able to put into one's own words. Appropriating and parroting the creation of others is now, according to Lessig, "free speech."

Lessig and his allies try to downplay what they are doing by making it an issue of finances. They say things like, "the copyright law used to restrict big business, which is fine—but now it restricts anyone who has access to the Internet." "Only 2 percent of works protected by copyright," they go on, "create a regular stream of income for their creators." Translation: only a small minority of "non-little" people will be hurt by repealing this law, so why not do it? This attack on money, success and big business—no doubt another symptom of the "Enron" era—is shameful and Marxist. How is the Court, as Lessig demands, to "balance the interests" of original thinkers against those for whom "creativity" consists of cannibalizing—and even vandalizing—the products of others' thought?

The government is expected to argue—properly—that the Supreme Court cannot arbitrarily impose a definition of "limited times." In other words, the power to set an appropriate time period for copyright protection lies with Congress. Congress has clearly been reasonable in its exercise of that power.

The other main argument offered by supporters of the 1998 law is that, in the long run, the law will promote creative work, and thus the national welfare, by offering higher profits to those who invest in it. This argument—based on the "public good" standard—is intellectually bankrupt and doomed to failure. Opponents simply counter that more creativity will be fostered by allowing people to obtain and build upon existing works. Many "conservatives," such as Milton Friedman, use the same "public good" standard to argue that the incremental economic payoff provided by the 1998 law is not significant enough to encourage creativity.

Anyone who raises the standard of "public good" in this context had better be ready to have his rights in any field adjudicated according to the latest iteration of Jeremy Bentham's utilitarian calculus. In practice, this means: according to the premises, preferences, and whims of the judge sitting before him.

An artist or intellectual is often not only or even primarily concerned with reaping the monetary benefits of his works; in addition, he wants to be that the integrity of the work is protected against mutilation as long as possible. This is especially true if the work conveys an important artistic or philosophic message. If those in the "digital liberties set" plan to have a field day with others' works of creative genius—bastardizing into whatever fragments they find appealing, adding any distorting content they choose, then blasting the results all over the Internet—what is the point of trying to convey to the world one's own vital viewpoint? What is the reward offered for trying painstakingly to create one's vision of truth or of an ideal universe, and to invite readers to share in it, if our nation's highest court gives Lessig's gang a formal sanction to practice intellectual vandalism on the finished product?

Topics for Reading and Writing

1. Peikoff charges that the limitation of copyright laws is "Marxist." Why does she choose this word? What does she mean? What is the rhetorical effect of using this word—both in terms of her ethos and in terms of the audience's emotions?

2. Although she supports the government's position on the law, she criticizes the "intellectually bankrupt" idea of the "public good" standard. What does she mean by the "public good" standard? If she is opposed to both Lawrence Lessig's side and to the government's side, how does she position herself on this question?

3. Given her position on this question, what do you think Peikoff's view of the Napster controversy would be?

Most of the pieces from the New York Times *included in this book have been signed opinion pieces or feature articles, but this editorial is unsigned, which indicates that the piece represents the opinion of the editorial board of the newspaper itself. (The* Times *editorial board is reliably liberal on most social questions, and many of the attacks on the paper as biased in favor of the liberal side rest on the extrapolated claim that since the editorial page is generally liberal, news coverage is biased that way as well.) A typical piece of editorial writing, this article takes a clear stand on an issue of the day—in this case, the January 2003 Supreme Court decision rejecting challenges to Congress' extension of copyright.*

New York Times
The Coming of Copyright Perpetuity

In 1998 Congress was the scene of a battle over public domain, the public right of common, free and unrestricted use of artistic works whose copyright has expired. Corporations like Disney, organizations like the Motion Picture Association of America, and dead artists' families wanted to extend copyright. Advocates of public domain wanted to leave copyright protection as it was, which would have allowed many early 20th-century works, including corporate creations like Mickey Mouse, to slip into the public domain. The copyright owners won, and yesterday they won again when the Supreme Court, by a vote of 7 to 2, decided that Congress was within its constitutional rights when it extended copyright. The court's decision may make constitutional sense, but it does not serve the public well.

Under that 1998 act, copyright now extends for the life of an artist plus 70 years. Copyrights owned by corporations run for 95 years. Since the Constitution grants Congress the right to authorize copyright for "limited times," even the opponents of an extended term were not hopeful that the Supreme Court would rule otherwise. This decision almost certainly prepares the way for more bad copyright extension laws in the future. Congress has lengthened copyright 11 times in the past 40 years.

Artists naturally deserve to hold a property interest in their work, and so do the corporate owners of copyright. But the public has an equally strong interest in seeing copyright lapse after a time, returning works to the public domain—the great democratic seedbed of artistic creation—where they can be used without paying royalties.

In effect, the Supreme Court's decision makes it likely that we are seeing the beginning of the end of public domain and the birth of copyright perpetuity. Public domain has been a grand experiment, one that should not be allowed to die. The ability to draw freely on the entire creative output of humanity is one of the reasons we live in a time of such fruitful creative ferment.

Topics for Reading and Writing

1. The editorial puts two terms into opposition: "copyright perpetuity" and "public domain." Is this a false dichotomy, as the editorial constructs it? Which side does the *Times* support?

2. What does the editorial mean by "the great democratic seedbed of artistic creation"? Why must works go into public domain for further creativity to take place?

The claims that music downloading will kill artists' livelihoods are no more than Chicken Little crying, according to **Siva Vaidhyanathan,** professor of media studies at New York University. Vaidhyanathan, author of Copyrights and Copywrongs (2000), counters in this article (written originally for this book) that the decline in music sales is not the fault of Napster and its brethren—in fact, sales declined even after the industry shut Napster down. Music is fundamentally a democratic product, one that is not well-served by the top-down distribution and ownership system devised by the recording industry. Record companies need to acknowledge this, Vaidhyanathan insists, rather than relying on the reactionary, short-sighted business model that has characterized their response to Napster, Gnutella, Kazaa and other file-sharing services.

Siva Vaidhyanathan
The Peer-to-Peer Revolution and the Future of Music

On a Wednesday afternoon in 2002, a couple of hours before the president of the Recording Academy used the 2002 Grammy Awards to berate music fans for downloading billions of music files from various peer-to-peer systems, I bought four compact discs and two box set collections—nearly $120 worth of music.

Why did I do this? I ask myself this question every time the credit card bill arrives. But I also ask it every time someone from the big record companies complains about decreasing music sales. After all, I spend hundreds of dollars per year on compact discs. I should be the record industry's dream customer. Instead, I'm a thief. See, I also download thousands of songs per year from Gnutella, a non-commercial peer-to-peer file sharing system built by volunteers who love music as much as I do.

On that Wednesday, in the middle of the 2002 Grammy Award show, Recording Academy president Michael Greene blamed the industry's woes on folks like me. He said it was a tough year for music sales because of "the unbridled advance of the Internet." Among all the problems facing the industry, Greene said, "the most insidious virus is piracy on the net." Greene claimed, "Ripping is stealing their livelihood one digital file at a time, leaving their musical dreams haplessly snared in this World Wide Web of theft and indifference."

Greene's tirade was not out of step with the messages his industry as a whole was sending. His complaints raised some important questions. Does each downloaded song equal a lost sale? I am not convinced. I would never consider buying 99 out of 100 songs I download. I get the songs to see if I want to buy stuff. I also get songs I can't buy, like out-of-print stuff from great bands like Too Much Joy and rare live cuts of "Jersey Girl" sung in concert by Bruce Springsteen and Tom Waits. Yet it's clear that the music industry has been losing sales in the years since it killed off Napster. Is this lull a historical anomaly? Is it the result of alienating consumers? Is it the result of fewer titles for sale? Has the price of compact discs made a difference? Do consumers have fewer marginal entertainment dollars to send to the recording companies, and do they have more entertainment options? And if downloading is this pervasive and detrimental to music sales, why aren't these companies doing worse than they are?

I suspect there is something more significant and interesting happening. There seems to be a serious abrogation of the presumed contract between a significant portion of music fans and the companies that distribute music. If so, which side broke the contract? When did we sign such a contract? Is copyright law at the foundation of that contract? Perhaps the contract itself is obsolete, or at least misplaced within cultural economies that involve such slippery, malleable, portable products. I suspect that this new consumer behavior is not so new. It's merely an amplification of old—ancient—habits that we never really gave up, despite the brief rise of a commercial music industry in the 20th century. We share music in a circle. Music doesn't work the same way if its piped to us, processed for us, and kept at a clean distance. We want to groove to it, mess with it, and remake it. Unfortunately, this urge does not meet the demands of the firms that produce and distribute the world's best-known music. At the Napster trial in 2001 both sides introduced shoddy studies purporting to show the effect that more than 70 million people sharing songs would have on the music market. Neither side convinced the appeals court of its position. Perhaps Napster retarded sales. Perhaps Napster sold discs. Perhaps it decreased sales of some artists and increased sales of others. We still don't know. But examining the political, technological, economic, and cultural dimensions of the battle over music can reveal some interesting things about the ways we use music in our lives and what we expect from our media and cultural systems. And by considering the cultural effects of free music flowing around the globe, we might learn something about the stability of cultures and the economic constraints that have rendered them inaccessible to each other.

In calendar year 2000, the only complete year in which Napster operated, compact disc revenue was up 3.1 percent from 1999. In 1999, the year Napster debuted and MP3s were widely available through various other means around the Internet, compact disc revenues were up more than 12 percent. In 2001, a year in which the music industry successfully shut down Napster, revenues were down 4.1 percent. In 2002, the number of sales of compact discs fell by between nine and 10 percent.

Since Napster went quiet, several other peer-to-peer services sprung up. Some are run by companies, and are destined to be shut down as well. Others, like Gnutella and FreeNet, are non-proprietary, fully distributed, and seemingly unstoppable. While millions of people trade billions of songs every month on these services, their popularity has surpassed that of Napster. Had the record industry cut a deal with Napster, it might have avoided the ungovernable chaos of decentralized peer-to-peer services now taking over the Internet. But it did not. Because the demise of Napster did not stem the tide of file-sharing, the music industry has shifted its tactics and targets from the peer-to-peer services themselves to the Internet Service Providers, colleges and universities, and the compact disc itself. Meanwhile, the industry tried to interest consumers in some pay-per-song services. What is most amazing about the recording industry reactions to the rise of peer-to-peer services is the fervent disrespect it shows for its fans. While avoiding direct confrontation with individual music fans, the industry through 2002 and 2003 was hinting at "making examples" out of a few, yet has consistently berated us all. But mostly, the industry has been trying to re-engineer the anarchy out of the music, and take the music out of the anarchy.

I suppose the recording industry thinks it can get away with such tactics because for so long it had almost complete control over how we use music in our lives. Peer-to-peer threatens its monopoly on control of marketing and distribution, even if it doesn't threaten its revenue. It certainly introduces a frightening level of uncertainty and unpredictability into what was already an unstable market. To reach fans, artists no longer have to go through the labels. To hear cool music, fans no longer have to turn on MTV or listen to a narrowing array of radio programs. So there is no telling what fans will find, and perhaps no clear feedback to the labels about what the people want.

It's important to note that the industries invested in the distribution of music are broad. They include much more than the major commercial recording companies. Doing my patriotic duty as a good American consumer, my music habits now enrich people far beyond the major labels. I'm also a dream customer for makers of compact disc burners, portable MP3 players, broadband Internet access, and faster personal computers. Not coincidentally, Sony is all of these, including a major record label.

Topics for Reading and Writing

1. How does Vaidhyanathan's article differ in approach, rhetorical appeal, and argument from the other anti-recording-industry articles included in this chapter? Outline each's thesis, intended audience, and primarily rhetorical appeal—which is most logically convincing? Which makes the best use of authority, and which appeals most to your emotions?

2. How does Vaidhyanathan use loaded language to characterize the recording industry and its spokespeople?

3. Vaidhyanathan ends his article on a note that seems to support the large media conglomerates such as Sony that dominate the music industry. Is Vaidhyanathan being ironic? What does he mean by "doing my patriotic duty as a good American consumer"? What is the relationship between consumerism and American patriotism, if any?

Jack Valenti
Testimony on Napster

*In most contexts, **Jack Valenti** and **Lars Ulrich** would be the strangest of allies. Valenti, CEO of the Motion Picture Association of America (MPAA), chairman of the Copyright Assembly and a powerful political insider since the Lyndon Johnson administration, is one of America's consummate political operators. Representing the interests of the major Hollywood studios, for decades Valenti has successfully defended the movie industry against government regulation. On the other hand, Lars Ulrich's perspective on the music industry comes from the bottom. The drummer for speed-metal band Metallica from that group's inception, Ulrich lived the rock-and-roll lifestyle—drugs, groupies, touring, tragedy (the band's*

The following is an excerpt of the declaration that Jack Valenti submitted on behalf of the recording industry in the case in which members of the industry are suing Napster. The full declaration and that of others are available at http:// www.riaa.com/napster legal.cfm.

The copyright community is the largest contributor to this nation's economy. The intellectual property created by these industries generates over $64 billion annually in *international* revenues alone—more than automobiles and auto parts, more than aircraft, more than agriculture. It produces jobs at three times the annual rate of the American economy as a whole.

The Copyright Assembly was formed because its members are deeply concerned about the future of creative works, particularly in light of the explosive growth of the Internet. All of the members of *The Copyright Assembly* are actively embracing new Internet opportunities for consumers, and are developing new, incentive business models

Reprinted with special permission, North America Syndicate, Inc.

bassist died in an automobile accident), money—for years. In the early 1990s Metallica began to achieve massive worldwide success, and by the end of the decade was the most popular metal band in the world.

Valenti and Ulrich have come together, though, over the issue of copyright violation. Valenti, usually an advocate for Hollywood, lent his considerable political savvy to a controversy that he saw would eventually touch upon his own industry. Risking the enmity of his fans, Ulrich became one of the dominant voices in the anti-Napster campaign, arguing forcefully that Napster robbed musicians of their livelihood. In the end, Valenti and Ulrich won the argument when Napster was forbidden to allow its users to download copyrighted material. Several other so-called

to deliver our creative works in a manner that can make them available to consumers via the Internet. Hundreds of millions of dollars are now being invested by our members to develop this new economy. They are all eager to be part of this revolutionary technology.

However, we also worry lest the great potential, the immense future worth of the Internet, becomes tangled by overt and covert piracy of copyrighted material. As legitimate businesses emerge on the Internet, illegitimate intruders find the Internet a haven. Piracy of copyrighted material is already a multi-billion dollar problem worldwide. For example, an estimated 38 percent of all software programs used worldwide in 1998 was pirated, at a market value of $11 billion and a loss of 109,000 American jobs. And, the economic impact of piracy stems well beyond the creative industries alone. It harms economies worldwide in the form of lost jobs and decreased tax revenues, and by inhibiting electronic commerce.

Napster has become a focal point for the unauthorized reproduction and electronic transmission via the Internet of copyrighted works in the form of audio recordings. It has gained enormous success by encouraging and facilitating *"peer-to-peer" networks have sprung up to take Napster's place (these services avoid the legal prohibition against providing users access to copyrighted material by making users contact each other directly), but the legality of these services is under attack.*

what amounts to piracy of copyrighted works. If Napster can encourage and facilitate the distribution of pirated sound recordings, then what's to stop it from doing the same to movies, software, books, magazines, newspapers, television, photographs, or video games? Literally, any intellectual property that can be digitized is vulnerable to the wholesale piracy enabled by Napster. The owners and creators of copyrighted material will of course be hesitant to offer their works over the Internet if they cannot be protected from this type of unauthorized duplication and dissemination.

Napster contributes to another very dangerous, though less tangible, problem for the members of *The Copyright Assembly*. If the courts allow Napster and services like it to continue to facilitate massive copyright infringement, there is a grave risk that the public will begin to perceive and believe that they have a *right* to obtain copyrighted material for free. This perception, of course, runs contrary to the entire complex system of copyright laws, which are designed to foster and encourage creativity and innovation by rewarding the creators. If the public believes that it ought to be able to obtain those materials for free, it will become more and more difficult to maintain legitimate markets for these materials, and the people and companies who provide the funds to create this material will have less and less incentive to do so.

Creative works do not spring from a void. The seed bed of this creativity lies within the imagination, artistry and ingenuity of a community of artists and craftspeople who provide Americans with most of what they read, hear and watch. It is the summation of massive infusion of risk capital that must be, for the most part, recouped else the risk becomes too large, the capital becomes too cautious, and the works dry up. The protection of Copyright and copyrights is not antagonistic to new technologies, such as the Internet. Not at all. But if we cannot protect what we invest in, create and own, then we really don't own anything.

Lars Ulrich
Testimony on Napster

Mr. Chairman, Senator Leahy, Members of the Committee, my name is Lars Ulrich. I was born in Denmark. In 1980, as a teenager, my parents and I came to America. I started a band named Metallica in 1981 with my best friend James Hetfield. By 1983 we had released our first record, and by 1985 we were no longer living below the poverty line. Since then, we've been very fortunate to achieve a great level of success in the music business throughout the world. It's the classic American dream come true. I'm very honored to be here in this country, and to appear in front of the Senate Judiciary Committee today.

Earlier this year, while completing work on a song for the movie *Mission Impossible-2*, we were startled to hear reports that a work-in-progress version was already being played on some U.S radio stations. We traced the source of this leak to a corporation called Napster. Additionally, we learned that all of our previously recorded copyrighted songs were, via Napster, available for anyone around the world to download from the Internet in a digital format known as MP3. As you are probably aware, we became the first artists to sue Napster, and have been quite vocal about it as well. That's undoubtedly why you invited me to this hearing.

We have many issues with Napster. First and foremost: Napster hijacked our music without asking. They never sought our permission—our catalog of music simply became available as free downloads on the Napster system.

I don't have a problem with any artist voluntarily distributing his or her songs through any means the artist elects—at no cost to the consumer, if that's what the artist wants. But just like a carpenter who crafts a table gets to decide whether to keep it, sell it or give it away, shouldn't we have the same options? My band authored the music which is Napster's lifeblood. We should decide what happens to it, not Napster—a company with no rights in our recordings, which never invested a penny in Metallica's music or had anything to do with its creation. The choice has been taken away from us.

What about the users of Napster, the music consumers? It's like each of them won one of those contests where you get turned loose in a store for five minutes and get to keep everything you can load into your shopping cart. With Napster, though, there's no time limit and everyone's a winner—except the artist. Every song by every artist is available for download at no cost and, of course, with no payment to the artist, the songwriter or the copyright holder.

If you're not fortunate enough to own a computer, there's only one way to assemble a music collection the equivalent of a Napster user's: theft. Walk into a record store, grab what you want and walk out. The difference is that the familiar phrase a computer user hears, "File's done," is replaced by another familiar phrase—"You're under arrest."

Since what I do is make music, let's talk about the recording artist for a moment. When Metallica makes an album we spend many months and many hundreds of thousands of our own dollars writing and recording. We also contribute our inspiration and perspiration. It's what we do for a living. Even though we're passionate about it, it's our job.

We typically employ a record producer, recording engineers, programmers, assistants and, occasionally, other musicians. We rent time for months at recording studios which are owned by small businessmen who have risked their own capital to buy, maintain and constantly upgrade very expensive equipment and facilities. Our record releases are supported by hundreds of record company employees and provide programming for numerous radio and television stations. Add it all up and you have an industry with many jobs—a very few glamorous ones like ours—and a greater number of demanding ones covering all levels of the pay scale for wages which support families and contribute to our economy.

Remember too, that my band, Metallica, is fortunate enough to make a great living from what it does. Most artists are barely earning a decent wage and need every source of revenue available to scrape by. Also keep in mind that the primary source of income for most songwriters is from the sale of records. Every time a Napster enthusiast downloads a song, it takes money from the pockets of all these members of the creative community.

It's clear, then, that if music is free for downloading, the music industry is not viable; all the jobs I just talked about will be lost and the diverse voices of the artists will disappear. The argument I hear a lot, that "music should be free," must then mean that musicians should work for free. Nobody else works for free. Why should musicians?

In economic terms, music is referred to as intellectual property, as are films, television programs, books, computer software, video games, and the like. As a nation, the U.S has excelled in the creation of intellectual property, and collectively, it is this country's most valuable export.

The backbone for the success of our intellectual property business is the protection that Congress has provided with the copyright statutes. No information-based industry can thrive without this protection. Our current political dialog about trade with China is focused on how we must get that country to respect and enforce copyrights. How can we continue to take that position if we let our own copyright laws wither in the face of technology?

Make no mistake, Metallica is not anti-technology. When we made our first album, the majority of sales were in the vinyl record format. By the late 1980's, cassette sales accounted for over 50% of the market. Now, the compact disc dominates. If the next format is a form of digital downloading from the Internet with distribution and manufacturing savings passed on to the American consumer, then, of course, we will embrace that format too.

But how can we embrace a new format and sell our music for a fair price when someone, with a few lines of code, and no investment costs, creative input or marketing expenses, simply gives it away? How does this square with the level playing field of the capitalist system? In Napster's brave new world, what free market economy models support our ability to compete? The touted "new paradigm" that the Internet gurus tell us we Luddites must adopt sounds to me like old-fashioned trafficking in stolen goods.

We have to find a way to welcome the technological advances and cost savings of the Internet while not destroying the artistic diversity and the international success that has made our intellectual property industries the greatest in the world. Allowing our copyright protections to deteriorate is, in my view, bad policy, both economically and artistically.

To underscore what I've spoken about today, I'd like to read from the "Terms of Use" section of the Napster Internet web site. When you use Napster you are basically agreeing to a contract that includes the following terms:

"This web site or any portion of this web site may not be reproduced, duplicated, copied, sold, resold, or otherwise exploited for any commercial purpose that is not expressly permitted by Napster."

"All Napster web site design, text, graphics, the selection and arrangement thereof, and all Napster software are Copyright 1999–00 Napster Inc. All rights reserved Napster Inc."

"Napster, the logo and all other trademarks, service marks and trade names of Napster appearing on this web site are owned by Napster. Napster's trademarks, logos, service marks, and trade names may not be used in connection with any product or service that is not Napster's." Napster itself wants—and surely deserves—copyright and trademark protection. Metallica and other creators of music and intellectual property want, deserve and have a right to that same protection.

In closing, I'd like to read to you from the last paragraph of a *New York Times* column by Edward Rothstein:

"Information doesn't want to be free; only the transmission of information wants to be free. Information, like culture, is the result of a labor and devotion, investment and risk; it has a value. And nothing will lead to a more deafening cultural silence than ignoring that value and celebrating..[companies like] Napster running amok."

Mr. Chairman, Senator Leahy and Members of the Committee, the title of today's hearing asks the question, "The Future of the Internet: Is there an Upside to Downloading"? My answer is yes. However, as I hope my remarks have made clear, this can only occur when artists' choices are respected and their creative efforts protected.

Thank you.

Topics for Reading and Writing

1. How do Valenti and Ulrich construct their respective ethos appeals? How does Ulrich walk the fine line between defending his interests and offending his fans—many of whom are heavy Napster users?

2. Valenti argues that Napster and similar services will encourage users to think that "they have a *right* to obtain copyrighted material for free." Is there an argument to be made for this? Given the ease of copying material, should we rethink the whole notion of copyright?

3. Where Valenti chooses to argue his case on a philosophical, long-term level, Ulrich makes a very simple case, using analogies (the carpenter and his table) and an ethos appeal (these people are stealing from *me*). What is the most effective—or is there an effective—counterargument to Ulrich's point?

Janis Ian, one of the most popular singer-songwriters of the 1960s and 1970s, writes here for USA Today *that the arguments made by the music industry against Napster are self-serving and disingenuous. Writing in the first person, Ian draws upon her experience with the industry and attempts to convince her audience that the industry is duplicitous and that the public should not take seriously any claims about "stealing" they made. Furthermore, she argues that the circulation of music facilitated by Napster and*

Janis Ian
Music Industry Spins Falsehood

The recording industry says downloading music from the Internet is ruining our business, destroying sales and costing artists such as me money.

Costing me money?

I don't pretend to be an expert on intellectual property law, but I do know one thing: If a record executive says he will make *me* more money, I'd immediately protect my wallet.

Still, the Recording Industry Association of America (RIAA) is now in federal court trying to gain new powers to personally target Internet users in lawsuits for trading music files online. In a motion filed with the U.S. District Court for the District of Columbia, the RIAA is *similar services is good for artists, and is fundamentally democratic, undermining the control of major-label executives who "twiddled their thumbs for years."*

demanding that an Internet service provider, Verizon, turn over the name and contact information of one of its Internet subscribers who, the RIAA claims, might have unauthorized copies of songs on a home computer.

Attacking your own customers because they want to learn more about your products is a bizarre business strategy, one the music industry cannot afford to continue. Yet the RIAA effectively destroyed Napster on such grounds, and now it is using the same crazy logic to take on Internet service providers and even privacy rights.

The RIAA's claim that the industry and artists are hurt by free downloading is nonsense. Consider my experience: I'm a recording artist who has sold multiple platinum records since the 1960s. My site, janisian.com, began offering free downloads in July. About a thousand people per day have downloaded my music, most of them people who had never heard of me and never bought my CDs.

Welcome to 'Acousticville'

On the first day I posted downloadable music, my merchandise sales tripled, and they have stayed that way ever since. I'm not about to become a zillionaire as a result, but I am making more money. At a time when radio playlists are tighter and any kind of exposure is hard to come by, 365,000 copies of my work now will be heard. Even if only 3% of those people come to concerts or buy my CDs, I've gained about 10,000 new fans this year.

That's how artists become successful: exposure. Without exposure, no one comes to shows, and no one buys CDs. After 37 years as a recording artist, when people write to tell me that they came to my concert because they downloaded a song and got curious, I am thrilled.

Who's really hurt by free downloads? The executives at major labels who twiddled their thumbs for years while company after company begged them to set up "micropayment" protocols and to license material for Internet-download sales.

Listen up

Many artists now benefit greatly from the free-download systems the RIAA seeks to destroy. These musicians, especially those without a major-label contract, can reach millions of new listeners with a downloadable song, enticing music fans to buy a CD or come to a concert of an artist they would have otherwise missed.

The RIAA and the entrenched music industry argue that free downloads are threats. The music industry had exactly the same response to the advent of reel-to-reel home tape recorders, cassettes, DATs, minidiscs, VCRs, music videos, MTV and a host of other products and services.

I am not advocating indiscriminate downloading without the artist's permission. Copyright protection is vital. But I do object to the industry spin that it is doing all this to protect artists. It is not protecting us; it is protecting itself.

I hope the court rejects the efforts of the music industry to assault the Internet and the music fans who use it. Speaking as an artist, I want us to work together—industry leaders, musicians, songwriters and consumers—to make technology work for all of us.

Topics for Reading and Writing

1. How would you characterize the tone of this article? How does it differ from the tone of the *New York Times* editorial? How does Ian use tone to achieve a rhetorical effect?

2. Ian argues that Napster got her music out to many consumers who wouldn't otherwise have heard her songs. Given that this is true, why should this be a convincing argument? Can we take one artist's experience as representative of a whole industry? And although Ian clearly sides with artists who are not currently popular in the mainstream music industry, should the law also side with these artists? What effect would this have on artists who, either by luck or talent, have become popular on radio and MTV?

3. Why does Ian bring up the industry's historic opposition to "reel-to-reel home tape recorders, cassettes, DATs, minidiscs, VCRs, music videos" and the like?

The Recording Industry Association of America (RIAA) is the trade group that represents the interests of the major recording companies. The RIAA was the most important force in opposing—and eventually shutting down—Napster, and continues to be proactive and aggressive in fighting against what it sees as the explosion of copyright violation facilitated by digital technology. Many people feel that the RIAA is fighting a losing battle, for its efforts to maintain control over music recordings may be doomed to failure as copying technology improves and spreads. Already the RIAA is seeing dramatic reductions in record-company revenues, which it blames on file-sharing services (and which many fans and musicians blame on corporate centralization and the focus on the bottom line, and on focus-group-tested, imitative music, that results). But even though the RIAA is often seen as the villain in the file-trading conflicts, the group has been remarkably successful, shutting down Napster and forcing Verizon (and other Internet service providers) to

Cary Sherman
Issue Is Piracy, Not Privacy

Ever since a federal court ordered Verizon to identify a subscriber who illegally distributed hundreds of hit songs on the Internet, the company has claimed the ruling somehow violates the individual's right to privacy.

Strangely, when it was arguing its case in court, Verizon never uttered a word about privacy. Indeed, Verizon acknowledged that it will identify certain infringers when it suits Verizon. That's because it knows the issue here isn't about privacy; it's about piracy.

The fact is, our right to privacy does not include a right to commit illegal acts anonymously. You or I may have a right to keep our banking transactions private, but when we stick a gun in a teller's face and ask for the contents of the cash drawer, the bank is more than entitled to take our picture with a security camera.

The same is true on the Internet. Offering to upload music files without permission so millions of strangers can copy them off the Internet is neither a private act nor a legal one. Should those who engage in this gratuitous giveaway of other people's property be able to conceal their identity behind computer numbers or made-up screen names?

The Recording Industry Association of America is a stalwart defender of the First Amendment. But music piracy is not the kind of expression the First Amendment seeks to protect. In the words of the opinion, we're not talking about a consumer who "is anonymously using *give up the names of users who trade music files. Although the economics of the music industry, the spread of technology, and the RIAA's fierce resistance to change may eventually weaken the big record companies, it is too early to view the trade group as irrelevant.*

the Internet to distribute speeches of Lenin, biblical passages . . . or criticisms of the government." Rather we're talking about someone who is distributing illegal copies of popular songs—the very antithesis of protected activity.

There is a good reason Congress enacted the Digital Millennium Copyright Act, the law that requires Internet service providers to promptly identify the infringer when copyright owners file a sworn declaration that a subscriber is illegally distributing copyrighted materials: In a digital age, when anyone with a decent computer and a shortage of scruples can instantaneously flood the world with an infinite number of perfect copies of any song, movie or text he can get his hands on, copyrights would be worthless without this most basic level of protection.

Topics for Reading and Writing

1. What does Sherman mean by "piracy"? Why does he choose this word instead of "stealing"? How does Sherman try to appeal to readers who might sympathize with Napster users—or who might illegally download songs themselves?

2. Is this an issue about privacy? What is the nature of the right to privacy? Should the right to privacy allow us to break the law?

In this commentary, the New York Times *writer* **John Leland** *examines the file-sharing phenomenon through a much larger lens. Americans are enamored of the idea of having copyrighted products for nothing when they can get them on the Internet, of course. But Leland argues that Americans want brand-name goods of all sorts for free or for a deep discount. Knockoff Louis Vuitton purses and Burberry scarves, movies based on television programs, college term papers bought on the Internet: it's all part of one giant culture of taking what's not really ours.*

John Leland
Beyond File-Sharing, a Nation of Copiers

The week the music industry brought suit against 261 users of Internet file-sharing services, Donald L. McCabe was in St. Louis to talk about a different form of digital copying. Mr. McCabe, a Rutgers University professor, has made a career of studying the cheating of American high school and college students. His most recent study found that cheating was spreading almost like file-sharing. Of more than 18,000 students surveyed, 38 percent said they had lifted material from the Internet for use in papers in the last year.

More striking to Mr. McCabe, 44 percent said they considered this sampling no big deal. Because the Internet makes it easy to copy information, he said, "it's made it much more tempting."

"I'm not sure it's shifted values yet," he continued. "But for a lot of students, it's heading in that direction."

In fact, for many people, that shift has already come. Like file-sharing—which 60 million Americans have tried—cutting and pasting from the Internet is just one part of a broader shift toward all copying, all the time.

Consider a night out in the wireless city: Throw on a faux-vintage sports jersey, grab a bootleg Prada bag and head to the Cineplex for the sequel to a movie based on a television show. Afterward, log on to KaZaA and download the movie's title song, based on a digital sample. While you're online, visit a blog with links to published movie gossip and use your pirated e-mail program to send tidbits to your hundred closest friends. Curl up with a best seller by Stephen E. Ambrose or Doris Kearns Goodwin, who last year admitted to slipping materials from other texts into their books.

Most of these activities would have been difficult or impossible a generation ago. They differ widely in their legal and ethical implications. (For example, you can't prosecute someone just for producing "Lara Croft Tomb Raider: The Cradle of Life.") But together they suggest a broad relationship between new technology and a value system that seems shaped to it. In a nation that flaunts its capacities to produce and consume, much of the culture's heat now lies with the ability to cut, paste, clip, sample, quote, recycle, customize and recirculate. It is tempting to ascribe the Culture of the Copy to college students, but its values run deeper. The United States economy shed 44,000 manufacturing jobs last month, continuing a long-running trend away from production. Since the 1980's, when liberalized trade laws made it easier to "outsource" manufacturing to subcontractors in the developing world, companies like Nike or Tommy Hilfiger have competed in what Naomi Klein, in her 2000 book "No Logo," described as "a race toward weightlessness," in which production is a hindrance, not an asset. In the brand market, value lies not in making things but in copying one's logo onto as many of them as possible.

D.J.'s, file sharers, handbag cloners, student plagiarists and some bloggers simply do what brand companies do: they reproduce work made elsewhere at lower rates, adding their own signature and mix. The legal ramifications may be different, but the action is the same.

"The quintessential American company was Enron, which made nothing," said Neal Gabler, author of "Life the Movie." In today's culture, he added, "the product is almost immaterial; it's the consciousness about it."

"What the Internet does is, it pries everything out of moral context and lets people feel knowing about it," he said, because the skills used to cut and paste something with a computer are more valued than those used to manufacture it.

"In a sense, Internet technology is a metaphor for the new morality. As long as you can get it, it doesn't matter how."

On a recent morning on Canal Street, crowds of shoppers, most past their undergraduate years, brought the metaphor to life, plucking up fake Louis Vuitton, Gucci and Kate Spade handbags. A New Jersey woman named Linda Dorian, plumping for two bootleg Vuittons, compared her purchases to downloading music. "Somehow everybody seems to be making out," she said. "I don't see any poor rock stars. I don't see any poor designers."

Besides, she added, buying the fake is cooler, just as Grokster, a file-sharing program, has a cachet the Wal-Mart CD counter cannot match. "Shopping for copies is getting to be a trend," she said.

As technology has produced a new ecology of copying, it has pushed into uncharted territories of ethics and the law, said Siva Vaidhyanathan, author of "Copyrights and Copy-wrongs: The Rise of Intellectual Property and How It

Threatens Creativity" and director of communication studies at New York University. He said he has had 10 percent of his students turn in whole papers copied from the Internet, not realizing that he could Google them into big trouble. "We're coming up on 10 years of widespread use of the Internet," he said. "We should have better discussions of a code of ethics for dealing with these materials. The rule of law will always incompletely and perhaps negatively affect the Internet."

Nearly 70 years ago, the critic Walter Benjamin addressed the aesthetic limitations of the copy in a famous essay about photography and authenticity, "The Work of Art in the Age of Mechanical Reproduction." Benjamin argued that even a perfect copy lacked the contextual meaning of the real thing. Since then, postmodern critics have developed dense theories of simulacra, bricolage and pastiche that could daze a tuna at 20 paces.

Now the bricoleurs are living next door, and they look nothing like the monographs said they would. "Somehow I don't think it comes from avant-garde theory," said Louis Menand, author of "The Metaphysical Club: A Story of Ideas in America." The KaZaA community can burn "All About the Benjamins," the song or the movie, without the endorsement of Walter.

"They wouldn't say it's all a simulacrum anyway," Mr. Menand said. "If they could say that they wouldn't need to copy their papers online."

In the current universe of the copy, the looseness of context is everything. Most users of music file-sharing services do not copy the products for sale by the music industry. While the industry sells albums, artificially shaped to the capacities of their commercial format, LP or CD, file-sharers tend to rip songs.

As their favorite musicians recombine digital samples to create new music, downloaders recombine digital songs in new contexts.

"I don't think they think of it as copying music," said Joe Levy, deputy managing editor of Rolling Stone. "It's a very individual experience for them. They want the songs they want in the order they want. Then it becomes not the new Mary J. Blige album, but their own mix. It's a much more individual package of music. Kids view it as an interactive and creative act."

Betsy Frank, the executive vice president for research and planning at MTV Networks, who studies young TV and music audiences, said the people in her focus groups tended to describe copying as an assertive act, a way of navigating a media environment that bombards them with information—some good, some bad, most of it a little of both. "They can rationalize downloading music or term papers extremely effectively as using their skills to select what works for them," she said.

The law, of course, will inevitably catch up. When rap acts started sampling James Brown records in the 1980's, complaints raged that they were violating copyrights and the principles of art. In a Bronx home studio in 1987, the producer Jazzy Jay described the law of the copy: "The laws on taking samples are, You take 'em until you get caught."

Two decades later, musicians usually pay for their samples, and the aesthetic argument—that sampling was theft, not music—has quieted. Now sample fees are part of the business model, and no one seems to worry about whether it is art.

At both stages, value judgments about copying followed technology and money, not the other way around.

In the culture of copying, technological considerations have trumped ethical ones: if you upload it, they will download.

Last week's lawsuits against file-sharers are an attempt to get the public to treat copying not as a question of technological possibility or moral implications, but as a threat to the wallet. A study by Forrester Research found that 68 percent of burners said they would stop if they thought they might get in serious trouble. As in sampling, the moral questions should follow the financial ones, said Josh Bernoff, the principal analyst covering media and entertainment at Forrester.

But the process still had some hurdles to get over, Mr. Bernoff admitted. Recently he was discussing his research with an executive at a media organization that has been very aggressive about trying to discourage file-sharing. When Mr. Bernoff asked the executive how he had gotten the report, which Forrester sells for $895, the man hesitated.

"They got a copy from one of the studios," Mr. Bernoff said. "Here is an organization that's saying that stealing hurts the little people, and they took our intellectual property and they shuttled it around like a text file."

The aesthetic fallout of all this copying will be harder to sort. In a culture that assigns diminishing value to production, can copying really fill the void? The hypothetical night out involves many aesthetic decisions but little that can be called art.

Mr. Menand noted that his students who downloaded papers from the Internet often picked mediocre work, perhaps thinking it would be less noticeable. The availability of obscure, non-Britney music on KaZaA—one of the justifications cited by users—has done nothing to stop Hilary Duff, the overpackaged star of the "Lizzie McGuire" movie and series, from having the No. 1 album in the country this week. If this is the democracy of the copy, it is enough to make one long for the elitism of creative genius.

Ms. Frank, the MTV executive, noted the limitations of unlimited customization, even amid unlimited access. For young Americans, she said, "because of the way they've trained themselves to use media, they never have to be exposed to an idea, an artist, or anything that they did not select for themselves."

Ruth La Ferla contributed to this article.

Topics for Reading and Writing

1. Is there a difference between copying—or stealing—music from an online file-sharing service and buying a knockoff brand-name item? Does buying a pirated DVD of a recently released movie differ from these?

2. Leland suggests that Americans are in the process of reevaluating their ethical stance toward taking things that aren't theirs. Do you think this is true? When we use Kazaa, do we really confront the ethical ramifications of our actions?

3. Apart from examining the ethical effects of our willingness to copy or pirate or steal, Leland alludes to the "aesthetic fallout of all this copying." What does he mean?

Neil Strauss and Bernard Chang
The Revenge of the Copyright Cops

Neil Strauss and *Bernard Chang's* cartoon asks us to think about the real nature of copyright and about how some of our most innocent-seeming daily activities could be construed as copyright violations. Although obviously hyperbolic, "The Revenge of the Copyright Cops" uses quotes from an intellectual property lawyer and from an RIAA spokesperson to spin a fantasy about copyright stormtroopers intruding on our lives.

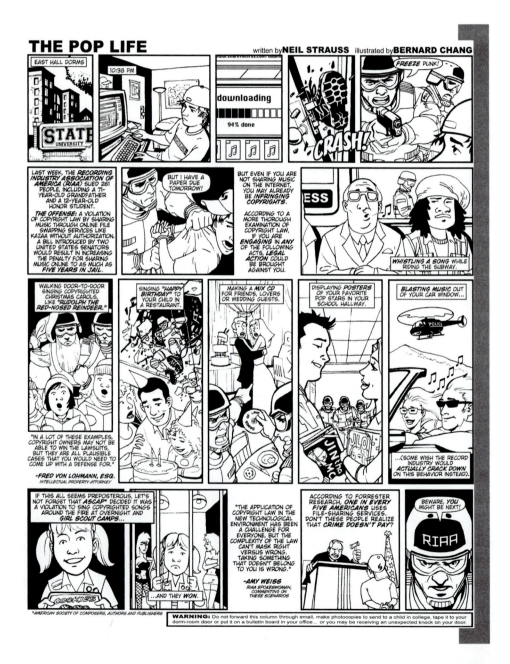

Neil Strauss is a journalist and writer with several books about rock-music figures such as Marilyn Manson and Mötley Crüe to his credit. Bernard Chang is an artist, comic-book illustrator, and former Walt Disney Company "imagineer."

Topics for Reading and Writing

1. Why do you think Strauss and Chang chose to use the comic-strip format to make this argument? What rhetorical effect does it have? Does it detract from the seriousness of their point?

2. If the activities depicted by Strauss and Chang amount to copyright violation, what other activities might, as well?

In another article from the Philadelphia Inquirer, University of Pennsylvania freshman **Emily Brill** alludes to a "revolution" on college campuses—a revolution against what she calls "Big Music," or the recording industry. Students don't feel guilty about downloading music for free, because the artists producing the music are so wealthy already—and students also don't feel that downloading MP3s qualifies as "stealing." Brill quotes several students who unapologetically talk about getting their music for free and who see this as a political act, taking power away from corporations and giving it to the people. But is this oversimplifying? Does Brill avoid answering the hard questions? Will this "revolution" really benefit artists, as she asserts? And how do services like Apple's iTunes Music Store (which offers songs for 99 cents apiece) play into Brill's argument that the music industry will never come up with a viable way to make a user-friendly download service?

Emily Brill
Empathy for Big Music? MP3s for Me

There's a revolution afoot—and if you're in doubt, go check out a typical college dorm. Almost all U.S. colleges and universities are now wired for high-speed Internet access, which means that students can download music files in matters of seconds (if they couldn't already at home). According to a recent study conducted by research firm Ipsos-Reid, 28 percent of the American population age 12 and over have downloaded a music file off the Internet. That translates to 60 million downloaders.

So here's a news flash for Big Music: It's over. We have cut you off, and guess what? We don't feel the least bit guilty.

Why? Because the overwhelming majority of the artists who fill our hard drives are considerably well off, as are the people and companies who manage them.

"Why should I feel guilty?" asks Princeton University freshman Molly Fay. "Most of the artists I download make more money than I ever will. Who am I to care if I cheat them out of a couple of bucks?"

But money isn't all of it. There's a big difference between stealing a hot dog from a street vendor and downloading an mp3 (a popular format for packaging and sending audio files). University of Pennsylvania freshman Malcom Dorson points out that "downloading something is way too impersonal to ever make me feel guilty." We don't have to look anyone in the eye, and when we "take" a file, we're not removing it; we're copying it.

Another reason there's no chance of us returning to the music stores: making our own CDs is just way too convenient.

"The majority of my CDs are definitely my own mixes," says University of Pennsylvania freshman Merrill McDermott, adding that since she likes a lot of different genres of music, "downloading is the only way to obtain that eclectic mix" she's after. And Merrill isn't alone. None of us want to have a decision as important as what to put on a CD made for us by a bunch of executives in a California conference room.

The Recording Industry Association of America is, of course, upset. And the organization's honchos seem to think that they're going to legislate their way out of this revolution by gaining access to private customer information held by Internet service providers. Haven't these guys heard of Web anonymizers—sites like SilentSurf.com, Anonymizer.com, and dozens more that will likely pop up? Such sites make anyone's presence on the Internet virtually ghostlike.

We aren't revolting against the artists. We are revolting against the non-artists, the people who take art and make it fit into a Doritos commercial. For those of us who have the money, supporting the little-known groups remains an important cause.

"The only reason I would ever buy a CD," says Brown University freshman Janis Sethness, "would be to support the music groups that I like [and that need supporting]. But if a group is on [the MTV Total Request Live] and I like what I hear, I go to Kazaa [a free downloading site], not Tower Records."

Music industry efforts to curtail our use of file-sharing programs will be futile for two reasons. First, kids are always one step ahead and can defeat almost any technology with another. Second and more important, the music industry gives us too great a reason not to buy music. They charge us $20 for albums that cost about 13 cents to make—albums that have, perhaps, two songs we actually want. That's a whopping 15,385 percent gross profit—and I mean gross.

New pay-per-download services—like one now in the news for which users pay $10 a month plus 49 cents per song—are probably still too expensive and won't work. Even if they did, it's hard to see how the music moguls would be able to keep their lifestyles on that kind of money.

Our revolution doesn't threaten the future of music. In fact, we have high hopes for what these changes could bring to our ears. University of Pennsylvania freshman Kevin Collins recently wrote in Wharton's First Call newspaper: "File sharing systems will force the resurrection of the album."

Programs like Kazaa, Collins argued, will "force the artists to return to the album to sell music" instead of going on MTV to promote a single song.

Fay captures a prevailing sentiment: "If having mp3s means that some [person] in a suit won't be able to buy that third BMW he was craving, along with the house in the Hamptons, because the rest of the population saves necessary money by not purchasing music from a store, then I'm all for it."

Topics for Reading and Writing

1. Brill is unapologetic about her willingness to download MP3s, but she seems unwilling to confront the real repercussions of her argument. Is she a thief? Why does she not address that issue? Why does she focus on "Big Music"

rather than on what she is doing? Does this weaken her article, or center it on what's really important?

2. How does Brill use ethos in this article?

3. Although when she wrote this article she was only a college freshman, Brill managed to get her article published in a major metropolitan daily, which happened to be the local paper in the city where her school is located. How might you go about publishing an article in your city's newspaper? Why do you think the *Inquirer* published Brill's?

How does DVD technology change the nature of a "film"? When viewers choose what parts of a movie to watch, can watch a film with director's commentary, or can shuffle the order of scenes, does this alter what we consider to be a movie? Does this make a movie just another consumer product, rather than a unified work of art that springs from the mind of a director? Or does this radically democratize the experience of art, allowing us to interact with the artwork in a way that makes it most relevant to our lives? In this article from the New York Times Magazine, *film critic **Terrence Rafferty** argues that the art form of film, which for over a century has determined the ways audiences can experience it, may not survive the technology of DVD.*

Terrence Rafferty
Everybody Gets a Cut

A kiss, all moviegoers know, is just a kiss, and a sigh, by the same inexorable logic, is just a sigh, but I'm starting to wonder whether in the age of the DVD a movie—even one as indelibly stamped on the collective memory as "Casablanca"—can ever again be just a movie. The DVD's that have been piling up in the vicinity of my TV seem to be telling me that a movie is not a movie unless it arrives swaddled in "extras": on-set documentaries, retrospective interviews with cast and crew, trailers, deleted scenes, storyboards, even alternate endings. These days, any film for which a studio's marketing department has sufficiently high commercial expectations is issued on DVD in a "special" or "limited" or "collector's" edition that makes an Arden Shakespeare look skimpy by comparison. The extras on the new double-disc Director's Edition of Brett Ratner's "Red Dragon" include such indispensable material as hair and wardrobe tests and one of the auteur's N.Y.U. student films, and take as long to watch as the movie itself. We all, in our 21st-century paradise of leisure, have too much time on our hands. But not that much.

Should some scholar of the future be insane enough to take an interest in "Red Dragon," however, the annotated variorum edition of this deeply mediocre picture could be useful. And the as-yet unborn author of "Unfaithful Cinema: The Art of Adrian Lyne" (2040) will need to consult the Special Collector's Edition DVD of "Fatal Attraction," which contains the film's original ending as well as the one moviegoers saw. It also includes the director's own helplessly revealing comment on the radical difference between the conclusion he chose and the one he discarded: "You can make up your mind which you like better."

I've always thought it was the *artist's* job to make that sort of decision, but as I watched Lyne smugly leaving it up to the viewer, I realized with a jolt that I had fallen behind the times. I still think of a film as a unified, self-sufficient artifact that, by its nature, is not interactive in the way that, say, a video game is. To my old-media mind, the viewer "interacts" with a movie just as he or she interacts with any other work of art—by responding to it emotionally, thinking about it, analyzing it, arguing with it, but not by altering it fundamentally. When I open my collected Yeats to read "Among School Children," I don't feel disappointed, or somehow disempowered, to find its great final line ("How can we tell the dancer from the dance?") unchanged, unchanged utterly, and unencumbered with an "alternate." For all I know, Yeats might have written "How can we tell the tailor from the pants?" and then thought better of it, but I'm not sure how having the power to replace the "dance" version with the "pants" version would enhance my experience of the poem.

And although "Among School Children" is divided into eight numbered stanzas and therefore provides what DVD's call "scene access," I tend to read them consecutively, without skipping, on the theory that the poem's meaning is wholly dependent on this specific, precise arrangement of words and images. If you read "Among School Children" in any other way, would it still be "Among School Children"? Would it be a poem at all?

The contemporary desire for interactivity in the experience of art derives, obviously, from the heady sense of control over information to which we've become accustomed as users of computers. The problem with applying that model to works of art is that in order to get anything out of them, you have to accept that the artist, not you, is in control of this particular package of "information." And that's the paradox of movies on DVD: the digital format tries to make interactive what is certainly the *least* interactive, most controlling art form in human history.

When you're sitting in a movie theater, the film is in absolute, despotic control of your sense. It tells you where to look and for how long, imposes its own inarguable and unstoppable rhythm, and your options for interaction are pretty severely limited. You can wise off quietly to your companion or loudly at the screen, or, in extremis, you can walk out, but nothing you can do, short of storming the projection booth, will affect the movie itself: it rolls on serenely without you, oblivious as the turning world.

It's that imperious, take-it-or-leave-it quality that, in the early days of cinema, aroused the suspicions of devotees of the traditional arts, who would argue that watching a film denied the audience some of the freedoms available to readers—who could set their own pace rather than meekly submit to a rhythm imposed on them by the creator of the work—and to theatergoers who were at liberty to look wherever they wanted to at the action on stage and whose reactions could actually affect the play's performance. Eventually, we all learned to stop worrying and love the art form, but the skeptics and reactionaries had a point: the techniques of film are unusually coercive, a fact quickly grasped both by the art's early masters, like D.W. Griffith, Fritz Lang, Sergei Eisenstein and Alfred Hitchcock, who reveled in their ability to manipulate the viewer's responses, and by the leaders of totalitarian states, who recognized the cinema's potential as an instrument of propaganda.

The manipulative power of cinema is neither a good nor a bad thing; it is what it is, and all movies partake of it in varying degrees. The films of Jean Renoir, for example, are markedly freer than those of Hitchcock, but the freedom they offer is relative; although the long takes, deep focus and improvisatory acting style of Renoir's "Rules of the Game" (1939) allow the viewer's imagination more room to roam, the director is nonetheless in complete control of what we see and what we hear. In fact, just about the only way a film artist can subvert his or her own authority is by significantly limiting the use of medium's expressive resources, as, for example, Andy Warhol did in the mid-60's. His eight-hour-long "Empire" (1964), a single shot at the Empire State Building, with no cuts, no camera movement and no sound, is about as uncoercive as a film can be. It's the most interactive movie ever made.

All I'm saying, really, is that watching a film is, and should be, an experience different from that of playing Myst or placing an order on Amazon. I suspect that many DVD owners use their players exactly as I do, as a way of recreating as nearly as possible at home the experience of seeing a film in a theater. The DVD picture is sharp, the sound is crisp and the film is almost invariably presented in its correct aspect ratio—i.e., letterboxed for movies made in wide-screen process, as all but a few since the mid-50's have been. The DVD player is, by common consent, the best-selling new device in consumer-electronics history. It's said that the "market penetration" of DVD players (which were introduced in 1997) into American homes is progressing at a rate twice that of the VCR. And the unprecedented "penetration" of this format cannot be attributed solely to the Rohypnol of advertising hype; the DVD is a distinct improvement over the videocassette, and even over the extinct laserdisc.

But the DVD is a gift horse that demands to be looked squarely in the mouth, because it has the potential to change the way we see movies so profoundly that the art form itself, which I've loved since I was a kid, is bound to suffer. What does it mean, for example, when a director recuts or otherwise substantially alters the theatrical-release version of his or her film for the DVD, as Peter Jackson did for the four-disc Special Extended Edition of "Lord of the Rings: The Fellowship of the Ring"? This cut, half an hour longer than the film that was shown in theaters and that sold millions of copies in the first two-disc DVD incarnation just four months earlier, is obviously the definitive version of "Fellowship": clearer: fuller, richer emotionally and kinetically. Better later than never, I guess, but I still felt a little cheated at having to watch this grand, epic-scale adventure on the small screen. And don't the hardy souls who every now and then peel themselves off their Barcaloungers, trek to the multiplex, stand in line for $4 sodas and dubious popcorn and then subject themselves to the indignity of sitting in a room with hundreds of rank strangers—don't *they* deserve the best version of the movie? At least when Steven Spielberg re-edited and digitally rejuggered his "E.T.: the Extraterrestrial," he had the decency to give it a brief stopover in movie theaters on the way to its final destination as a multidisc Limited Collector's Edition DVD.

It's thoughtful of Spielberg, too, to include in the DVD package, alongside the spiffy new "E.T.," a disc containing the original 1982 theatrical version of that justly beloved movie, which is not only the sole extra worth watching in the whole overstuffed grab bag of goodies—what viewers, I wonder are thrilled to discover therein a two-hour film of John Williams conducting the score at the

Shrine Auditorium?—but it is also a stern warning to filmmakers who might be tempted to tinker with their past work: in almost every respect the old version is better. Although the two brief scenes Spielberg has restored to the picture are nice, you wouldn't miss them it they weren't there (as the filmmaker evidently didn't when he left them on the cutting-room floor two decades ago), and the digital removal of the guns carried by the government agents in the original's climactic chase just seems silly.

What's most damaging to "E.T." is the way Spielberg has tampered with the movements and facial expressions of the eponymous alien itself. A team of computer wizards has labored mightily to make E.T. cuter—an undertaking that, as even those of us who admire the picture would have to agree, has a distinct coals-to-Newcastle quality.

I'm sure most filmmakers occasionally look at their past movies and wish they'd done one thing or another differently, but before the rise of the DVD, they rarely received much encouragement (i.e. financing) to roll up their sleeves, get under the hood and fine-tune or soup up their vintage machines. The state of affairs changed when the consumer-electronic industry discovered, to its delight, that many members of its affluent and highly penetrable market could be induced to buy the same entertainment product, with variations, over and over again. (One day you wake up to find you have 17 ways of listening to Elvis's "Heartbreak Hotel.") For movie lovers, a new DVD Director's Cut of "The Fellowship of the Ring" or "E.T." or "Apocalypse Now" or even "X-Men" can be powerful incentive to reach for the wallet yet one more time.

The restoration of older films that were mutilated before their theatrical release or that have suffered from disfiguring wear and tear is, or course, welcome. There's every reason to shell out for the DVD's of David Lean's "Lawrence of Arabia," Hitchcock's "Vertigo" and "Rear Window," with their images and sounds, which had faded badly over the years, not buffed by crack restorers, and Orson Welles's baroque 1958 noir "Touch of Evil," which replaces the distributor's release cut with a version that conforms more closely to the director's own extensive notes on the editing of the film. (Like the new "E.T.," all those restorations played briefly in theaters.) In each of those cases, the DVD allows us to see the film as its maker wanted it to be seen.

But most of the current mania for revision appears to be driven by motives other than a burning desire for aesthetic justice. It's not that I don't believe Steven Spielberg when he says that his "perfectionist" impulses were what spurred him to rework "E.T."; it's that I don't believe that without the financial incentive of DVD sales he would have given in to those impulses—or, perhaps, felt them at all. Although the film's 20th anniversary, last year, supplied a pretext for revision, nothing in the finished new version argues very strongly for its *necessity*. God knows, there are DVD packages far crasser than the Limited Collector's "E.T." (For an especially pungent recent example, see "X-Men 1.5.") I'm picking on Spielberg here because he's a great filmmaker and a man who loves and respects the history of his art; if even he can be seduced into tampering with his own work, then the innocent-looking little DVD is rolling us down a very steep slope indeed.

Revisiting past work is almost never a good idea for an artist. Every work of art is the product to a specific time and a specific place and, in the case of movies, a specific moment in the development of film technology. Sure, any movie made before the digital revolution could be "improved" technically, but the fact is that the choices that the director made within the technical constraints of the time *are* the movie. It wasn't so long ago, maybe 15 years, that filmmakers took up arms against Ted Turner and his efforts to "modernize" old black-and-white films by computer-coloring them. Colorization was an easy target, both because the process was surpassingly ugly and because it was inflicted on films without the consent of their makers. But would the principle have been any different if the colorization technology had been better, or if the directors had somehow been persuaded to perform the evil act themselves, on their own movies, of their own apparent free will? If Georges Méliès, the wizardly animator of silent cinema, were alive today, would he boot up his computer and take another crack at "A Trip to the Moon"? Would we think more highly of him if he did?

That's kind of where we are with DVD's today. We're all well past the point of being shocked at the compromises people make in the name of commerce, but I still wonder why filmmakers have been so meekly compliant with the encroaching revisionism and interactivity of the digital format. For many, I suppose, it's simply a matter of taking the bad with the good. The huge upside of the DVD's, for filmmakers, is that it makes their work widely available, in a form that more or less accurately reflects their intentions: they long ago learned to live with the reality that ultimately more people would see their films on a small screen than on a large one—the directors of Spielberg's generation themselves received a fair amount of their movie education from television—and at least on DVD the movies aren't interrupted by commercials or squashed into a "full-frame" presentation. So the filmmakers tell themselves, I guess that the more insidious features of the format don't really matter: that the making-of documentaries don't make them sound like hucksters and blowhards; that the deleted scenes and alternate endings don't subtly impinge on the formal unity of the work; that all the revisions of digital tweaks they agree on don't undermine the historical integrity of the picture; that voice-over commentaries don't drown the movie in a torrent of useless information; that scene access doesn't encourage viewers to rearrange the film to their own specifications; that the user-friendly conventions of the format will not steadily erode the relationship between movies and their audience.

The men and women who make films need to put more resistance to the rising tide of interactivity, because, "Casablanca" notwithstanding, there's no guarantee that the fundamental things will continue to apply as time goes by. The more "interactive" we allow our experience of art—any art—to become, the less likely it is that future generations will appreciate the necessity of art at all. Interactivity is an illusion of control; but understanding a work of art requires a suspension of that illusion, a provisional surrender to someone else's vision. To put it as simply as possible: If you have to be in total control of every experience, art is not for you. Life probably isn't either. Hey, where's the alternate ending?

There's not much point speculating on what the ending will be for the strange process of DVD-izing cinema. Many suspect that the DVD is already the tail wagging the weary old dog of the movies. Will the interactive disc ultimately become the primary medium, with film itself reduced to the secondary status of raw material for "sampling"? Maybe; maybe not. The development of digital technology, along with the vagaries of the marketplace, will determine the outcome, and neither of those factors is easily predictable. What's safe to say, I think, is that the DVD—at least in its current, extras-choked incarnation—represents a kind of self-deconstruction of the art of film, and that the DVD-created audience, now empowered to take apart and put together these visual artifacts according to the whim of the individual user, will not feel the awe I felt in a movie theater when I was young, gazing up at the big screen as if it were a window on another, better world.

I no longer look at movies with quite the wide-eyed innocence, of course, but it's always there somewhere in the background: an expectation of transport, as stubborn as a lapsed Catholic's wary hope of grace. Perhaps the DVD generation, not raised in that moviegoer's faith, will manage to generate some kind of art from the ability to shuffle bits and pieces of information randomly—the aleatory delirium of the digital. It just won't be the art of D.W. Griffith, Jean Renoir, Francois Truffaut, Sam Peckinpah, Andrei Tarkovsky and Roman Polanski.

Feeling slightly melancholy, I call up David Lynch, who is not only a director whose works—"Blue Velvet," "Mullholand Drive"—demand a pretty high level of surrender on the part of the viewer, but also who has in recent years refused to allow voice-over commentary or scene access on the DVD's of his movies. "The film is the thing," he tells me. "For me, the world you go into in a film is so delicate—it can be broken so easily. It's so tender. And it's essential to hold the world together, to keep it safe." He says he thinks "it's crazy to go in and fiddle with the film," considers voice-overs "theater of the absurd" and is concerned that too many DVD extras can "demystify" a film. "Do not demystify," he declares, with ardor. "When you know too much, you can never see the film the same way again. It's ruined for you for good. All the magic leaks out, and it's putrefied."

He's not opposed to DVD per se. Lynch is finished supervising the DVD of his first feature, "Eraserhead" (1976), which, while eschewing the usual commentary and chapter stops, will contain a few extras (the nature of his favorite DVD's, the Criterion Collection's "Complete Monterey Pop"), and agree that D.A. Pennebaker's groundbreaking concert film is the sort of movie the format serves well; even the scene access is, in this case, mighty useful. But Lynch says the filmmakers need to be very careful about the way they present their delicate, tender creations on DVD. "Don't do anything to hurt the film, and then you're rockin.'"

I hang up, leaving David Lynch to rock on, and find that I'm feeling more hopeful that the relationship between movies and their audience will survive the current onslaught of interactivity—that this need not be the beginning of the end of a beautiful friendship. So I dig out the no-frills DVD of "Mulholland

Drive," slide it into its little tray and pick up the remote. And I tell the machine to play it.

Topics for Reading and Writing

1. Rafferty argues that movies are "coercive," "the least interactive, most controlling art form in human history." What does he mean? Is he right?

2. David Lynch, director of *Blue Velvet, Mulholland Drive,* and *Twin Peaks* has refused to allow scene access on DVDs of his movies. Is Lynch sticking his head in the sand? Should we admire his stand on behalf of old-fashioned movie viewing? Or should he acknowledge that the days of the director as dictator are over?

Arguments About Definitions and Concepts

What Is an Argument About a Definition?

Is your dorm room a pigsty? Is Microsoft a monopoly? Does downloading traded MP3s constitute stealing? In order to answer these kinds of questions, writers must make arguments about the meanings of words. In the classical theories of rhetoric, these kinds of arguments are known as "definitional claims," but we'll just call them arguments about definitions and concepts.

"Who would argue about the meanings of words?" you might ask. Definitions can be easily found in any dictionary. While that is certainly true, arguments about concepts derive from two important and inalterable facts about language: language is a living, changing entity, and naming carries with it significant power. Language allows humans to make sense of the world; names, which are really nothing but designations for categories of things or actions or attributes, allow us to see the world not as a collection of singularities but as a vast network of categories. By using language we can talk about how many seemingly dissimilar things—you, me, Irving R. Levine, and Mother Teresa—all fit into one category: "human."

Whether or not something fits into a given category usually is obvious. *Moby Dick* is a book; *InStyle* isn't. Chicago is a city; Illinois isn't. The meaning of the terms "book" and "city" are so obvious to us that there doesn't seem to be any question about their meaning or about whether or not a given thing— especially these things!—might belong to that category. A reasonable person could not argue that *InStyle* is a book or Illinois is a city. But think about other examples that might be less clear-cut:

> the 600-page fall issue of *Vogue*
> a hardcover bound volume of all the 1998 issues of *Cook's Illustrated*
> all the book reports of Mrs. Channing's fourth-grade class, stapled
>   together and put in a spiral binding
> Chapel Hill, North Carolina
> Minneapolis-St. Paul, Minnesota
> Dancer, Texas—population 72

These examples aren't so easy to classify. Because they have some of the attributes that we know belong to the categories but others that don't, they cause us to question what we really mean by the words "book" or "city." Is a book bound between covers? Then the 1998 volume of *Cook's Illustrated* would qualify, even though it's really just several magazines. Does a book have to be published? Then Mrs. Channing's fourth-grade class reports aren't a book, but the fall *Vogue* is. If a city has to have at least 10,000 people, Dancer wouldn't qualify, but does that mean the large metropolitan area of Minneapolis-St. Paul can be thought of as one city? In order to make arguments about whether or not these specific examples fit into your categories "book" and "city," you make a claim about a word's definition.

There are other occasions that call for arguments about meaning. Sometimes, membership in a given category carries with it privileges or a stigma; in those cases, membership in that category becomes a point worth arguing about. Is your essay "above average" or "excellent"? Is a mobile home a house or a trailer? Do you attend a college or a university? Is Tiger Woods an African American or (as he termed himself, referring to his Caucasian and black and Asian heritage) "Cablanasian"?

Arguments about concepts and definitions become extremely important when the term being argued about carries political or social significance. Take the term liberal. From the 1940s to the 1960s, to be "liberal" in America meant to support freedoms: of the press, of religion, of personal lifestyle. A liberal opposed racial segregation in the South, was skeptical about the war in Vietnam, and wanted the government to provide social welfare programs for the poor. In those days, being a liberal was neither good nor bad; it was simply a description. However, beginning in the 1970s politicians and writers on the right of the political spectrum began to try and shift the definition of the term. They linked liberals to many of the social problems that were beginning to anger mainstream America: criminals being released from prison early, people on welfare refusing to work, and taxes being raised to pay for social programs that benefited few people. After years of constant work, these politicians and writers saw their efforts succeed as the American people began to reject politicians who carried the label "liberal." During the 1990s a liberal became a bad thing to be. Political candidates who clearly held liberal ideas denied being "liberals"; they called themselves "progressives," "New Democrats," or "centrists." Today, it's rare to find a politician who will admit to being a liberal.

"Liberal" isn't the only term that carries with it such power, of course. In fact, other terms used in public discourse are even more powerful. Among certain groups, to be designated a "feminist" is a terrible thing, while for others it's a badge of pride. "Right-winger," "environmentalist," "bleeding heart," "peacenik," "the rich," "fascist" and other terms get thrown around a lot. Some of these terms ("feminist" or "environmentalist" or "rich") can be either bad or good, depending upon the audience. Others—"peacenik," "fascist," "racist"— are almost never used positively.

So if these terms get used all the time, we are all clear on what they mean, right? Well, actually, no. And this is where questions of definition get interesting. We saw how a powerful group (right-wing politicians and writers) was able to shift the common understanding of the word "liberal" enough so that it went from being a neutral term to being a negative one. The term "feminist" has also seen its meaning shift. Because of the rhetoric about feminists produced by conservative commentators such as Rush Limbaugh, Bill O'Reilly, and Anita Bryant, for many people feminists are angry, furry-legged, man-hating lesbians. The leaders of today's feminist movement disagree; they view feminism as the quest for equal rights, equal pay, and self-determination for women. On the other side of the political spectrum, leftists viewed with alarm the growing influence of evangelical Christians in American politics starting in the 1970s and 1980s. Although the most important evangelical politician was actually a Democrat (President Jimmy Carter), people on the left rhetorically associated all politicians who talked about Christian values with the most extreme and reactionary members of their community. During the Reagan years in the 1980s, Christian evangelicals became known, pejoratively, as the "religious right," and left-wing groups warned that conservative Christians wanted to install a theocracy in America in which all students would pray to Jesus and birth control would be illegal. Evangelicals rejected these claims and argued that they were not the "religious right" but merely people of faith whose deeply held values informed their political beliefs. In this case, the attempt to redefine a political group seems to have failed: President George W. Bush identifies himself as an evangelical, as do many of the important figures in his administration.

Obviously, the act of naming is an exercise of power: by naming something we put it into a category that it may or may not belong to. More importantly, I may give something a different name than you might, or you might disagree about the name I gave to something or someone. Let's take an example from the readings in this chapter to illustrate this:

Is downloading MP3s from services such as Kazaa stealing?

First of all, we need to ask ourselves whether or not this is an arguable question. Could reasonable people answer "yes"? Yes, they could; in fact, there are several arguments for this side included in this book. Could reasonable people answer "no"? Again, reasonable people could feel, and in fact do argue, that this activity is not actually stealing. Finally, is this a question worth arguing? That, too, seems clear. The question touches on many issues that are of constant concern in our society: private property rights, the social effect of technology, copyright, the right to privacy, animosity toward large corporations, people's tendency to try to get things for free even if those things don't belong to them. So it does seem that this question is indeed arguable.

Now that we have determined that this is an arguable question, we go about constructing our argument. As you've probably figured out, this argument has to rest on the definition of the term "stealing." *Webster's New World Dictionary* defines "to steal" as

> to take or appropriate (another's property, ideas, etc.) without permission, dishonestly, or unlawfully.

That seems obvious, but it doesn't really get at the heart of our question. The way we use the word "stealing" transcends the very general definition given because that definition leaves unanswered many of the other questions we have about this issue: who actually owns those recordings? To whom do they belong legally, and to whom do they belong morally? Is it stealing when the act ultimately benefits the supposed victim?

This, then, is where you start writing an argument about meaning. Think about what you really feel about the question. Maybe your first impression is that downloading MP3s is, in fact, stealing. Make a list, then, of what characterizes "stealing."

- involves property that legally belongs to someone else

This works pretty well. The recordings legally belong to the record company. But this argument, it's important to keep in mind, might be an oversimplification. This isn't necessarily a bad thing—the Recording Industry Association of America (RIAA) has made this very simple and clear-cut claim the centerpiece of its argument—but it also doesn't answer the counterclaims of the pro-Kazaa, pro-Napster people. For those people, the recordings do legally belong to the record companies, but they also *should* belong to the artists, who have a moral right to their own recordings. Here, a responsible writer would start thinking about audience. Arguing to an audience of adults who don't really use MP3s and who tend to support private property rights, it would be smart to make the argument a simple one: the recordings belong to the record companies; stealing means taking something that belongs to someone else; therefore downloading those MP3s without the record company's permission is stealing.

But if you were arguing to an audience of college students or computer enthusiasts—that is, people who are likely to have downloaded these MP3s and who want a more equivocal definition of "stealing"—the writer would have to take that into consideration. Knowing these people often try to separate the ownership claims of record companies and of artists, you might try to yoke those two claims together *against* the "stealing" of downloaders by proposing a criterion like this one:

- even when there is an ethical question about ownership, we must defer to the claims of *all* possible owners before claiming ownership ourselves.

Finally, it's important to take into consideration your opponents' typical means of argument, especially when your claim is as much of a no-brainer as this one. Those who argue on behalf of MP3 sharing frequently go beyond just questioning the claim to ownership of record companies; knowing that it's hard to make a convincing argument that downloading isn't stealing, they will resort to demonizing the record companies (and sometimes even the artists who resist downloading). Just in the articles included in this chapter, artist Janis Ian suggests that record-company executives are thieves (an interesting rhetorical technique—she turns the question of "theft" around by alluding to the recording industry's historically poor treatment of artists), and student Emily Brill refers to the record companies as "Big Music," rhetorically lumping them together with such frequently reviled industries as "Big Oil." A responsible counterargument to this type of ad hominem or ad populem claim must be included in your argument; you might word it like this:

■ Even though the victims of this theft might not be the most admirable people in the world, and even though many of these artists are quite wealthy already, we must keep in mind that it's the principle—not the character of the people involved—that is important in making policy.

Most of the articles included with this chapter rely, to some degree, on claims about definitions or concepts. "Stealing," of course, is an important one when we talk about Napster and MP3 downloading. But many of our writers also rely on other terms they define—or fail to adequately define—as part of their arguments. The RIAA's Cary Sherman chooses an even more vivid word than "stealing"—"piracy." And all the sides in the debate chew over what might be meant by "privacy rights" (not surprisingly, for the right to privacy is one of the few rights the Supreme Court has enshrined even though it was not originally included in the Constitution).

IDEAS INTO PRACTICE 5-1

Come up with definitions for the following terms. Try to include several criteria—some that anything belonging to that category must have, some that many, but not all, members of the category will have, and at least one that members of this category will not have but that members of a closely related category will have.

1. Horror movie (differentiate from "suspense movie")
2. Sport-utility vehicle (differentiate from "truck")
3. "Reality" television program (differentiate from "documentary")
4. Hip-hop (differentiate from "rap")
5. Drug (differentiate from "food")

The Definitional Claim in the Real World

But most arguments about definitions and meanings don't start with a question about the category itself. Rather, these arguments usually begin when people try to place a particular item into a category. In fact, much of your classwork probably can be boiled down to claims of definition or meaning. Business classes will look at whether a company is financially healthy or not. Med school students, confronted by a set of symptoms, are asked to decide what disease or condition afflicts a patient. Much of the study of law revolves around questions of definition: is this illegal? Is this person liable for damages? Is this an actionable offense? Chemistry students decide whether an unknown substance is an alkane or alkene, and political scientists are asked to determine whether Great Britain is a social democracy or a constitutional monarchy. All of these are questions of definition; all ask us to decide whether or not a specific thing fits into a particular category.

Questions about definitions and naming characterize many of the debates that rage today. In the winter of 2002–2003, the most pressing issue was the impending conflict between the United States and Iraq over Iraq's refusal to disarm. The question whose answer would determine whether or not the United States would attack Iraq was itself a definitional question: was Iraq in "material breach" of the U.N. resolution that it had to disarm? In this case, the category in question is "material breach," while the specific example to be placed into or rejected from that category is "Iraq's actions to disarm or lack thereof." Another question that constantly recurs in American society centers on the proper relationship of church and state. In case after case, the Supreme Court is asked to decide whether specific actions—Nativity scenes on city hall lawns, nondenominational prayers at baccalaureate ceremonies—fit into the category "state-sponsored religion." Finally, the debate surrounding abortion, probably the most inflammatory and emotional political issue in America today, is essentially a debate about a definition: is a fetus a person?

IDEAS INTO PRACTICE 5-2

Construct your own definitional arguments for the following questions. Think about the typical arguments for the *other* side, and what important counterclaims you need to anticipate.

1. Downloading MP3s isn't stealing.
2. Sophisticated, open-ended video games like *The Sims* or *Grand Theft Auto* transcend the simplistic category of "game" and should instead be put in a new category: "digital simulation of reality."
3. When a movie is generated by teams of writers and marketing surveys and focus groups, it can no longer qualify as a creative work—it's simply a commercial product.
4. Degrees granted by online universities don't indicate that the graduate has had a real college education.
5. Gangsta rappers aren't really misogynists because their songs are told in the voices of characters, not in the voice of the artist himself.

Style Toolbox

Combining Sentences

The length of sentences within a paragraph can be an important part of that paragraph's rhetorical effect. A sequence of several short sentences followed by a long sentence often can have the effect of an argument building up to a forceful, logical conclusion. An unbroken series of short sentences can seem either plainspoken and clear or strident and patronizing. A series of long, complicated sentences strung together requires the audience to pay careful attention to what the speaker or writer is saying, and therefore can either draw the audience in (if the audience is willing and able to follow a complicated argument) or bore them.

Because the length of a sentence can have such a powerful rhetorical impact, a valuable tool for writers is the ability to combine sentences. Not only does sentence-combining give you more control over the rhythm of your prose, it allows you to associate concepts with each other without having to explicitly state you are doing so. For instance, the sentence

> I like dried apricots; they are really the best way I've found to eat
> enough servings of fruit in a given day.

is slightly different, conceptually, than if the same idea were stated like this:

> I like dried apricots. They are really the best way I've found to eat
> enough servings of fruit in a given day.

The first sentence, the one combined with a semicolon, conveys better the idea that the speaker likes dried apricots *because* they are the best way to get enough servings of fruit. The two ideas are more separate in the second example.

Sentences can be combined in a variety of ways. The simplest method of combining sentences is simply to use a *conjunction*—a word such as "and," "but," "or," "yet," "for," and "so." Sometimes sentences combined with conjunctions don't even require punctuation, as in the following examples:

> I like baseball <u>and</u> I like basketball.
> We're almost out of gas <u>but</u> I'm going to try to make it to Brockport.

These sentences can also be combined with a comma.

> I like baseball, and I like basketball.
> We're almost out of gas, but I'm going to try to make it to Brockport.

How does the rhythm of the sentence change its rhetorical effect?

Combining sentences with a comma, as in the second examples, always requires a conjunction. However, there are other choices for sentence combining that don't require conjunctions. Probably the most valuable of these is the semicolon. An ability to use the semicolon correctly is an extremely valuable tool for a writer to have, because it allows you to put ideas in complicated conceptual relationships to each other without having to tediously spell everything out to the audience. Sentences with semicolons stand out to a reader because they subtly make the writer's thoughts seem more developed or more nuanced—sentences with semicolons suggest that the writer has really thought through her argument.

Semicolons are used to indicate several kinds of conceptual relationships:

- either/or: "The Syrians might withdraw from their international obligations; they might, though, use this opportunity to rejoin the family of nations." The either/or relationship can be strengthened by use of words such as "though" or "however" that make it clear that the two are alternatives.

- on the one hand/on the other hand: "College gives you the chance to develop important intellectual and communications skills; but college also keeps you out of the job market and spending, not making, money for at least four years."

- closely related ideas: "By the end of 1967, the morass in Vietnam weighed heavily on President Johnson; it seemed as if the war was actually taking a physical toll on his once-robust body."

- an illustration of a concept: "Our society fears roving, anonymous child molesters far out of proportion to the actual danger they pose; in fact, the vast majority of child abuse is committed by a family member or close friend of the family."

Sometimes the sequence can be reversed, with the illustration of the point coming before the point itself, as in the following example from the great rock and roll writer Lester Bangs:

> Many of the Troggs' songs, aside from the fact that they were immediate come-ons and male self-aggrandizement, also seemed to have an extra-excited, almost celebratory quality about them, sexual anthems and sexual whoops that get banned from the radio and played by their proud owners never at parties for the titillation of giggling cases of arrested development but rather at home alone sitting in front of the speakers so you can pick up that full charge of bravado and self-affirmation even if the basic image is as corny at least as John Wayne; when you're a kid you need stuff like that. (Lester Bangs, "James Taylor Marked for Death")

Listen to the rhythm of Bangs's sentence, how it builds up and becomes almost breathless (he achieves this by eliminating the commas present in the earlier part of the sentence) before he reaches the climax of the first sentence. The semicolon steps in and gives the reader and writer a brief rest, allowing the writer to explain exactly what the point of all those preceding details were.

As you see in the examples provided, the semicolon does not necessarily have to use a conjunction. An important thing to remember about using the semicolon is that in standard American English, *whenever you use a semicolon in a sentence, there must be a complete sentence—with a subject and a conjugated verb—on each side of the semicolon.* This can be particularly confusing for students, because this grammatical rule was not fully established until the twentieth century; as a result, much writing that students read uses the semicolon in a way that would be considered incorrect today. The only exception to the complete-sentence rule with the semicolon is in the construction of a list: when the elements of a list themselves have commas, the semicolon should be used to separate out the elements of that list:

> Growing up where she did, my mother had to deal with cold, wind, and snow in the winter; brutal heat, a searing sun, and drenching humidity in the summer; tornadoes in the spring and floods in the fall.

The final method of combining sentences is with a colon. This is rarely used but can give a sentence a real punch, for the way that a colon abruptly stops a sentence makes an audience immediately start paying attention to what's coming next. For this reason, combining sentences with a colon can be especially effective when you precede the colon with a short general statement and follow it either with an illustration of your point, a restatement of your point in slightly different terms, or with a longer list of elements that illustrate your point. In fact, I've used two sentences in this chapter that fit into the first type of colon usage:

> At the same time, the *over*use of sentences with semicolons stands out, as well: such overuse can make the writer seem amateurish, as if she's learned a new trick and wants everybody to see it.

> The only exception to the complete-sentence rule with the semicolon is in the construction of a list: when the elements of a list themselves have commas, the semicolon should be used to separate out the elements of that list.

Using a colon to separate a general statement from a list of examples might produce a sentence like the following:

> Eminem's characters retain the ability to shock: they murder, they commit terrible acts of violence, they exemplify the narcissism, hatefulness, and self-pity of the young white men who grow up to become Rush Limbaugh or Sean Hannity.

How complicated can these sentences get? As complicated as the writer thinks the audience can accept. The Victorian novelist Henry James, renowned for the elegant, languid pace of his novels, partially created that pace in his very sentences, as in the following sentence composed of three increasingly long sentences joined by two semicolons:

> Nothing would have induced her, however, to encourage him; she was now conscious of having never in her life stood so still or sat, inwardly, as it were, so tight; she felt like the horse of the adage, brought—and brought by her own fault—to the water, but strong, for the occasion, in the one fact that she couldn't be forced to drink. (Henry James, *The Golden Bowl*)

How about a compound sentence separated by a colon whose second sentence has a list divided by semicolons (for categories) and commas (for elements within categories)?

> During those five years, I appeared, on the face of it, a competent enough member of some community, a signer of contracts and Air Travel cards, a cit-

izen: I wrote a couple of times a month for one magazine or another, published two books, worked on several motion pictures; participated in the paranoia of the time, in the raising of a small child, and in the entertainment of large numbers of people passing through my house; made gingham curtains for spare bedrooms, remembered to ask agents if any reduction of points would be *pari passu* with the financing studio, put lentils to soak on Saturday night for lentil soup on Sunday, made quarterly F.I.C.A. payments and renewed my driver's license on time, missing on the written examination only the question about the financial responsibility of California drivers. (Joan Didion, "The White Album")

Compound sentences are important tools for a writer, both in terms of conceptual and rhythmic control. However, the *over*use of these sentences can stand out even more than their judicious use. Writers who overuse compound sentences, especially sentences with colons and semicolons, seem amateurish, as if they've learned a new trick and want everybody to see it. As you decide whether or not to use these sentences, ask yourself: how much is the reader going to focus on *me,* and how much is the reader going to focus on what I'm saying?

WRITING WITH STYLE 5-1

For each of the following pairs or series of sentences, combine them in several different ways. Some will work equally well; others will make very little sense or actually be ungrammatical. After composing several sentences for each exercise, describe how each sentence differs from the others in terms of its rhetorical effect—when and with what audience you would use it.

1. I didn't know what to do about my problem. I called the psychic hotline.
2. Rousseau resented the fact that the *Essays* were not frank enough to suit him. But Montaigne was not writing confessions. (Donald Frame, introduction to *The Complete Essays of Montaigne*)
3. People with sunny natures do seem to live longer than people who are nervous wrecks. Yet mankind didn't evolve out of the animal kingdom by being unduly sunny-minded. (Edward Hoagland, "Heaven and Nature")
4. So let him march sometime. Let him have his prayer pilgrimages to the city hall. Understand why he must have sit-ins and freedom rides. (Martin Luther King, Jr., "Letter from Birmingham Jail")
5. In fact, it's sheer logic (if not poetry) in motion. When you're packed into a standing sweatshop with ten thousand other little bodies all mashed together, it stands to reason you can't dance in the traditional manner (i.e., sideways sway). (Lester Bangs, "The Clash")
6. There was no hardship. But there was no luxury. And he had thought that he could get back into training that way. (Ernest Hemingway, "The Snows of Kilimanjaro")

7. The terrible struggle that made me an American out of a potential slave said "On the line!" The Reconstruction said "Get set!" The generation before said "Go!" (Zora Neale Hurston, "How It Feels To Be Colored Me")

8. It was a period of religious tolerance. Trade and agriculture prospered. Palaces and temples multiplied. (Jason Elliott, *An Unexpected Light: Travels in Afghanistan*)

9. Meeting people has an overlay. I know what they notice first is that I am different. (Ynestra King, "The Other Body: Disability and Identity Politics")

10. Oppression—overwhelming control—is necrophiliac. It is nourished by the love of death, not life. (Paolo Freire, "The 'Banking' Concept of Education")

What's Real?

An explosion aboard the *USS Maine* leads to calls for the United States to go to war against Spain. The *National Enquirer* reports that Michael Jackson sleeps in a hyperbaric chamber so that he can live to be 200. The 2000 Republican Convention features one non-Caucasian speaker after another. An earnest Kuwaiti hospital volunteer, "Nayirah," testifies to Congress that she saw Iraqi soldiers pulling babies out of incubators and throwing them onto the floor. Fred Astaire dances with a Dirt Devil vacuum cleaner and Frank Sinatra sings "I've Got You Under My Skin" to a 2003 NBA audience. CBS News shows a panoramic view of New York's Times Square complete with a large CBS ad on the outdoor Jumbotron screen. And on *Blind Date,* one lonely heart has dinner with another.

All these disparate events have one thing in common: they aren't real. At least, they aren't "real" in the way we customarily understand the word. They all happened, yes, and they all

George W. Bush declares "Mission Accomplished" at what seemed like the end of the conflict in Iraq in 2003.

implicitly asked us to believe in them, but not one was actually "real" or "true" in any meaningful sense of the term.

■ In 1898, seeking to increase his newspaper's circulation by spearheading public outcry against a foreign enemy, *New York Journal* publisher William Randolph Hearst told his photographer, "You furnish the pictures and I'll furnish the war." Jingoistic coverage of the *Maine* incident by Hearst and his rival, *New York World* publisher Joseph Pulitzer, contributed to bringing about the Spanish-American War. Spain's defeat led to its expulsion from the last remnant of its New World empire, as well as the loss of the Philippines. However, in 1976 the U.S. Navy concluded that the *Maine* had exploded not from Spanish sabotage but as a result of spontaneous combustion in the coal chambers.

■ According to several sources, Michael Jackson's publicists planted the story about Jackson's hyperbaric chamber in the *Enquirer* to ensure that Jackson's name stayed in the headlines.

■ Many commentators remarked on the irony of the Republicans featuring non-white faces on the podium when the leadership of the party consists overwhelmingly of upper-middle-class white men, and argued that this was a cynical ploy to persuade Americans that the G.O.P. was really a "diverse" party.

- "Nayirah" was, in fact, the daughter of the Kuwaiti ambassador to the United States; her appearance in front of Congress had been orchestrated by Hill and Knowlton, a PR firm that represented the Kuwaiti royal family in Washington, in an effort to mobilize support for a war against Iraq. Nayirah had, in fact, witnessed no such events.

- The estates of Fred Astaire and Frank Sinatra granted permission for Dirt Devil and the NBA, respectively, to digitally insert old images of the dancer and singer into new film footage. The commercials were made after the deaths of Astaire and Sinatra and neither man granted permission for such use of his image.

- Not wanting to provide NBC, a competitor, with free advertising, CBS digitally altered the Times Square Jumbotron on its broadcast, covering up the NBC logo and a Budweiser advertisement. The fact that a news organization was altering pictures without informing the public was considered a serious breach of journalistic ethics.

- *Blind Date*'s "contestants" are hardly looking for love on the show. Rather, many of the daters are simply struggling actors and actresses seeking TV exposure of any kind.

Edward Bernays, the father of public relations, defined the work of his field as "creating circumstances," manufacturing events that do not seem staged but in fact are. The explosion of media outlets has provided public relations practitioners and ordinary citizens alike with many more opportunities to produce their own versions of reality for public consumption. Is this dangerous? What happens when "reality" is stage-managed? What is the public's responsibility to determine that what's real is . . . real?

▮▮ The Photo Opportunity

Conveying a message through language can be very effective, but this tends to invite the audience to respond to the message. Images—illustrations, photographs, logos—on the other hand, communicate a message without asking for an answer. A photograph also can distill complicated ideas and emotions into a very small piece of information. Originally just a chance for print and television journalists to take a picture (the "grip and grin," or the familiar smiling-handshake photo) of leaders at a high-level meeting, the photograph opportunity (or "photo op") has evolved into one of the most important weapons in a politician's arsenal. The photo op is especially valuable because it can't be disproven. A photo of an African-American speaker in front of a Republican National Convention banner provides viewers with a whole complex of ideas and associations, where the same idea stated verbally—"African Americans are welcome in our party and in fact hold many important national positions"—would invite a counterargument because relatively few African Americans are registered Republicans. It's hard to argue against a picture. Knowing that the presidency is always going to be news in itself, presidential advisers strive to make sure the pictures that journalists will broadcast on the evening news are not only as flattering to the president as possible, but that they also reinforce the message of the

The Nixon-Elvis Presley meeting on Dec. 21, 1970.

day. It's not just the president, either, who uses photo ops; candidates for county sheriff or school board also try to ensure that flattering pictures of themselves will appear in the press.

Journalists tend to be very cynical about photo opportunities—they know better than anyone that these are just publicity stunts—but the need for a picture for the front page or footage of any kind to fill the evening news trumps their desire not to be part of someone's PR machinery. Sometimes, though, the staged nature of the photo op becomes a story in itself. Making a 2003 speech in St. Louis promoting American industrial production, President Bush spoke before a backdrop of boxes labeled MADE IN U.S.A.: the boxes clearly were meant to provide a graphic reinforcement of his message. However, journalists later discovered that someone (journalists suspected a member of Bush's staff; the White House blamed it on an "overzealous office volunteer") had taped over the boxes' original Made In China label and had stamped the MADE IN U.S.A. logo on them afterward. The mainstream press treated this story as a humorous anecdote rather questioning the administration's honesty—clear evidence of just how much we assume these photo opportunities are staged PR.[1]

Politics isn't the only arena in which photo opportunities are invented in order to promote something. You have undoubtedly read the gossip or society pages of magazines like *People* or newspapers like the *New York Post,* in which a reporter covers parties thrown on behalf of movie premieres, product launches, or club openings. Although the coverage of these parties reinforces the notion

---

[1] Katy Textor, "American-Made Mystery." *ABC News.com* 22 Jan. 2003.
http://abcnews.go. com/sections/us/DailyNews/madeinusa_030122.html.

that celebrity life is just one endless parade of glamorous get-togethers, the truth is somewhat different. These events are motivated by nothing more than the desire to promote, and having glamorous celebrities come to the event is just a way to ensure that reporters will show up. Toby Young, a *Vanity Fair* writer from the 1990s, describes them this way:

> They weren't great parties that just happened to coincide with the opening of a film or a shop or an exhibition; they were organized solely for publicity purposes. The gossip columnists dutifully wrote about them the following day, as if they had some news value, when in fact they'd been organized precisely in order to produce this sort of coverage. They had no real point other than to generate column inches, yet in order to serve that purpose everyone had to pretend they were dazzling social occasions. They were the social equivalent of Potemkin villages, photo opportunities with nothing beneath the surface.[2]

Many observers of the media argued that the Pentagon orchestrated press coverage of the 2003 invasion of Iraq to such a degree that the entire war was a photo opportunity meant to promote the Bush administration and the military itself. The famous film of Iraqis pulling down the statue of Saddam Hussein in 2003, captured live, was the result of an organized attempt by the military to provide the press with appealing pictures. Soon after that war ended, moreover, the British Broadcasting Corporation questioned the Pentagon's version of events surrounding the capture and rescue of U.S. Army soldier Jessica Lynch (see John Kampfner's article "The Truth About Jessica" in this chapter). The fact that the Pentagon was simultaneously developing a "reality" show about military life with super-producer Jerry Bruckheimer (*Top Gun, Con Air, CSI*) made many people suspect that the military establishment is quite crafty about molding public opinion. President Bush received both plaudits and attacks for his stage-managed tailhook landing on the U.S.S. *Abraham Lincoln* after the end of the war. Critics pointed out that the carrier, after nearing San Diego harbor, actually had to be turned around and sent back out to sea in order to provide the best possible pictures for the Bush speech. Nonetheless, the landing and its accompanying speech (delivered in front of a banner reading "Mission Accomplished") provided fantastic visuals. Life imitated art imitating life, as the President pretended to be Tom Cruise in *Top Gun* (a movie made with the involvement and approval of the Pentagon) for an afternoon. You can even buy a George-Bush-as-Top-Gun action figure, just like he's a real movie star.

Appearances and the veneer of authenticity are also tools of political manipulators. Interest groups on all sides employ "Astroturf" campaigns, named after the artificial turf product used on sports fields, on behalf of their causes. These campaigns are called "Astroturf" because unlike grass-roots political move-

---

[2] Toby Young, *How To Lose Friends and Alienate People* (Cambridge, MA: Da Capo, 2001): 104.

The President George W. Bush in flight suit action figure.

ments, which genuinely come from ordinary people, "Astroturf" campaigns are initiated and controlled by professional lobbying groups (People for the Ethical Treatment of Animals, the National Rifle Association, the Sierra Club) but strive to *look like* grass-roots movements. These groups also produce "video news releases" (VNRs), TV clips filmed to look like news segments in order to fool viewers into thinking they are actually news. Although most reputable news organizations shun these VNRs, a few—through carelessness or lack of resources—even air these VNRs unedited as part of the news. (See the articles by William Klein and Eugene Marlow in this chapter for extended discussions of Astroturf campaigns and VNRs.)

⫼ Expert Testimony

"Nayirah" is not the only made-up expert who has ever testified to Congress. Interest groups seeking congressional support generally try to arrange for a hearing in front of the relevant subcommittee; most of the time, these hearings are open to the public. In the case of particularly pressing or hot-button issues, the news media will cover these hearings. It's especially important at those times for the interest groups to trot out testimony not just from experts, but from people who will appeal to the general public. Although this might at first seem strange—after all, it's Congress, not the public, who votes on these proposals or bills or resolutions—the Nayirah incident demonstrated yet again that public momentum can be mobilized by a particularly memorable piece of testimony, and that testimony can be made memorable not just by its content, but also by its packaging. Reacting to this, interest groups have recruited Hollywood celebrities to present their cases in front of Congress—not because those celebrities have any special insight about the issue, but because their star power might get the hearing on television and into American living rooms. Sometimes, the strategy backfires—the public often rejects arguments made by celebrities simply because those arguments are made by celebrities (who, the assumption goes, live a very privileged and sheltered life and don't understand the "real world"). It took former actor Ronald Reagan decades to be taken seriously as a politician, and liberal actors are frequently the target of derision from conservative political commentators. In fact, as recently as 2003, action hero Arnold Schwarzenegger took advantage of the California gubernatorial recall election to became the Republican governor of California. In winning the election, he overcame the same sneers and derision as his liberal Hollywood colleagues who try their hands at politics.

⫼ Bots and Plants

The Internet and the World Wide Web have provided ordinary citizens with many new ways to virtually congregate and converse about the issues of the day—in fact, the Internet is the most significant development in the public sphere since the invention of television. Via interactive forums such as bulletin boards, chat rooms, "blogs" with hyperlinked connections to e-mail addresses, or online polls, we can contribute to dialogues about pretty much anything: whether we should bomb North Korea, whether the Giants should trade Jeremy Shockey, whether the plot of last night's episode of *CSI* was plausible or not. These forums have been used, on occasion, to some effect. In February 2003, a group led by liberal actor Martin Sheen arranged for a virtual "march on Washington" consisting of a flood of e-mails and calls to protest plans to go to war against Iraq; as you read in "Smart-Mobbing the War" in Chapter 4, even teenagers can organize worldwide movements of shared interests. The causes around which these movements coalesce don't even have to be as serious as war; fans of TV shows have organized online efforts to persuade network executives not to cancel their favorite program, for instance. But perhaps more important, if less measurable, has been the Internet's ability to create communities. These communities can be based on anything—political opinions, medical conditions, a desire to find a date, a love for Hello Kitty paraphernalia—but they function in many ways like a "real" community based on geography or personal acquaintance.

There's a reason they call it "virtual" reality, though. As part of the seemingly unstoppable commercializing of the Internet, profit-oriented interests have invaded the world of online communities. One of the heroes of the early Internet was the Austin, Texas, movie fan Harry Knowles, whose "Ain't It Cool News.com" site collected gossip and insider information about films in progress. Even the studios had no idea who was leaking dirt to Knowles. Rather than fight him, though, they learned to play his game. Now, studios intentionally give out positive information about their productions through the same channels used for leaks, dressing up this PR as unauthorized secret scoops. These "plants" work like this: a corporate representative scouts the Internet for chat rooms in which their products or services are being discussed, then logs on as an ordinary user to praise the company, often in the vernacular of the chat room. Some companies (*Elle* magazine, for instance) have experimented with "bots" (short for "robots"), pieces of software that perform tasks automatically. These companies first harvest the e-mail addresses of users who log onto sites frequented by young or adolescent girls, then their "bots" will generate regular e-mails with beauty advice and advertising material to that girl. The problem is these bots can be quite deceptive—many unsophisticated young girls think they actually have made a friend, and do not realize they are interacting with a computerized advertising delivery system.

By far the most disturbing use of Internet bulletin boards and chat rooms, though, has been by pedophiles and sexual criminals. Like the corporate PR representatives discussed in the previous paragraph, these predators log onto sites popular with children and disguise themselves as genuine members of the online community. Their goal, frequently, is to find a vulnerable victim; to accomplish this, they pick out a member of the community and initiate one-on-one communication with that victim, then try to convince that victim to meet in person, at which time the predator can commit his or her crime. Although these kinds of horrific and terrifying crimes are rare, both in real terms and in terms of the percentage of incidents of sexual abuse, they underscore how responsible use of the Internet requires a critical stance and a determination to question the source of all information.

The vast virtual realm of the Internet provides us all with a place to be something other than ourselves. We might adopt personalities that are radically different than our real ones when we post on bulletin boards, or maintain a stable of e-mail addresses, each of which we use for a particular task. Marketers and spammers, lonely hearts, gamers, bloggers—with the internet we can pretend to be anything besides what we are and we can refashion ourselves in a way that might be much more difficult in the real world. This is both incredibly liberating and deeply frightening.

ⅠⅠⅠ Pictures Don't Lie

The June 27, 1994, cover photo of *Time* magazine was stark and striking: O.J. Simpson, a beloved athlete and pitchman and actor, the very embodiment of an America in which race was unimportant, stared impassively into the camera, his skin dusky and a five-o'clock shadow making his face look haggard and a little sinister. Below his chin were 15 numbers and the words "LOS ANGELES POLICE JAIL DIV."

People who passed newsstands that week understandably were startled by that photograph, and often had to look at it two or three times in order to believe it—and even then some couldn't. For next to *Time* on many of those newsstands sat *Time*'s major competitor, *Newsweek,* and *Newsweek* ran the same picture of Simpson. But *Newsweek*'s picture was different: Simpson's skin was lighter, he had no visible growth of beard, and the numbers below his name were larger. What happened?

To put it simply, *Time* altered the picture, and because *Newsweek* ran the same unaltered picture, *Time* got caught. The rationale behind *Time*'s decision was unclear; some civil rights activists blamed it on racism (theorizing that magazine editors feel that unshaven men with darker complexions appear more threatening) while others felt that *Time* simply wanted a more dramatic composition, whether or not it was ethical. *Time*'s managing editor, James Gaines, explained that the image was not a photograph, but rather a "photoillustration" and that the magazine had done this "numerous" times.[3] Gaines's explanation is worth quoting at length:

> To a certain extent, our critics are absolutely right: altering news pictures is a risky practice, since only documentary authority makes photography of any value in the practice of journalism. On the other hand, photojournalism has never been able to claim the transparent neutrality attributed to it. Photographers choose angles and editors choose pictures to make points, after all (should President Clinton be smiling this week, or frowning?). And every major news outlet routinely crops and retouches photos to eliminate minor, extraneous elements, so long as the essential meaning of the picture is left intact. Our critics felt that Matt Mahurin's [the photoillustration artist] work changed the picture fundamentally; I felt it lifted a common police mug shot to the level of art, with no sacrifice to truth. Reasonable people may disagree about that. If there was anything wrong with the cover, in my view, it was that it was not immediately apparent that this was a photo-illustration rather than an unaltered photograph; to know that, a reader had to turn to our contents page or see the original mug shot on the opening page of the story. But making that distinction clearer will not end the debate over the manipulation of photographs. Nor should it. No single set of rules will ever cover all possible cases. It will remain, as it has always been, a matter of subjective judgment.

Is Gaines being forthright here, or is he trying to weasel his way out of admitting *Time* committed a serious breach of journalistic ethics here? In either case his larger point is quite provocative. Language, as we learned in Chapter 2, is never purely objective; photographs, unable by definition to show more than one angle, are even more subjective. That they seem to capture life unmediated, "objectively," makes them even more potentially deceptive. Of course, there are

---

[3] James Gaines, "To Our Readers." *Time* 4 July 1994.

many layers of mediation that come between the action captured on film and the dissemination of that image to the public. The photographer must have access to the scene (think of all the photographs that might exist of wars, strikes, games, and the like if there were no restrictions!), he or she must choose an angle (thereby leaving out dozens of potential subjects of the photo), he or she must choose what part of the action to focus on and which to leave out of focus. Lighting, film speed, aperture, and choice of black and white or color all have significant implications for the resulting image. The photo is then developed or scanned (which can alter the image), cropped, and then must go through at least one and sometimes several editors before it is selected to be included in the newspaper or magazine. Finally, editors will decide where in the publication the photo will be printed. All these decisions and layers of mediation change how a photograph means.

Gaines is right, as well, that photo illustrations are widespread, even if his weak *mea culpa* really doesn't remedy the deep breach of trust that such images, unlabeled, represent. The National Press Photographers Association's (NPPA) code of ethics states

> **1.** It is the individual responsibility of every photojournalist at all times to strive for pictures that report truthfully, honestly and objectively.
>
> **2.** As journalists, we believe that credibility is our greatest asset. In documentary photojournalism, it is wrong to alter the content of a photograph in any way (electronically or in the darkroom) that deceives the public. We believe the guidelines for fair and accurate reporting should be the criteria for judging what may be done electronically to a photograph.[4]

Time's actions clearly violate these principles, but the magazine is by no means alone. The NPPA's web page on "Ethics in the Age of Digital Photography" details a few other instances as examples:

> *Newsweek* straightened the teeth of Bobbi McCaughey, the mother of the sextuplets; *Newsday* ran a photo supposedly showing Nancy Kerrigan and Tonya Harding skating together a day before the event really happened; *People* ran a photo of famous breast cancer survivors made from five separate negatives; The *St. Louis Post-Dispatch* removed a Coke can from a photo of their Pulitzer Prize winner. This just scratches the surface. How many cases have not become known? The cumulative effect is the gradual erosion of the credibility of the entire profession and I am not sure we can win this war. We are being bombarded from all sides, from movies, television, advertisements, the Internet, with images that are not real, that are created in computers and documentary photojournalism is the victim.[5]

---

[4] National Press Photographers Association, "Code of Ethics." http://www.nppa.org/members/bylaws/default.htm#_Toc2860711.

[5] National Press Photographers Association, "Ethics in the Age of Digital Photography." http://www.nppa.org/services/bizpract/eadp/eadp2.html.

Changing photographs for rhetorical purposes predates digital technology, of course. The famous photographer Matthew Brady, for instance, staged some of his well-known pictures of Civil War battlefields without making that clear to editors or readers. In the 1920s, the Soviet leader Joseph Stalin, seeking to efface the record of Leon Trotsky's role in the creation of the Soviet Union, had Trotsky's image erased from all pictures in which he appeared with Lenin. Before Photoshop made it unnecessary, pornographers glued celebrity heads on top of naked bodies and sold the photos as nude shots of famous people. But digital technology makes such alteration immeasurably more simple and more powerful. We must learn to question our almost-automatic trust in images and recognize there is almost no image that cannot be altered so well as to be unnoticeable.

Altering a still photograph so the change is invisible is time consuming. Altering moving images to achieve the same effect adds another layer of difficulty. In his 1983 film *Zelig,* Woody Allen inserted images of himself into older films—newsreels of Hitler and Woodrow Wilson and Babe Ruth—to make it appear that his character was present at all these historical events. Eleven years later, Robert Zemeckis's *Forrest Gump* took advantage of new digital technology to insert the actor Tom Hanks into old footage of John Lennon hosting a TV show (among other situations). The technology made it appear that Lennon was actually having a conversation with Gump—viewers unaware that this was a movie easily could have been fooled, so sophisticated was the melding of the two times. Advertisers, as well, have recently taken up this challenge, and have made the late Fred Astaire sell vacuums, John Wayne hawk beer, and Frank Sinatra sing the praises of the NBA. Although few would actually believe these commercials, it remains to be seen how easily we would be fooled if the two sets of images were not so disparate. Could someone put together 90 seconds of film in which Kim Jong-Il and Osama bin Laden appeared to be hatching plans? What effect would such footage have on public opinion regarding a war against North Korea? Could the Taliban create film footage showing American troops committing atrocities in Afghanistan, thus undermining public support for the war on terrorism? Although the digital alteration of film footage is generally used in ways that amuse us or try to sell us things, can you imagine more dangerous uses to which this technology can be put?

▮▮ The Search for the Real

Naturally, the proliferation of fake events, publicity stunts, altered photographs, staged photo ops, and the like helps create an atmosphere of cynicism in the target audience. Cultural critics and commentators describe Americans as jaded, as blasé, as world-weary about the pervasive presence of the unreal and the manufactured. Growing up in a media age can be a process of disillusionment, of learning that the cartoon characters on Saturday morning are just marketing devices, that pop stars don't usually write or play or sometimes even sing their own music, and that trusted leaders sometimes use the media to pretend to be

Soviet dictator Josef Stalin had the image of his rival Leon Trotsky (whom he later had assassinated) airbrushed out of this 1919 picture of Vladimir Lenin speaking. In the original, Trotsky is to the right of the podium; in the altered photo, a piece of the podium covers up Trotsky.

something they're not. Periodically, a small wave of "the real" will hit the culture. Arizona Republican Senator John McCain, in his 2000 run for president, charmed many cynical voters and not a few reporters with his refusal to package himself for media consumption. In 2002, the bluegrass and country soundtrack to *O Brother Where Art Thou* was the surprise winner of the Album of the Year Grammy award, and none of the other nominees could be called "prefab pop." A "slow foods" movement, begun in Europe but gaining popularity in America, seeks to promote traditional cooking and fresh local ingredients rather than standardized fast food menus concocted in a laboratory. Part of the popularity of blogs is a result of how real and unprocessed they feel in comparison to much public writing on politics, which feels as if it is generated in the central communications office of the Republican or Democratic Party. In Summer 2003, the democratic presidential hopeful Howard Dean, seen by many in the party as a "real" candidate, used the Internet to appeal directly to potential donors for contributions—and was extremely successful, easily outdistancing his competitors in terms of fund-raising. Dean combined the appeal of the "real"—or the seemingly real—with a cunning use of new communications technology to become the surprise frontrunner in the democratic field.

The return to the real will never be more than a small trend in a vast country. Ironically, the more popular this trendlet grows, the likelier it becomes that it will be co-opted by the very forces of marketing and advertising and promotion that try to sell S.U.V.s to environmentalists and try to convince parents that "homestyle" canned soups are home cooking. Our task as citizens and responsible consumers is simply to maintain our awareness: we need to know about all the ways reality can be created, staged, altered, manipulated, and erased, and understand that if technology makes something possible, someone will put that technology to use. We also must resist the temptation to entirely give in to cynicism, to say "nothing's real, everything's a scam." A democracy requires informed and critical citizens, certainly, but it also requires citizens whose passion or outrage persuades them to get and to remain involved.

A nalyzing the Message

1. Find five or six examples of the "unreal" in your daily life. How does technology make these unreal things possible?

2. Many philosophers feel that the proliferation of the "unreal" in contemporary society will be ultimately harmful for people's ability to interact—if we approach everything with skepticism, how can we ever be completely real with each other? Other philosophers welcome this development, arguing that the proliferation of the unreal made possible by technology just makes people more aware of what's always been the case—that those in power will always "create circumstances" or manufacture events to sway public opinion. What do you think? What effect will this have?

3. What other dangers to the "real"—and by extension, to the public sphere—does technology represent? Were you aware of the extent of alteration of photographs and filmed footage?

Readings

*In this piece from the conservative website townhall.com, writer **Armstrong Williams** questions the importance of images in the creation and maintenance of George W. Bush's presidency. Images have dominated Bush's first term, Williams points out; from the smoking World Trade Center to the entry into Iraq to the triumphant Bush on the aircraft carrier, images have played the central role in Bush's relationship with the American public. What's wrong with that? Williams here ponders where the Bush presidency can go with its images, and whether its reliance on images may end up being a problem in itself.*

Armstrong Williams describes himself as "one of America's leading black conservatives." He is a former clerk for Supreme Court Justice Clarence Thomas and author of Letters to a Young Victim: Hope and Healing in America's Inner Cities *(1996).*

Armstrong Williams
The Importance of Imagery in Modern Politics

It is a fact of modern politics that politicians must rely on image to carry the day. It's been that way since the first televised debates between Richard Nixon and John F. Kennedy in 1960. Watching the "great debates," political observer Daniel J. Boorstin complained that television was reducing complex political discussion to one-dimensional visual storytelling. "The television watching viewer was left to judge, not on issues explored by thoughtful men, but on the relative capacity of the two candidates to perform under television stress," he opined.

The vast increase in media outlets since then has only further trivialized the political process. Today, most voters grow up learning from television images, rather than words. The successful politician, therefore, must be more adept than ever at using images to solicit knee-jerk reactions from voters.

The arc of George W. Bush's presidency has proved no different. It began with thick plumes of smoke engulfing the Twin Towers. Then there was an image of the most powerful man in the world, dressed in plain clothes, standing amid the rubble and shouting into a megaphone. The image proclaimed simultaneously that he was one of us (necessary in a democracy) and that he had a sense of masculine defiance (necessary for a leader). Bush's presidency began there. Images of Gen. Colin Powell holding up a baggie of white powder followed. The war with Iraq came and went. Footage of Iraqis toppling statues was plastered all over CNN. Cut to our president striding victoriously across an aircraft carrier outfitted in full U.S. Air Force regalia.

With images like that, who needs words? Certainly not the president who has been careful over the past year not to usurp his own presidency by speaking too much. The poll numbers bear out this decision.

So what now?

Bush Sr. found himself in a similar predicament in 1990. The grainy black-and-white image of scud missiles held our attention. Once Desert Storm footage ceased, Bush had no new images to suggest his greatness. His presidency promptly fell into a black hole.

Unlike his father, George W. has prepared a whole storehouse of rousing images. Up next is North Korea (cue images of nuclear reactors), then Iran (cue images of repressed citizens). Meanwhile, the administration disseminates an endless loop of American forces uncovering vast, unmarked graves where hundreds of Iraqi corpses are stacked atop one another. That's good.

It helps sell the bottom line, which is war with Iraq made the world safer. It did so by toppling a tyrant who is evil; a man dedicated to manufacturing biological and chemical weapons and who was desperately trying to build a nuclear bomb; a man who has used weapons of mass destruction on his neighbor and against his own citizens. (Is there any doubt he would direct them at us, if given the chance?); a man whose government funnels money to the families of Palestinian suicide bombers; a man who nourishes hate and fanaticism in hopes that terrorism of the Sept. 11 variety will continue to replicate throughout the world. By toppling Saddam, we made the world safer and took the first crucial steps in engineering a new era of peace in the Middle East.

But American voters require something more. It is not enough to show that Saddam was a tyrant. The world is full of evil men. The administration desperately needs that image of uncovered weapons of mass destruction. Foreign affairs, which lack the immediacy of domestic issues, derive their legitimacy from the threat of clear and present danger. The administration understands this. That is why they sold the war with Iraq as a war to halt Saddam's weapons program. Without visual evidence to make this argument seem real, the administration will have difficulty making the case for strong action in North Korea or Iran. Every new foreign affairs agenda will be undercut by the failure to achieve visual closure in Iraq.

And that is a shame because we need to prevent North Korea from developing a cache of nuclear weapons and destabilizing the entire Asian continent. We need to liberate the citizens of Iran if we are to have any hope of achieving peace in the Middle East.

Sadly, American politics was long ago trivialized by television images. Should the administration fail to come up with the crucial image of Iraqi weapons of mass destruction, their foreign affairs agenda will recede in significance, and the nation will become suddenly susceptible to the next demagogue who immerses himself in domestic issues and popular culture.

Just like in 1992.

Topics for Reading and Writing

1. Williams's article is indistinguishable from an editorial in an opinion journal or a newspaper, but it appeared on townhall.com, a conservative news and opinion website. How does Williams establish his authority, given the fact that many people are suspicious of Web-only publications? How does Williams use the Web format to his own advantage?

2. Generally, it is liberals who bemoan the domination of images in political discourse. In fact, many of Williams's points could have been—and in fact have been—made by many liberal commentators. How does Williams make his conservative credentials and beliefs clear?

3. What is Williams's actual thesis? How can he be against the use of image in political discourse, when President George W. Bush has placed such great value on creating photo opportunities for the benefit of the media? Is he criticizing Bush or his advisers?

When is a trend really a trend, and when is it just a figment of a marketer's imagination? In this story from Advertising Age *on the "extreme" fad,* **Laura Petrecca** *sheds some light on marketers' need to be as cutting edge as possible, even to the extent of nursing a dying trend or even creating a trend that never really existed. How do we know when something is trendy? What role does the media have in creating a trend? Can trends exist without mass-media attention?*

Laura Petrecca
Going to Extremes

Everything from cheeseburgers to jeans is being dubbed "Xtreme," as marketers use "X" to get to Y—Generation Y, that is.

Gillette Co. just rolled out Right Guard Xtreme Sport deodorant. Pfizer's Schick edged into the trend by introducing the Xtreme III razor. Clairol turned up the color with Xtreme FX and Burger King Corp. beefed up its product line with an X-Treme double cheeseburger.

Extreme sports have boomed since the early '60s, but branding experts said most marketers only recently have realized the power the word "extreme" holds for teens.

Those same experts also said advertisers are way behind the cool curve if they're only now introducing Xtreme products.

"By the time it becomes mass, it's no longer a trend and kids are on to the next thing," said Alan Adamson, managing director at brand identity consultancy Landor Associates.

Five Years Behind

Bill Carter, president of Fuse Sports Marketing, agreed. "Madison Avenue is about five years behind, so a lot of brands are just now getting involved with [alternative] sports," he said.

Still, with U.S. teens spending more than $100 billion annually, according to Mr. Carter, Main Street marketers want to strike while extreme sports are still hot.

According to Fuse Sports, participation in alternative sports is up 35% since eggs, and still growing. The teen population is also increasing; Fuse Sports estimated the population of 12- to 17-year-olds will rise ion to 25 million by 2010.

"Researchers are telling clients, 'You better get involved, because the demographic is exploding. You better get involved now because five years from now could be too late,'" Mr. Carter said.

The extreme-theme newcomers follow the early success of teenoriented products in the soft-drink and athletic shoe categories.

Pepsi-Cola Co.'s Mountain Dew became the drink of a new generation after it embraced adrenaline athletes, both in its edgy advertising and event sponsorship. Shoemaker Vans, in turn, became the name sponsor of such events as skateboarding and snowboarding.

Lifestyle Appeal

While the pervasive new catchword is rooted in the popularity of alternative sports, marketers are drawn to it because it lends itself to a teen's entire lifestyle.

"Teens are naturally impelled to test limits," said youth marketing expert Julie Halpin of WPP Group's Geppetto Group. "Something extreme pushes the pre-existing boundaries and appeals to that part of a teen who fancies him or herself on the very edge of what the rest of the world considers normal."

With the extreme trend, more conservative brands—some tying in with extreme sports, while others are just leveraging the term—are using the label to give products a rebirth.

Clairol will brighten up its offerings next month with the launch of Xtreme FX hair color. The new line—targeted at 13- to 24-year-olds—comes in shocking shades of Blue Denim, Hot Red, Penetrating Purple and Smoldering Orange.

Even deodorant doesn't have to be a drag. Gillette recently gave its Right Guard brand a face-lift with bold neon packaging, a reformulated citrus scent and a new name: Right Guard Xtreme Sport.

"We got into this based fundamentally on demographic trends," said Bernadette King, Gillette director of global business management for deodorants and antiperspirants.

She cited the rapid growth of the teen population and the soaring participation rate in non-traditional sports as Gillette's impetus to go extreme.

Michael Wood, VP at Teenage Research Unlimited, said marketers such as Gillette are utilizing the term extreme because "it's safe but powerful."

"One of the biggest challenges is to get a message across to teens in a way that's relevant without talking down or trying too hard," he said. "Words like extreme or intense are safe and at the same time very descriptive."

But Mr. Wood warned companies to proceed with caution. "Teen-agers have a built in BS meter where they can tell if a company is trying too hard, or if it's an advertising gimmick."

Influx of X's

There might also be a danger of dilution. Marketers are lopping off the e in extreme in an attempt to emulate teenspeak in huge numbers. The U.S. Patent & Trademark Directory lists 296 filings for brands and products that include the word Xtreme. In this excess of Xs, there are even more popping up on the Internet and lining store shelves, including Xtreme American jeans and Xtreme Power Bars.

Branding experts advise an integrated, teen-oriented marketing approach for products even to be considered credible by their target market.

"If you don't layer your marketing plan to reach the grass-roots, core audience at the same time you reach the masses, your brand is going to get killed," said Fuse Sport's Mr. Carter. "You'll have millions of kids bashing your brand, saying it's not authentic."

In the case of Right Guard, Fuse Sports marketing helped the brand link with music festival Warped Tour and gain a presence on the Warped Tour Web site.

"No kids are going to go to a deodorant site to find out about sports, music and culture," Mr. Carter said.

Gillette anted up $61 million in a Right Guard Xtreme Sport marketing effort that also includes sponsorships of events such as BMX racing and snowboarding.

Teaming With Green

In an attempt to reach a broad teen audience, Right Guard's advertising features over-the-top MTV comedian Tom Green. The ads are running on youth-skewed programming such as "Angel," "Charmed," "Dawson's Creek" and World Wrestling Federation matches.

While marketers are investing millions to feed a teen's need for all things extreme, many experts said that's a risky proposition.

Marketers "think by picking up a word or idea that's relevant they can catch the wave, but this is the worst form of marketing. This could actually damage a brand because it's so me-too," said branding expert Mr. Adamson. "The first [company] out wins, the second one does OK, the third doesn't see a change and for the rest it's wasted money."

Topics for Reading and Writing

1. Why did marketers gravitate so quickly to the "extreme" trend? What was their target audience?

2. Compare Petrecca's article about the creation and maintenance of a trend (with its attendant music, buzzwords, and consumer products) with Malcolm Gladwell's discussion of the same phenomenon. How do the articles differ from each other? What do their respective forums (*Advertising Age,* the trade journal for professionals in the advertising field, and the *New Yorker,* a general interest magazine) have to do with this?

Eugene Marlow
Sophisticated "News" Videos Gain Wide Acceptance

What differentiates the news from advertising? To journalists and news producers, it's the process of creating the news: choosing stories to cover, assigning reporters and photographers and producers to cover the story, doing the reporting, editing the footage, checking the facts, airing the story. To audiences, it's often where and when the images air. If a story airs during the news program, it's news; during commercial breaks, it's advertising. In this article Baruch College professor of journalism and corporate

The use of video public relations vehicles, including video news releases (VNRs), has become widespread in the past five years. While many broadcast journalists claim to resist this type of publicity, there is hardly a TV news or entertainment show that does not air some material supplied by corporations or other sponsoring organizations.

Since the late '80s, VNRs have come under much scrutiny from the media, Congress, public relations practitioners, academics and even the clients who sponsor them. For example, an article in *TV Guide* calling VNRs "fake news" created a furor during the Gulf War of 1992.

communications veteran **Eugene Marlow** *examines the phenomenon of "video news releases," public relations videos intentionally made to look like segments on a local news channel. The companies that produce these videos send them to such news programs hoping that they spur the news producers to do a story on their product or service; sometimes, producers will actually air these VNRs as news themselves, assuming that viewers won't be able to tell the difference between them and the "real" news. Marlow's article raises questions about the authority of the news and about the blurry lines between "soft news" on a local broadcast and outright advertising.*

ID Sponsor

The major objection is that, very often, the VNR's sponsor is not identified in the telecast by a third party. While producers almost invariably identify the sources of supplied materials, including VNRs, broadcasters often do not acknowledge them. Unedited video footage, or "B-roll," as opposed to a fully edited VNR, called "A-roll," is gaining in popularity, because B-roll allows TV stations to edit the material as if it were shot by their own crews. The recipient may or may not use supplied scripts that can be read by the station's own announcer.

While VNR producers and most originators of video publicity adhere to codes of ethics, their practices do not guarantee that the public will know what is and is not a VNR when it plays on television. Meanwhile, quantitative measures by producers clearly show that very large numbers of VNRs are getting air play as news rather than sponsored programming.

Interactive video conferences, satellite links and even broadcast ads are all currently being picked up by TV news directors and programmers. Such value-added innovations have made video news more useful and effective as a public relations tool, according to video producers.

Resistance to VNRs, B-roll and other video programs has dwindled. The reason is simple: TV news and programming directors are often understaffed and lack the budget to cover many newsworthy stories. Companies or organizations that can provide videos about an interesting event, a breakthrough drug, a new product, or a subject of community interest will find a willing audience among broadcasters. This is true even for "soft" features, covering travel, food, fashion, and entertainment personalities, especially if the format allows a TV station to hold the stories for a slow news day.

"The future is now," said Dave Bartlett, who is president of the Radio and Television News Directors Association in Washington, DC. "Everybody gets material from syndicators and public relations firms. I doubt if any television news organization could say that it doesn't use some," he admitted.

Suit the Medium

The debate centers upon whether or not supplied video material is journalistically objective. "News is the VNR's middle name. It won't get on the air if it isn't newsworthy," observed Lew Allison former senior vice president at Hill and Knowlton, New York and now a Pelham, NY-based consultant. In fact, a VNR that's too commercial can be negative, because TV broadcasters won't heed the sponsor's organization and message, Allison said.

"If a company with a good solid reputation puts out a VNR that news editors scorn, that can really be a very bad thing. You've got to have a clear goal in mind and be sure there is a news angle to what you're offering," he advised.

For example, a financial institution might have a very big announcement that makes page one of the business section of the *New York Times*, but it will bomb as a VNR, he said. VNRs must be visually interesting, Allison concluded. "Television requires good strong images, as well as the news angle. If it's not a visual story, a VNR should not be used."

One Tool in the Media Mix

"We look at VNRs as one piece of the whole communications puzzle," reported Elizabeth Parkinson, a producer with Edelman Public Relations Worldwide in Chicago. "Press releases and various printed materials often don't have the same immediacy or visual effect as something that you see on television. So it's a very logical step for companies to put their message into some visual form."

On the other hand, Edelman often counsels clients not to do VNRs because they are not necessarily appropriate, she added. VNRs are most successful for "new product introductions that involve a very visual, unique event," Parkinson said. "It depends on whom the client is trying to reach. If theirs is a consumer message, then broadcast is often a good choice. We're going to have 500 channels soon, which means lots of messages will get lost. If you're trying to target a specific audience, such as physicians, then maybe a VNR isn't the way to go."

VNRs are not just for big companies, Parkinson added. "The cost of a VNR isn't expensive compared to advertising. Smaller companies, if they are interested in publicity component compared to the advertising component, probably get a much bigger bang for their buck if they do a VNR, as compared to advertising."

VNRs also work well in a crisis, when timely response to reach a large audience is important. In fact, two of the most important and widely seen video releases of the '90s involved corporations that were protecting their reputations and product positions.

For example, a VNR telling the Star-Kist "dolphin-safe" tuna story won a 1991 PRSA Silver Anvil award for H.J. Heinz Co. and Edelman. Designed to announce Heinz's new fishing policy, the campaign featured a VNR that reached 82 million viewers. Heinz and its Star-Kist Seafoods subsidiary had been under pressure from environmental groups, Congress and regulatory agencies because dolphins were killed when tuna were caught in certain types of nets.

Way to React Quickly

"Here was a message that had to go out immediately," recalled Parkinson. Edelman's Chicago, Washington, DC and Los Angeles offices were all involved in preparing press information on the "dolphin-safe" policy just before Earth Day 1990. "We were able to supply footage that a lot of stations didn't have the manpower to get," she said. "We interviewed spokespeople to whom the networks might not have had access."

More recently, video releases showing "stock" footage of Pepsi-Cola Co.'s bottling process were used very successfully to combat a product-tampering hoax. Two of the four VNRs produced by Robert Change Productions, New

York for Pepsi set new viewership records. One with B-roll of Pepsi bottling procedures was seen by a record 182 million viewers, according to Medialink, its distributor. A subsequent video release, showing surveillance camera footage of a suspect allegedly tampering with a can of Pepsi in Colorado, was viewed by at least 95 million, Medialink reported. The videos won Pepsi and Robert Change Productions a 1994 PRSA Bronze Anvil award. In addition, their entire response to the "Great Pepsi Hoax" earned them a 1994 Silver Anvil award for crisis communications not involving accidents or natural disasters.

B-Roll Gains Ground

The public relations team at Pepsi tends to prefer B-roll to a tightly produced, shorter VNR according to Rebecca "Betsy" Madeira, vice president, public affairs at the Purchase, NY-based company. Pepsi successfully used a mass release B-roll this past spring to introduce "freshness dating" on Diet Pepsi soft drinks.

Because B-roll allows TV news organizations to do their own editing, it is increasing in popularity, agreed Ron Sylvester, director of production at Edelman, New York. Often, the unedited B-roll, with full identification of the speakers and contents, is the only type of video sent to stations or cable networks, he said. "I usually include corporate and brand logos on B-rolls because stations collect them," added Sylvester. "News directors often use them in 'over the shoulder' windows while the anchor or reporter is telling the story." The narration or script for a VNR must also be non-commercial, he adds. "It can't be anything that you wouldn't hear an anchor or a reporter say on a daily basis."

"VNRs have a time and a place," added Pepsi's Maderia. "It's the responsibility of anyone charged with communication for a company, service or product to have some good, clear, basic materials that explain how the business works and what the product is," she said. You've got to be able to explain how things work visually, as well as have very detailed press kits with backgrounders and sheets and some of the more traditional tools," Madeira explained.

Help Position a Company

"3M uses VNRs to maintain an image and to position 3M as the most innovative corporation in the world," said Jim Schwinn, manager, broadcast media relations at 3M, based in St. Paul, MN. "Our thrust now is to shift focus to being more selective. We're targeting public relations efforts market by market," he said. The company's VNRs might show a product, a new technology, a manufacturing process, or people important to the real story, he explained.

"Our VNRs have included a third-grade class that sent us some suggestions for redesigning one of our overhead projectors," Schwinn said. "We also produced a VNR on the company's flood relief efforts in '93. We sent truckloads of relief materials to the Salvation Army and the American Red Cross distribution centers in St. Louis during the aftermath of the floods.

"I think you need to know what is acceptable in VNRs and what will sell," Schwin added. "Most distribution companies will give you a hand, but it's good to have somebody on staff who has been in television journalism and knows what makes a good news story in terms of visuals, information and flow. There are probably more instances where we would not use a VNR than there are when we would," Schwinn added. "A VNR is simply one mechanism for telling an otherwise good story."

VNRs grew out of the entertainment business, which is still an important outlet for certain kinds of material, observed Pepsi's Madeira. "B-roll VNRs are very popular when we are working on entertainment personality profiles," she explained. Such videos "give reporters a chance to go behind the scenes with a celebrity that they might not have access to, either because of time or location," she said. "We try to give the reporter many different angles, whether it's sports or entertainment or music or simply what one of the big names in Hollywood is doing in their off time.

"Reporters really like to see a celebrity up close and personal. B-roll, especially when it includes outtakes, flubs, or jokes off camera, is a lot more fun," Madeira added.

Started as Show Biz

Universal Studios in Florida uses VNRs for all major events and usually for the opening of new attractions and additions to the park, reported Jim Hampton, manager, publicity and public relations. For example, Universal recently hosted "Flintstones Weekend" in conjunction with the launch of Universal Pictures' new movie, *The Flintstones.* Actors John Goodman, Rick Moranis and Halle Berry, along with director Tom McLaughlin, talked with the entertainment press about the movie. They appeared at Universal Studios' new exhibition of sets from the movie.

"A VNR showing the film stars in our new exhibit was uplinked via satellite around the country," Hampton reported. Music videos are another source of promotion for the studios, he said. Universal often produces VNRs about music videos being made in the theme park and thereby gets low-key publicity.

"We're trying to give reporters something they can actually use on the news or on one of their talk or entertainment programs," summarized Hampton. We're getting the message across that something interesting and inviting is happening here, and we're also giving the stations something they can use that's entertaining. As long as we serve both those purposes, then it's a win-win situation."

In May, On the Scene Productions secured an unprecedented 3,000 air-dates for a video showing highlights of a concert tour and new album released by the rock group The Rolling Stones. The VNR reached a total of 63 million U.S. viewers, according to Nielsen tracking data.

Beyond Entertainment

Greg Albrecht, publicity manager, Walt Disney World, Lake Buena Vista, FL, was in TV news for 15 years. "From the side, I viewed VNRs in a very critical manner," Albrecht admitted. "First of all, I hated the term VNRs. For most news directors, this sends up a red flag. I felt VNRs were giant commercial endorsements for products and had very little to offer my news department. I was very suspicious of them." WDW has a 30-person broadcast division with full production facilities and uplink capabilities.

Disney is producing "news programming" that goes a step beyond VNRs, according to Albrecht. In a 26-piece series called *The 60-Second Tennis Tip*, tennis pros at Disney resorts give playing tips. The series, with very low-key Disney ID, is sent out to stations free of charge and is running in 50 markets across the nation, Albrecht said. The company is also producing training series of this type on golf and cooking.

In addition, Disney is packaging a series of expert talks about animals from Discovery Island Zoological Park at WDW. These 90-second segments, aimed at children, are being aired weekly in 70 markets across the United States. Stations receive exclusive rights in a market to *Animal Talk*, which focuses on endangered species and natural habitats. Customized weather reports are also available live from the nations represented in EPCOT center.

Albrecht emphasized the need for VNR producers to stay in touch with TV broadcasters. "We bring in news directors regularly to talk to us about what kind of material they would like. Often they come down to generate their own stories using our material. It may not have a Disney subtitle, but they can use [our park] as a backdrop, or they can use our experts on morning talk shows, for instance," he said.

If practitioners continue to provide valuable information in video format, the VNR and its cousins have a bright future, sources said.

"With the proliferation of cable and exploding visual media, there will be lots of opportunity to talk with customers through visual means," said Pepsi's Madeira. "Whether VNRs are the way to do it has a lot to do with the intelligence and good sense of the producers and their clients. VNRs could easily be banned from newsrooms if they become infomercials and are such heavily biased pieces that they serve no purpose other than as advertising."

VNRs are emerging as "a whole new concept of marketing," suggested 3M's Schwinn. "Commercial interests pitching corporations to put their story on the air in a video magazine format. Rather than buying air time, a sponsor will pay someone to produce a piece on the company for a specific show aimed at a specific audience."

"There's always going to be a demand for video material," stated WDW's Albrecht. "But the quality has to improve. The viewers out there are very sophisticated. They're very savvy."

Topics for Reading and Writing

1. Companies such as Disney spend vast amounts of time and effort and money in efforts at branding, or making sure the Disney name and logo is linked with emotional memories in consumers. If this is true, why does Disney downplay its brand identification in its own VNRs, as Marlow points out?

2. What is the ideal role of local television news? What information do you watch local news to obtain?

Skeptical media critics and leftists were immediately suspicious of the Pentagon's plans to "embed" reporters in combat units during the conflict in Iraq in 2003. After all, these critics charged, what reporter could be objective about the soldiers who were protecting that reporter's life? In this article from the liberal journal The American Prospect, though, Columbia University professor and corporate media opponent **Todd Gitlin** argues that the reporters themselves did "reasonably well" in their pursuit of the story. It's not the reporters Gitlin faults for the slant of the news coverage: it's the "network headquarters."

Todd Gitlin
Embed or in Bed?

In a standard supplement to their regular war package, mainstream media now occasionally feature—what else?—mainstream media criticism. This time around, the two prime subjects were (1) embedded reporters and (2) bombastic cable networks. Easier targets have never presented themselves. The cheerleaders of FOX News are surefire objects of scorn for networks and newspapers aiming to occupy the center. No complaint here: FOX's high-volume bluster and low-doubt punditry deserve all the criticism they get. FOX and MSNBC marinated their reportage in bathetic music and drum tattoos, binding their audience to the war effort and stifling thought.

As for the embeds, what a setup for easy cohabitation gags. Reporters in bed with the people they cover surely couldn't be intrepid independents. Who wouldn't favor the people who carry you around in their tanks? Who wouldn't hesitate to offend them? But in truth, many of these accusations were misplaced. Embedded reporters did reasonably well under what were surely confining circumstances. If most of the reporting was travelogue—desert expanses, puffs of smoke and occasional bang-bang, culminating in moments of toppled Saddam Hussein statuary—this was no fault of the embeds. They saw what they saw and couldn't see what they couldn't see. Nor was this the first time American reporters were life-and-death dependent on their subjects: In Vietnam it was customary for reporters to hitch rides in military helicopters; they knew who was watching their backs.

The prime deficiencies in the immense war reportage lay elsewhere, deep in the network headquarters where imagination was paralyzed, Washington deference was normal, and war coverage was (to paraphrase the title of Chris Hedges' recent book) a force that kept us mesmerized. Toward that end, the logoed, soundtracked war was sanitized. No doubt some viewers wanted it just that way. They wanted to "ooh" and "ah" at the glory of "shock and awe." The dirty little secret of much war "news" is that much of the audience wants to entrance itself into emotional surrender, and news officials want to elicit precisely that surrender. The spectacle is what both parties bargain for—an interest they share with the White House. Not surprisingly, the networks took to boasting of their technology, as when Charles Gibson, raving about ABC's "Saving Private Jessica" footage on *Good Morning America,* "ooh'd" and "ah'd" about "that nightscope video that is of course so captivating to watch." Note: He didn't tout the video because it was so informative or so significant but because it was so captivating. The secret was no secret. The point of the coverage was to win our attention, to hook us, to keep us connected to the war's emotional séance.

As many observers have noted (though not so many on American TV), corpses and human calamities were conspicuous by their absence—unless you were watching al-Jazeera, which much of the world was doing. In Europe, 10 days into the war, I saw in a single segment of Sky News more grotesque imagery—a wounded Iraqi child had lost his legs in a not-so-smart bomb blast—than in weeks of coverage by American networks. The networks surely had trouble counting casualties, but this should not have prevented them from saying and showing what they knew and explaining why they didn't know more. Much of the public is grown up and can handle the revelation that the networks are limited.

High among television's defaults was the endless recycling of euphemism. The small screen is over-renowned for indelible pictures—forgettable "wallpaper" takes up far more time—but at least as important is the way all media bend language. Even in the age of satellite telephones and uplinks, words come first. The power of the media is, crucially, the power to name. was the civil-rights movement the "freedom struggle" or the product of "outside agitators"? A name pulls a train of implications. A euphemism emits a haze of obfuscation.

Consider the terminology with which the Iraq War's heroes were designated (in print as well as electronically): "the coalition." The term radiated a certain grandeur. Trimmed back from its predecessor, the "Coalition of the Willing," it emitted a thumping sound: "the coalition," as if there could only be one. Surely "the coalition" sounded more prepossessing than "the United States, the United Kingdom, 2,000 Australians and various eastern European handfuls." Incessant use of the term "coalition," with "coalition forces" commanding "coalition-controlled territory," solidified and magnified the sense that the United States and its (few) allies were a multinational force of sweeping proportions. The term itself seemed instantly to refute the oft-heard charge that George W. Bush took the United States to war almost alone.

Refutation by vocabulary likely fooled no one outside the United States of America. But it did make the war a warmer, fuzzier affair for us, obscuring as it did the sorry history that left the United States, United Kingdom and a few friends defying the broad coalition of the unwilling. To say "the coalition" was to erase the diplomatic debacle wherein the Bush and Tony Blair governments objectly failed to recruit support for a war that most members of the United Nations Security Council, and most people in almost all countries, thought premature, unnecessary, misguided and/or downright wrong. So each repetition of "the coalition" amounted to an act of enlistment. Journalists who relayed the term in effect embraced the White House definition not only of the present war but its history. George Orwell, thou shouldst be living in this hour!

Reality, anyone? We heard so much about "the coalition" for two reasons. First, the U.S. government used the term routinely and incessantly—its idea of staying "on message" is to jump up and down in the same place until reporters weary. But second, the news anchors, correspondents and commentators echoed the euphemism. It was understandable that White House Press Secretary Ari Fleischer would not be totting up the population of the countries that opposed the war. But during their scads of on-air hours to fill, media commentators did not comment. They might have but didn't—out of fear, trembling or plain inertia. Indeed, when war burst forth on screen, the political and historical commentators, rare in the first place, were sent home. Thus it was in the Gulf War, thus it was again.

All the lavish sets, all the phalanxes of military commentators pointing their pointers and strolling over their floor maps were of no avail in reporting the war's political meanings (which will be, in the end, decisive to the nation's security). Just what was going on in Turkish politics? What did it signify that the largest demonstrations in Europe took place in countries that supported the war (Spain, Italy, Britain)? How was the war playing in Iran, Pakistan, India, Indonesia, China? How was it affecting the fight against terrorism? What were foreign police agencies up to? American TV displayed little interest in such reverberations. Foreign bureaus were emptied of correspondents, who were, of course, thin on the ground in the first place.

Also obscured was much of the war's domestic fallout. While embedded reporters paid tribute to American soldiers, House Republicans were voting to trim veterans' benefits, including free medical treatment and rehabilitation. Hell-bent on tax cuts, disproportionately for the rich, they would spend not a new nickel to secure U.S. ports against terrorist attacks. The networks did not illuminate such shocking and awesome developments. Occasional items of this sort popped up in staccato anchorman form and crawled across the screen beneath swatches of travelogue. That was that. Been near there, sort of done that and now for some guesswork about whether Saddam Hussein is alive.

Nor, in the course of hundreds of television hours from Qatar, Kuwait and Iraq, was much time spared to reexamine the case for the war. Been around there, kind of done that. So the question of weapons of mass destruction vanished as if in a sandstorm. Once Iraqi freedom was slipped back to the top of Bush's agenda, it might have looked unseemly to revisit the case the president had made for war, which, of course, rested on factual claims about the inadequacy of UN inspections. Perhaps the most shocking and awesome revelation during the war was the report that Bush had rested part of his case on a transparent fraud. In his State of the Union address, Bush, citing British intelligence, had claimed that Saddam Hussein "recently sought significant quantities of uranium from Africa." Interestingly, by the time Secretary of State Powell delivered his much-touted case to the UN Security Council, the African uranium claim had vanished. It didn't return—and the media didn't notice. Meanwhile, the International Atomic Energy Agency (IAEA) declared that the documents the United States and United Kingdom had brandished to make Bush's case were forgeries full of transparent errors. *The New Yorker*'s Seymour Hersh wrote that these fraudulent documents passed through CIA hands on their way to the IAEA.

Forgery. Intelligence agencies. Vanishing uranium deals. All this might have made for excellent television—but television largely absented itself. Don't blame the reporters. Don't even blame Ari Fleischer. The news organizations know how to tell such stories when they are of a mind to do so. Can't you just see the full-screen memos, the highlighted lines, the evidence of fakery? Can't you just hear the "aha"? Intelligence failures, disinformation, whatever this story turns out to be—the whole sordid thing would electrify. But the networks have decided that this sort of investigation is not their business. The sound emanating from network headquarters is the sound of suits walking on eggshells.

Thus does television's super equipment spew the pepper spray of war. History is toast.

Topics for Reading and Writing

1. Gitlin does not attempt to appear objective in his claim that the U.S. media's coverage of the 2003 conflict in Iraq favored the Bush administration's view of things. But even in his unabashed partisanship is he guilty of any logical fallacies? Does he "stack the deck" against his adversaries, either by slanted use of evidence or use of language? How? To what degree is it ethical to use inflated rhetoric and loaded language in making an argument, and when does it step over the line?

2. In Gitlin's opinion, why did media coverage of the war favor the Bush administration's view of the world? Is there a conspiracy among the corporations that cover the news to take the side of republicans—who, after all, defend the interests of large corporations? Or is this bias a product of fear? Laziness? Parsimony? Or is Gitlin just wrong about media bias?

3. Gitlin argues that the media coverage of the war created an alternate reality in which a "coalition" fought for freedom. He contrasts this reality to the coverage of the war airing on British television or on the Arab satellite network al-Jazeera. Do the other networks offer the real story? Or are these all just alternate realities, alternate versions of the truth competing for viewers? What does this mean for people's ability to understand and act in the real world?

In this article from the Christian Science Monitor, *William Klein (a veteran political consultant and writer) examines the phenomenon of "Astroturf" political campaigns. Taking their name from the artificial grass product used in indoor sports stadiums, "Astroturf" campaigns are centrally coordinated attempts by sophisticated, well-funded political groups to imitate the "grass-roots" (hence the name) movements that genuinely arise from ordinary people's concerns.*

Like Malcolm Gladwell, Klein maintains a website— www.headlineupdate.com—for his writings, most of which promise to "take you behind the headlines."

William S. Klein
Faking the Voice of the People

WASHINGTON—What happens when the voice of the people gets as fake as a television laugh track?

That's what's happening to the "letters to the editor" column in scores of newspapers today, thanks to a tactic known as "Astro Turf." Borrowing a trick from lobbyists, interest groups are using phony grass roots letter writing campaigns to puff up their support.

This week, the Republican National Committee (RNC) was caught distributing a form letter praising President Bush that ended up printed, often verbatim, in nearly 75 papers, according to "Fight Back Against Killer Astroturf," one of the many Internet "blogs" tracking this story.

Earlier, newspapers in Wisconsin received a number of letters supporting abortion rights that originated on a Planned Parenthood website.

The GOP letter, which begins, "When it comes to the economy, President Bush is demonstrating genuine leadership," was purported to be the genuine feelings of writers from Rutland, Vt., to Palo Alto, Calif. The truth, as Internet sleuths soon discovered, was that the text was posted on a RNC website that even included links to local news outlets.

The website (www.gopteamleader.com), is described as "an online toolbox for Republican activists." Once a visitor registers, they'll receive Republican e-mail updates and even the exciting opportunity "to collect 'GOPoints' by completing Action Items [e.g.: letters to the editor] and redeem them for collateral of your choice, ranging from coolers to mouse pads."

Well, that's OK then; if there's a tote bag in it, abusing news ethics isn't so bad.

But is it really so out of bounds to plant letters to the editor? After all, you can find the hidden hand of professionals just about anywhere in the newspaper. PR firms "place" their clients' messages in opinion pages and advice columns. Press releases get printed as news. Mass-produced letters flood Capitol Hill every day.

But the letters column is supposed to be a breath of fresh air, an open and genuine discussion that reflects the community's views.

Local newspapers, unlike the World Wide Web, link people together over narrow boundaries. Readers share their lives by writing letters about the home team, the new school, or the bears that are getting in peoples' garbage. They also tell the newspaper how it is doing in fulfilling one of the press' most vital functions—maintaining public trust.

If the letters space is put up for sale, that bond and sense of community is weakened.

Newspapers may or may not be going the way of the dinosaur, but in the meantime they still provide the lively forum for democratic expression Americans have always enjoyed. Since the days of Tom Paine, we have looked to the printing press to harness the power of an informed citizenry.

The danger is when powerful interests overwhelm ordinary citizens' voices. Politicians scheme over two kinds of publicity—paid advertising and "free media," or news coverage. Operatives see the letters to the editor column as one more way to influence the news cycle.

This may seem like good political strategy, but it's bad for democracy.

One of the reasons Americans are turned off by politics is because of the inherent cynicism they see in the political debate. Every position seems like a commodity, espoused not out of belief but for tactical advantage. It's bad enough when politicians do it.

We shouldn't let our views, and the places we express them, be so cravenly manipulated. Keep off the Astro Turf, and let the sun shine in!

Topics for Reading and Writing

1. Klein's article exhibits many of the typical rhetorical moves of the op-ed (opinion-editorial) page column. How does Klein's exposure of these "Astroturf" campaigns differ in terms of its rhetorical strategy from other pieces of writing (such as Laura Petrecca's article from *Advertising Age* or Patrick Goldstein's column from the *Los Angeles Times*) that also expose or profile behind-the-scenes creations of reality?

2. If "cool" is concocted in a marketing boardroom, if letters to the editor aren't actually from local people, if the news is using VNRs instead of reporting, and if even the government is resorting to publicity stunts in the course of fighting a war, how can ordinary citizens avoid just giving up and assuming that nothing's real or authentic?

3. What are the ethical ramifications of creating or altering the "real" for public consumption?

In one of the most dramatic human interest stories of the Iraq conflict, U.S. commandos liberated a hospital in which Private Jessica Lynch was being held after a fierce shoot-out with Iraqi forces. Ambushed near Nasiriya, Lynch's unit was decimated and Lynch herself was wounded. A week later, American soldiers stormed that hospital (a reputed stronghold of pro-Saddam Fedayeen forces) and rescued Lynch, filming the raid on a night vision camera. The story made for fantastic TV—a brave female soldier, a dramatic raid, unforgettable green-tinged footage—and after Lynch returned to the United States the major networks fell over themselves trying to land the "exclusive" interview with the brave soldier. (Demonstrating the advantages of conglomeration, Viacom eventually won the interview for its CBS news properties by also offering her a CBS TV movie, a chance to host MTV's TRL Live, a concert with TRL artists in her West Virginia hometown, and a book contract with Simon & Schuster.)

But the problem with the story is that questions about its truthfulness soon arose. In a story that immediately raised

John Kampfner
The Truth About Jessica

Jessica Lynch became an icon of the war. An all-American heroine, the story of her capture by the Iraqis and her rescue by US special forces became one of the great patriotic moments of the conflict. It couldn't have happened at a more crucial moment, when the talk was of coalition forces bogged down, of a victory too slow in coming.

Her rescue will go down as one of the most stunning pieces of news management yet conceived. It provides a remarkable insight into the real influence of Hollywood producers on the Pentagon's media managers, and has produced a template from which America hopes to present its future wars.

But the American media tactics, culminating in the Lynch episode, infuriated the British, who were supposed to be working alongside them in Doha, Qatar. This Sunday, the BBC's *Correspondent* programme reveals the inside story of the rescue that may not have been as heroic as portrayed, and of divisions at the heart of the allies' media operation.

"In reality, we had two different styles of news media management," says Group Captain Al Lockwood, the British army spokesman at central command. "I feel fortunate to have been part of the UK one."

In the early hours of April 2, correspondents in Doha were summoned from their beds to Centcom, the military and media nerve centre for the war. Jim Wilkinson, the White House's top figure there, had stayed up all night. "We had a situation where there was a lot of hot news," he recalls. "The president had been briefed, as had the secretary of defense."

loud objections from the Pentagon, **John Kampfner** *(political editor of the* New Statesman, *a British leftist journal) wrote that the Lynch rescue had been little more than a publicity stunt, and that the dramatic, frightening narrative provided by the Army was at best misleading and at worst simply fictional. Lynch herself, recovering in an American hospital, had amnesia and so could not confirm if the Army's version of events was true.*

The journalists rushed in, thinking Sadaam had been captured. The story they were told instead has entered American folklore. Private Lynch, a 19-year-old clerk from Palestine, West Virginia, was a member of the US Army's 507th Ordnance Maintenance Company that took a wrong turning near Nassiriya and was ambushed. Nine of her US comrades were killed. Iraqi soldiers took Lynch to the local hospital, which was swarming with fedayeen, where she was held for eight days. That much is uncontested.

Releasing its five-minute film to the networks, the Pentagon claimed that Lynch had stab and bullet wounds, and that she had been slapped about on her hospital bed and interrogated. It was only thanks to a courageous Iraqi lawyer, Mohammed Odeh al-Rehaief, that she was saved. According to the Pentagon, Al-Rehaief risked his life to alert the Americans that Lynch was being held.

Just after midnight, Army Rangers and Navy Seals stormed the Nassiriya hospital. Their "daring" assault on enemy territory was captured by the military's night-vision camera. They were said to have come under fire, but they made it to Lynch and whisked her away by helicopter. That was the message beamed back to viewers within hours of the rescue.

Al-Rehaief was granted asylum barely two weeks after arriving in the US. He is now the toast of Washington, with a fat $500,000 (£309,000) book deal. Rescue in Nassiriya will be published in October. As for Lynch, her status as cult hero is stronger than ever. Internet auction sites have listed at least 10 Jessica Lynch items, ranging from an oil painting with an opening bid of $200 to a $5 "America Loves Jessica Lynch" fridge magnet. Trouble is that doctors now say she has no recollection of the whole episode and probably never will. Her memory loss means that "researchers" have been called in to fill in the gaps.

One story, two versions. The doctors in Nassiriya say they provided the best treatment they could for Lynch in the midst of war. She was assigned the only specialist bed in the hospital, and one of only two nurses on the floor. "I was like a mother to her and she was like a daughter," says Khalida Shinah.

"We gave her three bottles of blood, two of them from the medical staff because there was no blood at this time," said Dr Harith al-Houssona, who looked after her throughout her ordeal. "I examined her, I saw she had a broken arm, a broken thigh and dislocated ankle. Then I did another examination. There was no [sign of] shooting, no bullet inside her body, no stab wound— only RTA, road traffic accident," he recalled. "They want to distort the picture. I don't know why they think there is some benefit in saying she has a bullet injury."

The doctors told us that the day before the special forces swooped on the hospital the Iraqi military had fled. Hassam Hamoud, a waiter at a local restaurant, said he saw the American advance party land in the town. He said the team's Arabic interpreter asked him where the hospital was. "He asked, 'Are there any Fadayeen over there?' and I said, 'No.' " All the same, the next day, "America's finest warriors" descended on the building.

"We heard the noise of the helicopters," says Dr. Anmar Uday. He says that they must have known there would be no resistance. "We were surprised. Why do this? There was no military, there were no soldiers in the hospital."

"It was like a Hollywood film. They cried, 'Go, go, go', with guns and blanks and the sound of explosions. They made a show—an action movie like Sylvester Stallone or Jackie Chan, with jumping and shouting, breaking down doors." All the time with the camera rolling. The Americans took no chances, restraining doctors and a patient who was handcuffed to a bed frame.

There was one more twist. Two days before the snatch squad arrived, Al-Houssona had arranged to deliver Jessica to the Americans in an ambulance. "I told her I will try and help you escape to the American Army but I will do this very secretly because I could lose my life." He put her in an ambulance and instructed the driver to go to the American checkpoint. When he was approaching it, the Americans opened fire. They fled just in time back to the hospital. The Americans had almost killed their prize catch.

A military cameraman had shot footage of the rescue. It was a race against time for the video to be edited. The video presentation was ready a few hours after the first brief announcement. When it was shown, General Vincent Brooks, the US spokesman in Doha, declared: "Some brave souls put their lives on the line to make this happen, loyal to a creed that they know that they'll never leave a fallen comrade."

None of the details that the doctors provided *Correspondent* with made it to the video or to any subsequent explanations or clarifications by US authorities. I asked the Pentagon spokesman in Washington, Bryan Whitman, to release the full tape of the rescue, rather than its edited version, to clear up any discrepancies. He declined. Whitman would not talk about what kind of Iraqi resistance the American forces faced. Nor would he comment on the injuries Lynch actually sustained. "I understand there is some conflicting information out there and in due time the full story will be told, I'm sure," he told me.

That American approach—to skim over the details—focusing instead on the broad message, led to a tension behind the scenes with the British. Downing Street's man in Doha, Simon Wren, was furious that on the first few days of the war the Americans refused to give any information at Centcom. The British were put in the difficult position of having to fill in the gaps, off the record.

Towards the end of the conflict, Wren wrote a confidential five-page letter to Alastair Campbell complaining that the American briefers weren't up to the job. He described the Lynch presentation as embarrassing.

Wren yesterday described the Lynch incident as "hugely overblown" and symptomatic of a bigger problem. "The Americans never got out there and explained what was going on in the war," he said. "All they needed to be was open and honest. They were too vague, too scared of engaging with the media." He said US journalists "did not put them under pressure."

Wren, who had been seconded to the Ministry of Defence, said he tried on several occasions to persuade Wilkinson and Brooks to change tack. In London, Campbell did the same with the White House, to no avail. "The American media didn't put them under pressure so they were allowed to get away with it," Wren said. "They didn't feel they needed to change."

He acknowledged that the events surrounding the Lynch "rescue" had become a matter of "conjecture". But he added: "Either way, it was not the main news of the day. This was just one soldier, this was an add-on: human interest stuff. It completely overshadowed other events, things that were actually going on on the battlefield. It overshadowed the fact that the Americans found the bodies of her colleagues. What we wanted to give out was real-time news."

Lockwood told *Correspondent:* "Having lost the first skirmish, they (the Americans) had pretty much lost the war when it came to media support. Albeit things had got better and everything came to a conclusion quite rapidly, but to my feelings they lost their initial part of the campaign and never got on the front foot again," Lockwood said. "The media adviser we had here [Wren] was an expert in his field. His counterpart on the US side [Wilkinson] was evasive and was not around as much as he should have been when it came to talking to the media."

The American strategy was to concentrate on the visuals and to get a broad message out. Details—where helpful—followed behind. The key was to ensure the right television footage. The embedded reporters could do some of that. On other missions, the military used their own cameras, editing the film themselves and presenting it to broadcasters as ready-to-go packages. The Pentagon had been influenced by Hollywood producers of reality TV and action movies, notably Black Hawk Down.

Back in 2001, the man behind *Black Hawk Down,* Jerry Bruckheimer, had visited the Pentagon to pitch the idea. Bruckheimer and fellow producer Bertram van Munster, who masterminded the reality show *Cops,* suggested *Profiles from the Front Line,* a primetime television series following US forces in Afghanistan. They were after human stories told through the eyes of the soldiers. Van Munster's aim was to get close and personal. He said: "You can only get accepted by these people through chemistry. You have to have a bond with somebody. Only then will they let you in. What these guys are doing out there, these men and women, is just extraordinary. If you're a cheerleader of our point of view—that we deserve peace and that we deal with human dignity—then these guys are really going out on a limb and risking their own lives."

It was perfect reality TV, made with the active cooperation of Donald Rumsfeld and aired just before the Iraqi war. The Pentagon liked what it saw. "What *Profiles* does is given another in depth look at what forces are doing from the ground," says Whitman. "It provides a very human look at challenges that are presented when you are dealing in these very difficult situations." That approached was taken on and developed on the field of battle in Iraq.

The Pentagon has none of the British misgivings about its media operation. It is convinced that what worked with Jessica Lynch and with other episodes of this war will work even better in the future.

Topics for Reading and Writing

1. Kampfner argues that the Pentagon "had been influenced by" the productions of Jerry Bruckheimer in its project for press coverage in Iraq. Is this a fair statement? What is Kampfner implying here that he doesn't say explicitly?

2. If Kampfner's story is true—and the Pentagon strenuously denies it—how does this change your view of the military? Of press coverage of the military?

Susan Faludi's book Backlash *(1991) created an immediate sensation upon its release. Arguing that well-organized conservative groups had systematically and successfully fed misinformation about the failures of the feminist movement to the media,* Backlash *sought to dispel many of these false reports about how feminism had failed women. Although later writers have faulted Faludi's research,* Backlash *is a model of a careful rhetorical analysis, grounded in facts and including important conclusions. Faludi has much to offer us: she describes the hidden workings of the creation of lifestyle features on television and in magazine journalism, and she describes the ways interest groups attempt to influence the press. Perhaps most importantly, she explodes many fictions that have grown up around popular understanding of feminist history (her debunking of the myth of the bra-burning feminist is both fascinating and quite telling).*

Faludi, a former Wall Street Journal *reporter, is also the author of* Stiffed: The Betrayal of the American Man *(2000).*

Susan Faludi
Introduction from *Backlash*

To be a woman in America at the close of the 20th century— what good fortune. That's what we keep hearing, anyway. The barricades have fallen, politicians assure us. Women have "made it," Madison Avenue cheers. Women's fight for equality has "largely been won," *Time* magazine announces. Enroll at any university, join any law firm, apply for credit at any bank. Women have so many opportunities now, corporate leaders say, that we don't really need equal opportunity policies. Women are so equal now, lawmakers say, that we no longer need an Equal Rights Amendment. Women have "so much," former President Ronald Reagan says, that the White House no longer needs to appoint them to higher office. Even American Express ads are saluting a woman's freedom to charge it. At last, women have received their full citizenship papers.

And yet . . .

Behind this celebration of the American woman's victory, behind the news, cheerfully and endlessly repeated, that the struggle for women's rights is won, another message flashes. You may be free and equal now, it says to women, but you have never been more miserable.

This bulletin of despair is posted everywhere—at the newsstand, on the TV set, at the movies, in advertisements and doctors' offices and academic journals. Professional women are suffering "burnout" and succumbing to an "infertility epidemic." Single women are grieving from a "man shortage." The *New York Times* reports: Childless women are "depressed and confused" and their ranks are swelling. *Newsweek* says: Unwed women are "hysterical" and crumbling under a "profound crisis of confidence." The health advice manuals inform: High-powered career women are stricken with unprecedented outbreaks of "stress-induced disorders," hair loss, bad nerves, alcoholism, and even heart attacks. The psychology books advise: Independent women's loneliness represents "a major mental health problem today." Even founding feminist Betty Friedan has been spreading the word: she warns that women now suffer from a new identity crisis and "new 'problems that have no name.'"

How can American women be in so much trouble at the same time that they are supposed to be so blessed? If the status of women has never been higher, why is their emotional state so low? If women got what they asked for, what could possibly be the matter now?

The prevailing wisdom of the past decade has supported one, and only one, answer to this riddle: it must be all that equality that's causing all that pain. Women are unhappy precisely *because* they are free. Women are enslaved by their own liberation. They have grabbed at the gold ring of independence, only to miss the one ring that really matters. They have gained control of their fertility, only to destroy it. They have pursued their own professional dreams—and lost out on the greatest female adventure. The women's movement, as we are told time and again, has proved women's own worst enemy.

"In dispensing its spoils, women's liberation has given my generation high incomes, our own cigarette, the option of single parenthood, rape crisis centers, personal lines of credit, free love, and female gynecologists," Mona Charen, a young law student, writes in the *National Review,* in an article titled "The Feminist Mistake." "In return it has effectively robbed us of one thing upon which the happiness of most women rests—men." The *National Review* is a conservative publication, but such charges against the women's movement are not confined to its pages. "Our generation was the human sacrifice" to the women's movement, *Los Angeles Times* feature writer Elizabeth Mehren contends in a *Time* cover story. Baby-boom women like her, she says, have been duped by feminism: "We believed the rhetoric." In *Newsweek,* writer Kay Ebeling dubs feminism "the Great Experiment That Failed" and asserts "women in my generation, its perpetrators, are the casualties." Even the beauty magazines are saying it: *Harper's Bazaar* accuses the women's movement of having "lost us [women] ground instead of gaining it."

In the last decade, publications from the *New York Times* to *Vanity Fair* to the *Nation* have issued a steady stream of indictments against the women's movement, with such headlines as WHEN FEMINISM FAILED or THE AWFUL TRUTH ABOUT WOMEN'S LIB. They hold the campaign for women's equality responsible for nearly every woe besetting women, from mental depression to meager savings accounts, from teenage suicides to eating disorders to bad complexions. The "Today" show says women's liberation is to blame for bag ladies. A guest columnist in the *Baltimore Sun* even proposes that feminists produced the rise in slasher movies. By making the "violence" of abortion more acceptable, the author reasons, women's rights activists made it all right to show graphic murders on screen.

At the same time, other outlets of popular culture have been forging the same connection: in Hollywood films, of which *Fatal Attraction* is only the most famous, emancipated women with condominiums of their own slink wild-eyed between bare walls, paying for their liberty with an empty bed, a barren womb. "My biological clock is ticking so loud it keeps me awake at night," Sally Field cries in the film *Surrender,* as, in an all too common transformation in the cinema of the '80s, an actress who once played scrappy working heroines is now showcased groveling for a groom. In prime-time television shows, from "thirtysomething" to "Family Man," single, professional, and feminist women are humiliated, turned into harpies, or hit by nervous breakdowns; the wise ones recant their independent ways by the closing sequence. In popular novels, from

Gail Parent's *A Sign of the Eighties* to Stephen King's *Misery,* unwed women shrink to sniveling spinsters or inflate to fire-breathing she-devils; renouncing all aspirations but marriage, they beg for wedding bands from strangers or swing sledgehammers at reluctant bachelors.

Popular psychology manuals peddle the same diagnosis for contemporary female distress. "Feminism, having promised her a stronger sense of her own identity, has given her little more than an identity *crisis,*" the best-selling advice manual *Being a Woman* asserts. The authors of the era's self-help classic *Smart Women/Foolish Choices* proclaim that women's distress was "an unfortunate consequence of feminism," because "it created a myth among women that the apex of self-realization could be achieved only through autonomy, independence, and career."

In the Reagan and Bush years, government officials have needed no prompting to endorse this thesis. Reagan spokeswoman Faith Whittlesey declared feminism a "straitjacket" for women, in the White House's only policy speech on the status of the American female population—entitled "Radical Feminism in Retreat." Law enforcement officers and judges, too, have pointed a damning finger at feminism, claiming that they can chart a path from rising female independence to rising female pathology. As a California sheriff explained it to the press, "Women are enjoying a lot more freedom now, and as a result, they are committing more crimes." The U.S. Attorney General's Commission on Pornography even proposed that women's professional advancement might be responsible for rising rape rates. With more women in college and at work now, the commission members reasoned in their report, women just have more opportunities to be raped.

Some academics have signed on to the consensus, too—and they are the "experts" who have enjoyed the highest profiles on the media circuit. On network news and talk shows, they have advised millions of women that feminism has condemned them to "a lesser life." Legal scholars have railed against "the equality trap." Sociologists have claimed that "feminist-inspired" legislative reforms have stripped women of special "protections." Economists have argued that well-paid working women have created "a less stable American family." And demographers, with greatest fanfare, have legitimated the prevailing wisdom with so-called neutral data on sex ratios and fertility trends; they say they actually have the numbers to prove that equality doesn't mix with marriage and motherhood.

Finally, some "liberated" women themselves have joined the lamentations. In confessional accounts, works that invariably receive a hearty greeting from the publishing industry, "recovering Superwomen" tell all. In *The Cost of Loving: Women and the New Fear of Intimacy,* Megan Marshall, a Harvard-pedigreed writer, asserts that the feminist "Myth of Independence" has turned her generation into unloved and unhappy fast-trackers, "dehumanized" by careers and "uncertain of their gender identity." Other diaries of mad Superwomen charge that "the hard-core feminist viewpoint," as one of them puts it, has relegated educated executive achievers to solitary nights of frozen dinners and closet drinking. The triumph of equality, they report, has merely given women hives, stomach cramps, eye-twitching disorders, even comas.

But what "equality" are all these authorities talking about?

If American women are so equal, why do they represent two-thirds of all poor adults? Why are nearly 75 percent of full-time working women making less than $20,000 a year, nearly double the male rate? Why are they still far more likely than men to live in poor housing and receive no health insurance, and twice as likely to draw no pension? Why does the average working woman's salary still lag as far behind the average man's as it did twenty years ago? Why does the average female college graduate today earn less than a man with no more than a high school diploma (just as she did in the '50s)—and why does the average female high school graduate today earn less than a male high school dropout? Why do American women, in fact, face one of the worst gender-based pay gap in the developed world?

If women have "made it," then why are nearly 80 percent of working women still stuck in traditional "female" jobs—as secretaries, administrative "support" workers and salesclerks? And, conversely, why are they less than 8 percent of all federal and state judges, less than 6 percent of all law partners, and less than one half of 1 percent of top corporate managers? Why are there only three female state governors, two female U.S. senators, and two Fortune 500 chief executives? Why are only nineteen of the four thousand corporate officers and directors women—and why do more than half the boards of Fortune companies still lack even one female member?

Nor is women's struggle for equal education over; as a 1989 study found, three-fourths of all high schools still violate the federal law banning sex discrimination in education. In colleges, undergraduate women receive only 70 percent of the aid undergraduate men get in grants and work-study jobs—and women's sports programs receive a pittance compared with men's. A review of state equal-education laws in the late '80s found that only thirteen states had adopted the minimum provisions required by the federal Title IX law—and only seven states had anti-discrimination regulations that covered all education levels.

Nor do women enjoy equality in their own homes, where they still shoulder 70 percent of the household duties—and the only major change in the last fifteen years is that now middle-class men *think* they do more around the house. (In fact, a national poll finds the ranks of women saying their husbands share equally in child care shrunk to 31 percent in 1987 from 40 percent three years earlier.) Furthermore, in thirty states, it is still generally legal for husbands to rape their wives; and only ten states have laws mandating arrest for domestic violence—even though battering was the leading cause of injury of women in the late '80s. Women who have no other option but to flee find that isn't much of an alternative either. Federal funding for battered women's shelters has been withheld and one third of the 1 million battered women who seek emergency shelter each year can find none. Blows from men contributed far more to the rising numbers of "bag ladies" than the ill effects of feminism. In the '80s, almost half of all homeless women (the fastest growing segment of the homeless) were refugees of domestic violence.

The word may be that women have been "liberated," but women themselves seem to feel otherwise. Repeatedly in national surveys, majorities of women say they are still far from equality. Nearly 70 percent of women polled by the *New*

York Times in 1989 said the movement for women's rights had only just begun. Most women in the 1990 Virginia Slims opinion poll agreed with the statement that conditions for their sex in American society had improved "a little, not a lot." In poll after poll in the decade, overwhelming majorities of women said they needed equal pay and equal job opportunities, they needed an Equal Rights Amendment, they needed the right to an abortion without government interference, they needed a federal law guaranteeing maternity leave, they needed decent child care services. They have none of these. So how exactly have we "won" the war for women's rights?

What actually is troubling the American female population, then? If the many ponderers of the Woman Question really wanted to know, they might have asked their subjects. In public opinion surveys, women consistently rank their own *inequality,* at work and at home, among their most urgent concerns. Over and over, women complain to pollsters about a lack of economic, not marital, opportunities; they protest that working men, not working women, fail to spend time in the nursery and the kitchen. The Roper Organization's survey analysts find that men's opposition to equality is "a major cause of resentment and stress" and "a major irritant for most women today." It is justice for their gender, not wedding rings and bassinets, that women believe to be in desperately short supply. When the *New York Times* polled women in 1989 about "the most important problem facing women today," job discrimination was the overwhelming winner; none of the crises the media and popular culture had so assiduously promoted even made the charts. In the 1990 Virginia Slims poll, women were most upset by their lack of money, followed by the refusal of their men to shoulder child care and domestic duties. By contrast, when the women were asked where the quest for a husband or the desire to hold a "less pressured" job or to stay at home ranked on their list of concerns, they placed them at the bottom.

As the last decade ran its course, women's unhappiness with inequality only mounted. In national polls, the ranks of women protesting discriminatory treatment in business, political, and personal life climbed sharply. The proportion of women complaining of unequal employment opportunities jumped more than ten points from the '70s, and the number of women complaining of unequal barriers to job advancement climbed even higher. By the end of the decade, 80 percent to 95 percent of women said they suffered from job discrimination and unequal pay. Sex discrimination charges filed with the Equal Employment Opportunity Commission rose nearly 25 percent in the Reagan years, and charges of general harassment directed at working women more than doubled. In the decade, complaints of sexual harassment nearly doubled. At home, a much increased proportion of women complained to pollsters of male mistreatment, unequal relationships, and male efforts to, in the words of the Virginia Slims poll, "keep women down." The share of women in the Roper surveys who agreed that men were "basically kind, gentle, and thoughtful" fell from almost 70 percent in 1970 to 50 percent by 1990. And outside their homes, women felt more threatened, too: in the 1990 Virginia Slims poll, 72 percent of women said they felt "more afraid and uneasy on the streets today" than they did a few years ago. Lest this be attributed only to a general rise in criminal activity, by contrast only 49 percent of men felt this way.

Some women began to piece the picture together. In the 1989 *New York Times* poll, more than half of black women and one-fourth of white women put it into words. They told pollsters they believed men were now trying to retract the gains women had made in the last twenty years. "I wanted more autonomy," was how one woman, a thirty-seven-year-old nurse, put it. And her estranged husband "wanted to take it away."

The truth is that the last decade has seen a powerful counterassault on women's rights, a backlash, an attempt to retract the handful of small and hard-won victories that the feminist movement did manage to win for women. This counterassault is largely insidious: in a kind of pop-culture version of the Big Lie, it stands the truth boldly on its head and proclaims that the very steps that have elevated women's position have actually led to their downfall.

The backlash is at once sophisticated and banal, deceptively "progressive" and proudly backward. It deploys both the "new" findings of "scientific research" and the dime-store moralism of yesteryear; it turns into media sound bites both the glib pronouncements of pop-psych trend-watchers and the frenzied rhetoric of New Right preachers. The backlash has succeeded in framing virtually the whole issue of women's rights in its own language.

But what has made women unhappy in the last decade is not their "equality"—which they don't yet have—but the rising pressure to halt, and even reverse, women's quest for that equality. The "man shortage" and the "infertility epidemic" are not the price of liberation; in fact, they do not even exist. But these chimeras are the chisels of a society—wide backlash. They are part of a relentless whittling-down process—much of it amounting to outright propaganda—that has served to stir women's private anxieties and break their political wills. Identifying feminism as women's enemy only furthers the ends of a backlash against women's equality, simultaneously deflecting attention from the backlash's central role and recruiting women to attack their own cause.

The antifeminist backlash has been set off not by women's achievement of full equality but by the increased possibility that they might win it. It is a preemptive strike that stops women long before they reach the finish line. "A backlash may be an indication that women really have had an effect," feminist psychologist Dr. Jean Baker Miller has written, "but backlashes occur when advances have been small, before changes are sufficient to help many people . . . . It is almost as if the leaders of backlashes use the fear of change as a threat before major change has occurred." In the last decade, some women did make substantial advances before the backlash hit, but millions of others were left behind, stranded. Some women now enjoy the right to legal abortion—but not the 44 million women, from the indigent to the military work force, who depend on the federal government for their medical care. Some women can now walk into high-paying professional careers—but not the more than 19 million still in the typing pools or behind the department store sales counters. (Contrary to popular myth about the "have-it-all" baby-boom women, the largest percentage of women in this generation remain typists and clerks.)

Women's advances and retreats are generally described in military terms: battles won, battles lost, points and territory gained and surrendered. The metaphor of combat is not without its merits in this context and, clearly, the same sort of martial accounting and vocabulary is already surfacing here. But by imagining the conflict as two battalions neatly arrayed on either side of the line, we miss the entangled nature, the locked embrace, of a "war" between women and the male culture they inhabit. We miss the reactive nature of a backlash, which, by definition, can exist only in response to another force.

In times when feminism is at a low ebb, women assume the reactive role—privately and most often covertly struggling to assert themselves against the dominant cultural tide. But when feminism itself becomes the tide, the opposition doesn't simply go along with the reversal: it digs in its heels, brandishes its fists, builds walls and dams. And its resistance creates countercurrents and treacherous undertows.

The force and furor of the backlash churn beneath the surface, largely invisible to the public eye. On occasion in the last decade, they have burst into view. We have seen New Right politicians condemn women's independence, antiabortion protesters firebomb women's clinics, fundamentalist preachers damn feminists as "whores" and "witches." Other signs of the backlash's wrath, by their sheer brutality, can push their way into public consciousness for a time—the sharp increase in rape, for example, or the rise in pornography that depicts extreme violence against women.

More subtle indicators in popular culture may receive momentary, and often bemused, media notice, then quickly slip from social awareness: A report, for instance, that the image of women on prime-time TV shows has suddenly degenerated. A survey of mystery fiction finding the numbers of female characters tortured and mutilated mysteriously multiplying. The puzzling news that, as one commentator put it, "So many hit songs have the B-word [bitch] to refer to women that some rap music seems to be veering toward rape music." The ascendancy of virulently misogynist comics like Andrew Dice Clay—who called women "pigs" and "sluts" and strutted in films in which women were beaten, tortured, and blown up—or radio hosts like Rush Limbaugh, whose broadsides against "femi-Nazi" feminists made his syndicated program the most popular radio talk show in the nation. Or word that in 1987, the American Women in Radio & Television couldn't award its annual prize for ads that feature women positively: it could find no ad that qualified.

These phenomena are all related, but that doesn't mean they are somehow coordinated. The backlash is not a conspiracy, with a council dispatching agents from some central control room, nor are the people who serve its ends often aware of their role; some even consider themselves feminists. For the most part, its workings are encoded and internalized, diffuse and chameleonic. Not all of the manifestations of the backlash are of equal weight or significance either; some are mere ephemera, generated by a culture machine that is always scrounging for a "fresh" angle. Taken as a whole, however, these codes and cajolings, these whispers and threats and myths, move overwhelmingly in one direction: they try to push women back into their "acceptable" roles—whether as Daddy's girl or fluttery romantic, active nester or passive love object.

Although the backlash is not an organized movement, that doesn't make it any less destructive. In fact, the lack of orchestration, the absence of a single string-puller, only makes it harder to see—and perhaps more effective. A backlash against women's rights succeeds to the degree that it appears *not* to be political, that it appears not to be a struggle at all. It is most powerful when it goes private, when it lodges inside a woman's mind and turns her vision inward, until she imagines the pressure is all in her head, until she begins to enforce the backlash, too—on herself.

In the last decade, the backlash has moved through the culture's secret chambers, traveling through passageways of flattery and fear. Along the way, it has adopted disguises: a mask of mild derision or the painted face of deep "concern." Its lips profess pity for any woman who won't fit the mold, while it tries to clamp the mold around her ears. It pursues a divide-and-conquer strategy: single versus married women, working women versus homemakers, middle- versus working-class. It manipulates a system of rewards and punishments, elevating women who follow its rules, isolating those who don't. The backlash remarkets old myths about women as new facts and ignores all appeals to reason. Cornered, it denies its own existence, points an accusatory finger at feminism, and burrows deeper underground.

Backlash happens to be the title of a 1947 Hollywood movie in which a man frames his wife for a murder he's committed. The backlash against women's rights works in much the same way: its rhetoric charges feminists with all the crimes it perpetrates. The backlash line blames the women's movement for the "feminization of poverty"—while the backlash's own instigators in Washington pushed through the budget cuts that helped impoverish millions of women, fought pay equity proposals, and undermined equal opportunity laws. The backlash line claims the women's movement cares nothing for children's rights—while its own representatives in the capital and state legislatures have blocked one bill after another to improve child care, slashed billions of dollars in federal aid for children, and relaxed state licensing standards for day care centers. The backlash line accuses the women's movement of creating a generation of unhappy single and childless women—but its purveyors in the media are the ones guilty of making single and childless women feel like circus freaks.

To blame feminism for women's "lesser life" is to miss entirely the point of feminism, which is to win women a wider range of experience. Feminism remains a pretty simple concept, despite repeated—and enormously effective—efforts to dress it up in greasepaint and turn its proponents into gargoyles. As Rebecca West wrote sardonically in 1913, "I myself have never been able to find out precisely what feminism is: I only know that people call me a feminist whenever I express sentiments that differentiate me from a doormat."

The meaning of the word "feminist" has not really changed since it first appeared in a book review in the *Athenaeum* of April 27, 1895, describing a woman who "has in her the capacity of fighting her way back to independence." It is the basic proposition that, as Nora put it in Ibsen's *A Doll's House* a century ago, "Before everything else I'm a human being." It is the simply worded sign hoisted by a little girl in the 1970 Women's Strike for Equality: I AM NOT A BARBIE DOLL. Feminism asks the world to recognize at long last that women aren't decorative ornaments, worthy vessels, members of a "special-interest group." They are half (in fact, now more than half) of the national population, and just as deserving of rights and opportunities, just as capable of participating in the world's events, as the other half. Feminism's agenda is basic: It asks that women not be forced to "choose" between public justice and private happiness. It asks that women be free to define themselves—instead of having their identity defined for them, time and again, by their culture and their men.

The fact that these are still such incendiary notions should tell us that American women have a way to go before they enter the promised land of equality.

Topics for Reading and Writing

1. This piece is an introduction to a much longer work. What strategies does Faludi use to lay out her argument? What is the thesis of the book? What methods and evidence does Faludi use to make her points?

2. One of the important rhetorical strategies Faludi uses is the identification and construction of a "villain": the backlash. In order to make her argument convincing, though, she must be careful not to make the backlash into a straw man. How does she establish that there has, in fact, been a backlash? Do you accept her argument? What criticisms do you have of it?

3. What is feminism? How is feminism described by the media—by television news, by radio talk show hosts, by opinion journals, by political websites? Is the image of feminism today as negative as the one Faludi identifies in 1991? If things have changed, how have they changed? If not, why?

Gladwell, a staff writer for The New Yorker *and author of* The Tipping-Point *(2000), profiles the ground-level marketing forces that seek out emerging trends among teenagers. Did you know large marketing and advertising companies have anatomized teenage social groups in terms of their relative "cool"? How does this affect the very notion of "cool"—can it still be rebellious? How quickly do trends move from the gritty streets of Brooklyn to suburban Wal-Marts? And what makes "cool" cool?*

Malcolm Gladwell
The Coolhunt

1.

Baysie Wightman met DeeDee Gordon, appropriately enough, on a coolhunt. It was 1992. Baysie was a big shot for Converse, and DeeDee, who was barely twenty-one, was running a very cool boutique called Placid Planet on Newbury Street in Boston. Baysie came in with a camera crew—one she often used when she was coolhunting—and said, "I've been watching your store, I've seen you, I've heard you know what's up," because it was Baysie's job at Converse to find people who knew what was up and she thought DeeDee was one of those people. DeeDee says that she responded with reserve—that "I was like, 'Whatever'"—but Baysie said that if DeeDee ever wanted to come and work at Converse she should just call, and nine months later DeeDee called. This was about the time the cool kids had decided they didn't want the hundred-and-twenty-five-dollar basketball sneaker with seventeen different kinds of high-technology materials and colors and air-cushioned heels anymore. They wanted simplicity and authenticity, and Baysie picked up on that. She brought back the Converse One Star, which was a vulcanized, suede, low-top classic old-school sneaker from the nineteen-seventies, and, sure enough, the One Star quickly became the signature shoe of the retro era. Remember what Kurt Cobain was wearing in the famous picture of him lying dead on the ground after committing suicide? Black Converse One Stars. DeeDee's big score was calling the sandal craze. She had been out in Los Angeles and had kept seeing the white teen-age girls dressing up like cholos, Mexican gangsters, in tight white tank tops known as "wife beaters," with a bra strap hanging out, and long shorts and tube socks and shower sandals. DeeDee recalls, "I'm like, 'I'm telling you, Baysie, this is going to hit. There are just too many people wearing it. We have to make a shower sandal.'" So Baysie, DeeDee, and a designer came up with the idea of making a retro sneaker-sandal, cutting the back off the One Star and putting a thick outsole on it. It was huge, and amazingly, it's still huge.

Today, Baysie works for Reebok as general-merchandise manager—part of the team trying to return Reebok to the position it enjoyed in the mid-nineteen-eighties as the country's hottest sneaker company. DeeDee works for an advertising agency in Del Mar called Lambesis, where she puts out a quarterly tip sheet called the L Report on what the cool kids in major American cities are thinking and doing and buying. Baysie and DeeDee best friends. They talk on the phone all the time.

They get together whenever Baysie is in L.A. (DeeDee: "It's, like, how many times can you drive past O.J. Simpson's house?"), and between them they can talk for hours about the art of the coolhunt. They're the Lewis and Clark of cool.

What they have is what everybody seems to want these days, which is a window on the world of the street. Once, when fashion trends were set by the big couture houses—when cool was trickle-down—that wasn't important. But sometime in the past few decades things got turned over, and fashion became trickle-up. It's now about chase and flight—designers and retailers and the mass consumer giving chase to the elusive prey of street cool—and the rise of coolhunting as a profession shows how serious the chase has become. The sneakers of Nike and Reebok used to come out yearly. Now a new style comes out every season. Apparel designers used to have an eighteen-month lead time between concept and sale. Now they're reducing that to a year, or even six months, in order to react faster to new ideas from the street. The paradox, of course, is that the better coolhunters become at bringing the mainstream close to the cutting edge, the more elusive the cutting edge becomes. This is the first rule of the cool: The quicker the chase, the quicker the flight. The act of discovering what's cool is what causes cool to move on, which explains the triumphant circularity of coolhunting: because we have coolhunters like DeeDee and Baysie, cool changes more quickly, and because cool changes more quickly, we need coolhunters like DeeDee and Baysie.

DeeDee is tall and glamorous, with short hair she has dyed so often that she claims to have forgotten her real color. She drives a yellow 1977 Trans Am with a burgundy stripe down the center and a 1973 Mercedes 450 SL, and lives in a spare, Japanese-style cabin in Laurel Canyon. She uses words like "rad" and "totally," and offers non-stop, deadpan pronouncements on pop culture, as in "It's all about Pee-wee Herman." She sounds at first like a teen, like the same teens who, at Lambesis, it is her job to follow. But teen speech—particularly girl-teen speech, with its fixation on reported speech ("so she goes," "and I'm like," "and he goes") and its stock vocabulary of accompanying grimaces and gestures—is about using language less to communicate than to fit in. DeeDee uses teen speech to set herself apart, and the result is, for lack of a better word, really cool. She doesn't do the teen thing of climbing half an octave at the end of every sentence. Instead, she drags out her vowels for emphasis, so that if she mildly disagreed with something I'd said she would say "Maalcolm" and if she strongly disagreed with what I'd said she would say "Maaalcolm."

Baysie is older, just past forty (although you would never guess that), and went to Exeter and Middlebury and had two grandfathers who went to Harvard (although you wouldn't guess that, either). She has curly brown hair and big green eyes and long legs and so much energy that it is hard to imagine her asleep, or resting, or even standing still for longer than thirty seconds. The hunt for cool is an obsession with her, and DeeDee is the same way. DeeDee used to sit on the corner of West Broadway and Prince in SoHo—back when SoHo was cool—and take pictures of everyone who walked by for an entire hour. Baysie can tell you precisely where she goes on her Reebok coolhunts to find the really cool alternative white kids ("I'd maybe go to Portland and hang out where the skateboarders hang out near that bridge") or which snowboarding mountain has cooler kids—Stratton, in Vermont, or Summit County, in Colorado. (Summit, definitely.) DeeDee can tell you on the basis of the L Report's research exactly how far Dallas is behind New York in coolness (from six to eight months). Baysie is convinced that Los Angeles is not happening right now: "In the early nineteen-nineties a lot more was coming from L.A. They had a big trend with the whole Melrose Avenue look—the stupid goatees, the shorter hair. It was cleaned-up aftergrunge. There were a lot of places you could go to buy vinyl records. It was a strong place to go for looks. Then it went back to being horrible." DeeDee is convinced that Japan is happening: "I linked onto this future-technology thing two years ago. Now look at it, it's huge. It's the whole resurgence of Nike—Nike being larger than life. I went to Japan and saw the kids just bailing the most technologically advanced Nikes with their little dresses and little outfits and I'm like, 'Whoa, this is trippy!' It's performance mixed with fashion. It's really super-heavy." Baysie has a theory that Liverpool is cool right now because it's the birthplace of the whole "lad" look, which involves soccer blokes in the pubs going super dressy and wearing Dolce & Gabbana and Polo Sport and Reebok Classics on their feet. But when I asked DeeDee about that, she just rolled her eyes: "Sometimes Baysie goes off on these tangents. Man, I love that woman!"

I used to think that if I talked to Baysie and DeeDee long enough I could write a coolhunting manual, an encyclopedia of cool. But then I realized that the manual would have so many footnotes and caveats that it would be unreadable. Coolhunting is not about the articulation of a coherent philosophy of cool. It's just a collection of spontaneous observations and predictions that differ from, one moment to the next and from one coolhunter to the next. Ask a coolhunter where the baggy-jeans look came from, for example, and you might get any number of answers: urban black kids mimicking the jailhouse look, skateboarders looking for room to move, snowboarders trying not to look like skiers, or, alternatively, all three at once, in some grand concordance.

Or take the question of exactly how Tommy Hilfiger—a forty-five-year-old white guy from Greenwich, Connecticut, doing all-American preppy clothes— came to be the designer of choice for urban black America. Some say it was all about the early and visible endorsement given Hilfiger by the hip-hop amateur Grand Puba, who wore a dark-green-and-blue Tommy jacket over a white Tommy T-shirt as he leaned on his black Lamborghini on the cover of the hugely influential "Grand Puba 2000" CD, and whose love for Hilfiger soon spread to other rappers. (Who could forget the rhymes of Mobb Deep? "Tommy was my nigga/And couldn't figure/How me and Hilfiger/used to move through with vigor.") Then I had lunch with one of Hilfiger's designers, a twenty-six-year-old named Ulrich (Ubi) Simpson, who has a Puerto Rican mother and a Dutch-Venezuelan father, plays lacrosse, snowboards, surfs the long board, goes to hip-hop concerts, listens to Jungle, Edith Piaf, opera, rap, and Metallica, and has working with him on his design team a twenty-seven-year-old black guy from Montclair with dreadlocks, a twenty-two-year-old Asian-American who lives on the Lower East Side, a twenty-five-year-old South Asian guy from Fiji, and a twenty-one-year-old white graffiti artist from Queens. That's when it occurred to me that maybe the reason Tommy Hilfiger can make white culture cool to black culture is that he has people working for him who are cool in both cultures simultaneously. Then again, maybe it was all Grand Puba. Who knows?

2.

If you want to understand how trends work, and why coolhunters like Baysie and DeeDee have become so important, a good place to start is with what's known as diffusion research, which is the study of how ideas and innovations spread. Diffusion researchers do things like spending five years studying the adoption of irrigation techniques in a Colombian mountain village, or developing complex matrices to map the spread of new math in the Pittsburgh school system. What they do may seem like a far cry from, say, how the Tommy Hilfiger thing spread from Harlem to every suburban mall in the country, but it really isn't: both are about how new ideas spread from one person to the next.

One of the most famous diffusion studies is Bruce Ryan and Neal Gross's analysis of the spread of hybrid seed corn in Greene County, Iowa, in the nineteen-thirties. The new seed corn was introduced there in about 1928, and it was superior in every respect to the seed that had been used by farmers for decades. But it wasn't adopted all at once. Of two hundred and fifty-nine farmers studied by Ryan and Gross, only a handful had started planting the new seed by 1933. In 1934, sixteen took the plunge. In 1935, twenty-one more followed; the next year, there were thirty-six, and the year after that a whopping sixty-one. The succeeding figures were then forty-six, thirty-six, fourteen, and three, until, by 1941, all but two of the two hundred and fifty-nine farmers studied were using the new seed. In the language of diffusion research, the handful of farmers who started trying hybrid seed corn at the very beginning of the thirties were the "innovators," the adventurous ones. The slightly larger group that followed them was the "early adopters." They were the opinion leaders in the community, the respected, thoughtful people who watched and analyzed what those wild innovators were doing and then did it themselves. Then came the big bulge of farmers in 1936, 1937, and 1938—the "early majority" and the "late majority," which is to say the deliberate and the skeptical masses, who would never try anything until the most respected farmers had tried it. Only after they had been converted did the "laggards," the most traditional of all, follow suit. The critical thing about this sequence is that it is almost entirely interpersonal. According to Ryan and Gross, only the innovators relied to any great extent on radio advertising and farm journals and seed salesmen in making their decision to switch to the hybrid. Everyone else made his decision overwhelmingly because of the example and the opinions of his neighbors and peers.

Isn't this just how fashion works? A few years ago, the classic brushed-suede Hush Puppies with the lightweight crepe sole—the moc-toe oxford known as the Duke and the slip-on with the golden buckle known as the Columbia—were selling barely sixty-five thousand pairs a year. The company was trying to walk away from the whole suede casual look entirely. It wanted to do "aspirational" shoes: "active casuals" in smooth leather, like the Mall Walker, with a Comfort Curve technology outsole and a heel stabilizer—the kind of shoes you see in Kinney's for $39.95. But then something strange started happening. Two Hush Puppies executives—Owen Baxter and Jeff Lewis—were doing a fashion shoot for their Mall Walkers and ran into a creative consultant from Manhattan named Jeffrey Miller, who informed them that the Dukes and the Columbias weren't dead, they were dead chic. "We were being told," Baxter recalls, "that there were areas in the Village, in SoHo, where the shoes were selling—in resale shops—and that people were wearing the old Hush Puppies. They were going to the ma-and-pa stores, the little stores that still carried them, and there was this authenticity of being able to say, 'I am wearing an original pair of Hush Puppies.'"

Baxter and Lewis—tall, solid, fair-haired Midwestern guys with thick, shiny wedding bands—are shoe men, first and foremost. Baxter was working the cash register at his father's shoe store in Mount Prospect, Illinois, at the age of thirteen. Lewis was doing inventory in his father's shoe store in Pontiac, Michigan, at the age of seven. Baxter was in the National Guard during the 1968 Democratic Convention, in Chicago, and was stationed across the street from the Conrad Hilton downtown, right in the middle of things. Today, the two men work out of Rockford, Michigan (population thirty-eight hundred), where Hush Puppies has been making the Dukes and the Columbias in an old factory down by the Rogue River for almost forty years. They took me to the plant when I was in Rockford. In a crowded, noisy, low-slung building, factory workers stand in long rows, gluing, stapling, and sewing together shoes in dozens of bright colors, and the two executives stopped at each production station and described it in detail. Lewis and Baxter know shoes. But they would be the first to admit that they don't know cool. "Miller was saying that there is something going on with the shoes—that Issac Mizrahi was wearing the shoes for his personal use," Lewis told me. We were seated around the conference table in the Hush Puppies headquarters in Rockford, with the snow and the trees outside and a big water tower behind us. "I think it's fair to say that at the time we had no idea who Issac Mizrahi was."

By late 1994, things had begun to happen in a rush. First, the designer John Bartlett called. He wanted to use Hush Puppies as accessories in his spring collection. Then Anna Sui called. Miller, the man from Manhattan, flew out to Michigan to give advice on a new line ("Of course, packing my own food and thinking about 'Fargo' in the corner of my mind"). A few months later, in Los Angeles, the designer Joel Fitzpatrick put a twenty-five-foot inflatable basset hound on the roof of his store on La Brea Avenue and gutted his adjoining art gallery to turn it into a Hush Puppies department, and even before he opened—while he was still painting and putting up shelves—Pee-wee Herman walked in and asked for a couple of pairs. Pee-wee Herman! "It was total word of mouth. I didn't even have a sign back then," Fitzpatrick recalls. In 1995, the company sold four hundred and thirty thousand pairs of the classic Hush Puppies. In 1996, it sold a million six hundred thousand, and that was only scratching the surface, because in Europe and the rest of the world, where Hush Puppies have a huge following—where they might outsell the American market four to one—the revival was just beginning.

The cool kids who started wearing old Dukes and Columbias from thrift shops were the innovators. Pee-wee Herman, wandering in off the street, was an early adopter. The million six hundred thousand people who bought Hush Puppies last year are the early majority, jumping in because the really cool people have already blazed the trail. Hush Puppies are moving through the country just the way hybrid seed corn moved through Greene County—all of which illustrates what coolhunters can and cannot do. If Jeffrey Miller had been wrong—if cool people hadn't been digging through the thrift shops for Hush Puppies—and he had arbitrarily decided that Baxter and Lewis should try to convince non-cool people that the shoes were cool, it wouldn't have worked. You can't convince the late majority that Hush Puppies are cool, because the late majority makes its coolness decisions on the basis of what the early majority is doing, and you can't convince the early majority, because the early majority is looking at the early adopters, and you can't convince the early adopters, because they take their cues from the innovators. The innovators do get their cool ideas from people other than their peers, but the fact is that they are the last people who can be convinced by a marketing campaign that a pair of suede shoes is cool. These are, after all, the people who spent hours sifting through thrift-store bins. And why did they do that? Because their definition of cool is doing something that nobody else is doing. A company can intervene in the cool cycle. It can put its shoes on really cool celebrities and on fashion runways and on MTV. It can accelerate the transition from the innovator to the early adopter and on to the early majority. But it can't just manufacture cool out of thin air, and that's the second rule of cool.

At the peak of the Hush Puppies craziness last year, Hush Puppies won the prize for best accessory at the Council of Fashion Designers' awards dinner, at Lincoln Center. The award was accepted by the Hush Puppies president, Louis Dubrow, who came out wearing a pair of custom-made black patent-leather Hush Puppies and stood there blinking and looking at the assembled crowd as if it were the last scene of "Close Encounters of the Third Kind." It was a strange moment. There was the president of the Hush Puppies company, of Rockford, Michigan, population thirty-eight hundred sharing a stage with Calvin Klein and Donna Karan and Issac Mizrahi—and all because some kids in the East Village began combing through thrift shops for old Dukes. Fashion was at the mercy of those kids, whoever they were, and it was a wonderful thing if the kids picked you, but a scary thing, too, because it meant that cool was something you could not control. You needed someone to find cool and tell you what it was.

3.

When Baysie Wightman went to Dr. Jay's, she was looking for customer response to the new shoes Reebok had planned for the fourth quarter of 1997 and the first quarter of 1998. This kind of customer testing is critical at Reebok, because the last decade has not been kind to the company. Somewhere along the way, the company lost its cool, and Reebok now faces the task not only of rebuilding its image but of making the shoes so cool that the kids in the store can't put them down.

Reebok has its headquarters in Stoughton, Massachusetts, outside Boston—in a modern corporate park right off Route 24. There are basketball and tennis courts next to the building, and a health club on the ground floor that you can look directly into from the parking lot. The front lobby is adorned with shrines for all of Reebok's most prominent athletes—shrines complete with dramatic action photographs, their sports jerseys, and a pair of their signature shoes—and the halls are filled with so many young, determinedly athletic people that when I visited Reebok headquarters I suddenly wished I'd packed my gym clothes in case someone challenged me to wind sprints. At Stoughton, I met with a handful of the company's top designers and marketing executives in a long conference room on the third floor. In the course of two hours, they put one pair of shoes after another on the table in front of me, talking excitedly about each sneaker's prospects, because the feeling at Reebok is that things are finally turning around. The basketball shoe that Reebok is brought out last winter for Allen Iverson, the star rookie guard for the Philadelphia 76ers, for example, is one of the hottest shoes in the country. Dr. Jay's sold out of Iversons in two days, compared with the week it took the store to sell out of Nike's new Air Jordans. Iverson himself is brash and charismatic and faster from foul line to foul line than anyone else in the league. He's the equivalent of those kids in the East Village who began wearing Hush Puppies way back when. He's an innovator, and the hope at Reebok is that if he gets big enough the whole company can ride back to coolness on his coattails, the way Nike rode back to coolness on the coattails of Michael Jordan. That's why Baysie was so excited when the kid said Reebok was trying to get better when he looked at the Rush and the DMX RXT: it was a sign, albeit a small one, that the indefinable, abstract thing called cool was coming back.

When Baysie comes back from a coolhunt, she sits down with marketing experts and sales representatives and designers, and reconnects them to the street, making sure they have the right shoes going to the right places at the right price. When she got back from the Bronx, for example, the first thing she did was tell all these people they had to get a new men's DMX RXT out, fast, because the kids on the street loved the women's version. "It's hotter than we realized," she told them. The coolhunter's job in this instance is very specific. What DeeDee does, on the other hand, is a little more ambitious. With the

L Report, she tries to construct a kind of grand matrix of cool, comprising not just shoes but everything kids like, and not just kids of certain East Coast urban markets but kids all over. DeeDee and her staff put it out four times a year, in six different versions—for New York, Los Angeles, San Francisco, Austin-Dallas, Seattle, and Chicago—and then sell it to manufacturers, retailers, and ad agencies (among others) for twenty thousand dollars a year. They go to each city and find the coolest bars and clubs, and ask the coolest kids to fill out questionnaires. The information is then divided into six categories—You Saw It Here First, Entertainment and Leisure, Clothing and Accessories, Personal and Individual, Aspirations, and Food and Beverages—which are, in turn, broken up into dozens of subcategories, so that Personal and Individual, for example, includes Cool Date, Cool Evening, Free Time, Favorite Possession, and on and on. The information in those subcategories is subdivided again by sex and by age bracket (14–18, 19–24, 25–30), and then, as a control, the L Report gives you the corresponding set of preferences for "mainstream" kids.

Few coolhunters bother to analyze trends with this degree of specificity. DeeDee's biggest competitor, for example, is something called the Hot Sheet, out of Manhattan. It uses a panel of three thousand kids a year from across the country and divides up their answers by sex and age, but it doesn't distinguish between regions, or between trendsetting and mainstream respondents. So what you're really getting is what all kids think is cool—not what cool kids think is cool, which is a considerably different piece of information. Janine Misdom and Joanne DeLuca, who run the Sputnik coolhunting group out of the garment district in Manhattan, meanwhile, favor an entirely impressionistic approach, sending out coolhunters with video cameras to talk to kids on the ground, that it's too difficult to get cool kids to fill out questionnaires. Once, when I was visiting the Sputnik girls—as Misdom and DeLuca are known on the street, because they look alike and their first names are so similar and both have the same awesome New York accents—they showed me a video of the girl they believe was the patient zero of the whole eighties revival going on right now. It was back in September of 1993. Joanne and Janine were on Seventh Avenue, outside the Fashion Institute of Technology, doing random street interviews for a major jeans company, and, quite by accident, they ran into this nineteen-year-old raver. She had close-cropped hair, which was green at the top, and at the temples was shaved even closer and dyed pink. She had rings and studs all over her face, and a thick collection of silver tribal jewelry around her neck, and vintage jeans. She looked into the camera and said, "The sixties came in and then the seventies came in and I think it's ready to come back to the eighties. It's totally eighties; the eye makeup, the clothes. It's totally going back to that." Immediately, Joanne and Janine started asking around. "We talked to a few kids on the Lower East Side who said they were feeling the need to start breaking out their old Michael Jackson jackets," Joanne said. "They were joking about it. They weren't doing it yet. But they were going to, you know? They were saying, 'We're getting the urge to break out our Members Only jackets.'" That was right when Joanne and Janine were just starting up; calling the eighties revival was their first big break, and now they put out a full-down videotaped report twice a year which is a collection of clips of interviews with extremely progressive people.

What DeeDee argues, though, is that cool is too subtle and too variegated to be captured with these kind of broad strokes. Cool is a set of dialects, not a language. The L Report can tell you, for example, that nineteen-to-twenty-four-year-old male trendsetters in Seattle would most like to meet, among others, King Solomon and Dr. Seuss, and that nineteen-to-twenty-four-year-old female trendsetters in San Francisco have turned their backs on Calvin Klein, Nintendo Gameboy, and sex. What's cool right now? Among male New York trendsetters: North Face jackets, rubber and latex, khakis, and the rock band Kiss. Among female trendsetters: ska music, old-lady clothing, and cyber tech. In Chicago, snowboarding is huge among trendsetters of both sexes and all ages. Women over nineteen are into short hair, while those in their teens have embraced mod culture, rock climbing, tag watches, and bootleg pants. In Austin-Dallas, mean-while twenty-five-to-thirty-year-old women trendsetters are into hats, heroin, computers, cigars, Adidas, and velvet, while men in their twenties are into video games and hemp. In all, the typical L Report runs over one hundred pages. But with that flood of data comes an obsolescence disclaimer: "The fluctuating nature of the trendsetting market makes keeping up with trends a difficult task." By the spring, in other words, everything may have changed.

The key to coolhunting, then, is to look for cool people first and cool things later, and not the other way around. Since cool things are always changing, you can't look for them, because the very fact they are cool means you have no idea what to look for. What you would be doing is thinking back on what was cool before and extrapolating, which is about as useful as presuming that because the Dow rose ten points yesterday it will rise another ten points today. Cool people, on the other hand, are a constant.

When I was in California, I met Salvador Barbier, who had been described to me by a coolhunter as "the Michael Jordan of skateboarding." He was tall and lean and languid, with a cowboy's insouciance, and we drove through the streets of Long Beach at fifteen miles an hour in a white late-model Ford Mustang, a car he had bought as a kind of ironic status gesture ("It would look good if I had a Polo jacket or maybe Nautica," he said) to go with his '62 Econoline van and his '64 T-bird. Sal told me that he and his friends, who are all in their mid-twenties, recently took to dressing up as if they were in eighth grade again and gathering together—having a "rally"—on old BMX bicycles in front of their local 7-Eleven. "I'd wear muscle shirts, like Def Leppard or Foghat or some old heavy-metal band, and tight, tight tapered Levi's, and Vans on my feet—big, like, checkered Vans or striped Vans or camouflage Vans—and then wristbands and gloves with the fingers cut off. It was total eighties fashion. You had to look like that to participate in the rally. We had those denim jackets with patches on the back and combs that hung out the back pocket. We went without I.D.s, because we'd have to have someone else buy us beers." At this point, Sal laughed. He was driving really slowly and staring straight ahead and talking in a low drawl—the coolhunter's dream. "We'd ride to this bar and I'd have to carry my bike inside, because we have really expensive bikes, and when we got inside peo-ple would freak out. They'd say, 'Omigod,' and I was asking them if they wanted to go for a ride on the handlebars. They were like, 'What is wrong with you. My boyfriend used to dress like that in the eighth grade!' And I was like, 'He was probably a lot cooler then, too.'"

This is just the kind of person DeeDee wants. "I'm looking for somebody who is an individual, who has definitely set himself apart from everybody else, who doesn't look like his peers. I've run into trendsetters who look completely Joe Regular Guy. I can see Joe Regular Guy at a club listening to some totally hardcore band playing, and I say to myself 'Omigod, what's that guy doing here?' and that totally intrigues me, and I have to walk up to him and say, 'Hey, you're really into this band. What's up?' You know what I mean? I look at everything. If I see Joe Regular Guy sitting in a coffee shop and everyone around him has blue hair, I'm going to gravitate toward him, because, hey, what's Joe Regular Guy doing in a coffee shop with people with blue hair?"

Picking the right person is harder than it sounds, though. Piney Kahn, who works for DeeDee, says, "There are a lot of people in the gray area. You've got these kids who dress ultra funky and have their own style. Then you realize they're just running after their friends." The trick is not just to be able to tell who is different but to be able to tell when that difference represents something truly cool. It's a gut thing. You have to somehow just know. DeeDee hired Piney because Piney clearly knows: she is twenty-four and used to work with the Beastie Boys and has the formidable self-possession of someone who is not only cool herself but whose parents were cool. "I mean," she says, "they named me after a tree."

Once, I was visiting DeeDee at her house in Laurel Canyon when one of her L Report assistants, Jonas Vail, walked in. He'd just come back from Niketown on Wilshire Boulevard, where he'd bought seven hundred dollars' worth of the latest sneakers to go with the three hundred dollars' worth of skateboard shoes he'd bought earlier in the afternoon. Jonas is tall and expressionless, with a peacoat, dark jeans, and short-cropped black hair. "Jonas is good," DeeDee says. "He works with me on everything. That guy knows more pop culture. You know: What was the name of the store Mrs. Garrett owned on 'The Facts of Life'? He knows all the names of the extras from eighties sitcoms. I can't believe someone like him exists. He's fucking unbelievable. Jonas can spot a cool person a mile away."

Jonas takes the boxes of shoes and starts unpacking them on the couch next to DeeDee. He picks up a pair of the new Nike ACG hiking boots, and says, "All the Japanese in Niketown were really into these." He hands the shoes to DeeDee.

"Of *course* they were!" she says. "The Japanese are all into the tech-looking shit. Look how exaggerated it is, how bulbous." DeeDee has very ambivalent feelings about Nike, because she thinks its marketing has got out of hand. When she was in the New York Niketown with a girlfriend recently, she says, she started getting light-headed and freaked out. "It's cult, cult, cult. It was like, 'Hello, are we all drinking the Kool-Aid here?'" But this shoe she loves. It's Dr. Jay's in the Bronx all over again. DeeDee turns the shoe around and around in the air, tapping the big clear-blue plastic bubble on the side—the visible Air-Sole unit—with one finger. "It's so fucking rad. It looks like a platypus!" In front of me, there is a pair of Nike's new shoes for the basketball player Jason Kidd.

I pick it up. "This looks . . . cool," I venture uncertainly.

DeeDee is on the couch, where she's surrounded by shoeboxes and sneakers and white tissue paper, and she looks up reprovingly because, of course, I don't get it. I can't get it. "Beyooond cool, Maalcolm. Beyooond cool."

Topics for Reading and Writing

1. Gladwell's piece differs from Petrecca's in that Petrecca's is almost straight reporting, while Gladwell's is a profile. How does Gladwell make an argument about "coolhunting"? About advertising in general? What do you think Gladwell's opinions of advertising and marketing are?

2. How does Gladwell's article throw into doubt the status of the "real"? Think about what Gladwell's "coolhunters" seek out, and what happens to urban, African-American culture when it is commodified. How does this affect the urban notion of "keeping it real"?

3. In addition to writing about the conjunction of media, culture, and capitalism, Gladwell is somewhat of a pioneer in the field. His website (www.gladwell.com) is an attempt to come to take advantage of the freedom that new technologies give individuals—no longer does Gladwell have to be at the mercy of his employer (*The New Yorker*) and publisher (Little, Brown): he has become a brand himself. How will the Web change the nature of writers' work—who they work for, what freedoms they have, what restrictions are placed upon them?

*University of Southern California student **Aron Flasher** here profiles the career of singer Mariah Carey, and calls into question any claims for authenticity or "the real" that Carey or her representatives might make. Focusing on Carey's well-publicized 2001 breakdown and her disastrous film debut* Glitter, *Flasher makes arguments about the nature of celebrity, the relationship of a celebrity to her publicity team, and whether or not "the truth" or "the real" is even a meaningful concept when discussing the promotion and branding of a celebrity.*

Aron Flasher
Glitterless (Student Essay)

In a controversial interrogation tactic that one prominent human-rights organization says 'borders on torture,' CIA operatives in Afghanistan have been showing Al Qaeda prisoners the Mariah Carey film Glitter. *The film usually induces prisoners to talk after 10 or 12 minutes. 'They usually crack during the scenes in which Mariah Carey plays herself as a teenager . . .'*

—Humorist Andy Borowitz,
winner of the 2001 Dot-Comedy Award for
best humor columnist on the net (Borowitz).

On July 25, 2001, vocal star Mariah Carey, 31, the highest selling female musician of the nineties, was admitted to a Westchester County hospital in New York (Corliss). She was suffering from what her publicist called "an emotional and physical breakdown," as reported in the August 13, 2001, issue of *Time*. Tabloid versions of the incident state that Carey was seen entering the hospital with her hands bandaged, thus insinuating that she may have attempted suicide; however, this account is denied by Carey's ambulance driver (Corliss).

Another version of the incident, a version supported by Carey's PR consultants, is that Carey, while staying at the Tribeca Grand Hotel in Manhattan, "became severely agitated." (Corliss). She reportedly was tossing crockery about and stepped on the shards, cutting her bare feet. After this, she was taken to her mother's house, and it was there that she suffered a nervous breakdown (Corliss). Her mother then called 911 and got Mariah to the hospital where she was treated for "exhaustion" (Corliss).

Despite these varying claims of what happened on July 25, 2001, since that date Mariah Carey's career has taken a turn for the worse; the lackluster sales of her latest album combined with the critical and commercial failure of her film have led to what may have been the most humiliating consequence of the period. Last year, record labels Virgin and EMI had signed the star to a reported $80 million, five-album deal, according to the March 2 issue of *Entertainment Weekly* (Serpick). On January 23, 2002, six months after her breakdown, Virgin and EMI paid the star $28 million to buy her out of her contract (Bonin). Essentially, Mariah Carey, an artist who in just 13 years had sold over 140 million albums, had 15 number one singles, and trails only the Beatles and Elvis Presley in record sales, was "finally being paid not to sing" (Serpick). So how did this happen? Stated simply, Mariah Carey lost her core audience in an effort to broaden it by changing her image.

Carey's image has changed radically over her 13-year career, and so has her audience. Where she began as an icon of innocence and fluff, today she embodies the modern, Britney Spears/N'Sync pop culture, where everyone is young, beautiful, sexually aware, and consequence free. This metamorphosis has not been a slow and natural change, but rather a well-orchestrated public relations action as part of an effort to capitalize on the growing success of these younger pop artists. Mariah's image change was an attempt to expand the singer's audience, while at the same time retaining her following of diehard fans who stuck with her since the start of her career.

According to a *Rolling Stone* biography, Mariah Carey was born on March 27, 1970, in Huntington, NY, to an Irish opera singer and an African/Venezuelan engineer (RollingStone.com). Carey was exposed to music at an early age. By the time she was 15, she was performing in New York City nightclubs and making rough demo tapes (RollingStone.com). She eventually landed a job as a backup singer for Brenda K. Starr, an established musician, who in turn introduced her to many music executives, one of whom—Tommy Mottola—was then the president of Columbia Records (RollingStone.com). Carey gave Mottola her demo tape and within a month she had a record deal (RollingStone.com). She was only 19 at the time (RollingStone.com). Carey's debut album *Vision of Love* was released in 1990 (RollingStone.com). It was an instant success, spawning four number 1 singles. The album sold over 6 million copies in the U.S. alone, and won two Grammys (RollingStone.com). Her follow-up albums, *Emotions* in 1991, and *Music Box* in 1993, were also largely successful and produced some of Carey's most popular singles (including the songs "Hero" and "Dreamlover") (RollingStone.com). 1993 was also the year that Carey, then 24, married Mottola who was 43 at the time (RollingStone.com). This was the height of Carey's career commercially; however, this would soon change.

For the majority of Carey's career, her music had been mostly made up of sappy love songs, often with simple lyrics and rhythms. An example of this is her hit single "Dreamlover":

Dreamlover come rescue me
Baby take me up take me down
Take me anywhere you want to baby now.

Like "Dreamlover", Carey's songs are usually about love and for a good reason: these songs have a wide audience. Carey herself says, "everyone can pretty much relate to songs about love . . . Love is something that everyone has experienced" (official website). Consequently, her songs and lyrics often receive a critical bashing for their simplicity, yet Carey believes that her songs touch a chord with the public. In defense of her song "Hero," Carey says, "one person could say 'Hero' is a schmaltzy piece of garbage, but another person can write me a letter and say, 'I've considered committing suicide every day of my life for ten years until I heard that song and I realized after all I can be my own hero.' . . . it meant something to someone." (Singapore's Passion For Mariah). This makes it apparent that, according to Carey, there is a following that connects to her music.

This following was initially made up of mostly preteen and teenage girls. Carey herself comes from a racially mixed background, but at the onset of her career, she did not attempt to make an issue of it. Says the star, "my mother is Irish, my father is black and Venezuelan, and me—I'm tan, I guess" (Singapore's Passion For Mariah). A reason for this approach is that her initial fan base was mostly composed of white, middle and upper class consumers, who may not have warmed to a more urban musician.

Also, one must remember that Carey's career took off at a time when grunge rock and gangster rap were booming. Her fan base was nourished by those who did not fit in with this music of angst and anger. Carey fans enjoyed the fact that her music was happy, and her image was wholesome. There were no curse words in her lyrics, no distortion in her instruments, and no political messages in her songs. This formula worked extremely well throughout the early nineties; however, toward the end of the decade, a new form of pop music surfaced. There was an explosion of very attractive, very manufactured, and very young talent, who sold tremendously well. Carey began to feel that this new wave of music was detracting from her own audience, as well as that these new pop icons were younger, and perhaps better looking than her.

Carey's 1995 album *Daydream* began to illustrate the change in the artist's image. On the album Carey collaborates for the first time, both in songwriting and in singing. She performs duets with gangster rapper Ol' Dirty Bastard, of Wu-Tang Clan, and also with the well-established R&B group Boyz II Men (Bonin). Both songs reached the number one spot on the pop charts. Also during this period, Carey's physical appearance begins to change. During the *Emotions* years, Carey was always fully clothed and glamorous; yet, as her albums progress, Carey begins to appear in more revealing and more urbanized outfits. In fact, up until the release of the *Butterfly* album, Carey's full body had never been shown on an album cover (RollingStone.com). Since *Butterfly*, Carey has appeared in a skimpy tube-top, a bikini, and in a strategically cropped, bare shoulder photo, that leads the potential consumer to believe that singer is naked in the picture (RollingStone.com). All of this illustrates the process by which Carey's image was changed, for what initially appeared to be a profitable reason.

Where her earlier work was being purchased by mostly white, female audiences, after *Butterfly* her music became more acceptable both to a suburban audience who wanted to be urban and to urban audiences who wanted something other than gangster rap (RollingStone.com). This was the first time that Carey began to noticeably exploit her mixed-race heritage. Also, her new image was now gravitating much more towards the male audience than ever before. In her earlier work, Carey's sex appeal was always limited, but now, it was wide open. All of these marketing strategies appeared to be working well—that is, until recently.

The first signs of faltering in Carey's career began in the years just before her breakdown. In 1998, Carey divorced Tommy Mottola, then the boss at Sony Records (Corliss). From there, Carey made the record deal with Virgin and EMI, but according to the *Time* article, Carey began to believe that Mottola was attempting to sabotage her image (Corliss). She went so far as to hire private investigator Jack Palladino, a man who has worked for both Jeffrey Wigand in the *Insider* Tobacco case, and for Bill Clinton in his series of sex scandals (Corliss).

What followed in the months just before the breakdown can only be described as a series of eccentric episodes. On the set of the upcoming film *Wisegirls* Carey reportedly got into a fight with costar Mira Sorvino (Singapore's Passion For Mariah). Conflicting accounts about the extent and severity of the fight have surfaced. *People* reported that the two "threw things at one another," but Carey's publicist will only acknowledge that "words were exchanged" (Singapore's Love For Mariah). This event was followed by a frazzled BET interview and a bizarre *Total Request Live* taping where the star stripped down to a sports bra. According to the *Entertainment Weekly* article, while appearing at a mall in Westbury, New York, Carey began to ramble to a crowd of onlookers about "Positivity" (Bonin). Her incomprehensible rant went on until her publicist, Cindi Berger, attempted to grab the microphone from her (Bonin). A brief struggle occurred of which Berger says, "I won." (Bonin). This led to an intense exchange between the star and her publicist (Bonin). Says Berger, "She was upset, . . . I did not want her to air her frustrations publicly on camera. Never on camera." (Bonin). Despite all of these efforts by Carey's camp to help salvage her image, the worst was yet to come.

To promote Carey's upcoming film *Glitter*, the soundtrack album—which featured songs with more rappers such as the Da Brat, Ludacris, Ja Rule, and Nate Dogg—was released months before the movie was to open (official website). Again this album was geared toward a more urban audience in an attempt to widen Carey's fanbase. However, the album's first single, "Loverboy," received weak airplay, and remained frozen in the mid-60s on the Billboard hot 100 chart. The single eventually ascended to the number two slot, but could not surpass a single by the R&B/rap girl band Destiny's Child (featuring a young Beyoncé Knowles). This upset the star a great deal. One close friend of Carey's said that she was "very concerned" about the star (Serpick). Then, less than a month before the release of her film, Mariah Carey suffered a breakdown. On her official website, this message was posted the next day: "I'm trying to understand things in my life right now and so I really don't feel that I should be doing music right now. I'm gonna take, like, a minute off . . . Nothing's wrong" (official website). (These messages soon disappeared, and no trace of them can be found on the website today.)

What happened to Mariah Carey exemplifies one of the saddest stories in the entertainment world: a star who tries to become someone they're not in order to remain who they want to be. In short, the audience that Carey attempted to reach did not accept her new persona, despite the best intentions of her PR campaign; and in this attempt, she lost part of her core fanbase. As one music marketing executive states, "we aren't idiots in this field. It happens all the time that, once they're stars, musicians believe they're right and everyone else is full of shit. That works if you have good taste, like Madonna. But from what we've been seeing, Mariah doesn't" (Bonin).

Mariah's campaign to change her image was multipronged. She reconstructed her image to appear younger, in an attempt to make herself more accessible to a younger audience. However, the star herself is well into her thirties, and has been competing with well-conditioned, aesthetically chosen twentysomethings and teenagers. On this point, Carey has been making attempts at showing off her physical appearance, but with mixed results. As one music executive puts it, she looks like a "shrink-wrapped cheesecake" (Bonin). DoublXXposure consultant Angelo Ellerbee, whose clientele includes DMX and Mary J. Blige, says of Mariah's physical appearance that "the body is not that booming. She should work with a classy designer . . . so we notice the voice and not the sex" (Bonin).

This leads into the question of her music style. Her original fan base was sold on her wholesome image and sheer vocal talent. "What made her was the strong ballads, not 200 duets with every rapper under the sun," says Ellerbee (Bonin). "She needs MTV to sell large numbers, and she's not twenty anymore," says an established music manager (Goodman). Where she has gone, her audience has not followed, yet Carey has not been counted out just yet.

Since her breakdown, Carey has kept up a number of public appearances, perhaps to make it appear like nothing was wrong. She sang the national anthem at the 2002 Super Bowl, and has visited her own summer camp, Camp Mariah, to pass out copies of her single "Loverboy" (Singapore's Passion For Mariah). She has been on the cover of countless teenybopper magazines and performed in the most successful telethon of all time, *America: A Tribute to Heroes*, a fundraiser helping New York City after the September 11, 2001, attacks (RollingStone.com). Her website also continues to post positive reviews of both the film and the album *Glitter*. *Glitter* features 12 tracks that run the musical gamut, from Mariah's highly stylized dramatic pop ballads to straight-up urban-orientated party tunes (official website). All of this shows that Carey's PR people are still working to help the star recover, but what remains to be seen is whether or not the star will resurface as the Carey of old, or as something brand new.

Over her 13-year career, Mariah Carey drastically transformed her public image, going from a naive young teenager to a thirty-something sex goddess. The levels of success have varied, but like any public relations battle, Carey's camp continues to try and guess the newest direction of public opinion. Whatever the next move for Carey will be, one thing is for certain: her next image will be part of a PR campaign that is as well-orchestrated as her previous one.

Works Cited

1. Bonin, Liane. "Just Duet." *Entertainment Weekly*. EW.com. March 2, 2002.
2. Borowitz, Andy. "The Borowitz Report: CIA Using Mariah Carey Movie in Al Qaeda Interrogations." *Newsweek*. Newsweek.com. January 2, 2002.
3. Corliss, Richard. "A Diva Takes a Dive." *Time*. TIME.com. August 13, 2001.
4. Goodman, Fred. "Mariah: What's Next?" *RollingStone*. RollingStone.com. March 28, 2001.
5. MariahCarey.com. Official Website.
6. RollingStone.com. Mariah Carey Biography.
7. Serpick, Evan. "Money Honey." *Entertainment Weekly*. EW.com. March 2, 2002.
8. Singapore's Passion For Mariah. http://www.geocities.com/mariahcareysg.com.

Topics for Reading and Writing

1. Flasher seems implicitly to be criticizing Carey for her changes and her efforts to alter her appearance and music for different audiences. What, though, is wrong with that? Shouldn't a pop singer try to reach the largest and most lucrative audiences possible?

2. How does Flasher's rhetorical strategies differ from those of the editorial writers? What are the characteristics of the academic paper that appear in his article? How does he use source material differently than Petrecca or Gladwell? Why?

3. Do you think Mariah Carey is the exception or the rule when it comes to the promotion of celebrity? Do her handlers treat the public unethically? Do they treat her unethically? Does the public treat her unethically?

4. How has Flasher conducted the research for his paper? What evidence does he use? Can you think of other conclusions one might draw from that evidence, or of other kinds of evidence that Flasher might also have used? Does Flasher's dependence on Internet sources weaken his credibility? Which sources are credible, and which might lack credibility?

The Writer at Work Arguments About Evaluations and Judgments

Chuck Berry was the greatest rocker ever, but the Beatles are the best musicians of the rock era.

Putting marijuana smokers in jail is a terrible response to teenage drug use.

The "C" I received on my last paper wasn't fair—this was clearly a "B" paper.

You'll definitely want broadband DSL rather than a cable modem.

The Ford El Camino combines the comfort of a pickup truck with the payload of a passenger car.

There is no way that *Titanic* was the best picture of 1997!

All of us go through our lives making evaluations and judgments about everything we encounter. If we make initial sense of the world through those definitions and categories we discussed in the previous chapter, evaluations and judgments help us understand what we want and love and appreciate in the world—what's a good thing and what's a bad thing, to put it in its simplest terms. Already you've probably constructed and accepted or rejected dozens of evaluative arguments today: Do these shoes look good with this skirt? Yes they do, but are they going to be good in the rain? Should I take the bus or drive to work? Should I walk up the stairs to class or take the elevator? Am I going to take better notes on my laptop or with paper? Even though these questions seem to be of very different types, the decisions you made rested on claims of evaluation or judgment. In your mind you have learned what makes a good shoe-skirt combination; you look at these particular shoes and this particular skirt and try to evaluate it according to guidelines you have developed over your life. Today you want to get to school as quickly as possible because you're running late, so you evaluate each mode of transportation (in the car I might get stuck in freeway traffic, which will be worse because of the rain; the bus is usually slow but might still be faster than the freeway in this weather). Without even being conscious of it you're constantly making judgments about choices of action, and when confronted by new objects or experiences you evaluate them according to your ideas about that kind of object or experience.

Most of the evaluative arguments we encounter in our daily lives take place internally—we make these judgments often without having to think about them.

But other acts of evaluation—including many of the questions examined by the writers included in *Media and Messages*—are nowhere near so clear or easy. Is the media biased—and if so, is that a bad thing or is that just something we need to accept? What's so wrong about a few large corporations owning most of the major media outlets in America? And what's so valuable about the "community" having a voice? What's wrong with copyright perpetuity? Even such apparently simple claims as *"Charlie's Angels: Full Throttle* isn't as good as the first *Charlie's Angels* movie" rely on complex acts of evaluation.

An evaluative claim must go through almost all the same steps as a definitional claim: make an argument about why something is good or bad (or why something is a good or bad example of a larger criteria—a great horror film, a terrible way to deal with the health care system in the United States, an acceptable way of financing your own higher education), devise criteria about the larger category, and take into consideration the audience's prejudices and preexisting ideas about the meaning or purpose of the larger category. An evaluative argument differs from a definitional argument largely in that one (the definitional) says that item X does or does not fit in category Y, while the other (the evaluative) makes a claim about how much of a Y item X is. How good of a rocker is Chuck Berry? How smart a television show is *The Simpsons?* How reasonable are the Japanese trade delegation's requests?

Obviously, the most important task in making a claim of evaluation or judgment is to come up with criteria for your category—criteria your audience will accept. Always keeping your audience in mind is crucial, for if you want to argue to a group of television critics that *American Idol* is great TV, your criteria will be very different than if you are making that argument to a group of high school students. Each group will have a different idea of what makes "great TV," and if the audience doesn't accept your criteria your argument will not be convincing at all. What criteria might you use to evaluate great TV to a group of teenagers?

- attractive people
- fast-moving, but still easy to follow
- has people you can relate to
- music
- it has a game, a competition, people we root for and against
- it's interactive—the audience helps decide the winner

According to these criteria, *American Idol* certainly would be a hit with teenagers. Would the TV critics accept these criteria? It's unlikely. This is not to say they reject these criteria—who doesn't like attractive people and music and competitions?—but that to a group of critics the term "great TV" signifies something else entirely.

- has both emotional and intellectual components
- is both immediately compelling and retains the ability to surprise us
- features good writing, good direction, and good acting
- makes us think about important things in different ways
- if it includes music, it should include sophisticated music used well

For our hypothetical teenagers, then, the most important factor here is entertainment. This makes sense: teenagers like to be entertained; their intellectual experiences happen in school and in their extracurricular activities. For the critics, though, that something is merely "entertaining" isn't enough: TV must be doing new things, pushing intellectual and artistic envelopes, exploiting the possibilities of the genre.

A similar instance of differing criteria emerges every year in March, when the Academy Awards are presented to the best movies of the previous year. Film lovers and filmmakers annually wait to see if experimental, artistic, innovative films will be rewarded for their daring and quality, and annually these Oscar-watchers are disappointed when the Academy gives its awards to safe, uplifting, family-friendly crowd pleasers. Why does this happen? Again, it's a matter of audience. The Academy voters tend to be older, more traditional, and more conservative. Many of them don't understand the appeal of movies like *Pulp Fiction, Natural Born Killers,* or *Bamboozled,* but they do see why people want to see *Titanic* or *A Beautiful Mind* or *Erin Brockovich.* For them, "Best Picture" means the movie that best combines technical excellence, great acting, an appealing and moving script, and wide audience appeal. For our younger, edgier audience, the criteria will be much more heavily weighted on the side of innovation, experimentation, and "making it new."

That said, the most important and interesting part of an evaluative argument (just as with a definitional argument) is often the criteria, which represent the ideas of the writer or speaker. I'm probably less interested in my friend's opinion of *Titanic* than I am in what she thinks makes a "great film." The criteria that a writer or speaker proposes for his or her argument are often the actual point of the argument. You've probably had an argument similar to this with a friend:

> Angus Young of AC/DC is the greatest rock guitarist ever.
> You're a moron. I can name 30 better guitarists off the top of my head.
> Just listen to me. Being a great rock guitarist doesn't mean being a
> super-virtuoso. In fact, I think that hurts. A great rock guitarist
> makes things as simple as possible. A great rock guitarist comes up
> with basic 5 or 10-note riffs. Chuck Berry does this. Keith Richards
> does this. But Angus Young does it better than any of them. When
> you hear the first three notes of an AC/DC song, you instantly recog-
> nize it and it makes you want to ROCK!

The preceding argument wasn't really about Angus Young—it was about the speaker's idea of what makes a good rock guitarist. This speaker feels that he has an original, unique idea about that, and was just using the specific example of Angus Young to make his larger point: we should rethink what we usually mean by "great rock guitarist."

IDEAS INTO PRACTICE 6-1

Come up with at least three criteria for the following categories. Try to make your criteria as flexible and nuanced as possible—include a few things that a good X must have, one or two that it cannot have, and one or two that it might, but is not required to, have.

1. A good suspense movie.
2. A terrible place to take a vacation.
3. A good date.
4. A good company homepage.
5. A good dentist.
6. The best cartoon ever.
7. The most important issue facing America today.
8. A feasible solution to global warming.
9. An acceptable compromise between an older sister and a younger brother.
10. An unsuccessful party.

IDEAS INTO PRACTICE 6-2

What common evaluations would you like to change? Choose a few from the following list. Think of what the commonly held idea of what makes a good or the best example of each of the following categories might be—come up with a few criteria you think most people would easily accept. Then propose your own new, different criteria, and explain why they make more sense than the ones they're replacing.

1. An opera singer.
2. A notebook computer.
3. A political system (democracy, republic, monarchy, dictatorship).
4. A university education.
5. A pet.

Let's look at an example of an evaluative claim. Read Eugene Marlow's article on video news releases included in this chapter. In his piece, Marlow doesn't really take an explicit ethical stand on whether or not these VNRs are a good or bad thing; he does use some language that might suggest he's opposed to the spread of using VNRs in place of "real" news, but this isn't really the thesis of his argument. Let's say, for the sake of argument, that in watching the local news last night you saw a segment that was clearly a VNR: the segment was a puff piece for a new pharmaceutical technology, the reporter was not one of the familiar reporters for the local station or its network affiliate, and the anchors thanked a company called "Pharmaceutical Information Services" for the report. Irritated because you feel that the use of VNRs masquerading as news is a dangerous thing, you write a letter to the station's news director. How do you make your argument? Is it sufficient to say "You shouldn't use VNRs because they're bad?" Does this argument work logically? What components does your claim have to have in order to be convincing?

You've probably already spotted the main problem with your claim: it's not enough to say that something is "bad." To make a persuasive argument, you must say *why* it's bad and *for whom*. Let's sketch out a fuller claim:

> The use of video news releases in the news is a bad thing, and as the news director you should ensure that you don't use video news releases in place of reported news.

Why is it a bad thing? Here, as in the definitional claim you learned about in the previous chapter, you need to brainstorm criteria. "Bad" for what? Bad for the reliability of the news? Bad for people's trust in the news? Bad for the news' mission of providing a fair and balanced view of the issues?

All these criteria rely on one proposition: that the point of the news is to provide the people a reliable, trustworthy, balanced source of information. Is this the kind of statement that the news director—who is, after all, your audience—might accept? Yes—in part. For the news director, the purpose of the news *is* to provide viewers with a reliable, trustworthy, balanced source of information. However, for the news director (and his boss, the station manager) the purpose of the news is *also* to bring in viewers and to earn a profit for the station. But let's start with our first proposition, and deal with those potential objections later. Our revised thesis now looks like this:

Using video news releases in place of real news is a bad practice because it goes against the whole purpose of the news: providing people with a reliable, trustworthy, balanced source of information.

Now, as with the arguments about meanings and definitions discussed in the previous chapter, we need to explain our criteria. What do you mean by "reliable"? Do people actually rely on TV news, or do they assume that it is unreliable? Is there a history of TV news being reliable? And given this, how exactly do the VNRs damage the reliability of the TV news? Do they damage the news' reliability if nobody knows they're there—that is, if the news director can completely disguise their provenance, does this undermine our criteria? And what about the other criteria? Do "reliable" and "trustworthy" mean the same thing? How can we pry apart their meanings? And if no news can ever be fully objective, can any news actually be truly balanced? If not, why shouldn't we just embrace that lack of balance? Or, on the other hand, why can't a VNR be balanced?

IDEAS INTO PRACTICE 6-3

Take the argument we sketched out and flesh it out. Outline the entirety of your letter to the news director of the local TV station, detailing your criteria for "good quality news programming" or "bad TV news" (word it in a way that works best for your argument). Make sure to anticipate the news director's objections or counterarguments.

Style **T**oolbox ▌ Sentence Rhythm

Describing his victory over the feared Gauls, the ancient Roman general Julius Caesar summed things up memorably: *Veni, vidi, vici* ("I came, I saw, I conquered"). Caesar's statement embodies much of what we remember about him: determination, an almost swaggering confidence, and the ability to accomplish what he set out to do. The rhythm of his sentence, with its one-word clauses and simplified grammatical structure, counters our expectation that he would describe a long, arduous campaign with a long, drawn-out sentence. Without having to actually say it, Caesar uses the rhythm of his sentence to express the idea "this campaign was quite simple—but what would you expect? I'm Julius Caesar!"

Writers don't use words alone to convey meaning. Surprisingly, the way a sentence is constructed—where the emphasis falls, what parts are accented and what parts aren't, whether the essential information of the sentence is presented immediately or saved until the end—is part of the rhetorical structure of the argument. For instance, the following paragraph—

Fast Times at Ridgemont High is the best teen movie ever. It's got the best cast. Many of them went on to become big stars. It's well-written. Cameron Crowe, the writer, went undercover as a high school student to write it! Amy Heckerling's direction is poignant and very funny. And the character of Jeff Spicoli—has there ever been a better surfer dude?

—has a very different feel than this one:

> *Fast Times at Ridgemont High,* brilliantly written by Cameron Crowe (who actually impersonated a high school student in order to write it!) and sensitively directed by Amy Heckerling, easily ranks as the best example of the "teen movie" genre. It's hard to believe that that cast (Jennifer Jason Leigh, Phoebe Cates, Judge Reinhold, Anthony Edwards, Eric Stoltz, Forrest Whittaker, Nicolas Cage) were all unknowns at that time. But the crowning glory of the film has to be Sean Penn's Jeff Spicoli, a character that has certainly become the paragon of the surfer dude in American popular culture.

Of the two, the second paragraph just sounds . . . smarter. Both give almost exactly the same information, but because of the longer, more complex sentences the writer of the second paragraph appears more authoritative. Often, in making an argument, longer or better-crafted sentences are more persuasive than short ones, probably because a series of short sentences can sound stilted, like the writer or speaker isn't particularly deft at using language.

The reverse, though, can be the case if the audience is likely to respond better to conviction or strong emotion, both of which come through much more clearly in short declarative statements. A series of short sentences (used judiciously and sparingly) also works well to motivate or warm up an audience. Speaking to a right-to-life group, an orator might use the following paragraph:

> We must overturn *Roe* v. *Wade.* We cannot allow more babies to die. We cannot allow this culture of death to continue in this country. We must continue to fight!

The short sentences and the repetition of the "We must . . . We cannot" construction reflects passion. On the other hand, a more subtle or reasoned argument such as the following,

> It's imperative that we confirm a Supreme Court judge who will overturn the *Roe* v. *Wade* decision, for if we don't do that we will continue to allow babies to die. This culture of death that predominates in this nation, exemplified by legal abortion, has to end, and it's necessary for us to fight in order to accomplish that.

while seemingly more intellectually solid, is less likely to rouse a group to action.

Generally, writers accomplish rhythmic effects not by using only one type of sentence, but by using several kinds of sentences in a sequence intended to achieve a specified effect. A writer might begin a paragraph with long, running sentences and then conclude with a very short sentence meant to sum up the previous information and pass judgment on it, as in the following passage from the American novelist Thomas Pynchon:

> One summer afternoon Mrs Oedipa Maas came home from a Tupperware party whose hostess had put perhaps too much kirsch in the fondue to find out that she, Oedipa, had been named executor, or she supposed executrix, of the estate of one Pierce Inverarity, a California real estate mogul who had once lost two million dollars in his spare time but still had assets numerous and tangled enough to make the job of sorting it all out more than honorary. Oedipa stood in the living room, stared at by the greenish dead eye of the TV tube, spoke the name of God, tried to feel as drunk as possible. But this did not work. (Thomas Pynchon, *The Crying of Lot 49*)

Pynchon's paragraph mirrors the rhythm of formal oratory, in which a speaker lays out many details and claims and sums it all up at the end with a snappy demand. This kind of sentence rhythm makes the audience wonder what the point of all of the running narration is (she did this, she did that, she heard this, she learned that), and then gives us a very short stop at the end, a sentence with a pronoun ("this") that makes us look back to find its antecedent. All of the clauses and phrases, moreover, tend to make us a little dizzy and confused—just as Mrs. Oedipa Maas feels after having "too much kirsch" in her fondue.

Another well-known American novelist, Ernest Hemingway, is known for his use of the very short, simple, declarative sentence. Hemingway breaks many of the rules of "good" prose—his rhythm tends not to vary and thus can irritate the reader, he overuses "to be" verbs to such a degree that his prose loses much of its life, he rarely inverts sentences or strays from the subject-verb-object sequence of construction. However, he does this for a purpose: most of his characters (in whose minds the narration takes place) are shell-shocked, world-weary men who have seen a great deal and simply want to rest for a while. The monotony of Hemingway's rhythm lulls us into the minds of the protagonists, and then Hemingway will throw in a long sentence that (like Pynchon's short sentence) jerks us out of our rhythm:

> There was a log house, chinked white with mortar, on a hill above the lake. There was a bell on a pole by the house to call the people in to meals. Behind the house were fields and behind the fields was the timber. A line of lombardy poplars ran from the house to the dock. Other poplars ran along the point. A road went up to the hills along the edge of the timber and along that road he picked blackberries. Then that log house was burned down and all the guns that had been on deer foot racks above the open fire place were burned and afterwards their barrels, with the lead melted in the magazines, and the stocks burned away, lay out on the heap of ashes that were used to make lye for the big iron soap kettles, and you asked Grandfather if you could have them to play with, and he said, no. (Ernest Hemingway, "The Snows of Kilimanjaro")

The long sentence marks the point in this memory-voyage at which the character stops thinking just about the setting and begins thinking about people and events.

There are no hard and fast rules about the rhetorical effects of particular rhythmic patterns. Sometimes a series of short, staccato sentences can be extremely powerful and motivating; sometimes that same series of sentences will sound like simplistic pep-rally language. As you have heard before in this book, rhetoric is radically situational, and the rhetorical effect of almost every use of language is the product of the interaction of the audience, the speaker, the situation, and the speaker's argument. Fortunately, because we are such experts at communicating in language, we are pretty good at predicting what the effect of any given use of language might be, even if we can't actually verbalize why that is. As you learn to write for this new academic audience, doubtless you'll misjudge the appropriateness of your diction, vocabulary, sentence rhythm, and the like more than once. However, understanding that all these are tools that can be used to give your writing a more calculated effect is the first step in learning precisely how to use those tools.

WRITING WITH STYLE 6-1

Experiment with sentence rhythm. In response to one of the following prompts, write three or four paragraphs that use different rhythmic patterns. In one, write exclusively short subject-verb sentences. In another, perhaps alternate short/long sentences. In the third, perhaps write three or four very long, running sentences (such as sentences that tack on clauses and prepositional phrases one after the other) and finish with a short sentence. In the final paragraph, reverse that pattern. Or make up your own variety! Just be sure to try at least three or four different kinds of patterns, and focus on the *rhetorical effects* of each.

1. The most important issue facing America today, and what we should do about it.
2. Whether or not your university should require community service as a prerequisite for graduation, and why.
3. The inherent conflicts and synergies between media companies such as Viacom or News Corp. and technology companies such as Microsoft or Qualcomm.
4. Your opinion of the increasingly mainstream use of cosmetic surgery and medical procedures such as collagen injections, Botox, pectoral implants, and the like.
5. The educational benefits of taking a year off before attending college.

What Should I Say, and How Should I Say It?

Chapter 7

"**P**olitical correctness." You've certainly heard about it. You might have even experienced it. Just by the name you know it can't be a good thing—who wants to be "politically correct"? But what does it really mean, and how has it affected the ways that individuals communicate with each other, or the ways that the mass media communicates with all of us?

The term "politically correct" came into common usage in the 1980s. Initially, to call someone politically correct was an act of humorous or ironic praise—that person was so careful to be sensitive to all groups and to hold all the "right" opinions that he or she could be dubbed "correct." Arising among the groups of the political left, the correctness in question generally referred to small acts of linguistic sensitivity—using the appellation "Native Americans" rather than "Indians," or "African Americans" instead of "blacks." As the civil rights struggle demonstrated to the

Howard Stern (center), the controversial radio host.

culture at large, one important way that groups in power maintain their control over other groups is by determining the names to call those groups, and so an important early act of resistance was to reclaim the name. Among other groups, the process of determining a name was even more complicated. Before the 1960s, all people of Latino descent in the United States tended to be called "Mexicans" or "Spanish." Activism among these groups made their differences plain: people of Mexican descent who were born in the United States had different experiences and interests than people born in Mexico, and so used the term "Chicanos" to describe themselves. Other Hispanic groups also made their unique identities known: Puerto Ricans, Dominicans, Peruvians, Guatemalans, and many others. In recent years, society is starting to recognize that it's too simple even to break down people's ethnicity into these groupings, because so many of us come from mixed backgrounds. The golfer Tiger Woods, for instance, referred to himself as "Cablinasian"—Caucasian, black, American Indian, and Asian.

While these changes in nomenclature were generally accepted, others were not. Some feminists, wanting to ensure that women's separate identity from men was reinforced linguistically, began spelling the word "women" "womyn" and substituting the neologism "herstory" for history. These proposed changes were widely ridiculed. Other groups, too, wished to have their common names changed so they could define themselves more positively—"crippled people" became "the disabled" and, later, "the differently abled." The term "mentally retarded" (which itself had replaced uglier terms like "cretin" or "feeblemind") became "mentally challenged" or "developmentally delayed."

Political correctness wasn't just about naming, either. In order to be politically correct, one had to support an array of social policies intended to help disadvantaged groups—the Equal Rights Amendment, affirmative action, bilingual education, the revision of college curricula to include the study of non-Western cultures. Most of these changes were efforts on the part of activists to make society less cruel to nondominant groups and to make society recognize the unique contributions of all its members. However, the occasionally excessive zeal of many such activists to convert people to their way of thinking met with great resistance, and the term "politically correct" quickly became a term of attack. Stories—some true, some probably apocryphal—detailing the horrors and excesses of political correctness (especially on college campuses) made the rounds of the culture through talk radio, conservative magazines, and word of mouth. By the mid-1990s, many people were convinced that American college campuses were ruled by a cadre of intensely disciplined intellectual stormtroopers, led by a corps of Marxist professors, who were determined to stomp out any dissent. Although this impression was vastly exaggerated, it is true that political correctness thrived in the college and university setting.

Always minutely sensitive to public opinion, the corporate media have responded in their own way to the political correctness (PC) movement. News producers have become much more sensitive about the images they put on television, and make an effort not to show young black men in handcuffs, young black women with several children, poor white people living in trailers, and other stereotypical images. Education scholar Diane Ravitch has studied another branch of the corporate media—the publishers of school textbooks—and shown that hundreds of images, ideas, and phrases are now banned from those books. On that list: "Adam and Eve" (should be "Eve and Adam," to show that men aren't superior or primary), depictions of Irish-American policemen (stereotypical), "anchorman" (sexist), "Founding Fathers" (same), African-American athletes (racist), and even a story about forest animals living in a rotted tree trunk (could be interpreted as offensive to people who live in shoddy apartments). Textbook publishers are sensitive, as well, to the often right-wing committees and boards of education that purchase books for large states like Texas and California, and so will also delete references to evolution or the scientifically hypothesized age of the Earth.[1]

Entertainment has also been affected by PC. Until the late 1960s the sight of a nonwhite person on television was relatively rare, but in the 1970s, television producers such as Norman Lear began to develop programs about nonwhite families. Such programs as *The Jeffersons, Good Times, Sanford and Son,* or *Chico and the Man* depicted African-American and Latino life, and can proba-

---

[1] Ravitch's book *The Language Police* (2003) describes these incursions into textbooks in great detail; for her, contemporary textbooks "combine left-wing political correctness and right-wing fundamentalism, a strange stew of discordant influences." Included in this chapter is a short editorial by Ravitch on this very subject.

The Huxtable family from
The Cosby Show.

bly be understood as precursors of the desire for "diversity" (a central term in the political correctness debate) in the media. The television networks tended to try to include at least one nonwhite cast member in all their shows, leading to the concept of the "token" black actor. (Robert Townsend's hilarious film *Hollywood Shuffle* (1987) depicts, in several comic vignettes, his struggles as a black actor faced with an endless series of roles as a pimp, mugger, street hoodlum, or servant in the 1970s and 1980s.) Things seemed to change in the 1980s, when *The Cosby Show,* a situation comedy about a highly educated and affluent African-American family, achieved enormous popularity for years. After *Cosby,* though, few similar shows were produced, and those that were produced were nowhere near as successful. In the 1990s, responding to increased pressure from advocacy groups, the networks attempted to develop more shows featuring nonwhite casts. Some, like *Martin* or *The Fresh Prince of Bel Air,* were quite popular; others, like the short-lived situation comedy *All-American Girl* starring the Korean-American comedienne Margaret Cho, lasted only a short while. When such shows fail, the networks generally argue that white audiences (which still form the majority of the U.S. population) are not interested in programs about nonwhite people, while the cast members and show creators generally argue that the networks meddled too much with the show and did not allow it to develop an individual voice or style. In the case of *All-American Girl,* for instance, the network executives insisted that Cho had to slim down significantly to be appealing to mainstream audiences; her crash diet landed her in the hospital with liver failure, and the show declined along with Cho's health.

Interestingly, smaller stations took up where the networks would not. For years, big cities had supported small UHF stations (UHF, or ultra-high frequency, refers to the broadcast spectrum above channel 13 on a normal television) that catered to specific ethnic populations. Chicago had Polish television, Miami had a Cuban station, New York had Russian and Italian channels, and Southern California supported several Spanish-language stations. In the 1990s, two companies (Telemundo and Univision) developed nationwide Spanish-language cable networks. As the Latino population in the United States has grown—and grown wealthier—the large networks have begun to cater to that large market, running Spanish-language commercials during sporting events. Recently, the broadcast network NBC bought a large interest in Telemundo. At the same time, Latino faces are starting to be seen even on the mainstream networks: the Mexican-American comedian George Lopez headlined his own show on ABC during the 2003–2004 season, and CBS makes a point of including Cuban-American characters on its *CSI: Miami* crime drama.

Hollywood movies, too, have responded to the pressure of so-called political correctness. For decades, the only roles African Americans could play in mainstream cinemas were servants or criminals; notwithstanding these limitations, the African-American actress Hattie McDaniel won an Academy Award for her portrayal of "Mammy" in *Gone with the Wind* (1939). Other pioneering black actors followed—Sidney Poitier, Bill Cosby, even Nichelle Nichols of *Star Trek*—until by the 1970s it was no longer remarkable to see black characters on television or in the movies treated just like white characters. Although it's considered politically correct to include people of color in the casts of movies and television shows, many activists have argued that the positions behind the camera are more important. On-camera diversity for its own sake has been attacked as "tokenism"—making sure that a member of each minority group is represented as a way of avoiding criticism without really relinquishing the control that the dominant group—white men—maintains.

Many other minority groups have also objected to their portrayals in the movies and on television, and those concerns are increasingly taken seriously. In the 1970s, the Italian-American Anti-Defamation League protested that the *Godfather* movies gave the false impression that all Italians were embroiled in organized crime; similar protests met the popularity of the recent HBO drama *The Sopranos*. Movie studios have to be careful about the foreign villains in thriller or action movies, as well—villains must be of a nationality that Americans can get worked up against, but they cannot be from a group that actually is experiencing real discrimination or prejudice. In pre-1970s Westerns, for example, the "Indians" were always the villains, and were almost always depicted as brutal savages. Later movies looked at the myth of the West through indigenous eyes, though—such films as *Dances with Wolves* (1990) or *Smoke Signals* (1998) have been much more sympathetic to the "natives" than to the white settlers. Arabs were frequently villains in the 1970s and 1980s, but in the 1990s and especially after the September 11 attacks Hollywood has shied away from making films in which Arabs or Muslims are demonized.

Similar issues arise when talking about the representation of almost any other historically oppressed or marginalized group. In her extensive discussion of the homosexual text and subtext on the very mainstream situation comedy *Seinfeld* (included in this chapter's readings), Katherine Gantz brings up some very provocative questions about what's acceptable to portray on television, what's acceptable to suggest, and what's just unacceptable. Another recent NBC sitcom, *Will and Grace,* deals much more forthrightly with male homosexuality—the title character, Will, is openly gay, and his friend Jack is stereotypically flamboyant—but many people suspect that neither the Will nor the Jack character will ever be allowed to have a real relationship because that would make the portrayal of homosexuality "too real" for network executives or middle America. But is the only reason that Will and Jack appear on television NBC's desire to be politically correct? It's not just historically marginalized groups who feel slighted by the entertainment industry, either. Conservative groups charge that the last group that can be regularly shown in a negative light are religious people, who are portrayed as closed-minded, discriminatory, killjoy Philistines.

If political correctness is no longer the consuming preoccupation it was 10 years ago, that can partly be attributed to its success. It is no longer acceptable to call all people of Asian descent "Chinese" or "Orientals," for instance, and casual slurs against gays are no longer a part of public discourse. After the civil rights movement forced the United States to change its legal and official systems of discrimination, in recent years the political correctness movement has, at least, forced us to think about how the language we use can be harmful—not just by hurting individuals' feelings, but by maintaining *de facto* structures of repression and discrimination against people of different religions, races, gender, or economic status. And although the "PC police" have argued that "angry white men" who complain about political correctness are only motivated by resentment about their diminishing supremacy, as students of rhetoric you should keep in mind just how off-putting and *un*persuasive a self-righteous nag can be.

A nalyzing the Message

1. Does mainstream American society "owe" something to the groups it has historically oppressed—African Americans, Latinos, women, homosexuals? What? Does the PC movement address that obligation or not? How do we determine who is an "oppressor" and who is a "victim"?

2. What is the proper way to portray homosexuality on television? Should there be more of it on television? Less?

3. Most of the PC debate centers on the idea that language and naming have power. Is this a false assumption? What harm does language do? How does that harm compare with the harm done by legal discrimination or by personal persecution?

4. Many conservative groups argue that PC has become its own form of oppression and prejudice—people who don't use the "right" terms or have the "right" ideas are ostracized or persecuted. Do you agree? What examples of this do you see in contemporary America?

Readings

Conservative writer and radio talk show host **Larry Elder** writes here about what he sees as the media's politically correct bias in covering crime stories. The murders of Matthew Shepard and James Byrd, Elder argues, both became causes celèbres for liberals in the media, for both played into important master narratives about racist, homophobic white males who must resort to violence when their superiority is questioned. However, the media was not so eager to cover the story of two black police officers in a Chicago suburb who forced a white man to walk home through some tough neighborhoods, where he was assaulted and fatally burned. Nor did the media cover a companion crime to Byrd's murder that occurred in the same small Texas town, the killing of a white man (Ken Tillery) allegedly by three African-American men. This article appeared in Capitalism Magazine, a small conservative magazine inspired by the writings of the novelist Ayn Rand.

Larry Elder
Politically Correct Murder and Media Bias: Some Murder Victims Are "More Equal" Than Others

On Oct. 7, 1998, two thugs killed gay University of Wyoming student Matthew Shepard. HBO recently moved up the airdate for "The Laramie Project," its Matthew Shepard movie, in order to beat NBC's soon-to-air movie about the same murder.

Killers kidnapped and robbed Shepard, apparently because of Shepard's sexual orientation, tied him to a fence, beat him into a coma, then left him to die. This shocking killing made international headlines.

Given Hollywood's interest in, call it, sexual orientation murder, we might then soon expect a Hollywood feature called "The Jesse Dirkhising Story." Who is Jesse Dirkhising?

Approximately one year after the abduction and murder of Matthew Shepard, two gay men abducted, tied up and raped Jesse Dirkhising. The *Denver Post*'s Sue O'Brien describes the killing, "Police say the 13-year-old was drugged and blindfolded, gagged with underwear, strapped to a mattress and then brutally and repeatedly sodomized by one of his killers while the other watched. Ultimately, the seventh-grader died of suffocation because of the position he was in."

On June 7, 1998, three white racists abducted and dragged James Byrd, a black man of Jasper, Texas. This killing properly provoked international outrage. Jesse Jackson, Al Sharpton, NAACP President Kweisi Mfume, Houston Mayor Lee Brown and Rep. Maxine Waters (D-Calif.) came to Jasper to condemn the killing and express condolences to the Byrd family.

Sen. Kay Bailey Hutchison (R-Texas) said that Byrd's death and his family's way of coping served as an example to others. "We are diminished by this act," said Hutchison, "but from the depths of our pain, the fog of all our disbelief, we are going to emerge stronger . . . .We have seen a family tested. We are better today because we have seen a family tested like no other family has been tested." President Bill Clinton, in a letter to the Byrd family, said, "People across our nation have been shocked and saddened by this tragedy. Violence and hatred in our society hurt us all, but few have had to endure its effects as personally as have you and your loved ones."

But how many presidential letters went out to the family of Ken Tillery? Who is Ken Tillery?

Tillery, approximately a month ago, walked down a Jasper, Texas, road. Three men offered him a ride. But the men kidnapped Tillery, driving him to a remote location. John Perazzo of FrontPageMagazine.com, describes what happened: "When the terrified Tillery jumped out of the vehicle and tried to flee, the kidnappers caught up with him, beat him, and finally ran over him—*dragging* (emphasis added) him to his death beneath their car's undercarriage." How much coverage did the case get? An online search of 557 newspapers found that 22 covered the story.

Why the deafening silence?

Well, Tillery is white, and the three suspects in the case—Darrell Gilbert, Blake Little and Anthony Holmes—are all black.

No story.

In 1995, the late *Chicago Tribune* columnist Mike Royko wrote about a tragedy that took place in a Chicago suburb. According to Royko, the police stopped two black men in a car and arrested the driver for outstanding warrants. They towed the driver's car, leaving the passenger to fend for himself in a tough, predominantly white Chicago neighborhood. "Please don't leave me," the black man begged the cops, to no avail. Fifteen minutes later, this same black man was found suffering third-degree burns. Just as the man feared, apparently someone in this tough neighborhood doused him with some inflammable liquid and set him on fire. He later died.

But then Royko threw us a curve. He wrote that, yes, he factually described the incident, but with one small wrinkle. He reversed the races of the cops and the drivers. Royko said, "Would this create much of a public uproar? Demands by community and political leaders for a full investigation? Based on past events, yes, there could be quite an outcry. Assuming, of course, that this story is factual. But it isn't entirely true. I changed a few facts. Such as race. In reality, the two cops were black and the two men they stopped were white." Again, no story. Never mind that where violent crime takes place between blacks and whites, the cases overwhelmingly involve a black perpetrator and a white victim.

In "Coloring the News: How Crusading for Diversity Has Corrupted American Journalism," journalist William McGowan exposes modern mainstream journalism's let's-emphasize-racism-while-minimizing-minority-crime bias. *New York Times* publisher Arthur Sulzberger Jr., according to McGowan, said, "If being labeled PC is the burden we must carry for offering readers a broader, more complete and therefore more accurate picture of the diverse world around us, it is one I bear proudly."

Mainstream media continue to deny their liberal bias. It's just that mainstream media consider some murder victims more equal than others.

Topics for Reading and Writing

1. Elder's rhetorical approach is anecdotal: he uses the media coverage of two representative crimes to argue that the media rarely covers such crimes honestly. How effective can an anecdotal argument be? Are there kinds of arguments that lend themselves more to anecdotal evidence? What kinds of arguments don't work well with anecdotal evidence? Identify other articles in this book that rely on anecdotal evidence.

2. Why do you think the media covered Tillery's case so differently than they covered Byrd's? Is there an important difference in those crimes, or does this coverage prove Elder's point that the media shies away from covering crimes with African-American perpetrators?

*Political correctness has seen few successes more total than in the arena of school textbooks, writes the educational historian **Diane Ravitch**. In this editorial from the* Wall Street Journal, *Ravitch details some of the more ridiculous examples of political correctness and excessive "sensitivity" in the production of public-school textbooks. Publishers provide writers with guidelines for how to represent almost everything so as to avoid any possible offense to anyone. Of course, Ravitch feels, with so much attention to sensitivity it is almost impossible to accurately teach American history—or much else.*

Ravitch, currently Research Professor of Education at New York University and a Brookings Institution Fellow, is the author of The Language Police: How Pressure Groups Restrict What Students Learn *(2003),* Left Back: A Century of Battles over School Reform *(2000), and* The Schools We Deserve *(1985), among many other publications. Ravitch also served as assistant secretary of education in the administration of George H.W. Bush.*

Diane Ravitch
Cut on the Bias

Students across the state of New York recently took their Regents' examinations, the tests that they must pass in order to get a high school diploma. A year ago, the state education department was embarrassed when Jeanne Heifetz, a vigilant parent in Brooklyn, announced her discovery that state officials had expurgated literary selections on the English examination. Words and sentences that might offend anyone had been quietly deleted from passages by writers such as Elie Wiesel, Isaac Bashevis Singer, and Franz Kafka.

New York's penchant for bowdlerizing literature, it turns out, was not unique to the Empire State. The educational publishing industry follows very specific guidelines to ensure that school children are not exposed to words or topics that might be controversial, especially those that are related to gender, race, religion, or sex. I compiled a list of over 500 words that are banned by one or more publishers. Some are relatively obsolete, like "authoress" or "geezer," but others are everyday words that one is likely to encounter in the newspaper, like "landlord," "senior citizen," "dogma," "yacht" or "actress" (what would the late Katharine Hepburn have made of that?).

Since my book appeared, I have received a large number of letters from people in the educational publishing industry, offering fresh material about the sanitizing that occurs on a regular basis. In Michigan, the state does not allow mention of flying saucers or extraterrestrials on its test, because those subjects might imply the forbidden topic of evolution. A text illustrator wrote to say that she was not permitted to portray a birthday party because Jehovah's Witnesses do not believe in celebrating birthdays. Another illustrator told me that he was directed to airbrush the udder from his drawing of a cow because that body part was "too sexual."

A review of my book in "The Scotsman" (Edinburgh) said that a well-known local writer for children sold a story to an American textbook company, along with illustrations. The U.S. publisher, however, informed her that she could not show a little girl sitting on her grandfather's lap, as the drawing implied incest. So, the author changed the adult's face, so that the little girl was sitting on her grandmother's lap instead. A contributor to a major textbook series prepared a story comparing the great floods in 1889 in Johnstown, Pa., with those in 1993 in the Midwest, but was unable to find an acceptable photograph. The publisher insisted that everyone in the rowboats must be wearing a life vest to demonstrate safety procedures.

A freelance writer sent me the "bias guidelines" for a major publisher of texts and tests. The "bias guidelines" consist of advice to writers and editors about words and topics that must be avoided, as well as specifications for illustrations. Like other publishers, this one requires adherence to gender and ethnic balance. All lessons, test questions, and illustrations must reflect the following ratios: 50-50 male-female; 45% Caucasian; 25% African American; 22% Hispanic American; 5% Asian American; 5% American Indian and others; and 3% "persons with disabilities." These figures do not total 100%, nor do they represent actual U.S. Census numbers, but the principle of representation is well understood by writers and editors. American society, as represented in the textbooks, is perfectly integrated by race, ethnicity, gender, age, and disability.

When it comes to illustrations in textbooks, certain images—women cooking, men acting assertive, scenes of poverty, and old people walking with the aid of a cane or a walker—are likewise considered unacceptable. The specifications for photographs, I have learned, are exquisitely detailed. Men and boys must not be larger than women and girls. Asians must not appear as shorter than non-Asians. Women must wear bras, and men must not have noticeable bulges below the waist. People must wear shoes and socks, never showing bare feet or the soles of shoes, and their shoelaces must be solid black, brown, or white. People must never gesture with their fingers, nor should anyone be depicted eating with the left hand. Things to avoid: holiday decorations and scenes in which a church or a bar appears in the background.

There are so many rules, one wonders how they manage to keep track of them. Even after its national humiliation a year ago, the New York State Education Department still manages to make mistakes. On the last administration of the Regents' English examination in January, the state asked high school seniors to write about a poem by Matthew Arnold. However, the examination did not mention the name of this famous poem ("Dover Beach"); it inexplicably offered only one stanza of the four-stanza poem; and it changed or misquoted an important line. Instead of Arnold's exclamation, "Ah, love, let us be true to one another!" it stated, "Ah, friend, let us be true to one another!"

As the example shows, bowdlerization is not only dishonest, it leads to dumbing down of language and ideas. And of one thing I am convinced: The widespread censorship of language and ideas in education caused by the demands of advocacy groups will not end unless it is regularly exposed to public review and ridicule. The next time someone in a publishing office or a state education agency suggests deleting a literary passage from a test or textbook because it contains the word "anchorman" or shows a witch flying around on a broomstick, perhaps someone in the room will say, "Wait, if we do that, people will laugh at us."

Topics for Reading and Writing

1. Is Ravitch guilty of "stacking the deck" (see the Writer at Work section of Chapter 3) by relying so much on the most excessive examples she can find?

2. Is there a happy medium of "sensitizing" school textbooks? What kinds of guidelines can we create to avoid the egregious examples Ravitch describes but still pay attention to the sensitivities of various groups?

3. What examples of "sensitivity" in your own high school textbooks do you remember? How did your textbooks handle touchy subjects like the civil rights movement, the westward expansion, or the Vietnam War?

Boondocks © 2000 *Aaron McGruder. Dist. by Universal Press Syndicate. Reprinted with permission. All rights reserved.*

Bumfights, a crudely produced video featuring homeless men fighting each other and performing Jackass-like stunts, was made by two student filmmakers, and quickly gained the attention of radio personality Howard Stern, who promoted it on his show. Selling on the Internet for $19.95, the video quickly became popular among young men. The problem was that the video featured a great deal of footage that almost crossed the line from filmmaking into illegal exploitation. After the video gained popularity, some of its "performers" began telling journalists they had been coerced into performing the dangerous antics (which included punching each other, ramming their heads into walls, and extracting their own teeth) by the filmmakers. The "performers" also testified that

Derek Shaw
Punks, Bums, and Politicians

Love it or hate it, the shocking video "Bumfights" has sold hundreds of thousands of copies over the Internet and invaded the living rooms of countless American homes.

Thanks to a storm of international media coverage since the video's release in mid-April, "Bumfights" has caught the attention of everyone from Howard Stern to the F.B.I. The outrageous video, which features such gratuitous violence as school-yard fights and a homeless man ramming his head into a metal garbage dumpster, has received both praise and contempt from the American people.

As a close friend of the primary producer of the video, I have seen what lies on the other side of the camera. Over the past few months, I have watched his name being thrown around national television, radio and the internet with such labels as "uncaring, unfeeling individual" and "criminal."

I would simply like to tell some basic facts about the video, most of which goes unreported by the media and unrecognized by the general public.

the filmmakers took advantage of their alcoholism, and gave them liquor in exhange for their performances. Three of the filmmakers were convicted in June 2003 of conspiring to stage an illegal fight and fined $500 apiece, but according to the Los Angeles Times, *rather than seeming chastised by the lecture from Superior Court Judge Charles Ervin or relieved at being sentenced to probation instead of jail, the three left the courtroom smiling, laughing, and vowing to produce an equally outrageous video soon.*

In a guest editorial from the University of Southern California Daily Trojan, one of the film's self-described "creators" (**Derek Shaw**) argues that there is nothing wrong with the video, while an opposing piece from the daily newspaper of **California State University, Long Beach** counters that the video is simply "exploitation." Who's right? Who has the right to determine what's acceptable for consenting adults to do? To watch? To buy? Finally, the third contribution to this debate comes from U.S. Representative **Earl Blumenauer,** a Democrat from Oregon. Blumenauer uses his position and the powerful forum of the floor of the U.S. House to argue for criminal prosecution of the filmmakers responsible for Bumfights.

I remember meeting Rufus Hannah and Donnie Brennan, two of the homeless men featured in the film, when I was a junior in high school. At the time, my friends and I were working on a video entitiled "Afro" that later became the foundation for what is known today as "Bumfights."

We first approached Rufus and Donnie out of curiosity and compassion. A few months later, they had become more than stars in our video: they were our friends. Granted, we were interested in filming them because there was something unmistakably intriguing about the things we were catching on tape. I am not justifying the violence and destruction that ensued, but I am challenging the many public attacks on the morality and rights of the filmmakers.

Simply put, there are many things that the viewer does not see on the video. We've always treated these men with respect. They practically consider us family. On Thanksgiving and Christmas every year, my friends and I would collect food and clothing for the men and surprise them with the gifts. We tried to help the men with housing and invited them to our own homes on occasion. I can't count the times we purchased food for both Rufus and Donnie, and we couldn't buy them alcohol even if we wanted to since we were all underage. Once the "Bumfights" project began, my friend rented out a place for them to temporarily stay, and both men were compensated for their efforts in the video.

Does this sound like the same vicious, inhumane people that were portrayed so harshly in the news?

The truth is that they have done more for the homeless people in "Bumfights" than law enforcement and the federal government combined. Rufus and Donnie are all too used to people sneering out of their periphery as they stroll back to their luxury cars and return home to loving families. These men have been ignored and spat upon their whole lives. But look how many humanitarians and friends they have on their side now.

I'm not going to try to deny the fact that there are some disturbing, controversial images in "Bumfights." The video even shocked me with its vulgarity. However, one must realize that much of the film is about challenging taboos and drawing new boundaries for what is considered immoral and entertaining. Obviously the footage in "Bumfights" was edited to make it seem as extreme as possible. This video was created to evoke emotional reactions. Reality is exaggerated. Limits are pushed. In many respects, it is a sick reflection of the social degradation surrounding us every day.

One well-known homeless activist, Ted Hayes of the homeless shelter, Dome Village, in Los Angeles, supports the underlying purpose of "Bumfights." "What they're doing is bringing homelessness to the consciousness of America," said Hayes. "It's the best thing that has happened to the homeless movement in the 17 years I've been involved" for the widespread attention it has brought to the harsh reality of street life.

Others have come to the defense of the homeless people portrayed in the video. Some have called it "exploitation." Rep. Earl Blumenauer spoke in front of the House of Representatives in July saying, "(We should) punish those who would torture, degrade and exploit some of our most vulnerable citizens."

And maybe that's true. Let's say, for the sake of discussion, that these homeless men were indeed "exploited" in the filming of "Bumfights." How are we then to draw the distinction between this brand of exploitation and that of say, pornography or the midget in an elf costume at the mall? It's simple; if you don't like it, don't watch it.

The bottom line is that "Bumfights" is hardly illegal. Las Vegas law enforcement and the F.B.I. investigated the case thoroughly, only to find that there were no substantial charges to be filed. My friends' eventual arrests were little more than a publicity stunt—a feeble attempt by a small town cop and district attorney to make the public believe that justice was being served.

The fact remains that all of the participants in "Bumfights" signed consent forms and were compensated. And despite the many inaccurate claims from the media that "the men allegedly were paid in alcohol, doughnuts and cash" and that they were "drugged and intoxicated," the homeless people were usually sober and always knew exactly what they were getting involved in.

Critics of "Bumfights" have openly perpetuated the stereotypes that all homeless men are mentally unstable drug and alcohol addicts. The media's overly broad, often fabricated assumptions about the condition of these men have only added to an already misunderstood case.

Fortunately for my friends, negative publicity is often the most effective means of advertising, especially when your product's target consumer is a beer drinking male prone to liking violent or seemingly offensive material. But I guess it always boils down to the almighty dollar anyway. My friends were consummate capitalists in an unorthodox, but apparently effective, manner.

Call it disgusting. Call it hilarious. "Bumfights" has proven that America has an insatiable desire for violence. So what's more sickening? The fact that some kids and bums made a brutally outrageous movie, or that hundreds of thousands of people think it's worth paying $19.95 for?

California State University, Long Beach *Daily 49er*
Homeless Face Exploitation

The producers of the infamous online video, "Bumfights," which invoked a large amount of controversy this summer, are currently facing felony charges in San Diego County for allegedly offering transients money, alcohol and housing to physically assault each other and to perform other outrageous stunts on film.

The "Bumfights" video, if you haven't already heard, depicts obviously intoxicated "bums" not only beating each other up but also doing things similar to what can be seen on the MTV show "Jackass," which is probably where the producers originally got the idea for the film.

One videotape shows a homeless man ripping out his own tooth with a pair of pliers. Another shows someone smashing a candy machine with a sledgehammer.

The most disturbing thing about "Bumfights," and the reason for the massive amount of criticism, controversy and felony charges against the four young producers, is the fact that they exploited the needs of the transients.

Although shows like "Jackass" may not necessarily be considered in good taste by all, they at least involve people who are performing because they want to be on film and they want to shock people, not because they need the money.

On the contrary, the transients in "Bumfights" are desperate for money, a place to stay and perhaps alcohol. The producers preyed on people who were vulnerable to exploitation and they exploited them. They promised to provide them with basic needs for dangerous, disgusting actions in return.

What may be even more disturbing, but sadly unsurprising, is the fact that many people bought this video as a form of entertainment.

According to the *Christian Science Monitor*'s Web site, more than 250,000 copies of the hour-long movie have sold since it debuted in April. The producers have become millionaires.

The four producers, Zachary Bubeck, 24, Daniel J. Tanner, 21, Ryan Edward McPherson, 19, and Michael J. Slyman, 21, profited from the exploitation of other human beings. Although this sort of exploitation is unfortunately not an uncommon occurrence in our world, it should definitely not be rewarded. These producers should not only pay the consequences of their crime by being charged with felonies, but they should also be forced to give their profits to the people they exploited to get it.

Representative Earl Blumenauer
Speech to the House of Representatives, Jan. 23, 2002

Mr. Speaker, one of the most troubling problems for our communities facing the struggle for liability deals with our homeless population. The problem of homelessness, if not worse today, is certainly more complex. As a result of deinstitutionalization, many of these people now live on the streets; and one of the most serious consequences is violence against the homeless.

Stories of the abuse of homeless and the mentally ill are appearing with stark and frightening regularity, setting a homeless woman on fire, random beatings, even murders. We know last year there were 18 murders and dozens of assaults on the homeless.

These are the stories that were reported to the authorities and found their way into the media. Because of the hidden, often forgotten, world these people inhabit, we know that incidents are underreported and that the known violence is just the tip of the iceberg.

I have been appalled at the people who would not just avoid helping but actually are seeking to exploit the homeless, and the worst example I have seen is a recent video entitled "Bumfights" that films the abuse and violence against the homeless. "Bumfights," the brain child of two recent graduates of the University of California and USC film schools, sets a new standard for the cruel exploitation of damaged human beings. In less than a month, these people have sold 10,000 copies of a video depicting homeless men assaulting each other on the streets of Las Vegas.

A vagrant struggles to escape the punishing punches, kicks and body slams of his attacker. Another scene with a man standing in a dark alley, hitting himself on the head as he realized that his hair is on fire. A purported crack addict smoking the drug and defecating on the sidewalk, and then there are films of a homeless man extracting his own teeth with a pair of pliers.

A segment entitled "Bumhunter" parodies television's *Crocodile Hunter,* with a man in safari clothing binding, gagging and measuring and marking various homeless men on the streets of Las Vegas before releasing them to their national habitat. These sad, pathetic images are described as hilariously shocking. I call it criminal.

They say it is voluntary, since they reward the men with food, clothing, shelter and small change. I charge them of preying on the despair of those without the basic necessities to sustain life or the facilities to cope. Who among us would willingly be filmed extracting our teeth with a pair of pliers? Of course, the film makers are already planning a sequel.

When I read about this video, I was appalled. Not surprisingly, it was promoted on Howard Stern's television show and soon being shipped to people nationally and internationally.

This is not about committee jurisdiction or the geography of the people we represent. It is about our basic humanity. If we cannot act to protect our most vulnerable, what does this say about us all? We need to fix this problem.

I have started with inquiries to the heads of the Las Vegas Federal investigative offices of the FBI, Customs and the U.S. Postal Service. I have asked them specifically to explain what steps they intend to take, and if they decline to open a case, whether it is because they lack resources, they have other priorities, or whether there simply is not a legal action.

I believe that this is already criminal conduct. First of all, in their own press releases, the film makers admit that they are paying homeless actors to commit crimes such as assault and kidnap. They are, therefore, accessories or aiders and abettors. This activity is not protected by the first amendment anymore than the so-called "snuff flick" might be protected pornography. All three of the Federal agencies investigate pornography, and they know the difference.

The FBI should have jurisdiction because of the interstate nature of the business and the possible conspiracy to violate State laws. Customs should have jurisdiction because the material is being distributed internationally, and the postal service should have jurisdiction because the mails are being used to further the distribution.

If these agencies claim they do not have the resources, then perhaps Congress should act to earmark funds, because this is a serious public safety issue. If these agencies claim they have other priorities, then perhaps we should examine the setting of their priorities; and if they claim that there is no specific law that authorizes them to investigate this activity, then perhaps we should enact one.

A Congress that will push the constitutional limits on fighting pornography and that will appropriately outlaw crush videos that depict the torture of animals should do no less for our fellow human beings. This violence against the homeless is not just a crime against them. It is an assault against us all. We should do all we can to stop this outrage and punish those who would torture, degrade and exploit some of our most vulnerable citizens.

Topics for Reading and Writing

1. Shaw seems to have read a great deal of movie publicity and advertising language, to the degree that this article reads more like a press release than an editorial. Look at this article in terms of its language—what tools of the advertiser or publicist that you learned about in Chapter 3 does Shaw use? Is this a responsible or ethical argument? How?

2. What is the *Daily 49er's* argument? How is this article different, in terms of rhetorical strategy, than Shaw's? Does freedom of speech enter into this question?

3. How does Rep. Blumenauer's piece differ from the others in its rhetorical strategies, in its use of the rhetorical triangle, and in what it is intended to accomplish?

4. Because videotapes are so inexpensive to produce and duplicate, a growing number of young entrepreneurs—not just the *Bumfights* team but, most notably, the *Girls Gone Wild* owners—have experienced rapid success from their productions. Is this evidence of the democratization of filmmaking? Does this just demonstrate that one can never lose appealing to the lowest common denominator? Or does it indicate something else about American society today?

If the media is liberal, college media—dominated by wild-eyed, radical student activists—is the most liberal media of all, one could naturally assume. But that assumption is increasingly outdated. In this feature article from the Los Angeles Times, *staff writer **John Johnson** profiles several student activists who align themselves with the conservative side of debates and who have helped to spearhead a new era of conservative newspapers on college campuses.*

John Johnson
Campus Ink Tanks: Conservatives Make Their Voices Heard with a Rising Tide of Hard-hitting Student Newspapers

WINGATE, N.C.—More than a dozen earnest college students gathered in the marshy meadowland of rural North Carolina recently to plot the overthrow of campus liberalism.

Their weapon of choice? The newspaper.

"People complain about the media," said Joshua Mercer, the pink-cheeked director of the seminar held at the Jesse Helms Center in the heart of chicken-growing country. "Our philosophy is, 'Be the media.'"

In an eight-hour session that bore little resemblance to a traditional journalism class, the students were taught how to start their own conservative newspapers and opinion journals. And how to pick fights with lefty bogeymen on the faculty and in student government.

By the end of the day, the student journalists were fired up for battle—determined not only to change the tenor of notoriously liberal campus dialogues, but also, in the long run, to alter the basic makeup of the nation's professional news outlets.

"What do you want professors to feel when you call them up?" asked Owen Rounds, a former speechwriter for Rudolph Giuliani.

"Threatened," replied Duncan Wilson, a tousle-haired 19-year-old from the University of North Carolina, Charlotte.

In the wake of Sept. 11 and the war on Iraq, seminars such as this one are brimming with recruits to the battle for the hearts and minds of America's college students. There are now more than 80 right-leaning newspapers and magazines circulating on campuses from Stanford to Yale. That's the most ever, and 50% more than just two years ago.

"This year alone we've had 35 inquiries for starting new papers," said Brian Auchterlonie, executive director of the Collegiate Network, which trains conservative journalists. "That's double what we usually have."

The reason, the students say, is a mad-as-hell feeling among campus conservatives that they are the only ones in academia who seemed to notice that the world changed after the Sept. 11 attacks on America. They say they have watched aghast as left-leaning professors and student leaders blamed America for the attacks. So now they're starting their own guerrilla publications, often styled as unbridled opinion journals, to drum up support on campus for President Bush and the Iraq war.

"Conservative students have felt shut out on campus," explained Vince Vasquez, 22, college field director for the Leadership Institute, which sponsored the North Carolina seminar. "9/11 motivated them to say, 'If this is the case, we'll start our own newspapers.'"

Though most of these boot-strap affairs cannot compete in the finer points of writing and editing with better-funded campus dailies, they make up for these deficiencies with passion and combativeness. They gleefully ridicule student government antiwar measures and lampoon baby boomer professors and their teach-ins.

"How many sides are your professors teaching?" asked UC Santa Barbara's incendiary *Gaucho Free Press,* one of six new conservative publications on University of California campuses. "Hint: One."

The *Free Press,* whose front page features the slogan "We Do Not Apologize," is among the newest members of the fraternity, having begun this year. But its bite-the-ankles approach is typical of the breed. The *Free Press* prints embarrassing e-mails from faculty members and taunts the administration with surveys showing that most professors are Democrats.

"A lot of my professors don't try to hide the fact they are outright Marxists," said Nicholas Romero, 20, the feisty editor of the *Free Press.*

Romero, whose father is a doctor, became a convert to the conservative cause when the school asked him if he wanted to live in one of the "minority-interest" floors that concentrate minority students in parts of some residence halls. He said he was appalled at what he viewed as an implication that, as a Latino, he didn't "have the social skills" to interact with other ethnic or racial groups.

Romero and co-editor Gretchen Pfaff, 21, had no interest in writing for the main campus newspaper, the *Daily Nexus,* which they say too often glamorizes drug use and promiscuity. "It's offensive," Pfaff said.

The confrontational tactics encouraged in the seminars have inspired opposition on campus, ranging from vandalism to death threats. Seth Norman, managing editor of the *California Patriot,* said the magazine's Berkeley office was broken into and copies stolen. Distributors have been spit on.

When the UC *Irvine Review* called it "sheer lunacy" to create a Filipino studies department during a budget crisis, Filipino activists threatened advertisers with a boycott, said Editor Nathan Masters. Two companies stopped advertising.

Some conservative editors confess to being nervous about the opposition, but most are defiant. Staffers at the Patriot helped publicize the in-your-face flag-waving march by Republicans in Berkeley late last month. At UC Irvine, Masters said: "Our opponents' bully tactics will not silence the *Irvine Review.*"

The modern swashbuckling style of right-wing publications is often traced to the *Dartmouth Review,* which began publishing in 1979. Over the years, the Review has sometimes been accused of stumbling over the line of good taste. In one of its more egregious episodes, it inserted a quote from Adolf Hitler into the paper's mission statement on the eve of Yom Kippur.

Today's publications share some characteristics with the conservative tracts that sprang up in the 1980s. The staffs remain all-volunteer and money is always short. The *Free Press* survives on private donations to pay the $1,400 it costs each month to print its run of 6,000 copies.

But there are important differences. Besides Sept. 11 and the Iraq war, new technology has made it easier than ever to spread ideas on campus.

Computers and publishing software are so sophisticated that, in days, a lone student can become a subversive Citizen Kane, spreading a message to hundreds and, often, thousands of readers. The *Gaucho Free Press* is full of graphics and cartoons, yet Pfaff does it all in her dorm room, on her laptop.

Another difference: The conservative political organizations that train the right-wing editors are better organized than ever. The Leadership Institute, which sponsored the North Carolina seminar, is one of three organizations that train and fund conservative journalists. Founded by Morton Blackwell, a former Reagan White House operative, the institute offers to pay the costs of printing first issues.

The Collegiate Network sponsors its own competition to honor journalism excellence. And in April, it announced its sixth annual Polly awards, recognizing "the excesses of college administrators and professors."

The organizations boast that their graduates have gone on to some of the most prestigious media outlets in the nation, including *Esquire* magazine, *CNN*, *Time* and *Newsweek*, as well as major metropolitan papers. Some see such "seeding" of the news media with conservatives as a welcome check on the liberalism of mainstream papers.

"I think it's great if more young conservatives are going into journalism," said Howard Kurtz, the *Washington Post*'s media critic. Noting that journalism has traditionally attracted liberal students "who want to change the world," he said, "we can definitely use people who have different political and cultural points of view."

Others see a dangerous attempt to politicize the media.

David Brock, the onetime conservative author who has become a born-again Democrat, said campus conflicts are "phony wars instigated by conservatives. They introduce division and polarity where none exist."

Don't tell that to the students at the North Carolina seminar. Virtually all had stories about some campus outrage perpetrated by student government or gray-bearded professors who regard the Iraq war as Vietnam II.

Duncan Wilson, the UNC Charlotte student, complained that college Republicans got less than $500 in student fees this year. The campus gay club got $2,241, which was used partly to put on a show featuring drag queens, he said.

Wilson, who started college at 16, was particularly incensed at his "Marxist" sociology professor. Would it be all right, he asked, to label the man "Public Enemy No. 1?"

That was probably going too far, seminar teachers warned.

One thing seems clear from the furor surrounding the right-leaning publications: Conservatives no longer feel outshouted on campus. "I take perverse pleasure in getting hate mail," said Andrew Jones, who edits *The Criterion*, an online UCLA publication that takes shots at the American Civil Liberties Union and even urges donors to stop giving money until the college changes its liberal policies.

The thought of right-wing students attacking their leftist professors in print is richly rewarding to some observers.

"The left is going to have a rude awakening here," said David Horowitz, a onetime campus radical who became an outspoken conservative. Professors "have politicized the university" and students are right to rebel.

Despite occasional incidents, most students at UC Santa Barbara have been receptive to the new voice on campus, Pfaff said. Even Brendan Buhler, the 22-year-old *Nexus* editor, said "it's good for them to try to get their viewpoint out there."

But Buhler, who wears T-shirts and flip-flops around the office, thinks it's a mistake to compare a general-interest paper to the *Free Press*. "When you come out and say you are the conservative voice on campus, you are automatically saying you are not going to cover the news in a fair manner," he said.

The *Free Press* has a roster of 20 writers, but most of the work falls on Romero and Pfaff. And that can be a problem. Depending on committed individuals leaves a publication vulnerable when the founders graduate. Many of the papers started in the 1980s later folded.

But Pfaff said she and her colleagues are in it for the long haul.

"My boyfriend is bummed," she says, at all the hours she spends putting the paper together, "but he knows I'm passionate about this."

Topics for Reading and Writing

1. If these magazines are given seed money and funded by conservative foundations or conservative activists, can they really be considered "student" newspapers? How are they different from a truly student-run periodical—or are they?

2. How would one start a newspaper on your campus? What would the practicalities of production and distribution be? Would it be more effective for activists just to start a website? How does a newspaper reach a different audience, and how does an audience respond differently to a printed newspaper than to Web-based content?

Rob Long
Jerry Built

Looking at Seinfeld *from a surprising point of view, the television producer **Rob Long** here argues (in an article that appeared in the conservative journal* National Review*) that the show is a welcome respite from the politically correct pieties of most network television: Jerry and the gang are unrepentant narcissists, selfish and self-interested and not in the least inclined to help others. In this, Long feels, the show rejects the lessons of the 1960s that we should all just get along and accept each other in all of our lovely diversity.*

*In another article from the same journal, writer **David Klinghoffer** looks at another television comedy that responds to the effects of political correctness on the media. Of all the critics of political correctness, one of the most relentless and funniest over the last few years has been the cartoon* South Park. *It's also one of the crudest programs*

Years ago, at lunch with an NBC executive, I happened to mention a promising new series on his network. *The Seinfeld Chronicles*, it was called. It had aired three times in a terrible time slot in the middle of summer—the boneyard, the death trap, the place, in other words, where networks dump their least promising shows.

"Oh, that," he said, with a dismissive swat of his hand. "That show is dead. We shoulda just flushed the money down the john. Woulda been faster."

Nine years and billions of dollars later, *Seinfeld*, as it was renamed, has not only made its eponymous star a centimillionaire, but it has noticeably buoyed the balance sheet of its network, NBC, and that network's owner, General Electric. The executive who dismissed it so haughtily in 1991 was promoted.

That, of course, is standard Hollywood procedure.

Hits aren't created; they're stumbled into. *Seinfeld* is, essentially, a show about four desperately selfish and ludicrously childish friends who behave in a way that can be described, in clinical terms, as sociopathic. They fall in and out of bed with a gaggle of partners, none of whom measure up, and spend a good portion of each episode in a local coffee shop, kvetching. Who could like these people?

ever televised. Its creators, Trey Parker and Matt Stone, gleefully take on almost every PC piety: race, sexual orientation, parent-child relationships, earnestly liberal celebrities. But the show never seems to be a shrill conservative backlash to the PC movement, because those on the right (the police, the church) also get a good skewering. Klinghoffer, though, reviles South Park *for its potty humor and its general offensiveness.*

Who would want to have them as friends? They wear life like an itchy sweater—grumbling, grouchy, and always trying to wiggle out of responsibility.

The show is also a pretty smutty little half-hour, which is one of the reasons conservatives are uneasy about it. Conservatives have a hard time with smut, sadly. They associate it with the excesses of the 1960s and 1970s—young people grooving on sex and drugs and tinny music, bad haircuts, that sort of thing. But the true legacy of those years wasn't music or intoxicants, it was piety. Insufferable, caring, toasty-warm piety. The adjective "nurturing" to describe a relationship between adults; the phrase "handicapped"; the smoothing out of all the rough edges of life— "challenged" for slow, "homeless" for alcoholic, "white wine" for bourbon-rocks, and "life partner" for . . . well, you know.

Seinfeld is gleefully free of cant. There are no messages, positive or otherwise, delivered in an episode except the only one that matters: Laugh. Enjoy. And tune in next week. We are the kings; they are the clowns. Implicit in the series is the understanding that our moral and spiritual life is our own affair. Jerry and friends are strictly for laughs.

The most revolutionary aspect of *Seinfeld* was how easily it confounded the prevailing wisdom. What you need to have a hit, the networks will tell anyone who listens, is a core group of likable characters. They can't be mean or caustic. They need to love one another. They need to be the kind of people the audience can rely on. They cannot be, in other words, the cast of *Seinfeld.* (Early on in the series, the rumor goes, an NBC executive suggested that Jerry get engaged to Elaine, his platonic friend played by Julia Louis-Dreyfus. "What you need here," he is reported as saying, "is a reason to care about these characters. Otherwise, the show will die. No one will watch." He has also, presumably, been promoted and given a large raise.)

The year the show broke out and became a certified smash, Hollywood flew into a frenzy of copy-cat development. "Get me young people talking," went the morning line. And so the following autumn, a dozen or so young-people-talking series went on the air. Most were canceled in a few weeks. It escaped attention that the cast of *Seinfeld* wasn't particularly young—Jerry's got fifty on the horizon, at least. Michael Richards, who plays Kramer, isn't much younger.

"It's a show about nothing," was also part of the prevailing wisdom.

Not so. *Seinfeld* is the most intricately plotted, self-conscious situation comedy ever broadcast on American television. In 21 minutes of storytelling time, *Seinfeld* could cram twenty or more scenes, some barely five seconds long, to keep the story moving.

They were wrong when they said it wouldn't work, and they're wrong when they try to explain why it does. This, too, should cheer conservatives. The market-tested, focus-grouped, top-down, bureaucratically administered conventional wisdom was spectacularly mistaken. *Seinfeld* is a plot-heavy show about unlikable adults in their forties. If you pitched it to a network today, they wouldn't even offer you coffee.

Why, then, does it work? Why is Jerry Seinfeld, comedian, richer than Jack Welch, corporate titan? Perhaps because there is something in the American spirit that loves a misfit. Perhaps because *Seinfeld* once produced an episode in which the central characters disrupted the life of a handicapped—and insufferable—boy. Perhaps because after years of pious liberal nonsense, the American viewing public relished the naughty pleasure of apolitical laughter. *Seinfeld* isn't a show about nothing; it's a show about nothing pompous.

In one episode, a local reporter mistakes Jerry and George's bickering friendship for a longstanding homosexual marriage. Jerry and George are horrified. A dozen or so times during the episode they proclaim their heterosexuality. "We're not gay!" they shout, followed quickly by a robotic, "not that there's anything wrong with it." That, in a nutshell, is the average American's typical response to homosexuality: "I'm not but if you are, well, what the hell can I do about it, anyway?"

The American character is made up of equal parts preacher, bartender and Huckleberry Finn. We are a cynical, maudlin, gluttonous, parsimonious, practical, extravagant people—sometimes all in the same day. We should savor these contradictions, if for no other reason than because they terrify the rest of the world. Europeans, especially, are bewildered by us.

"How on earth," a French critic once asked me, "can a country so religious and conservative support a show like *The X Files?*"

I shrugged. "We like monster movies," I said.

"But *The X Files* is so much more," he protested.

"Actually," I replied, "it's so much less."

When a show like *Seinfeld* slips through the cracks and becomes a hit, it reinforces our unpredictable, iconoclastic spirit. Here, finally, is the real reason why conservatives should lament the passing of *Seinfeld:* no episode ever ended in a hug.

David Klinghoffer
Dirty Joke

Warning: There's no way to write about the cartoon series *South Park* without alluding to things that would make any normal person queasy: flatulence, flatulence that causes flames to burst from a character's rear end, an anal probe, more flatulence, a talking mound of excrement, explosive diarrhea, plus from the third-grade protagonists, unrelenting vulgar language that can't be reprinted in *NR*. Such stuff is the very point of this, the hottest show on television.

"Hottest" doesn't mean "most watched." But the 4.5 million souls who clicked on to the Christmas special are nothing to sneeze at (31.3 million typically watch *Seinfeld*), and from a marketing viewpoint *South Park* is a weighty phenomenon. Since it premiered in August, fans have bought $30 million worth of *South Park* T-shirts alone, along with quantities of refrigerator magnets, greeting cards, calendars, and bumper stickers. You see the T-shirts on sale everywhere in Manhattan.

Nor does "hottest" mean "best," since *South Park* is just a more obscene knock-off of *Beavis and Butt-head* mated with a much less funny knock-off of *The Simpsons,* the best show on television. (Though *South Park*'s Valentine's Day special, with many smirking references to lesbianism, had moments as funny as anything on *The Simpsons.*) What it means is that, God help us, *South Park* has managed to generate excitement among TV viewers like nothing since the early days of *Beavis and Butt-head* and *The Simpsons.* Recently it was on the covers of *Rolling Stone* and *Spin* magazines simultaneously.

Thought up by a couple of twentysomethings, Trey Parker and Matt Stone, the show recounts the adventures of four cute little boys. The setting is perpetually snowed-in South Park, Colorado. Artistically speaking, paper cutouts of kids bundled in parkas have been scanned onto computers; the images are then moved across a static background for a naïve look that's actually charming.

In one episode, the fat kid, Cartman, is abducted by space aliens, who perform an anal probe on him. At the climax, an eighty-foot radar dish emerges from his rear orifice and beams a signal to flying saucers.

In another, the mother of Cartman's buddy Kyle is offended by a TV cartoon show that has won the devotion of all the kids in South Park. This idea was swiped from the cartoon-within-a cartoon on *The Simpsons,* "Itchy & Scratchy," except on "Terrance & Phillip" the characters do nothing but break wind or talk about breaking wind. Kyle's mom leads a protest outside the headquarters of the cable channel that produces the cartoon—Cartoon Central, a reference to Comedy Central, the TV home of *South Park.* The protest succeeds when an epidemic of explosive diarrhea among the protestors overwhelms the portable toilets—and, well, you get the picture. As stated by one boy, Stan, the moral is: "Damn it! You know, I think that if parents would spend less time worrying about what their kids watch on TV, and more time worrying about what's going on in their kids' lives, this world would be a much better place."

The depiction of gross bodily functions upsets normal people. That's because drawing a decorous curtain around things like that is one way we confirm for ourselves that we're not animals. In a weird way, the fact that so many people find *South Park* hilarious is good news. Outrageousness makes us laugh, and it comes as something of a relief that explosive diarrhea on TV is still considered outrageous. Despite the efforts of secularists to convince us that we're all animals anyway, with everything that implies by way of loosened standards of what's proper and improper, Americans still resist the idea. For now.

Of course people find humor in all sorts of things besides outrageousness. It's just the lowest, easiest way to get a laugh. The not-very-good news is that so many Americans evidently find outrageous humor funnier than any other kind. What a person laughs at is the most accurate intelligence test ever invented. Since August, our estimated national IQ has dropped a few points.

But that's not what is really regrettable about the show. The other source of *South Park* amusement is that prized, aggravating quality of the Nineties sensibility: irony.

Creators Stone and Parker specialize in it. As film students they made features titled *Cannibal: The Musical* and *Giant Beaver of Southern Sri Lanka.* The two came to the attention of Hollywood by producing a five-minute short, "The Spirit of Christmas." In this, Santa Claus and Jesus fight each other "Mortal Kombat"-style while the South Park kids stand by cursing ("Dude, don't say 'pigf____' in front of Jesus!"). According to *Rolling Stone,* they'll soon have their first real movie out: *Orgazmo,* about "an earnest, soon-to-be-married, martial-arts-obsessed Mormon who gets caught up spending boogie nights in the porn game in order to pay for a church wedding."

The formula for ironic humor is numbingly ironclad. You just take one concept suggestive of convention and normality (a musical, a Mormon), and link it with an unrelated, somehow transgressive concept (cannibals, pornography). Thus half the laughs in *South Park* are supposed to come from the fact that we're watching adorable animated children talk the way these talk, and do other things children don't normally do on TV, like die gruesomely. The show's famous tag line is "Oh my God! They killed Kenny!" which Stan blurts out every episode after his friend Kenny has been impaled on a flagpole, crushed by hot lava, whatever. Then rats come and devour him. By the start of the next episode, he has been restored to life.

When a *Rolling Stone* writer accompanied Stone and Parker to an appearance on the *Tonight* show the pair bumped into Jerry Springer on the NBC lot and proceeded to ironically fawn on him. They exclaimed that they watch his schlocky talk show for inspiration: "Oh, my God! It's Jerry Springer! Now everything's been worthwhile!"

The appeal of irony is simple. By chuckling at it you remind yourself what a jaded, cynical—i.e., cool—person you are, how high you fly above the dowdy heads of those old folks and others squares who find irony mystifying or offensives. As Susan Sontag once explained, homosexuals love camp—defined as the juxtaposition of heightened emotion with cheesy art (as in Barbra Streisand's music)—because it affirms that life isn't to be taken seriously. Thus their characteristic activity needn't make them feel guilty. Irony is camp for heterosexuals, although its payoff is to set you above conventionality in general, not just conventional sex rules.

Of course some irony is cleverer than other irony. *South Park* is irony for dumb-dumbs, the worst kind.

Topics for Reading and Writing

1. Is *Seinfeld* as relentlessly anti-PC as Long argues? Or are we meant (in good liberal fashion) to see these selfish characters as ultimately unlikable? In the final episode of the show, the main characters are put on trial for their self-indulgence, their inability to be socially responsible, and found guilty. Does this affect Long's argument?

2. How might Rob Long respond to Katherine Gantz? Do they agree on any level?

3. Do you see any contradiction in Long's love of *Seinfeld* and Klinghoffer's attack on *South Park?* Or are the two compatible?

In this very academic paper, Katherine Gantz engages in a "queer" reading of the situation comedy Seinfeld, pointing out that a very strong gay subtext underlies the friendship between Jerry and George, even considering the fact that most of the episodes concern their short-lived relationships with women. Television's long history of including characters who are "coded" gay but who are never explicitly said to be so reaches a pinnacle with Seinfeld, Gantz argues—do you agree?

Katherine Gantz
"Not that there's anything wrong with that": Reading the Queer in *Seinfeld*

The world of mass culture, especially that which includes American television, remains overwhelmingly homophobic. Queer theory offers a useful perspective from which to examine the heterosexism at the core of contemporary television and also provides a powerful tool of subversion. The aim of this article is twofold: first, it will outline and explain the notion of a queer reading; second, it will apply a queer reading to the narrative texts that comprise the situation comedy *Seinfeld.*

In the summer of 1989, NBC debuted a tepidly received pilot entitled *The Seinfeld Chronicles,* a situation comedy revolving around the mundane, urbane Manhattan existence of stand-up comic Jerry Seinfeld. Despite its initially unimpressive ratings, the show evolved into the five-episode series *Seinfeld* and established its regular cast of Jerry's three fictional friends: George Costanza (Jason Alexander), ex-girlfriend Elaine Benes (Julia Louis-Dreyfus), and the enigmatic neighbor Kramer (Michael Richards). By its return in January 1991, *Seinfeld* had established a following among Wednesday-night television viewers; over the next two years, the show became a cultural phenomenon, claiming both a faithful viewership and a confident position in the Nielsen ratings' top ten. The premise was to write a show about the details, minor disturbances, and non-events of Jerry's life as they occurred before becoming fodder for the stand-up monologues that bookend each episode. The show's characters are modeled on real-life acquaintances: George is based on Seinfeld's best friend (and series cocreator) Larry David; Elaine is an exaggeration of Seinfeld's ex-girlfriend, writer Carol Leifer; Kramer's protoype lived across the hall from one of David's first Manhattan apartments.[1] To further complicate this narcissistic mirroring, in the 1993 season premiere entitled "The Pilot" (see videography for episodic citations), Jerry and George finally launch their new NBC sitcom *Jerry* by casting four actors to portray themselves, Kramer, and Elaine. This multilayered Möbius strip of person/actor/character relationships seems to be part of the show's complex appeal. Whereas situation comedies often dilute their cast, adding and removing characters in search of new plot possibilities, *Seinfeld* instead interiorizes; the narrative creates new configurations of the same limited cast to keep the viewer and the characters intimately linked. In fact, it is precisely this concentration on the nuclear set of four personalities that creates the *Seinfeld* community.

If it seems hyperbolic to suggest that the participants in the *Seinfeld* phenomenon (both spectators and characters included) have entered into a certain delineated "lifestyle," consider the significant lexicon of Seinfeldian code words and recurring phrases that go unnoticed and unappreciated by the infrequent or "unknowing" viewer. Catch phrases such as Snapple, the Bubble Boy, Cuban cigars, Master of My Domain, Junior Mints, Mulva, Crazy Joe Davola, Pez, and Vandelay Industries all serve as parts of the group-specific language that a family shares; these are the kinds of self-referential in-jokes that help one *Seinfeld* watcher identify another.[2] This sort of tightly conscribed universe of meaning is reflected not only by the decidedly small cast but also by the narrative's consistent efforts to maintain its intimacy. As this article will discuss, much of *Seinfeld*'s plot and humor (and, consequently, the viewer's pleasure) hinge on outside personalities threatening—and ultimately failing—to invade the foursome. Especially where Jerry and George are concerned, episodes are mostly resolved by expelling the intruder and restoring the exclusive nature of their relationship. The show's camera work, which at times takes awkward measures to ensure that Jerry and George remain grouped together within a scene, reinforces the privileged dynamic of their relationship within the narrative.

Superficially speaking, *Seinfeld* appears to be a testament to heterosexuality: in its nine-year run, Jerry sported a new girlfriend in almost every episode; his friendship with Elaine is predicated on their previous sexual relationship; and all four characters share in the discussion and navigation of the (straight) dating scene. However, with a viewership united by a common coded discourse and an interest in the cohesive (and indeed almost claustrophobic) exclusivity of its predominantly male cast, clearly *Seinfeld* is rife with possibilities for homoerotic interpretation. As will be demonstrated, the construction, the coding, and the framing of the show readily conform to a queer reading of the *Seinfeld* text.

The show is laden with references and plot twists involving gay characters and themes. In separate episodes, Elaine is selected as the "best man" in a lesbian wedding ("The Subway"); George accidentally causes the exposure of his girlfriend Susan's father's affair with novelist John Cheever ("The Cheever Letters"); and, after their breakup, George runs into Susan with her new lesbian lover ("The Smelly Car"). At its most playful, *Seinfeld* smugly calls attention to its own homosexual undercurrents in an episode in which Jerry and George are falsely identified as a gay couple by a female journalist ("The Outing").[3] Due to the direct nature of such references to homosexuality, these are episodes that slyly deflect queer reading, serving as a sort of lightning rod by displacing homoerotic undercurrents onto a more obvious target.

Even if the pink triangle's proactive gay recoding remains obscure to the "unknowing" viewership (i.e., unfamiliar with or resistant to queerness), *Seinfeld* also offers a multitude of discursive referents chosen from a popular lexicon of more common gay signifiers that are often slurs in use by a homophobic public.

In an episode revolving around Jerry and Kramer's discussion of where to find *fruit*—longstanding slang for a gay man—Jerry makes a very rare break from his standard wardrobe of well-ironed button-up oxfords, instead sporting a T-shirt with the word "QUEENS" across it. Although outwardly in reference to Queens College, the word's semiotic juxtaposition with the theme of fruit evokes its slang connotation for effeminate gay men.

Narrative space is also queerly coded. Positioned as Jerry and George's "place" (or "male space"), the restaurant where they most often meet is "Monk's," a name that conjures up images of an exclusively male religious society, a "brother-hood" predicated on the maintenance of masculine presence/feminine absence, in both spiritual and physical terms.

Recurring plot twists also reveal a persistent interest in the theme of hidden or falsified identities. As early as *Seinfeld*'s second episode ("The Stakeout"), George insists on creating an imaginary biography for himself as a successful architect before meeting Jerry's new girlfriend. Throughout the *Seinfeld* texts, the foursome adopts a number of different names and careers in hopes of per-suading outsiders (most often potential romantic interests) that they lead a more interesting, more superficially acceptable, or more immediately favorable exis-tence than what their real lives have to offer: George has assumed the identity of neo-Nazi organizer Colin O'Brian ("The Limo"); Elaine has recruited both Jerry and Kramer as substitute boyfriends to dissuade unwanted suitors ("The Junior Mint" and "The Watch"); Kramer has posed as a policeman ("The Statue") and has even auditioned under a pseudonym to play himself in the pilot of *Jerry* ("The Pilot"). Pretense and fabrication often occur among the foursome as well. In "The Apartment," Jerry is troubled by Elaine's imminent move into the apartment above him. Worried that her presence will "cramp his style," he schemes to convince her that she will be financially unable to take the apart-ment. In private, Jerry warns George that he will be witness to some "heavy act-ing" to persuade Elaine that he is genuinely sympathetic. Unshaken, George answers: "Are you kidding? I lie every second of the day; my whole life is a sham." This deliberate "closeting" of one's lifestyle has obvious connections to the gay theme of "passing,"[4] the politically discouraged practice of hiding one's homosexuality behind a façade of straight respectability. One might argue that *Seinfeld* is simply a text about passing—socially as well as sexually—in a repres-sive and judgmental society. It must be noted, however, that George and Jerry are the only two characters who do not lie to each other; they are in fact engaged in maintaining each other's secrets and duplicities by "covering" for one another, thus distancing themselves somewhat from Kramer and Elaine from within an even more exclusive rapport.[5]

Another thematic site of queerness is the mystification of and resulting detachment from female culture and discourse. While Jerry glorifies such male-identified personalities as Superman, the Three Stooges, and Mickey Mantle, he prides himself in never having seen a single episode of *I Love Lucy* ("The Phone Message"). Even Elaine is often presented as incomprehensible to her familiar male counterparts. In "The Shoes," Jerry and George have no problem creating a story line for their situation comedy, *Jerry*, around male characters; however, when they try to "write in" Elaine's character, they find themselves stumped:

Jerry: [In the process of writing the script.] "Elaine enters." . . . What
  does she say . . . ?
George: [Pause.] What *do* they [women] say?
Jerry: [Mystified.] I *don't know.*

After a brief deliberation, they opt to omit the female character completely. As
Jerry explains with a queerly loaded rationale: "You, me, Kramer, the
butler. . . . Elaine is too much." Later, at Monk's, Elaine complains about her
exclusion from the pilot. Jerry confesses: "We couldn't write for a woman." "You
have *no idea?*" asks Elaine, disgusted. Jerry looks at George for substantiation
and replies: "None." Clearly, the privileged bond between men excludes room
for an understanding of and an interest in women; like Elaine in the pilot, the
feminine presence is often simply deleted for the sake of maintaining a stronger,
more coherent male narrative.

  Jerry seems especially ill at ease with notions of female sexuality, perhaps
suggesting that they impinge on his own. In "The Red Dot," Jerry convinces the
resistant George that he should buy Elaine a thank-you gift after she procures
him a job at her office. Despite George's tightfisted unwillingness to invest
money in such social graces as gift giving, he acquiesces. The duo go to a department store in search of an appropriate gift for Elaine. Jerry confesses: "I never
feel comfortable in the women's department; I feel like I'm just a *little* too close
to trying on a dress." While browsing through the women's clothing, George
describes his erotic attraction to the cleaning woman in his new office:

  George: . . . she was swaying back and forth, back and forth, her hips
    swiveling and her breasts—uh . . .
  Jerry: . . . convulsing?

George reacts with disdain at the odd word choice, recognizing that Jerry's
depiction of female physicality and eroticism is both inappropriate and unap-
pealing. (It should be noted that the ensuing sexual encounter between George
and the cleaning woman ultimately results in the loss of both their jobs; true to
the pattern, George's foray into heterosex creates chaos.)

  "The Boyfriend" explores the ambiguous valences of male friendships. Celebrated baseball player Keith Hernandez stars as himself (as does Jerry Seinfeld
among the cast of otherwise fictional characters), becoming the focal point of
both Jerry's and, later, Elaine's attentions. Despite Elaine's brief romantic
involvement with Keith, the central narrative concerns Jerry's interactions with
the baseball player. Although never explicitly discussed, Jerry's attachment to
Keith is represented as romantic in nature.

  The episode begins in a men's locker room, prefiguring the homoerotic
overtones of the coming plot. The locker room is clearly delineated as "male
space"; its connection to the athletic field posits it as a locale of physicality,
where men gather to prepare for or to disengage from the privileged (and predominantly homophobic) world of male sports. The locker room, as a site of
potential heterosexual vulnerability as men expose their bodies to other men, is
socially safe only when established as sexually neutral—or, better still, hetero-
sexually charged with the machismo of athleticism. This "safe" coding occurs

almost immediately in this setting, accomplished through a postgame comparison of Jerry's, George's, and Kramer's basketball prowess. As they finish dressing together after their game, it is the voracious, ambisexual Kramer who immediately upsets the precarious sexual neutrality, violating the unspoken code of locker-room decorum:

> **Kramer:** Hey, you know this is the first time we've ever seen each other naked?
> **Jerry:** Believe me, *I* didn't see anything.
> **Kramer:** [With disbelief.] Oh, you didn't sneak a peek?
> **Jerry:** No—did you?
> **Kramer:** Yeah, I snuck a peek.
> **Jerry:** Why?
> **Kramer:** Why not? What about you, George?
> **George:** [Hesitating] Yeah, I—snuck a peek. But it was so fast that I didn't see anything; it was just a blur.
> **Jerry:** I made a conscious effort *not* to look; there's certain information I just don't want to have.

Jerry displays his usual disdain for all things corporeal or carnal. Such unwillingness to participate in Kramer's curiosity about men's bodies also secures Jerry firmly on heterosexual ground, a necessary pretext to make his intense feelings for Keith "safe." The humor of these building circumstances depends on the assumption that Jerry is straight; although this episode showcases *Seinfeld's* characteristic playfulness with queer subject matter, great pains are taken to prevent the viewer from ever believing (or realizing) that Jerry is gay.

After Kramer leaves, Jerry and George spot Hernandez stretching out in the locker room. With Kramer no longer threatening to introduce direct discussion of overtly homoerotic matters, the queer is permitted to enter into the narrative space between Jerry and George. Both baseball aficionados, they are bordering on giddy, immediately starstruck by Hernandez. Possessing prior knowledge of Keith's personal life, Jerry remarks that Hernandez is not only a talented athlete but intelligent as well, being an American Civil War buff. "I wish *I* were a Civil War buff," George replies longingly. Chronically socially inept, George is left to appropriate the interests of a man he admires without being able to relate to him more directly.[6]

Keith introduces himself to Jerry as a big fan of his comedy; Jerry is instantly flattered and returns the compliment. As the jealous and excluded George looks on (one of the rare times that Jerry and George break rank and appear distinctly physically separated within a scene), Keith and Jerry exchange phone numbers and plan to meet for coffee in the future. Thus, in the strictly homosocial, theoretically nonromantic masculine world of the locker room, two men have initiated an interaction that becomes transformed into a relationship, consistently mirroring traditional television representations of heterosexual dating rituals. The homoerotic stage is set.

Later, at Monk's, Jerry complains to Elaine that three days have passed without a call from Keith. When Elaine asks why Jerry doesn't initiate the first call, he responds that he doesn't want to seem overanxious: "If he wants to see me, he has my number; he should call. I can't stand these guys—you give your number to them, and then they don't call."

Here, in his attempts not to seem overly aggressive, Jerry identifies with the traditionally receptive and passive role posited as appropriate female behavior. By employing such categorization as "these guys," Jerry brackets himself off from the rest of the heterosexual, male dating population, reinforcing his identification with Elaine not as Same (i.e., straight male) but as Other (Elaine as Not Male, Jerry as Not Straight). Elaine responds sympathetically:

Elaine: I'm sorry, honey.
Jerry: I mean, I thought he liked me, I really thought he liked me—we
were getting along. He came over to *me*, I didn't go over to *him*.
Elaine: [Commiserating.] I know.
Jerry: Here I meet this guy, this *great* guy, ballplayer, best guy I ever
met in my life . . . well, that's it. I'm *never* giving my number out
to another guy again.

Jerry is clearly expressing romantic disillusionment in reaction to Keith's withdrawal from their social economy. Elaine further links her identity—as sexually experienced with men—to Jerry's own situation:

Elaine: Sometimes I give my number out to a guy, and it takes him a
month to call me.
Jerry: [Outraged.] A *month?* Ha! Have him call *me* after a month—
let's see if *he* has a prayer!

Thus, Jerry's construction of his relationship with Keith is one bound by the rules of heterosexual dating protocol and appropriate exchange; the intensity of his feelings and expectations for his relationship with Keith have long surpassed normative (that is, conventional, expected, tolerable), straight male friendship. By stating that Keith's violation of protocol will result in Jerry's withdrawal, it is clear that Jerry is only willing to consider any interactions with Keith in terms of a romantic model—one that, as suggested by Keith's relative indifference, is based in fantasy.

Elaine suggests that he simply put an end to the waiting and call Keith to arrange an evening out. Jerry ponders the possibility of dinner but then has doubts:

Jerry: But don't you think that dinner might be coming on too strong?
Kind of a turnoff?
Elaine: [Incredulous.] Jerry, it's a *guy*.
Jerry: [Covering his eyes.] It's all very confusing.

Throughout the episode, Jerry is content to succumb to the excitement of his newfound relationship, until the moment when someone inevitably refers to its homoerotic nature (terms such as "gay" and "homosexual" are certainly implied but never explicitly invoked.). Elaine's reminder that Jerry's fears about a "turnoff" are addressed to a man quickly ends his swooning, he covers his eyes as if to suggest a groggy return from a dream-like state.

To interrupt and divert the narrative attention away from Jerry's increasingly queer leanings, the scene abruptly changes to George at the unemployment office, where he is hoping to maneuver a thirteen-week extension on his unemployment benefits.[7] There, George evades the questions of his no-nonsense interviewer Mrs. Sokol until she forces him to provide one name of a company with which he had recently sought employment. Having in truth interviewed nowhere, he quickly concocts Vandelay Industries," a company, he assures her, he had thoroughly pursued to no avail. Further pressed, he tells Mrs. Sokol that they are "makers of latex products." His blurting-out of the word "latex" must not be overlooked here as a queer signifier directly associated with the gay safe-sex compaigns throughout the last decade. Whereas "condoms" as a signifier would have perhaps been a more mainstream (straight) sexual symbol, latex evokes a larger category of products—condoms, gloves, dental dams—linked closely with the eroticization of gay safe-sex practices. When Mrs. Sokol insists on information to verify his claim, it is telling that George provides Jerry's address and phone number as the home of Vandelay latex. George's lie necessitates a race back to Jerry's to warn him of the impending phone call; once again, he will depend on Jerry's willingness to maintain a duplicity and to adopt a false identity as the head of Vandelay Industries.

As if to await the panicked arrival of George, the scene changes to Jerry's apartment, where he is himself anxiety ridden over his impending night out with Keith. In a noticeable departure from his usual range of conservative color and style, he steps out of his bedroom, modeling a bright orange and red shirt, colors so shocking that they might best be described as "flaming." "Pivoting slightly with arms outstretched in a style suggesting a fashion model, he asks Elaine's opinion. Again, she reminds him: "Jerry, he's a guy." Agitated (but never denying her implication of homoerotic attraction), he drops his arms, attempting to hide his nervous discomfort.

Jerry's actual evening out with Keith remains unseen (closeted) until the end of the "date"; the men sit alone in the front seat of Keith's car outside of Jerry's apartment. In the setup that prefigures the close of Elaine's date with Keith later in the episode, Jerry sits in the passenger seat next to him; a familiar heterosexual power dynamic is at play. Keith, as both the car owner and driver, acts and reacts in his appropriate masculine role. Jerry, within the increasingly queer context of an intimate social interaction with another man, is left to identify with what we recognize as the woman's position in the car. As the passenger and not the driver, he has relinquished both the mechanical and social control that defines the dominance of the male role. In a symbolic interpretation of power relations, Jerry's jump into the feminized gender role is characterized by the absence of the steering wheel:

Jerry: [Aloud to Keith.] Well, thanks a lot, that was really fun.
[Thinking to himself.] Should I shake his hand?

This anxiety and expectation over appropriate and mutually appealing physical contact expresses the same kind of desire—that is, sexual—that Keith will express with Elaine later on; whereas Keith will long for a kiss, Jerry's desires have been translated into a more acceptable form of physical contact between men. It would seem that part of Jerry's frustration in this situation comes from the multiplicity of gender roles that he plays. Whereas in his interactions with George, Jerry occupies the dominant role (controlling the discourse and the action), he is suddenly relegated to a more passive (feminine) position in his relationship with the hypermasculine Keith Hernandez. Part of the tension that comprises the handshake scene stems not only from Jerry's desire to interact physically *and* appropriately but also from wanting to initiate such an action from the disadvantaged, less powerful position of the (feminine) passenger's seat. I would suggest that the confusion arising out of his relationship with Keith is not strictly due to its potentially homosexual valences but is also the result of the unclear position (passive/dominant, feminine/masculine, nelly/butch) that Jerry holds within the homoerotic/homosexual coupling.

Once again, the humor of this scene is based on the presupposition that Jerry is straight and that this very familiar scene is not a homosexual recreation of heterosexual dating etiquette but simply a parody of it. Nonetheless, Jerry's discomfort over initiating a handshake betrays the nature of his desire for Keith. From behind the steering wheel (the seat of masculine power), Keith invites Jerry to a movie over the coming weekend. Jerry is elated, and they shake hands: a consummation of their successful social interaction. However, Keith follows up by telling Jerry that he would like to call Elaine for a date; the spell broken, Jerry responds with reluctance and thinly veiled disappointment.

Back in Jerry's apartment, George jealously asks for a recounting of Jerry's evening with Keith. Again, the handshake is reinforced as the symbol of a successful male-to-male social encounter:

George: Did you shake his hand?
Jerry: Yeah.
George: What kind of a handshake does he have?
Jerry: Good shake, perfect shake. Single pump, not too hard. He didn't have to prove anything, but firm enough to know he's there.

George and Jerry share a discourse, laden with masturbatory overtones, in which quantifying and qualifying the description of a handshake expresses information about the nature of men's relationships. This implicit connection between male intimacy and the presence and quality of physical contact clearly transcends the interpretation of the handshake in a heterosexual context. Upon hearing that Jerry had in fact shaken hands with Keith, George follows with the highly charged question: "You gonna see him again?" Here, the use of the verb "to see," implying organized social interaction between two people, is typically in reference to romantic situations; George has thus come to accept Jerry in a dating relationship with Keith.

Elaine enters and immediately teases Jerry: "So, how was your date?" Not only has she invaded Jerry and George's male habitat, but she has once again made explicit the romantic nature of Jerry's connection to Keith that he can only enjoy when unspoken. Jerry is forced to respond (with obvious agitation): "He's a guy." Elaine quickly reveals that she and Keith have made a date for the coming Friday, perhaps expressing an implicit understanding of a rivalry with Jerry. Realizing that such plans will interfere with his own "date" with Keith, Jerry protests with disappointment and resentment. Elaine mistakes his anger as being in response to some lingering romantic attachment to her:

> **Elaine:** I've never seen you jealous.
>
> **Jerry:** You weren't even *at* Game Six—you're not even a fan!
>
> **Elaine:** Wait a second . . . are you jealous of *him* or are you jealous of *me?*

Flustered and confused, Jerry walks away without responding, allowing the insinuation of a queer interpretation to be implied by his silence.

Jerry steps outside of the apartment just as Kramer enters; he sits alone with Elaine as George disappears into the bathroom. Predictably, it is just as Kramer finds himself next to the phone that the call from the unemployment bureau arrives; Kramer, the only one uninformed about George's scheme, answers the phone and responds with confusion, assuring the caller that she has reached a residential number, not Vandelay Industries. Having overheard, George bursts from the bathroom in a panic, his pants around his ankles. Despite his frantic pleading with Kramer to pass him the phone, Kramer is already hanging up; the defeated George collapses on the floor. Precisely at this moment, Jerry reenters the apartment. In a highly unusual aerial shot, the camera shows us Jerry's perspective of George, face down, boxer shorts exposed, and prone, lying before him on the floor in an obvious position of sexual receptivity. Jerry quips: "And you want to be my latex salesman." Once again, Jerry's reinvocation of latex has powerful queer connotations in response to seeing George seminude before him.

The next scenes juxtapose Elaine and Keith's date with Jerry's alternate Friday night activity, a visit to see his friends' new baby. Elaine, the focal point of a crowded sports bar discussing Game Six of the World Series with Keith, has occupied the very place (physically and romantically) that Jerry had longed for. In the accompanying parallel scene of Jerry, he seems both out of place and uncomfortable amid the domestic and overwhelmingly hetrosexual atmosphere of the baby's nursery. The misery over losing his night on the town to Elaine is amplified by his obvious distaste for the nuclear family, the ultimate signifier of "straightness."

The scene again changes to Keith and Elaine alone in his car, this time with Elaine in the passenger seat that Jerry had previously occupied. Elaine, comfortable in her familiar and appropriate role as passive/feminine, waits patiently as Keith (in the privileged masculine driver's seat) silently wonders whether or not he should kiss her, mirroring Jerry's earlier internal debate over suitable intimate physical contact. Although they kiss, Elaine is unimpressed. Later, just as George had done, Jerry pumps Elaine for information about her date. When Elaine admits that she and Keith had kissed, Jerry pushes further: "What *kind* of kiss was it?" Incredulous at Jerry's tactlessness, Elaine does not respond. Jerry at last answers her standing question: "I'm jealous of everybody."

Keith calls, interrupting one of the few moments in the episode when Jerry and George share the scene alone. After hanging up, he explains with discomfort that he has agreed to help Keith in his move to a new apartment. George seems to recognize and identify with Jerry's apprehension over this sudden escalation in their rapport. "This is a big step in the male relationship," Jerry observes, "the biggest. That's like going all the way." Never has Jerry made such a direct reference to the potential for sexual contact with Keith. Of course, Keith has by no means propositioned Jerry, which makes the queer desire on Jerry's part all the more obvious in contrast with the seemingly asexual nature of Keith's request. However, Jerry has made clear his own willingness to homo-eroticize his friendship with another man. By likening "going all the way" to moving furniture, Jerry is able to fantasize that Keith shares Jerry's homosexual desire. Ingeniously, he has crafted an imaginary set of circumstances that allow him to ignore Keith's preference for Elaine as a sexual object while tidily completing his fantasy: Keith has expressed desire for Jerry, but now Jerry has the luxury of refusing his advance on the moral ground that he will not rush sexual intimacy. Once Keith arrives, Jerry tells him that he cannot help him move, explaining that it is still too soon in their relationship. Again, by positing Keith in the masculine role of sexual aggressor, Jerry in turn occupies the stereotypically feminine role of sexual regulator/withholder.

Kramer and Newman arrive just as Jerry declines Keith's request; not surprisingly, Kramer jumps at the opportunity to take Jerry's place. As he and Newman disappear out the door to help Keith move his furniture, Jerry commiserates with Elaine over the phone: "You broke up with him? Me too!" Even as Jerry's homoerotic adventure has drawn to a close, Kramer's last-minute appearance lends an air of sexual unpredictability to end the episode on a resoundingly queer note.

Seinfeld's narrative design would, at first glance, seem to lack the depth necessary in character and plot to facilitate a discussion of the complexities of homoerotic male relationships. The sort of nonspecific, scattered quality of the *Seinfeld* text, however, makes it well suited to the fluid nature of a queer reading, whose project is more concerned with context than fixity, more with potential than evidence. Nonetheless, *Seinfeld* is full of both context and evidence that lead the text's critics toward a well-developed queer reading. *Seinfeld* enjoys a kind of subculture defined by a discursive code that unites its members in a common lexicon of meaning. The narrative restricts its focus to the foursome, containing, and maintaining the intimate bonds between the show's three men and its one woman (the latter being clearly positioned as sexually incompatible and socially separate from the others). Directly related to this intense interconnection, the foursome often causes each member's inability to foster outside heterosexual romantic interests.

Jerry and George share the most intimate relationship of them all; they aid each other in perpetuating duplicities while remaining truthful only with one another. They are the two characters who most frequently share a frame and who create and occupy male-coded narrative spaces, whether in the domestic sphere of Jerry's apartment or in the public sphere at Monk's.

All of these relationships are in motion amid a steady stream of other discursive and iconic gay referents. Their visibility admits the "knowing" viewer into a queerly constructed *Seinfeld* universe while never being so explicit as to cause the "unknowing" viewer to suspect the outwardly "normal" appearance of the show.

Reading the queer in *Seinfeld* sheds a revealing light on the show's "not that there's anything wrong with that" approach to representations of male homo-eroticism. While sustaining a steadfast denial of its gay undercurrents, the text playfully takes advantage of provocative semiotic juxtapositions that not only allow but also encourage the "knowing" spectator to ignore the show's hetero-sexual exterior and instead to explore the queerness of *Seinfeld.*

Notes

All dialogue quoted in this essay, unless otherwise indicated, comes from my own transcriptions of the television programs in question.

1. Bill Zehme, "Jerry and George and Kramer and Elaine: Exposing the Secrets of *Seinfeld*'s Success," *Rolling Stone* 660–61 (6–22 July 1993): 40–45, 130–31.
2. As evidence of this Seinfeldian shared vocabulary, I offer one of my primary resources for this paper, The *Entertainment Weekly* "Seinfeld" Companion. Author Bruce Fretts creates a partial glossary of these terms, situating them in their episodic contexts, cross-referencing them with the episodes in which the term recurs, and finally providing a chronological plot synopsis of episodes 1–61, ending with the 1993 season premiere, "The Pilot."
3. My essay takes its title from this episode; while combating the rumor of their homosexuality, the phrase "not that there's anything wrong with that" serves as Jerry and George's knee-jerk addendum to their denials. The catchphrase becomes a running joke through the episode, being echoed in turn by Jerry's and George's mothers and, later, by Kramer as well.
4. A particularly useful example of this theme occurs in "The Café," in which George, terrified of his girlfriend Monica's request that he take an IQ test, fears that he will not be able to pass. Out of desperation, he arranges for the more intelligent Elaine to take the test for him by passing it out to her through an open window. Jerry too has approved their secret plan to pass George off as an intelligent, appropriate partner for Monica: "Hey, I love a good caper!" Despite their best efforts to dupe Monica by presenting George in a false light, she discovers their duplicity and breaks up with him.
5. When questioned, Jerry makes no secret about the intensity of his "friend-ship" with George; in "The Dog," he confesses that they talk on the phone six times a day—coincidentally, the same number of times a day that he gargles.
6. A queer reading of the social differences between Jerry and George reveals a substratum of conflict: within the homoerotic dynamic that groups them together as a couple, George is constantly portrayed as crude, unrefined, and in need of direction. When George is paired with Jerry in the intimate, caretaking relationship they share, their connection suggests a domestic partnership in which Jerry, the more successful and refined of the duo, acts

as their public voice, correcting George's social missteps, allowing them to "pass" less noticeably through acceptable, urban, upper-middle-class society.

7. It should be noted that George's presentation as both unemployed and desperate accentuate the clear class differences between him and Jerry, the successful stand-up comic being courted by a celebrity athlete.

Topics for Reading and Writing

1. What does Gantz mean by "queer"? How does this term differ from "gay" or "homosexual" or "lesbian"? How does she use this term to make her argument? What does she mean by a "queer reading" of the TV show?

2. Is Gantz arguing that Jerry and George are actually gay? If they are, why wouldn't the show make that explicit? How else does the show play with the idea that George and Jerry are lovers of a sort?

3. Gantz's article is an academic paper. How does it differ in its rhetorical strategies from, say, the article on Philip Morris's marketing included in Chapter 3?

4. Is it silly to take apart a television show in such detail, seeing it as important that Vandelay Industries works with "latex"? Is Gantz just reaching? Or are these details actually meaningful to a "reading" of the show? Do the intentions of the creators and writers of the show matter? Should they play into our reading of the show?

The Writer at Work: Arguing About Causes and Effects

In 1999, in a pleasant suburban community, two heavily armed teenage boys, bullied outcasts, roamed through the halls of their high school, murdering students and teachers. In the wake of the Columbine High School shootings in Littleton, Colorado, American society painfully turned inward to ask itself "why?" Eric Harris and Dylan Klebold's actions were only the most recent in a spate of school shootings committed by middle-class white teenage boys. What caused these boys to kill? The boys, the public learned in the ensuing investigation, were obsessive fans of the violent videogame *Quake,* in which the characters wander through halls, slaughtering enemies. How much responsibility did the video game bear for their rampage? How much responsibility did the school bear for allowing the bullying that apparently filled these boys with self-righteous rage? How much responsibility do the gun makers bear? How responsible is society, for making those guns available? What about the violent images in movies and on television? What about the boys' parents? What about the boys themselves?

No clear answer emerged from the convulsive societal argument that followed the Columbine shootings. Ironically, the difficulty of definitively assigning a cause to Columbine made many of the pundits, commentators, and talking heads that populate the American media chew over another, perhaps more valuable topic: the idea that making indisputable arguments about causes may be impossible.

Of course, like any other philosophical debate this one isn't new. The Greeks puzzled over causality, while Enlightenment thinkers posited a "Great Chain of Being" in which God was the ultimate cause of everything, from the existence of evil to the fact that Shakespeare's plays remained unaccountably popular. The Scottish philosopher David Hume, watching one billiard ball strike another, insisted that nobody could make an ironclad case that ball 2 moved solely because ball 1 hit it. (Samuel Johnson, another leading intellectual figure of the eighteenth century, when asked about Hume's argument kicked a rock in the road and proclaimed "I refute him thus!")

Arguing about billiard balls or stones in the road is one thing, but arguing about social issues is another. Why do high school boys bring guns to school, intending to kill? People tend to gravitate toward the causes that confirm prejudices they already hold: gun control advocates blame America's relaxed or even glorifying attitude toward firearms, conservatives blame the disappearance of values-based education, critics of the entertainment industry blame the celebration of violence in video games and movies. Other, more complex problems have even more causes assigned to them. Why does poverty seem so intractable in America's inner cities? Thousands of sociologists have worked for centuries on that problem, but nobody has ever proposed a cause everyone could agree upon.

That, in essence, is the problem. Social problems aren't like scientific or engineering conundra—what caused the space shuttle to explode, why the World Trade Centers collapsed, what creates the aurora borealis. These questions can be answered by factual evidence. Although this factual evidence might not be enough to convince David Hume, it is enough for most of us. On the other hand, explanations for social problems rely, like all the other kinds of arguments discussed in this book, on arguments that are not only factually supportable but also convincing to the audience being addressed, largely because the proposed causes themselves are debatable propositions. Think back to the Columbine example for a minute. The vast majority of members of the National Rifle Association, strong supporters of the right to bear arms and generally socially conservative, will never accept that the availability of guns caused Harris and Klebold to murder. They would be far more open to the argument that the lack of "morality" in the schools was an important or perhaps even the most important cause. Liberals, on the other hand, who generally oppose such "morality education" as prayer or the Ten Commandments in schools, would be happy to blame Columbine on guns. Both audiences, also, would be open to an argument that put some of the blame on the media— conservatives feel the media lacks morality, while liberals dislike the media's glorification of violence.

IDEAS INTO PRACTICE 7-1

Propose a cause or several causes for each of the following societal phenomena. Then, taking into consideration the audiences listed for each social phenomenon, choose which cause would best fit their preconceptions.

1. The popularity of "reality" television.
   a. High school history teachers.
   b. A high school football team.
2. The persistence of segregated public schools in many cities.
   a. A group of republican businessmen.
   b. A group of civil rights activists.
3. Global warming.
   a. Automakers.
   b. Members of the Sierra Club (an environmental group).
4. The increasing narrowness of the playlists on many commercial radio stations.
   a. Fans of Britney Spears.
   b. Fans of underground "alt-country" music.

Constructing a Causal Claim

Making an argument about what causes something is one of the most difficult tasks a writer can undertake. The writer must first decide what *kind* of argument about cause he or she wants to make. Sometimes, for instance, we start with the cause and want to make an argument about what the effect is going to be—your parents might have argued to you that dropping out of high school (the known cause) would result in you "ruining your life" (the presumed effect). Other causal arguments go the other way, like the Columbine question. Another kind of causal argument interrogates the actual relationship between a known cause and a known effect. We know, for instance, that media conglomeration has resulted in the movie industry relying on tried and true franchise movies and sequels rather than taking chances on new ideas. But why?

Even if there are three different varieties of arguments about causes, all of them rely on the same logical structure. Let's try out a causal argument of the first variety (known cause, unknown effect) using an idea from this chapter:

> The media's growing tendency to be politically correct is limiting societal discourse about important issues.

This is a good, controversial question to tackle. Most of us would agree that the media are changing the way they treat minority groups, but to designate that change with the pejorative term "politically correct" is itself an arguable point. (This calls for a claim about meaning!) You might think this change is a great thing; in that case you might change the first idea to "The media's growing sensitivity to minority groups" or "The media's commitment to inclusion and diversity" or some other positive way to state a similar idea. In either case, this causal argument is going to start out with a claim or argument about naming that will rely on concrete evidence of how the media are more "sensitive" or "politically correct." (To an especially skeptical audience, you might also have to prove that the media are more "politically correct" or "diverse" than they were 20 years ago—this probably wouldn't be difficult.)

Having established that the way the mass media treat issues of ethnicity or gender or sexual orientation (for these are the central concerns of the diversity/

political correctness movement) differently today than it used to, you now have to move to the heart of the argument: the actual argument about what effect this cause is going to have. Here, you'd need to come up with some evidence. You could rely on conjecture and analogy:

> It's like putting blinders on a horse. When you limit the way that people *see* the outside world—when you only talk about ethnicity and gender and sexual orientation in one way—you limit the ideas people can have about those issues.

Or you might rely on an emotional claim:

> The media only allow us to think *in one way* about these things—they try to control our minds so we can't generate ideas outside of their preconstructed box.

You could even rely on humor and hyperbole, as have many opponents of the political correctness movement.

> Eventually, we are going to refer to every group by some sort of victimhood affiliation as a way of "affirming" or "validating" their experiences: instead of "George Drakoulian, driving without his glasses, ran a stop sign and hit Nerese Woods," we'll have "The visually challenged George Drakoulian, a descendant of victims of the Armenian genocide, was involved in a traffic communication breakdown with alter-abled lesbian of color Nerese Woods."

It's probably most effective, though, to come up with some actual evidence. Here, Larry Elder's article might help. Elder argues that the media is so afraid of showing black perpetrators of crime (because the media don't want to be accused of furthering the stereotype of the criminal black male) that we are no longer able to honestly confront the facts that some black males do commit crimes. Elder brings up several highly publicized actual cases in which the perpetrators were white males and another similar case (which was not covered much at all) in which the aggressors were African Americans. Elder's example seems to indicate that the media does, in fact, treat these crimes differently because they fit into the priorities of the PC crowd differently.

Is one example enough to prove a causal relationship? Generally, no. The causal claim here is so big—it's about all of American society, after all—that you'd need an enormous amount of anecdotal evidence to even suggest a circumstantial link. Elder's evidence certainly helps flesh out the argument; it's vivid, based in provable historical fact, and speaks directly to our claim. But it's not enough, even if bolstered with the arguments by analogy, emotion, and hyperbole we've sketched out.

What we need is a logical chain. How does the media's growing "PCness" or "sensitivity" result in a limited ability to discuss issues? Let's think about how this might happen.

1. The media grow more "sensitive" or "PC."
2. The media begin to cover issues of ethnicity, gender, sexual orientation—everything that we might call "identity politics" (although that's also a loaded term) carefully.

3. Worried about offending "victim" groups, the media downplay stories that appear to confirm stereotypes about those groups.
4. Many societal issues do, in fact, touch on the concerns of these minority or marginalized groups.
5. When the media cover those issues, then, it will go out of its way to not offend those groups.
6. Inevitably, a conflict will arise between covering a story honestly and covering a story without offending an involved party or the group he or she represents.
7. Because of its growing PCness, the media will cover that story in the inoffensive way.
8. The media will then not be covering stories honestly.
9. Citizens rely on honest and accurate media coverage of issues in order to have an open and realistic discussion about these issues.
10. Because they are not receiving this from the media, they will not be able to have an open and realistic discussion.

So what we seem to have here is what seems to be a solid logical case. Is it that simple? Unfortunately, no. Although the chain works well—few people would deny that each proposition leads to the next proposition—many of the propositions themselves are debatable. Here is where questions of audience come into play. People who are already skeptical about the media would be very likely to agree with Propositions 2, 6, and 8; media officials and many others would disagree. Some audiences would argue that the media is irredeemably racist and will never err on the "sensitive" side. Other audiences would argue with Proposition 9, and counter that this gives the media too much power in public discourse, that citizens can discuss the issues without the media being involved.

Most arguments about social problems, in fact, work this way. Causal arguments often rely on so many factors—so many of which are themselves debatable—that it's very difficult or even impossible to make the kind of iron-clad causal argument that a scientist might make (that smoking causes cancer, for instance). The rhetor must construct a logical chain that works, but must also keep in mind that the individual links in that causal chain might themselves be called into question. It's here that the effective writer will rely on his or her skill in appealing to the audience, and keep in mind which propositions will be appealing to the audience—and which propositions that audience will reject.

IDEAS INTO PRACTICE 7-2

Construct a causal chain for each of the following cause-effect relationships. For each link in the chain, indicate what evidence a writer would need to prove that link

Example: The low pay offered by careers in journalism causes the media to be liberal.

 a. Careers as a reporter or even an editor don't offer much in the way of money, especially considering the amount of time and professional preparation they demand. (Evidence: actual salaries offered by television, radio, and print journalism organizations.)

b. Although this isn't always the case, conservative people frequently value monetary and material success more than do liberals. (Evidence: that wealthy people tend to be conservative, that many professions that pay little but require a great deal of education and commitment are populated by liberals.)

c. Because of the two previous propositions, we can posit that liberals gravitate toward the media. (This is a syllogism, although certainly a tenuous one—Proposition 2 appears quite shaky and overly general. One could also cite here the Media Research Center's statistics about the political leanings of journalists.)

d. Since it is impossible to report the news entirely without bias, the news media will reflect the biases of the people who create its content—who are, as we have just proven, largely liberal. (Again, this proposition depends upon another generalization that one could refute.)

1. The growing presence of commercialism in public schools—Channel 1, exclusive contracts with soda companies, classes or after-school programs sponsored by corporations—causes students to believe that commercialism is the natural order of things.
2. The decreasing quality of network and cable news programming is causing young people to get their news from late-night comedy shows.
3. Watching a great deal of television when they are toddlers will cause children to have short attention spans.

Style
Toolbox **Transitions and the "Known-New Contract"**

You learned in the previous Style Toolbox that the rhythm of sentences—their length, their pattern of stresses, the placement of essential information within the sentence—is a crucial tool for writers in bringing readers along through an argument. Effective use of sentence rhythm engages readers in an argument and can reach them emotionally. Just think of the most effective arguments you're read: they probably made good use of rhythm both within each sentence and within paragraphs.

Perhaps more important than the rhythm of the language you use within and among sentences is the rhythm of the *concepts* within and among sentences. What does the rhythm of concepts mean? Just as sentence rhythm relies on a regular pattern of stresses (short sentence—short sentence—short sentence—long sentence), conceptual rhythm relies on a regular pattern of ideas being introduced and explained. Well-constructed paragraphs tend to introduce their concepts and details in a regular "rhythm." In a descriptive essay, for instance, the writer will probably write a general topic sentence or two that will encompass all the details that will be presented in the paragraph; the rest of the sentences of the paragraph will color in the space drawn by the topic sentence(s), as in the following excerpt from an essay about rats by *New Yorker* writer Joseph Mitchell:

The brown rat is distributed all over the five boroughs [of New York City]. It customarily nests at or below street level—under floors, in rubbishy basements, and in burrows. There are many brownstones and redbricks, as well as many commercial structures in the city, that have basements or sub-basements of dirt floors; these places are rat heavens. The brown rat can burrow into the hardest soil, even tightly-packed clay, and it can tunnel through the kind of cheap mortar that is made of sand and lime. To get from one basement to another, it tunnels under party walls; slum-clearance workers frequently uncover a network of rat tunnels that link all of the tenements in a block. (Joseph Mitchell, "The Rats on the Waterfront")

Outlined conceptually, this paragraph might look like this:

Main concept: The brown rat is distributed all over the five boroughs [of New York City]. It customarily nests at or below street level—under floors, in rubbishy basements, and in burrows.

Illustrations of main concept:
1. There are many brownstones and redbricks, as well as many commercial structures in the city, that have basements or sub-basements of dirt floors; these places are rat heavens.
2. The brown rat can burrow into the hardest soil, even tightly-packed clay, and it can tunnel through the kind of cheap mortar that is made of sand and lime.
3. To get from one basement to another, it tunnels under party walls; slum-clearance workers frequently uncover a network of rat tunnels that link all of the tenements in a block.

Illustration Sentences 1–3 really could go in any order; we don't need Sentence 2 in order to understand Sentence 3.

Another effective type of conceptual rhythm or structure, one used frequently in persuasive writing or in writing intended to explain a process or concept, is called the "known-new contract." In this type of paragraph structure, each sentence incorporates an idea from the previous sentence, then introduces a new idea that relies on the previous sentence to make sense. (It's called a "contract" because the writer and reader implicitly agree that any new concepts in a sentence will be linked to and explained by a concept the reader already knows.) In paragraphs structured by the known-new contract, the topic sentence is less a general summation of the paragraph as a whole than a general lead-off statement for the chain to follow. The following sentence from Annie Dillard's essay "Total Eclipse" provides an excellent example of the known-new contract as a structuring principle for a paragraph:

The Crab Nebula, in the constellation Taurus, looks, through binoculars, like a smoke ring. It is a star in the process of exploding. Light from its explosion first reached the earth in 1954; it was a supernova then, and so bright it shone in the daytime. Now it is not so bright, but it is still exploding. It expands at the rate of seventy million miles a day. It is interesting to look through binoculars at something expanding seventy million miles a day. It does not budge. Its apparent size does not increase. Photographs of the Crab Nebula taken fifteen years ago seem identical to photographs of it taken yesterday. Some lichens are similar. Botanists have measured some ordinary lichens twice, at fifty-year intervals, without detecting any growth at all. And yet their cells divide; they live.

Dillard's paragraph actually includes two separate conceptual chains, the sentences of each of which are linked by the known-new contract. In the following breakdown, the "known" part of each sentence is in **bold,** the "new" is *italicized.*

> **Conceptual Chain 1: The Crab Nebula,** in the constellation Taurus, looks, through binoculars, like a smoke ring. **It** is a star in the *process of exploding.* Light from **its explosion** first reached the earth *in 1954;* it was a supernova **then,** and *so bright it shone in the daytime.* **Now** it is not so bright, but it is *still exploding.*

> **Conceptual Chain 2: It expands** at the *rate of seventy million miles a day.* It is interesting to *look through binoculars* at something expanding **seventy million miles a day.** *It* **does not budge.** *Its apparent size* **does not increase.** *Photographs of the Crab Nebula* taken fifteen years ago **seem identical** to photographs of it taken yesterday. *Some lichens* are **similar.** *Botanists have measured* **some ordinary lichens twice,** at fifty-year intervals, *without detecting any growth at all.* And **yet** *their cells divide; they live.*

The links proceed by several principles. Many sentences are linked to one another by the relationship of a pronoun and its antecedent: "The Crab Nebula" becomes "it" in Sentence 2; Sentence 2's introduction of the explosion becomes "its explosion" in Sentence 3. Time, specifically the opposition of past and present, is also an important conceptual structure in Dillard's paragraph: the final sentences of Conceptual Chain 1 are related conceptually through time (then . . . now). What are the conceptual relationships in Conceptual Chain 2?

The known-new contract can be a great way to structure a paragraph, but it relies on a very informed and confident writer. In order to lead the reader though a tightly linked chain of ideas, the writer must be very clear in his or her own head about how they all relate to each other, and must carefully reread the paragraph after initially composing it in order to make sure that each sentence (excluding the first) draws upon an idea of the previous sentence and introduces a new idea that will appear in the following sentence. As you saw in the Writer at Work section of this chapter, one weak link in your causal chain causes the whole argument to collapse; this is also true on the much smaller scale of the known-new contract.

WRITING WITH STYLE 7-1

Diagram the conceptual relationships in the following paragraphs. What new idea is introduced in each sentence? How is it used in the following sentence(s)?

1. Even some of the mass-market publishing houses were trying to broaden the boundaries, to seek new readers, and to raise general levels of literacy

and knowledge. The most notable of these was the New American Library of World Literature, where I began my own work in publishing. NAL was initially the American branch of the British Penguin, to whom its general approach to publishing owed a great deal. Penguin was the most successful and influential of the early mass-market publisher, and its policies were emulated throughout Europe and the Americas. (André Schiffrin, *The Business of Books*)

2. Welcome to post-liberal Los Angeles, where the defense of luxury lifestyles is translated into a proliferation of new repressions in space and movement, undergirded by the ubiquitous "armed response." This obsession with physical security systems, and, collaterally, with the architectural policing of social boundaries, has become a zeitgeist [the spirit of the times] of urban restructuring, a master narrative in the emerging built environment of the 1990s. Yet contemporary urban theory, whether debating the role of electronic technologies in precipitating "postmodern space," or discussing the dispersion of urban functions across poly-centered metropolitan "galaxies," has been strangely silent about the militarization of city life so grimly visible at the street level. (Mike Davis, *City of Quartz*)

WRITING WITH STYLE 7-2

Now, practice the known-new contract in a paragraph of your own composition. Write one paragraph about one of the following topics, making sure that each sentence introduces one new concept and that the following sentence uses that concept as a jumping-off point (referring back to the original concept by a pronoun or conjunction such as "Yet" or "However" or "Moreover").

1. How to drive from this campus to your family's home.
2. Why teen sex comedy movies are adversely affecting the sexual morality of high schoolers.
3. The process of photosynthesis.
4. A summary of the plot of your favorite novel.
5. A genealogical discussion of one branch of art or music, in terms of how particular artists influenced others.

What's out of Bounds?

Chapter 8

"*Kangaroo Jack* wasn't really a kids' movie—it was far too raw for that. I felt that the advertising was very misleading."

"After so many children have been hurt imitating stunts, it's time to take *Jackass* off the air."

"I find it comical that Howard Stern gets fined for saying offensive words that everyone already knows, when his real problem is that he's a racist."

"Hollywood films glorify cigarette smoking. In response, our coalition is going to boycott movies that glamorize tobacco."

"TV shows like *Friends, King of Queens,* and *Grounded for Life* have too much sex in them to be shown at 8 p.m.—and as for *Will and Grace,* that raunchy show shouldn't be on network TV at all!"

"It's a disgrace that children can access pornographic websites on public library computers."

The University of California at Berkeley was the home to the Free Speech Movement in the mid-1960's.

"People who sell *The Turner Diaries* or *Protocols of the Elders of Zion* should be prosecuted. And we need to keep an eye on anyone who'd buy those books, too."

"Eminem, 50 Cent, Snoop Dogg, I don't care—it's all garbage that teaches young men crass materialism, violence, and misogyny."

You've probably heard these or similar complaints being made by politicians, teachers, even your parents. Older people and authority figures in a society tend to worry about the messages circulating around society, fearing that impressionable, easily influenced young people lack the critical faculties to fully understand those messages or to resist their negative content. The funny thing about these complaints is that they've been made for centuries. Ever since the printing press enabled information to be reproduced in large quantities and distributed to anyone who could afford it, society has bemoaned how information or entertainment corrupts the youth and coarsens the intellectual atmosphere. In the early 1800s, parents fretted about the craze for rebellious Romantic writers like Byron and Goethe that resulted in a rash of faddish suicides of young men imitating the melancholy heroes of literature. The "penny-dreadful" newspapers that appeared in the late nineteenth century, with their lurid woodcuts of crime scenes and scantily clad actresses, were assigned at least some of the blame for the perceived increase in urban crime and degradation at that time. In the 1920s, such an outcry rose against Hollywood's low moral standards that movie producers established an agency (the Hays office) to create and enforce a code for movies. The system of film ratings we have today—G, PG, PG-13, and R—was adopted in the 1960s after another period of anger at the movie industry for the sexually explicit films of the late 1960s. The terrorist attacks of Sept. 11 spawned a collateral controversy about what kinds of messages were out of bounds—White House spokesman Ari Fleischer warned that domestic critics of the U.S. government's security efforts should "watch what they say," and talk-show fixture Ann Coulter earned criticism even from her right-wing colleagues when, on the website of conservative magazine *National Review,* she called for a "crusade" to forcibly convert Muslims to Christianity.[1]

Moral standards, though, don't just loosen; at times morality even gets stricter. The Puritans who settled this country, with their draconian standards of behavior and belief, were in many ways reacting against the easy sexual morality of the Renaissance. In more modern times, the Roaring 1920s saw standards about what can be expressed in public change dramatically; the following three decades, though, tightened moral strictures again. Many observers of these phenomena suggest that the occupant of the White House sets the tone for the nation, and certainly the laid-back, easygoing Bill Clinton was an inspiration for, and embodiment of, the good economic times the nation enjoyed in the 1990s. According to these observers, the election of the much more conservative (politically and morally) George W. Bush signaled the counterswing of the moral pendulum—many voters were appalled at President Clinton's personal behavior and sought to elect a man who embodied a different, stricter personal morality.

Arguments about what kind of information is "out of bounds"—and for whom—take place in every society and every culture. For each society, moreover, the kind of information that is prohibited differs. In some societies—the Stalin-era Soviet Union, Saddam Hussein's Iraq, Nazi Germany—any information that criticized the government or questioned its leaders was prohibited. Taliban-ruled Afghanistan, Inquisition-era Spain, and Puritan America reserved their heaviest sanctions for information that challenged the official line on religious doctrine. Today in the United States and Western Europe, the type of information or content that is considered the most dangerous is probably child pornography—depictions or descriptions of sexual acts involving children. But child pornography is by no means the only kind of information whose dissemination is prohibited in American society today. Broadly stated, information that is either restricted or completely off limits falls into one or more of the following categories:

- depictions or descriptions of sexuality.
- explicit threats to public safety or to individuals.
- "sedition," or encouragement to rebel against or overthrow the government.
- invective or threats against a racial, ethnic, or religious group.

---

[1] "This Is War." *National Review Online* 13 Sept 2001. (www.nationalreview.com/coulter/coulter091301.) Because of this column, the editors of the *National Review Online* declined to continue running Coulter's pieces.

- discussions or depictions of certain functions of the human body (chiefly sexual or eliminatory).
- language that is considered "obscene."
- insults to or attacks on a religion.
- insults to or attacks on a revered public figure (Martin Luther King, Jr., or George Washington).
- advocacy of political opinions—white supremacy, communism, radical Islam—deemed dangerous or fundamentally opposed to American values.
- information about how to construct or use certain kinds of weapons.
- information about how to produce or distribute illegal substances.

There are probably several more categories of frequently restricted information, but this list encompasses the majority of such topics. To say that these topics are restricted or prohibited, though, is not specific enough; each type of problematic or transgressive information is restricted according to *what* group or groups it endangers, the nature of that danger, and the nature of the media through which that information is communicated. Take sexuality, for instance. For many reasons, American society is more conservative or "puritanical" about sexuality than are other, similar societies. Information about children and sexuality is often completely prohibited, while other kinds of sexual information are partially restricted—parents must give their consent for students to attend sex education classes in school; pornographic images cannot be sold or distributed to people under the age of 18; movies depicting sexuality are forbidden to children under 17 completely (the X or NC-17 ratings) or unless their parents are present (the R rating). Television's and radio's restrictions on sexuality are much more stringent than the restrictions placed on films, while the restrictions on personal communications are much looser. These standards, moreover, are constantly changing.

It might be valuable, just as an intellectual exercise, to break down all these types of transgressive information into two different categories: information that threatens public order and stability, and information that threatens public morality. (We are artificially separating these categories here when many conservatives and some liberals would see them as essentially interdependent.) Into the first category would go anything that questions the government, that questions laws, that questions the basic ideological consensus about the value of democracy, freedom, and free enterprise most of us share. In this model, communications that target certain racial or religious groups must be restricted because a working democracy cannot scapegoat or devalue groups of people based on permanent characteristics. Obviously, this category must prohibit those messages that explicitly seek to damage or overthrow public order—calls for revolution, advocacy of political parties that would fundamentally change the nature of our government, information about how to avoid the law. Societies and governments naturally seek stability and self-preservation, and will always pass laws and enforce restrictions that ensure their own survival. As James Gleick points out in his article "Tangled up in Spam," the "national interest" can also involve crucial economic activities. While we probably wouldn't consider e-mail a necessary resource or service for public safety, Gleick points out that so much commerce and communication now takes place on the Internet and via e-mail that not just our convenience and sanity but also our nation's economic health depends on eradicating the problem of e-mailed spam.

Closely related to questions of public order are questions of public morality. In fact, the two are probably impossible to disentangle, for governments often are the entities that define public morality. However, it is rare that a government is the *only* force determining the meaning of "public morality" in a society; morality defined by religion, family, cultural inheritance, and tradition is generally more powerful than morality legislated by a government. (Totalitarian governments in Nazi Germany, the Soviet Union, and Khmer Rouge Cambodia sought to replace the morality of each culture with an entirely new code based on that government's desires, but the pull of centuries of tradition was almost always too strong.) In the United States, public morality determines restrictions on information about and depictions of sexuality, the body, religion, obscene language, and attacks on revered public figures. Public morality also was a driving force behind the outrage sparked by the *Bumfights* videos you read about in Chapter 7.

Because morality is generally a more compelling and powerful basis for an argument than governmental self-preservation, restrictions that are in reality based on the latter will often be explained as being based on the former. For example, advocacy of communism in America has generally been characterized as a moral problem (communism, the argument goes, is evil and godless) rather than as a political problem (because it threatened the American system of government). Stalin's Soviet Union and its satellite states took this a step further, educating young children that turning in one's own family for seditious statements was a laudable, moral act. And in ancient Athens, Socrates was sentenced to death on charges of "corrupting the youth"—his crime was encouraging them to question governmental policy.

Rhetoricians took a great deal of interest in President Bush's decision to characterize the September 11 hijackers, the Taliban, and Al Qaeda as "evil" rather than as rational people who were devoted to the destruction of the United States and of Western-style freedom. As the writer Susan Sontag and the television comedian Bill Maher learned, the presidency's power to determine the terms of argument made it impossible to discuss the hijackers' motivations in any but the most theological language—Sontag was attacked for her writings in *The New Yorker* and Maher lost his television show *Politically Incorrect* in part because he denied that the suicidal terrorists were "cowardly," as Bush had stated. (ABC and Disney executives, nervous about public and governmental backlash against Maher, cancelled the program soon after he said this.) Moreover, the debate about the 2001 USA Patriot Act—a package of new laws that relaxed restrictions on law enforcement officials and tightened restrictions on foreign nationals entering and living in the United States—illustrates the importance of language in controlling what's out of bounds. "USA Patriot," "Operation Iraqi Freedom," "Operation Enduring Freedom" (the 2001 invasion of Afghanistan), "Operation Infinite Justice" (the original name for the 2001 invasion of Afghanistan, changed so as not to play into Afghan animosity toward outsiders and "crusaders"). What is the rhetorical effect of those names on public sentiment toward the operations and laws themselves?

So how does all this play out in the contemporary media? Primarily, these questions of statements or ideas or information being "out of bounds" or "off limits" determine what can be transmitted in the media. Agencies and offices and boards—some governmental, some not—write the regulations about what can be disseminated, where, and when. Television programs that air at 8 p.m. are allowed less leeway than are the programs in the 10 p.m. lineup, and programs that air from midnight to early in the morning have even more freedom. Local standards also come into play; television and radio stations in more conservative parts of the nation may choose to air such programs as *NYPD Blue* at 11 p.m. rather than 10 p.m., and some radio stations may simply not play suggestive music that dominates the hit parade in other markets. The broadcast networks and the cable networks have more stringent restrictions placed upon them by the FCC and by their own "standards and practices" departments than do such pay channels as Showtime or HBO, presumably because consumers must make an active choice to allow the pay networks into their houses. The uproar caused by singer Justin Timberlake exposing Janet Jackson's breast during the halftime show of the 2004 Super Bowl—a stunt broadcast live to an enormous television audience—demonstrates that standards may be changing but are still present and powerful. The radio is much the same: the time and type of station determine what can be aired. Moreover, the intent of the information matters: the Federal Communications Commission will fine a radio station for airing a profanity-laced song or a "shock jock's" show that uses one of the forbidden words (which were memorably lampooned in comedian George Carlin's routine "Seven Dirty Words"), while an NPR documentary using those same words with the intent of educating is exempted from such fines.

Other media, as well, experience restrictions. The Internet has been the most important battleground of recent years. Laden with pornography and opportunistic marketers, not to mention actual sexual predators, the Internet can be a dangerous place for children. Because our society has determined that children should not see depictions of sexual acts, Internet pornographers are required to provide at least some kind of barrier preventing children from entering their sites or accessing their merchandise (although that "barrier" is often no more than an "AGREE" box stating that "I am 18"). Companies have developed software for parents that attempts to block access to sites containing pornography, but it is very difficult to block pornographic materials without filtering out all sorts of other, nonpornographic sites: health-related sites about breast cancer, for instance, or literary criticism about novels such as James Joyce's *Ulysses* that depict masturbation. The Children's Internet Protection Act of 2001 mandated that public libraries had to install such filters on public Internet terminals, but the American Library Association has protested the law on the grounds that such filters block vast amounts of legitimate, nonpornographic information. (The Supreme Court, in 2003, upheld the law.) In an article included in this chapter, the Watergate figure turned conservative minister Chuck Colson attacks the American Library Association for its willingness, as he sees it, to put the free speech rights of pornographers and predators above the public interest of protecting children from dangerous information. What do you think should be allowed in libraries? What principles can we devise for what should and shouldn't be available on your library's shelves or Internet terminals?

"Censorship" or "filtering" or "protection" (the word used to describe the action varies according to the political stance of the speaker) doesn't just occur with information transmitted over the air or on wires. Even what you choose to buy or rent may have had its content altered. Several companies have recently started producing "cleaned-up" versions of popular movies, with pro-fanity and sexual content excised from the films. The films' directors have, in many cases, protested what they see as a violation of their works' integrity, but many conservative parents have praised companies like CleanFlick for allow-ing them to control the content of their children's viewing. (See Patrick Gold-stein's article "This Dad Demands Final Cut" in the readings for this chapter.) Acting as a filter on behalf of parents, retailers such as Blockbuster and Wal-Mart stock sanitized versions of movies and CDs—in many cases, these com-panies *only* stock the censored version, causing other consumers to complain about the retailers making their choices for them. On occasion, an artist's work will be so trangressive or "dangerous" or "immoral" that parents and authority figures will go so far as to attack the company that produced it. In 1992, rap star Ice-T endured massive criticism from police groups, parental groups, and even Vice President Dan Quayle for his song "Cop Killer." Targeting Ice-T's record company, these groups' relentless attacks forced the company to with-draw the record from the market, release Ice-T and his group Body Count from their contract, and even renege on its own statement defending Ice-T's artistic freedom.[2]

Many of us growing up in this society start out as absolutists on this ques-tion, vehemently opposed to any kind of censorship or restriction on the flow and dissemination of information. After all, when we are children *we* are the ones who don't get to stay up to watch late-night television or see R-rated movies or listen to the latest hip-hop songs. However, as we grow older we become more resigned to these restrictions, and even begin to accept the idea, which seemed so patronizing earlier, that some segments of the population need to be "protected." Generally, this change of heart comes about partly as a result of our growing realization of just how naíve children can be when faced with shrewd marketers or predators, and partly as a result of what almost every-one ends up seeing as the growing coarseness of society. For centuries, adults have lamented that children are allowed to see or read or hear or believe or learn things that would have been completely off limits earlier, and for cen-turies young people have explained to their elders that the world is different today. Undoubtedly, the proliferation of media outlets and the explosive devel-opment of communication technologies will only accelerate this age-old dynamic—you might find yourself saying "When I was your age . . ." to your younger sibling, thinking about how different things were only last year. In reading and writing about these questions, though, it is of central importance to

---

[2] Barry Shank, "Fears of the White Unconscious: Music, Race, and Identification in the Censorship of 'Cop Killer'." *Radical History Review* 66 (1996).

keep in mind those things that change much more slowly: the arguments about the *actual* underlying grounds on which particular information needs to be censored or restricted.

The development, management, establishment, and control of public morality is a vastly complicated topic; especially in a society as diverse as the United States, there are hundreds of powerful influences on public morality. For every George W. Bush fighting for "family values," it seems, there is a Madonna or Johnny Knoxville seeking to expand the bounds of what's permissible. Most bodies or agencies or individuals with power seek to have some influence on the setting of the boundaries about what can and can't be said or depicted in public. Certainly such traditional powers as the church and the government still carry a great deal of influence on these questions. But who else influences the tone and boundaries of public discourse? Actors and entertainers? The public school system? Corporations? Television producers? Politicians? And how do they exert this influence—how are the restrictions, written or unwritten, formal or informal, on what can be expressed in public created and disseminated and enforced? It's very tempting to think of these questions in simplistic terms: "society" won't let me say what I want to say, "the government" will stop me from making the film I want to make, "they" will prevent me from truly expressing myself. However, in reality the maintenance of standards for public discourse is handled by thousands of different people and groups with thousands of different agendas and values and hundreds of ways of enforcing their desires. It's worthwhile to give the questions the kind of nuanced, subtle thought and investigation they deserve.

Analyzing the Message

What kinds of information should be restricted? For whom? Why? What kind of access to this information should be allowed? Who should determine this? For each of the following examples, answer these questions, thinking about how you could explain the necessity of these restrictions to various audiences.

1. The movie *Titanic,* which depicts two characters under the age of 18 having sex.
2. Pornographic films made by Traci Lords when she was under the age of 18.
3. *The Anarchist's Cookbook,* an underground book detailing how to make molotov cocktails and pipe bombs.
4. Information about how to modify a legally purchased and registered shotgun in order to make an illegal sawed-off weapon.
5. A website produced by American associates of Al Qaeda urging terrorist attacks against the United States.
6. A website produced by overseas Al Qaeda operatives urging terrorist attacks against the United States.
7. The film *Jackass,* showing stunts that can result in injury.
8. The violent gangster film *Scarface,* starring Al Pacino.
9. The videotape *Faces of Death,* a collection of filmed images of people dying violently.

10. Televised images of American prisoners of war being interrogated by Iraqi troops during the Iraq invasion of 2003.

11. Televised images of dead American soldiers during the Iraq invasion of 2003.

12. *Will and Grace,* a network television situation comedy depicting homosexual characters as ordinary people.

13. A film in which a character says "motherfucker."

14. A newspaper produced by the American Nazi Party.

15. A movie starring Orlando Bloom and Mandy Moore that glamorizes smoking and drug use.

Readings

Michael Medved
The Infatuation with Foul Language

*One of the best known TV-based film critics, over the last decade **Michael Medved** has differentiated himself from his peers by reviewing films from a political stance—a conservative one. His 1992 book* Hollywood vs. America *was an important contribution to the growing anger against the entertainment industry, a sentiment endorsed by both the Democratic and Republican candidates for the Presidency and Vice-Presidency in 2000. This anger is based on the sense that the products of the entertainment industry— movies, television programs, music, videogames, and the like—relentlessly glorify irresponsible sexuality, violence, materialism, misogyny, disrespect for religion, and a general atmosphere of aggression and crassness. In this excerpt from Medved's book, he speaks specifically about crude language.*

For many members of America's mass audience, a low-frequency tone is hardly necessary to produce gut-churning results: they are already ill over the foul language that pervades our popular culture.

It may seem anticlimactic to discuss the excessive use of four-letter words after covering the current fascination with vomit and urine, roaches and maggots. Audiences are so energetically assaulted with every manner of maiming and mutilation, every imaginable approach to sexual exploitation and debasement of the human spirit, that one might well expect them to overlook the nasty language that usually accompanies the ugliness.

The public, however, remains surprisingly sensitive to the verbal obscenities that have become such a common-place aspect of our movies, popular music, and even prime-time TV. All public opinion surveys measuring attitudes toward the media report a remarkable unanimity behind the idea that Hollywood should clean up the language in the products it offers to the people.

A well-publicized 1989 poll by Associated Press/ Media General asked its respondents: "Overall, do most movies that come out nowadays have too much profanity in them, or not?" An astonishing 80 percent cited "too much" profanity; *not one* of the 1,084 survey participants endorsed the idea that movies today contained "not enough" harsh language.

This sort of statistical response conforms to the strong impressions I've received during more than seven years of communicating with the public as a nationally televised film critic. Among thousands of letters complaining about one or another new movie release—or about the sad state of films in general— foul language is *by far* the most commonly mentioned offensive element, well ahead of excessive violence, graphic sexuality, racial and gender stereotyping, or any other grounds for objection.

Anyone who bothers to listen to the public must come to understand that the explosion of verbal obscenities on screen has contributed powerfully to the sense of many moviegoers that a visit to their local theater has become a demeaning experience.

Ann Landers, whose nationally syndicated column provides a popular forum for the sentiments and values of Middle America, reports a huge volume of mail expressing outrage on this issue. On May 15, 1989, she ran a sampling of these letters under the headline "Filthy Talk Tarnishing the Silver Screen." Among the comments she included:

- from Oxnard, California: "I'm sick to death of crude and vulgar language. How much more explicit can it get? . . . Why must decent people be embarrassed in front of their children by obscene words . . . ?"
- from Vancouver, British Columbia: "My wife and I have walked out of so many movies because of the dirty language . . ."
- from Panama City, Florida: "Amen to your comments about gutter talk in movies. . . . Rock bottom, I call it."
- from Palo Alto, California: "I'm a sixty-four-year-old male who has been around. Nothing shocks me, but some things offend me. I'm talking about the F-word in the presence of my fifteen-year-old grandson. I'm afraid to take the boy to the movies again."
- from Kansas City, Missouri: "You said it wouldn't hurt Hollywood to clean up its mouth. I agree. In fact, I'll go further and say it would help the box office. My husband and I go to very few movies these days because of the dirty talk. I'll bet millions of Americans feel the same way."

Hollywood's refusal to face the sincere hurt and disappointment behind such statements represents an especially appalling illustration of the industry's underlying contempt for its audience.

Even if one insists that all survey results are overstated, and that letter writers are unrepresentative, it still makes little sense to give needless offense to any significant segment of the moviegoing public. I've heard industry defenders make the argument that among the 80 percent of all Americans who tell pollsters of their annoyance at the street language in films, only a minority are *seriously* alienated by the obscenities. Even so, what producer in his right mind would unnecessarily and knowingly write off 30 percent, or 20 percent, or 10 percent of potential patrons for his movie?

What makes Hollywood's self-destructive obsession with the language of the sewer even more difficult to understand is the total lack of countervailing pressure on this particular issue. Where are the advocacy groups, or even individual members of the audience, who clamor for the industry to maintain its impressive quota of F-words. S-words, and other expletives in film after film? Richard Pine, one of the most savvy and respected literary agents in the business, addresses the situation with common-sense clarity: "Nobody ever walked out of a movie and said, 'Gee, that was a great picture, but the only problem was they didn't say "Fuck" enough.' Who thinks like that?"

Who indeed? Who dictates the idiotic overrepresentation of a few crude Anglo-Saxonisms in today's movie dialogue—especially in the absence of any discernible audience demand for the inclusion of such words?

As with the gratuitous vomit and urine scenes, the utterly gratuitous use of obscene language stems in part from the filmmakers' adolescent insistence on thumbing their noses at all conventional notions of propriety. Many of the major decision-makers in Hollywood can recall a time when even the use of "hell" and "damn" was strictly limited; their current opportunity to pepper their pictures with literally hundreds of far harsher words represents a recently won and deeply cherished freedom. At times, they seem determined to use that freedom simply because it is *there.*

This attitude appears at every level of the production process, from producers to screenwriters to directors to the actors themselves. Certain performers are notorious for their insistence on inserting their favorite words in every film in which they are cast, even when those expletives never appeared in the script. According to veteran observers, Oscar winners Robert De Niro and Joe Pesci are among those who are especially apt to increase the intensity of their characterizations with an abundance of unscripted, improvisatory obscenities.

Significantly, both men appeared in *GoodFellas* (1990), one of Hollywood's all-time champions when it comes to expletives per minute. The Entertainment Research Group of Boca Raton, Florida, which devotes itself to the unenviable (and exhausting) task of counting the obscene words in new movie releases, certified this film's remarkable achievement. With a total running time of 146 minutes, director Martin Scorsese and his cast managed to pack in some 246 F-words, fourteen S-words, seven A-words ("asshole"), and five "slang terms for parts of the male anatomy." This means that viewers of *GoodFellas* heard a major obscenity nearly twice every minute; or, to be more precise, once every 32.2 seconds of the picture's running time.

Brilliantly well-acted, emotionally gripping, and critically overpraised, Scorsese's stylish triumph gave bad language a good name. When this veritable festival of foul speech won an Oscar nomination for Best Picture of the year and swept the leading awards from all the major critics' organizations, it only served to reinforce the idea that the finest in cinematic artistry requires a wealth of obscene dialogue. According to this reasoning, Scorsese needed every one of his hundreds of expletives in order to treat his subject with uncompromising integrity. After all, how can he be expected to shape a convincing film about murderous Mafia hoods without reproducing the filthy language such thugs would surely use in real life?

This argument displays not only a childish literalism but also an ignorance of cinema history.

The mere existence of some unpleasant aspect of reality—say, the morning constipation and hemorrhoidal pain that afflict a significant percentage of our fellow citizens—does not create an obligation to portray that situation on the screen. The failure to focus on the moments that a character spends grunting on the commode does not necessarily betray the truth of his existence, nor imply a lack of integrity on the part of the filmmaker. Despite the professed enthusiasm for the subject matter from bands like the Toilet Rockers and performers like Shane Embury of Napalm Death (mentioned above), mainstream filmmakers have—so far—chosen to ignore defecation as a major focus for their artistry. Every movie is inevitably selective in those elements of an individual, or a story, it chooses to convey. Artistic restraint—and consideration for the sensitivities of the audience—do not always amount to dishonesty.

Anyone who remembers *White Heat*, the great Jimmy Cagney film from 1949, knows that the portrayal of a psychopathic gangster can be just as convincing, and just as terrifying, without obscene language. Somehow, director Raoul Walsh managed to bring to life the cruel realities of his main character's world, both inside and outside of prison, while using 246 fewer F-words than Martin Scorsese employed in *GoodFellas*. Can any fair-minded observer watch *White Heat* and honestly declare that its effectiveness has been compromised by the restraint of its language?

In this regard, as in so many others, the classics of Hollywood's Golden Age could provide an education for many of today's filmmakers. Consider John Ford's *The Grapes of Wrath* (1940), with its harrowing tale of embittered farmers (one of them an ex-con) fleeing the horrors of the Dust Bowl in Oklahoma for exploitation in the fruit orchards of California. While real-life "Okies" may well have employed extremely salty language in their moments of rage or pain, the impact of this noble film is hardly reduced by its characters' failure to reproduce those curses.

The same point might be made for the masterful *Paths of Glory* (1957) with its grim, nightmarish account of the fate of three ordinary French soldiers in World War I who are sacrificed by vainglorious higher-ups. The battlefield, and the military prison, as rendered by director Stanley Kubrick, are no less horrifying for their absence of expletives. When viewing this stunning film alongside Kubrick's more recent antiwar epic *Full Metal Jacket* (1987), it is hard to see how the bountiful use of abusive language in the latter project makes it in any way a better film.

While arguments may reasonably rage over the appropriateness of including verbal obscenities in movies about the mob, or migrant farm workers, or long-suffering soldiers in the heat of battle, no one can make a convincing case that those words are essential in lighthearted comedies, or sentimental romances, or adventure movies for kids.

Nevertheless, the Hollywood establishment inserts vile speech in nearly all such projects, without rhyme, reason, or proper warning to the public.

A simple word count on 282 major movie releases from 1991—performed by the aforementioned Entertainment Research Group—proves that the public is correct in its assumption that it is virtually impossible to escape street language in today's films.

A breakdown of 1991 releases according to their MPAA ratings shows that the *average* R-rated movie contains twenty-two F-words, fourteen S-words, and five A-words—providing its viewers with a major obscenity every two and half minutes. Keep in mind that these figures represent an average—indicating that half the films in this category provide even heftier doses of foul talk.

Far more surprising is the ubiquity of harsh language in films deemed more appropriate for youthful audiences. I am almost amazed at how many parents still cling to the notion that a PG or PG–13 rating for a film means that their children will be spared the most intense obscenities. This supposition hardly squares with the fact that 39 percent of 1991 PG–13 films used the F-word, 66 percent used the A-word, and an amazing 73 percent used the S-word!

Even among PG movies—films to which parents eagerly bring their six- and seven-year-old children—58 percent use the A-word, and 46 percent use the S-word. Insisting on this sort of language in so many films for kids is not only unnecessary; it is insane.

Similarly insane is the dramatic drift toward dirty words on prime-time TV; increasingly, Americans find themselves assaulted by crude language in their own living rooms. Bill Bruns and Mary Murphy lamented this trend in a November 1990 article in *TV Guide:*

> Try explaining to your six-year-old, for example, what six-year-old Maizy on CBS's "Uncle Buck" means when she tells her brother, "You suck." Or what fourteen-year-old Darlene Conner on ABC's "Roseanne" is talking about when she brags to her sister that she was "felt up" by her boyfriend. . . . Other words on other shows are coming across loud and clear. Sharon Gless, in the title role on CBS's "The Trials of Rosie O'Neill," candidly tells how "I'm thinking about maybe having my tits done" to cope with her divorce. . . . NBC's "L.A. Law," meanwhile, has attorney Grace Van Owen upset because her former boss, the DA, is "pissed at me." On ABC's "Cop Rock," a judge calls a defendant a "scumbag"—a vulgarism for a condom.

One 1990 scene in "The Trials of Rosie O'Neill" helped to define the new freedom for prime-time producers to use harsh language. In the midst of an argument with her office mate Hank Mitchell (Dorian Harewood), Rosie blows her stack. "I've had it with the Beverly Hills *crap.* You elitists *son of a bitch!* You're worse than any snob in my mother's club," she snaps.

"I couldn't get into your mother's club," he shoots back. *"So kiss . . . my . . . ass!"*

Producer Barney Rosenzweig fought passionately to keep this scene as written and considered it a major victory for creating freedom when, after a extended battle, CBS gave him his way.

As a result of his triumph, millions of American kids had the opportunity to hear role models on television engage in precisely the sort of crude and abusive exchange that most parents try hard to discourage in their children.

Not everyone in the television industry is convinced that the medium's new tolerance for explicit language represents progress. Delbert Mann is one of the great directors in TV history, with credits including the original, televised version of *Marty, The Bachelor Party, The Man Without a Country,* and *Playing for Time.* As he reflected on the current dilemma of the networks he has served so well, Mann told the *Los Angeles Times* in 1991: "I get a real sense of America being turned off by the network television we see, and that the language is one reason for the lost network audience. The language is still important to people in this country."

Other television veterans agree with him. "I wish we could go back to the innocent days of television," says distinguished producer David Gerber, chairman of the MGM/UA Television Production Group. "Looking at some of the current shows, I wonder: how far can we go before the audience is offended and turns off? The pendulum always swings back. People in the industry just forget that."

Topics for Reading and Writing

1. Is Medved too puritanical? What is the problem with using the kind of language that real people use in the real world?

2. How does Medved's decision to use euphemisms ("the F-word," "the S-word") rather than "street language" itself affect his argument?

3. Although he spends most of his energy discussing "gutter language," how do you think Medved might feel about the proliferation of racially based slurs in movies such as *Pulp Fiction?*

4. How does Medved counter the impression that what he'd really like to see on TV and in the movies are a bunch of childish, simplistic, Disney-like stories? What do you think he would consider to be "good" movies? And why does he feel that the coarsening of movie language is "self-destructive" on the part of Hollywood?

The *New York Times*
Censoring the Internet

The Children's Internet Protection Act, upheld by the Supreme Court in 2003, held that libraries that received federal funding had to install filters on their public Internet terminals in order to "protect" children from pornographic websites. In this editorial (written before the court handed down its decision), the **New York Times** *argued that the law should be struck down. Internet filters are instruments far too blunt to accomplish the task with which they are charged; many legitimate websites are rendered inaccessible by filters that block words like "breast." Ultimately, the* Times *argued (unsuccessfully), this legislation is well-intentioned but flawed, and a major infringement upon the right to free speech.*

Countering the New York Times' *argument is* **Charles Colson,** *former Nixon aide (and*

The Supreme Court heard arguments last week in a case that will help shape the degree to which free speech prevails in cyberspace. To qualify for federal funds, libraries are required to block access to pornographic Web sites. This means that the law, in effect, coerces libraries to deny access to constitutionally protected materials. The libraries are rightly challenging the law. The court should strike it down.

The First Amendment guarantees freedom of expression on the Internet. The Supreme Court made this clear in 1997 when it invalidated portions of the Communications Decency Act that made it illegal to post sexually explicit material online without restricting minors' access to it. But the Internet's technology poses an array of legal issues that do not occur offline, such as the question of filtering.

The Children's Internet Protection Act requires that libraries receiving federal aid for Internet access install filters that block material considered obscene or, in the case of underage users, "harmful to minors." Libraries regard the law as an infringement on their ability to provide information freely to their users. They say it requires them to use *imprisoned Watergate figure) turned evangelist. In his articles, appearing as a part of his "BreakPoint" commentaries for Christian radio, Colson insists that these filters accomplish precisely what they are intended to do. Furthermore, Colson attacks the American Library Association (ALA) for its adamant refusal to "protect" children from sexual predators. In Colson's view, child molesters wait in the library for children, force them to look at Internet pornography, and then might even take those children away to assault them sexually. The ALA, cloaking its irresponsibility in "free speech" arguments, is actually a danger to children.*

software that erroneously blocks access to many inoffensive sites. A group of libraries sued, and last year, a three-judge court unanimously held the law unconstitutional.

It is clear that the software being forced on libraries prevents their patrons from seeing a large amount of constitutionally protected material. By one estimate, it "overblocks" by 15 percent or more, meaning that untold hundreds of thousands of Web sites that should be accessible to library users are not. The trial court found that the software blocked the Web sites of political candidates and sites discussing such topics as sexual identity and abstinence.

The government argues that librarians can remove the filters when asked to do so. But the unblocking technology is itself flawed. There was testimony at trial that only one person in a library system, no matter how large or busy it is, can have access to unblock the software. And as the lower court found, patrons may be unwilling to ask librarians to unblock sites if they cannot do so anonymously. Forcing users to specifically request information about subjects like sexually transmitted diseases or homosexuality may, in some cases, effectively deny them access to it.

The Children's Internet Protection Act is the first federal law ever to impose free-speech restrictions on local libraries, and it does so in a constitutionally unacceptable way. If there is a problem with library terminals being used to gain access to inappropriate Web sites, it is a problem the court should trust local libraries to solve.

Charles Colson's Prison Fellowship Ministries
The ALA's Addiction to Porn

Predators in Your Neighborhood

The citizens of Greenville, South Carolina, were shocked last December to read a story in the local newspaper reporting that their tax dollars were being used to fund obscenity in, of all places, the public library.

The article documented that on one randomly selected day, adult men took up more than half the library's computers, prowling through online pornography. And one of them, it turned out, had been convicted for distributing obscene material to minors.

In graphic detail, the report told of children attempting to complete school projects while men beside them gawked at all forms of perversion. But every American should take note of what happened next. When citizens complained, the library director shrugged it off, saying that the First Amendment gives people the right to see anything they want on the Internet, including pornography.

Well, a firestorm erupted. Church and civic leaders organized, determined to take back their library. Congressman Jim DeMint urged citizens to flood the library board with complaints. But despite the uprising, the board and its director balked, refusing to install software to filter obscene material from computers.

This time the citizens turned to the Greenville Country Council, which appoints the library board, and they got action. Six of the eleven library board members were replaced. The new board fired the director and launched a study to find out how bad the situation really was. What they found should send shivers through every community in America.

Their report showed that in one nine-month period more than 100 complaints were made about incidents arising from library patrons using the Internet for pornography. The library's own investigation had reported far less.

In one case, a man grabbed a seven-year-old boy and forced him to view pornography. When the boy turned away, the man laughed. "Ten years from now, he'll be begging for it," he said. On another occasion, a staff member watched as a man and three 13-year-old girls viewed a website offering "sex with snakes."

When these appalling facts, long covered up by the library director and board, became public, it galvanized the new library board. This month (August 2000), new software is being installed to block pornography in the Greenville County Public Library—another hard-won victory by citizens who refused to let their tax money fund moral rot.

But their fight may not be over. The board is anticipating lawsuits, perhaps from the ACLU, claiming violation of the First Amendment. But State Attorney General Charlie Condon has offered to defend the library if they are sued. In Condon's words, "A library is an information storehouse, not an Internet Penthouse."

This case is a textbook example of what citizens can accomplish when they work together within the political system.

But it also offers a warning. Across America, library boards are refusing to block Internet porn, under the misguided belief that patrons, even minors, have a constitutional right to view obscene material, no matter how revolting it may be.

And sadly, their defense of pornography is orchestrated by the American Library Association, which has become an advocate for radical causes in America.

Tomorrow, I'll tell you more about what's going on with the American Library Association and its agenda to turn our culture on its head, starting with your kids.

Beware, Public Library: The ALA's Agenda of Porn

Are you ready for this?

One of the most dangerous places you can send your child today may be the public library. That's right, the public library.

Why? Well, under the guise of free speech, many librarians have decided it's their duty to permit patrons to explore the underworld of virtual perversion by logging onto pornographic websites. And your tax dollars are paying for it.

It's not a local problem but a nationwide campaign, and nobody knows the full extent because some libraries cover it up. A Minneapolis study documented only three cases of pornographic Internet use. But, off the record, library staffers admitted that its use was widespread.

And its use leads to incidents with children being victimized. In Greenville, South Carolina, a man forced a seven-year-old boy to view pornography on the library's computer. In Denver, a woman was briefly distracted, only to find her seven-year-old daughter viewing pornography with a stranger.

While some libraries have installed software to filter this trash, others simply refuse. And you should know that the librarians who insist on public access to porn aren't just the misguided few; they're the intellectual mainstream, trained and accredited by the American Library Association.

The ALA, in league with the ACLU and the Gay and Lesbian Alliance, has embraced pornography as "free speech." They say everyone, minors included, has a right to unrestricted access to it.

But most disturbing, according to Robert Marshall, a member of the Virginia House of Delegates who has become an expert on the subject, parents' wishes are often dismissed. He says the ALA frowns on efforts by schools to require age-level restrictions, or even permission from parents before children can gain unlimited access to pornography in books or on the Internet.

In the ALA's view, parents have the right to control what their children can access only while they are with them. If no parent is present, children can get anything they want.

Think about that!

It's illegal for minors to buy pornography at magazine stands, but librarians will look the other way, under orders from the American Library Association.

The ALA's own website illustrates that uncontrolled Internet access is just part of their larger agenda: to radicalize society, starting with our kids.

The website invites kids as young as 13 to log on to "Go Ask Alice," a so-called advice column sponsored by Columbia University. But bluntly put, it encourages teenage sex. The column even explained to one teen how to have "safe sex" with animals. Other topics include first-time sex, love toys, and sado-masochistic role-playing. Yes, you heard it right. And that's just for starters.

The ALA aggressively promotes homosexuality, sponsoring an annual "Gay, Lesbian, Bisexual and Transgendered Book Awards," and it opposed the Boy Scouts for refusing to allow gay scoutmasters. It has challenged statutes to limit obscenity in libraries and elsewhere.

Tomorrow, I'll tell you how you can speak up and counter the ALA's influence in your community. But whatever you do, don't assume your public library is a safe place for your kids.

Perils of the Public Library

Putting Our Kids at Risk

"Picture this. You are a librarian who sees a ten-year-old boy not two feet from a man viewing a full screen of sexual intercourse. Or you see a young woman, who happens to walk by a porn-viewing Internet user, become visibly upset, throw down her books and run from the library. When you retrieve the books, you find they are on recovery from rape."

These are the heartbreaking words of Heidi Borton, who resigned from a Seattle library because she could not stomach the library's policy of open access to Internet porn. Heidi was one librarian the American Library Association wasn't able to brainwash.

The past two days, I've described how the ALA, along with radical groups, has been working to make Internet pornography freely available in libraries everywhere. They insist that everyone, minors included, has a constitutional right to Internet porn.

The ALA's dirty little secret should light a fire in every community. Grassroots groups should be indignant that their tax dollars are subsidizing, not only pornography, but a left-wing agenda bent on turning our moral standards upside down.

But what can you do? Well, first, find out if your local library has open access to the Internet, but you should know that the ALA trains its members to evade these kinds of questions. You may be told, for example, that the Constitution doesn't allow computer software that filters pornography. That's not true. No law has ever required a library to include smut in its collection.

Librarians make judgments every day. Some libraries, as you well know, ban Christian books. And indeed, librarians have the right to screen out vulgar websites, just like they screen anything else.

You might be told that filtering software is unreliable, that it can't distinguish between legitimate health information, like breast cancer, and pornography. But a study of Utah public schools that use filtering devices found only one site in a million was ever blocked in this way. Some libraries that do reject the ALA's dictates are already banning obscenity from their computers, while maintaining legitimate links to the Internet.

If your library insists on an open-access policy, I suggest you organize your friends and neighbors and church and take action. Library boards are usually appointed. Some communities have successfully lobbied to get intransigent boards fired and replaced with citizens who understand the social consequences of taxpayer-financed smut.

The ultimate answer, of course, is in the state legislatures. To date, only a handful of states have laws mandating that tax-financed libraries install filtering devices. When such bills are proposed, state library associations encouraged by the ALA work hard to defeat them.

And too often, citizens don't get involved—but we need to.

The American Library Association, and its supporters in libraries across this country, has perverted the meaning of free speech. Too often, they block books that portray Christian values and beliefs while defending with all their might the right to view obscene and immoral material.

If Christians don't stand up against such decadence, then we become willing slaves to the counter-cultural values of the American Library Association and its friends.

Topics for Reading and Writing

1. What is the *logos* of each piece? What is the heart of the logical chain of each argument?

2. How might these two rhetors speak to each other about this issue? Is there any point at which they agree?

3. Is there any kind of information that should not be available at a public library? Does this violate the Constitution's guarantee of freedom of speech?

In the first piece—from the University of Southern California Daily Trojan— *editorial writer **Katie Dunham** discusses the phenomenon of services that "censor" or "clean up" Hollywood movies. Dismissing the objections of the movie studios and of the Directors Guild of America (DGA), Dunham argues that movies, once purchased by an end user,* belong *in the most meaningful sense to that owner. Why shouldn't parents have the right to buy cleaned up versions of movies, versions that omit problematic content? **Patrick Goldstein**, writer of the "Big Picture" column in the* Los Angeles Times, *agrees with Dunham, but adds the perspective of a parent.*

Katie Dunham
Censoring Is A Choice

Recently, the Director's Guild of America took steps toward shutting down companies experimenting with technology that can edit out sex, violence and profanity from home videos. The DGA, along with Hollywood big names such as Martin Scorsese and Steven Spielberg, claims companies such as ClearPlay, Principle Solutions and CleanFlicks are illegally altering copyrighted movies.

The DGA's suit hinges on copyright law, which says that while viewers can mute, skip or fast-forward offensive or mature material, it is unlawful for companies to sell software that could do it for them. Of course, they can sell us the remote controls, VCRs and DVD players complete with "pause" and "stop" buttons, but everything's dandy just so long as Sony, Toshiba or RCA aren't doing the clicking for us.

While I don't think I'll ever invest in any of these new upstart editing systems, I don't understand why it should be any director's business what viewers do in the comfort and privacy of their own homes. If a concerned father wants to use ClearPlay to remove an all-too-spooky scene from "The NeverEnding Story" so that his toddler can sleep at night, it's no filmmaker's place to stop him. If I need to baby-sit and I decide to buy an edited version of "Spiderman" from CleanFlicks, does injuring the artistic integrity of the film really matter to me?

This isn't an issue of censorship by any means, but rather one of viewers' rights. Rating boards and studios can cut foul language and excessive blood-spurting till the day is done, but allow the audience one shred of freedom and autonomy over their own viewing experience and the fat cat directors start crying out for artistic freedom. Just another example of greed propelling the movie industry, if you ask me.

This new software doesn't change the fact that the complete and intact version of the director's movie is out there somewhere, it just allows people who don't want to see the gruesome war scenes or hardcore sex scenes to do just that. If you're exhausted and fatigued from a long, hard day at the office, you should be allowed to watch whatever will bring you relief and fulfillment when you come home at night. I'm sure Steven Spielberg isn't always in the mood for the first 20 minutes of "Saving Private Ryan," and Martin Scorsese certainly has the right to skip from scene to scene when watching "Taxi Driver" or "Goodfellas." It's hardly comparable to walking into the Louvre and painting a mustache over the Mona Lisa. It's more like taking a print of the Mona Lisa and cutting it up to decorate your dorm room walls.

Are ClearPlay or CleanFlicks going to hinder a director's chances at taking home the Oscar? Are they setting boundaries on the great things directors can do through the art of filmmaking? Are they keeping some masterpiece work hidden from the eyes of the American public? Not at all. These companies are just making it easier for parents and other mild-mannered citizens to make their own decisions about what they watch or don't watch.

It isn't any filmmaker's place, regardless of artistic integrity or feeling of ownership, to tell viewers that they can't do that. By the time I pop a Blockbuster New Release into my VCR, the director will have already received all the acclaim and self-fulfillment he or she is going to for that particular movie. He or she has released it to the world and can't take it back. The efforts of DGA in trying to do that just proves how vanity, pure and simple, is still at work in Hollywood.

Patrick Goldstein
This Dad Demands Final Cut

If you were looking for a knee-jerk defender of artists' rights, you'd find me first in line. So when I started hearing about CleanFlicks, ClearPlay and the other Utah companies that have developed technology to edit out profanity, sex and violence from home videos, I was appalled by the idea of people chopping up movies simply to fit their moral sensitivities. As director Michael Mann recently told a Times reporter: "The idea that somebody else can arbitrarily take our works apart and destroy them . . . there's no polite word for it—it's stealing."

Right on, Michael. When it comes to attacks on artistic freedom by a bunch of philistines, I'm on your side. And then I had an unsettling little epiphany.

When it came to watching movies with my 4-year-old son, Luke, I was— ahem—something of a philistine myself. One of Luke's (and my) favorite movies is "The Lion King." But the film has one scene, in which Mufasa dies trying to save his son in a stampede, that was simply too intense for him to watch. "Dada!" he would shriek, holding his ears. "Skip! Skip!" At first, we'd simply fast-forward to the next scene. Then I had a friend dub a copy of the video with the scene edited out.

Since then, Luke has watched "The Lion King" about 900 times without incident. But what about me? Have I painted a mustache on a masterpiece? The Directors Guild of America firmly believes I have. Joined by a group of prominent Hollywood directors that includes Steven Spielberg and Martin Scorsese, the DGA has taken legal action to shut down a host of companies they say are illegally altering movies. The DGA suit casts a broad net, going after such companies as CleanFlicks, which sells reedited versions of Hollywood films, as well as firms such as ClearPlay and Principle Solutions, which sell software that operates more like a remote-control clicker, giving parents the option of sanitizing otherwise unaltered DVDs and videos.

According to DGA consultant Lon Sobel, who teaches entertainment law at the Berkeley Center for Law and Technology, my "Lion King" analogy is imprecise. Copyright law, he says, allows individuals to fast-forward, skip or mute scenes, but companies can't sell software that does it for us. But, I asked, doesn't Sony sell clickers that fast-forward and mute for us? Yes, Sobel says, "but it's still the consumer who's doing the fast-forwarding, not Sony doing it for us."

He adds that according to a federal trademark statute known as the Lanham Act, an outside company can't edit or create new versions of someone's work without permission. "These companies are either editing or creating software that reflects the editing made by the company, not by an individual," Sobel says. "So when you see one of their videos, the editing is so seamless that if you don't understand [the narrative logic of the film], you have no idea whether the editing was done by their program or by the original filmmaker."

The DGA believes it has legal precedent on its side. But with nearly every advance in entertainment technology geared to consumer choice, it becomes more of a struggle to put the genie back into the bottle.

And when it comes to an intellectual debate over artistic integrity, the entertainment business, having made so many craven concessions to self-censorship and commerce in recent years, has a weak case. Parents are tired of being played for suckers. The more I talked to my friends, especially parents who've spent years diving for the clicker to fast-forward through a scary scene in a movie or a repellent commercial on a kids' TV show, the easier it was for me to side with consumer rights over copyright protection.

When a studio buys a popular novel, as Universal did with Thomas Harris' "Red Dragon," it's entitled to create or eliminate as many scenes as it sees fit. Yet if I buy a copy of the same movie and use a program to fast-forward through the scene in which a serial killer tortures Philip Seymour Hoffman, rips out his tongue and set his corpse on fire, it's suddenly a heinous trampling of artists' rights.

Pleasing the Ratings Board

I might be more sympathetic to the DGA's case if someone were willing to acknowledge the vast abandonment of artistic principles that occurs daily in the movie business. Michael Apted, one of the many distinguished directors who has joined the DGA's suit, recently told The Times that if "any small interested parties are entitled to change anything to suit their own particular will . . . that leaves you in anarchy and chaos. It's fascism to me."

With all due respect to Apted, if he wants to point fingers at small interested parties that change film content to suit their own particular will, why not start with the 13 anonymous parents who make up the Motion Picture Assn. of America ratings board? Thanks to the failure of studios or filmmakers to challenge their judgments, the ratings board enjoys the absolute power to arbitrarily force filmmakers to mutilate delicate works of art by cutting out scenes that somehow offended the rating board's sensibilities.

As far as I can tell the filters designed by companies such as ClearPlay simply deputize parents to be ratings board surrogates. With a flick of a switch, they can jettison sex or profane language, instantly transforming an R-rated movie into a PG-13 film, or a PG-13 film into a PG. Here's the DGA voicing outrage over a digital tool that gives parents the ability to cut out dirty words, and yet most of these same filmmakers meekly kowtow to the capricious judgments of a roomful of anonymous overseers, slicing and dicing their beloved works of art to earn a PG-13 rating, giving their film infinitely more profit potential.

It's hard to sympathize with the DGA's efforts to prevent parents from cleaning up movies when it allows studios to do it every day. As long as there's a buck in it down the line, filmmakers allow studios to reedit their films for TV and airplane broadcast. If studio research numbers come in low, filmmakers willingly change endings, reshoot scenes, tone down sex and violence, cut out entire characters and subplots, and even change the whole tone of a film to make it more commercially salable.

Filmmakers aren't the only ones who've ceded their right to the moral high ground by placating moralists or grandstanding politicians with self-censorship. When family-values activists attacked smutty lyrics in the 1980s, the music business began labeling potentially offensive CDs with parental warning stickers. And when Wal-Mart and other retailers told record companies they wouldn't carry stickered CDs, the record companies agreed to make "clean" CDs that had been laundered of enough foul language to be sold without a warning sticker. Nearly every artist has agreed to sanitize records, even though it's Wal-Mart that sets the rules, not the artists—no doubt because Wal-Mart accounts for roughly 10% of CD sales.

Interestingly, you can find plenty of "uncensored" versions of popular films in video stores, meaning that studios have discovered the value of offering dirtier edits. If studios, backed by filmmakers, also provided "clean" versions of their big movie hits, they might not be faced with such a grass-roots parental rebellion. In today's culture, everything is about choice—our national motto should be "Have it your way." It comes as no surprise that ClearPlay chief Bill Aho used to be a brand manager at Procter & Gamble; he recognizes the power of a consumer-friendly product.

"If anyone thinks Americans are going to allow film directors to rip the remote control out of their hand, you're underestimating the desire people in this country have for personal choice," Aho says. "Technology enables lots of things that people don't like. I'm sure directors would love to outlaw the mute button and the fast-forward button if they could. But in the living room, it's Mom and Dad's call, not the film director."

In fact, this skirmish between the DGA and parent-friendly filtering devices represents only the latest salvo in a much bigger war—the ongoing battle between media companies and the technology industry. Whether the war is over Internet filesharing, MP3s or CD burning, the fight essentially boils down to people who profit from copyright (media conglomerates, filmmakers and recording artists) versus people who profit from serving consumers (electronics firms and Internet mavens). For the past several decades, the most popular new technologies—from the VCR, the CD and the Sony Walkman to the DVD, MP3, iPod and TiVo—have been designed to give consumers more control and convenience in experiencing entertainment.

When I play music on a CD or computer or MP3, I can reconfigure it any way I want, adding or skipping tracks, mixing and matching music from different artists. Thanks to DVDs, I can watch a movie in an entirely different order than the artist intended, skip scenes I don't like or listen to the director's commentary instead of the original dialogue.

If ClearPlay had a program letting you skip all the Jar Jar Binks scenes in "Star Wars," wouldn't you jump at the chance to try it?

For years, MPAA czar Jack Valenti and his counterparts in the record business have provided ratings information and warning stickers, but insisted that it's ultimately parents' responsibility to monitor what their kids are watching. But now that someone has come up with a way to make that unenviable task a little easier, filmmakers are crying foul.

They argue that if parents are given any control over the process, their artistry will be threatened by chaos and fascism.

My advice to the DGA: Watch your step. Whoever thought I'd be paraphrasing Charlton Heston? But if you tell parents they're lawbreakers when they try to do right by their kids, you're going to find a lot of people daring you to rip those family-friendly filters out of their cold, dead hands.

Topics for Reading and Writing

1. Read Dunham's and Goldstein's articles while thinking about the issues of ownership brought up in Chapter 5. How do these viewpoints contribute to the debate about what, exactly, an end user owns when he or she buys a DVD?

2. What might be the counterarguments to Dunham's and Goldstein's points? Why do the studios and the directors have a claim to what version of their films are sold?

3. Both of these articles are opinion pieces: one was written for the editorial page of a college newspaper, while the other was written as a column for a major national newspaper. What different rhetorical strategies might these writers adopt if they were to address Congress? If they were to speak directly to the DGA or the studios?

*A profile of a baseball player in the dead of winter, when only die-hard fans are paying any attention to the sport, is generally unlikely to generate much heated discussion. However, **Jeff Pearlman's** article on fastball pitcher John Rocker (appearing in the December 27, 1999 issue of* Sports Illustrated*) sparked a storm of controversy. In the article, Atlanta Braves reliever Rocker sounded off on his many opinions about "other" types of people: Asian women, Atlanta drivers, immigrants, and especially New Yorkers. Embarrassed by their employee's ideas and comments, both Major League Baseball and the Atlanta Braves took strong sanctions against Rocker. In the years following this profile, Rocker's pitching career has taken a nosedive; he has bounced around with four teams in the last three years and only pitched in two games in 2003.*

Jeff Pearlman
At Full Blast

You are a disgrace to the game of baseball. Maybe you should think before you shoot off your big fat mouth. You are an immature punk who is lucky to be in the majors. Get some class!

—A posting by "Metsfan4Life" on
www.rockersucks.com

A minivan is rolling slowly down Atlanta's Route 400, and John Rocker, driving directly behind it in his blue Chevy Tahoe, is pissed. "Stupid bitch! Learn to f---ing drive!" he yells. Rocker honks his horn. Once. Twice. He swerves a lane to the left. There is a toll booth with a tariff of 50 cents. Rocker tosses in two quarters. The gate doesn't rise. He tosses in another quarter. The gate still doesn't rise. From behind, a horn blasts. "F--- you!" Rocker yells, flashing his left middle finger out the window. Finally, after Rocker has thrown in two dimes and a nickel, the gate rises. Rocker brings up a thick wad of phlegm. *Puuuh!* He spits at the machine. "Hate this damn toll."

With one hand on the wheel, the other gripping a cell phone, Rocker tears down the highway, weaving through traffic. In 10 minutes he is due to speak at Lockhart Academy, a school for learning-disabled children. Does Rocker enjoy speaking to children? "No," he says, "not really." But of all things big and small he hates—New York Mets fans, sore arms, jock itch—the thing he hates most is *traffic.* "I have no patience," he says. The speedometer reads 72. Rocker, in blue-tinted sunglasses and a backward baseball cap, is seething. "So many dumb asses don't know how to drive in this town," he says, Billy Joel's "New York State of Mind" humming softly from the radio. "They turn from the wrong lane. They go 20 miles per hour. It makes me want— Look! Look at this idiot! I guarantee you she's a Japanese woman." A beige Toyota is jerking from lane to lane. The woman at the wheel is white. "How bad are Asian women at driving?"

Two months have passed since the madness of John Rocker was introduced to the world. In the ninth inning of Game 3 of the National League Championship Series, Atlanta Braves manager Bobby Cox called for his closer—Rocker, a hard-throwing 6'4", 225-pound lefthander who would turn 25 two days later and who had 38 regular-season saves, a 95-mph fastball and an unhittable slider—to seal a 1–0 win over the Mets. The Shea Stadium bullpen gate opened. A smattering of boos. Louder. Louder. Then, on the fourth or fifth stride of Rocker's dash toward the mound, it started: "A--hole! A--hole! A--hole!" Fifty-five thousand nine hundred eleven fans—black, white, brown, whatever—united by a common bond: hatred of John Rocker.

"You are a low-class, ignorant piece of scum who doesn't care about anything or any-body. You are the Neanderthal. Maybe this upcoming season Mike Piazza or any other Mets player will hit you in the head with a line drive."

—A posting by "Ed" on
www.rockersucks.com

John Rocker has opinions, and there's no way to sugarcoat them. They are polit-ically incorrect, to say the least, and he likes to express them.

■ On ever playing for a New York team: "I would retire first. It's the most hectic, nerve-racking city. Imagine having to take the [Number] 7 train to the ballpark, looking like you're [riding through] Beirut next to some kid with purple hair next to some queer with AIDS right next to some dude who just got out of jail for the fourth time right next to some 20-year-old mom with four kids. It's depressing."

■ On New York City itself: "The biggest thing I don't like about New York are the foreigners. I'm not a very big fan of foreigners. You can walk an entire block in Times Square and not hear anybody speak-ing English. Asians and Koreans and Vietnamese and Indians and Rus-sians and Spanish people and everything up there. How the hell did they get in this country?"

But Rocker reserves a special place in his heart for Mets fans, whom he began bad-mouthing during the regular season when the Braves were battling the Mets for the National League East title eventually won by Atlanta. Although the Braves beat the Mets in a grueling six-game Championship Series (and thus reached the World Series, in which they were swept by the other New York team, the Yankees), Rocker has not allowed himself to let go of the bitter-ness. You try to find different topics—hunting, women, family—but it always comes back to three cold nights at Shea, when bottles whizzed past his head, beer was dumped on his girlfriend and 2,007 sexual positions involving him and a sheep were suggested.

Like many Americans nowadays, Rocker is not one to look on the bright side. He likes to bitch and moan and shred things, and his voice—deep, intimidating—is naturally suited for the task. So are the thick eyebrows, the killing-spree scowl. Want to know how Atlanta will play in 2000? Ask later. Want to know why he has Manson-like feelings toward the Mets and every-thing remotely blue and orange? *Heeeeere's Johnny.* . . .

■ On Mets manager Bobby Valentine: "The guy is not professional. Could you see [Yankees manager] Joe Torre or Bobby Cox getting thrown out of a game and then putting on a Groucho Marx disguise and sneaking back into the dugout? If a player got kicked out of a game and did that, Joe Torre would probably suspend him for a week. Bobby Cox would probably demand that the player be traded and tell him not to come back to the team. The Mets' *manager* did it! That, and his col-lege rah-rah s---? I don't like it."

■ On Mets fans: "Nowhere else in the country do people spit at you, throw bottles at you, throw quarters at you, throw batteries at you and say, 'Hey, I did your mother last night—she's a whore.' I talked about what degenerates they were, and they proved me right. Just by saying something, I could make them mad enough to go home and slap their moms."

Much of Rocker's rancor traces to Game 4 of the NLCS, when the fans were especially harsh, the night especially frigid and the Braves one win from reaching the World Series. Rocker entered in the eighth inning to protect a 2–1 lead, with two outs and runners on first and second. After a double steal, John Olerud, the Mets' dangerous-but-struggling first baseman who was 0 for 7 lifetime against Rocker, rapped a bouncer up the middle, slightly to the left of second base. Atlanta reserve shortstop Ozzie Guillen, who had just replaced starter Walt Weiss as part of the double switch that brought Rocker into the game, lunged awkwardly for the ball. It hit his glove, then dribbled into the outfield. Two runs scored, and the Mets won. Afterward an angry Rocker called Olerud's single "one of the more cheaper hits I've given up my entire life." In retrospect he doesn't even allow that much credit. "If Walt is playing shortstop instead of Ozzie, that's not a hit, and we win," says Rocker. "But we had a 38-year-old guy [actually 35] playing shortstop, and he can't make that kind of play."

That's not all. At Shea, Rocker was a one-man psycho circus. He spit at Mets fans. He gave them the finger. During batting practice he would shag a ball in the outfield, fake a toss to a throng of waving spectators, then throw it back to the pitcher, smiling wickedly. Once he took a ball and chucked it as hard as he could at a net that separated fans from the field. "If there wasn't a net there, it would have smoked 'em right in the face," he says. "But they're so stupid, they jumped back like the ball would hit 'em."

Cox, who was routinely asked about Rocker's behavior, told the media before Game 3 against the Mets that he had spoken with the pitcher, requesting that he tone down the act. "That never happened," Rocker says now. "Bobby never talked to me about it, and I never talked to him. Why would he? We were winning."

"You are the most hideous man I have ever laid eyes on. Hope your baseball career is short . . . just like your intelligence."

—A posting by "Michelle" on
www.rockersucks.com

Rocker bemoans the fact that he is not more intelligent, and though his father says John graduated with a 3.5 GPA from Presbyterian Day High in Macon, Ga., in 1993, sometimes it's hard to argue. In passing, he calls an overweight black teammate "a fat monkey." Asked if he feels any bond with New York Knicks guard Latrell Sprewell, notorious for choking coach P.J. Carlesimo two years ago, Rocker lets out a snarl of disgust. "That guy should've been arrested, and instead he's playing basketball," he says. "Why do you think that is? Do you think if he was Keith Van Horn—if he was white—they'd let him back? No way." Rocker is rarely tongue-tied when it comes to bashing those of a race or sexual orientation different from his. "I'm not a racist or prejudiced person," he says with apparent conviction. "But certain people bother me."

Rocker was into sports from the get-go; if it wasn't baseball, football or basketball, it was hunting and fishing. (He has gone hunting more than 40 times during this off-season.) His passion, though, was baseball. By his senior year at Presbyterian in 1993, Rocker—who threw three high school no-hitters and a pair of 16-strikeout games—was reaching 91 mph on the radar gun, drawing as many as 15 scouts per game.

Rocker was the Braves' 18th-round selection in the June '93 amateur draft, lasting that long because many clubs thought he'd enroll at Georgia. A starter who threw hard but was wild, Rocker was also nervous and sometimes eccentric. At Class A Danville in '94 he earned a mutant Fidrychian reputation for biting baseballs and letting throws from the catcher nail him in the chest. "He can get crazy," says Atlanta reliever Kerry Ligtenberg, who missed last season with a torn right elbow ligament. "I've played with John since '96. He's got a real short fuse. When it goes off, it's probably better not to be around."

When he signed with the Braves, Rocker and his parents, Jake, an executive at Georgia Farm Bureau Insurance, and Judy, who runs an ad agency out of her home, agreed on a five-year plan. If things weren't looking good, he would use the education clause in his contract and finish college. (Rocker has completed two semesters at Mercer.) By the end of the '97 season things weren't looking good—5–6, 4.86 ERA at Double A Greenville—and the Braves mentioned turning him into a reliever. "It didn't sound too great to me," Rocker recalls. "I was a starter my whole life." The Braves sent Rocker to the Arizona Fall League to pitch exclusively from the pen. There, "I learned that everything's about attitude," says Rocker. "I used to worry over every pitch, every batter. The coaches in Arizona talked to me about just going out and throwing. Don't worry, throw."

The following season Rocker stuck with the big club and appeared in 47 games, mostly as a long reliever. During spring training last year, after Ligtenberg got hurt, Cox named Rocker the closer, and he amassed those 38 saves (in 45 opportunities) with a 2.49 ERA and 104 strikeouts in 72 1/3 innings. Still it is his mouth, not his arm, that has won him Rodmanesque notoriety. "Some of the more stoic guys on the team probably get annoyed by me," he says. "But the younger, fiery guys—we get annoyed at their stoicism. There needs to be more atmosphere in our clubhouse. I don't mean loud music and hooting and hollering. But I don't think having the atmosphere of a doctor's office helps."

In the locker room at Shea following Game 4 of the National League Championship Series, as Rocker ranted and raved, fumed and fussed, Mike Remlinger, a 33-year-old lefthanded reliever with six years of major league experience, was asked whether Rocker had gone too far. Remlinger—quiet, thoughtful—paused. "The thing is," he said, "baseball is a game of humility. You can be on top one minute, as low as possible the next. When you're young, you don't realize it. But sooner or later you learn—we all do. Be humble."

"My mouth is watering for that day when Rocker steps foot in Shea once again. (This time I'm bringing D batteries.)"

—A posting by "Metswin" on
www.rockersucks.com

Topics for Reading and Writing

1. Is this a fair portrait of Rocker? Did Pearlman "poison the well" here— that is, did he intentionally construct a negative portrait of Rocker rather than attempt to depict him fairly?

2. What responsibility does Rocker bear for his portrayal in this article? Is it possible for the subject of a profile to manage how that profile might appear? Think of this in the light of some of the articles in Chapter 3 about publicists and celebrities.

3. Rocker's ugly comments, the writer suggests, are at least partially motivated by the treatment he has received from fans, especially in the New York Mets' Shea Stadium. How would you respond to tens of thousands of fans screaming obscenities at you? Is it Rocker's job to deal with this kind of pressure, or is this excessive?

4. The comments that received the most negative reaction were Rocker's statements about immigrants, "foreigners," and the experience of riding the New York City subway. Do you think that Rocker is just a bigot? Or might there be other reasons for his strongly negative reaction to what many of us consider a very positive facet of America: the "melting pot" quality of our cities?

5. Rocker's opinions may not be the kinds of opinions our society exalts, but does he have the right to express them? Should he have been punished for speaking his mind?

Quickly responding in an unsigned editorial to the firestorm surrounding John Rocker's comments in Sports Illustrated, *baseball commissioner Bud Selig suspended and fined Rocker and "ordered him to undergo sensitivity training." Later the next season, Rocker's team (the Atlanta Braves) released Rocker after many of his teammates responded poorly to the relief pitcher's statements. In this editorial, the* **Chicago Tribune** *argues that the punishment Rocker received was just.*

Chicago Tribune
John Rocker Gets His Due

John Rocker got what he deserved Monday when Baseball Commissioner Bud Selig suspended him, fined him and ordered him to undergo sensitivity training.

Rocker, the fastball phenom closer for the Atlanta Braves and an equal-opportunity bigot, got in trouble over a Sports Illustrated interview published last December. In it he disparaged Asian women, blacks, gays, foreigners in general and teammates individually. Nobody ever said pitching makes you smart.

Selig's ruling, which will cost Rocker $20,000 and keep him out of spring training and the Braves' first 24 games, was right on the money. The sanctions against Rocker are what any employee representing his company could fairly expect after spouting off in so offensive and public a manner.

Make no mistake: This is not a 1st Amendment issue and John Rocker's free-speech rights have not been violated. If he had expressed his views privately in a personal conversation, he would be no less a jerk but he would have a stronger basis for his argument that he should not be punished for his words.

As it is, he spoke publicly in his role as a member of Major League Baseball, and Major League Baseball has both a right and a responsibility to protect itself from such a "spokesman." Selig set the record straight Monday, saying Rocker had set a terrible example and "brought dishonor" to himself, to his team and to the institution of baseball.

This punishment makes a lot more sense than Selig's previous order, immediately after the article appeared, that Rocker undergo psychological evaluation. He may be intolerant, but he's not crazy.

What's more, John Rocker has every right to think what he wants about anybody he wants. Bud Selig can't control what Rocker thinks—but he can sanction him for what he says.

Rocker has indicated that he may appeal the ruling; that would be a big mistake.

The suspension gives him an opportunity to make peace with his teammates, whom he has insulted both personally and professionally. It also offers some buffer time before Rocker, whose popularity rating these days is about on a par with Linda Tripp's, faces the players and fans of a new season.

More to the point, though he has apologized, accepting his punishment with good grace would be a far more effective way to express remorse. And good grace is something this young pitcher desperately needs to practice.

Topics for Reading and Writing

1. Unsigned editorials represent the opinion of a newspaper's editorial board. Why would a large metropolitan newspaper care about a sporting controversy in a city thousands of miles away?

2. How does the editorial writer present his logical case? What might be some of the obvious objections to Rocker's punishment, and how does this editorial defuse those objections? Does it do that effectively, in your opinion?

---

*Looking at the Rocker controversy with a cynical eye, Salon.com writer **Allen Barra** here argues that the Atlanta Braves pitcher's punishment was only incidentally a result of his inflammatory comments. "Rocker got toasted," Berra argues, "for saying the same things about New York in*

Allen Barra
John Rocker, Whipping Boy

June 9, 2000

I must be the only person in America who believes the Atlanta Braves. I think the only reason John Rocker is currently pitching for East Podunk is because he has been

Sports Illustrated *that a lot of baseball executives say about New York in private." The* outrage showed by Major League Baseball Commissioner Bud Selig truly amounted to nothing, for his punishment cannot be upheld—and Rocker would never have been punished by his team if he were still performing at a high level. Barra's argument has a lot to say about how organizations respond to and use the media to construct their own images.

pitching lousy for the Braves. Never, ever forget that professional athletes are property, and as long as a property has value its owner isn't going to discard it.

Ask Latrell Sprewell. Here's a guy who tried to kill his coach—twice!—just a couple of years ago. By the end of the playoffs this season, New York call-in radio fans had gone from asking why the Knicks had ever acquired such a thug to praising him for not letting all the past turmoil interfere with his jump shot. The bottom line, the only line, with the Knicks' front office and the majority of New York area fans and sportswriters was that Sprewell was valuable to his team.

Rocker didn't even choke anybody: He just choked. He couldn't handle all the post-apocalyptic flak. If Rocker had been throwing strikes this season, I guarantee you that by fall we'd be seeing editorials on his "newfound maturity" and "how good a job he did putting it all behind him."

Essentially Rocker got toasted by the media for saying the same things about New York in Sports Illustrated that a lot of baseball executives say to each other about New York in private. Which, I have no doubt, is one reason why baseball executives weren't more vocal about punishing him.

Many were speculating on what a tough spot commissioner Bud Selig was in: how to reconcile his phony job as Major League Baseball's P.R. man with his real job of protecting his employers' property? The truth is that there was never really a conflict in the first place, but Selig handled the situation brilliantly. He immediately took the high moral ground by announcing a substantial suspension and fine—not much of a risk, really, since he knew very well he had no real authority to take any such action. But it got him off the hook with the press and a public that demands a "tough" commissioner.

In point of fact, and despite the image as baseball's "czar" and the rhetoric about "the power to act in the best interests of baseball," the commissioner's power to act in such matters is severely limited by two factors. The first is the basic agreement with the Players Association, which doesn't give the "czar" any power to clamp down hard on a player who happens to state offensive or unpopular views in public, and the second is the personal services contract Selig signed with Major League Baseball, which means that, yes, he can come to almost any decision he wants regarding the property of his employers, the team owners, but that if they don't like it they can buy off his contract, fire him and hire someone to reverse the decisions (as they did with Fay Vincent a few years ago). In other words, the commissioner has no power with the players to make arbitrary punishments, and even if he did, no owner is going to allow him to mess with a valuable piece of property.

Selig made his decision to punish Rocker in full knowledge that no arbitrators would uphold it, but what the heck, he could now say to the cameras, "Hey, I tried." That Major League Baseball had absolutely no business restricting Rocker from pursuing his livelihood because he is a bigoted asshole went curiously unremarked on by the mainstream media. The people who should have come down hard on Rocker—the executives of the Atlanta Braves baseball club—did nothing (except, eventually, to work out a small face-saving deal with the union and Major League Baseball in which all parties agreed to allow the commissioner's power to slap Rocker's wrists).

The Braves, of course, were primarily interested in maintaining the value of their property. Now, with Rocker giving up about a run per inning over his last nine appearances—not exactly what a contending team looks for in a closer— the Braves' front office is ready to cut its losses. Officially, he is simply being demoted to the parent club's minor-league teams. Realistically, Rocker has roughly the same chance of appearing again in a Braves uniform that he does of hosting "Saturday Night Live."

If anyone has come out of the Rocker mess looking good, it's Sports Illustrated's Jeff Pearlman, who wrote the Rocker piece last year. When approached by other media members for a comment after Rocker threatened him last week, Pearlman turned from the cameras and said, "Leave me out, I don't want to be part of the story." If Pearlman's story didn't deserve a prize, his behavior in refusing to exploit it does. Pearlman's behavior has set an admirable pattern for the rest of the media. From here on in, let's all agree that there's nothing positive to be gained from following John Rocker around with a pencil.

Topics for Reading and Writing

1. What role did the media play in the drama of John Rocker—in his construction as a villain, in his own self-immolation, in the righteous responses of baseball executives and team owners? How does Barra interpret the media's role?

2. Do you agree with Barra that if Rocker had been pitching well, his team and baseball's power structure would not have attacked him? What does this have to do with the basketball player Latrell Sprewell?

A growing number of university campuses now boast conservative student newspapers, self-proclaimed "alternatives" to the official college newspapers. In Austin, Texas, home to the University of Texas's well-respected and historically liberal Daily Texan, *the* Austin Review *fills this role. In March 2000,* Austin Review *writer **Randy Samuelson** weighed in with his opinion of the John Rocker controversy.*

Randy Samuelson
MLB and Braves Are
off Their Rockers

As many know, Atlanta Braves pitcher John Rocker made several controversial remarks about New York City in a December Sports Illustrated interview. His comments, dealing with racial issues, consisted of observations about certain subpopulations in New York City. For example, he commented about Times Square's Puerto Ricans and Cubans inability to speak English and the "queers with AIDS" on the Number 7 train to Shea Stadium. His opinions sent shock-waves through Major League Baseball and the Atlanta Braves organization, reviving racial issues that Major League Baseball has long tried to suppress.

Like any other American, John Rocker has the right to speak his mind on any issue he wishes and to hold any opinion he so desires. Housed in the First Amendment, these free speech rights are the same rights liberals love to reference regarding art, journalism, and speech. Perhaps the way he phrased his comments could have been more tactful, but he broke no law by saying them.

But MLB has labeled Rocker a racist, and the Braves have suspended him. Nobody wants to associate with this man because he expressed his opinions about race. Paradoxically, though, when Louis Farrakan denounces white men as devils or when Jim Brown comments about the power aristocracy of the white men in football team ownership, the media praises them for standing up to the white man. This the media does to keep itself from being labeled racist.

There is a definite double standard in the media and society in dealing with the issue of race. It is trendy to blame heterosexual, white males for all society's problems. Blaming the white man for racism makes the accuser look good to his friends, family and co-workers. It supposedly proves that the accuser is not racist by pointing out how much of a racist somebody else is. John Rocker is a scapegoat for baseball and society.

MLB has asked Rocker to get psychiatric help for his problem with racism. Unfortunately, racism in baseball has a history that far precedes Rocker or even the last generation of baseball greats. Some of the best players to ever the game never were allowed to play in the Majors because they were black or Hispanic. They were relegated to the Negro Leagues until Jackie Robinson tore down the color barrier.

As recently as April 6, 1987, Al Campanis, then an executive with the Los Angeles Dodgers, said blacks did not have the necessities to be in MLB managerial positions. His statement set baseball afire, and many blacks were subsequently elevated into executive and managerial positions by order of Commissioner Giamatti so that baseball could claim to be diverse. The Dodgers terminated Campanis on April 7, 1987, for his comments. Campanis was a lifetime Dodger, having played in the 1950s and 60s with the likes of Jackie Robinson and Sandy Koufax. The Dodgers said there is no place in baseball for racism, yet it continues today because owners have done nothing to change their practices.

Most of the black executives in baseball are still "token blacks," and it's been thirteen years since Campanis' comments. There are many more black executives in baseball today, but most of them are there to make the team and the sport look good and have no legitimate power with the organization. Typically, offices such as "Assistant Executive Vice President for Player Relations" are created to give a Hall-of-Fame black player an executive position. Frank Robinson, former manager of the Baltimore Orioles, had three straight bad years managing the team. Instead of firing him, the Orioles "promoted" him to an "executive position" to keep him in the organization.

Baseball and sports in general does everything it can to look politically correct. That is not to say that blacks are unqualified for substantive positions, but that baseball is trying to put on a politically correct facade for the media concerning race relations. Rather than rapidly trying to desegregate its upper echelons, baseball should allow all managerial candidates, including minorities and other high-profile candidates, to hone their skills in the minor leagues before being thrown into the big time, just like players must do.

John Rocker will be analyzed by probably 15 different psychiatrists, who will all come to the same conclusion: "He's a jerk." Rocker has done nothing illegal; the real crime has been committed by MLB and the Braves, who have blown the ordeal out of proportion. But if Atlanta cuts Rocker for politically correct reasons, 27 other teams will line up to sign him, including the Mets and Yankees. Rocker is 25, left-handed, and throws 100 mph. His talent precludes Baseball's ostracizing him completely.

The Atlanta Braves and Major League Baseball, not John Rocker, are off their rockers for race relations in this sport. John Rocker has simply expressed his opinions by stereotyping a city and its inhabitants. If stereotyping is a crime, then we are all guilty because we all do it, even Ted Turner and other bleeding-heart liberals.

Perhaps, once and for all, this incident will lead sensible Americans to look elsewhere than professional sports for guidance on political and social issues. After all, John Rocker is not the only professional athlete who is better inside the lines than outside.

Topics for Reading and Writing

1. How does Samuelson's take on the Rocker controversy differ from the position that Allen Barra takes in Salon.com? How does each construct and appeal to his specific audience?

2. Samuelson sees hypocrisy in the way that "the media and society" attacked Rocker for his comments while ignoring or downplaying similarly inflammatory, bigoted comments by African American figures such as Jim Brown or Louis Farrakhan. What evidence does he have for this double standard? Does he need evidence—is this a clearly-established fact?

3. Our society places a great deal of importance on sports, obviously; what is often surprising to people from other cultures, though, is how we often displace our anxieties and conflicts about race and ethnicity onto sports. How does Samuelson feel about this? Should our racial conflicts be played out on a playing field? Does this make these debates safer for us and less dangerous to our society's stability?

Censorship has always existed on high school campuses. One of the most important Supreme Court decisions on First Amendment issues, Tinker v. Des Moines Independent Community School District *(1965), established that students did not shed their*

Jill Rosen
High School Confidential

Katy Dean, science buff and student journalist, knew this could be good. Though fellow reporters at Utica High School had passed on it, a story about a lawsuit against the district lit Dean's fuse. People who live near the district bus garage alleged that diesel fumes from revving buses were making them sick. One man said unrelenting exhaust gave him throat and lung cancer.

"I'm definitely doing this," the 16-year-old junior said to herself—with the emphasis on definitely. "I don't think anyone else realized how much this could affect our community." So Dean and Dan Butts got on the case, spending weeks phoning officials in the suburban Detroit district, digging for chemical information through the Environmental Protection Agency and eventually knocking on the door of the family that was suing. As the students were leaving after an interview that lasted a few hours, the wife of the sick man asked, "Are they really going to let you run this?" Dean didn't even think about it. No one had ever censored the *Arrow*. "Oh," she said with the breezy sureness only a 16-year-old who has never been let down could have, "they have to let us."

A couple of weeks later in March, after her principal demanded the story be pulled from the front page, Dean merely said, with the disgust only a 16-year-old who has been let down can muster, "Uh, I guess I was wrong on that one."

More than 30 years of shepherding student publications and teaching high-school kids English and journalism have left Gloria Olman, adviser to the *Arrow*, with a crisp yet patient voice and an easy, knowing laugh. With the exception of a few timeouts to have children, Olman has been up to her ears in high-school newsprint since the early 1960s. The staffs under her watch have brought Utica High hundreds of awards, while Olman's own shelf is heavy with honors, including 1992's Dow Jones Newspaper Fund National High School Journalism Teacher of the Year and a place in the Michigan Journalism Hall of Fame. Her write-up by the Hall of Fame says, "Gloria Olman is scholastic journalism."

When Olman joined the *Arrow* in 1977, she had her work cut out for her. "It was not a solid journalism program," she says. "They were reporting, you know, fluff, restaurant reviews, light things. It wasn't serious journalism." And serious was all she would settle for. "As a journalist, I wanted to train my students for their roles as reporters and as consumers of media in society," she says. "We would cover issues, all sides of the story, and they would dig."

Through the years they certainly dug, into issues as thorny as teens getting pregnant and having abortions, kids taking drugs. These stories would now and again make administrators wince, Olman says, but until this March, they never—not once—said a topic was too hot to touch. No one ever told her not to put a story in the paper.

"I was shocked, OK? I was stunned," Olman says, recalling how the principal called her to the office to say, "I'm directing you not to print this." And she said, "You are censoring us." He repeated, "I am directing you not to print it."

The kids, angry and upset, thought she was kidding. "I am not," she said. "I am his employee and I follow orders." "But Mrs. O," they said, "We should print it anyway. You always taught us to stand up."

Though this was happening within hours of press time, the *Arrow* staff pulled the story from the front page. Then, where an editorial saying the district should move the bus garage would have appeared, the students quickly wrote a piece on censorship. In place of an accompanying cartoon went a black box stamped in white lettering: "Censored."

Yanked newspaper stories, disappointed student journalists and resolute administrators are an unfortunately common part of the high-school experience. Censorship occurs so consistently, so ubiquitously that it's almost clichéd, no more eyebrow-raising than the cafeteria serving mystery meat or a nerd getting books smacked out of his arms in the hallway. And those are only the cases where conflict has erupted. How many student papers don't even try to print controversial topics because they know they can't, where it's all pep rallies and teacher profiles all the time?

Though censoring of student content probably started about the time when cavekids first scribbled something on the wall that ticked off tribal elders, what's new is the frequency with which it's occurring and, more interestingly, how often students are contesting it. In 2000, the Student Press Law Center logged 518 calls for help with censorship from high schools. The advocacy group reports that's up 41 percent from the year before—a year that also broke a record. The number of calls has increased every year for six years, and when the center counts again this year, it expects the trend to continue.

Schools can be tense in these post-Columbine years, as those in the education world call the times since the spring of 1999, when two troubled students stormed Colorado's Columbine High School, killing a teacher and 12 students before turning the guns on themselves. There's the basic fear of anything like that happening again, compounded by increasingly tight education budgets and increasingly rigorous standards to test both students and teachers. The more pressure administrators feel, the less edgy journalism they're willing to tolerate, speculates Mark Goodman, executive director of the Student Press Law Center.

"They feel less able to allow controversy and criticism," he says in his Arlington, Virginia, office, messy with paper evidence of student battles past and ongoing. "And they're less likely to tolerate dissent and debate. . . . They really have to run their operations like generals."

Administrators with a militaristic bent have no better weapon in their arsenal than the Supreme Court's 1988 decision in Hazelwood School District vs. Kuhlmeier. Up until then, papers operated under the premise that a student's right to free speech should only be limited in cases where it could disrupt school or invade the rights of others. The Supreme Court reached that conclusion in 1969's *Tinker* vs. *Des Moines Independent Community School District,* a case of students suspended for wearing black armbands to school to protest the Vietnam War. Hazelwood, however, set more limits on expression, particularly at papers deemed not "forums for public expression," meaning that students don't typically make content decisions. The court found administrators could censor a St. Louis student paper that wanted to run articles about teen pregnancy and the effects of divorce. The court's definition of when such intervention is allowed is so hazy that school officials can easily make cases to squash challenging stories or any copy that otherwise rocks the boat.

Consider:

- In March, the principal at Illinois' Huntley High School confiscated an issue of the *Tribe* that included stories about students who've suffered depression, attempted suicide and dropped out of school. The *Tribe* got the idea for the piece after more than 400 worried parents attended a January meeting about those problems. The principal told the Chicago *Tribune* it wasn't the content that bothered him, but rather the paper's inclusion of anonymous sources and former students.
- In February the principal at Cheyenne, Wyoming's East High School wouldn't allow the *Thunderbolt* staff to run a story about debate team members being arrested for vandalizing police cars. The principal said the students didn't need further embarrassment.
- Tampa's Plant High School paper, *Pep O' Plant*, planned a column in March endorsing condom availability at the prom. Because the school's curriculum promotes abstinence, officials stopped distribution of the paper, considered reprinting several pages, but in the end let the column, headlined "Face It; Sex Happens," run.
- When reporters at Saluda, Virginia's Middlesex High School put together a safe-sex spread for the Valentine's Day issue, the principal refused to let it run in the *Big Blue Review,* which is circulated as an inset in the local paper. When the *Review* tried a spread on censorship the following month, the principal at first nixed that too, although it eventually ran.

Rebecca Gates, Middlesex High's principal and a 26-year educator, says she simply cannot allow just anything to go into a school paper that's circulated to the community where much younger kids could see it. As she puts it, her superintendent has a daughter in middle school and he certainly wasn't comfortable with her seeing a piece on contraceptives. District policy grants her this authority, decreeing Gates the "final editor."

"We work very, very hard to build a positive image of this high school in this community," Gates says, recalling a recent issue of the paper that included a story about drug use at the school. "Now the community feels the school's just full of drugs. There are a lot a retired folks around here who look forward to the paper coming out so they can get the dirt on the high school. Those are their words—the dirt."

Flag-waver for student press rights Tom Eveslage teaches journalism ethics and law at Temple University. But back in the day he did time teaching English and advising a high-school paper in Minnesota. His flag was out in earnest earlier this year when education officials in Pennsylvania, a rare state where the burden is on administrators in questions of student speech, wanted to "streamline" the state code, essentially removing much of the protection student journalists work under.

Though the code changes were back-burnered, Eveslage worries about the message this sort of thing sends young journalists, the kids who he thinks are, more often than not, the best and the brightest. "A lot of people think what they're doing is just Mickey Mouse stuff, they're just playing around," Eveslage says. "But more and more dedicated advisers with sharp kids are really doing impressive things. These are the ones I don't think we want to step on."

Goodman from the Press Law Center says, "You don't want to teach them in their formative years, 'Oh, always be worried about what the powers that be will do if you print that.'"

This spring in Little Rock's bedroom community of Bryant, Margaret Sorrows, adviser to Bryant High School's Prospective, began walking a fragile line between pleasing her boss and standing up for what she believed were her students' First Amendment rights.

Last fall a reporter she considers one of her best—and her paper has snagged the state press association's top award for five years straight—pitched an idea for a three-part series on discrimination. Installment by installment, she'd tackle race issues, then religious topics, and then wrap up with sexual orientation. When the first package was ready to run in November, Sorrows let the principal see it to make sure he was OK with the sensitive material, which included racial slurs. She wasn't asking his permission but rather giving him a heads-up, a courtesy call. Principal Danny Spadoni was fine with it, as he was with the next piece on religion.

Not so part three. As the reporter was gathering sources, students, faculty and parents besieged the principal's office with complaints that the paper was singling kids out, targeting them as gay. To get sources, the reporter typed out questions, sealed them in envelopes with students' names on them, and asked teachers to pass them out before class. This is how the Prospective does most of its reporting because reporters aren't allowed to interview on class time—only before school, at lunch, or after school. Usually this is not a problem. This time, kids who got envelops worried other students would assume they were homosexuals.

Spadoni collected the surveys and put the kibosh on the final article. Not long after, he presented Sorrows with new rules for the newspaper, rules that if she didn't abide by, she could lose her job. Highlights of The New Deal: Spadoni would see all story ideas and questions reporters planned to ask and he would preview the paper 48 hours before it went to press. No matter that this conflicted with the school's policy that the principal is not part of editorial decisions unless the editor and the adviser disagree and request a judgment call. The rules were scrapped after two issues.

Spadoni, who's been a principal for 24 years, says he had no choice but to step in. One student who got a survey came to him in tears, he says, while another was thrown out of the house after her parents saw the survey and assumed she was gay. The same policy that keeps him away from editorial decisions, he says, also states that the paper is not to disrupt the educational environment or invade people's privacy. "I'm here to keep everyone safe and protected from being harassed," he says. "Imagine sitting in an English class and all of a sudden, bang, everybody thinks you're a homosexual. No one has right to subject you to that."

Spadoni says the current staff of the Prospective sacrifices propriety in the name of winning awards. The same student who was doing the discrimination series won an award this year for a story headlined, "My Cup Runneth Over."

"Can you guess what that was about?" he dryly asks. "Going shopping for a double-D bra. We're in the Bible belt here. Talk about getting phone calls."

So, Spadoni is tightening the reins. "I know what censorship is. I'm not going to try to censor," he says. "I'm just going to make sure we do what's appropriate."

Despite Spadoni's concerns, Sorrows is sticking with the district rules already on record: No prior review. "I'm willing to support my students. These aren't my First Amendment rights," she says, "these are the students'."

Embattled high-school journalists around the country would envy the paper/school relationship at Lakewood High School in Lakewood, Ohio. At the award-slathered *Times*, it's a veritable lovefest between the kids, longtime adviser John Bowen and principal Vincent Barra. That's not to say that the paper doesn't question Barra and the administration. As Bowen puts it, "They will report whatever they think is of interest to students."

For instance, the Times recently did a story on the possibility of teaching creationism. Another questioned the school's policy of using Social Security numbers as Internet log-ons when hacking is so common. Still another reported on the football coach's son, a member of the team, who was caught with beer but still allowed to play. The paper, which comes out once a month, used the incident to get into a bigger piece about athletic code enforcement. The story won an award—not a student award, but the Ohio Society of Professional Journalists' second place honor for sports coverage. It beat out professional papers. "That," Bowen says, "is what kids can do when given the chance to be journalists."

Barra says the student body trusts and enjoys the paper because it covers issues that matter to them. "I don't want [the paper] to be seen only as a PR vehicle for the school where nothing but achievements are covered. This gives them a reason to think and look at things critically . . . . You can't teach kids about the First Amendment, then deny them their First Amendment rights— that's inconsistent, and they can see through that."

But a hard-driving high-school press isn't usually the stuff authority figures smile upon. Goodman of the Student Press Law Center says it's often the best student journalism that gets censored. If it pushes buttons, if it challenges authority, if it highlights the unsavory truths about life at school, it's often a matter of time before someone wants to put a lid on it. Administrators act more like corporate CEOs than lead educators, Goodman says. "First and foremost is image, everything else be damned. [Papers] can cause lots of headaches for a lot of people, but that's why they're there, to encourage debate, discussing and thinking."

Willing Wakefield, principal of Indianapolis' Plainfield High School, was likely reaching for the Excedrin after a lambasting by *Indianapolis Star* editorial writers in March. When kids on a senior prank decided to jump into the school pool in the middle of the day with their clothes on, Jason Pearce, editor of the school's *Quaker Shaker*, jumped himself—at the chance to photograph it as a news event. Wakefiled suspended everyone found at the pool, Pearce included, though he was only shooting the action from the sidelines. "We strenuously object to the sanctions imposed on [Pearce] whose on-the-scene photographs would have earned him praise had he been working at this or any other newspaper," the *Star* editorial read.

Wakefield, who says he would never censor the paper, calls this nothing more than a case of kids being in an unauthorized place—the pranksters, the journalist, all of them. "It was dark, the room wasn't being used, you couldn't see who was in the pool; they could have jumped on each other," he says. Plus, he says the presence of someone with a camera just made the pranksters act that much sillier. "Just because they're in a journalism class, they think they're the *Washington Post*—I don't agree with this."

The soft-spoken, 17-year-old Pearce, much to the dismay of his *Quaker Shaker* adviser, didn't fight Wakefield's ruling after school officials knocked his punishment down from five days to three and a paper on censorship. Had he not accepted the suspension deal, he would have missed a choir competition that weekend. Pearce balanced the choir gig on one hand and a journalism rights showdown on the other, and the singing won. He liked the attention, though, while it lasted. "We were all talking about it," he says, "Was it right? Was it wrong? Was it infringing on my student press rights, or uh, whatever?"

Pearce didn't fight his administration's judgment. Maybe with enough spit and fire, the endorsement of local media and a dollop of community outrage, he could have had his punishment stricken. Or maybe not. Either way, his was not exactly the censorship case to mold a journalism martyr.

The Student Press Law Center is the only organization in the country—and director Goodman believes, the world—that exists solely to defend the First Amendment rights of student journalists. When student journalism is under the gun, the center doesn't quibble about quality. Be it Pearce's picture or the high-school equivalent of Watergate, if a school is quashing expression, the center opens its arms to the silenced. "Students can say what they want," Goodman says, "even if they say a stupid and an offensive thing."

Besides educating people about their rights and being an outspoken advocate for them, the center also hooks students up with attorneys prepared to take on their cases pro bono. About 150 lawyers are in the network nationwide.

Katy Dean, back in Utica, Michigan, plans to fight. She and the *Arrow* have enlisted the center, and not only do attorneys think there's a case, they think it's the one-in-a-million that could set precedent.

"This is the best case I have seen post-Hazelwood," says Goodman. Not only has the Arrow been, unquestionably, a public forum for 25 years, he says, but the story about the bus garage lawsuit was evenhanded and well-reported. "It's as strong as any case we'll ever find."

Utica High's principal, Richard Machesky, declined to comment for this story, though he wrote in a letter to the *Arrow* staff, "In a professional setting, the editor . . . is obligated to make sure that stories that appear in the paper are both complete and accurate. In the case of a student newspaper, that responsibility falls to the journalism adviser. Again, at a professional newspaper, if the editor has failed to catch errors and omissions, the task becomes the publisher's responsibility. In the case of the *Arrow*, the school principal acts as the newspaper's publisher and the appropriate action was taken."

Machesky went on to fault the story's use of pseudonyms for "no appropriate reasons," hearsay, unidentified sources and "scant scientific evidence." All arguably legitimate points. But Gloria Olman, the adviser, says, "I felt it was well-written and accurate to the best of our ability."

Olman, who says "the kids are now carrying this battle on their own," is supportive, even while she steps aside. For more than 30 years she's taught kids what the First Amendment entitled them to. Now is hardly the time to change her message. "If not," she says, "how do I look my former students in the eyes? How do I look myself in the mirror?"

Dean heard all of Olman's lessons and bought in. If a reporter had all the facts, she thought that was enough. And she saw "complete freedom of the press" as something nonnegotiable, set in stone. Now, "I realize it's all politics," she says. And she's thinking about her future. Earlier this year, her list of career maybes might have included being a journalist. Now, she's got other ideas. "This whole thing," she says, "has made me want to be a First Amendment attorney."

Topics for Reading and Writing

1. Is this a persuasive piece? Does Rosen attempt to convince us to believe something about these cases of censorship? Or is this just a descriptive feature? Describe the rhetorical strategies of the article.

2. Did you experience censorship from your school authorities? Did this censorship fall on the newspaper? On the drama department? Where? What was the issue? What kind of expression and what type of content was being censored? What was the administration's fear? What was the outcome?

Few uses of the Internet have produced more frustration and fury than "spam," those endless sales pitches for mortgage refinancing, "natural Viagra," or other products and services. In recent months the spam "epidemic" has gained the attention of Congress, which had almost a dozen different proposals for dealing with spam on the table in its 2003 session. In this article from the New York Times Magazine, *the well-known science and technology writer* **James Gleick** *(author of* Chaos: Making a New Science *(1987) and* Genius: The Life and Science of Richard Feynman *(1992)) attempts to devise a simple, common-sense answer to the plague of spam.*

James Gleick
Tangled up in Spam

I know what your in-box looks like, and it isn't pretty. It looks like mine: a babble of come-ons and lies from hucksters and con artists. To find your real e-mail, you must wade through the torrent of fraud and obscenity known politely as "unsolicited bulk e-mail" and colloquially as spam. In a perverse tribute to the power of the online revolution, we are all suddenly getting the same mail.

The spam epidemic has just a few themes and variations: phone cards, cable descramblers, vacation prizes. Easy credit, easy weight loss, free vacations, free Girlz. Inkjet cartridges and black-market Viagra, get-rich-quick schemes and every possible form of pornography. The crush of these messages on the world's networks is now numbered in billions per day. One anti-spam service measured more than five million unique spam attacks in December, almost three times as many as a year earlier. The well is poisoned.

Spam is not just a nuisance. It absorbs bandwidth and overwhelms Internet service providers. Corporate tech staffs labor to deploy filtering technology to protect their networks. The cost is now widely estimated (though all such estimates are largely guesswork) at billions of dollars a year. The social costs are immeasurable: people fear participating in the collective life of the Internet, they withdraw or they learn to conceal their e-mail addresses, identifying themselves as user@domain.invalid or someone@nospam.com. The signal-to-noise ratio nears zero, and trust is destroyed.

If your own experience doesn't seem this bad, just wait. You may be a recent convert to e-mail; your address may not yet have percolated through the deep swamp of spammer databases (truly a land of no return). Quantity matters, psychologically. If five daily spams seem merely annoying, 20 or 30 will be maddening, creepy—and chilling. Some avid Internet users report a hundred or more a day.

The harvesting of e-mail addresses by spammers is relendess and swift. Investigators for the Federal Trade Commission recently posted some freshly minted e-mail addresses in chat rooms and news groups to see what would happen; in one case, the first spam came in nine minutes. Addresses are sold and resold on CD-ROM's in batches of millions. If you have ever revealed your e-mail address in a public forum, or allowed it to appear on a Web page, or used it in buying merchandise online, your experience of the online world is sure to sound like this: "Looking for love?" "$900 weekly at home." "Fwd: Your winning lottery ticket." "Biggee your penis 3 inches in 22 days." "Have you received your cash?" "Hard core so intense it's sinful." "Advanced degree = advanced career." "Natural enlargement where you need it." "Live chat room with real women!!"

Parents panic when they discover that their teenagers have mail from "Mellisa" at Sex Affair.org: "Hi there! I got your e-mail from Jennifer and I just wanted to tell you strait up, I really like—! She told me u're into—too. Lets hookup for a juicy weekend." Does this mean the kids are checking out porn sites? (No, it does not.)

How this bane came to sully the greatest revolution in personal communication since the telephone makes for a complex and troubling story, with no promise of a happy ending. From the beginning, the Internet has tried to fight spam with grass-roots vigilantism. Software companies now routinely build spam-filtering technology into their e-mail programs, and independent programmers are struggling to devise more creative methods for separating wheat from chaff. Millions of individual e-mail users are trying to devise coping strategies of their own. Consumer advocates are working mostly in vain to persuade lawmakers to take action in what should, after all, be a popular cause.

Each in its own way, for different reasons, these efforts are failing.

Long, long ago, in a previous century, when the Internet was young, people discovered both the power and danger of mass e-mail. One online pioneer, Brad Templeton, says he believes he has pinpointed the first e-mail spam: in 1978, a Digital Equipment Corporation salesperson typed several hundred addresses by hand—those of scientists and researchers on the Arpanet, the predecessor of the Internet—and sent them an announcement of a product presentation. A small furor erupted. "Where is the line to be drawn between this sort of thing (if it is to be allowed at all) and advertising?" a recipient at Stanford University asked plaintively. The Net was a scientific and military enterprise—most emphatically noncommercial.

The modern epidemic began 15 years later, coinciding with the explosive popularization of e-mail in 1993 and 1994. A chain letter began to spread, titled "MAKE MONEY FAST." And a pair of Arizona immigration lawyers, Laurence Canter and Martha Siegel, bombarded the Internet with a notorious advertisement about the "Green Card Lottery." Angry recipients counterattacked, overwhelming the lawyers' service provider with complaints. But these proto-spammers were unrepentant. Eventually they tried marketing a book, "How to Make a Fortune on the Information Superhighway: Everyone's Guerrilla Guide to Marketing on the Internet and Other On-Line Services."

Frauds and cons from the horse-and buggy world quickly adapted to the new technologies. One of the most shameless is the so-called Nigerian spam. The subject is "Urgent/Confidential" or "Assistance Required." The sender confides that he is a bank manager or political exile or son of the late commander in chief of the armed forces in Lagos. He explains that he needs your help in transferring $21.5 million in cash out of the country. "I will like you as an foreigner to stand in as the next of kin. If only you will send your bank-account information, you have a 40 percent cut." It's always the same letter, more or less. "Should you can not be in a position to assist, this deal has to remain a secret till the end of time." Sure. Some secret.

Few Internet users realize that this particular con began with handwritten letters and only recently grew into a mass-market business, in the category of World Gone Mad. Perhaps there's a reason for one con artist to "solicit for your assistance in this mutually benefiting business transaction"; surely it defeats the purpose when they all send this same e-mail several times a day, week in and week out. Today it's from Dominic Tutu and Dominic Egbu, separately. Before that it was Dr. Lawrence Adu and Dr. Francis Oputa and Dr. Williams Ossai and Dr. Shuaibu Hamza. There can hardly be any unsuspecting victims left, so you have to wonder—what's the point?

Early Internet users reacted so angrily to commercial mass mailings that fake return addresses became a necessity. America Online and other large service providers began closing accounts used for spam. The next big step—indispensable to the spam epidemic—was the rise of free mail services: Hotmail, now owned by Microsoft, and Yahoo. Two features of the modern Internet (both more or less accidental) make spamming easy: service providers desperate for market share at all costs; and an architecture of relatively open and insecure mail gateways. Together these enable hit-and-run e-mailers to create quick, disposable, false identities. It's why so many of your correspondents have addresses like "buffy0412xxxmeb13mxy@hotmail.com"—though that one, offering me "eBay insider secrets," day after day, turns out to be not just a pseudonym but also a forgery, not a real Hotmail account at all.

For that matter, anyone named Buffy who sends me e-mail is a spammer, judging from my experience. A suspicious number of my correspondents now seem to be called James. It seems safe to assume that a sender named NoMore-Constipation68487 is a spammer. Likewise for Persondude1—but no, that turns out to be my 11-year-old nephew. Sorting the good from the bad looks easy, but it's a real problem, both for humans trying to manage their in-boxes and for artificial intelligence.

A human being, looking at a sender called "Ug56miZ5w@msn.com," can guess it's not a real person. Looking at subjects like "Do your butt, hips and thighs embarrass you" and "My husband's not home, come and have me!" and "Make money fast" (yes, this ancient artifact still makes the rounds), a human being knows enough to press the delete key. Why can't a computer be that smart?

Many programmers are working to automate the filtering of spam. The spammers, of course, are working to stay ahead. They forge identifying headers; some of your spam now appears to have been sent to you by you. They continually change the content, even adding random text. They make their subject lines sound real, or at least plausible:

- How are you?
- Thanks for requesting more information.
- Error in your favor.
- It is critical that your Internet connection is fixed.
- Someone is waiting for you.
- Listen to what people are saying about you.
- Pentagon readies war plans. (This one was an attempt to sell heating-oil options: "$5,000.00 minimum investment.")

Another gambit is to have their computers insert your name:
- James, is this still your e-mail?
- James, your paycheck has just increased!
- Hello, Gleick, darling.

All this in the name of tricking you into opening the message. "Baby you're so strange"—can you resist?" "Do you remember me?"

Every major e-mail program now comes with filters meant to spare you the trouble. The idea is for the computer to detect spam and delete it, or at least move it into a separate folder where you can while away your time examining it later. Microsoft's e-mail clients use simple rules. If the first eight characters of the sender's name are digits, they guess the mail is spam. Likewise if the subject contains dollar signs and exclamation points, or if the message contains "money back" or "check or money order" or "over 21" or "Dear friend."

This approach catches less and less spam as time goes on, because the spammers buy the same software and test their mail in advance. If you're an enthusiastic computer user, you can add filters of your own. You can even download interesting filters from sites organized by other spam victims. You can't expect perfection. There will always be false negatives—junk mail that manages to sneak through.

More troublesome, however, is the problem of false positives—legitimate mail that is blocked. If you filter deletes what it thinks is spam, you may never see the message from your long-lost high-school sweetheart, who finally wants to make contact but uses too many exclamation points, or calls you a dear friend, or mentions sex.

Most corporate networks use spam filters, and many Internet service providers are also installing them, in response to pressure from their customers. The effectiveness varies widely. People use whitelists (friends) and blacklists (known spammers). People get frustrated and overcompensate, putting all of hotmail.com and yahoo.com and aol.com on their blacklists. "Am I likely to miss important e-mail?" writes Michael Fraase, a Minnesota Web consultant who goes to these extremes. "Probably, but I have no way of knowing. Unfortunately the spam problem has become so bad that it's on the verge of rendering e-mail useless."

The newest approach to a technological solution is a different kind of filtering, based on statistics. A computer scientist, Paul Graham, caused a stir in the online world last summer with a proposal for adaptive, probabilistic filtering. The idea is to give up trying to list specific features of spam, to quit trying to get inside the mind of the spammers. "Over the past six months, I've read literally thousands of spams, and it is really kind of demoralizing," Graham declared. "Norbert Wiener said if you compete with slaves you become a slave, and there is something similarly degrading about competing with spammers."

Instead, the new software keeps track of all the words in every e-mail, calculates their statistical probabilities as spam-indicators and adjusts these with experience. With his new method, he claims to be catching more than 99 percent of spams, with no false positives.

Graham's screed inspired many independent programmers to work on statistical filters. You train the software with a few hundred examples of good and bad mail, and the software starts to get smart. If you're curious, you can study the details. In my case, for example, the word "Viagra" appears almost exclusively in spam. The word "vanilla" appears almost exclusively in real mail. "Awesome" is bad; "awful" is good. "Fraction" is bad; "fragment" is good. I don't know why, and it doesn't matter.

"I was skeptical of filters, too, but in my case there wasn't much of a choice," says Michael Tsai, the author of SpamSieve, one of the more effective statistical filters. "I don't have time to categorize my mail by hand, and if I did I'd probably get trigger-happy with the delete key."

If you wonder why words like "Viag.a" and "pen-s" have started appearing in your spam, this is why. It's the spammers trying to outwit the filters. They have also begun appending random chunks of innocent text.

After weeks of training, my spam filter didn't see a problem with a letter titled "See what hot girlz do behind closed doors!" To a wary human, just the word "girlz" would be a giveaway. The filter didn't suspect anything unwelcome about a letter from Ivanna Come titled Obscene Facial Pictures. You can't say these spammers are brilliantly concealing their intentions. A human being gets the point. Yet none of these words, singly or in combination, triggered the alarm in my filtering software. The filter still thought this might be legitimate e-mail:

Looking for a good time?
Want some FREE ladies?
Then click here!

Deep inside the majestic Pennsylvania Avenue headquarters of the Federal Trade Commission lies the control center for the government's battle against spam, such as it is. This is the grandly named Internet Lab. It turns out to be eight PC's on desks.

"It's a great resource," says Brian Huseman, the F.T.C. lawyer assigned to tell me about the commission's spam-fighting. "I don't know how we would do our spam investigations without it." While I watch, three young staff members surf the Web.

During the Clinton administration, the commission set up an e-mail address, uce@ftc.gov, for consumers to forward samples of their spam. The database now contains 27.5 million of these, and 85,000 more arrive daily. Every month or so, the commission files an enforcement action against someone, leading to a warning letter, or a promise by the spammer to cease and desist, or even, occasionally, a "disgorgement of ill-gotten gains." No one really imagines any of this makes a dent.

The agency can't help noticing that, by and large, spam is not illegal. Its enforcers can go after only the most obvious forms of fraud, of which there is, after all, no shortage. The fact that you may not want to get this stuff is not their problem. "From the F.T.C.'s point of view, whether it's wanted or unwanted, what we're concerned about is whether it's deceptive," Huseman says.

In reality almost all spam qualifies as deceptive. Junk messages typically come with false return addresses. The Internet headers are typically forged to falsify the mail servers, relays and other data that could help trace the source. Instructions for removing your name from their lists are typically false; your name won't be removed, and the spammer will know you're alive and reading the mail. In theory, any of these lies could justify action by the commission. "Maybe there's a deceptive statement about how your name was acquired," Huseman says. Why, yes!

In practice, it's hopeless. You can't prove that you never clicked a button marked "O.K." after failing to read the fine print of a privacy agreement, thus unwittingly giving someone a sort of authorization to sell your e-mail address. The F.T.C. is a strong believer in these lawyerly privacy statements, but how many people read them?

You don't want to test the Click Here to Be Removed link, because you suspect it will just lead to more spam. This is just another in the series of spam Catch-22's.

The spammers are elusive and hidden—one reason Barry Shein compares their operations to organized crime. "These are not legitimate businesspeople," he said. "These are people who are acting in a way that society does not accept." Yet it is often possible for a determined victim to track them down. Although headers will be forged, inspecting the HTML source of junk mail usually reveals a genuine domain name, because, after all, you are meant to visit some Web site. Domain names are required to list publicly a technical contact and an administrative contact. For example, SexAffair.org, which sends a torrent of spam from supposedly willing maidens called "Erica" and "Jen" and "Katie," turns out to be Sobonito Investments Ltd., at 10800 Biscayne Boulevard in Miami. They handle Sex2go.com, too. I'd like to talk to them about this, but they don't return my calls. Anyway, until Congress sees fit to make their activities illegal, tracking down spammers provides little satisfaction.

Yet the perpetrators are not just misfits and pornographers. Real companies send spam, too—because they don't know any better, or because they don't care, or just in rote obeisance to the gods of marketing.

E-mail marketers, from the sleazy to the near-legitimate, defend their behavior by citing postal junk mail and unsolicited telemarketing. These irritate consumers but are tolerated, up to a point. Spam is different. It is intrusive because, in the nature of e-mail, it arrives round the clock, demanding attention. It lacks even the modest checks and balances of traditional marketing: to print letters and send them through the post costs money; likewise to make telephone calls. A direct mailer can't afford a pitch so shabby and fruitless that it will produce a one-in-a-thousand rate of return. A spammer can, because sending a million more copies is practically free.

We citizens and consumers have more points of contact with the world then ever before; more points of exposure. Our front doors and mailboxes are one kind of interface; our telephones and fax machines another; our televisions and radios still another. Because networked computers open a pathway wider and faster and more fluid than all these combined, the spam epidemic will prove a need for new kinds of locks and new kinds of rules.

Many people who hate spam believe, honorably enough, that it's protected as free speech. It is not. The Supreme Court has made clear that individuals may preserve a threshold of privacy. "Nothing in the Constitution compels us to listen to or view any unwanted communication, whatever its merit," wrote Chief Justice Warren Burger in a 1970 decision. "We therefore categorically reject the argument that a vendor has a right under the Constitution or otherwise to send unwanted material into the home of another."

Odd forces have conspired to create paralysis in the government on the matter of spam. Corporate marketers and Internet traditionalists have found themselves in an accidental alliance. The marketers, particularly the powerful Direct Marketing Association, have lobbied hard to preserve their ability to send cheap messages to potential customers; "self-regulation" has been the industry's watchword. And the Internet's culture, too, lines up against government intervention. The word "clueless" might have been invented to describe legislators with an urge to meddle in the high-tech arena. In cyberspace, policy and rulemaking have come from the bottom up, and the benefits have been spectacular. Time and again, the online world has behaved like a self-healing organism, outwitting authorities who tried to impose structure from above.

But cyberspace belongs to the world of human beings, who rely on laws to discourage the worst behavior and to protect the powerless. The grass roots have not solved the problem—indeed anti-spam posses have often caused trouble of their own, with blacklists that block mail from legitimate sources. And even the Direct Marketing Association has come to believe that spam hurts its members. "I've got caught in the vicious cycle," says Regina Brady, an e-mail marketing consultant who works with the association. "All of a sudden your e-mail address is spun out into cyberspace. This is a real problem for legitimate marketers trying to do the right thing." This fall, after fighting it for years, the association came out in favor of federal anti-spam legislation in some form.

Arguments about such legislation tend to focus on the issue of "opt in" versus "opt out." In opt-out schemes, which the marketers favor, consumers have to take action to declare their unwillingness to receive unsolicited bulk mail. If the system is opt-in, then marketers have to be able to show that consumers have given their consent to receive solicitations. The European Parliament recently voted to adopt opt-in requirements, putting Europe far ahead of the United States in acting against spam.

As remote as an effective solution seems, the spam problem might not be so intractable after all. The Telephone Consumer Protection Act of 1991 made it illegal to send unsolicited faxes; that law passed with strong backing from manufacturers of fax machines. It should be extended to include unsolicited bulk e-mail.

For free-speech reasons, any legislation should avoid considering e-mail's content; trying to define key words like "commercial" and "pornographic" only leads to trouble. And it isn't necessary. For that matter, even short of outlawing spam, two simple measures might be enough to stem the tide:

1. Forging Internet headers should be made illegal. The system depends on accurate information about senders and servers and relays; no one needs a right to falsify this information.
2. Unsolicited bulk mail should carry a mandatory tag. That alone would put consumers back in control; all the complex technological challenge of identifying the spam would vanish.

We need to be able to say no. No, I'm not looking for a good time. No, I don't want to "e-mail millions of PayPal members." No, I don't want an anatomy-enlargement kit. No, I don't want my share of the Nigerian $25 million. I just want my in-box. It belongs to me, and I want it back.

Topics for Reading and Writing

1. One of the problems with legislating against "spam" is defining it. No marketer admits to being a "spammer"; even the most egregious violator of responsible marketing practices will claim not to be a spammer and point to another marketer who is worse. What is spam? How can we define spam? Is it any unwanted advertising? Any advertising we haven't specifically asked for? Any advertising that clearly isn't targeted at our own needs? Can spam be differentiated from "legitimate" advertising come-ons? The more reputable advertising and marketing firms who harvest Web visitors' e-mail addresses on behalf of large companies claim that they don't spam—is that true? What about companies like Travelocity, Amazon, or Entertainment Weekly.com who send e-mail to those who have visited their own sites?

2. Underlying the spam controversy is a deeper, more enduring question about free speech versus commercial speech. Advertisers claim that the Consti-

tution gives them the right to contact potential consumers to inform them about products, and for the most part U.S. law has upheld companies' rights to advertise freely. However, more and more consumers are claiming that the Constitution also provides a right of privacy—a right to be left alone, an assumption that one's own private information (telephone numbers, e-mail addresses, credit records, medical history) should not be used by people who are just trying to sell things. Where should the line be between privacy and the legitimate right to advertise?

3. Gleick's article—appearing in the Sunday magazine of the most important newspaper in the United States—makes some quite radical suggestions for what to do about spam. Are these suggestions workable? Are they fair to "legitimate" marketers?

4. Is there a difference between e-mail spam and telephone solicitations? Should one be regulated differently than the other (based on degree of annoyance? level of privacy invasion? legitimacy of the originating company)?

5. Is this a fair article? Where are the opposing views? Why do we not hear from Internet marketers—spammers or reputable Internet marketers?

The Writer at Work: Proposing a Solution

In previous chapters, you have learned how to effectively argue some of the most common kinds of claims: claims about meanings, claims about judgments and evaluations, and claims about causes and effects. These claims are used, generally, to *explain* something to an audience. But in a society in which citizens have to be convinced not just to think but to *do* things, writers must also be capable of making arguments that motivate people to act—or, at the very least, to accept that one proposed solution to a problem is the best one, and that one should pursue that solution.

Not surprisingly, such arguments are generally known as "proposal claims." Some sample proposal claims you have read just in the last few chapters include:

- The clergy of Birmingham should accept and even endorse Martin Luther King, Jr.'s, crusade to end segregation in the South.
- Students should be aware of the commercial messages embedded in the content provided by Channel One.
- Citizens should oppose the loosening of restrictions on media ownership.
- Congress and the courts need to recognize that copying and trading music and movies is piracy and should be prosecuted.
- We should oppose the video *Bumfights*.

Other proposal claims that circulated in the culture at large in the last few years include:

- The United States needs to attack Iraq in order to eliminate its weapons of mass destruction.

- The United States needs to attack Iraq and depose Saddam Hussein because he has links with the Al Qaeda terrorist group.
- SUVs should be regulated under the rules for cars, not for trucks.
- We need a tax cut to stimulate the economy.

You probably have encountered some proposal claims in your own personal life in the last few months:

- You should study two hours for every hour of class.
- Let's go out to the taquería tonight instead of eating at the dorm.
- You should go to a state school instead of an expensive private college.
- I think we should get married.

A proposal claim, in its simplest form, is just a statement asserting that someone—you, we, the citizens of the United States, the state legislature, the National Rifle Association, the United Nations—should or should not pursue a particular action. Of course, an effective proposal argument is more complicated, not least because it's *hard* to spur people to action—it's much more difficult to persuade someone to do something than it is to persuade them that a concept is true. In fact, a proposal argument involves two crucial parts: first, you have to convince people there is a problem that needs to be addressed; then, you have to propose the solution that will actually solve that problem.

Identifying the Problem

Before proposing a solution to a problem, you have to convince your audience that a problem exists. This task can be more complicated than it seems; sometimes a situation is more of a problem for some people than for others, and sometimes a situation might exist that one group sees as a problem but another group doesn't mind at all. Let's look at a few examples of potential problems, and think about which audiences would see them as problems.

- There are giant potholes on the freeway between Seattle and Tacoma.
    Who would find this to be a problem: Commuters who use that road.
    Who would not care: People who do not use that road.
    Who might see this as a good thing: Nobody.

- North Korea has several atomic weapons and is threatening to use them.
    Who would find this to be a problem: Nations that are threatened (South Korea, Japan, the United States).
    Who would not care: Nations that don't believe North Korea would use those weapons; nations far enough away from East Asia that such actions would not threaten them.
    Who might see this as a good thing: Nations friendly to North Korea; North Korea.

■ People are copying music from CDs and trading it among themselves.

　　Who would find this to be a problem: Those, such as musicians and record companies, who profit from record sales.

　　Who would not care: People who have no interest in music or property rights.

　　Who might see this as a good thing: Music fans who don't have to pay for music; musicians who feel that the exposure created by music trading outweighs the loss of income from people not buying their music.

Before ever proposing a solution to these problems, a writer must first take into consideration his or her audience. Arguing to an audience of truckers that the potholes should be repaired will likely be a simple task—their livelihoods and safety depend on well-maintained freeways. This audience is likely to be so concerned about this issue that they might even be motivated to such actions as contacting state or federal transportation authorities. Convincing a group of residents of southern Washington state that this is a problem is more difficult. They probably don't use these roads very frequently, and it's likely that there are road problems in their area, as well. Faced by this kind of reluctance, an effective writer must change his or her argument and show the audience how this seemingly remote problem actually affects them. Goods coming from Seattle will take longer to arrive and be more expensive since many truckers will use other roads. Transportation costs in general will rise because of damage to trucks. This audience will never respond with the passion of the audience of truckers, but a writer must keep in mind that audiences will have varying degrees of response and acceptance of a speaker's point.

The case is the same with the much more grave issue of North Korean arms. Most nations in the world see this as a very serious problem: North Korea has generally behaved erratically and at times very aggressively, and it's frequently difficult to understand that nation's motivations. A nuclear-armed North Korea threatens its neighbors as well as the United States; moreover, every nation has the responsibility to try to prevent the use of nuclear weapons. But while North Korea's few friends—China, for one—might fear the unpredictability of North Korea's actions, they might also endorse the change in the balance of power in the region. Arguing to China that North Korea must be disarmed would be very difficult. Finally, nations in regions such as Africa or South America just might not care. Such a conflict would not involve them, and even the environmental damage from nuclear conflict would be, they might reason, minimal.

Establishing that there is a problem isn't so simple, is it? In addition to finding arguments that convince particular audiences, a good writer will even have to select different kinds of evidence for different audiences. Let's look at our third example (about MP3 copying) and try to come up with a proposal argument there. Start with the first part of a proposal: convincing the audience that it's a problem. Some audiences will be very open to this argument—record company employees, many musicians, people who put a high value on private property, probably many older people who aren't familiar with the idea of computer file swapping. Other audiences wouldn't. Let's make our argument to an audience of college students.

We've come up with the first part (file sharing is a problem); now let's generate a solution. There are many solutions to this "problem" floating around.

- Record companies should freely release music to be traded on the Internet; that way, loyal fans can get a taste of the music they like and then buy the CDs of their favorite artists.
- Record companies should sell MP3 files to users and rely on consumers' ethical obligation not to circulate those files.
- Record companies should work on better encryption techniques so that MP3s can't be traded.
- Computer companies should phase out music software so that computer users can't take advantage of MP3s.

While all these proposals would remedy the problem in some way, for the sake of this heuristic let's argue the most inflexible position—the position, in fact, that record companies have taken.

- Law enforcement agencies should actively pursue and prosecute computer users who illegally trade copyrighted music files, and should levy legal sanctions against the Internet service providers that allow the users to engage in illegal activity.

Arguing this position to an audience of college students (many of whom have become accustomed to getting their music for free) is a tough assignment. What are some of the possible rationales we can use just for the first part of this argument—convincing the students that file sharing is a problem?

> When you trade music files, you rob struggling musicians of their livelihood. Without initial success through record sales, musicians will give up music, depriving us of the art they might create in future years. (Music fans might respond to this argument, as might people who are fans of underground or alternative bands.)

> Yes, many of the musicians (such as Metallica) who complain about file sharing are themselves very wealthy, and the loss of revenue to them hardly seems a problem. What about other, poorer musicians? What about the older musicians who foolishly signed abusive contracts long ago and only today profit fairly from their music? (This argument might appeal to those who pull for the underdog.)

> Trying to finesse the definition of "stealing" is disingenuous. When you download copyrighted files without paying, you're stealing just as much as if you shoplifted CDs from a record store. (This might appeal to more conservative students.)

To each of these three audiences, you have to make a different appeal just to convince them there is a problem that needs addressing. After all, if you're proposing a solution and nobody thinks there's a problem, you're not going to get very far. It's extremely important to take into consideration all the arguments that this problem isn't in fact a problem. You can't just rely on your own forceful thesis and rugged good looks to sell your argument; you've got to explicitly address those people who say that Problem X isn't actually a problem, and show why their arguments are insufficient or just wrong—making sure to do so in a way that will be convincing to them. Tough task!

IDEAS INTO PRACTICE 8-1

Sketch out strategies for convincing the following audiences of these problems.

1. There is too much sex on television shows during the "family hour" of 8–9 p.m.
   Audiences: a) An elementary school parents' group; b) A congressional subcommittee; c) executives at NBC, ABC, CBS, and Fox.
2. The media, in general, are too liberal.
   Audiences: a) The membership of the National Rifle Association; b) Reporters at your local daily newspaper; c) A democratic party meeting.
3. The consumption of fossil fuels is having a serious effect on our climate.
   Audiences: a) "Soccer moms"; b) the Senate Commerce Committee; c) the membership of the National Rifle Association.

Proposing a Solution

Obviously, once you've established that there is a problem your audience should care about, you need to suggest a solution. But it's not enough to simply state "We should prosecute people who trade MP3s." If the explanation of why the problem is a problem is intended to overcome your audience's inertia, the proposed solution then channels their nascent energy. You need to make sure your solution works and, perhaps more important, that it is the best solution available.

Any proposal argument will have an explanation of exactly what this solution is and of how this solution addresses the problem in question. A humorous series of television commercials for the technology company IBM recently depicted an anxious team of information technology officers at a corporation listening to a salesman's presentation of his company's product: magic pixie dust that heals computer servers. The ad was funny, of course, because the salesman explained very well how the pixie dust would solve all the company's problems—but he neglected to explain how it worked. A convincing proposal must do both.

A recent proposal argument that hinges largely on the feasibility of the solution centers on the question of what to do about poor quality or dangerous public schools. "School vouchers," a program whereby parents are granted governmental credits to be used toward private-school tuition, are intended to address the problem of these substandard public schools. Advocates of vouchers explain that the vouchers solve both the problem of individual students receiving a poor education (their parents transfer them to better schools) and the problem of poor public schools (faced with declining numbers of students, public schools will be forced to shape up in order to compete). Voucher opponents rebut not that "there is no problem with public schools," but with the notion that encouraging students to leave those schools solves that problem. The environmental issue of global warming is somewhat different. Environmental activists argue that "greenhouse gases" emitted by industry and consumer products are changing the climate, and that restrictions on the consumption of fossil fuels must be put into place to counter this climatic change. The counterarguments to that point attack both the establishment of the problem ("there's no long-term evidence that the climate is changing," "the effects of climate change are miniscule and will be offset by other trends," "it's all made-up science anyway") and the proposed solution ("fossil fuels aren't the worst problem," "restricting fossil fuel use in the industrialized world will just cause it to explode in the developing world"). As you go about constructing your proposal argument, make sure your explanation of the problem does indeed convince your audience of the nature of the problem before you even propose your solution.

Once you have convinced the audience that the problem is in fact a problem, it's important to explain your solution in detail and to be honest about what this solution will cost in terms of money, effort, or sacrifice. At the very least, your explanation should include details about the following:

■ How the solution works.
■ Who will implement this solution.
■ How the solution addresses the problem—does it eliminate it, does it attack the root causes of the problem or just its symptoms, is it a permanent or temporary solution.
■ What this solution will cost.
■ Who will have to pay that cost, in terms of money or time or energy or lost resources.
■ How long this solution will last.
■ Whether this solution has negative ramifications, and if so, how to keep them in check.

In addition to explaining how the solution works and how it addresses the problem, a proposal must also take into consideration the counterarguments. In the first section of your argument, you've persuaded us that Problem X is actually a problem, and you've gone so far as to counter all the objections that Problem X isn't a problem at all. Showing that you understand that there are legitimate objections to your point, and respectfully and responsibly defusing those objections, adds immensely to your *ethos:* you look like you've thought through this issue, and that you respect and have seriously considered the ideas of others, but have arrived at your own conclusion through careful study and contemplation. The proposal section of a proposal argument must do the same thing. Admit that there are other possible solutions to the problem, and even briefly explain those possible solutions, giving credit to their spokespeople. After doing this, though, point out—using specifics and facts—how these solutions are not as good as yours. They might be only temporary. They might cost more. They might bring with them the potential for collateral dangers. They might be unproven. They might be insufficiently or excessively ambitious. Explain how those solutions that ask less of the audience (in terms of money or time or effort) don't do enough to solve the problem, or how those solutions that are more elaborate and far-reaching will cost too much to be worthwhile.

In the end, the outline for a proposal argument should look something like this:

- Statement of the problem that needs to be addressed.
   Explanation of why this is a problem to your audience.
   Explanation of other communities or groups that are affected by this problem, and why your audience should care about these other communities or groups.

- Statement of the proposed solution to the problem.
   Explanation of the proposed solution: who has to expend effort or money, who is affected, exactly how this addresses the problem.
   Explanation of why this is the best solution possible: comparison of this proposal with others and description of how it is the superior choice (because it most completely solves the problem, requires the least investment of effort or money, has the fewest adverse side effects, etc.).

IDEAS INTO PRACTICE 8-2

For the problems in Ideas into Practice 8-1, come up with solutions. How should we deal with these problems? Make arguments to each of the audiences in the questions in Ideas into Practice 8-1, outlining a proposal argument that takes into consideration *ethos, pathos,* and *logos* appeals geared to the audience. Finally, be sure to research some of the alternate solutions to the problem, and make explanations—explanations that will appeal specifically to that audience!—as to why your solution is superior.

Style
Toolbox

Sentence Fragments

Sentence fragments. All of us have received papers back from writing teachers with the word "frag" scribbled on almost every page. Most of us know what a sentence fragment is: an incomplete sentence, generally lacking either a subject or a conjugated verb. Although many sentence fragments are "correct" in the sense that the reader will understand what the writer is saying, sentence fragments are generally considered nonstandard, and thus undesirable in formal written English.

As you have probably seen in the previous chapters' Style Toolboxes, this book makes a differentiation between "incorrect" usage and "nonstandard" usage. Incorrect usage, for our purposes, describes the type of ungrammatical statements that competent speakers would never construct, whereas nonstandard usage describes the kind of constructions that competent speakers might use and that any competent speaker would understand, but that are generally considered "wrong." Some incorrect grammatical constructions are so incorrect as to be essentially meaningless, and competent speakers of any language are able to distinguish grammatical sentences from ungrammatical ones without even thinking because the rules of grammar are so deeply ingrained in us once we learn our native languages. Confusing? Let's look at a couple of examples. In English, "I'm going to the library" is correct, while "To are me library goes" isn't; no native speaker of English would ever construct that second sentence and think it is correct. However, what about the sentences "I is going to the library" or "I be going to the library"? Are they incorrect or just nonstandard? Can a competent speaker of English immediately understand what the speaker is saying? In both of these cases, yes. In addition, these constructions are characteristic of Southern American English and Ebonics; both of these sentences follow the internal rules of those dialects although they violate the rules of standard English. Therefore, they are *correct* in that they can be understood, but they are *nonstandard.*

This distinction has ideological freight: the differentiation of nonstandard from incorrect recognizes that people who speak varieties or dialects of the English language (American Ebonics, London cockney, Scots, West Indian patois, Appalachian and Southern American dialects) don't go through their daily lives saying everything wrong; rather, each dialect has internal rules, many of which are different from standard English, these speakers follow. "Standard English," in turn, doesn't have any set rules, as French does (the Académie Française in Paris sets the rules for standard French; English, with many geographic centers—London, New York, Singapore, Los Angeles, New Delhi, Sydney, Johannesburg, among others—has no central body that acts as rule keeper for the language). Instead, the rules of standard English come from various authorities: English teachers, influential writers, dictionary editors, widely read journalists, newspaper editors, and others. Standard English is important because the powerful bodies in public life—the government, the media, businesses, educational institutions, foundations and nonprofit organizations—use that dialect, and in order to accomplish anything in those worlds people must communicate in standard English or risk their audiences finding them "ignorant," "uneducated," "provincial," "foreign," or even "stupid." Again, whether or not a particular use of language is right depends entirely on the rhetorical situation.

Back to fragments (now, that's a fragment itself). Most sentence fragments are pretty easy to identify.

> Sure.
> The love shack.
> Hell yeah!
> Goin' mobile.
> So what?

In these examples, the fragments consist either of interjections (words or phrases that convey surprise or strong emotions), or of simple noun phrases lacking verbs or verb phrases lacking nouns. Those fragments are easy to spot, and when writing for an academic audience most writers know to avoid them. Not all very short sentences, though, are fragments. Some sentences don't need subjects—verbs in the *imperative mood* (i.e., commands) have an implied subject ("you"). Thus, "Getting paid" is a sentence fragment (the word "getting" is a gerund form of the verb, and therefore not eligible to be the main verb in a sentence) while "Get paid" is a complete sentence (the speaker is ordering the hearer to do something).

Things get more complicated, though, when the fragments get longer.

> If you can handle the pressure.
> Which is what I was worried about: whether or not that radiator leak
> would get worse.
> All over but the crying, my friend.

All of these are sentence fragments, but each feels like it could be a sentence. In the first two, there is a subject—"you" and "I"—and there is a verb—"can handle" and "was." However, both of those examples are actually *dependent clauses*—in other words, they are clauses (a grammatical construction that includes both a subject and a verb) that are *subordinated* to a main sentence by the *subordinating conjunction* "if" or the *relative pronoun* "which." Both of these words indicate that these clauses aren't the main sentence, but are instead branches off the main sentence. The third example lacks both a subject and a verb, but it sounds like a sentence both because it's relatively long and because we can easily imagine someone saying that in informal conversation as a sentence in itself.

Each of these fragments can be turned into complete sentences, of course. For the first two, we need to add a main sentence to the dependent clause:

> If you can handle the pressure, *working as an air-traffic controller can
> be very lucrative.*
> *The car ended up overheating as we crossed the Rockies,* which is what
> I was worried about: whether or not that radiator leak would get
> worse.

For the third, we need a subject and a verb.

> *It's* all over but the crying, my friend.

Writing with Style 8-1

Indicate whether each of the following is a complete sentence or a sentence fragment. For the fragments, explain why it is a fragment—is it a dependent clause lacking a main sentence, is it an interjection, is it a verb without a subject or a noun phrase without a verb? Then, rewrite the fragments as complete sentences.

1. Because I really just don't want to.
2. If I don't return these library books pronto I'm going to owe some serious cash.
3. Move!
4. Moving on up, to the East Side, to a deluxe apartment in the sky.
5. If I could, I would.
6. If I could, if I only could.
7. Whether or not it rains, and if the ground is sufficiently dry to allow play on this field.

8. A brand new Cadillac Escalade, with alloy rims and a sound system that will shake every window on Wilshire Boulevard.
9. Several people asked me my opinion on the matter.
10. That's what I asked her; if she was going to come to the movies tonight or not.

Identifying sentence fragments can be difficult, but with a little practice it will become second nature to you—you'll be able to sense that the sentence you just wrote has something important missing. Eventually, though, as you become a more confident and skilled writer, you're going to start writing for occasions in which sentence fragments can be perfectly acceptable, or even desirable.

It's not the case that sentence fragments never occur in formal writing. Because they are so short and abrupt and because their very incompleteness makes them stand out, sentence fragments are an important part of formal oratory and speechmaking. Imagine the leader of a group speaking on the Washington Mall:

> We have come a long way to be here today. We have come from the suburbs of this city. From the hills of West Virginia and from the plains of Indiana. From the desert of Texas and from the mountains of Washington. From jail cells and mansions. In cars, in buses, on airplanes, and even on bicycles.

Hearing that paragraph in your head, you can probably sense the pauses that the orator placed between each sentence fragment. Imagine how the paragraph would sound if the fragments all began with the phrase "We have come"—that phrase is powerful when repeated twice, but repeated six times, it would just be pretentious.

But sentence fragments can also appear even in formal written English. Maureen Dowd of the *New York Times* ended her column of April 20, 2003, with this:

> Instead of hectoring those who expressed any doubt about the difficulty of occupying Iraq, the conservatives should worry about their own self-parody: pandering to the base by blessing evangelical Christians who want to proselytize Muslims; protecting their interests by backing a shady expat puppet; pleasing their contributors by pre-emptively awarding rebuilding contracts to Halliburton and Bechtel; and swaggering like Goths as Iraq's cultural heritage goes up in flames.
>
>   Talk about a baptism by fire.

(You might also notice how this sentence is an example of using a colon to start a list and using semicolons to separate long elements within that list.) Her final sentence isn't really a sentence. Of course, in some rhetorical contexts this fragment could be a sentence in the imperative mood (imagine Mike Myers's *Saturday Night Live* character Linda Richman saying "Talk amongst yourselves!") but this isn't what Dowd intends. Her final fragment is an ironic statement saying that the "conservatives" have made choices that will make their ultimate tasks difficult (a "baptism by fire" is an expression indicating a very difficult test one must go through at the beginning of a process or when joining a group). We're all familiar with the common slang expression "talk about a . . .", used when a speaker wants to draw attention to a great example of an ironic contrast. It's an informal expression, often accompanied by eye-rolling and a world-weary expression. Dowd could have chosen to use standard formal written English, and ended her column by making the same point like this:

> These conservatives have certainly set themselves a difficult task, because their actions tend to confirm their opponents' worst suspicions about them.

This sentence, although it explains Dowd's point just as well, lacks the snap, the sarcastic attitude, the verbal eye-rolling, the sense of the personality of the author that Dowd wants to convey. Her choice to use a fragment in such a prominent place in the essay—as the only sentence in the final paragraph—gives it even more punch, as does the fact it follows a very long, complicated and well-constructed sentence.

Look at the following excerpt from Elizabeth Wurtzel's *Prozac Nation.* What does Wurtzel accomplish here with sentence fragments? And how does she combine sentence fragments with a control of sentence rhythm?

> Summer of 1987. Dallas, Texas. The Oak Lawn section, to be precise. I have finished my sophomore year at Harvard. Somewhere down the road I managed to pick up the 1986 *Rolling Stone* College Journalism Award for an essay I wrote about Lou Reed for the *Harvard Crimson,* and now I have a summer job at the *Dallas Morning News* as an arts reporter.

Sentence fragments are best used when a writer wants to convey strong emotion (as in the previous fictional example of the orator), surprise, breeziness and informality, or sarcasm. When used well, they can give academic or formal writing more personality. When used poorly, they make the writer look unwise or just sloppy. And of course, one needs to know what audience the speaker is addressing before being able to judge whether or not the fragments are used well or poorly!

WRITING WITH STYLE 8-2

Write two paragraphs responding to an editorial in the newspaper. In the first paragraph, use no sentence fragments; write as formally as possible, assuming that your audience consists of the best educated, most powerful, most established people in the community served by that newspaper. In the second paragraph, try using a fragment or two, thinking about how you can take the formality of your voice down a notch or two without losing any of your *ethos.*

Credits

Text Credits

Adams, Lorraine, "The Write Stuff." Reprinted with permission from *The American Prospect,* Volume 14, Number 2: February 1, 2003. The American Prospect, 5 Broad Street, Boston, MA 02109. All rights reserved."

Alterman, Eric and Bozell, Brent, "Are the Media Liberal? /Response from Eric Alterman and Brent Bozell" from *The National Review Online,* February 5, 2003. Reprinted with permission of Eric Alterman and Brent Bozell.

Barra, Allen, "John Rocker, Whipping Boy." http://archive.salon.com/news/sports/2000/06/09/rocker/print.html. This article first appeared in Salon.com, at http://www.Salon.com An online version remains in the Salon archives. Reprinted with permission.

Boehlert, Eric, "Radio's Big Bully." http://dir.salon.com/ent/feature/2001/04/30/clear_channel/index.html. This article first appeared in Salon.com, at http://www.Salon.com An online version remains in the Salon archives. Reprinted with permission.

Brill, Emily, "Empathy for Big Music? Mp3s for Me" from *The Philadelphia Inquirer,* 2/20/03. Reprinted by permission of the author.

Cary, Sherman, "Issue Is Piracy, not Privacy" from *USA Today,* posted 1/25/2003. http://www.usatoday.com. Reprinted by permission of the author.

Colson, Charles, "The ALA's Addiction to Porn, Pts. 1–3." Commentary #000809, 8/9/2000. Copyright © 2000 Prison Fellowship Ministries. Reprinted by permission. http://www.safeplace.net/ccv/docs/alaadporn/htm

Didion, Joan, excerpt from "Quiet Days in Malibu" from *The White Album.* Copyright © 1979 by Joan Didion. Reprinted by permission of Farrar, Straus and Giroux, LLC.

Dionne, Jr., E. J., "The Rightward Press" from *The Washington Post,* December 6, 2002. Copyright © 2002, The Washington Post Writers Group. Reprinted with permission.

Dunham, Katie, "Censoring is a choice" from *The Daily Trojan,* November 5, 2002. Reprinted with permission of the author.

Elder, Larry, "Politically Correct Murder and Media Bias: Some Murder Victims Are "More Equal" Than Others" from *Capitalism Magazine,* March 4, 2002. Reprinted by Permission of Larry Elder and Creators Syndicate, Inc.

Neuharth, Al, "Why your news is sometimes slanted." *USA Today.* Copyright February 27, 2003. Reprinted with permission.

O'Neill, Charles, "The Language of Advertising." Reprinted by permission of the author.

Orwell, George, "Shooting An Elephant" from *Shooting an Elephant and Other Essays.* Copyright © 1950 by Harcourt, Inc., and renewed 1979 by Sonia Brownell Orwell, reprinted by permission of Harcourt, Inc.

Orwell, George, "Shooting an Elephant" from *Shooting an Elephant and Other Essays.* (Copyright © George Orwell, 1936) by permission of Bill Hamilton as the Literary Executor of the Estate of the Late Sonia Brownell Orwell and Secker & Warburg Ltd.

Packer, George, "Smart-Mobbing the War" from *The New York Times Magazine,* March 9, 2003. Copyright © 2003, George Packer. From *The New York Times Magazine.* Reprinted by permission.

Pax, Salam, *Salam Pax.* Copyright © 2003 by Salam Pax. Used by permission of Grove/Atlantic, Inc.

Pax, Salam, "Excerpt from Friday, May 29, 2003" from http://www.dear_raed.blogspot.com. Reprinted by permission of McArthur & Company.

Pearlman, Jeff, Reprinted courtesy of *Sports Illustrated:* "At Full Blast" December 27, 1999–January 3, 2000. Copyright © 1999, Time Inc. All rights reserved.

Peikoff, Amy, "Would-Be Intellectual Vandals Get Their Day in the Supreme Court." Copyright © 2002 Ayn Rand Institute. All rights reserved. Reprinted by permission of the Ayn Rand Institute.

Petrecca, Laura, "Excess of X's: Marketers Are Testing the Limits of Hot Teen Buzzword." Reprinted with permission from the July 24, 2000 issue of *Advertising Age.* Copyright Crain Communications, Inc. 2000.

Pollard, Timothy D., "Yo, yo, yo! This is the hip-hop CNN" from *Philadelphia Inquirer,* Wednesday, October 9, 2002. Reprinted by permission of the author.

Pynchon, Thomas, *The Crying of Lot 49.* Philadelphia, PA: Lippincott, 1966.

Rafferty, Terrence, "Everybody Gets a Cut" from *The New York Times Magazine,* May 4, 2003. Copyright © 2003, Terrence Rafferty. From *The New York Times Magazine.* Reprinted by permission.

Ravitch, Diane, "Cut on the Bias," July 1, 2003. Reprinted from *The Wall Street Journal.* Copyright © 2003 Dow Jones & Company, Inc. All rights reserved. Reprinted by permission of the author.

Rodriguez, Richard, from *Hunger of Memory.* Reprinted by permission of David R. Godine, Publisher, Inc. Copyright © 1982 by Richard Rodriguez.

Rosen, Jill, "High School Confidential" from *American Journalism Review,* June 2002. Reprinted by permission of American Journalism Review.

Saffo, Paul, "Quality in an Age of Electronic Incunabula" from *Liberal Education,* 79: 1, Winter 1993. Reprinted by kind permission of the author.

Samuelson, Randy, "MLB and Braves Are Off Their Rockers" from *The Austin Review,* March 1, 2000. Reprinted by permission of *The Austin Review.*

Saunders, Debra J., "Conservatism Can Survive Legal Bias" from *San Francisco Chronicle,* May 5, 2002. Reprinted by permission of the Copyright Clearance Center.

Seipp, Catherine, "The Puppet Masters" from *American Journalism Review,* October 1999. Reprinted by permission of American Journalism Review.

Shafer, Jack, "The Varieties of Media Bias, Pt. 2" from *Slate,* Wednesday, February 12, 2003. Copyright © Slate/Distributed by United Feature Syndicate, Inc.

Shaw, Derek, "Punks, Bums and Politicians" from *The Daily Trojan,* October 25, 2002. Reprinted by permission of the author.

Smith, Ph.D., Elizabeth and Malone, Ph.D., Ruth E., "The Outing of Philip Morris: Advertising Tobacco to Gay Men." RN from *American Journal of Public Health,* June, 2003. Vol. 93. Reprinted by permission of The American Public Health Association.

Staples, Brent, "The Trouble with Corporate Radio: The Day the Protest Music Died" from *The New York Times,* Opinion Editor, February 20, 2003. Reprinted by permission of *The New York Times.*

Steinem, Gloria, "Sex, Lies and Advertising" from *Ms. Magazine,* July-August, 1990. Copyright by Gloria Steinem. Reprinted by kind permission of the author.

Stewart, Ian, "Judge: Bonds' Home Run Ball Must Be Sold" from Associated Press, December 18, 2002. Reprinted with permission of The Associated Press.

Tomorrow, Tom, "Who's Watching the Watchers? A Tale of Diminishing Returns" from The Back Page. *New Yorker,* September 30, 2002. Reprinted by permission of the author.

Trudeau, G. B., Doonesbury © G. B. Trudeau. Reprinted with permission of Universal Press Syndicate. All rights reserved.

Vaidhyanathan, Siva, "The Peer-to-Peer Revolution and the Future of Music." http://SIVACRACY.NET Reprinted by permission of the author.

Williams, Armstrong, "The Importance of Imagery in Modern Politics." Published on June 18, 2003. Copyright © 2003 Tribune Media Services. Reprinted with permission.

Zehme, Bill, "Portrait of the Actor as Two Men" from *Esquire,* September 2002. Reprinted by permission of the author.

"U.S. not saying Iraq in 'material breach'" from cnn.com, December 18, 2002. Copyright © 2004 Cable News Network LP, LLLP. Reprinted by permission.

"Media Bias Basics" from Media Research Center, http://www.mrc.org/biasbasics. Reprinted by permission of the Media Research Center.

"Oh the good ole days of simple commercials" from *Jackson Clarion Ledger,* December 12, 2001. Reprinted by permission of the *Jackson Clarion Ledger.*

"Who's wearing the trousers?" September 8, 2001. Copyright © 2001 the *Economist* Newspaper Ltd. All rights reserved. Reprinted with permission. Further reproduction prohibited. http://www.economist.com

"The Case for Brands" September 8, 2001. Copyright © 2001 the *Economist* Newspaper Ltd. All rights reserved. Reprinted with permission. Further reproduction prohibited. http://www.economist.com

"The Coming of Copyright Perpetuity" from Editorial from *The New York Times,* January 16, 2003. Reprinted by permission of *The New York Times.*

"Declaration of Jack Valenti Filed in Support of the Plaintiffs' Motion for Preliminary Injunction in A&M Records v. Napster." Reprinted by permission of the Motion Picture Association of American, Inc.

"Code of Ethics" National Press Photographers Association.
http://www.nppa.org/members/bylaws/default.htm#_Toc2860711.
Reprinted by permission.

"Ethics in the Age of Digital Photography"
http://www.nppa.org/services/bizpract/eadp/eadp2.html Reprinted by permission.

"Homeless face exploitation" from *The Daily 49er,* October 7, 2002. Vol. X, No. 21.
Reprinted by permission of *The Daily 49er.*

"Rep. Earl Blumenauer (D-OR) speaks to the House of Representatives about the "bumfights" video. January 23, 2002.
http://www.nationalhomeless.org/civilrights/blumenauer.html
Reprinted with permission.

"Censoring the Internet" from *The New York Times,* Op Ed, March 10, 2003. Reprinted by
permission of *The New York Times.*

"John Rocker Gets His Due" February 2, 2000, *Chicago Tribune.* Copyright © 2000, Tribune
Media Services. Reprinted with permission.

Photo Credits

Page **1:** Karim Shamsi-Busha/The Image Works;   **6:** NewsCom;   **7:** Bettmann/Corbis;
57: Ann Johansson/Corbis;   **58:** Copyright 2003 ABC Photography Archives;   **59:** Copyright 2003 ABC Photography Archives;   **123:** Bernd Oberman/Corbis;   **162:** © The New
Yorker Collection 2002 Barbara Smatler from cartoonbank.com. All Rights Reserved.;
229: Robert Holmes/Corbis;   **235:** AP/Wide World Photos;   **237:** AP/Wide World Photos;
245: Clay Bennett/2003 © The Christian Science Monitor;   **303:** AP/Wide World Photos;
304: AP/Wide World Photos;   **334:** Written by Neil Strauss. Illustrated by Bernard Chang.;
355: AFP/Getty Images;   **357:** AP/Wide World Photos;   **359:** Blue Box Toys/Getty Images;
365: Time LIfe Pictures/Getty Images;   **365:** Sovfoto/Eastfoto;   **410:** Barry Blitt;
412: Jim Huber;   **421:** Reuters/Corbis;   **423:** NBC/Globe Photos;   **465:** The Oakland
Tribune Collection, the Oakland Museum of California, Gift of the Alameda Newspaper
Group.

Index